D1707506

OBITUARIES FROM TENNESSEE NEWSPAPERS

Compiled By:
Jill L. Garrett

Please Direct all Correspondence & Orders to:

Southern Historical Press, Inc.
P.O. Box 1267
Greenville, S.C. 29602-1267

Originally published: Easley S.C., 1980
Reprinted by: Southern Historical Press, Inc.
Greenville, S.C., 1995
Copyright 1980 by:
The Rev. Silas Emmett Lucas, Jr.
Easley, S.C.
All Rights Reserved.
ISBN # 0-89308-174-4
Library of Congree Card Catalog # 80-51025
Printed in the United States of America

INTRODUCTION

A word about nineteenth century newspapers--they are a delight.

This was a time when a newspaper writer called a spade a spade, often with adjectives. There were no alleged murderers in this era. Instead, a suspected murderer was a blackhearted knave whose guilt was not questioned once he had been arrested. There was no unwritten rule about speaking evil of the dead. When William T. Sherman died, no Southern editor hesitated a moment to write that he was a man who lacked the milk of human kindness. Or when the son of General Gideon J. Pillow died, it was written that he might have been as great as his father except for a total lack of ambition. What modern editor would describe Judson Kilpatrick an "imbecile libertine, who has disgraced his uniform by cowardice, society by indecency, and mankind by his existence" without a regiment of lawyers behind him?

In these entries the language of the time has been retained, often entire phrases and paragraphs are just as they appeared at the time. Original spelling has also been retained in the spelling of names, towns, diseases, and other things, as has capitalization and often punctuation. This will account for men being hanged while others were hung, people came from Pittsburg as well as Pittsburgh, and the cause of death will often not be found in any known dictionary.

Some entries are not obituaries but have been included for interest or for vital information. Notes or comments by the compiler will be in parenthesis, so that all comment made in an entry will be that of the editorial writer of the time.

Only Union newspapers were available for the Civil War period--and the word "rebel" refers to Confederate soldiers or those with Southern sympathies. It will come as a surprise to some to read the comments made about the Confederates in these newspapers.

Many of these newspapers are from my own personal collection of over 80 bound sets for the nineteenth century or from microfilm in my possession. The majority of the papers has been microfilmed by the Tennessee State Library and Archives, but a large number have never been. Some newspapers are not complete volumes as often only one or two papers might have survuved.

Newspapers represented in this book: Academist, Lawrenceburg, TN; Bakerville Review, Humphreys County; Birmingham News, Birmingham, Ala.; Clarksville Gazette, Clarksville Chronicle, Clarksville Weekly Chronicle, Clarksville Jeffersonian, Clifton Mirror, Columbia Herald, Columbia Herald and Mail, Columbia Observer, Columbia Beacon, Central Monitor, (Murfreesboro), Columbia Sentinel, Columbia Journal, Daily Herald (Columbia), Dover Courier, Dickson County Press, Dickson County Herald, Democrat-Sentinel (Waverly), 83d Illionisan (Clarksville), Erin Review, Florence, Ala., Times, Florence, Ala., Gazette, Florence, Ala., Herald, Free Press (Murfreesboro), Hohenwald Chronicle, Humphrey County News, Houston County Review, Houston County Times, Huntsville (Ala.) Democrat, Hickman Pioneer, Huntsville (Ala.) Advocate, Home Press (Franklin), Linden Times, Lawrenceburg Democrat, Lincoln County Herald, Lawrenceburg Times, Memphis Appeal, Memphis Avalanche, Maury Democrat, Maury County Herald, Middle Tennessean (Pulaski), Murfreesboro Courier, Murfreesboro News, Nashville Republican Banner, Monitor (Murfreesboro), Nashville Daily Union, Nashville Daily Gazette, Nashville Whig, Nashville Union and American, Nashville Dispatch,

The Sentinel (Paris), Seventh Brigade Journal (Columbia), Tenn-
essee Watchman (Clarksville), Town Gazette & Farmers Register
(Clarksville), Times-Journal (Waverly), Western Mercury (Colum-
bia), Western Weekly Review (Franklin), Whig & Tribune (Jackson),
Waynesboro Tribune, West Tennessee Whig (Paris), Weekly Register
(Paris), Rutherford Telegraph (Murfreesboro), The Columbian,
Columbia Review, and The Current (Columbia).

   This information was abstracted from the newspapers to help
those doing research in both the historical and genealogical
fields.

A

ABBEY, Negro, belonging to Mr. Abbey of Nashville, died on the 7th of
cholera. (Western Weekly Review, Franklin, TN, 13 Sept. 1833.)

ABERNATHY, William, of Giles County, committed suicide on Bradshaw's
Creek on June 29; cut throat with butcher knife. (Whig and Tribune
Jackson, TN, 12 July 1873.)

ABERNATHY, Miss, daughter of Elias Abernathy, Esq., committed suicide
by hanging herself on Saturday night in the southern part of Giles
County. (Nashville Republican Banner, 24 Dec. 1870.)

ABERNATHY, Colonel G. T., died 4 Dec. 1888 of tyhpoid fever in Montgomery County. (Houston County News, 7 Dec. 1888)

ABRAHAMS, Frederick, second lieutenant in the 44th Illinois Volunteer
Infantry, died 18 March 1870. (Nashville Republican Banner, 19
March 1870.)

ACTOR, Mattie, age 1 year 4 months 2 days, daughter and only child of
B. F. and Lucille Achor, died 4 September 1874. (Nashville Union and
American, 6 Sept. 1874. N. B., Name spelled both ways in this
obituary.)

ACREE, Dr. G. W., 53, died 16 Jan. 1870 in Memphis. (Memphis Daily
Appeal, 17 Jan. 1870.)

ACREE, Dr. John R., of Arkansas, was shot and killed by a band of ruffians; brother of Dr. G. W. Acree of Memphis. (Memphis Daily
Appeal, 21 Jan. 1869.)

ACREE, Sam Lee, little son of Dr. Acree, having been in the river for
2½ months, body was taken up 150 miles below Memphis in a mutilated
condition. Five people were drowned at the same time. The body of
Dr. Garhey has not been found. (Memphis Daily Appeal, 25 July
1869.)

ADAMS, John Quincy, great-great-grandson of President John Adams, died
near Quincy, Mass., Thursday. In 1872 he was Democratic candidate
for vice-president. (Maury Democrat, Columbia, TN, 23 Aug. 1894.)

ADAMS, Mrs. J. J., killed near Trezevant in her buggy while crossing
the railroad, at noon Sept. 30 when returning from Sunday School.
(Maury Democrat, 4 Oct. 1888.)

ADAMS, Lottie Putnam, wife of B. H. Adams, daughter of Col. A. W.
Putnam, died in Uniontown, Alabama, on the 8th. (Nashville Republican Banner, 9 Sept. 1868.)

ADAMS, E. W., old citizen of Nashville, died yesterday of flux. (Nashville Union and American, 21 June 1873.)

ADAMS, Capt. James W., born in Kentucky, died 30 March 1913, member of
UCV 1577, George E. Pickett Camp, Tacoma, Washington. (Confederate
Veteran Magazine, Oct. 1913, page 497.)

ADAMS, Mrs. Louis, 56, only woman who held commission in Confederate
Army, died Friday in New Orleans; native of England; she was married
1856 and her husband went into army; she organized relief association and was commissioned lieutenant in Confederate Army by Jefferson Davis. (Daily Herald, Columbia, TN, 3 Sept. 1901.)

ADCOCK, Jennie, three weeks old, funeral to be held today. (Nashville
Republican Banner, 21 April 1870.)

ADCOCK, Katy, died on the 7th on Leatherwood in Hickman County and
taken to Columbia, TN, for burial. (Columbia Herald, 18 July 1873.)
Mrs. Catherine Adcock, 78, died 7 July 1873; mother of Houston and
Ab Adcock. (Columbia Herald, 11 July 1873.)

ADCOCK, Marshal, a Union man of worth and respectability, living four miles north of Columbia on the Franklin turnpike, was shot by some of Forrest's men some days ago. His body remained five days unburied when his wife sent a negro man to search for him, and with his assistance only she buried her husband. (Nashville Daily Union, 5 March 1863.)

ADE, old man, his wife, children, and Rosa Morier of Paradise Ridge, Davidson County, were murdered March 1897 and their house burned. Thomas O'Bryant and George Newland, serving three years for cattle stealing in Cheatham County, have been indicted for this murder; robbery was the motive. (Daily Herald, 12 June 1900)

ADKISSON, Miss Pig, died 13 May 1877 in Maury County of consumption; she was buried beside her father; mother survives. (Columbia Herald and Mail, 22 June 1877)

AKIN, Caleb F. Eagan, 17 months, died on the 12th, son of Capt. M. and H. Akin, died in Nashville. (Nashville Dispatch, 14 Sept. 1862.)

AKIN, Aaron J., born 18 April 1801, died in Texas of congestive chill; came to Maury County early in his life; married Mary Caldwell; had son James Akin, who died as prisoner of war during Civil War; died on August 20 in Palestine, Texas. (Columbia Herald and Mail, 27 Aug. 1875)

AKIN, James, died a few weeks ago in Maury County of stroke of paralysis. (Memphis Daily Appeal, 22 April 1870)

AGEE, H. L., late editor of the Paris, TN, Republic, died in Paris on the 17th, age 22 years. (Nashville Daily Gazette, 1 Oct. 1852)

ALCOTT, Louisa M., instructed or directed in her will that all her manuscripts be burned. (Maury Democrat, 22 March 1888)

ALEXANDER, Mrs. J. N., 60, died Saturday in District 6, Maury County, and buried at Reese's Chapel. (Columbia Herald, 9 Jan. 1891)

ALEXANDER, Polly, has left bed and board of her husband John Alexander of Rutherford County. (Murfreesboro Courier, 7 Sept. 1827)

ALLEN, Lewis, 53rd Tennessee Regiment, CSA, died in prison at Indianapolis, July 7. (Nashville Dispatch, 15 July 1862)

ALLEN, General W. W., who has been buried in the Florence Cemetery for 23 years, was disinterred Wednesday and taken to Birmingham; he died 24 Nov. 1894 in Sheffield, Alabama; a child of his kinsman Wade Allen was also moved, the child being his grandchild. Wade Allen was in charge of the old North Alabama Furnace Company. (Florence, Ala., Times, 16 Feb. 1917)

ALLEN, Mrs. Maria, 83, died on the 3rd in Montgomery County, widow of William Allen; sister of A. B. Skelton; connected with the new Cumberland Presbyterian Church; lost her eyesight several years ago. (Erin Review, 8 Jan. 1887)

ALLEN, James M., 65, died Sunday in New Orleans, La., left Maury County about 40 years ago as a poor man, now very wealthy, and believed to be a millionaire; brother of John M. Allen of Maury County. (Columbia Herald and Mail 11 Jan. 1878) In his will he left $350,000; $222,250 to go to people in Maury County. (Columbia Herald and Mail, 18 Jan. 1878) James M. Allen, 63, died on the 6th; native of Maury; in 1836 settled in Yazoo County, Mississippi; in 1854 went to New Orleans. (Columbia Herald and Mail, 15 Feb. 1878)

ALLEN, Lt. Samuel M., formerly of Nashville, son of Joseph W. Allen of Nashville; fell victim to robbers and was murdered near home of Mr. Jamison about 12 miles from Memphis about 17 March 1864. (Nashville Daily Union, ___ March 1864.)

ALLEN, Rev. Van, and wife, of Iowa, were killed on board the steamer
Brazil near Donaldson, La., on 11 Dec. 1863, by a shot from a rebel
battery on shore as they were going South as teachers of and to freed-
men. (Nashville Daily Union, ___ Dec. 1863.)*

ALLEN, Horace, private, died at Huntsville, Alabama, about 13 April 1864
when a caisson of the 1st Illinois Battery exploded. (Nashville
Daily Union, ___ April 1864.)

ALLEN, Dr., an army surgeon in charge of one of the hospitals at Jackson,
Mississippi, committed suicide on 23 Oct. 1862 by inflicting three
wounds in his breast with a lancet. (Nashville Daily Union, 1 Nov.
1862.)

ALLEN, Mrs. Fannie E., wife of M. W., died yesterday in Nashville.
(Nashville Republican Banner, 29 Nov. 1870.)

ALLEN - In July 1865 Col. B. H. Payne shot and killed Capt. M. S. Allen
for "having various times had illicit intercourse with the former's
wife." She had obtained a divorce on 24 May 1865. She was his
second wife. He had divorced his first wife, a Kentucky lade; he
went to Texas during the Mexican War. (Nashville Republican Banner,
17 June 1868) Col. Payne was acquitted of the murder. (Nashville
Republican Banner, 24 June 1868)

ALLEN, Miles, died in Nashville. (National Intelligencer, 1 July 1833.)

ALLEN, George C., well-known broker of Nashville, died in Augusta, Ga.,
23 Jan. 1873. (Whig and Tribune, Jackson, TN, 1 Feb. 1873.)

ALLEN, William, was killed by Tobe Moore in Rutherford County a week or
two ago. (Paris, TN, Gazette, 30 May 1878.)

ALLEN, Dr. James H., funeral was held yesterday. (Nashville Union and
American, 24 Oct. 1874.) James H. Allen, 41, died on 22 Oct. 1874,
son of Mrs. Kate Allen. (Nashville Union and American, 23 Oct. 1874)

ALLEN, Mrs. Margaret R. M., formerly Mrs. John M. Kirby, died 7 Nov.
1874 in Edgefield, age illegible. (Nashville Union and American,
8 Nov. 1874.) (N. B., Edgefield is now East Nashville.)

ALLEN, William B., Lawrence County - "Capt. William B. Allen, of Lawrence County, who was killed in the late brilliant action at Monterey.
We hope our respect and friendship for that brave young officer, will
be considered a sufficient apology for the appearance of the above
Poem, though to say sooth, we would have wished the tribute had fallen
from an abler man. Signed, D. R. A." (N. B., Poem entitled Death of
Allen by David R. Arnell, published in paper.) (Columbia Beacon,
25 Nov. 1846.)

THE LAST LETTER OF WILLIAM B. ALLEN - Seralvo, Mexico, 14 Sept. 1846
My dear Parents,
I never wanted to see you so badly in my life--I arrived here yesterday with my company together with the 1st Regiment Tenn. Volunteers.
We leave here in the morning for Monterey. We are about 60 or 70
miles from Monterey and about the same distance from Camargo. They,
(the enemy) are fortifying the place. They are reported as being 10
or 12 thousand strong. Give my love to all my friends.

I have this day sent my resignation to the President, who appointed
me Quarter Master. The boys are unwilling to be commanded by any
body else. By the grace of God, I will try and lead them without
dishonor to victory.

*The term "rebel" in the papers published from 1861 to 1865 refers to
the Confederate Army as the majority of the newspapers available for
research were published by Union sympathizers.

I have a sword that was worn by my father, which shall not be dis-
honoured in my hands. Your son, Wm. B. Allen.
(Columbia Beacon, 25 Nov. 1846.)

(N. B., A Tennessee Historical Commission marker placed at the site
of Captain Allen in Lawrence County reads: "Allen's Stand. A stage-
coach tavern was kept here by Gen. Richard H. Allen, veteran of the
War of 1812. His son, Capt. William Allen, raised a company of
Lawrence countians for the Mexican War. He was killed, leading his
troops with his father's sword, at Monterey. He is buried in the
garden behind the house.")

"We learn from the Nashville papers of yesterday that the remains of
Capt. W. B. Allen, Peter H. Martin, Robt. W. Green, Julius C. Elliot,
and Inman Elliot, who fell at Monterey reached that place on the 9th
of this month. On yesterday they were taken to the First Presbyterian
Church, Nashville, where a funeral discourse was delivered by the
Rev. Dr. Edgar." (Columbia Beacon, 12 March 1847.)

"We learn from the Lawrenceburg Times that the remains of the late
Capt. W. B. Allen were consigned to their long resting place a few
days ago, at the residence of his father with becoming and appropriate
ceremonies. Two military companies and about 1000 of the friends of
the deceased were present on the occasion." (Columbia Beacon, 26
March 1847)

"Cornerstone to the Mexican War monument at Lawrenceburg to be laid
Sept. 21st. By order of the building committee the cornerstone of the
Monument to be laid is designed to enclose in a crypt, under the
column, copies of newspapers, documents, coins, lists of officers,
&c...The inscription is on the north face of the column as follows:
To the memory of Capt. Wm. B. Allen, J. B. Burkett, W. M. Alford,
F. Glover, W. Rhodes, G. W. Wilson, J. M. Campbell &c, of the
Lawrenceburg Blues, Company K, 1st Regiment Tennessee Volunteers, who
fell at the capture of Monterey, by the American Army under the command of Maj. Gen. Z. Taylor, and all Tennesseans who died of wounds
or disease, received or contracted during their service in the war
with Mexico. The monument will cost something about $1,500 which
is and is to be raised by contribution...(Columbia Weekly Recorder,
31 August 1849.)

Inscriptions made from the monument made in 1977: "Let Posterity
remember that the Valor of the Citizen Soldier scaled the Rocky
Mountains, Planted our eagles on the shores of the Pacific, Doubled
our Country's Area and opened a new Path to the commerce of Asia.
Erected by L. W. Kirby 1849. Rebuilt by Jas. E. Sloan Co. under the
resolution of the Gen. Assem. of Tenn., A. D. 1895 (South Side).

"Erected to the Memory of Capt. W. B. Allen, J. C. Burkitt, W. M.
Alford, F. Glover, W. Rhodes, A. J. Pratt, A. J. Gibson, A. J. Eaton,
Lt. L. M. Putman, J. H. Sanders, J. A. Hill, O. E. Porter, E. W.
Thomas, J. F. Coffee, A. D. Willis, J. C. Turner, D. H. Dolton, J. H.
Johnson, P. H. Martin, J. H. Elliot, B. Soaper, E. Prior, J. H. Alli-
son, H. Collins, W. H. Robinson, J. M. L. Campbell, of the 1st Regi-
ment Tennessee Volunteers who fell on the 21st Sep. 1846 at the Cap-
ture of Monterey. By the American Army under the command of Maj.
Gen. Z. Taylor and of all Tennesseans who died of wounds or diseases
received or contracted due to their service in the War with Mexico.
(North Side)

"Died of Diseases: S. H. Allen, A. Boswell, J. Dillingsly, J. Farris,
L. Garrett, J. Goodson, J. M. Gray, S. G. Keltner, M. W. Lindsey,
T. Tucker, J. W. Walker. How sleep the Brave who sink to rest by all
their Country's Wishes Blest. Lieut. G. H. Nixon died July 4th,
1887. (East Side)"

Daily Herald, 17 Sept. 1977: "When the Civil War was at its height
in this section, a troop of Federal soldiers invaded Lawrenceburg and
began shelling the courthouse and the downtown area. In the middle

of the firing, the major in command noticed the tall shaft on the
square and asked what it was. He was told that this was a monument
to Captain William B. Allen and his fallen comrades in the war with
Mexico, men who had died for the same flag that the major was serving. Immediately, the Federal leader ordered that the firing cease,
remarking that he had heard of Capt. Allen and his bravery at Monterey. The courthouse was saved from destruction and the Federals
entered the town without opposition..."

ALLEN, Samuel Houston, the brother of Wm. B. Allen, died in New Orleans
on his way home from the army. The state of his health rendered him
unable to perform the duties of a soldier, and he was honorably discharged from the service. He was unable to get farther than New Orleans and whilst there he heard of the death of his brother. Although
weak at the time the news reached him and he exclaimed, "I would
rather have died than to have heard that news. Oh, that I had not
been taken sick and had been by his side. I would rather have fallen
with my brother than to have died any other death." They have fallen
one with disease, and the other from a cannon ball, far away from
their father's house, in a strange land, but many have been the tears
shed over their graves...Both of them were members of the Cumberland
Presbyterian Church and were exemplary Christians." (Columbia
Beacon, 25 Nov. 1846.)

ALLENDER, William, old gentleman, who lived with Henry Hill family for
four years, died July 18 in Nashville of congestive chill; said he
was born and reared in Maryland and resided in Kentucky where he has
a brother living; nothin else known of his history. (Nashville
Dispatch, 20 July 1862.)

ALLENER, Frank, of Nashville, died on 21 June 1873 in San Francisco;
had gone west for his health. (Nashville Union and American, 23
June 1873)

ALLEY, Miss Emma, died of scarlet fever in Montgomery County. (Clarksville Weekly Chronicle, 3 Feb. 1860.)

ALLIN, Major Philip T., died on 25th in Memphis; member of 154th Regiment
CSA. (Memphis Daily Appeal, 25 Feb. 1870.)

ALLISON, Russell, of Putnam County, TN, shot and killed by disguised men
recently; one Braswell and brother are suspected. (Columbia Herald
and Mail, 24 Dec. 1875)

ALLISON, Mrs. Polly, 95, who died at her home hear Wingo, KY, last week
had a unique record; she was widow of War of 1812 soldier, who died
45 years go, and she had drawn a pension for 30 years; never had any
children, never joined a church, never cooked on a stove, and never
rode on a train. (Daily Herald, Columbia, TN, 17 Jan. 1902.)

ALLISON, Matthew, citizen of Knoxville, died a few days ago in military
prison at Alton, Illinois; had been arrested 6 or 8 weeks ago.
(Nashville Daily Union, 26 Feb. 1863.)

ALLISON, Major Alexander, funeral today in Nashville. He died on 3d at
the age of 63; was elected mayor in 1847 and accepted no salary while
mayor. (Nashville Dispatch, 4 Nov. 1862.)

ALLISON, Judge, killed by George K. Whitworth in Nashville. Whitworth,
until recently clerk and master, killed Chancellor Allison and then
himself. Allison appointed his own son clerk and master, and ousted
Whitworth. Judge Allison was buried Nov. 17 at Mt. Olivet and the
killing is the talk of the town. According to a letter left by Whitworth, the killing was over a shortage of funds--Allison had said he
did not run for office for the salary alone. (Maury Democrat, Columbia, TN, 15 Nov. 1894, 23 Nov. 1894, 29 Nov. 1894.)

ALLMAN, Major George T., of Cornersville, died a few days ago; a stock
man. (Columbia Herald and Mail, 18 April 1878.)

ALLRED, Mrs. John L., formerly of Williamsport, TN, died in Arkansas a few days ago of fever. (Columbia Herald, 1 March 1872.)

ALSTON, Skidmore, 85, died recently in Rolesville, NC, father of 24 children, and he had so many grandchildren he was never able to recognize them all. (Maury Democrat, Columbia, TN, 28 Feb. 1895.)

ALTMAYER, Conrad, funeral to be held today. (Nashville Republican Banner, 9 Oct. 1868.)

AMERICAN HORSE, a Canadian Indian, 65, has been laid to rest in Evergreen Cemetery in New York City. (Maury Democrat, 7 March 1895.)

AMES, Nathaniel, Revolutionary War soldier, died at home of his grandson in the town of Oregon, Daine Co., Wisconsin, on the 27th ultimo; age 102 years 4 months 2 days; served under Washington and was present at the execution of Andre; last Revolutionary War soldier in the state. (Nashville Daily Union 17 Sept. 1863.)

AMIS, Joe, killed at Williamsport, Maury County, TN, 1889 by H. E. Rucker, who got two years in penitentiary, being found guilty of manslaughter. (Columbia Herald, 30 Jan. 1891.)

AMIS, John, deceased, his estate is insolvent; Asa Hardison is executor. (Columbia Herald, 22 April 1870.)

AMIS, Mrs. Thomas, died in her 70th year; funeral preached Sunday in Culleoka Methodist Church, Maury County. (Columbia Herald and Mail, 8 March 1878.)

AMOS, Joseph, of Haywood County, TN, born 1760 in Virginia, is the oldest man in the state and lives near Bell's Depot. (Nashville Republican Banner, 22 Dec. 1868.)

ANDERSON, Willie Munford, 7, youngest daughter of Thompson Anderson, died Friday last. (Clarksville Weekly Chronicle, 1 March 1861.)

ANDERSON, Sam. "This community was deeply saddened on Tuesday last, by the announcement made about noon that a fight had occurred at the Fair Grounds, an hour or so before, between Bailey Brown and Sam Anderson, both of this city (Clarksville) in which Anderson was almost immediately killed. The circumstances of this painful affair, as reported by men who were on the spot, are as follows, and are, no doubt, correctly stated: Anderson and Brown both belonged to Capt. Forbes Company of Volunteers, which has been in camp at the Fair Grounds for some two weeks past, and Anderson had been acting as Provisional Orderly Sergeant of the corps. An election of permanent officers was held Tuesday morning, and, Mr. Anderson was elected Orderly Sergeant by a very large, if not an unanimous, vote. It has been both asserted and contradicted, that Mr. Brown was a candidate for this office. Whether this is true or not we cannot say.

"After the election, Brown indulged in certain ungenerous remarks respecting Anderson, and reflecting upon his character, which were reported to the latter and led to an altercation between them, in the course of which Anderson struck Brown with his fist, and knocked him down, and was, himself, down on him, when Brown stabbed him with a pocket knife twice, it is said--once in the side and again in the heart; and Anderson exclaiming, "I am stabbed to my heart, and am a dead man!" fell and in a few moments expired.

"Brown attempted to make his escape, but was taken by some of the camp officers, who, it is said, had to protect him from violence at the hands of some of Anderson's friends. He was brought into town and surrendered to the legal authorities; and on being taken before a Justice of the Peace, he waived an examination, and was held for appearance at Criminal Court in a bond of $2,000...he was discharged." (Clarksville Weekly Chronicle, 10 May 1861)

ANDERSON, General J. R., of Tredegar Iron Works, is mortally wounded. (Nashville Dispatch, 4 July 1862.) (N. B., Joseph Reid Anderson, known as "the Krupp of the Confederacy" survived this wound and died 7 Sept. 1892 and was buried in Hollywood Cemetery, Richmond, Va.)

ANDERSON, Andrew, 72, died Monday in Nashville; once mayor of Nashville and on city council for 20 years. (Memphis Avalanche, 21 Apr. 1867.)

ANDERSON, Col. Scott, brother of Major General Patton Anderson, died on the 25th ult. in Eagle Lake, Texas, also brother of Butler Anderson; formerly of Hernando, Mississippi; was colonel in CSA; died of congestive fever. (Memphis Daily Appeal, 13 Oct. 1868.)

ANDERSON, Thomas, 82, died 1 Oct. 1869 at home of son Van A. W. Anderson in Memphis. (Memphis Daily Appeal, 2 Oct. 1869.)

ANDERSON, Capt. Samuel S., CSA - Tribute of respect on his death published by Memphis bar. (Memphis Daily Appeal, 20 Feb. 1870.)

ANDERSON - $100 REWARD - on 25 April 1862, Marion Anderson, 30, 5 ft. 10 in., his brother Nathan Anderson, 22; Samuel Jones, 22; and Henry Noland, all in jail for crimes, broke jail in Bedford County and made their escape. Signed, R. B. Blackwell, sheriff. (Nashville Dispatch, 2 May 1862. N. B., Physical descriptions given on all these men.)

ANDERSON, Mrs. Hannah Jene, died 17 Jan. 1863 of pulmonary tuberculosis; wife of Robert S. Anderson; native of Columbia, KY; Baptist; married (1) Lindsay Watson in 1844 and lived in Tompkinsville, KY. He died in 1847 and left her with two children; she married 1850 to Mr. Anderson and they had four children. (Nashville Daily Union, __ Jan. 1863.)

ANDREWS, Jimmie, school boy, died recently at Rock Spring, Maury County. (Columbia Herald, 8 May 1885.)

ANDREWS - has been brought to Atlanta from Chattanooga; native of Hancock County, VA, where he was born 1829; lived in Fleming County, KY, and was to be married this month; he was leader of engine thieves and was launched into eternity yesterday. Item dated the 8th. (Nashville Dispatch, 26 June 1862.)

Tennessee Historical Commission highway marker, 1.8 miles east of Shelbyville, TN, has marker to ANDREWS' RAIDERS: "On this knoll, members of the Federal party which attempted to destroy the Western & Atlantic RR in 1862, assembled before starting their foray. It started with seizure of the engine "General" and ended with recapture of the engine at the Georgia state line the same day. Several of the party were subsequently hanged."

Nashville Tennessean Magazine, 12 Feb. 1956, "The Great Train Chase", by Hugh Walker, identifies this man as James J. Andrews, contraband runner and Federal spy. Andrews was tried by a Confederate military court in Chattanooga and sentenced to death as a spy. He made his escape from the jail but was recaptured and taken to Atlanta where he was hanged and buried in an unmarked grave. Years later, his body was moved to Chattanooga and buried with honor in the National Cemetery.

APPLEGATE, Elijah, "oldest man in Louisville and first white child born in the county" died yesterday at 93 years. (Nashville Union and American, 24 May 1874.)

ARCHER, Old Aunt Phoebe, of Washington County, TN, died on the 19th. (Nashville Union and American, 3 March 1873.)

ARGO, Mrs. Emma, funeral notice published in paper. (Nashville Republican Banner, 7 Sept. 1870.)

ARGO, Mrs. Julia M., died in Nashville on the 29th instant, age 45; Methodist. (Nashville Republican Banner, 1 Aug. 1869.)

ARMSTRONG, General Robert, his remains were deposited in their last
resting place at Nashville on Monday; died in Washington City last
spring. (Clarksville Jeffersonian, 17 Jan. 1855.)

ARMSTRONG, little daughter of James L. Armstrong, drowned this Thursday
at Fairfield; fell into a tub of water. (Nashville Republican
Banner, 1 Aug. 1868.)

ARMSTRONG, Col. Charles G., former citizen and member of the Memphis
bar, died a few days ago in Insane Asylum at Jackson, Miss.; he was
originally from Yalobusha County, Miss., and was in the legislature
before the war; commander of 17th Confederate Cavalry, severely
wounded and his wound never healed; practiced law in Memphis until
friends were forced to send him to asylum at Nashville, and since
removed to Jackson; died on the 28th ult. (Memphis Daily Appeal,
2 July 1869.)

ARMSTRONG, Samuel Henry, Sr., died Monday night of apoplexy near Ashwood in Maury County. (Columbia Herald, 3 Dec. 1869.) (N. B.,
his antebellum home, The Pines, is currently being restored by Mr.
and Mrs. Z. V. Jasaitis of Piedmont, California.)

ARMSTRONG, Captain, formerly of Knoxville, and another rebel Jenkins
were killed near Warrensburg a few days ago by the 18th Tennessee
Cavalry under Lt. Bibb. (Nashville Dispatch, 21 Feb. 1865.)

ARMSTRONG, Maria, late wife of General Frank Armstrong, daughter of the
late Col. Knox Walker, died in Springfield, Missouri, after a long
illness. (Columbia Herald, 30 August 1872.)

ARNOLD, Mrs. Margaret, 40, wife of policeman J. M. Arnold, died on the
9th of tuberculosis; native of Nashville. (Nashville Republican
Banner, 11 Aug. 1870.)

ARP, Hezekiah, nephew of the original Bill Arp, shot two men to death
near the state line in Fannah County, Ga., recently. (Florence, Ala.
Times, 29 Aug. 1891.) (N. B. Bill Arp (Charles Henry Smith) was
author and "benign cracker-barrel philosopher," who enlisted in 1861
in Confederate Army in Georgia.)

ARROWSMITH, William, 68, of Giles County, died of paralysis. (Whig
and Tribune, Jackson, TN, 5 Oct. 1872.)

ARTHUR, Hugh, old citizen of Baltimore, Maryland, died last week at 90
years, came from Londonderry, Ireland, in 1798; many of the finest
flouring mills in Baltimore and vicinity were built by him. He
aided Fulton in building the first steamboat and was with him on his
first trip up the Hudson. (Memphis Daily Appeal, 8 July 1869.)

ARTHUR - On the 2d ultimo, three young men, named Benjamin Arthur, Leonidas Bouris, and John K. Morris, of Company A, 5th Ohio Cavalry, went
outside the Federal pickets near Huntsville, Alabama, to visit several lady acquaintances. During the evening they were pounced upon by
a detachment of the enemy who summarily threw them all into a well,
and covered them up with about 12 feet of earth. After two days absence, a force went out in search of them, and found a well partially
filled with dirt. After digging down, they found the bodies of three
young men, and from a neighbor they learned the facts connected with
their death as above stated. One hundred and thirty-five dollars was
taken from one of the young men. All three of the young men were residents of Clarmont County, Ohio. (Nashville Daily Union, 16 March
1864.)

ASHBY, General Turner, who was killed in one of the recent battles in
Shenandoah Valley, was buried at Charlottesville, Va., on the 8th.
(Nashville Dispatch, 24 June 1862.) Ashby was leading a cavalry
charge near Harrisburg when killed. (Nashville Dispatch, 25 June
1862.) The remains of the famous General Ashby have been re-interred
at Winchester, Va., on Oct. 25. At the same time Capt. Richard
Ashby and Lt. Col. Thomas Marshall were placed in the soil they

loved until death. (Memphis Avalanche, 5 Nov. 1866.)

ASHWORTH, C. A., 53rd Tennessee Regiment, died July 3 as prisoner of
war in Indianapolis. (Nashville Dispatch, 15 July 1862.)

ATKINS, Miss Ion, only daughter of Peyton R. Atkins, of Pine Bluff,
Arkansas, died at the Clarksville Female Academy. (Clarksville
Weekly Chronicle, 18 March 1859.)

ATKINS, James, 18, son of J. and Virginia Atkins, died 12 July 1861
in Knoxville and brought back to Clarksville for burial; was in
Captain Lockhart's company, and was the first from Montgomery County
to die. (Clarksville Weekly Chronicle, 26 July 1861.)

AUDUBON, Mrs. John J., widow of the eminent naturalist, died in Shelbyville, KY, 18 June 1874; since his death she has lived with his
relatives in Kentucky. (Nashville Union and American, 20 June 1874.)

AUSTIN, Mrs. Mary Ann, 69, died 1 June 1868. (Nashville Republican
Banner, 2 June 1868.)

AUTEN, Mary, sister of William T. Auten, to be buried in Nashville this
afternoon. (Nashville Republican Banner, no date.)

AYRES, Bruce - it is rumored that Bruce Ayres, formerly of Williamsport
in Maury County was killed in West Tennessee a few days ago.
(Columbia Herald, 20 June 1873.)

B

BACH, Adam, was murdered in Wheeling, West Virginia, recently by Robert
Pool, who was found guilty of murder in the first degree. (Nashville
Dispatch, 26 Oct. 1862.)

BACIGALUPO, James, infant son of Vincent and Mary Bacigalupo, died
20 Feb. 1870. (Memphis Daily Appeal, 21 Feb. 1870.) Madame Vincent
Bacigalupo, who runs a restaurant featuring oysters, large attendance at her son's funeral. (Memphis Daily Appeal 23 Feb. 1870.)

BACIGALUPO, Antonio, 90, died on 12th in Memphis; father of Vincent
Bacigalupo. (Memphis Daily Appeal, 13 Aug. 1869.)

BACKUS - Two children, boys aged 11 and 12, son of Edward Backus of near
Boster, Maine, went fishing and did not come home; search was made
and their bones were found near a ledge of rocks long known as a
wolf's den; it was thought they were killed and eaten by wolves.
(Maury Democrat, Columbia, TN, 20 June 1889.)

BADGER, Mrs. John H., 87, died on 14th four miles north of Williamsport
in Hickman County; nee Nancy Beakley; survived by husband who is
91 years old; born 17 April 1792 while her parents were en route
from Virginia to Tennessee; married 28 Aug. 1811; Free Will Baptist.
(Columbia Herald and Mail, 24 March 1876, 7 April 1876.)

BADOUX, Frank, native of Switzerland, died yesterday after a brief illness; had lived on Union Street in Nashville 15 years; left a large
family. (Nashville Republican Banner, 4 Aug. 1870.)

BAILEY, William A., CSA, 51st Mississippi, died at hospital in Nashville between 1st and 15th of month. (Nashville Daily Union, 25 May
1865.)

BAILEY, Rupert, infant son of Robert S. and M. Bailey, died on the 21st.
Springfield and Holly Springs papers, please copy. (Nashville Union
and American, 22 Oct. 1874.)

BAILEY, Mrs. Elizabeth, widow of Jesse Baily, died 5 Jan. 1862 in Montgomery County. (Clarksville Weekly Chronicle, 10 Jan. 1862.)

9

BAILEY, Jesse, administrator's notice for him in paper. (Clarksville Weekly Chronicle, 23 Jan. 1857.)

BAILY, Col. W. C., of Macon, TN, was killed 10 April 1862, 4 miles east of Grand Junction when several railroad cars thrown from track while train was moving very fast. (Nashville Dispatch, 8 May 1862.)

BAIN, Fanny E., 16 months, daughter of John M. and Sarah L. Bain, died on the 5th in Nashville. (Nashville Republican Banner, 6 July 1870.)

BAIRD, Rev. Robert, D. D., well known author, preacher, traveller, and linguist, died at his home in Yonkers, NY, on 15th, age 65. (Nashville Daily Union, 24 March 1863.)

BAKEMAN, Daniel F., 106, last survivor of the Revolution, died 5 April 1869 in New York State. (Clarksville Leaf Chronicle, 15 Nov. 1901.)

BAKER, R. A., late of Clarksville, has died. (Nashville Republican Banner, 31 Oct. 1869.)

BAKER, Johnnie, infant son of L. D. and Lamira D. Baker, funeral to be held today in Nashville. (Nashville Dispatch, 16 May 1862.)

BAKER, S. E., of Company E, 44 Indiana Volunteers, was killed near Cleveland, TN, in railroad accident; Asa Bills, Company B, had leg broken in same accident. (Nashville Daily Union 3 Feb. 1865.)

BAKER, Samuel, aged, of Rhea County, TN, died last week. (Memphis Daily Appeal, 8 June 1870.)

BAKER, Van Buren - Anyone who knows the fate of Van Buren Baker, formerly of Cass County, GA, but who was living in Marion County, Ark. at the beginning of the war, will greatly oblige his distressed relatives by communicating such fact to G. W. Baker, Rome, GA. He was in Confederate cavalry in the Trans-Mississippi Department in the war and has not been heard from since. (Memphis Daily Appeal, 4 June 1869.)

BAKER, Captain, a "gentle" man died yesterday in Memphis. (Memphis Avalanche, 18 Jan. 1866.)

BAKER, J. M., 96, died recently in Gibson County; old and prominent citizen. (Maury Democrat, 21 Aug. 1890.)

BAKER, Pitts, son of J. W. Baker, of Baker's Station, killed when he fell from train; member of the Pale Faces; buried at Baker's Station. (Nashville Republican Banner, 16 Feb. 1869.)

BAKER, Giles, shot fatally by Alexander Donelson in Old Hickory, TN; Donelson is grand-nephew of Mrs. Andrew Jackson; the Baker buggy was demolished by Donelson and they quarreled over it; he was shot several times, one time in the head. (Daily Herald, Columbia, TN, 23 March 1900.)

BAKER, John, ex-sheriff of Hickman County, is very low of cancerous affection of left eye and head. (Columbia Herald, 11 April 1873.) John Baker, ex-sheriff of Hickman County, died 24 July 1873 at Shady Grove of cancer of head. (Columbia Herald, August 1873.)

BALES, Mr. and Mrs., of Seville, Ohio, just measure 8 feet in height each, or 16 feet between them. It is said that the China giant Chang has become jealous of them and has quit the U. S. in disgust. (Erin Review, 17 Dec. 1881.)

BALL, Stephen F. -- Information wanted on Stephen F. Ball, Orderly Sergeant, Company G, 22d Regiment Wisconsin Infantry, said to be sick in one of the hospitals in Nashville. (Nashville Daily Union, 17 April 1863.)

10

BALLARD, Milton J., 54, died on 2d at Covington, TN. (Memphis Daily Appeal, 10 Aug. 1869.)

BALLARD, John, tribute of respect to him on his death by Lodge 89 AL 5861. (Clarksville Weekly Chronicle, 8 Feb. 1861.)

BALLEW, Leonard G., jailor of Williamson County, was seized by an attack of vertigo, fell, struck his head against table, and broke his neck. (Whig and Tribune, Jackson, TN, 9 Aug. 1873.)

BALLINGER, David, bugler to Capt. Allison's company of cavalry from Smith County, "The American Guards", died of short illness of fever on the 2d instant at Camp Carroll. (Tennessee Democrat, Columbia, TN, 23 July 1846.)

BAMBER, John, an old soldier and member of GAR, died 24 Nov. 1889 in Lakeview Hotel, Peoria, Ill. No one seems to know him. (Maury Democrat, Columbia, TN, 28 Nov. 1889.)

BANCROFT, George, the venerable historian, is reported as seriously ill and near the close of his life. (Florence, Ala., Times 7 Nov. 1890.)

BANG, Ella, 18, young daughter of William F. and Jane Bang, died on the 26th. (Nashville Republican Banner, 27 Feb. 1870.)

BANKHEAD, James, old and well known, died yesterday of violent attack of jaundice; native of Ireland; came to Nashville at 16 years of age and before the war was successful merchant; funeral to be at the Cathedral. (Nashville Union and American, 21 June 1873.)

BANKHEAD, General Smith P., born Fort Moultrie, S.C., 28 Aug. 1823, died 31 March 1867 in Memphis; CSA general; editor of the Whig; was brutally beaten on sidewalk in Memphis and died 25 hours later; was buried Elmwood Cemetery. (Memphis Avalanche, 2 April 1867.)

BANKHEAD, Mrs. Ada Clark, wife of late General Smith F. Bankhead, died 26 Feb. 1873 in Charlottesville, VA; buried in Memphis at Elmwood Cemetery on 1 March 1873. (Nashville Union and American, 3 Mar. 1873.)

BANGS, Rev. Nathan, one of the fathers of American Methodism, died at his home in New York on the 3d instant. (Nashville Dispatch, 6 May 1862.)

BANKSTER, Theodore Hicks, 13, died 3d instant of pneumonia in Clarksville. (Clarksville Weekly Chronicle, 6 Sept. 1861.)

BAPTISTE, Mary Ann, died at Prairie du Chien Friday, aged 129 years. (Memphis Daily Appeal, 22 Feb. 1869.)

BARBER, W. T., deceased; E. A. Land appointed guardian of Martha, Mary, Fannie, Joseph, and Jacob Barber, minor children of W. T. Barber. (Linden Times, 5 Feb. 1880.)

BARFIELD, Dr. W. B., died 1 March 1873. (Columbia Herald, 7 March 1873.)

BARHAM, John A., 2d lieutenant, Company I, 13th Tennessee Regiment, Preston Smith's Brigade, CSA, drowned on the 9th at Frankfort, KY, while bathing in river; seized with a cramp; native of Henderson Co., Tennessee. (Nashville Dispatch, 26 Sept. 1862.)

BARHAM, William, and Thomas Elbeck, were murdered in Williamson County on Sunday last by persons unknown. (Nashville Daily Gazette, 26 Feb. 1850) Elbeck and Barham were severely cut; one in heart which caused instant death. (Nashville Daily Gazette, 27 Feb. 1850.)

BARINDA, Edward, of Memphis, old citizen, will revisit Russia, his native country. (Memphis Daily Appeal, 17 May 1870.)

BARKER, James S., of Missouri, is the sole survivor of an expedition formed in 1847 for the relief of General Zachary Taylor in Mexico

City; he rode from Missouri to Austin, Texas, to enlist in Capt. Hayes' regiment. (Daily Herald, Columbia, TN, 28 Aug. 1900.)

BARKLEY, Oscar Judson, died 13 July 1877, age 31; ate hearty meal, then lapsed into unconsciousness; born in North Carolina; at the age of 5 months moved to Florida; in March 1868 came to Maury County; 1870 he married Fannie Gray. (Columbia Herald and Mail, 27 July 1877.)

BARKSDALE, Thomas W., resolution of respect on his death passed by Lodge 89 in Clarksville. (Clarksville Weekly Chronicle, 29 Oct. 1857.)

BARKSDALE, Mrs. Sarah W., 30, wife of T. W., died on THursday in Clarksville. (Clarksville Jeffersonian, 24 August 1844.)

BARMORE, Seymour.
"Feb. 20.--A Negro called on Major Fredericks, commander of detachment stationed at Columbia and told him that the dead body of a white man had been found 2½ miles SW from Columbia and he sent a squad to the spot; proved to be Barmore, who was taken from train at Columbia a month ago by masked men; there was rope around neck, the end of it forming a noose. His hands tied back with linen handkerchief...and a valuable diamond ring was on one finger..." (Memphis Daily Appeal, 22 Feb. 1869, Monday.)

Barmore was killed by a pistol shot through top of head after having been shot, his hands were tied behind him...KKK rig was found in his carpet sack. (Memphis Daily Appeal, 26 Feb. 1869.)

Estate of Seymour Barmore being settled. (Nashville Republican Banner, 7 Feb. 1869.)

A business letter to the Banner from Columbia, under the date of the 13th, states that the writer visited the depot that morning, but he could not discover any of the tracks of the horses said to have been heard tramping the earth and champing their bits by fellow passengers of Barmore on train, the morning that he was removed.

Yesterday the body of an unknown man was found floating in Duck River about 12 miles below Columbia. The Coroner of Maury County started from Columbia for the purpose of holding an inquest over the corpse. It was not expected that he would return to Columbia before this morning, and we have, therefore, no means of knowing whether the body found, has been identified as that of the lost detective.

Barmore had received a notice to go to Pulaski and had remarked, "I hate to make this trip; I do not like to go out there and leave my business; though, if I do not, the Negro will not be convicted, because I have the evidence in my own hands..." (Nashville Republican Banner, 15 Jan. 1869.)

Captain Seymour Barmore, before his extraordinary abduction from a railway train by the Tennessee Kuklux was a man who had made some little reputation as a detective and a great deal more as a dead beat, but the unpleasant little circumstances which is alleged to have recently happened to him may send his name down in history as one of the martyrs and the mystery which enshrouds his fate will draw the sympathy of at least all who did not know him. It was, at any rate, bad taste in the Kuklux to make a martyr of Seymour Barmore, or to meddle with him in any way.

Poor Barmore. The kicks and cuffs he has received on all hands during his career as a detective, whether deserved or not, was enough to have made a misanthrope of the best man that ever lived.

People seemed to think he had no business to live, and even now that he is dead--or supposed to be--they are not willing to let him rest.

12

The New Albany Commercial which applauded the Indiana Kuklux yesterday gave Barmore a parting kick. It did up his obituary in a hurry.
It says of him: "Barmore the detective captured by the Tennessee
Kuklux is the man in velvet, and a great humbug. It's hard to tell
which has the worst of the bargain--the detective or the Kuklux.
Barmore figured around New Albany until his trunk was sold to liqui-
date an unpaid board bill."

Some time ago a reporter in Madison, Indiana, worked up a story about
Barmore which might or might not have been true. There was an injured female in the case, and the odium which this publication brought
upon him no doubt had much to do with his emigration to Tennessee.
He went to Nashville about the time of its capture by the valorous
Joe Blackburn and the debut of the Radical Metropolitan Police. It
was said he had an eye to a position on the police force, but this he
never received and some of the Metropolitans were proverbially down
on Barmore from their first sight of him.

Some of Barmore's enemies subsequently fabricated a story of his seizure by the Kuklux and of his initiation into the padlock degree.
The story was generally believed, and brought him into ridicule,
though there was not a word of truth in it, as, on the night it was
said to have occurred, he was in Nashville. Altogether the man in
velvet led a very unenviable life, and if the Kuklux have really had
to do with his taking off, they only freed a poor persecuted soul
that will cry out to God against them in the day to come. Louisville
Courier-Journal. (Nashville Republican Banner, 17 Jan. 1869.)

Detective S. Barmore's gold-headed cane, which has been stored in the
baggage room of the Decatur depot since the night of his mysterious
abduction, has been attached for debt.

Letter from Coroner of Maury County, date 18 Jan. 1869:
Dear Sir--Having seen in your two or three last issues a statement
relative to the Coroner of Maury County holding an inquest over the
supposed body of one Barmore, etc., now I beg leave to say that your
informants were in error as to my going to Williamsport to hold an
inquest, or being sent for to do so. I have not held an inquest over
anyone in the last three months, and as to the report about Barmore
being taken from the cars, I strongly suspect from all that I can
learn, that the whole thing has been adroitly conceived for purposes
to answer the ends of persons in no way connected with a klan called
Kuklux, but by evil minded persons to answer their own ends. These
reports are well calculated to do us a county much injury, and I hope
to see the day when men and parties can effect their purposes without
circulating stories of murders and assassinations said to have taken
place in this county. I have been Coroner of Maury County now for
four years, and will here state that I have held in that time but four
inquests upon the bodies of persons supposed to have been killed by
the so-called Kuklux Klan, and there were doubts as to who killed two
of them. The murderer of Bicknell was hung by persons in disguise
(from fifty to one hundred in number) some of whom I saw in town the
night of the hanging. A negro by the name of Raney, for attempting
to murder a white man, was also hung by parties in disguise. Of the
other two, there are many doubts as to who killed them. They were
all bad men. Respectfully, Wm. Wood, Coroner, M. C.
P.S. I believe that Barmore will turn up when it suits his purpose
to do so to serve the ends of his employers.
(Nashville Republican Banner, 20 Jan. 1869.)

THE QUIET TAKING OFF OF A DETECTIVE NAMED BARMORE.--One of the most
quiet killings that ever occurred in this county (Maury) was the
killing of a Federal detective named Barmore. As little is known at
this day, as then, of the particulars of the killing, I have never
had the least hint of the name of any participants in the affair.

The first intimation of the occurrence among our citizens was the
receipt of two dispatches from the city, one of John A. Engle, then

Mayor, and the other to your writer from Major Henry Heiss, requesting me to furnish him with full details of the capture. The dispatches were received between 4 and 5 p.m.

When I received mine, I passed it to W. M. Street, now of Murfreesboro, and asked if he knew anything of it. He replied that he did not. I then called upon Mayor Engle, who informed me that he was in receipt of a similar telegram, but he knew nothing. I then called on Black Thompson, and he knew nothing. While talking to the latter, Len Davy, then engineer of the Columbia accommodation, had just arrived from Nashville and informed us that it was the topic in the city (Nashville).

The facts as they developed were about as follows: Barmore was on his way on a morning train to Pulaski, which train stopped here for a short while, and it was said he had a conversation with J. B. Woodside and R. H. Jamison, with whom he was acquainted and to whom he said he was after a negro on charge of larceny.

In reply to the question of his return, he stated perhaps not for several days, but he started on his return the same night arriving here about midnight. When the train stopped, one or more took charge of the conductor, Thomas Moore, now in Texas. Others passed through the cars, jabbing the passengers with their pistols to arouse them, all being in slumber, among whom was Mr. Nelson of Murfreesboro, who remarked on awaking that he was not the person they were looking for. This remark placed suspicion upon him of having some knowledge of whom they were searching for. He was arrested, but very soon released.

They finally reached Barmore and informed him "that he was the man they were after." He insisted, it is said, on taking his valise with him, but was assured that he would have no further use for it, and he did not take it with him. They took him out of the rear and to the opposite side of the cars from the one on which passengers alight. They came up on the same side, being the south side, and departed the same way.

Barmore's valise was taken off at Nashville, where it was opened and said to have contained a full suit of Kuklux garments. It was said that he publicly avowed in Nashville that he intended to capture some of the klan and secure the reward of $500 offered by Gov. W. G. Brownlow.

Many weeks after his body was found in Duck River, near the railroad bridge by a fisherman. There was a rope around the neck to which a heavy stone or rock was attached. His remains were brought in town and placed in the hearse-house of Lamb and Boyd, now owned by F. H. Smith, when an examination was made by the surgeon of the 14th Michigan, assisted by Dr. H. S. Cox, which examination showed that a bullet entered the top of his head and passed through his head and lodged in the body below the neck.

Coroner Wm. Wood held an inquest, making a very thorough investigation. Among others examined was a Mr. Wilbert, a Northern man and telegraph operator, who testified no dispatchers had passed over the wire indicating Barmore's return from Pulaski.

The verdict was, "Came to his death by unknown hands," being certainly a true verdict to all except those who participated in the killing. (Signed) Wm. J. Andrews. (Nashville Banner, 26 March 1897.)

From Secretary Fletcher's testimony given before the Reconstruction Committee in Congress in 1870: In 1869 Capt. Barmore was taken from the train at night at the Columbia depot, by men in mask, and a month afterward his body was found in Duck River, his head and body perforated with bullets, a rope about his body which had been fastened to a stone. When the conductor on the train returned to Nashville,

he told the particulars of his taking off the train, as did the
engineer and other attaches of the train, but they subsequently
denied all knowledge of the case. The newspapers at Nashville made
merry over this case, and said Barmore ran away. Barmore was a
detective, and was said to have designs to ferret out the secrets
of the Ku Klux. (Columbia Herald, 13 April 1870.)

DO YOU REMEMBER WHEN - When Barmore, the great Yankee detective, was
killed by the Ku Kulx on the site of the old lime kiln on the banks
of Duck River? Our informant saw his body later at Noah's Ark
(i.e. store) on South Main Street and recalls that Barmore was sent
from Washington to spy into the activities of the Ku Klux Klan, a
powerful organization at that time. He, it is said, succeeded in
joining the order at Pulaski and in getting the desired information
as well as the names of the leaders. The South was infested with
Yankees at that time. The story goes on, upon accomplishing his
mission, Barmore went to the telegraph office in Pulaski and wired
Washington of his success and advised them that he was leaving on
an evening train. The telegraph operator seems to have been a klans-
man, as were all good men in those days, and thus was Barmore's down-
fall. The operator wired the klan in code to meet the
train at Columbia and take charge of Mr. Barmore. Three men entered
the car and escorted the detective from the train and thence to the
river bluff where he was relieved of the papers and given a chance to
utter a prayer. Whereupon his body was riddled with bullets. The
episode was devoid of excitement and ended the chapter. (Maury
Democrat, Columbia, TN, 5 Nov. 1931.)

BARNER, Capt. Sterling M., 71, died on the 21st ult. at Smithland, KY.
(Nashville Dispatch, 9 July 1862.)

BARNER, Mary E., 21, daughter of late Capt. S. M. Barner of Smithland,
KY, died 1 Dec. 1862 of typhoid; graduate of Nashville Female Academy.
(Nashville Daily Union, 2 Dec. 1862.)

BARNES, Alfred, 98, died in Mexico, Missouri, today; had been a Mason
for 75 years and is said to be the oldest member of the order in the
world. (Maury Democrat, 6 May 1888.)

BARNES, Mrs. Sarah, 82, widow of John Barnes, died 29 Oct. 1871 in
Williamson County. (Whig and Tribune, 11 Nov. 1871.)

BARNES, Mrs. Nettie, wife of John W. Barnes, died on 19th in Columbia;
buried at Zion; daughter of A. M. Wingfield. (Columbia Herald,
21 March 1873, 28 March 1873.)

BARNES, John F., 58, died in Warm Springs, Virginia, while visiting his
sons in the army; inflammation of the stomach; died 1 Dec. 1861;
Baptist; buried Trinity Cemetery, Montgomery Co., TN. (Clarksville
Weekly Chronicle, 13 Dec. 1861.)

BARNES, W. W., 60, of Verona, Marshall County, drowned in Duck River at
Lillard's Mill while attempting to cross river and boat was drawn
against the dam by a strong current. (Columbia Herald, 17 April
1891, 24 April 1891.)

BARNES, Major General James R., of Springfield, Mass., died Monday; he
was native of Mass.; graduate of West Point in 1829 along with Gen.
Robert E. Lee and Gen. Joe Johnston; commanded the 18th Massachusetts
in the Army of the Potomac in 1862; commanded the 5th Army Corps;
brigadier general in 1863; retired to private life and was special
commissioner of Union Pacific Railroad. (Memphis Daily Appeal,
18 Feb. 1869.)

BARNETT, Charles, colored septagenarian, died Saturday of congestive
chill; he was a hack driver in Nashville for quarter of a century;
his was one of the largest funeral processions ever in Nashville.
(Nashville Daily Union, 23 Dec. 1862.)

BARNETT, Benjamin, of Memphis, died at Bailey Springs at Florence, Ala., on 28 Dec. 1868 of dropsy. (Memphis Daily Appeal, 1 Jan. 1869.)

BARR, Mrs. Ida, wife of A. E. Barr, died in Edgefield yesterday; her remains sent to Brooklyn for interment. (Nashville Union and American, 8 July 1874.)

BARR, Martha, rumor says she has committed suicide...notorious character; had been a wanderer; no friend, no home. (Columbia Herald and Mail, 28 May 1875.)

BARROW, Mrs. Patsy, daughter of John Childress and wife Nancy Hickman, was born 30 Oct. 1789 in Nashville and married 3 July 1808 to Matthew Barrow, who died 28 May 1855. She was one of those who attended the Claiborne reunion in 1869. (Nashville Republican Banner, 17 Feb. 1869.)

BARROW, Alexander, 38, of Louisiana, died of yellow fever at Homestead Plantation, West Baton Rouge, La.; nephew of Washington Barrow of Nashville and son-in-law of Sterling R. Cockrell of Nashville. (Nashville Republican Banner, 5 Dec. 1867.)

BARROWS, Washington, 98, died in county poorhouse in Nashville on Saturday; drove the stage between Louisville and Nashville; was the last survivor of those who drove stages. (Clarksville Leaf Chronicle, 8 Nov. 1901.)

BARRY, Henry Baldwin, died 14 April 1868 of inflammaton of brain; son of Priscilla Jane and John W. Barry, age 11 months 3 weeks. Editor expresses sympathy to family who "four times have been called upon to mourn the loss of their offspring at nearly a similar age." (Nashville Republican Banner, 15 April 1868.)

BARRY, Mrs. Frances, 72, wife of late John Barry, died May 24 in Dublin, Ireland. (Nashville Daily Union 21 June 1865.)

BARRY, James T., 45, died on the 18th at his brother-in-law's James L. Haynes, Esq., of Lebanon; was in Mexican War under Capt. Cheatham and also in Confederate Army in Wheeler's Cavalry. (Nashville Republican Banner, 20 Feb. 1869.)

BARRY, Miss Annie, of Stewart County, hanged herself a few days ago; insane; "amiable and beautiful." (Nashville Republican Banner, 27 Aug. 1869.)

BARRY, John G., 84, a printer, who in 1800 set up announcement of the death of George Washington, took part in the funeral of a Mr. Barrett at Holly Springs, Mississippi, recently. (Memphis Daily Appeal, 26 May 1870.)

BARRY, Nancy Harriet, 25 months 21 days, daughter of John W. and P. J. Barry, died Oct. 31 in Nashville. (Nashville Dispatch, 1 Nov. 1862.)

BARTLEY, Joe, son of A. W. Bartley of Wayne County, resolution of respect on his death published in paper. (Hohenwald Chronicle, 15 Dec. 1899.)

BARTON, Clara, goes to her reward, dies at home, Red Cross, in Glen Echo, Maryland, age 90, on 12 April 1912. (Maury Democrat, 18 April 1912.)

BARTON, Mrs. Thomas, died at home of W. C. Sellars on Knob Creek in Maury County Monday at 73 years; mother of C. W. Irvine and was buried in old Irvine Cemetery. (Columbia Herald, 16 Jan. 1891.)

BARTON, Jo., cut throats of his wife and three children; the murder took place before daylight on Sunday; lived on Clarksville Pike near Nashville; formerly of Clarksville. (Nashville Republican Banner, 23 Nov. 1869.)

BASKETTE, Col. Gideon P., leading merchant of Shelbyville, died at his home a few days ago. (Nashville Union and American 3 March 1873.)

BASS, Mrs. Nicey, 81, mother of H. C. Bass, died in Shelbyville last week. (Whig and Tribune, Jackson, TN, 20 July 1872.)

BASS, Dr. William, of Nashville, son of John M. Bass, who has been connected with guerrilla parties in this area, has met a violent death. Soldiers guarding the home of Mrs. General Harding in the country fired on the guerrillas of Bass's, he attempted to escape and was shot. (Nashville Daily Union, 3 Oct. 1862.) Dr. William J. Bass was killed Thursday; son-in-law of William Watkins; arrested by the Federals and attempted to escape, he ran and guard shot and killed him; son of John M. Bass, who is in the south on his plantation. (Nashville Dispatch, 3 Oct. 1862.) William James Bass, 32, died 2 Oct. 1862. (Nashville Dispatch, 8 Oct. 1862.)

BASS, John D., deceased, notice published to Nancy Jane Bass, Mary Duke Gilford Bass and the children of John D. Bass, deceased, living in West Tennessee, all are heirs of John Y. Smith of Wilson County and they are to appear and receive their portion of estate. (Nashville Daily Union, 15 March 1865.)

BASS, Mr., of Kentucky Central railroad division, division overseer, was struck by lightning near Demasville, Pendleton Co., Ky. on Saturday during a thunderstorm and was instantly killed. (Memphis Avalanche, 7 Nov. 1866.)

BATEMAN, Capt. Morgan M. died yesterday; pioneer boatman and was among the first settlers on the Bluff, steamboating for 20 years. At the breaking out of war, he raised a cavalry company at Jacksonport, Arkansas, and served in Trans-Mississippi department, and came out of the war penniless. (Memphis Daily Appeal, 24 April 1870.)

BATES, Alexander, of Bolivar, Missouri, claims to be 120 years old and has applied for pension for service in Mexican War; enlisted 1845 at Lexington, Missouri; came to U. S. in 1812 with General Pakenham and was with General Gibbs when he was killed and fought at New Orleans against Andrew Jackson; later became naturalized citizen. (Maury Democrat, 1 July 1915.)

BATTLE, Joel A. - At the battle of Shiloh, Joel A. Battle, Jr., son of Gen. Joel A. Battle, was killed; on his person was a plain gold watch, bearing his name engraved on the shield. A Federal soldier got possession of it and sold it to Col. W. H. Heath of the Federal Army. This gentleman met General Battle and learning from him the real ownership of the watch, returned it to him. (Memphis Daily Appeal, 29 June 1869.) Joel A. Battle, ex-Treasurer of Tennessee, was sent to Military Prison yesterday until further orders on charge of treason. (Nashville Daily Union 1 June 1865.) Joel A. Battle, Jr., son of Col. Joel Battle of the City Hotel, was killed 7 April 1862 at Shiloh; also had brother killed in war; was adjutant in father's regiment; left wife in Ohio to serve; lawyer. (Nashville Republican Banner, 22 June 1869.)

BATTLE, Col. William M., died at his residence near this place on the 18th of the month and last day of year; a man of exalted worth. (Nashville Daily Gazette, 29 Jan. 1850.)

BATSON, Thomas H., Esquire, 62, died of apoplexy on Monday in Clarksville. W. B. and Smith Batson were his administrators. (Clarksville Weekly Chronicle, 22 Nov. 1861.)

BATSON, Theodore Hicks, 31, died on 3d; husband, father, and brother; tribute of respect by rifle company at Camp Mills. (Clarksville Weekly Chronicle, 13 Sept. 1861.)

BAUER, G. P., In Memoriam published by Typographical Union in the paper. (Nashville Republican Banner, 31 March 1870.)

BAUGH, James, private, Company K, 5th Tennessee Cavalry (Federal) was killed 22 Feb. 1864 on Calf Killer near Sparta, TN. (Nashville Daily Union, ___ Feb. 1864.)

BAXTER, Mrs. James, died Christmas; widow. Isom news. (Columbia Herald and Mail, 12 Jan. 1877.)

BAXTER, Mrs. Nancy, wife of Joseph Baxter, of near Caledonia, Henry Co., TN, stricken with paralysis last week and there is no hope of her recovery. (Whig and Tribune, 21 Dec. 1872.)

BAXTER, John Ewen, infant son of Edmund and Eliza P. Baxter, died on the 8th instant. (Nashville Union and American, 9 Sept. 1874.)

BAYNE, Sarah, 4, died 19 June 1862; funeral to be at home of John Q. Dodd. (Nashville Dispatch, 20 June 1862.)

BEACH, G. C. Tobett, 10½ days, died on 17th, son of W. J. and Emma Lou Beach. (Nashville Republican Banner, 18 June 1869.)

BEADLE, Mr., wealthy man of Humboldt, piloted a party of Jackson's cavalry to a bridge. A slave of his went to Federals and told them. His house was burned as well as those of four others taken with him and he was hanged on 29 July 1862 at Trenton. (Nashville Dispatch, 3 Aug. 1862.)

BEALL, Malvina Grundy, youngest daughter of William N. R. and P___ Beall, died in St. Louis on Sunday the 28th; infantile bronchitis. (Nashville Republican Banner, 6 April 1869.)

BEAN, M. L., of Crittendon, Arkansas, says he is only living son of Russell Bean, first white man born in Tennessee. (Memphis Daily Appeal, 31 Aug. 1869.)

BEAN, Hannah Elizabeth, 16 years 19 days, daughter of Joseph W. and Mary Ann Bean, born 3 Aug. 1853, died 12 Aug. 1869, Maury County. (Columbia Herald, 17 Sept. 1869.)

BEAN, Samuel, died 1836 in Mississippi; was first jailor of Hickman County. (Hickman Pioneer, Centerville, TN, 22 Feb. 1878.)

BEARD, Capt. David R., 85, died of dropsy Wednesday night, wealthy citizen of Hopkinsville, Kentucky. (Maury Democrat, 4 Nov. 1899.)

BEARD, Justice William D., of the Supreme Court, dropped dead in the lobby of the Hermitage Hotel on 7 Dec. 1910, Confederate veteran, to be buried in Memphis. (Daily Herald, 7 Dec. 1910.)

BEARD, Lewis M., of Campbell County, TN, is amongst the prisoners in Castle Thunder, an old man and is gradually sinking under his sufferings; has 5 sons and 8 grandsons in the Federal Army; prisoners here suffer much and in need of food. (Nashville Daily Union, 9 Dec. 1863)

BEARD, Thomas, deceased, estate insolvent in Maury County. (Columbia Herald and Mail 19 Feb. 1875.)

BEASLEY, Charles M., infant son of George H. and S. F. Beasley, died yesterday. (Nashville Republican Banner, 21 July 1869.)

BEATY, C. M., died Tuesday the 21st; brother of William Beaty of South Nashville. (Nashville Republican Banner, 23 Jan. 1868.)

BEATY, John, 83, died yesterday, well known citizen; born in County Dungannon, Ireland; come to U. S. when he was 14; lived in New York four or five years, moved to Lexington, KY, where he resided until 1820; then came to Nashville; lived here 55 years; had considerable fortune; buried City Cemetery today. (Nashville Union and American, 3 Dec. 1874.) Mr. Beaty came to Nashville in 1820; Jacob McGavock came in 1808; Joseph Vaulx came in 1818; James Woods came in 1815; Francis B. Fogg came in 1817; James B. Knowles came in 1817; Willoughby Williams came in 1815; M. M. Howard came in 1818; Samuel Watkins was then a grown man having been born and reared in Nashville. (Nashville Union and American, 6 Dec. 1874.)

BEATY, James W., of Trace Creek, Lewis County, died on the 18th of consumption. (Linden Times, 1 July 1880.)

BEAUMONT, Thomas. The remains of Col. Thomas Beaumont and Capt. George Williams of the 50th Tennessee Regiment, who fell at Chickamauga, were reinterred at Clarksville yesterday. (Memphis Daily Appeal, 26 Aug. 1868.)

BEAUMONT, Capt. Frank S., died 9 Oct. 1861 in Warm Springs, Virginia, Captain of Company H, 14th Regiment of Volunteers; survived by widow and children. (Clarksville Weekly Chronicle, 10 Oct. 1861.)

BEAUREGARD, P. G. T. In 1960 there was a bronze tablet in the tomb of Army of Tennessee in vault 10 at Metaire Cemetery, New Orleans, La., which had the following inscription on it: P. G. T. Beauregard, General, CSA, born in the Parish of St. Bernard, La., 28 May 1818, died in the city of New Orleans, 20 Feb. 1893. (N. B., Some say that his remains were removed from this tomb many years ago, but no one knew where he was reburied. (However, reputable scholars on the Civil War believe that he is still entombed in vault 10.)

BECK, Mrs. Judith, of Turnbull Creek, Dickson County, is 91 years old, being born 7 Sept. 1796; mother of 11 children, 42 grandchildren, 99 great-grandchildren and 1 great-great-grandchild; she remembers all of them by name and can give their age; remarkably preserved lady. (Houston County News, 14 Oct. 1887.)

BECK, George, compositor of the Nashville Union and American, died yesterday at 4 o'clock in North Nashville. (Nashville Union and American 9 May 1873.) George Beck, well known Nashville printer died May 8 age 45. (Whig and Tribune, Jackson, TN, 17 May 1873.)

BECK, Mrs. Eliza A., wife of George, died 7 Feb. 1864 at 35 years. (Nashville Daily Union, 8 Feb. 1864.)

BECKUM, Abe, died at home in Texas recently; reared in Mt. Joy, Maury Co. area; moved to Texas about 8 years ago. (Columbia Herald, 6 Feb. 1891.) Abe Beckum's funeral to be at Mt. Joy Cumberland Presbyterian Church. (Columbia Herald, 13 March 1891.)

BECKUM, Mrs. Ruth, died Sunday at home of Jabe King at Rockdale in Maury County. (Columbia Herald, 13 March 1891.)

BECKWITH, Hugh, son of George and Fannie H. Beckwith, died on the 10th in Coffee County; age 13 months 2 days. (Nashville Republican Banner, 15 Aug. 1869.)

BEE. The mother of Tom Bee (c), died last week in Corpus Christi, Texas, age 133; born in Virginia in 1737; had lived in Texas for 50 years; she had been servant of George Washington's mother. (Memphis Daily Appeal, 26 June 1870.)

BEELER, Mr., died on Feb. 25 at Bardstown, KY; was of Red Hill, Grainger County, TN, died of relapse of measles; belonged to the 1st East Tennessee Cavalry; Methodist; wife and child survives. (Nashville Daily Union, 29 March 1863.)

BEHRENS. A very old trunk arrived at Castle Garden recently. It arrived with William Behrens on the Fulda and had date 1667 on it; made of black oak. He was bound for Monticello, Iowa, and the trunk had been in his family 220 years. (Maury Democrat, 4 Oct. 1888.)

BEIRMAN. Harry Powers, captain of the steamer Clarksville, is being held in the sum of $7000 at Memphis to answer charges of hanging a young Hebrew, S. Beirman, to make him confess to robbing a female passenger and putting him ashore with his hands tied behind him.

(Nashville Union and American, 14 May 1874.)

BELL, Sarah, living in a millinery establishment on College Street, burned to death yesterday when clothes caught fire from lamp. (Nashville Union and American, 2 April 1873.)

BELL, W. D., a blacksmith, who lived 8 miles south of Nashville on Owen and Winstead Pike, was killed by a drunken Robert Reams, who kicked in door and shot him. (Nashville Republican Banner, 28 Feb. 1869.)

BELL, Mrs. Eliza Jane, 64 years 10 months, died on Saturday at Tulip Grove. (Nashville Republican Banner, 31 Jan. 1869.)

BELL, George and Robert Bell (brothers) were gentlemen of means and leisure, and were "fighting friends" of General Jackson. They owned Capitol Hill, which they sold to George W. Campbell with three or four acres adjoining for $6,000. They delighted in horse-trading but were the very "soul of honor". Judge McNairy married a sister of these gentlemen. (Nashville Republican Banner, 2 July 1869.)

BELL, Philip. Jim Morrow and Chambliss, his nephew, went to the house of Philip Bell in Knox County and attempted to rob him. His daughter begged for her father's life and they shot her in head, an instant death. Citizens went after them and found one of them in a still-house and shot him to pieces; the other was put in jail last week. (Nashville Daily Union, 21 March 1865.)

BELL, Dr. W. S., chief of medical department of the Confederate Army in Mississippi, died in Memphis on the 15th ult; formerly lived in Chattanooga; son of Capt. James Bell of Knoxville. (Nashville Dispatch, 14 April 1862.)

BELL, Elmina, 7, daughter of R. F. Bell, died on 28th in Nashville. (Nashville Dispatch, 30 Aug. 1862.)

BELL, Robert C., Adjutant of the 14th Regiment, was wounded in seven days fight at Chickahominy and has died; brother of James T. Bell of Nashville; he was of Clarksville, where he was a druggist. (Nashville Dispatch, 1 Nov. 1862.)

BELL, Susan Mary, age 1 year 3 months 21 days, youngest daughter of R. P. Bell, died on 28th in Nashville. (Nashville Dispatch, 30 Oct. 1862.)

BELL, Ida, eldest daughter of John M. and Francis B. Bell of New Orleans, age 2 years 10 months 5 days, died on June 28 at the home of her grandfather Dr. Gilbert D. Taylor near Pulaski. (The Academist, Lawrence County, 12 August 1846.)

BELL, Honorable John, died at Cumberland Iron Works this morning at 2 a.m. (Nashville Republican Banner, 10 Sept. 1869.) He had been quite feeble for some time; weaknesses of respiratory organs, producing suffocation. (Nashville Republican Banner, 11 Sept. 1869.) An account of his imposing funeral may be found in the Memphis Daily Appeal, 15 Sept. 1869.

BELL, Montgomery, Esquire, an old and well known resident of this county met with an accident Tuesday evening which it is feared will prove fatal; he left town for his residence about ten miles from town and his horse became frightened, ran away, threw him out of the buggy, and down a precipice, breaking his shoulder bone and severely injuring his back. He lay helpless for several hours before any help came to him. A negro woman passing heard his calls and gave information, which brought him relief. Nashville Whig, 25th. (Clarksville Jeffersonian, 7 May 1851.)

M. B. This accident was not fatal. His tombstone in Cheatham County in the family cemetery reads: Montgomery Bell, born 3 Jan. 1769 in Chester County, Pa., died 1 April 1855 in Dickson County, he was one of the earliest and most successful ironmasters in the State; this

20

monument erected by his ex'crs, W. E. Watkins, J. L. Bell, O. P. Roberts, 1855. (At the time of his death this was Dickson County.)

NARROWS OF HARPETH.--Mysterious footprints have been found on wall at Narrows of Harpeth when the late Montgomery Bell, pioneer iron manufacturer in Tennessee, pierced it with two tunnels, the first of which was completed the fourth of July 1818 and celebrated with a great festival and cost $8,000. It was unimproved until 1830 when Mr. Bell built a large forge with four large tilt hammers for making hammered iron about 1830 or 1831 he pierced the second tunnel about 60 yards south of the first; the second tunnel was 16 feet wide, 6 feet high, and cost $6000. The property was willed to his nephew James Bell. Several human footprints may be seen imbedded in the rock--two pairs of children and one adult. (Nashville Union and American, 2 Aug. 1874. Long account of this in this paper.)

BENNETT, Dr. John D., well known physician of Culleoka, Maury County, died Sunday last week of flux. (Whig and Tribune, Jackson, TN, 20 Sept. 1873.)

BENNETT, Mrs., of Giles County, married on 12 Dec. 1828 in Roanoke Co., Va., still has a piece of her wedding cake. (Nashville Union and American, 7 June 1873.)

BENSON, Captain Henry, of Battery M, 2d Regiment USA Regulars, died on the 11th instant on board the Spaulding, on which he was returning home, suffering from shell wound received from one of his own guns at the battle of Malvern Hill. (Nashville Dispatch, 26 Aug. 1862.)

BENNETT, Samuel, was killed Wednesday by firing of the cannon on Capitol Hill, during the marching of procession in honor of late Henry Clay, who died yesterday. George Johnson had left thumb blown off at the same time; they were endeavoring to fire three rounds a minute. (Nashville Daily Gazette, 30 July 1852.)

BENTON, Honorable Thomas H., died of cancer of stomach. (Clarksville Jeffersonian, 14 April 1858.) The statue of Benton will be erected in Missouri Park at St. Louis. (Memphis Avalanche, 8 Nov. 1866.) Madame la Baronna Gauidres Boileieau, daughter of Thomas H. Benton, was buried in France on March 10 at St. Philippe d'Roche. (Nashville Union and American, 4 April 1874.)

BENTON, Samuel, of Holly Springs, Mississippi, nephew of old Tom Benton, lawyer, died in battle around Atlanta in 1864. Benton County, Miss., a new county is to be named for Col. Benton. (Memphis Daily Appeal, 5 June 1870.)

BENTON, Mrs. Nancy P., 36, of Limestone County, Alabama, died on the 6th in Nashville at home of her father Rev. J. Rains. (Nashville Dispatch, 7 June 1862.)

BENTON, Mrs. Sallie, 25, who lived 2½ miles from Garland, near Covington, TN, has had four children, 3 girls and a boy; one boy and one girl have died; father is 60 years old; they are poor. (Daily Herald, 29 Aug. 1901.)

BERNHARDT, Joseph, half-brother of Sarah Bernhardt, told the press that he was brought to Columbia, TN, by his guardian Professor Toeffel, a teacher in a Columbia school; no one here remembers him. (Daily Herald, 12 April 1923.)

BERMAN, Samuel, is suing Capt. Reese Pritchard, commander of the steamer Clarksville for damages; Pritchard was not on board at the time of the hanging. (Nashville Union and American, 17 May 1874.)

BERRY, William, living near Cross Plains in Robertson County, blew his brains out; insanity. (Nashville Republican Banner, 6 March 1868.)

BERRY, William T., funeral to be held today in Nashville. (Nashville Republican Banner, 7 Nov. 1869.)

BERRY, Addie F., only child of Mrs. Augustus D. Berry, died March 12 in
New York City. (Nashville Republican Banner, 15 March 1871.)

BERRYMAN, General Mason, 81, ex-Governor of Idaho, and formerly associated with Abraham Lincoln in the practice of law, died in Kansas
City last week. (Maury Democrat, 7 March 1895.)

BEST, little boy, was drowned in Lewisburg, KY, a few days ago by falling in a tub of water. (Nashville Daily Union, 25 March 1863.)

BETHELL, Colonel P. C., of Memphis is visiting his son Capt. W. D. Bethel
in Columbia. (Columbia Herald and Mail, 23 June 1876.) The following tombstones are in Elmwood Cemetery in Memphis:
BETHELL, Pickney C., born in Rockingham County, N. C., 3 May 1816,
died in New Orleans, 18 Feb. 1884.
BETHELL, Harriet E., 24 Sept. 1819 - 2 June 1858.
BETHELL, Pickney S. (Buddy), son of Pickney and Harriet, born
14 April 1852, died 11 Aug. 1867.
(Tombstone inscriptions listed by Mrs. Paul McAnally, Columbia, TN.)

BIBB, Porter, of Limestone County, Ala., died on the 8th; buried with
Masonic honors. (Nashville Daily Union, 16 July 1865.)

BICKNELL, John. Walker, about 25, committed a cold-blooded murder 10
miles from Mt. Pleasant day before yesterday. His victim was John
Bicknell, 22, son of Col. Bicknell of Columbia "who fled from East
Tennessee to avoid vindicative persecution visited upon him by loyal
neighbors." The Pale Faces of which young Bicknell was a member have
sworn that Walker, if caught, will meet with swift and terrible retribution. (Nashville Republican Banner, 1 March 1868.)

Watts, Walker, or Powell, "lynched at last." Lynched on Tuesday by
the Kuklux; taken from Columbia jail by 60 to 100 men to a point on
railroad, 1 mile south of town and hung on tree; left hanging for
considerable portion of day; he at one time lived with Ben Harlan in
Maury County and had a mistress named Hays; he was living at Wayland
Springs, TN, at the time of the murder. (Nashville Republican
Banner 5 March 1868.)

Twenty horsemen, well mounted and disguised, went to the jail and
seized the murderer, Walker, who in some way made his escape from his
captors; he swam Duck River, got on Bear Creek, and entered the home
of Mr. Dooley to dry himself. Mr. Dooley became suspicious and got
his gun and his father-in-law who had come into the house, Mr. Loftin,
and they took him back to jail. Bicknell's corpse was escorted to
the grave by the Pale Faces and about 20 Kuklux, who kneeled down and
swore vengence. (Nashville Republican Banner, 4 March 1868.)

About two and one half miles beyond Summertown, there are five trees
on the roadside with crosses made of oak lathes nailed on them, marking a circle in which the noble John Bicknell was murdered. (Columbia Herald, 19 August 1870.)

Bicknell Stand is located in the Barrens...John Bicknell killed in
cold blood in 1868 here. (Columbia Herald, 24 Oct. 1871.)

Captain James Craig lives and owns place where Bicknell was killed
several years ago. The tree stands in his front yard that was marked
so the place could be identified. Summertown was not here then.
(Maury Democrat, 26 March 1896.)

Soon after our organization (i.e. The Pale Faces in Maury County)
one of our original members, John Bicknell, was murdered in Lawrence
County. Bicknell's family were from East Tennessee and were in sympathy with the South. The feelings just after the war, between the
Unionists and the Southerners in that section of the state was said
to be very bitter and many Southerners were driven from their homes
and located in Middle Tennessee, a number of others, besides the
Bicknell family, locating in our town and county. (Columbia and
Maury County.)

22

Young John Bicknell procured the agency for some Southern books and was canvassing for their sale. He borrowed from T. Jeff Coleburn (at present a Justice of the Peace here) a horse, and from John Pickard (now at Murfreesboro) a revolver.

He set out for and arrived in Lawrenceburg, at which place he made some sales. There he met a man with whom he had some conversation and informed the man that he was going to return to Columbia that evening. This man set out on foot and got several miles out from Lawrenceburg on the road leading to Columbia.

Anyone who ever traveled the road know it passes through a barren country with but few houses upon it. The man took his seat on a log on the roadside, a few miles west of Summertown, and awaited the arrival of young Bicknell, whom, as afterward learned, he prevailed upon to dismount and take a seat by his side. After gaining the attention he secured Bicknell's pistol and killed him. The man took from Bicknell his horse and pocketbook and mounting the horse, rode on to Mt. Pleasant, where he entered a business house, purchased some cheese and crackers and made a lunch of them.

In the meantime Dr. Long of Mt. Pleasant had received a call towards Lawrenceburg and came up with the remains of Bicknell on the roadside. On his return to Mt. Pleasant, he made known his discovery, upon which it was remarked about the stranger being in Mt. Pleasant, the color of the horse he was riding, and the pair of boots which were hanging to his saddle. Suspicion was at once aroused that he was the murderer.

A posse formed and went in pursuit. They kept trail of him to within 5 miles of Columbia and there the trail was lost. He had left the pike and taken a road to the South. The pursuing party came to Columbia, arriving early in the morning, and the news of the murder was soon generally known, and soon runners were dispatched in every direction to effect the murderer's capture.

Several of the pursuing party returned to the point where they had lost the trail and took it up again on the road leading South, following him to Bigbyville and pursuing him on to Culleoka, at which place fresh men and horses took up the pursuit, stopping occasionally to dismount and remount fresh horses.

They continued on until within a few miles of Shelbyville where they were overtaken by darkness. The residence of a Mr. Thompson was near.

Dismounting and holding a council, they decided that it was best not to seek shelter in Mr. Thompson's house as the murderer might be putting up with him and might become alarmed and make his escape in the darkness.

They placed guards around the house and kept watch till morning. Entering the house, they were informed by Mr. Thompson that a stranger had put up with him during the night. Informing Mr. Thompson of their object, he showed the party up to the room where the man slept and was probably still sleeping.

In the room was a pile of wheat. After searching the man, Mr. T. suggested that they had better examine the wheat, as he might have secreted something in it. On doing so they found a revolver and a pocket-book. None of the party had any evidence or knowledge to satisfy them that they had the right man, but they returned with him to this place on the same afternoon a procession of eight Pale Faces marched to the residence and took charge of young Bicknell's remains and while on the way, the funeral procession was joined by about thirty Kuklux, arrayed in red silk gowns and black cowls or masks over their faces.

They were drenched with water, it having been raining nearly all day.

Arriving at the grave the Pale Faces read the funeral rites of the order, some friends standing by and holding upraised umbrellas over them while reading. The Kuklux standing around, the rain pouring down on them.

23

After the conclusion of the ceremony of the Pale Faces, a member of the order advanced to one whom he took to be the leader of Grand Cyclops of the Kuklux and inquired of him if they wished to go through any ceremony, which was answered by the nod of the head. The members of the Pale Faces stepped back a few paces from the grave.

The Cyclops of the Kuklux raised his right hand and made a circular motion, whereupon the members of that order formed a circle around the grave. The Cyclops then knelt upon both knees followed by the others, then raising his right hand with all but the first or index finger closed and it outstretched, he said, "We solemnly swear with uplifted hand to avenge the death of our brother." They then arose, proceeded to a grove near by, mounted their horses and were soon lost to sight.

While the burial was going on, unknown to those present, the party which had captured the murderer, was entering town upon the same road, which they had just taken to the graveyard, and though not in sight they could not have been very far in the rear for they had reached the jail but a few minutes ahead of those who had attended the funeral.

Arriving at the jail, Squire Jeff Coleburn at once recognized the horse which he had loaned Bicknell, and upon which the murderer was seated, and Mr. Pickard identified the pistol which he had lent him. Other circumstances soon fixed the guilt upon the murderer beyond any question of doubt. Had the band of Kuklux who attended the burial not made their departure so soon or had the fact of the capture been known to them no doubt there would have been a lynching that night.

There was great excitement during the night among all the male citizens, nearly all being up and out on the street, the elderly portion all of whom were exerting themselves to quiet the excited ones, urging that the law be allowed to take its course. So matters existed until after midnight, when the word passed from lip to lip, "Let's retire for the night." Soon the streets were deserted and all was quiet.

The following day was another of excitement. The town was thronged with country people, a number visiting the jail to look upon the prisoner. All were expecting an attack upon the jail at any moment. The prisoner was called upon and spent some time with the Rev. Mr. Otts, the Presbyterian minister here at that time. The day passed off.

Soon after the night came on, a body of Kuklux entered the Public Square and compelled all the outsiders to enter the houses. While they were doing this, another squad went to the jail where they secured the prisoner, placed him behind a horse with a man in front and moved out of town, taking an eastern course. They were soon joined by those on the square. Many citizens remained up until after midnight, in hope of receiving some news of the lynching, but nothing was heard until the following morning when it was currently reported that the murderer had made his escape, which was not believed by anyone until later in the day, when several countrymen rode in with the culprit and again landed him in jail.

It was learned that while passing along a high bluff overlooking Duck River which was out of its banks, the prisoner made a leap from the horse, dashed into and swam across the river, followed by a hail of lead. The weather was quite cool, and, being drenched with water and also having frostbitten feet, he did not journey far until he sought shelter in the residence of a farmer who recognized him, having seen him in jail during the day. The farmer called in some of his neighbors who kept watch over him during the night and returned him to jail the next morning.

The day passed without any manifestation of his being again interrupted. Many concluded that no further effort would be made to lynch him, while others kept a lookout for the appearance of the Kuklux. The weather was so cool that one could not remain long from the fire, consequently many went to their homes. Near midnight, while in a store-house, someone exclaimed that the town was full of Kuklux. Reaching the front door with a friend and seeing none, we inquired where they were and were informed that they were at the jail.

They had entered the town so quietly very few were aware of their presence. Wending our way towards the jail and taking a position on the
platform of the Nelson House, we had a sight, of the surroundings.* A
platoon of some twenty or twenty-five men were in line, reaching from
one side to the other of North Main Street. Another was further down
the same street and below the jail, and still others on Sixth Street,
both to the east and west of the jail, and others in and around the jail.
A fence ran from the north end of the hotel to Sixth Street, and east
along Sixth Street. My friends and I steathily made our way inside of
the fence, hoping to get near Sixth Street and the jail, so as to hear
and see what was going on.

We had not proceeded far when we were ordered back with half a dozen revolvers drawn upon us. We retreated and again took positions on the
hotel porch. Very soon the prisoner was mounted upon a white horse,
with a man behind him this time, to whom he was tied and his feet were
tied together under the horse. They made him so secure that he would
not escape again.

He was brought up and in the rear of the first squad, the rear coming up
from behind, and those on the east and west ends of Sixth Street, taking
places on his right and left sides, forming a hollow square. The order
to forward march was given, and thus they moved across the square. A
deafening yell arose as they moved south on the Pulaski turnpike, followed by a large crowd of citizens until they reached Eighth Street,
where the rear squad wheeled their horses in about face, drew their revolvers and ordered all citizens not to proceed further. The main
squad moved on until they reached Eleventh Street, when the rear squad
again wheeled and rode rapidly on and joined the others.

We have an old darky whom we call Bragg, who claims to have been the servant during the war of Gen. Braxton Bragg. He also claims he was a Rebel
and a Democrat, and always voted the Democratic ticket. At the time of
the foregoing occurrence he was living in the country south of here.**
He was not so well known then as now. Many threats of violence were
made against him on account of his politics by other negroes, so in order to protect himself he always went armed with a revolver and sword
which was then very dangerous for a negro, too, as he might be shot or
whipped.

Bragg very luckily came in on the Bigbyville pike, which runs somewhat
parallel with the Pulaski pike, consequently did not encounter the Kuklux. When informed by Dr. Sam Frierson of the narrow escape he had
made in not meeting them and the danger he would place himself in were
he caught with his weapons on, he quickly disarmed himself and retired
for the night.

---

*The Nelson House, then a hotel, but an office building in 1978, still
stands on North Main Street in Columbia; the present jail is located on
the same site as the jail standing in 1868.

**Braxton Bragg (colored), died 17 Jan. 1900 in Columbia, body servant
of General Braxton Bragg; Leonidas Polk Bivouac and William H. Trousdale Camp, Confederate veterans passed tributes of respect to him on his
death; his pallbearers were former Confederate soldiers and were: H. A.
Brown, H. G. Evans, W. J. Whitthorne, J. T. Williamson, H. L. Hendley,
A. N. Akin. There was a large attendance at his funeral. (Confederate
Veteran Magazine, May 1900, page 233.)

Bragg's father came from region near Lake Victoria Nyanza where he was
a war chief; kidnapped and brought to this country; born in Africa.
(Columbia Herald and Mail, 18 May 1877.)

No news was heard from the Kuklux as to what they had done until the
following morning when it became generally known that they went out
about a mile from town and entered a woods lot, where they held a leng-
thy interview with the murderer, who admitted the killing, giving as his

reason for committing the crime that his feet were badly frostbitten, that being very footsore he was not able to tramp much, and that he slew Bicknell in order to secure his horse, and continue his journey on horseback, that he was a native of South Carolina, and had been a Confederate soldier through the war; that his mother was a very worthy woman; that he had committed but one other crime and that at home; that a negro had insulted his mother and he slew him with a hatchet for which he had no regrets, but feared that his life was in danger and left home. The only request he made of the crowd, it was said, was that they would not insist upon his giving his true name and his residence for it was his dying hope that his mother would never know of his final end.

To the Rev. Mr. Otts he made a full confession, but the latter would not impart it, only saying that he went under the name of Pitts. Dr. Otts also stated that he was highly educated and spoke seven different languages.

His remains were taken down by the Coroner, Wm. Woods, about 10 o'clock a.m. and placed in a coffin brought to town and laid in the market-house during the day, and they fell into the hands of the medical fraternity during the night. (Signed) Wm. J. Andrews, Columbia, TN. (Nashville Banner, 10 March 1897.)

Letter to the Editor:
I see in Wednesday's Banner an article from W. J. Andrews of Columbia, being an account of the murder of Bicknell in Lawrence County by a man named Pitts. Pitts was captured at Thomas Baxter's about three miles east of this place. He passed here the evening before, stopped and bought a piece of tobacco.

A while after night the pursuing party came along making inquiry for such a man. I informed them of what I new about him; that he was riding a certain kind of horse and had a pair of boots tied to his saddle. They were then sure they were after the right man, and told me of the murder he had committed, and that the boots belonged to the man he had killed.

I told them if he did not travel at night he was not more than three miles ahead of them. They went on, and I heard no more of them until next morning, when they passed back and had the man a prisoner. I was told where they captured him and that they had waited till daylight to make the capture. I learned through the Nashville papers that he was taken from jail at Columbia, that he made his escape but was recaptured and summarily dealt with.

The next spring I visited my old home in South Carolina, which was in 1869, and while there I was aksed by an old friend B. J. Ramage, how far I lived from Columbia. I told him about 25 miles. He then asked if I knew anything about a young man being lynched there the year before and I told him I did, and all I new about it. He asked if I knew who killed him. I told him he was killed by the Kuklux. He then wanted to know of me what the Kuklux were. I told him that from all I could learn about them they were members of a clan, and might be called regulators.

He then said, "Bob, do you know that man was a son of Reuben Pitts?" I told him I did not, and was truly sorry that a son of as good and influential a man as Reuben Pitts should come to such an end. Ramage told me that from they had seen in the papers that the people of Newberg were satisfied it was young Pitts.

He also spoke of him being such a fine scholar, but did not tell me why he left that country. His mother was then alive, his father having died several years before the war. Ramage also told me that it was agreed by everyone who had seen or heard of the fate of the young man not to let it go to the ears of the mother.

Preacher Otts of whom Mr. Andrews writes, being from South Carolina, must have known or heard of the Pitts family and therefore would more

willingly keep the man's confession. Reuben Pitts and my father were
boys together and I new him well myself before I left the old state
in 1865. (Signed) R. S. Montgomery, Palmetto, Tennessee.
(Nashville Banner, 15 Mar. 1897)

Letter to the Editor:
...A few days after the appearance of my letter I received from a gentleman in your city (Nashville), one whom I knew to be a leading and influential citizen, who imparted to me considerable information regarding
a man by the name of Charley Pitts, but added that he was not writing
for publication. I answered him and requested his permission to make
known his statements to which he consented with the condition that his
name be withheld.

He wrote: "Pitts, the man you referred to in yesterday's Banner, was an
acquaintance of mine. At the time he was lynched, his home was in White
County, Tenn., where he bought a farm. He paid for the place in part,
went off to get money to complete payment, and was lynched as you detail. He was a man rather slight in size, freckled face, and of a
quite pleasant address.

"He told some tale about being a South Carolinian, and, having killed a
negro. As a matter of fact, he was a guerrilla and had been one of
Quantrell's men, afterward with Jesse James. I think he had been on a
raid with them and was unsuccessful, or rather they were successful,
but were so pressed that they scattered out. He lost his horse, weapons and money, and was trying to get back to White County when lynched.

"I also knew Jesse and Frank James very well having had business with
both of them, particularly with Jesse when I knew him as J. D. Howard...
who was in jail here for assaulting one Steven Jackson, a noted guerrilla. Jesse, then lived in Humphreys County on Big Bottom of Duck
River and was a farmer at home. Frank was a teamster, hauling logs...
They had previous to this time, a partner named Charles Pitts, whom I
am satisfied is your man. I have often thought I would write Frank
James and ask him about Pitts, but have not done so. Pitts was a very
intelligent man and a well educated man, and made himself agreeable to
his neighbors, though all knew that there was a mystery about him. I
was not a bushwhacker myself, but a boy, at the time, living in DeKalb
County, and after the war was right smart of a hunter and fisherman and
went into the hills and hollows."

This gentleman in his second letter to me says, "I am in some doubt
about Pitts being the Charley Pitts of James notoriety but I believe it.
No one ever made any inquiry about him from South Carolina, and there is
every evidence that he was the man I suppose him to be. There is no
doubt, however, that the man lynched is the same man I knew. I remember the lynching well, and took steps at the time to satisfy myself of
his identity."

In conversation with an acquaintance and ex-official of this county
last night, he informed me that he had recently read the history of the
James boys and he could not believe that the Pitts referred to could be
the same Charley Pitts who operated with the James gang, as Charley
Pitts was spoken of as the man who led the gang to a raid in which
Cole Younger was seriously wounded, and supposed to be mortally wounded,
and supposed that they were being pursued and that their trail was
being followed from the loss of blood by Younger. Charley Pitts insisted that Younger was past hope--that their safety depended on the slay-
ing of Younger, and that he, Charley Pitts, wanted to slay and leave
him, but Bob, brother of Cole, would not consent but determined to en-
deavor to save his brother by remaining with him, which he did, and
they were both captured, tried and imprisoned and are now in prison.
That this occurred in 1870, while Pitts was lynched in 1868. Which is
correct?

Another acquaintance informed me that he was knowing to Pitts'
confession; that he had murdered six persons; that he could not call

27

all to mind, but one case in which he slew a washwoman at Memphis, TN, and took from her person the sum of 50 cents. (Signed) William J. Andrews, Columbia, TN, 16 March 1897. (Nashville Banner, 17 March 1897.)

Chick Watson is building a house in Columbia where the murderer of Bicknell was hung. (Columbia Herald, 17 Jan. 1873.)

Maury County appropriations show that the county paid for a coffin on 2 March 1868 and for an inquest on 4 March 1868 for "John Pitts, murderer."

BICKNELL, Colonel Samuel P., father of the murdered man, died Saturday night; said to be colic, but really believed to be distress over his son's murder. (Nashville Republican Banner, 3 March 1868.)

BIDDOX, Susan, oldest daughter of Ceily Biddox of Williamsport, Maury County, died Wednesday of last week and buried in the neighborhood. (Columbia Herald and Mail, 21 Jan. 1876.)

BIFFLE, Jacob. DEATH OF COLONEL JACOB BIFFLE - Gainesville, Texas, 7th Jan. 1877: Letter to Mr. Wm. Biffle. Dear Uncle--It is with grief that I write to you of pa's death. He left home in his usual health, and was brought home a corpse, Thursday evening. Pa and his partner, Mr. Belcher, carried their cattle west, and located their ranch on the Pease River, 100 miles from here. Pa left on the 15th of October and did not expect to be gone longer than three weeks. Mr. Belcher was to go up in two weeks and relieve him, so he could come home; but he seemed very indifferent about getting off, and finally sent a man to boss the cattle until he got there, so that pa could leave.

Pa started with three wagons and six or seven of the herders; and when they had traveled 50 miles, they had stopped to camp over at night, on the Washita River, when some of the men went out and killed a deer. Pa told the cook he wanted the hind quarters saved to bring home. All of the hands seemed perfectly satisfied that he should do so, except a man by the name of Waters, who began cursing; pa spoke to him and told him he was not armed, but if he wanted a fight, to wait till he could take his coat off; at this, Waters drew his revolver, and fired twice, and would have fired again if he had not been stopped. Pa dodged the first shot, but the second passed throug his right arm into the shoulder.

He started a man here immediately for Uncle Fletcher and Mr. Belcher; also sent for Brother John and Dr. Barnett; they moved him to Henrietta immediately. Dr. Barnett sent us word that he would be able to be moved home the next week, and they thought he was doing fine. He was shot on the 15th of Dec. The last message we got, the man left them on the 1st of Jan. and arrived here the next evening. He stated he was improving fast, and Uncle Fletcher would start home the next morning to get a feather-bed and half a dozen pillows to bring him home on. Uncle Fletcher started and got 3 or 4 miles, when pa began complaining of something in his throat. They sent for him to come back, and pa died that evening at dusk.

The second night afterward, when we were looking for Uncle Fletcher, so expectantly, hoping to hear some good news, they arrived with the corpse. He was very rational until the last. He was very much interested in his salvation. When first shot, he asked several to pray for him; also sent for a preacher. Just before he breathed his last, he began praising the Lord. The evening he died, he sent out for a lawyer and had his business fixed up. He was buried on the 5th. As soon as Waters shot the last time, he mounted his horse and left. There has been a reward of $500 offered for him. Signed, Mary Ann Biffle. (Columbia Herald and Mail, 9 Feb. 1877. N. B. This article notes that the murderer's name was really Wallace and that Col. Biffle was a native of Wayne County, TN.)
(N. B. This was the Colonel Biffle, who served in Confederate Army as leader of a cavalry group.)

BIGGER, Mrs. Eliza, an old lady, living on Paradise Hill Turnpike, near the Cheatham County line, was found dead in road on 14th. (Nashville Republican Banner, 20 April 1869.)

BIGGS, Mrs. Sarah, 54, died on 16 Dec. 1870. (Nashville Republican Banner, 17 Dec. 1870.)

BILBO, Mary Agnes, youngest child of Mr. and Mrs. W. N. Bilbo, died on the 11th. (Nashville Dispatch, 12 Oct. 1862.)

BILES, R. M., of Pulaski, TN, died at Kansas City on the 4th instant. (Columbia Herald, 20 Dec. 1872.)

BILLINGS, James J. S., funeral to be held this evening in Nashville. (Nashville Dispatch, 27 June 1862.)

BINGHAM, Thomas M., was murdered by one of his own slaves, who has been missing, but has been found and confessed. They strangled him with a rope and put body in sack, weighted with rocks, and threw him in a creek. Two men, a boy, and a woman have been arrested and put in irons; mob took them from jail and hanged them. Grenada, Miss., Republican (newspaper). (Clarksville Jeffersonian, 20 March 1852.)

BINGHAM, Mrs. Myra, died last week of consumption; sister-in-law of Squire Jesse S. Bingham, Maury County. (Columbia Herald and Mail, 7 Dec. 1877.)

BINGHAM, Nelson, "aged" of Shady Grove, Hickman County, died Wednesday of last week. (Columbia Herald and Mail, 4 Feb. 1876.)

BIRD, Lewis, Private, Company H, 5th Tennessee Cavalry, was murdered in 1862 while making his way to the Federal lines; murdered by one Emory Kiker, who was found not guilty in Greeneville, TN, in 1868. (Memphis Daily Appeal, 18 Nov. 1868.)

BIRD, Mrs. Ann, died March 2 near Enterprise, Maury County; had been in bad health for several years and was perfectly willing to die; her aged father and brother survive. (Columbia Herald and Mail, 10 Mar. 1876.)

BIRGE, Private Joseph, of Northampton, Mass., was killed July 24 when lightning struck his tent on the fairgrounds at Newbern, NC; he was in Company A, 27th Massachusetts. (Nashville Dispatch, 3 Aug. 1862.)

BISHOP, Madame Anna, was burned on the 15th ult. by her clothes taking fire from effects of which she died Friday morning at St. Paul, Minnesota. (Nashville Dispatch, 4 Nov. 1862.)

BIZWELL, Joseph A., died 15 June 1876 near Primm Springs; was an eccentric; Hickman County. (Columbia Herald and Mail, 30 June 1876.)

BLACKWELL, __, was shot and killed at Hiwassee Gap, Polk County, TN, by unknown person while he was eating supper. His wife went for help and the murderers robbed the house while she was gone. (Memphis Daily Appeal, 18 April 1870.)

BLACK, Mrs., mother-in-law of Gosh White of Columbia, has gone back to Hickman County; she was born 1799 in Orange Co., NC, and is the mother and stepmother of 18 children. (Columbia Herald and Mail, 1 Feb. 1878.)

BLAIR, Robert, was murdered 22 Aug. 1863; Andrew Johnson offers $300 reward for William T. Holmes, 21, and Andrew Huggins, between 35 and 40, for the murder; they have fled and running at large. (Nashville Daily Union, 23 Sept. 1863.)

BLAKE, Amos S., 83, died recently at Waterbury, Conn., builder of the first locomotive in New England in 1832. (Maury Democrat, 7 March 1895.)

BLAKELY, Lt. John D., Company B, 1st Tennessee Regiment, has been repor-
ted as killed at Perryville. (Nashville Dispatch, 21 Oct. 1862.)
The remains of Lt. Col. John Petterson, Lt. Thomas B. Lanier, and
Lt. John Blakely (Son of Mr. Peleg Blakely) arrived in Nashville on
Thursday; all were killed at Perryville. (Nashville Dispatch,
8 Nov. 1862.)

BLAKESLEA, Seth, one of the drafted soldiers in Royalton, Ohio, cut off
his great toe to gain an exemption. He performed this brilliant operation in surgery with a dull axe and was obliged to hack and man-
ble the member frightfully before he succeeded in getting it off.
(Nashville Dispatch, 28 Oct. 1862.)

BLANCHARD, General Albert G., 81, died at New Orleans, Louisiana, on
Sunday. He was at West Point and was a classmate of Generals Robert
E. Lee and Albert Sidney Johnson and graduated in 1829. (Florence,
Ala., Times, 4 July 1891.)

BLAND, Mrs. Henrietta, 27, buried today, died on the 23d in Nashville.
(Nashville Daily Union, 25 Jan. 1863.)

BLAND, Mrs. DEATH OF NOTED WOMAN. Jackson, TN., March 5.--News was received here today of the death, in Chester County, of Mrs. Bland,
formerly the wife of the "Great Land Pirate" John A. Murrell, who was
a leader of one of the most daring gangs of murderers, horse and negro slave thieves. The operation of which extended over several
Southern states 40 years ago and one of the most successful operations
in this country. Murrell was finally captured and sentenced for horse '
stealing and after serving his sentence he moved to the mountains of
East Tennessee and died a reformed man. His wife was a quiet and most
estimable woman, and married a man named Bland after her husband's
imprisonment. The history of Murrell reads like a romance, our older
citizens will readily recall incidents of his life in this section.
The death of the wife at this late day, probably closes the history
of this once bold, bad man. (Florence, Ala., Times, 14 March 1891.)
(Refer also to John A. Murrell entry.)

BLANKENSHIP, T., died on the 23d ult; had been sick three weeks; lived
at Napier, Lewis County. (Maury Democrat 7 Feb. 1895.)

BLEDSOE. On Wednesday last, A. W. Smith, late probate judge, and Israel
Bledsoe were sitting on porch of Townsend House in Covington, TN,
joking one another about taking the oath of allegiance. Smith made
remarks which offended Bledsoe and he slapped Smith. Smith stabbed
Bledsoe, who died the next day. (Nashville Daily Union 9 Oct. 1863.)

BLUM, Pauline, 13 years 9 months, died on Sept. 29 in Nashville of rheu-
matic fever; daughter of Mr. and Mrs. R. D. Blum. (Nashville Dispatch, 1 Oct. 1862.)

BLUNT. Henry Blunt's eight year old child was buried Monday at Summertown, TN. (Maury Democrat, 26 April 1894.)

BLYTHE, Colonel, of Mississippi, was killed at Shiloh; was formerly the
Consul to Havana. (Nashville Dispatch, 30 April 1862.)

BODINELLI, Antonio's wife Catharina to be buried in Memphis today.
(Memphis Daily Appeal, 9 Nov. 1868.)

BODWIN. At Timmonsville, SC, is grave of Mrs. Florence Bodwin of Philadelphia, Pennsylvania. She was a member of a Federal regiment and as
she was dressed as a soldier, her sex was not discovered until her
death. (Memphis Daily Appeal, 21 April 1870.)

BOGGIOMO, John, funeral to be held today at his home on Horn Lake Road
at Memphis. (Memphis Avalanche, 15 Nov. 1866.)

BOGGIANO, Victorio C., 23 months, funeral today in Memphis; son of Mr.
and Mrs. James Boggiano. (Memphis Avalanche, 22 Dec. 1866.)

BOHLEN, John Borie, died at Baden Baden, Germany; was of Philadelphia and son of late General Bohlen; father and son died the same day, Aug. 22; one in battle and the other in a foreign land. (Nashville Dispatch, 30 Sept. 1862.)

BOLTON, Wade, was killed last spring by Col. Thomas Dickens; Dickens has been found not guilty. (Memphis Daily Avalanche, 14 Feb. 1870.)

BOLYER, Mr., died in a well in Memphis on the 29th ult., inhaling noxious gas. He had descended for the purpose of cleaning out a well. (Nashville Dispatch, 7 Aug. 1862.)

BOND, little daughter of James Bond, age 2, died December 27 in District 2 of Maury County. (Columbia Herald and Mail, 15 Jan. 1875.)

BOND, Mrs. Sarah B., died last Wednesday in Columbia; mother of Captain John B. Bond. (Columbia Heraldn and Mail, 31 Aug. 1877.)

BOOTH, John Wilkes, is playing an engagement in Washington. His Richard Third is very favorably criticized. (Nashville Daily Union, 13 Nov. 1863. (N. B. He appeared in Nashville, TN, on 1 Feb. 1864 in the same play.) J. Wilkes Booth and Harrold were chased from the swamp in St. Mary's County in Maryland to Garrett's farm near Port Royal on the Rappahannock by Colonel Baker's force. The barn in which they took refuge was fired. Booth was shot and killed and Harrold was captured. Booth's body and Harrold are now here. (Signed, Edwin M. Stanton, 27 April.)(Nashville Daily Union 28 April 1865.)

Booth's body was buried without disfigurement. It was buried in secret and in the night, and no stone marks or ever will mark the spot, but this was the choice of the family. The body was given to them. They had it carried far away to the North, away beyond New York. (Nashville Daily Union 30 May 1865.)

Three trunks, packed, belonging to J. Wilkes Booth have been found in Canada. (Nashville Daily Union, 14 June 1865.)

The spirit of John Wilkes Booth has informed a Brooklyn spiritualist that he is having a good time in the other world with St. Paul and St. Peter, the former of whom he knows very well. He complains that Michael keeps him pretty close in Heaven--or wherever he is. That ought to be tolerably conclusive that he is not still in the land of the living, and put at rest doubts of his identity; although the persistent refusal to give up his remains to his friends tends to divide the public mind on the subject. (Memphis Avalanche, 18 Oct. 1867.)

———

IS J. WILKES BOOTH DEAD?--The statement which appeared in your paper of Sunday last in regard to the point as to whether J. Wilkes Booth still lives, calls to mind other publications that have heretofore appeared in print about the same subject...Early in the spring of 1866 a letter was received from one of the West India islands, by a correspondent of a New York paper, stating that J. Wilkes Booth had been seen and recognized on the Island of Cuba a short time previous to the writing of the letter. This letter was noticed by some, if not all the Memphis papers. Not long after this publication a statement appeared in some of the papers of this country, to the effect that Booth had been seen in Europe, in one of the Italian states.

Some time last summer a man was arrested in Kentucky on a charge of horse-stealing, and lodged in jail. If my memory serves me right he gave his name as King. He wrote to Gen. Jefferson C. Davis, of the U. S. Army, stating that he desired to make a confession to him of importance to the country. General Davis, accompanied by another officer of the army, a general, went to the prison and the newspaper stated at the time that they were occupied nearly an entire day in taking down in writing the confession of the man.

The newspapers also stated that the substance of the confession was, that Booth was not the assassin of Lincoln, but that the man King committed the crime--that after the shooting of Lincoln he leaped upon the stage of the theater and passed out to the back door where Booth was with the horses.

The two rode rapidly to the residence of Mr. Seward. King dismounted and went in and attempted to kill Seward. He then returned to Booth and the two made their escape through Maryland on horseback, and thence to Cuba where he separated from Booth in the spring of 1866 and came to Kentucky.

He called the attention of the two generals to the fact that no proof had ever been made identifying Booth with the killing except the testimony of Laura Keene, an actress, who he stated was a personal enemy of Booth. She stated she recognized Booth as the man who jumped upon the stage with the drawn dagger.

King said it was not Booth, but him. He also said that Mrs. Surratt knew nothing of the conspiracy, and he gave information to the said official where certain papers could be found that would throw light upon the subject. All this has appeared in the newspaper heretofore, and may be taken for what it is worth.

Now, as one who is somewhat in the habit of looking closely into facts and the circumstances surrounding complicated cases, I propose to call your attention to certain facts that have an important bearing upon the whole question as to the probability of Booth not having been the man who was shot in the barn when Harrold was arrested.

The history of the matter, as given to the public at the time, is that Harrold was arrested and Boston Corbett had shot Booth. They put the dead body in a wagon and proceeded with it toward Washington City, the news of their success having reached Washington before them.

Baker, the Chief Detective of the Secretary of War, Mr. Stanton, went to meet the party who had killed Booth and captured Harrold. Upon meeting them, Baker and Corbett took possession of the reputed body of Booth, and as they say, buried it in some secret place, that is known to no person living except Baker and Corbett, and they both took a solemn oath over the grave that they would never reveal the burial place.

A large reward had been offered by the Government for the apprehension of Booth, and this being the case, does it not seem most natural that if the man who was killed in the barn was Booth, that Baker and Corbett would have carried the body to Washington City, where the body, if that of Booth, could have been identified by thousands who knew him and thus shown to all that the captors had shown themselves entitled to receive the reward. (Memphis Avalanche, 26 Jan. 1867.)

The remains of John Wilkes Booth were to be buried today in New York in presence of Mrs. Booth, Edwin and Junious Booth. The skeleton had been put in a metallic coffin. Hundreds viewed the remains in New York on the 16th. There is nothing but bones left. Upon one foot was an old army shoe and on the other a boot, cut open at the top. This covered the left foot, the leg having been broken in his leap from the stage box of the theater after he killed President Lincoln. Arrangements have been made to bury him beside his father. (Memphis Daily Appeal, 18 Feb. 1869.)

McHENRY - A MYSTERY - Late one evening, in the fall of the year, back in the early 80's, there came to the door of W. C. Pullen, who lived six miles south of McEwen (in Humphreys County, TN), a man about sixty years of age, who afterwards gave evidence of being the possible assasinator of Abraham Lincoln. He gave his name as Charles McHenry and asked to spend the night with them.

The man was courteously welcomed by the family, and accorded the usual Southern hospitality, so well known.

Mr. McHenry was dressed rags and tatters, and wore a shoe on one foot and a boot on the other. He made no apology for his dress, however. He was very reserved and spoke only when spoken to. He had a courtly and distinguished manner, yet there was a reserve and aloofness about his personality that created a feeling of awe. The visitor evidently like the country, the people, and the seclusion--for he stayed on several days.

Then he announced the fact that he was a school teacher, and wished to teach a subscription school. Mr. Pullen was a school director, so he assisted McHenry in securing the school at Shiloh. In a short time he had his school well under way. He continued to stay at Mr. Pullen's home, paying board.

Mr. McHenry, being well educated and highly intelligent, proved to be a splendid teacher, and the school progressed rapidly under his leadership. In a few months the success of his school became known in the adjoining communities, and pupils came from a distance to attend the school, boarding in private homes.

Mr. Gordon Pullen, son of Mr. W. C. Pullen, attended the McHenry School, and it is through his courtesy that much of this information has been obtained.

His patrons were highly pleased with the school, praising and commending it. But when they wished to advertise it, and bring in more pupils, he curtly refused.

The schoolmaster was a strange fellow, and full of superstition. He made few friends, keeping mostly to himself. He would not meet strangers if he could possibly avoid it. If a stranger came to see him, Mr. Pullen stated that McHenry would not go out, until he had learned who the man was and what he wanted.

Mr. McHenry had a square head, and an intelligent face, with graying hair and beard. He would not look a person straight in the eye, but had a sidewise, cutting look.

He never talked about himself, never told a thing of his past life, except that his native home was Virginia, and that he had a brother living in New Orleans. On a few occasions he came under the influence of intoxicating liquor, and would begin to loosen up. Then evidently realizing what he was doing, he would soon close up like a clam, and not say another word.

His chief recreation was playing croquet. He enjoyed the game immensely and would play for hours at a time. He once made a croquet ball from an apple tree know, so it would not split.

The whole time McHenry stayed at Shiloh he wrote no letters and received none. He claimed to be a bachelor. He was not fond of children, even avoided them. They would group around and stare at him, until he angrily told them to go away.

About the close of his third year of teaching at Shiloh, he went to New Orleans, or so he said--to visit his brother, where he stayed for some time. He promised to return in the spring to teach a term of school, but did not come for two or three months.

When he finally showed up, he was greatly dissatisfied and was even more restless, and acted more strangely than ever before. He stayed only a few months, going from Shiloh to Bodine, on Buffalo River, another section of the county, where he began another school. After teaching there for a short time, and building up a good school, he left, going to Dickson County, where he taught for a time.

One story about him is that he bought a place in Dickson County, about ten miles south west of Dickson, where he died and was buried.

Another is that he died on Buffalo and is buried there. On his death-bed he asked for a close friend to come to him, saying that he had something to tell him. When the friend arrived, however, McHenry was too far gone to speak, and died without divulging his secret. The story goes on, Mr. Pullen stated, that the schoolmaster had said that when he died, he wished no one to know where he was buried, except the person who attended the burial. And no one knows where his grave is.

It was thought that McHenry was John Wilkes Booth, Abraham Lincoln's assassinator, living under an assumed name. Several similarities were noted between the two men. Like Booth, McHenry claimed to have been an actor, and quoted Shakespeare freely. McHenry was crippled in the same leg and in the same manner that Booth was. Then his aloofness, his silence, his dread of publicity, caused people to think that for some reason he was in hiding.

But whether he was the notorious Booth who killed our great Civil War president, remains a mystery. (Democrat-Sentinel, Waverly, TN, 23 Aug. 1934.)

Apparently there is disagreement on this McHenry story. The follow-ing is from a clipping from the Nashville Tennessean Magazine, no date, found in a file belonging to the late Mildred S. Gambill of Waverly, TN: "L. J. Browning of Charlotte, TN, commenting on the 60-year-old Hickman County mystery raised in the November 15 magazine about the identity of Charles McHenry, writes that in January, 1885, when he enrolled as a pupil in Shiloh academy on Hurricane creek in Humphreys County, Charles McHenry was principal.

"'He was the finest teacher I ever knew,' says Browning. 'He was a great historian and a master mathematician. I was informed by the citizens in that community that McHenry came whence nobody knew about the year 1883 or 84 and opened a school composed of young men and girls. About the last of April, 1885, he gave a two-weeks vacation that he might attend the exhibition then in progress in New Orleans. At the end of two weeks he failed to return. A few weeks later he returned with the excuse that he left Memphis on a boat and for safe-keeping he deposited his money in the boat's safe and that while at anchor the boat sank. The boat was finally raised, and he claimed his money and returned.

"'During his stay at Shiloh, he boarded with Billie Pullen, and I have been informed that he told Pullen he had a past history that he wanted to tell but that he never revealed his secret. Charles McHenry could have been the assassin of James A. Garfield.'"*

Old Buckskin, the horse rode by Lt. Baker of Lansing, Michigan, in the capture of John Wilkes Booth, died in that city a few days ago. His skin will be mounted and placed on exhibition in the state museum. (Maury Democrat, Columbia, TN, 10 Feb. 1888.)

BOOTH, Edwin Thomas, born 13 Nov. 1833 near Bel Air Maryland, died 7 June 1893 in New York City; actor. "Edwin Booth was a very wealthy man. He left all to his daughter and to her children. The property given by Mr. Booth to the Players' Club, which he gave before his death, was free of all encumbrances and is alone worth $90,000." (Maury Democrat, Columbia, TN, 8 Feb. 1894.) "Edwin Booth cast a vote for Abraham Lincoln for President, but never voted before that occa-sion or after...leaves half million to his daughter." (Maury Demo-crat, 29 June 1893.) Edwin Booth's estate is worth $672,000, after all debts are paid. (Maury Democrat, 28 March 1895.)

*Stories and legends of Booth's survival began soon after the assassina-tion and historians still write trying to disprove Booth's survival.

34

BOSLEY, Mrs. Ellie, 50, died on 27th in Nashville; funeral to be held at Caper's Chapel. (Nashville Daily Union, 1 Dec. 1863.)

BOSTICK, Lt. F., of Yazoo, Mississippi, was wounded at Leesburg, Va., and killed in one of the battles before Richmond. (Nashville Dispatch 31 July 1862.)

BOURNE, Capt. W. F., and Lt. Otes Smith, buried at Elmwood Cemetery in Memphis; flower crosses to their memory have been placed on their graves. (Memphis Daily Appeal, 8 May 1870.)

BOWEN. The widow of Gen. John Bowen is making efforts to have the remains of her husband removed to Port Gibson, Miss., cemetery over which the 23rd Miss. Regiment of Bowen's Brigade intend to erect a suitable monument. (Memphis Daily Appeal, 20 Feb. 1870.)

BOWEN, Col. Cody, 94, the oldest ex-Union soldier in Kentucky, died in Anderson County on Friday. (Maury Democrat, 7 Nov. 1895.)

BOWERS, W. D., of Colonel James E. Rains' Confederate Regiment, has been arrested as a spy. (Nashville Dispatch, 26 July 1862.)

BOWMAN, George W., 22, died 31 Dec. 1861, at his father's in Christian County, KY, member of the 3d Kentucky Regiment. (Clarksville Weekly Chronicle, 10 Jan. 1862.)

BOWMAN, James N., died on the 16th in Panola County, Texas, formerly of Maury County; "espoused the cause of Texas Independence." (Nashville Republican Banner, 8 Dec. 1867.)

BOYD, Sarah, an old Irish woman, whose husband left a short time ago, was found dead on the 19th in Nashville; she died of starvation. (Memphis Daily Appeal, 20 Dec. 1868.)

BOYD, Belle, notorious female spy and mail carrier, has been captured near Warrenton and sent to Washington on the 2d and is now in the Old Capitol Prison; for some time now has carried rebel mails to Richmond and beyond. (Nashville Dispatch, 7 Aug. 1862.) Belle Boyd has been discharged from the California Insane Asylum and is in a pitiable state of poverty and sickness. (Memphis Daily Appeal, 16 March 1870.) Belle Boyd, rebel spy, is making a tour of the south and is now 51; still as piquant and vivacious as she was at 16 when she first entered the "service". (Maury Democrat, 12 Sept. 1895.)

BOYD, John, an old citizen of Breckenridge County, KY, was murdered near his home near Hardinsburg on the 29th ult.; the murderers West, Scott, and Northern locked Boyd in his room, stabbed him three times, then beat him to death with a maul. (Nashville Dispatch, 6 June 1862.)

BRADFORD, Capt. John, noted guerrilla, arrested in Jackson, TN, recently while on the way to Henderson County; he was taken from the hands of the sheriff and killed; he had been charged with murder and counterfeiting and was a bold, bad man. It is said to have been done by the Loyal League. (Memphis Daily Appeal, 16 June 1869.) Jack Bradford was 26 at his death, began his career as guerrilla at 17 years; he was native of Jackson, TN; his father died before the war; in 1862 the Yankees plundered his mother's home and he vowed vengeance against the whole race; waylaid and killed couriers, picking off every man who straggled his way; was soon joined by other youths and soon had 60 in his group. He was the terror of the Yankee Army at Jackson. Often disguised himself as chicken peddler and entered the enemy lines. (Memphis Daily Appeal, 18 June 1869.)

BRADFORD, Captain Simon, old and respected, died at Memphis 16 Feb. 1865. (Nashville Daily Union, 26 Feb. 1865.)

BRADFORD, Benjamin J., Esquire, editor of "Nashville Examiner" died Thursday last of long and lingering illness. (Nashville Whig, 2 March 1814.)

BRADLEY, John, an old man of Lincoln County, was killed last week near the Alabama line; called out of house before day by some unknown; bullet through head and heart. (Nashville Republican Banner, 12 May 1868.)

BRADSHAW, Armistead, 83, died last Monday in Maury County. (Columbia Herald, 10 Jan. 1873.)

BRADSHAW, Rev. James N., died 21 Jan. 1895 in Madison, Florida, age 77; President of Southern Methodist Female College many years; he was buried at Covington, Ga., in the City Cemetery; was reared at Campbell Station in Maury County.

BRADY, Mrs. Catherine, age 100 years 7 months 13 days, died yesterday at City Hospital in Memphis and buried in Elmwood Cemetery. (Memphis Avalanche, 11 Feb. 1866.)

BRAGG, Braxton. Galveston, Texas, Sept. 27.--General Braxton Bragg dropped dead while crossing Twentieth Street in front of the Post Office. He was 61 years of age. The body lies in state and will be taken to Mobile if arrangements can be made at New Orleans for conveyance. General Bragg's health was good up to the moment of death. The cause of his death was a fatal syncope induced by organic disease of the heart. (Columbia Herald and Mail, 29 Oct. 1876.)

General Braxton Bragg, who died last week in Galveston, Texas, was born in Warren County, NC, 1815 and was admitted to West Point 1833, graduating in 1837. He was appointed second lieutenant in the 3rd Artillery and served under General Taylor in the Mexican War and in 1855 was offered a commission in a new regiment which he declined and entered private life. At the commencement of the Civil War he became a brigadier general in the Confederate Army, being stationed at Pensacola to act against Fort Pickens. He was not generally successful while in this command. In 1862, having been appointed a general of division under orders to serve under General Albert Sidney Johnston in the Army of the Mississippi, he took part in the two days battle of Shiloh. On the death of Johnston, he was appointed to the command of the entire force with the full rank of general in which position he conducted a brilliant campaign against the forces of General Buell...His chief exploit was at Chickamauga, when he defeated the army of General Rosecrans, though afterwards he was defeated by General Grant, which led to his removal from command in January 1864 and was appointed Chief of Staff by President Davis, in November 1864 he succeeded to the command of the Department of North Carolina but having been defeated at Fort Fisher, Wilmington, and Kingston was superseded by General Joe Johnston with whom he surrendered to General Sherman 26 April 1865. Since then he has not appeared before his countrymen, preferring the quiet of private life to the turmoil of public. (Columbia Herald and Mail, 6 Oct. 1876.)

BRAGG, Mrs. Elese, wife of General Braxton Bragg, died a few days ago and buried beside her husband at Mobile, Ala. (Linden, TN, Mail, 2 Oct. 1908.)

BRAGG, Joseph, was murdered recently; three guerrillas, Davis, Schaegger, and Clark went to his house in Tipton Co., TN, and hanged Bragg. A few days ago Schaeffer and Clark were captured and one of them hanged; Davis is still at large. (Nashville Dispatch, 20 Nov. 1863.)

BRANNON, James, business man of Louisville, died in Nashville on Friday; his remains are to be taken to Louisville. (Nashville Daily Union, 4 March 1865.)

BRATTON, George, died 17 Jan. 1889 in Memphis where he was undergoing treatment; brought back to Leatherwood Creek, Hickman County, for burial. (Maury Democrat, 31 Jan. 1889.)

BRAZIER, William, of Maury County, is confined to his bed with cancer on left side of his head. (Columbia Herald and Mail, 15 May 1874.)

BREATHED, Dr. James, of Hancock, Maryland, died a few days ago; he was
known during the war as "Heroic Major Breathed of Stuart's Horse
Artillery". (Memphis Daily Avalanche, 4 March 1870.)

BRECKENRIDGE, General, will return to Kentucky from exile soon. He
stands foremost in affections of people of Kentucky. (Memphis Daily
Appeal, 1 Feb. 1869.) One of the successful lawyers of the Pacific
slope is a son of the famous John C. Breckenridge, and a brother of
the Kentucky congressman, bears the curious name of "Owen County"
Breckenridge. (Florence, Ala., Times, 12 Dec. 1891.)

BREECE, Mrs. Alva, and Mrs. Miller (D. C. Miller's mother) died a few
days ago in Hickman County; also Mrs. John Burchett, died Oct. 23 on
Swan Creek. (Columbia Herald and Mail, 5 Nov. 1875.)

BRICKFORD, age 14, young boy, committed suicide by shooting himself in
Waterbury, Vermont, on the 14th; no cause assigned. (Nashville
Dispatch, 1 June 1862.)

BRIDGEFORTH. "Information sought on Benjamin Bridgeforth's connection
with the Confederate Army." (Daily Herald, Columbia, TN, 22 April
1917.)

BRIEN, Marsh Howard, 1 year 7 months, died April 16 in Edgefield; son
of Carl D. and Luzette Brien. (Nashville Daily Union, 21 April
1865.)

BRIGGS, Laura, daughter of W. W. Briggs, granddaughter of Esquire
Grimmet, age 15, died on the 15th on Pine River, Hickman County.
(Columbia Herald, 21 Nov. 1873.)

BRIGHT, James L., 21, died April 18, at home of father in Ashland City,
age 21 years 8 months 18 days. (Nashville Dispatch, 26 April 1862.)

BRIM, Miss Ellen, died Monday of consumption at Sawdust, Maury County,
buried at Nebo. (Columbia Herald and Mail, 2 March 1877.)

BRITTON, Mr., who lived 12 miles south of Columbia, hung himself near
railroad at Brentwood, Williamson County, on Tuesday, by using a lin-
en duster as rope; had been drinking and lost quite a sum of money.
(Whig and Tribune, Jackson, TN, 14 June 1873.)

BROADWAY, John, died sometime before June 1843 in Wayne County, when a
non-resident notice published; Benjamin and John Broadway had land
on Second Creek; his heirs were Thomas Lanear, Smith Broadway, a
minor, John Broadway, and Benjamin Broadway. (Columbia Observer,
20 July 1843.)

BROOKS, H. Clay, died Oct. 29 at Brooklyn, Alabama; married Elizabeth
Cook, daughter of John M. Cook of Columbia, TN. (Columbia Herald
and Mail, 13 Nov. 1874.)

BROWN, Ex-Senator Joseph E., of Georgia, died Friday at home in Atlanta.
He was Governor of Georgia during the war; one of the wealthiest men
in the South and is gratefully remembered by the Southern Baptists
for his gift of $50,000 to the Southern Baptist Seminary in Louis-
ville. (Maury Democrat, 6 Dec. 1894.) The will of Joseph Brown was
sent to probate in Georgia; he left property worth $1,500,000; he
owned 30,000 acres in Texas, 3 farms in Georgia, and lots in Georgia
and Colorado. (Maury Democrat, 14 Feb. 1895.)

BROWN, William, died in Columbia recently; his brother R. S. Brown of
Martinsville, Indiana, was in town for funeral. (Columbia Herald
and Mail, 18 Jan. 1878.)

BROWN, Mrs. Mary E., age 20, died May 6 of consumption in Hickman County
and was survived by her husband Thomas H. Brown and two children;
daughter of Clagett Primm and granddaughter of Mr. Gray. (Columbia
Herald and Mail, 24 May 1878.)

BROWN, Mrs. Henry, has died; lived on Turkey Creek in Maury County and was buried at Goshen Church, where she had been a member for 34 yrs. (Maury Democrat, 8 Aug. 1895.)

BROWN, Capt. A. C., was among those killed at the fight at Lebanon on May 5; son-in-law of Major Vannoy of Nashville; in Louisiana Cavalry. (Nashville Dispatch, 15 May 1862.)

BROWN, Granville D., only son of late Governor A. V. Brown, age 16, went to Arkansas to see about his mother's business; he was shot and killed by overseer for interferring with his duties; shot in the eye and killed instantly. (Nashville Dispatch, 27 May 1862.) Granville Pillow Brown, 16, died April 28 in Arkansas. (Nashville Dispatch, 8 June 1862.)

BROWN, Joseph, 84, of Columbia, died last week in Vincennes, Indiana; has son Charles Brown living in Columbia; well traveled and well educated. (Columbia Herald, 23 Jan. 1891.)

BROWN, Thomas, 65, died Monday 7 miles northwest of Franklin. (Memphis Daily Appeal, 24 Jan. 1870.)

BROWN, Miss Jennie, died on 31st near Zion, Maury County; daughter of Caldwell Brown. (Columbia Herald and Mail, 26 Feb. 1875.)

BROWN, Mrs. Sarah W., wife of Honorable A. V. Brown, died on the 14th in Pulaski. (Tennessee Democrat, Columbia, TN, 23 May 18-4.) (N. B., She was Sarah Burrus before her marriage, daughter of Joseph Burrus and his wife Sophia Rucker of Rutherford County, TN.)

BROWN, well known scout, belonging to Home Guards in the upper end of Hamilton County, TN, was found dead in road about a mile out of Harrison on the 28th; shot through head; body was buried a short distance from where it was found. (Nashville Daily Union, 1 Feb. 1865.)

BROWN, Gen. Allen, 80, one of the oldest and best known men in Maury County, died at his home January 17 in Columbia; settled here in 1813. (Whig and Tribune, Jackson, TN, 1 Feb. 1873.)

BROWN, Mrs. Lucy Draper, died 14 Dec. 1884 on White Oak Creek, wife of Dr. John Brown. (Times-Journal, Waverly, TN, 2 Jan. 1885.)

BROWN, Dr. John, 84, died 10 May 1888. (Houston County News, 24 May 1888.)

BROWN, Judge William T., old and highly esteemed member of the Memphis bar died near Memphis on the 18th. (Nashville Dispatch, 25 July 1862.)

BROWN, Joseph. "We heard it reported yesterday that the veteran pioneer and Indian fighter, Colonel Joe Brown of Giles County, died during the morning at the advanced age of 96 years." (Nashville Republican Banner, 6 Feb. 1868.)

BROWN, Bedford. "From Memphis Argus of the 26th ult. Bedford Brown, son of the late Judge Brown of Memphis, who resides on his plantation 18 miles above Memphis on the Tennessee side was aroused from his sleep by continued knocking on the front door of his residence. He arose, went to the door, opened it, and asked who was there. A man named Allen was standing immediately in front of the house, and Mr. Brown had no sooner appeared in the doorway than the former advancing a step or two, and drawing a repeater, demanded his money. The demand was refused, and Allen at once fired at Brown, the shot taking effect, the ball piercing his heart. He fell dead at his murderer's feet. Allen did not remain to search for money, but immediately fled, and up to yesterday noon had not been apprehended. A metallic case was sent from the city for Mr. Brown's remains yesterday and they will doubtless be brought to the city for interment." (Nashville Daily Union 6 March 1864.)

BROWN, James, was killed May 29 in Franklin County by members of Capt. Rickman's group of Brownlow militia; they said he was a bushwhacker and belonged to Rodgers guerrillas and had bragged of how many Federal soldiers he had bushwhacked. (Memphis Avalanche, 4 June 1867.) There is a reign of terror in Franklin County by the Brownlow militia; they shot a man named Brown and also a Tullahoma man. The President has been petitioned for protection. (Memphis Avalanche, 31 May 1867.)

BROWNLOW, Lt. Columbia Sentinel, Sat., 21st inst.--On Wednesday last at 8 p.m., Major Fitzgibbon, at the head of 80 men, started for the immortal Cooper and his comrades. Crossing Duck River, eight miles below town, came upon the rear of Cooper's camp, who, as usual, led the Major, however, losing five of his men as prisoners; the Major still pursuing him through the cedars. Cooper camped three times during the night, in order to elude his pursuers, but in vain. On the run through the cedars, one of Cooper's men was wounded in the back. Cooper, still on the run, went through the mountains and crossed Anderson's creek. There he lost one man killed, supposed to be Lt. Brownlow.

At length Cooper, thinking himself safe, halted, but the Major coming upon his rear guard, they again "skedaddled," but keeping up a running fight some eight miles below Mount Pleasant--the Major capturing four more of the guerrillas. Some of Cooper's men wore the Federal uniform. The result of the scout foots up as follows: Major capturing 22 prisoners belonging to the 9th Tennessee Cavalry, Col. Biffle, and 47 horses. The Major and his little band deserve high praise for the gallantry displayed, and the good done. With his indomitable courage and great skill in a military point, he will soon rid the country of so great a pest as guerrillas, thieves and robbers. May success attend him. (Nashville Daily Union 27 Nov. 1862.)

BRUNTON, William Russell, 8 years 1 month, drowned on 2d while bathing in river; son of W. H. and J. E. Brunton. (Nashville Dispatch, 6 Aug. 1862.) Little son of W. F. Brunton drowned in Cumberland River near Brown's Landing on Sunday, was an only child, between 10 and 12 years. (Nashville Dispatch, 5 Aug. 1862.)

BRYAN, Willis, infant son of J. J. and Zulinah Bryan, died on 12 Aug. 1864. (Nashville Daily Union, 21 Feb. 1865.)

BRYAN, Zulinah, wife of J. J., age 35 years 8 months 16 days, died on 23 Jan. 1865; gone to join her dear little children in heaven; died of consumption. (Nashville Daily Union, 21 Feb. 1865.)

BRYAN, James T., druggist at Spring Hill, TN, died on 2d of typhoid; (Columbia Herald, 18 Nov. 1870.) To be buried November 5 at Spring Hill. (Columbia Herald, 4 Nov. 1870.)

BRYAN, Mrs. Sarah, wife of W. D. Bryan, died last week in Hickman County. (Columbia Herald, 29 Sept. 1871.)

BRYANT, Mrs. Hannah M., 59, died at Andrews, Maury County, on June 23; widow of William D. Bryant, who was killed in war in Georgia; died of tuberculosis of bowels; buried Rock Springs Cemetery. (Maury Democrat, 27 June 1895.)

BRYANT, John, of the revenue department of Bedford County, was shot twice in side by D. P. Brown of Fairfield, while trying to arrest Brown for "violating the revenue law." Badly wounded. (Columbia Herald and Mail, 29 March 1878.)

BUCKLEY, Joseph, deckhand on the Lady, fell overboard and drowned Thursday night while boat backing away from Fulton Landing. (Memphis Avalanche, 17 Nov. 1866.)

BUDDEKE, Bernard, 8 years 9 months, son of John H. and Mary Jane, died on the 20th in Nashville. (Nashville Dispatch, 22 July 1862.)

BUFORD, Col. N. C., leading citizen of Giles County, age 61, died on Monday. (Nashville Republican Banner, 28 Nov. 1869.)

BULLOCK, Ralph, favorite young jockey, associated with career of horse Tim Whiffles, died Jan. 28 at Middleham, England. (Nashville Daily Union, 4 March 1863.)

BUNDY, Dr. Z. T., formerly of Wayne and Hardin Counties, TN, is now surgeon in the Confederate home in Austin, Texas; Confederate veteran, he was born Olive Hill, Hardin County, on 27 Feb. 1849, the son of John and Nancy Bundy, natives of North Carolina, who came to Tennessee in 1826. Many wrongs and outrages were perpetrated upon the residents of his section by the bushwhackers, who pretended to be Union sympathizers and from which his father did not escape, so incensed the lad that at the age of 15 he left home and joined Company F, 9 Tennessee Cavalry, Capt. John Johnson's company under Colonel Biffle; later he went to Texas and joined the Texas Rangers and fought the Indians; in 1875 returned to Tennessee to study medicine and married Patty Fariss; has twice been mayor of his home town in Texas. (Clifton Mirror, 10 May 1907.)

BUNTING, Thomas W., a Confederate soldier, died in general hospital at Louisville last week. (Nashville Dispatch, 27 July 1862.)

BURDON, J. W., killed during the war by George W. Shackelford in Yazoo County Mississippi; Shackelford has been convicted of manslaughter and sentenced to four years. (Memphis Avalanche, 29 Dec. 1866.)

BURFIELD, also BIERFIELD. In Franklin, TN, on 15th masked horsemen broke open the store of a Prussian Jew, Burfield, a Radical; he tried to get away but was killed by five bullets; his negro servant was mortally wounded. (Memphis Daily Appeal, 17 Aug. 1868.) Bierfield was the leader of a group of assassins who killed Jeremiah Ezzell. Bierfield was from Russia and had lived in Franklin one year...he was determined to make a fortune out of these troubles. (Memphis Daily Appeal, 20 Aug. 1868.)

BURKE, John, Englishman, drowned in Cumberland River Sunday, about five or six miles below Nashville. (Memphis Avalanche, 7 July 1867.)

BURNETT, Gen. Ward B., of New York, is only surviving graduate of West Point who was a general in the Mexican War. (Erin Review, 10 Sept. 1881.)

BURNETT, Isaac, Wayne County, was shot and killed by Louis Coffey. Burnett's 13 year old daughter eloped with Coffey and married him recently. (Maury Democrat, 15 Aug. 1895.)

BURNS, Anthony, fugitive slave who was arrested 1854 in Boston and remanded into bondage and afterwards redeemed, died on July 27 in St. Catharines, Canada West. (Nashville Dispatch, 14 Sept. 1862.)

BURNS, John, was shot dead on Saturday night by Dr. J. C. M. Rankin at Ashland in Wayne County, TN. (Columbia Herald, 2 Nov. 1871.)

BURNS, Elijah, was killed three miles below Fayetteville on Elk River; KKK items found in pockets. He had said he was a member of KK. (Memphis Daily Appeal, 17 Sept. 1868.) Body of Elijah Burns, once noted horse thief of Middle Tennessee, was found recently in Elk River; evident marks that he had been lynched for his crimes. (Memphis Daily Appeal, 6 Sept. 1868.)

BURR. Monument erected mysteriously at midnight over grave of Aaron Burr at Princeton, New Jersey, by relatives. (Memphis Avalanche, 6 April 1867.)

The attorney general Bates has decided against claims of the widow of Aaron Burr for a pension. They were married 1833, divorced in New York 1835, and he died 1836. (Nashville Dispatch, 2 Dec. 1863.)

BURROUGHS, George, formerly of Chicago, but recently of Memphis, was arrested on the 17th at Cario, Illinois, on charges of being a spy. Medicine and papers found in his trunk. (Nashville Dispatch, 27 July 1862.)

BURROW, Nimrod, old and eccentric farmer of Carlisle County, Kentucky, was shot and killed by his tenant Jack Russell a few days ago; there had been a fuss and feud for some time. (Houston County News, 28 July 1887.)

BURROW (also BURROWS), Rube. The history of Rube Burrows, the notorious murderer and robber, reads like a romance of the olden time. Bold, brave and brutal, for years he has defied the laws of the land, and his exploits have paled into insignificance the deeds of his most daring predecessors in crime. Pursued with relentless vigor, he at last falls prey to two negroes, and then in a characteristic break for liberty, he is shot down, and pays with his life the penalty of his misdeeds. The Times here briefly records the incidents of his capture and death.

HIS CAPTURE

DEMOPOLIS, A., Oct. 7.--This afternoon at Myrtlewood, in South Marengo, Mr. John McDuffie and others, sent out by the Southern Express company captured the real, genuine Rube Burrows.

As reported in the daily papers heretofore, he was working his way back to Lamar county, had passed through Monroe, and had been in Marengo the past few days.

Detectives in numbers, assisted by deputy sheriffs, have been close behind him in this county since Sunday.

Today McDuffie came upon Rube who had stopped out of the rain in a house. McDuffie arranging with two colored men to go in the house, ostensibly for some other purpose. Burrows had placed his rifle in the corner of the room, but had his revolvers on him. The darkies engaged him in conversation and then grabbed him by the hands, preventing his shooting. He fought the darkies furiously until McDuffie and others got in and after a desperate struggle they succeeded in conquering and securely tieing the great desperado.

McDuffie went to Linden jail this afternoon with his famous prisoner strapped hard and fast in front of him on his horse, his body being across, head on one side and feet on the other. His position was very painful but he had to be allowed no chances. The great Rube is now in jail in reality. He had only $178 on his person.

HIS ESCAPE AND DEATH

Demopolis, Oct. 8.--Rube Burrows is dead. He died with his boots on. In the last moments of his life he manifested that desperate courage and reckless daring which has made him the most notorious character in the annals of Alabama crime. Bound and guarded by armed men, his attempt to regain liberty showed the cunning and coolness of a devil. Last night, for safe keeping, Burrows was placed in the sheriff's office inside the jail at Linden. McDuffie and a negro named Marshall were put to guard him. The three men sat there through the still watches of the night, keeping vigil while the world slept, unconscious that a great desperado was at last in the coils of the law. Midnight had sounded four hours before, when the prisoner complained of hunger and asked for food.

"Nothing can be obtained at this hour," said Guardsman McDuffie.

"But I must eat," responded Burrows. "Hand me that old sack of mine there are some crackers in it." And he pointed to an old cloth bag that he carried when captured. The bag was passed to him. With manacled hands he stooped down, opened it and taking out some crackers, gave them to the guards. Bending once more to the bag he arose with a revolver in each hand.

"Now untie me," he demanded of the astonished guards.

They per force obeyed.

"Unlock the door," was the stern demand. And with their eyes on the cold, steady steel that glittered in the flickering light of the oil lamp the guards unbarred the door and the wide world lay before the freed bandit.

"Now handcuff that man," he said to Marshall, referring to McDuffie, and again the desperate man's stern bidding was obeyed. "Now you come with me," he said to the negro guard, and with a key in his hand and the negro in front he passed out of the door, locking it behind him, and holding McDuffie fast a prisoner.

Being aware that J. D. Carter, one of his captors, had his money, $178, Burrows commanded Marshall, the negro, to take him to Carter's room at the hotel. Arrived at the hotel, it was ascertained that Carter was not there, but was sleeping in the back room of P. B. Glass's store. Thither the two hurried, and Burrows knocked loudly on Carter's door. Carter arose and opened the door.

"Give me my money instantly," demanded the desperado, covering the man with his revolvers.

Carter quickly stepped back in the dark room, got his revolver, returned to the door and he and Burrows opened fire at the same moment. Burrows retreated at once, but keeping up his firing all the while. Carter followed him and his revolver answered that of Burrows. Each fired five shots and each fell, Burrows mortally wounded and Carter badly hurt.

Burrows was hit but once, that in the bowels, and died without a word.

Carter was hit but once, and that making a flesh wound in the shoulder. Marshall, the negro, received a slight wound from one of Burrows' bullets.

Circuit Clerk C. B. Cleveland, who resides near the scene of the tragedy, says that he was awakened about 4 o'clock by a loud knocking on the door of Glass' store. He got up, dressed, and then heard rapid reports of firearms and hurried in the direction of the noise, and near the gate leading to the jail yard he saw a man lying. His attention being attracted by a groan, he approached the prostrate form, which shook with convulsive shudders, and he saw Rube Burrows lying there dead. He, who for long years outraged and defied the law, died with a groan upon his lips. Immediately Cleveland heard a voice on the opposite side of the street in the direction of Glass' Store, cry out, "Oh, my mother." The voice was that of J. D. Carter, who Cleveland at once attended to

The rewards which will go to his captors are as follows:

By the Mobile & Ohio railroad and the Southern Express company, $2,000.
By the United States government $1,000 for each member of the Burrows band.
By the Illinois Central railroad and Southern Express company, $1,000.
By the state of Mississippi, $500.
By the state of Arkansas and the St. Louis, Arkansas & Texas Railway company, $500.
By the state of Alabama, $500.
Total reward, $7,500.

BIRMINGHAM, Ala., Oct. 9.--In a little graveyard among the hills of Lamar county this afternoon, all that was mortal of Rube Burrows was laid in the grave by the side of his wife, who died six years ago. Hundreds of men and women, who had been the playmates and friends of the dead outlaw came for a last look at his face, and one and all recognized him at once. The last link in the chain of his complete identification had been forged, his relatives, friends, and neighbors who have known him from childhood, said without hesitation that the dead man was Rube Burrows. A gray-haired man of 70 years was the last to look upon the face of the dead, and when he turned from the coffin a sigh of relief came from his lips while tears flowed from his eyes. The old man was Allan Burrows, the father of Rube, an honest citizen, known and respected by all who know him.

The body of Burrows arrived here from Demopolis, Ala., at 3:30 o'clock this morning. Even at that hour thousands of people were gathered about the depot, hoping to catch a glimpse of the body or at least the coffin containing it. At every station along the road where the train stopped hundreds had gathered out of morbid curiosity.

The coffin was opened here, and all who cared to were allowed to see the body. Placing the open coffin on an end, and arranging the outlaw's rifle and pistols at his side, a flash-light photograph was taken.

One of the first men who pressed forward for a look at the body when it arrived here was Neil Bray, who was shot by Burrows when he was escaping from the police in Montgomery, Ala., three years ago.

"That's the man who shot me," said Bray. "I shall never forget that face."

Among the articles found on the outlaw when captured were the railroad checks and vouchers for $2000 and the lottery tickets taken from the express car at the Flomaton train robbery. He also had the pistol he took from the express messenger the same time.

There was nothing of the dime novel style of bandit in the appearance of Burrows. He was a typical backwoodsman in appearance, and his face was expressive of only low cunning and cruelty. He was six feet tall, very slender, and would not weigh over 150 pounds.

This morning Superintendent Agee and detective Jackson of the Southern Express company took the body to Sulligent, Lamar County, where it was delivered to his father and brother. It was immediately taken to the burying ground and interred without any religious ceremony. Several parties in the city wired the family offers of a large sum for the body, which they wanted to embalm and place on exhibition, but the offers were all refused. (Florence, Ala., Times, 17 Oct. 1890.)

"Allen H. Burrow, the father of Rube Burrow, was born in Maury County, Tennessee, 21 May 1825, his parents moving to Franklin County, Alabama in 1826, and who, in 1828, settled within the vicinity of his present home in Lamar County, Alabama." (From "Rube Burrow, King of Outlaws and His Band of Train Robbers" by G. W. Agee of Memphis, 1890, no page number.)

OUTLAW'S FATE - The story of the capture of Rube Burrows, the famous train-robber and murderer, in a lonely cabin near South Marengo, Ala., by two deputies, assisted by two colored men, was supplemented Wednesday by the killing of the outlaw after he had wounded one of his captors. The deputies, strapping him to a horse, carried him 12 miles to Linden jail, where they arrived late Tuesday night, and placed him in the wooden structure. It was agreed that Detective McDuffie and one of the colored men named John Marshall should stay in the jail with the prisoner, still handcuffed and securely bound, until daylight while Detective Carter and the negro went off to get a brief nap before day. A short time before day Wednesday morning he complained of being hungry, and asked for something to eat. McDuffie answered he had nothing to eat.

A sachel of Burrow's was lying in one corner of the room "I have some crackers in my bag there, if you will hand it to me," said the

43

prisoner. McDuffie handed the bag to Burrows without opening it, and Burrows put manacled hands in the bag for a moment and brought out two pistols, covered McDuffie and the negro, and ordered them to untie him, which they did.

Keeping the negro in front of him, Burrows disarmed both men and unlocked the front door and asked where Carter was with his money. When told that he was at the hotel he ordered the negro to show him the way, remarking that he was going to have the money back or kill somebody. He locked McDuffie in the jail and with the negro for a guide went to Carter's room, and getting the drop on him, demanded his money. Carter sprang to one side and drawing a pistol fired at Burrows. The outlaw fired at the same instant.

Carter's sudden movement probably saved his life. He received the outlaw's bullet. The bullet from Carter's pistol struck Burrows in the middle of the abdomen and passed through his body. Carter is badly wounded. (Maury Democrat, 16 Oct. 1890.)

BURTON, Eddie, son of E. H. and Susan Hill, age 2 years 2 months 8 days, died on the 2d in Edgefield. (Nashville Dispatch, 7 June 1862.)

BUSBY, Benjamin. Information wanted on Benjamin Busby, age 19, 5 ft. 9 in., blue eyes, light hair; since Dec. 1862 in the 81st Indiana Volunteers; took sick, sent to Nashville in ambulance, and nothing heard from him since; son of John Busby of New Albany, Indiana. (Nashville Daily Union, 9 April 1863.)

BUSHY HEAD, ex-chief of Cherokee Nation, died recently. (Florence, Ala., Times, 23 Jan. 1892.)

BUSSELL, Kennett B., formerly of Davis County, Indiana, and a private in Company D, 44 Indiana Volunteers, died of apoplectic convulsion and inquest held yesterday. (Nashville Daily Union, 18 June 1865.)

BUTLER, Benjamin F. "The proper text for the funeral of General Butler is Jeremiah III, 19." (Memphis Daily Appeal, 5 Nov. 1868.) General Benjamin F. Butler died 11 Jan. 1893 in Washington of heart failure. Ben Butler's career is too well known in the South to require extended comment. If he had any good traits they are yet to be discovered. (Maury Democrat, Columbia, TN., 19 Jan. 1893.) General Butler's will has been filed, dated 1854 and with codicil added in 1862. All his real and personal property has been left to relatives, including a wife and mother since deceased. (Maury Democrat, 9 Feb. 1893.) Beast Butler appointed a negro boy of Salem, Mass., to cadetship at West Point, first one ever appointed. (Memphis Daily Appeal, 12 Mar. 1870.) General Butler lives on a scale that most millionaires would regard extravagant, keeping up establishments in Washington, Boston, and Lowell. Despite a belief to the contrary, he is a remarkably generous man and gives away more money than do many people who have reputations for philanthropy. (Florence, Ala., Times, 16 May 1891.) (N. B.--Butler is buried in Lowell, Mass. While in New Orleans during the Civil War, he was accused of stealing the silverware from the house in which he made his headquarters and was given the nickname of Spoons. Also while there, he gave his order against the women of New Orleans, which outraged the South. The 1863 Nashville papers have almost daily "outrages" by Butler reported. One person offered $50,000 to the person who would kill Butler.)

BUTLER, Col. S. F., 11th Mississippi CSA, who was killed at Sherosburg, his remains have been buried in the Odd Fellow Cemetery at Columbus, Mississippi. (Memphis Daily Appeal, 6 Nov. 1868.)

BUTLER, Mrs. Julia, relict of Col. P. M. Butler, of Edgefield, S. C., died of grief at the death of her youngest son, E. J. Butler, who was killed in battle on the 1st near Richmond. (Nashville Dispatch, 26 July 1862.)

BUTLER, John, will be 92 next December; lives on Bear Creek in Maury
County. (Columbia Herald, 18 Feb. 1870.) Was 93 last December.
(Columbia Herald, 24 March 1871.) Died Tuesday, would have been 93
on December 19; built the house he lived in in 1808. (Columbia
Herald, 17 November 1871.)

C

CAHAL, Miss Dee, born in Columbia, TN, died 23 July 1909 in Nashville;
teacher; her father was from Virginia and was chancellor; her mother
was Ann Saunders; she had a sister Mrs. Hoggatt of Cloverbottom farm;
brother Lt. Terry Cahal, who was in Confederate Army; and a sister
Mrs. William Osborn; through a family disagreement "she was left
practically penniless." (Confederate Veteran, August 1909, page 424)
(N. B., She was daughter of Judge Terry Cahal of Maury County, whose
home still stands in Columbia and is presently owned by Mr. and Mrs.
Newsom Cooper.)

CAHIL, John, the poor man, who was stabbed seriously at his own door
about three weeks ago is still alive but in dangerous state...he can
scarcely live this week out; family is in very destitute condition.
(Nashville Dispatch, 4 Nov. 1862.) John Cahil, poor hard-working
man, died on the 6th at home on Pearl Street; wife and two children
in very destitute circumstances. (Nashville Dispatch, 7 Nov. 1862.)

CAHANIN, Gustave, a resident of Opelousa, Louisiana, for the past fifty
years, died on the 9th instant. (Memphis Daily Appeal, 25 July 1869)

CALDWELL, John S., 80, of Blanton Chapel area in Maury County, died and
buried Blanton Chapel Cemetery; member of Lasea Church of Christ.
(Columbia Herald, 9 Jan. 1891.)

CALDWELL, Mrs. Mary Pointer, died Wednesday, lived in Maury County almost 50 years; relict of Dr. St. Clair F. Caldwell; member of the
Presbyterian Church for 40 years; buried by husband, daughter and
step-daughter in family burying ground; has one daughter Mrs. M. L.
Stockard of Mt. Pleasant. (Columbia Herald and Mail, 18 Jan. 1878.)

CALDWELL, John S., 90 years 90 days, elder of Presbyterian Church, died
on the 29th ult. (Tennessee Watchman, Clarksville, TN, 7 Dec. 1821.)

CALDWELL. Non-resident notice for Mary E. Caldwell and her husband
Alexander Caldwell. (Columbia Herald and Mail, 6 Nov. 1874.)

CALLAGHAN, Isaac, employee of H. C. Jackson, found in store Tuesday in a
speechless condition; died during the day; fell through a scuttle in
second floor to the first floor. (Nashville Daily Union, 26 Nov.
1863.)

CALLIS, C. M., 55, born in Louisa Co., Virginia, dropped dead with apoplexy on Friday last on streets of Hopkinsville, KY, where he was a
leading citizen. (Nashville Daily Union, 12 Feb. 1863.)

CALLOM, D. C., foreman, died of injuries when graining mill at Sycamore
Powder Company in Cheatham County, blew up last week. (Maury Democrat, 4 June 1891.)

CALHOUN, Col. W. R., of 1st South Carolina Artillery Regiment, was killed recently in duel with Major Alfred Rhett of same regiment; he
challenged Rhett; the disagreement had its origin in April 1861 at
the time of the bombardment of Fort Sumpter. (Nashville Dispatch,
6 Nov. 1862.)

CALHOUN, James C., 35, died 29 Dec. 1866 in Texas; he had gone west for
his health; lawyer; son of John A. Calhoun of Abbeville, South Carolina; grand-nephew of John C. Calhoun; Confederate soldier; he was
married eight years ago to the daughter of I. B. Kirkland; buried in
Elmwood Cemetery, Memphis. (Memphis Avalanche, 25 Jan. 1867.)

CALHOUN. From the Yazoo Banner: A citizen brought a white rose taken from John C. Calhoun's body when it lay in state in Charleston nearly twenty years ago. The rose was planted and it grows luxuriously. (Memphis Daily Appeal, 14 June 1870.)

CAIN, Francis D., Company C, 18th U. S. Infantry, sentenced to be shot at Murfreesboro, for mutiny; Cain to be shot on the 10th. Ezekiel Inman, 6 Kentucky, sentenced to be shot for desertion at Murfreesboro on the 14th; James Welsh, 40th Indiana, sentenced to be shot at Murfreesboro, on the 14th for desertion. (Nashville Daily Union, 8 April 1863.)

CAMERON, Colonel John F., formerly first lieutenant of the famous Chickasaw Guards, and afterwards captain of Bluff City Greys, died March 10 of tuberculosis. (Erin Review, 25 March 1882.)

CAMERON, Mrs. Sarah, 76, died on the 27th; old resident of Nashville; came here 1820. (Nashville Dispatch, 28 Aug. 1862.)

CAMPBELL, Major William, killed at Perryville, Ky., was member of the 15th Kentucky (U.S.) (Nashville Dispatch, 18 Oct. 1862.)

CAMPBELL, Andrew, died in Nashville on the 18th. (Nashville Dispatch, 21 Oct. 1862.)

CAMPBELL, Bob, his remains brought from Nashville and buried in Lasting Hope Cemetery in Maury County on Tuesday. (Columbia Herald, 10 Apr. 1891.)

CAMPBELL, Miss Sallie, granddaughter of Col. A. P. Hughes, died in Culleoka, Maury County, on Saturday. She is the fourth member of her family to die in last few weeks. (Columbia Herald and Mail, 16 June 1876.)

CAMPBELL, John, 90, died Sunday near Spring Hill, Maury County, and buried in Spril Hill Cemetery. (Columbia Herald, 3 April 1891.)

CAMPBELL, Lucius, died on the 17th of cholera in San Antonio, Texas; was member of Company G, Terry Rangers. (Memphis Avalanche, 21 Nov. 1866)

CAMPBELL, Thomas, died Saturday of typhoid fever at home on Cedar Creek in Perry County. (Linden Times, 12 Feb. 1880.)

CAMPBELL, Mrs. M. J., 72, died Saturday in Houston County; wife of Isaac Campbell. (Houston County Times, 12 May 1892.)

CAMPBELL, Dr. P., died recently in Texas; son of Mrs. R. Campbell of Culleoka, Maury County. (Maury Democrat, 9 Aug. 1894.)

CAPPS, Captain, "leader of stampeders" of Grainger County, was killed on the 16th. (Nashville Dispatch, 29 April 1862.)

CARMICHAEL, ___, died at city poor house in Quincy, Illinois, a few days ago; among his effects was found $1294.50 in gold. (Nashville Daily Union, 26 Feb. 1863.)

CARNEY, Peter, of Hopkinsville, Kentucky, on Jan. 10 went to meeting of the Order of Red Men in Columbia and then went to "Flat Rock"; he had $600 on him when he was last seen; believed to have been thrown into Duck River; citizens are dragging the river for him. (Nashville Republican Banner, 20 Jan. 1871.)

CARNEY, Nick, was shot dead by barkeeper in Jack Hall's restaurant in Clarksville; Carney had been drinking and the barkeeper shot in self defense; during the war he was a member of one of the partisan bands who won a terrible name in the annals of guerrilla warfare. (Memphis Avalanche, 26 July 1867.)

CARNEY, C. N., deceased, administrator's notice published. (Clarksville Weekly Chronicle, 17 Jan. 1862.)

CARNEY, Mrs. Elizabeth, 39, died on the 31st ult.; wife of Captain
Christopher N. Carney. (Clarksville Jeffersonian, 7 Sept. 1844.)

CARNOTER, Charles, died March 19 of pneumonia; from Vincennes, Indiana;
employee of Quartermaster shop in Nashville. (Nashville Daily Union,
21 March 1863.)

CARR, Willie, a little six year old boy, who was brought away by some
Federal soldier from the vicinity of Murfreesboro, TN, has been taken
into the family of J. W. Conway of Madison, Indiana, where he will be
well cared for. The Courier says that he had on, when found, a suit
of soldier clothes, which were rather large for him; that he said he
went to school to "Miss Mary" and that the father of the children,
Julia and Emma Cassida, with whom he used to play, was a dealer in
furniture. The above paragraph from the Louisville Journal will be
of deep interest to someone in Murfreesboro. (Nashville Daily Union,
18 Feb. 1863.)

CARR, John, justice of the peace of District 21 in Maury County, is a
bachelor, born in Bedford County, but cannot recall date of his birth.
(Maury Democrat, 4 July 1895.)

CARRIGAN, Leonidas M., of Tennessee, was arrested July 14 at Cairo as a
spy; confined at Alton prisoner, but ordered released to stay in St.
Louis...he is sick and dying of consumption and is to be allowed to
live in St. Louis and be nursed. (Nashville Dispatch, 10 Sept. 1862.)

CARRELL, Judge S. A., 79, died Saturday in Lawrenceburg, TN; born 15 Mar.
1817 in Maury County; married 3 Feb. 1842; had 12 children, 8 of whom
are living; had lived in Lawrence County for 70 years; at one time
was county court clerk of Lawrence County. (Maury Democrat, 6 Feb.
1896.)

CARROLL, Kile Taylor, son of Mr. and Mrs. Frank Carroll, of Newburg,
Lewis County, has died. (Maury Democrat 27 Sept. 1894.)

CARSON, Kitty, notorious courtezan and keeper of house of ill-fame, died
on Saturday night; leaves several small children to inherit her shame.
(Nashville Daily Union, 28 Feb. 1865.)

CARSON, Augustus, (c), died Monday at Franklin, TN; early in the war
attached himself to Confederate cause and followed it to the end; was
buried in Confederate gray. (Memphis Daily Appeal, 17 Aug. 1868.)

CARTER, Private Julius, member of Governors Guard (Richmond), was killed
in Malvern Hill skirmish. (Nashville Dispatch, 2 Aug. 1862.)

CARTER, Peter J., (c). one of the most prominent colored men in Eastern
Virginia, died recently at Onancock; for 45 years he had been a mem-
ber of State Legislature and had frequently presided over Republican
State conventions. (Erin Review, 7 Aug. 1886.)

CARTER, John W., vs Mary Carter, non-resident notice in suit for divorce
in Rutherford County. (Murfreesboro News, 26 Sept. 1860.)

CARTER, child of James Carter of Montgomery County, drowned in wash tub
last week. (Nashville Republican Banner, 23 July 1869.)

CARTER, Rev. D., of Wayne County, died on 2d of cholera; funeral to be
first Sunday in April next. (Columbia Observer, 19 Nov. 1840.)

CARTER, Mrs. Mit, died Tuesday night last at her home on Knob Creek in
Maury County. (Columbia Herald and Mail, 7 Dec. 1877.)

CARTER, Mit, killed last October by John R. Holcomb, who got 20 years
for the crime; Maury County. (Maury Democrat, 13 May 1881.)

CARUTHERS, Honorable Ab, of Lebanon, died recently in Marietta, Georgia.
(Nashville Dispatch, 16 May 1862.)

CASE, Mrs. M. E., funeral to be held today. (Nashville Republican Banner, 15 Nov. 1870.)

CASKEY, three weeks old son of James Caskey, died Saturday and buried Sunday at Kettle Mills. (Columbia Herald, 26 June 1896.)

CASSERATTA, Catherine Rosa, 20 months, daughter of John Casseratta of Memphis, funeral to be held today. (Memphis Daily Appeal, 25 April 1870.)

CASSARETTO. Motto Piccin was found murdered at old Borrow place, some miles northeast of Memphis; was an Italian and killed by negroes for his money; it was reported that he had some stored away, an amount of specie. (Memphis Daily Appeal, 10 May 1870.) The man's name was Cassaretto and he was shot by John Miller at the old Borrow place; the wound was painful but not dangerous. (Memphis Daily Appeal, 11 May 1870.)

CASTIEL, Martha, deceased, Wayne County; Thomas S. Carr was administrator of her estate as of 4 Feb. 1873; estate insolvent. (Columbia Herald, 14 Feb. 1873.)

CATES, Mrs. George, was buried at Pisgah Cemetery in Maury County last Saturday. (Columbia Herald and Mail, 14 April 1876.)

CATES, Mrs. Lewis, was killed recently in Carter County, TN, by Powell Phillips. Phillips was going to see Miss Britt, who lived with her sister Mrs. Cates. Mrs. Cates dressed up as a young man and pretended to be courting Miss Britt. Phillips was so exasperated he shot Mrs. Cates and she died in 20 minutes. (Nashville Dispatch, 6 May 1862.)

CATHEY, Emily, relict of William Cathey, died March __, age 55 on Love's Branch in Maury County. (Columbia Herald, 21 March 1873.)

CATRON, Honorable John, associate justice of Supreme Court of United States, died at his home in Nashville last evening; his health had been rapidly declining for 12 months past. (Nashville Daily Union, 31 May 1865.)

CAUGHRON, Mrs. Louise, of Santa Fe, Maury County, died. She was wounded when husband James Caughron was murdered: "The ball taking effect in her mouth and passing into her neck, where it lodged and remained." Many thought the wound was the cause of the paralysis which killed her. (Columbia Herald, 30 Jan. 1891.)

Our community (Santa Fe) was somewhat excited this week by a report given by a young Mr. Wade. He was coming to Santa Fe, when he was overtaken by a tall man on horseback, a stranger, who had a large navy pistol hanging to his saddle. When passing Mrs. Caughron's dwelling, he asked Wade who lived there and on being told said, "I knew who lived there, I killed the damned old rascal and shot his wife." He then asked where Dr. Sam Godwin was, when told that he had moved to Obion County, he said he must never cross his path again. The fellow, whoever he was, passed in the direction of Spring Hill. Our citizens were all off attending the burial of Mr. Latta, and no one was here to follow the armed stranger, who did not know the war was over. Old Squire Caughron was killed in his own house about the close of the war, by a party of ruffians, and his wife shot down and badly wounded. The ruffians are yet at large and if this is one, he ought to be caught. (Columbia Herald and Mail, 16 Oct. 1874.)

The following sketch comes from a brief history of Santa Fe, by Marise Lightfoot (based on work done by Charlotte Forgey Shenk):

"James Caughron had his home just outside of Santa Fe on the Fly Road. His first wife was Sarah Brooks and his second wife was Louisa Penelope Witherspoon, daughter of David and Penelope Gee Witherspoon. During the Civil War bushwhackers had paid several visits trying to get Mr. Caughron's money. One night near the end of the war, they called him and he went to the door and talked to them, but he refused to go out in the yard or tell them where the money was buried. With that they shot him in the heart.

"Mrs. Caughron cried out, "You have shot my husband." They shot at her and hit her in the mouth. She survived and the thieves did not get the money. It was buried in the path between the negro quarters and the big house. Sarah Ann Witherspoon and two of the Caughron girls happened to be in the house at the time. They ran to the next neighbor's Epp Miller and asked for help."

James Caughron is buried in the Cook-Caughron Cemetery on Fly Road out from Santa Fe and his stone reads:

JAMES CAUGHRON, born 8 March 1800, died 20 January 1865.

Penitentiary records in State Archives show that James Garner of Maury County got two years because on 20 Jan. 1865 he killed one Caughron and set fire to the house.

CAVENDER, ___, a Methodist minister in Van Buren County, TN, Union man, was taken out of his house, rope tied around his neck, and told to renounce Union; he refused; he was hanged and left to rot, flesh was torn from his body; this happened early in the war. (Nashville Daily Union, 6 March 1863.)

CAWHORN, Miss, of Carroll County, TN, has never learned to walk and has to be carried like a baby; weighs 160 pounds; is not lame, just does not know how to use her limbs. (Houston County News, 7 Oct. 1887.)

CEARLY, Sam H., 40, of District 15, Hardeman County, TN, was returning from mill, when his horse stumbled and fell on him; he was found unconscious and later died. (Columbia Herald, 6 March 1891.)

CHALMERS, James Ronald, born 11 Jan. 1831 in Halifax County, Virginia, died 9 April 1898, Memphis, Tennessee. (Tombstone inscription in Evergreen Section, Lot 448, Elmwood Cemetery, Memphis, Tennessee.) Brigadier general in the Confederate Army. "Called 'Bun' Chalmers because he was so small, according to his cousin Emily Ledford. (Confederate Veteran Magazine, July 1909, page 344.) General Chalmers had a good voice and was fond of singing, composed several songs which he would sing for the men, one veteran recalled hearing him sing as they lay in camp or rode along the march. (Confederate Veteran Magazine Aug. 1906, page 352.) Letter from General Chalmers: "...alarmed that rumor that he had left the country to avoid being arrested by U. S. Government: 'I have settled here to practice law... I am not prepared to desert my friends who have suffered and fallen, too.'...did nothing that he was ashamed of..." Office at 262 Front Street, Memphis. (Memphis Avalanche, 7 Feb. 1866.) (N. B., married 7 June 1854 to Rebecca Jones Arthur, daughter of William Arthur and his wife Susan Hill Peters; niece of Dr. George B. Peters.)

CHAMBERS, William, of Chatham, Ontario, who is claimed to be a survivor of the Battle of Waterloo, is reputed to be well and hearty at the great age of 107 years. (Maury Democrat, 17 May 1894.)

CHAMBERS, Dr. William H., died in Shelby County on the 15th. (Memphis Avalanche, 17 Nov. 1866.)

CHAMP, John W., formerly sheriff of Marshall County, died recently in Texas. (Columbia Herald and Mail, 16 July 1875.)

CHANDLER, James, of Lyon County, Kentucky, is 79 years old. He lives on farm on which his grandfather settled 109 years ago and has never been away from home more than 10 days at a time. (Maury Democrat, 7 Feb. 1895.)

CHANNEY, Joseph, has been the postmaster at Bristol, Anne Arundel, Co., Maryland, since the administration of President James K. Polk, by whom he was appointed. (Maury Democrat, 14 June 1894.)

CHAPMAN, ___, from near Mt. Pleasant, was shot by Tom Hatch and is in critical condition. (Nashville Republican Banner, 10 Sept. 1869.) Chapman died on Wednesday and Hatch fled. (Nashville Republican Banner, 22 Sept. 1869.) Tom Hatch, murderer of Chapman, has been arrested in Nashville. (Nashville Republican Banner, 26 Sept. 1869.)

CHARD, Mrs. Hanna, nearly all of whose 48 grandchildren and 142 great-grandchildren helped to celebrate her 105th birthday last week at Ferrel, NJ, takes a great comfort in her pipe, but she doesn't over indulge in it. She allows herself just four smokes a day. (Maury Democrat, 17 May 1894.)

CHARTER, J. R., 74, died March 20 of heart disease; lived on Leatherwood Creek, Maury-Hickman County line. (Columbia Herald, 11 April 1873.)

CHARTER, William, drowned on the 14th at the mouth of Leatherwood Creek; had been seining fish, river swollen, and he drowned in deep hole; was unable to swim; body was found the next day when a thunderstorm brought it to the surface; served in Company C, 9th Tennessee Cavalry in Confederate Army; (Columbia Herald, 20 June 1873, 27 June 1873.) (N. B., the paper also says he drowned on the 11th.)

CHEATHAM, Alexander, is dead, leaving widow Emma H., and son John L., a minor, who are non-residents; chancery court notice in paper. (Columbia Herald and Mail, 9 Oct. 1874.)

CHEATHAM, John, 76, died at home near Culleoka of flux. (Whig & Tribune Jackson, TN, 9 Aug. 1873.)

CHEATHAM, Lenora, daughter of L. P. Cheatham, funeral to be held today in Nashville. (Nashville Daily Union, 26 Feb. 1863.)

CHEATHAM, Dr. William A., married Mrs. Adelina Acklin last week. (Memphis Avalanche, 26 June 1867.)

CHEATHAM, Bertie, alias Bertie Stokes, who tried to commit suicide by drowning herself in Duck River a year or so ago, has been arrested for co-habiting with a negro; she was an illegitimate child; her mother lived some 9 miles this side of Nashville; she married railroad conductor Worthington and he died; she came to Columbia and entered a house of ill-fame; two years ago began living with Tom Powell (c). (Columbia Herald and Mail, 22 March 1878.)

CHERRELLA, Stephen, deceased. Letters of administration on his estate have been given on May 5 to Stephen Fransioli in Memphis. (Memphis Daily Appeal, 24 May 1870.)

CHERRY, infant of Mr. and Mrs. Kin Cherry, died Oct. 3 and buried at Rose Hill in Columbia. (Maury Democrat, 10 Oct. 1895.)

CHERRY, Mrs. William, Sr., died Saturday on the Sowell Mill Turnpike, and buried at Rose Hill in Columbia. (Columbia Herald, 3 April 1891.)

CHESSOR. Infant of Mr. and Mrs. J. H. Chessor of Lewis County died on June 6 and buried in Rock House Cemetery. (Maury Democrat, Columbia, TN, 20 June 1895.)

CHILES. Negro to be tried next week for the killing of his master Dr. Chiles in Todd County, KY. (Clarksville Weekly Chronicle, 8 May 1857.)

CHILTON, ___, A. Huddleston, and John Brown, Union citizens, were all shot by rebels at Liberty, Casey County, KY; Chilton, who was of Clinton County, KY, had five balls in him. (Nashville Dispatch, 9 Sept. 1862.)

CHOLERA DEATHS. The following have died of cholera at Paris, KY, up to Thursday night: William Ford, Charles Atternall, Mrs. Elizabeth Rains, Nat. Roark, F. Scherrer, and five Irishmen also. (Nashville Daily Gazette, 31 Aug. 1852.)

CHOERMAT, Rebecca, sues Charles Choermat for divorce in circuit court in Davidson County, January rules. (Nashville Daily Union, 21 April 1865.)

CHRISMAN, James F., shot and killed Friday night at Lancaster, Garrard County, KY, by his partner; they quarreled about a piece of silk. (Memphis Avalanche, 7 Nov. 1866.)

CHRISTY, E. P., founder of the famous Christy's Minstrels, who is worth $200,000, has for several months been possessed with the idea that the Confederates will invade the North and he will lose everything, has been insane over the subject for some time. On the 9th he jumped out of a window of his house in New York and at last accounts was in a dying condition. (Nashville Dispatch, 17 May 1862.)

CHUMLEY, Thomas Edward, 14 years 8 months, son of Henry Chumley of Battle Creek Mines, died Dec. 19 and brought to Maury County for burial in the family burying ground. (Columbia Herald, 3 Jan. 1873.)

CHURCH, Mrs. Charles, had twins last week and one has died; Maury County. (Columbia Herald and Mail, 14 Jan. 1876.)

CHURCH, J. N., living between Pulaski and Elkton, shot and killed a few days ago by Oliver Powell. (Nashville Republican Banner, 24 Dec. 1870.)

CHURCH. Elder Boyle, a Latter Day Saint, preached at Leatherwood Chapel last Sunday on "Plural Marriage", and will preach the funerals of Elder Church and his wife at the Methodist Church in Shady Grove on Sunday. (Columbia Herald, 22 March 1872.)

CHURCHILL, Lord Randolph, died last Thursday morning. (Maury Democrat 31 Jan. 1895.) Lord Randolph Churchill has had a large estate and fine country home left to him by an eccentric maiden lady, Miss Charlott Rose Raines, who had never set eyes on him, but who enriched him because of her admiration of his genius and service to his country. The only other beneficiaries under her will were 13 cats, who are to be maintained in comfort all their lives at the expense of her estate. $60 per cat is to be the annual allowance. Kittens which might appear upon the scene were not to be heirs-at-law. (Maury Democrat, 27 Dec. 1894.)

CISNEY, Theophilus, 104, died on the 20th ultimo in Hill Valley, Huntington, Pennsylvania; managed his farm until he was 94. (Memphis Avalanche, 16 April 1867.)

CLAGETT, Mrs. Rebecca, died at home of her son Mr. H. Clagett in Centervill, 24 Feb. 1876; born 7 Aug. 1788 in Maryland near Washington City; 1817 came to Hickman County; Methodist; raised seven children to maturity; mother of W. G. and H. Clagett. (Columbia Herald and Mail, 3 March 1876.)

CLAPP, Henry, formerly of Maury County, but now of Marshall County, is 104 years old; he doesn't believe he'll live past Christmas. (Columbia Herald and Mail, 27 Oct. 1876.) There is now living and has been living near Rally Hill (Maury County) ever since the oldest inhabitant can recollect, Henry Clapp, who according to his account is getting very old. He says he was 38 years old in the war of 1812, and drew for a draft, but was not taken as he drew a blank. With the exception of rheumatism in one leg, he is in good health, and can walk easily several miles a day, and bids fare to live several years longer. (Columbia Herald and Mail, 5 June 1874.)

CLARK, James P., funeral to be today in Nashville. (Nashville Daily Union, 8 Feb. 1863.)

CLARK, Tom. Alabama.--Last Monday night two burglars went into eight or
ten houses at Athens, Alabama, robbed the people of watches, jewelry,
money, and other valuables. The next day they left Athens for Florence in a buggy and robbed the people there.

That night they were pursued by the marshal and others, and with the
assistance of officers of Limestone County and Florence were caught
22 miles below Florence and brought back and placed in jail Wednesday
evening.

We learn by telegraph that they with a man named Clark, who was implicated in the burning of a house and other lawless acts, were taken
from the jail on yesterday (the 5th) and hung by a mob on the public
swuare in Florence.

In Columbia there was a burglary one night last week; attempts were
made to rob F. H. Wakins, R. G. Harris and A. Barr; it is believed
to be the ones who were hanged in Florence. (Columbia Herald,
6 Sept. 1872.)

A HANGING BEE IN FLORENCE YEARS AGO.--The annoying robberies that have
taken place in Florence during the past two weeks recalls to the minds
of our older citizens an event that occurred in this city soon after
the war, in which two bold, bad men paid the penalty of their acts
at the hands of the outraged people for offenses similar to those just
lately occurred.

At the time mentioned the people had been greatly annoyed by robberies and other grave misdemeanors, aggravated, no doubt, by the fact
that then the machinery of civil government had not yet got into perfect working order, owing to the eruptions and disturbances of the
"reconstruction" period. In this condition of things two professional burglars struck the town. Their coming had been heralded from
Athens and Rodgersville, where their depredations had been a grievous
sin upon the people. Their presence here was not known by the people
until the next morning after their exploits, when a number of our citizens awoke to the fact that while they and their families were
peacefully sleeping, their houses had been robbed and valuables of
all kinds--money, watches, silverware, etc.--had mysteriously disappeared.

The work of the robbers showed they were experts. They aroused nobody, and "went through" the different houses like old familiar
friends, in some instances lighting lamps, and after accomplishing
their purposes, leaving them brightly burning, apparently boastful
of their skill and dexterity in their nefarious work.

The next morning the city was astir early and the mysterious and
general robbery of the citizens was the talk of the town. A large
number of persons were sufferers.

In the meantime two well dressed strangers, dandies in appearance,
with stove-pipe hats setting off their handsome general get-up, had
been observed in town; and after a brief stay here they departed in a
buggy westward, taking the Waterloo road. Upon these men suspicion
rested. It was determined to follow them. Mr. Ed. Blair with a small
posse of brave men undertook the job. They came up with the dandy
outfit near Waterloo and their object was made known to the travellers.

The latter were very indignant. They threatened damage suits--and
their virtuous indignation and shiny silk ties discomfitted the posse
comitatus. They disclaimed any disrespect and were about to depart
(providing their indignant dude travellers would allow them)--when lo,
and behold, Mr. Blair happened to spy, sticking out from the top
lining of their buggy a part of the booty they had captured at
Florence.

The tables were turned--the thieves were arrested and brought to jail,
it may well be understood that excitement run high. The citizens

were made--and some of them mortified, at the slick manner in which they
had been robbed. A deep under current of feeling set in against the
robbers, but so far as the general public knew no serious trouble was
anticipated.

The next morning, however, when the town awoke, it found three men hanging to the limbs of the trees in the old Masonic Hall lot, on the corner
of Court and Tombigbee streets. During the night a large crowd of well
organized citizens placed the robbers in a position that gave assurance
that they would rob no more houses.

And there, hanging beside the two thieves, was the notorious Tom Clark,
a man who for years had been the terror of the rural district circumja-
cent to Florence, and against whom most grievous charges existed. Clark,
it was said, in his wild career as a bushwhacker, had cut out the tongue
of a Confederate soldier and had in the presence of its helpless mother
deliberately shot an infant to death, besides doing other things equally
atrocious.

He had been captured and lodged in jail here; and along with the two well
dressed thieves, attended the midnight picnic which for years afterwards
had a most salutary effect in preserving order and suppressing evil-
doers.

Florence is now in no humor to palliate the crime of the deliverate and
continuous robbery of her citizens. (Florence, Ala., Times, 10 Dec. 1892)

(N. B.--Memory is a tricky thing at best. The above account was written
many years after the event. The following account is from a contemporary
newspaper.)

GREAT EXCITEMENT IN FLORENCE/SUMMARY Punishment Visited Upon the Guilty!/
Crime and Punishment/THREE MEN HUNG ON ONE TREE!/Thomas Clark, the Notorious Outlaw, Executed!/Robbers captured and Hung by outraged Citizens!--
We give below the facts as we father them, of the hanging of Tom Clark
and the Burglars in our town last night.

Tuesday evening, a gentleman of Athens, came to this place and brought
information that on the night previous, nine houses had been burglarously
entered in the town of Athens, and much valuable property stolen therefrom. He stated that the parties supposed to have committed the burglary were coming towards this place, and advised the citizens to be on
the alert. But no one thought anything of it; and retired as usual, little suspecting burglars in our quiet town. During the night, the houses
of Judge Allington, Jas. Hancock and R. T. Simpson were entered, gold
watches stolen from the latter two.

About half past two o'clock that night two men were seen on the streets
driving a sorrel mare to a buggy.--Suspicion was at once fixed upon these
as the guilty parties, and at sunrise yesterday morning four men went in
pursuit. It was ascertained that they had gone in the direction of
Waterloo.

THE CAPTURE.--The capture of the robbers was effected by Messrs. Wm. E.
Blair (City Marshall), Wm. Barks, Wm. Joiner and W. B. Warson. The robbers had stopped for dinner and were about unhitching their horse near
the residence of Esq. Pettypool, a few miles below Gravelly Springs.
They offered little resistance, but expressed much surprise as Mr. Blair
and others rode up, and the Marshall demanded their surrender. A search
of their persons discovered nothing, but on examining the buggy, the pin
of a breastpin was observed sticking through the lining of the buggy top.
The party immediately went "upstairs", in the language of one of the gallant gentlemen, and found there eight watches, and a handful of breast-
pins, &c. On opening a drummer's satchel, which was in the buggy, files,
saws, and other burglarious instruments were found, amongst which was a
murderous sling-shot.

At this part of the game the countenances of the robbers fell. They
seemed to give up all thought of escape and to make up their minds to

suffer the penalty of the law, (if they could not by some ingenious trick manage to break jail). Their arms having been taken, they were placed in the buggy and with their captors, before and behind, turned toward Florence.

Just above Gravelly Springs, the party was joined by one of the many ubiquitous candidates, now canvassing the county, and further on, by the marshall of Athens and his companion.--The prisoners, who were elegantly dressed, expressed much annoyance at the heat and dust, seeming not to care much for anything else.

Florence turned out en masse, as the party rode in town, much excitement prevailed.

At night it culminated in THE HANGING.

The jail being insecure, Sheriff Hudson had summoned eight men, in addition to the jailer, to guard the prisoners. About midnight a great crowd came to the jail and demanded the keys. The guard refused to give them up, and fire on the mob. It is said that the fire was returned. At any rate, the jail doors were broken and the guard disarmed. The cells wherein Tom Clark and the robbers were confined, were also broken into, and the three men taken out and carried immediately to an adjoining square, and hanged by the neck until they were dead. The three were suspended from a tree, which stands in the rear of the site of the old Masonic Lodge.

In the morning the citizens found them there. One was identified as Tom Clark; one was a short, stalwart man, with the initials F. R. and a star in Indian ink, on his right arm, and two hearts pierced by an arrow on his left hand; and one is supposed to be ___ Gibson.

We understand that one of the robbers directed his portion of the $365 in money, which was found on their persons, to be sent to his sister, Miss Kate Schilee, of Indianapolis, Indiana. The same man attempted to escape, was shot by some person, unknown, recaptured, and hung with the others. It is the opinion of Dr. Hannum, who examined his wound, that death would have resulted from the postol shot. The younger robber marched up boldly to the tree and requested the executioners to hold him up and drop him, instead of drawing him up. The prayers of Clark were agonizing, and were heard by the citizens living near. Clark is said to have killed sixteen men during his life.

The indignation of the citizens at the outrages of these men, was so great that, the ladies of the community, and many of the colored people requested the Mayor to have the bodies buried outside of the cemetery.

Esq. Rice, in accordance with this request, has ordered that the bodies be interred in one of the old fields near our town.

Messrs. Hancock and Simpson identified their watches among those found in possession of the burglars.

We hope that people at a distance will not accuse our citizens of lawlessness for this act. We are as lawabiding as any people in the land; and only, when driven by the highest law of natures God, self preservation, would our community take the law in their own hands, and met out to these murderers and robbers, the just punishment for their enormous crimes.

If ever Mob Law was justifiable, it was in this instance. Tom Clark, who boasted that he had murdered, in cold blood, sixteen men, deserved hanging sixteen times over. The others, no doubt, would have slain their scores if they had found it necessary to cover their villiany. They were murderers at heart, and entered our dwellings with the formed design to slay every man who might be awakened, and attempt to defend his household.

These men have only met their deserved end. Let all such take warning. This was no Ku-Klux affair, but simply the legitimate effect of an indignant and outraged public feeling. Fearfully and quickly has the hand of retribution overtaken them, but it was only justice asserting her claims upon three of the most heartless villains that ever cursed the world.

We are opposed to mob law, but these men met a death richly deserved, and over their fate we shed no tears.

The thanks of the community are due Messrs. Blair, Joiner, Barks and Warson, for their prompt action in making the capture.

Coroner Ed. Brown, summoned a jury and held an inquest this morning. The verdict was that the parties came to their death on the night of the 4th inst., by strangulation by hanging at the hands of persons unknown.

Messrs. L. E. Powers, John T. Petty, Joseph Milner, Andrew Brown, J. T. Westmoreland and A. W. Porter composed the jury. (Lauderdale Times Extra, 5 Sept. 1872. This clipping was sent to the writer in 1970 by the late Dr. Maurice Pruitt of Chattanooga, TN.)

CLARK, Mrs. Latitia, 87, died near Buffalo Ridge in Washington County, TN on last Saturday at the home of her daughter Mrs. Amanda Bacon. (Columbia Herald, 27 Sept. 1872.)

CLARK, Mrs. Mary, relict of Henry C. Clark of Memphis, age 35, died in Nashville on the 14th. (Nashville Dispatch, 15 Nov. 1863.)

CLARK, Andrew, 92, was recently found dead in his apple orchard in Hardin County. (Nashville Union and American, 29 March 1873.)

CLAY, eldest daughter of James B. Clay, died a few days ago of diptheria in Ashland, KY. (Nashville Daily Union, 12 March 1863.)

CLEAR, Charles, "known as the marrying squire in Maury County, TN." (Columbia Herald, 13 Jan. 1871.)

CLEBURNE, Major General Pat, was killed on the top of the breastworks leading his division on. (i.e., at Battle of Franklin.) Brig. Gens. Granberry, Gist, and Strahl were killed nobly leading their brigades to victory...Brig. Gen. Carter was mortally wounded. Gen. Gordon was captured. Every member of Strahl's staff was killed. Mobile Advertiser, Dec. 17. (Nashville Daily Union, 7 Jan. 1865.)

At the Jan. 1908 meeting of the Maury County Historical Society, Capt. R. D. Smith "read the paper for the evening concluding his biography of Gen. P. R. Cleburne. The article dealt with the search for the general's body on the battlefield of Franklin and how from the mistaken information of an escaped Confederate prisoner the search had been stopped; the finding the body and laying it out on the back porch of the McGavock house, every room being filled with wounded soldiers; the bringing of the remains to Mrs. Dr. Polk's (where the Elks Home is now), the walnut casket made by Elijah Neelley, who is yet a cabinet maker here; the funeral services by Rev. C. T. Quintard, afterwards Bishop of Tennessee; the mistake in burying among the Federal soldiers at Rose Hill and the second burial a few days later at Ashwood with so many other Confederate officers who had fallen at Franklin; the removal of the remains to Helena, Arkansas, in April 1870, and the honors paid here and at Memphis; the dedication of the monument at Helena in 1891--these and other facts and incidents were all told in graphic detail by the author." (Daily Herald, Columbia, TN, 15 Jan. 1908.)

Mr. Boyd (of Lamb & Boyd) being in the army as Ordnance Sergeant of the 2nd Tennessee, the factory was run by Mr. Lamb as opportunity offered and as material could be obtained. Much of the work done was on coffins for the soldiers who had died here in hospitals or who were killed in the various skirmishes about Columbia. These coffins were generally made by Mr. Elijah Neely, who tells me that when lumber was scarce he often made them all of one size, 6 feet long, with plain

swell sides and at top. Of course, there were many fine coffins made,
as the old account book now in my possession will show, notably those
for Generals Van Dorn, Lieut. Wills Gould, Generals Pat Cleburne, Granberry, Strahl, and many other officers and citizens. (Columbia Herald,
26 Sept. 1904.)(N. B.--The account book of Lamb & Boyd was published in
recent years in "Frank H. Smith's History of Maury County, TN, by the
Maury County Historical Society.)

REMOVAL OF CLEBURNE'S REMAINS.--Last Tuesday morning it was announced in
our city that a couple of gentlemen from Helena, Arkansas, Dr. L. H.
Grant and Judge Mangrum had come here with the purpose of taking the remains of Gen. Pat R. Cleburne from their resting place at Ashwood, TN,
to Arkansas, his adopted home. About 11 o'clock those gentlemen, accompanied by a number of our citizens, proceeded to St. John's Church, in
the princely country of Ashwood, and soon exhumed the body, or rather
what was left of the body of one of the bravest soldiers and grandest
heroes of our war for independence.

The coffin was very much decayed, and not a particle of flesh was remaining on the skeleton. The General was buried in a new gray uniform, and
much of it was in a good state of preservation. A number of the citizens
of the neighborhood were present, and followed the remains to Columbia,
where the coffin was placed in St. Peter's Church.

At the solicitation of Col. J. W. Dunnington and Capt. Rufus K. Polk,
some of our most prominent citizens, both young and old, sat up all
night with the returning dust of the immortal Cleburne.

Gen. Cleburne had no family of his own in America, and made his home with
Dr. Grant of Helena. He was at one time a druggist, but quit for the
practice of law. He had a personal difficulty in Helena, and was wounded almost in the same spot where he was struck when killed at Franklin,
which was through the body just below the heart. At Franklin he was also
wounded in the heel.

After his death he was brought to Columbia and buried at Rose Hill Cemetery, and by mistake was placed among the Federal dead. He was afterwards taken up and buried at Ashwood, where his grave has been bedecked
with flowers by the lovely and beautiful ladies of the neighborhood on
every return of Spring.

Last Wednesday evening a large procession of Masons proceeded to the
Episcopal Church for the purpose of escorting the remains of their brother to the Depot. All the business houses were closed and the people
joined in the procession. At the church the Masons opened ranks on
each side of the entrance, and sent a detail inside for the coffin, one
of whom, Capt. R. D. Smith, was on Gen. Cleburne's staff during the war.

Under the impulse of the monotone swinging of the bell, the procession
started, the Masons in front of the hearse, which was followed by Gen.
Lucius J. Polk's carriage, in which were General Polk, General John C.
Brown of Giles, and Judge Mangrum of Arkansas, next came Gen. Pillow's
carriage, in which were members of his family. A large crowd of citizens followed on foot...(Columbia Herald, 29 April 1870.)

MEMPHIS.--The remains of Gen. Cleburne will be received here Thursday at
2:30 p.m. and will be received with honor. Jefferson Davis and G. J.
Pillow will be in procession. (Memphis Daily Appeal, 27 April 1870.)

A niece of General Cleburne's in Dublin, Ireland, is seeking information
on her uncle; she is Nameo Cleburne, daughter of the only brother and
is seeking information on his estate; she recently wrote the mayor of
Helena, Arkansas. (Maury Democrat, 28 Aug. 1913.)

FALLEN HEROES.--Through the kindness of Maj. Will Polk the Democrat presents this week a list of Confederate soldiers buried in the graveyard
at St. John's Church, Ashwood:

   Lieut. Harper, Company K, 30th Ala. Regiment, wounded at Columbia,
   TN, Nov. 20, 1864, died at St. John's Church hospital Dec. 6, 1864.

J. A. Seymore, Barber's Co., Forrest's Old Reg't., Fayette Co., TN, died Nov. 21st, 1864.

Col. Robert F. Beckham, chief of artillery of Lt. Gen. Stephen D. Lee's corps, born in Culpeper County, Va., May 6, 1837; mortally wounded at Columbia, TN, Nov. 29, 1864, died Dec. 5, 1864.

Joel Dubose wounded in battle at Columbia, TN, Nov. 29th 1864, died Dec. 1864.

Andrew J. Comer, of Capt. Higg's Scouts, Forrest's cavalry, killed near Ashwood on the morning of the 29th Nov. 1864.

Brig. Gen. O. F. Strahl of Confederate Artillery, born in Ohio, June 30th, 1834; killed at Franklin, TN, Nov. 30th, 1864.

Lieut. J. H. Marsh of Hardeman County, TN, aid to Gen. Strahl, killed at Franklin, TN, Nov. 30th, 1864.

Col. ___ Young of Texas, killed at Franklin, TN, Nov. 30th, 1864. (Will someone give us Col. Young's regiment, etc.?)

Lieut. Welborn S. McMaury, born in Columbus, Ga., Nov. 24th, 1843, died Feb. 25th, 1864.

Gen. Pat Cleburne, killed at Franklin, TN, Nov. 30th, 1864, was buried here but after several years was removed to Helena, Ark., his old home.

Gen. Granbury, who was killed at Franklin, TN, Nov. 30th, 1864, was also removed last year to his old home, Granbury, Texas.

There were also other Confederates buried in private plots:
George S. Martin, born Jan. 3rd, 1840, died Sept. 23rd, 1863.
George M. Pillow, born July 19th, 1839 in Maury Co., TN, died Aug. 30th, 1872.
Brig. Gen. L. E. Polk, died Dec. 1st, 1892, age 59 years.
Maj. Campbell Brown, died Aug. 31st, 1893, age 58.
(Maury Democrat, 18 Oct. 1894.)

CLEBURNE BURIAL. A member of General Cleburne's staff writing from Columbia, TN.: "I had his remains brought to this place and buried at Ashwood, 6 miles distant, the private graveyard of the Polk Family. I met with great kindness from the people here in the performance of my sad duty. His coffin was strewn with flowers by the ladies..." (The Monitor, Murfreesboro, TN, 4 Nov. 1865.)

CLEM, Johnny, the youngest soldier in the Army of Cumberland, age 12, in Company C, 22d Michigan Infantry, was from Newark, Ohio; he first attracted General Rosecrans attention during a review in Nashville when he acted as marker for his regiment; called by the Confederates "that little Yankee devil." (Nashville Daily Union, 10 Dec. 1863.)

CLEMENTS, William, Esquire, died on the 4th in Montgomery County; he was native of Scotland; Presbyterian. (Tennessee Watchman, Montgomery County, 15 Feb. 1822.)

CLEMENTS, William, died on the 9th instant; lived on Yellow Creek in Montgomery County; came to America at the end of the Revolution with his parents. (Tennessee Watchman, 22 Feb. 1822. See one above.)

CLEVELAND, notorious jayhawker of Kansas, who has kept that state in continual alarm for four months past, died on the 11th; he was at Ossawattomie, Kansas, raising troops, was taken prisoner, tried to make his escape, and guard shot him through the heart. (Nashville Dispatch 23 May 1862.) His real name was METZ, but he use to drive stage out of Cleveland, Ohio, and adopted that name. (Nashville Dispatch, 30 May 1862.)

CLIFF, Dr., Union man of Franklin, TN, had home burned a few days ago by some of Forrest's men. (Nashville Daily Union, 14 Jan. 1863.)

COBB, General Howell, was standing in corridor of a Fifth Avenue Hotel in New York City, talking to his wife, put hand to head, gasped, "I am ill, very ill," sank to floor and died; of Athens, Ga.; age 53 yrs. 1 month, 2 days. (Memphis Daily Appeal, 13 Oct. 1868.)

COBB, Gideon Clark, 9, died 19 Dec. 1860 in Clarksville, son of Dr. Joshua and Marina Cobb. (Clarksville Weekly Chronicle, 4 Jan. 1861.)

COCKE, Mrs. Sarah, 98, died 14 Oct. 1861 at home of G. W. Bradbury in Montgomery County, TN. (Clarksville Weekly Chronicle, 1 Nov. 1861.)

COCKRELL, Gran, drowned Thursday a few feet below the bridge in Columbia; was in a canoe which overturned; subscription raised for his burial. (Nashville Republican Banner, 1 March 1868.) (N. B.--buried in Greenwood Cemetery in Columbia, grave never marked.)

COGGSWELL, Congressman, of Massachusetts, who died recently in Washington had a remarkable career in the army during the Civil War. Before his 22nd year he had risen to the grades of captain, lieutenant colonel and colonel to brigadier general. (Maury Democrat, 6 June 1895.)

COFFEE, John. In 1818 Mrs. Anne Royal, the wife of Captain Royal, who had fought in the Revolution and became a resident of Alabama, made an extensive tour through the South, writing letters to her friends many which are as rich in pleasant personalities and descriptions as in some instances, they are, in keen, cutting sarcasm and scathing criticism. These "Letters from Alabama" were afterward put into book form and published, and from this the following extract was made:

Huntsville, Alabama
1st January 1818
General Coffee. Last evening I had the pleasure of seeing this renowned soldier and companion of General Jackson. This hero of whom you have heard so much is upward of 6 feet in height and proportionately made. No did I ever see so fine a figure. He is 35 or 36 years of age. His face is round and full, features handsome. His complexion is ruddy, though sunburnt. His hair and eyes are black and a soft serenity suffuses his countenance. His hair is carelessly thrown to one side, in front, and displays one of the finest foreheads in nature--high and smooth.

In General Coffee, I expected to see a stern haughty, fierce warrior. No such thing.

You look in vain for that rapidity with which he marched and defeated the Indians at Tallashatches, nor could I trace in his countenance the swiftness of pursuit and sudden defeat of the Indians again at Emuckfau; much less his severe conflicts at the head of his gallant men in New Orleans. He is as mild as the dewdrops; but deep in his soul you see very plain that deliberate, firm, cool and manly courage which has covered him with glory. He must be a host when he is aroused. All These Tennesseans are mild and gentle except when they are excited, which is hard to do; but when they are once roused, it is victory or death. Weekly Democrat, Huntsville, Ala., Wed., 26 May 1897. (Florence Times, 23 August 1918.)

General Coffee, the savage assassin of the Indians during the Seminole War died on the 7th July near Florence, Ala. He fought the first battle, that of Tullshatchez under the orders of Gen. Jackson, but not in his presence. This was the prelude to the glorious succession of victories; which terminated before New Orleans. General Coffee signalized himself by his valor and commanding powers in the hard fought battles of Talledega, Emuckfaw, Enotichopco and Tohopeka. At Emuckfaw he was shot through the body and although suffering under the dreadful wound, when the Indians attacked the retiring army at Enotichopco Creek, and threw it into panic and confusion, General Coffee

rose from the litter on which he was borne and greatly aided the commander-in-chief in restoring order and retrieving the day.

On the summons of General Jackson, without the orders of the Government, General Coffee raised the 2,000 volunteers that enabled the
commander-in-chief to storm Pensacola, drive out the British, to rescue the whole southern frontier, and finally to triumph in the succes-
sive conflicts upon the plains of New Orleans.

He died the death of the righteous and manifested true faith of a
Christian...(Central Monitor, 18 Jan. 1834, Murfreesboro, TN)

COFFEE, Mary. The widow of General John Coffee, Old Hickory's bower,
now 77, still lives in Lauderdale County, Alabama, at the place where
she and her husband settled on removing to Alabama in 1818. (Memphis
Daily Appeal, 10 June 1870.) The first flag of Stars and Bars to any
military organization was presented to the Florence Guards on 1 April
1861--unfurled by Mrs. John Coffee. (Confederate Veteran, Dec. 1915,
page 548.) On the 27th of April there was a war meeting at Wesleyan
and the ladies gave a flag to the Lauderdale County Volunteers. Mrs.
Coffee came on the stand and unfurled the banner, which features the
seven-starred flag of the Confederacy. (Florence Gazette, Florence,
Ala., 1 May 1861.) (N. B.--Her tombstone in the Coffee Cemetery,
Cloverdale Road, reads: born 13 June 1793, died 11 Dec. 1871.)

COFFEE, Colonel Andrew Jackson, born 20 August 1819 near Nashville; died
Wednesday. (N. B.--place of death not given in account, possibly in
California.) He entered West Point as a cadet in 1837 where he remained several years, resigning to become a civil engineer, with which
he alternated with being a cotton planter until 1846 when he was appointed paymaster in army and assigned to duty on Gen. Taylor's staff
in the field, serving during the Mexican War up to the Battle of Buena
Vista, 23 Feb. 1847, where his actions were so conspicuous as to win
him promotion from major to lieutenant-colonel. General Taylor selected him to bear message to President Polk, going over the battlefield with him before his departure, pointing out and describing various positions; he stayed in army and in 1853 was assigned to duty
"in this city" July 1859. At one time with Col. John Hayes and several others owned nearly the whole site of Oakland, California, but
he lost the property.

His paternal grandfather was Joshua Coffee, who served in Revolutionary Army, and his father was General John Coffee, distinguished soldier of the War of 1812 and General Jackson's most trusted friend and
lieutenant.

General Jackson selected General Coffee to make the night attack on
the British soon after they landed, which resulted in the memorable
hand-to-hand combat on the night of 23 Dec. 1814, with the Tennesseans
used their hunting knives, as they had no bayonets.

His mother was Miss Mary Donelson, whose family have borne a prominent
part in the history of Tennessee. Her aunt Rachel Donelson was the
wife of General Jackson...

On his death, General Jackson bequeathed the sword presented to him
by citizens of New Orleans to Colonel Coffee. Unfortunately, it was
accidentally destroyed by fire during the Civil War, while in possession
of Colonel Coffee's mother near Florence, Alabama.

Colonel Coffee married 3 April 1839 Miss Elizabeth A. Hutchings of
Huntsville, Alabama. He took no active part on either side during the
Civil War, but had he entered the Confederate Army a brigadier general
commission would have been offered him. (Florence, Ala., Times,
18 April 1891.) (N. B.--The blade of the sword presented to General
Jackson by the citizens of New Orleans and bequeathed to Colonel
Andrew Jackson Coffee was presented to the Hermitage, near Nashville,
Tennessee, by Alexander D. Coffee and is displayed there.)

COFFEE, Colonel John, son of General Coffee of War of 1812 fame, was murdered by Zack Taylor in Arkansas near Surrounded Hill; he had married
a step-daughter of Dr. James Brown; wife and two children brought his
body to Memphis where he was buried Friday; was shot in the mouth;
shot mutilated the face, fell dead from horse with buckshot in back
and in heart. Memphis Avalanche, 26 April. (Nashville Union and
American, 28 April 1874.) (N. B.--There is a stone for him in the old
Coffee Cemetery near Florence, Ala.)

COFFEE, Rachel Jackson, wife of Alexander J. Dyas, born 3 Nov. 1823 at
her father's home near Florence; died 8 Sept. 1892 at Nashville, TN;
married 23 Oct. 1857; in 1843 under Dr. Daniel Baker, evangelist,
joined the Presbyterian Church. (Florence, Ala., Times 17 Sept.
1892.)

COFFEY, Rosa Hudson, 3, died Saturday at Campbell Station, Maury County.
(Maury Democrat, 24 May 1894.)

COKER, Nathaniel,82, died in Conecuh County, Alabama, recently. (Memphis
Daily Appeal, 8 July 1870.)

COLBERT, Samuel, his funeral to be held at the Christian Church on Big
Creek, Giles County. (Maury Democrat, 24 May 1888.)

COLE, Colonel James, died Friday, served with distinction in the Confederate Army; almost fatally wounded at Chickamauga, lay six months in
a hospital, shot in mouth and the ball lodged among the nerves of the
left cheek; wife and child survive. (Memphis Daily Appeal, 5 Sept.
1869.)

COLEMAN, Edmund Daniel, only son of P. B. and Martha Jane Coleman, died
on the 19th in Nashville. (Nashville Dispatch, 20 April 1862.)

COLEMAN, John, Esquire, lawyer of Memphis, native of Kentucky, died in
Memphis recently. (Nashville Dispatch, 16 Aug. 1862.)

COLEMAN, Alexander, Esquire, age 40, died on the 9th in Humphreys County;
served 1839 in the General Assembly for Benton and Humphreys counties;
wife and several children survive. (Clarksville Jeffersonian, 21
Sept. 1844.)

COLEMAN, Captain Booker W., 38, grocer of Memphis, died yesterday; he was
unmarried; gallant Confederate soldier. (Memphis Daily Appeal, 25
Aug. 1869.)

COLEMAN, Mrs. James, of Mousetail, Perry County, died on the 14th.
(Linden Times, 18 Aug. 1880.)

COLLEY, William, an eccentric, died in Lower Village near Lockport, Ohio;
kept grocery; willed property valued at $18,000 to relatives in Eng-
land. He kept his specie in an old boiler buried in the cellar and
among the deposits were 50,000 three cent pieces. (Nashville Daily
Union, 4 Jan. 1865.)

COLLIER. Son of Dr. Collier of Williamsport, Maury County, was shot and
killed Friday at Santa Fe by George F. Stone; they were at a dance at
Mr. Lewis's on the Columbia Road; Stone was shot by Collier and hurt;
Stone is 30 and unmarried. (Columbia Herald and Mail, 11 Dec. 1874.)

COLLIER, Matthew, died 15 Jan. 1897. (Waynesboro Tribune, 21 Jan. 1897.)

COLLIER, Mrs. Ruth E., died Friday and buried at Rose Hill, Columbia;
wife of John A. Collier; four children survive; parents are dead; she
was a Daimwood. (Columbia Herald, 9 Jan. 1891; 16 Jan. 1891.)

COMPTON, Mrs. Martha Atlanta Lumpkin, died recently at Decatur, Georgia;
Atlanta was named for her; it was first known as Marthasville, but
later changed. (Florence, Alabama, Times 2 March 1917.)

COMSTOCK, Sallie, infant daughter of Mr. and Mrs. S. G. Comstock, one of twins, died in Columbia on Wednesday of cholera infantum. (Columbia Herald and Mail, 3 Aug. 1877.)

CONNELLY, Mrs. Hannah, 65, found yesterday in her room suspended by a short rope to a clothes line across the room; neck broken; her husband said she had been out of her mind; buried Elmwood Cemetery in Memphis. (Memphis Avalanche, 13 Feb. 1866.)

CONNERS, Patrick, fireman, killed by 18 year old E. W. Ferguson, late of Nashville on Adams Street in Memphis; he took umbrage at something Conners said, beat him up, and later shot him. (Memphis Avalanche, 16 Dec. 1866.)

CONNOR, Mat A., was killed at McKinnon, Houston County, last Friday; he married daughter of McKendree Hollister. (Houston County Times, 23 May 1890.)

CONRAD, Mrs., 106, lives in Cedar Grove, Gilmer County, West Virginia, was baptised May 12 in the Southern Methodist Church; she lives on a pension for her husband's War of 1812 service. (Maury Democrat, 16 May 1889.)

COOLEY, Reuben Ford, infant son of Theodore and Eugenia P. Cooley, age 2 months 3 weeks, died yesterday in Nashville. (Nashville Republican Banner, 29 July 1869.)

COOLEY, Jim, noted desperado of East Tennessee, Roane County, demolished the home of his enemy Mack Brown with dynamite, and after he was arrested drew pistol against the first witness called against him, and he was shot by deputy sheriff, but made his escape. Mrs. Brown was so severely injured that her recovery is in doubt. Cooley escaped to North Carolina, and if caught will be lynched. (Maury Democrat, 28 March 1889.)

COOK, Annie, died 1878, buried Howard Association lot in Elmwood Cemetery in Memphis. From the Memphis Appeal, no date: Annie Cook, the woman who after a long life of shame, ventured all she had of life and property for the sick, died 11 Sept. 1878 of yellow fever which she contracted while nursing her patients. "If there was virtue in the faith of the woman who but touched the hem of the garment of the Divine Redeemer, surely the sins of this woman must be forgiven her."

COOK, Alexander, 30, died 16 Oct. 1867 of the prevailing fever; steamboat clerk for several years; boats in port at Memphis lowered their flags in his honor; buried Elmwood Cemetery, Memphis. (Memphis Avalanche, 18 Oct. 1867.)

COOK, Dr. Philip H., 40, well known physician of Williamson County, died two weeks ago. (Whig and Tribune, Jackson, TN, 24 Feb. 1872.)

COONEY, Terence, 79, old resident of Paris, TN, died a few days ago. (Memphis Daily Appeal, 11 Aug. 1868.)

COOPER, Samuel, was shot on the 28th by a pistol by William H. Hunt at Culleoka and died short time later; Cooper had been drinking. (Columbia Herald and Mail, 3 August 1877.)

COOPER, Mrs. Sarah M., widow of General Sam Cooper, late adjutant general of the Confederate Army, died at her home in Fairfax County, near Alexandria, Virginia, on July 29 at 90 years; she was the daughter of late John Mason of "The Island" and a sister of James M. Mason, ex-U. S. Senator and Confederate States commissioner to England with John Slidell. (Florence, Ala., Times, 8 Aug. 1890.)

COOPER, Colonel James Fairlie, died in Atlanta, Ga., recently, the son of Thomas A. Cooper, tragedian; grandson of Major James Fairlie of the Revolutionary War; grandson of Chief Justice Yates of New York; he was graduate of West Point and in same class with Joe Johnston and Meade;

was Lt. Colonel of 7th Georgia Infantry, CSA. (Memphis Daily Appeal, 31 Oct. 1869.)

COOPER, Mr., of Hampshire, Maury County, died a few days ago over 100 years; buried at Jones Church. (Columbia Herald and Mail, 26 Jan. 1877.)

COOPER, Mrs. Eleanor, died 19 Jan. 1877; born 1870 in North Carolina in the midst of the Revolution; daughter of Samuel McAdams, who moved when she was young to Smith County, TN. There she married John Cooper and her older sister married the Rev. John Gwin, noted Methodist minister (whose father was onetime senator from California); they moved to Maury County where they were among the earliest settlers along Duck River and lived near Mt. Pleasant. He died many years ago. She has two sons living, one in Mt. Pleasant, and one in Weakley County, TN. She died near Mt. Pleasant at the home of Mr. Williams, who married her granddaughter. (Columbia Herald and Mail, 15 June 1877.)

COOPER, Duncan. "Duncan Cooper, entering the Confederate Army while a mere boy attained to the rank of colonel in his 19th year..." (Columbia Herald and Mail, 7 Oct. 1870.)

A citizen of Hickman county informs us that a recent raid of a battalion of the 14th Michigan Mounted Rifles struck terror into the hearts of the guerrillas and thieving bands that infest that and adjoining counties. The Federals, he says, were in command of Major Fitzgibbon, and were reputed to be 800 strong by the fleeing enemy. Our informant was conscripted the day before the Federals came, but in their haste to get away from the terrible Yankees, his captors left him to take care of himself.

Col. Duncan Cooper, successor to Dick McCann, sent word to the Federals that he would fight them at Bigby River, but though the Federals numbered 80, and Cooper had nearly 300, he fled at the first fire, leaving three of his men prisoners. The pursuit was rapid and exciting, the Federals keeping close on their heels for 12 miles, through mountain defiles and ravines, till they reached Centreville, when Cooper, finding himself sorely pressed, had his force scattered in all directions to avoid death or capture.

Cooper himself went ten miles further before he halted. The Federal commander, then headed to the east, and striking in the rear of Mt. Pleasant, the morning following routed the commands of Captains Williams and Barnes, of Biffle's regiment, capturing 13, killing two, and wounding one, without the injury of man or horse to himself. The Federals destroyed a tannery and its contents, used by the rebels at Bigbyville.

To give an idea of the terror our force inspires, our informant says that he had heard Major Fitzgibbon's command estimated at 1500. Our force carried neither blankets nor rations, but lived upon prominent rebels. They were well mounted, and looked the manliest and healthiest set of fellows that ever visited that part of Dixie.

We are proud and glad that such a live Colonel as Henry R. Mizner is in command of such an important post as Columbia, and under his directions we are sure the 14th Michigan will give little rest to guerrillas in Maury, Hickman, Giles and Lawrence counties.
(Nashville Daily Union, 30 Oct. 1863.)

Quoting the Columbia Sentinel, Sat., 21st inst.,: "On Wednesday last at 8 p.m., Major Fitzgibbon, at the head of 80 men, started for the immortal Cooper and his comrades. Crossing Duck River eight miles below town, came upon the rear of Cooper's camp, who, as usual, led the Major, however, losing five of his men as prisoners; the Major still pursuing him through the cedars. Cooper camped three times during the night, in order to elude his pursuers, but in vain. On the run through the cedars one of Cooper's men was wounded in the back.

62

Cooper, still on the run, went through the mountains and crossed Anderson's Creek. There he lost one man killed, supposed to be Lt. Brownlow.

At length Cooper, thinking himself, safe, halted, but the Major coming upon his rear guard, they again "skedaddled," but keeping up a running fight some 8 miles below Mount Pleasant--the Major capturing four more of the guerrillas. Some of Cooper's men wore the Federal uniform. The result of the scout foots up as follows: Major capturing 22 prisoners belonging to the 9th Tennessee Cavalry, Col. Biffle, and 47 horses. The Major and his little band desire high praise for the gallantry displayed and the good done. With his indomitable courage and great skill in a military point, he will soon rid the country of so great a pest as guerrillas, thieves, and robbers. May success attend him." (Nashville Daily Union 27 Nov. 1863.)

Colonel Duncan Cooper, notorious rebel guerrillas, burnt 150 bales of cotton last Tuesday in Lawrence County, the property of W. J. Porter, who owns a cotton mill in that county, one miles southwest of Lawrenceburg. (Nashville Dispatch, 31 Dec. 1863.)

The notorious guerrilla Lt. Col. Duncan B. Cooper was yesterday captured by Col. Mizner's command. The dispatch which conveys this information says the railway bridges will be a little safer now. (Nashville Daily Union 17 Feb. 1864.)

We mentioned yesterday the capture of the notorious guerrilla, Lt. Col. Dunc B. Cooper. He was brought in this city yesterday, in company with some sixteen other prisoners, rebel soldiers, horse thieves, etc., by Lt. Finn of the 14th Michigan. We are informed that he was captured on Swan Creek, some 21 miles west of Columbia, in Lewis County, by a portion of the 7th Iowa Infantry, who met with him unexpectedly. Cooper says he owes his capture to the falling of his horse. (Nashville Daily Union, 18 Feb. 1864.)

CAPTURE OF MASTER D. B. COOPER.--Master D. B. Cooper, who figures in this neighborhood as a harmless guerrilla for the last 18 months, was captured on Bigby by Sergeant Haney of the 50th Illinois on Tuesday last. He was brought in by a detachment of the 14th Michigan and confined in jail over night, when he was sent to Nashville. He was much talked of by foolish girls and brainless boys of his own age and mental calibre. He was the most insignificant thing it has been our fortune or misfortune to get possession of bearing a commission in any army since the war began. He would not pass muster among third class drummer boys.

FALSE.--A feminine phleghotomist of this city writes to protest against Major Fitzgibbon's ill treatment of Col. Cooper, after he was captured and his prisoner, and adds that "that is not the proper way to treat a noble (?) enemy."

The accusation that Major Fitzgibbon insulted or maltreated any prisoner is false; and as our looking upon Mr. Cooper "as an enemy," that is a mistake. His case and ours was like that of the mother who was asked by her husband to chastise and quiet her crying babe. Rolling the child all over her lap, she turned to her husband and said, "I can't beat him; I can find no place large enough to lay a hand on."

TAKE NOTICE.--The patriotic citizen who offered to give $50,000 bonds for the "freedom of the city" to Dunc Cooper is hereby notified that the authorities would deem it more becoming his loyalty, honesty, and humanity (if he is troubled with such follies) if he would visit the orphans and widows left helpless and disconsolate through the agency of said Cooper, and dispense part of his charity among them. He and his gang of rebel worshippers and sympathizers will have to do it. We are growing sick and weary with the hollow-heartedness of these conspirators who are growing fat. (The Sentinel, Columbia, TN, 20 Feb. 1864.)

CAME OUT O' THE WET.--Tom Moss, for sometime Acting Adjutant of the late "Lieut. Col." D. B. Cooper, came inside the Federal lines here and took the oath of allegiance. It was he who rode his horse to death in Novem-

ber to inform Col. Albert Cooper of Major Fitzgibbon's intended
attack upon Lawrenceburg, thus giving ample time for preparations and
defense. Cooper prepared the defense but abandoned his command on
being attacked. Moss was a daring and vigilent scout. (The Sentinel
Columbia, TN, 27 Feb. 1864.)

Alfred Horsely, onetime editor of the Columbia Herald, wrote: "Billy
Hughes named his gun Florence for Miss Florence Fleming, who he admired greatly before the war he clerked for John F. Morgan. Though
his home was Stokes Co., N.C...His father was brother of A. M. Hughes
of Columbia. Billy Hughes was shot in the hand (at Dead Angle on
27 June 1864), sent to Griffin, Ga., got gangrene, though it was amputated he died from it. He was a fine man. He and Ed W. Voss were
about the only men whose guns were bright and perfect for inspection."
(Maury Democrat, 18 June 1896.)(N. B.--After the war Duncan Cooper
was married to Florence Fleming, daughter of W. S. Fleming. Samuel
Watkins in his book "Co. Aytch" recalled that a fellow in his outfit
had a gun called Florence Fleming--this being Bill Hughes, who died
in Georgia.)

COOPER, Mrs. Florence Fleming, wife of Col. D. B. Cooper, died Friday;
    wife and mother. (Columbia Herald, 9 Sept. 1870.)

Married at Ewell Farm, home of Major Campbell Brown, on the 18th, Col.
Duncan B. Cooper and Miss Mary P. Jones, eldest daughter of Mrs. Sa-
rah P. Jones and granddaughter of late General Lucius J. Polk.
(Columbia Herald and Mail, 19 Jan. 1877.)

Col. D. B. Cooper with his lovely bride was on a visit to her mother
at Spring Hill last Sunday. (Columbia Herald and Mail, 23 Feb. 1877.)

Duncan Cooper is moving to the old Cooper place on the Hampshire Pike.
(Columbia Herald and Mail, 22 June 1877.)

Colonel Dunc Cooper of Maury had his right hand badly crushed and
lacerated in a cider-mill last week. (Nashville Republican Banner,
26 July 1868.)

Colonel Duncan Cooper, widely known Nashvillian, died Saturday night,
79 years; former editor and publisher of Nashville American; he died
at the home of his daughter Mrs. Lucius E. Burch; was son of Matthew
D. and Mary Ann Cooper, born at Mulberry Hill, 7 miles from Columbia,
on 21 April 1843; grandson of Rev. Duncan Brown; early education in
Maury Co.; attended college in Cannonburg, Penn., a Presbyterian in-
stitution and while he was in college the Civil War began, whereupon
he left class room at 16 and enlisted in the Confederate Army; he
served on staff of General Nathan B. Forrest on the state raid and
later organized a regiment within the Federal lines; was captured and
imprisoned at Fort Delaware and figured in the last exchange of prisoners between the contending forces; after the war Col. Cooper was admitted to the bar in Columbia, later moving to Nashville where he made
his home for many years, the last 15 at the home of his daughter,
Mrs. Burch. He married (1) Miss Florence Fleming of Columbia; married
(2) Miss Mary Polk Jones of Maury County...He is said by friends to
have been a man of much brilliance; personal friend of Theodore Roosevelt, President Grover Cleveland, and Vice-Pres. Adley E. Stevenson,
who visited Col. Cooper in his home here; he was buried in Maury Co.
in his native soil. (Nashville Banner, 5 Nov. 1922.)

N. B.--Colonel Cooper, an intimate friend of Governor Patterson, became active in the Patterson-Carmack campaign for Governor of Tennessee. Despite his persuasive powers, Edward Ward Carmack was defeated
for governor and following his defeat he became editor of the Nashville Tennessean and continued his fight--the liquor question was the
raging issue.

Carmack possessed a remarkable vocabulary and command of language, and
Colonel Cooper was much incensed by some of Carmack's embittered and
strong editorials, particularly one entitled "Across the Muddy Chasm"
on the 8th of November 1908.

64

On the afternoon of 9 November 1908, Cooper and his son Robin Cooper encountered Senator Carmack on Vine Street (now 7th Avenue) in Nashville. Carmack was killed and Robin was wounded. Robin fired the fatal shot. Both father and son were tried and convicted. The case was appealed to the Supreme Court which affirmed the colonel's verdict. Cooper was immediately pardoned by Patterson. Robin Cooper got a new trial which was nolle prossed.

Maury Democrat, Columbia, TN, 4 Sept. 1919: Robin J. Cooper found murdered August 30; had been lured from his home; his blood-stained car was found and his body had been thrown in creek in Belle Meade park section of Nashville. His skull had been crushed and there were signs of a violent struggle; he had been struck in head three times by a stone and part of his clothes had been torn off in the fight; he had married daughter of Milton H. Smith, President of L&N Railroad; body found in Richland Creek beneath Nc&StL railroad trestle at Harding Road.

N. B.--Mulberry Hill, the old Matthew D. Cooper home and where Duncan Cooper moved in 1877, still stands on the Hampshire Pike out from Columbia. The house was built in 1828 by Royal Ferguson, a pioneer in the iron industry. It was purchased in 1978 by Mr. and Mrs. Jimmy Mayes of Columbia.

CORBETT, Ida Frances, age 2 years 5 months 25 days, infant daughter of Ephraim F. and Frances E. Corbett, died on 16th of Nashville. (Nashville Dispatch, 18 Aug. 1863.)

CORBIN, William, and J. H. McGraw, were shot to death on the 15th at Johnson's Island as rebel spies. (Nashville Dispatch, 14 May 1863. N. B.--This was reported as having taken place.)

CORCORAN, Mrs. Elizabeth, 35, wife of Brig. Gen. Michael Corcoran, died on the 4th inst., in New York of congestion of the brain; native of Ireland. (Nashville Dispatch, 9 Aug. 1863.)

CORNYM, Florence M. During a court martial at Corinth, Mississippi, on the 10th, there was an altercation between Col. Cornwyn and Lt. Col. Bowen, both of the 10th Missouri Cavalry. Cornwyn struck Bowen and the latter shot Cornwyn in three places killing him instantly. (Nashville Dispatch, 13 Aug. 1863.) The court martial which tried Lt. Col. W. D. Bowen for killing Col. Florence M. Cornym of the 15th Missouri Cavalry at Corinth last August acquitted him. (Nashville Daily Union, 13 Feb. 1864.)(N. B.--His surname spelled various ways in these reports.)

COUSINS, Mrs. Emily, wife of Thomas Cousins of the 4th Florida Regiment, CSA, was sent from Murfreesboro to Nashville; she came to see her husband and when the rebels retreated she was left destitute. Army police have placed her with Mrs. Winburn at the City Hotel. (Nashville Dispatch, 8 April 1863.)

COUTTS, Miss Letitia, age 95, died in Nashville on the 22d. (Nashville Dispatch, 24 Jan. 1863.)

COVINGTON, Thomas, died on the 25th instant of consumption in Clarksville (Clarksville Weekly Chronicle, 26 June 1861.)

COWARD, William, shot and killed by Capt. James McFerrin in a difficulty at Atoka, Tipton County, TN, on Sunday the 1st. (Paris Gazette, 19 Dec. 1878.)

COWAN, Old Man, of Union County, Kentucky; on April 24 his house was entered by armed, disguised outlaws, who dragged him from his bed and carried him into the woods about two miles, stripped him, pinioned him to ground and with hickory withes lacerated his body until one mass of wounds and blood. They left him helpless and alone in woods. He had given information to Union soldiers in relation to movements of guerrillas in his area. (Nashville Dispatch, 7 May 1863.)

COWAN, James H., old and respected merchant of Knoxville, died last week. (Columbia Herald, 3 Nov. 1871.)

COWLES, Annie, age 11 months, daughter of Macon and Frances Cowles died at home of grandfather Richard Porter in Maury County of cholera infantum. (Columbia Herald and Mail, 31 Aug. 1877.)

COWSERT, James, of Spring Hill, TN, died on 18th; Cumberland Presbyterian and buried in Spring Hill Cemetery; lived at Spring Hill for 50 years. (Columbia Herald and Mail, 23 Feb. 1877.)

COX, Nancy Clarke, "The Lady of St. Clair". We never supposed that Congress had any right to give the peoples' money to the multitudes of widows on the pension rolls.

General Fremont's widow has no more "right" to $2,000 a year, taken from the poor toilers of all the states, that the poor widow of St. Clair County, Ala., whose husband was permanently injured by a musket ball at Chickamauga.

He lay in bed 23 years, perfectly helpless. The brave wife cultivated the little farm and garden and planted the little cotton patch and picked the cotton and carried it on her back in bags-full to her neighbor's gin, who charged her no toll. And this was the only charity she ever knew.

In a deep glen, in the midst of the mountains of St. Clair, she lived, shut out from intercourse with all the world, except her helpless husband. He died one day, blessing her with his expiring breath...

She still lives, unpensioned though her splendid virtues are recognized by neighboring farmers and their wives.

But she is only a poor woman of the common people, and the poor have no friends among the gilded rulers of the empire. Fremont's widow who never knew want or sorrow or hunger or harshest exactions of servile toil and penury, is entitled, we suppose, to $2000 a year.

The faithful widow of St. Clair, whose life story is exceeded in beauty and sublimity of virtues by no dream of poets--or of sages-- is unhonored, unpensioned and uncared for. She cultivates her little farm today. The sun now shines less fiercely on her gray hairs and furrowed brow than when anxiety for the helpless soldier was tugging at her heart-strings. She will not accept charity, and would refuse a pension. She says, "I prefer to support myself."

But then, she is only a poor, unlettered, simple, honest woman of the mountains of Alabama, and it is strange that she should be too proud, poor as she is, and growing old and helpless, to accept charity, even from a king.

The women of Alabama, as a lesson to their children, should build a monument in attestation of the heroism and sublime devotion and inextinguished pride of race and character of Nancy Clarke Cox.

We are always building monuments to perpetuate the names and deeds of men, whose worth and courage and splendid virtues do not outshine those of the poor soldier's widow of St. Clair. Birmingham News. (Florence, Ala., Times, 15 Aug. 1890.)

COX, Laura, infant, of Pisgah, Maury County, died Sunday; she was reared by Leonard Newton. (Columbia Herald, 4 March 1871.)

COX, Mr. Dobe, of District 16 in Maury County, and one of the old landmarks, died last week; highly respected. (Columbia Herald, 3 July 1891.)

CRAIG, David J., 68, died last night at 11 p.m.; had been sick since Christmas; Cumberland Presbyterian; of Maury County. (Columbia Herald, 4 July 1873.)

CRAIG, W. B., 65, died on the 3d inst. at Mt. Pleasant. (Columbia Herald, 7 March 1873.)

CRAIG, Sam, 75, of Cranford Hollow, Maury County, has been crippled for 35 years and for 12 months has been helpless; he injured himself in fall Friday night, and it is feared fatally. (Maury Democrat, 8 May 1885.)

CRAIG, N. H., deceased, estate is insolvent; W. R. Covey, administrator, April 15. (Maury Democrat, 20 May 1886.)

CRAWFORD, C. D., of Columbia, TN, died of smallpox in Columbia night before last...a true patriot. (Nashville Daily Union, 7 Nov. 1863.)

CRAWFORD, Thomas E., blacksmith of Spring Hill, TN, found guilty of rape on Emma McKee on Feb. 19 in Franklin and given life imprisonment; attack took place in the Snow Creek area of Maury County. (Columbia Herald and Mail, 25 Feb. 1876.)

CREADY, Hugh Daniel, 2 years 3 months, son of John W. and Ellen Cready died on 16th in Nashville. (Nashville Dispatch, 17 June 1863.)

CREEK, William, killed in 1865; Mitchell Pearson convicted in Bedford County for his murder and got 10 years. (Columbia Herald and Mail, 6 Oct. 1876.)

CREEL, notorious character from Mississippi, killed his daughter with a pine knot in Louisiana because she refused to work in the field. (Memphis Avalanche, 14 June 1867.)

CRENSHAW, James, 21, died July 4 in Atlanta, Georgia, and his sister Miss Mattie Crenshaw died July 20, age 23, at Beech Grove, Williamson County. (Nashville Dispatch, 5 Sept. 1862.)

CRENSHAW, John R. J. (or Jr.), Captain of Bluff City Guards, 18th Regt., CSA, who fell at Murfreesboro, 31 Dec. 1862, is to be buried at Elmwood Cemetery, Memphis, on the 10th in the family vault. (Memphis Avalanche, 9 Feb. 1867.)

CRITTENDEN. Bills have passed in the Senate to grant pensions of $100 a month to Mrs. Katharine Todd Crittenden, widow of General Thomas Crittenden of Kentucky and widows of Major General Nathaniel P. Banks and Major General John A. McClelland. (Maury Democrat, Columbia, TN, 20 Dec. 1894.)

CROCKETT, Col. John W., died at Henderson, KY, Tuesday of Pneumonia, age 47, once represented Kentucky in Confederate Congress. (Memphis Daily Appeal, 7 March 1869.)

CROCKETT, Mrs. Elizabeth, died of poison given to her by two slaves who were owned by William Sullivan; slaves to be executed in Montgomery County on the 8th. (Tennessee Watchman, Clarksville, TN, 1 June 1821.)

CROCKETT, Dr. B. F., old, formerly of Rally Hill area in Maury County, died in Williamson County; a Root Doctor. (Columbia Herald and Mail, 16 July 1875.)(N. B.--His old home still stands on Kedron Road, but is not occupied in 1978.)

CROCKETT, David. San Antonio has fallen. And the Gallant Band of Patriots who defended the walls with undaunted heroism have been inhumanely butchered. Col. David Crockett is among the slain.

Among the slain at San Antonio, we regret to record the name of John M. Hayes of this place, Mr. Washington and Mr. Thomas of Robertson Co., Mr. Haskell of Jackson, and Mr. Autry, formerly of this county; but late of Jackson...Mr. Cloud of Kentucky and Mr. Bonham of S.C., young gentlemen, it is said, of great promise were also among the dead. National Banner. (Columbia Observer, 14 April 1836.)

...Mr. Childress said he heard a list read of those killed; the following only he recollects: Charles Haskell, son of Judge Haskell of Jackson, this state, a brave young man; Maj. Autry of the same place; John M. Hays of Nashville; Young Washington of Robertson County; Young Thomas of Robertson County; Cloud of Kentucky, most intrepid soldier; Lieut. Dickinson; Col. Bowie was sick in his hammock; the negro saw him murdered; Col. David Crockett is also among the fallen, it is said he fought with heroic desperation to the last, and was one of the last that perished, almost burying himself with the slain.

We fear our young friend from Randolph, David Murfee, as noble and daring a spirit as ever marched to the field of battle, poured out his youthful blood on the walls of the Alamo. Capt. Peacock was there sick, and young Murfree, at last account was attending him, the Captain died, and the brave young hero we are pained to think has fallen...A gentleman from Texas a day or so since says he saw Charles Haskell, Esq., two days after the battle, but we fear not... (Columbia Observer, 14 April 1836.)

Five thousand people gathered at Lawrenceburg last week to see the cornerstone laid of the David Crockett monument there. W. R. King of Lawrenceburg is president of the Davy Crockett Monumental Association. (Maury Democrat, Columbia, TN, 28 Aug. 1890, 11 Sept. 1890.)

DAVID CROCKETT'S OLD FLINT-LOCK RIFLE FOUND.--San Antonio, Texas.--David Crockett's old flint-lock squirrel rifle, presented to him in Nashville, TN, in 1822, is still owned by Capt. J. S. Taylor of Bermuda.

"A Texan never asks another Texan where he got a thing," Captain Taylor remarked when he was asked about the history of the gun. "Possession is nine-tenths of the law," he added. "Here is the gun with David Crockett's likeness etched upon the plate and here is a letter giving its history."

This gun which fell from the hands of Crockett, one of the defenders of the immortal Alamo were massacred at San Antonio 6 March 1836, was recovered many years later in Dimmit County following the capture and rescue from a band of Mexicans of Sheriff Gene Buck.

According to a letter received by Captain Taylor, written in 1910 by W. H. Barnett of Braddus, Ga., to Judge John W. Crockett of Little Rock, Arkansas, Barnett says he bought the rifle from the son of Wade Hall in Jan. 1890. Hall and Crockett were inseparable companions and owned guns of a similar make back in Montgomery County, Alabama, with which they hunted constantly.

During the war of 1861-1862 while Barnett was at the front, the gun was sold by Barnett's wife to a Mr. Whitton, who refused to sell it back to Barnett. After Whitton's death Barnett again bought the gun.

In 1886 the weapon had become so rusted at each end that Barnett cut off the ends of the barrel and changed the gun from a flint-lock to a percussion-lock, half-stock, of American black walnut, replacing the brass and silver trimmings, tallow box and nameplate as they were before.

A silver plate on the barrel bears the inscription: "Presented to David Crockett at Nashville, Tenn., 5 May 1822 by James M. Graham." This inscription is hand-engraved. A brass plate on the stock bears an etched likeness of Colonel Crockett, while the brass tallow box at the butt of the stock was used to hold the molded bullets. Silver halfmoons and stars adorn the stock toward the barrel and lock.

Captain Taylor also has the bullet mold, powder horn, measuring cup and leather pounch with shoulder straps which was a part of Crockett's equipment.

Captain Taylor came from California to Laredo, Texas, later moving into the Nueces river valley in Dimmit County, where he built the Bermuda dam, the first irrigation project in the southwest, to aid onion growers. He also founded the town of Bermuda. The project built more than 25 years ago is still in use today. (Perry Countian, Linden, TN, 19 Sept. 1924.)

In recent years the manner of Crockett's death has been in controversy, following a translation made in 1975 of a diary of one of the staff members of Gen. Santa Anna's staff. The diary of Lt. Jose Enrique de la Pena included a paragraph that indicated Crockett surrendered or was captured and then executed when the Alamo was seized.

The de la Pena account: "Some seven men had survived the general carnage and under the protection of General Castrillon, they were brought before Santa Anna. Among them was one of great stature, well proportioned, with regular features, in whose face there was the imprint of adversity, but in whom one also noticed a degree of resignation and nobility that did him honor. He was the naturalist David Crockett, well known in North America for his unusual adventures..."

The account went on to say that Santa Anna ordered the immediate execution of Crockett and the other six prisoners. "Several officers with swords in hand fell upon these unfortunate and defenseless men just as a tiger leaps upon his prey. Though tortured before they were killed, these unfortunates died without complaining and without humiliating themselves before their torturers."

De la Pena, described as a "sensitive lieutenant colonel" kept a diary, which was written in Spanish and was in private hands for years but has now been translated into English. The diary was given to the University of Texas at San Antonio by the late John Peace, a regent for the University and a collector of Texas historical items. (Nashville Banner, 21 April 1978; Nashville Tennessean, 20 Oct. 1975; Longview, Texas, Daily News, 9 Sept. 1975.)

Apparently there was some delay in the Crockett Monument from 1890 until 1922 as the following inscription on the monument on the public square in Lawrenceburg indicates:

South side--Erected by gift of the people and the Legislature of Tennessee, to the memory of Col. David Crockett. Born in East Tennessee 17 Aug. 1786 and gave his life for Texas liberty amid the smoking walls of the Alamo Sunday morning 6 March 1836.

East side--Justice of the peace for Lawrence County 1818. Member of the first commission of Lawrenceburg, 1819. Represented Lawrence-Hickman Counties in the State Legislature 1821-22; Congressman from West Tennessee 1827, 1831, 1833-1835.

West side--Path-finder, Pioneer, Hunter, Patriot, Statesman and Soldier. His fame is immortal with the story of his state, and the Glory of his death. "Thermoplyae had its messenger of defeat, The Alamo had none."

North side--"Be sure you are right, then go ahead." David Crockett. State aid and gifts secured by Sen. C. C. Kelley. Committee: Robert B. Williams, C. C. Kelley, John C. Crews. Erected 1922 by W. M. Deans Marble Co., Columbia, Tenn.

CROFFORD, James T., born 11 Dec. 1796, died 17 Feb. 1883, buried on the Looney lot, 146-149, Elmwood Cemetery, Memphis, Tennessee.

CROFFORD, Jane B., born 30 Dec. 1800, died 30 Aug. 1874, buried on the Looney lot, 146-149, Elmwood Cemetery, Memphis, Tennessee. (These tombstone inscriptions were copied by Mrs. Evelyn B. McAnally, Columbia, TN.)

CROFFORD, James M., who left Maury County 37 years ago has been here on a visit and has returned home today taking his brother Silas J. Crofford with him; Silas has been somewhat demented since his wife died and county court declared him a lunatic. (Columbia Herald and Mail, 16 Oct. 1874.)(N. B., earlier newspapers show that Mrs. S. J. Crofford of Bigbyville died 27 March 1874. Silas J. Crofford, born and reared in Maury County, died 4 March 1889 at the age of 68 and was buried in the Odd Fellow Cemetery in Denton, Texas.)

CRONK, Hiram, of Ava, New York, last veteran of the War of 1812, died 13 May 1905 at the age of 105 years. (Tri-State Trader, 9 Dec. 1972.)

CROOK, General George, died suddenly in his parlor at the Grand Pacific Hotel in Chicago, 21 March 1890, shortly after 7 a.m. He had occupied a box at the Columbia Theater the night before and witnessed Mr. Mansfield's portrayal of the dual role of Dr. Jekyll and Mr. Hyde, returning to the hotel shortly after 11 o'clock, retired, and was apparently in the best of health. He arose at 6:30 on March 21, dressed and commenced to exercise with dumb bells.

About 15 minutes later his wife in an adjoining room heard him call in a faint voice, "Mary! Mary!" She found him reclining on a sofe and evidently in pain. His hands were pressed over his heart and he said, "Mary, I can hardly breathe." She got assistance, but he died at 7:15 o'clock. Mrs. Crook and her sister Mrs. Reid were the only members of family present. He had no children. He died of affection of the heart and had complained of a bearing down sensation in the neighborhood of the heart recently.

General Crook was born near Dayton, Ohio, 8 Sept. 1828; graduated from the U. S. Military Academy 1852; was assigned to duty with the 4th infantry in California 1852-1861; on Rouge river expedition in 1856; commanded Pitt river expedition 1857 where he was wounded.

When Civil War began he became a colonel in the 36th Ohio and in 1862 was wounded at Lewisburg, West Virginia; brevetted lieutenant colonel for his service at Antietam, later brevetted brigadier general and major general.

In 1872 he quelled disturbances in Arizona; in 1875 at Powder river, Wyoming, defeated the Sioux and Cheyenne; conducted campaigns until May 1877 when all hostile tribes yielded; in 1882 he was sent to Arizona to force squatters off Indian lands; in 1883 he pursued the Chiricahuas and took 400 prisoners; in 1886 he forced the surrender of the Indians under Geronimo; Geronimo escaped and he was relieved from this duty by General Miles; Geronimo was later captured and was taken to Florida where he now is.

(Paper was torn at this point)...5,000 filed by his casket in Chicago where he was given a great military funeral; to be interred in Oakland, Maryland. (Maury Democrat, Columbia, TN, 27 March 1890.)

Mrs. General Crook has made a visit to Arlington Cemetery for the purpose of selecting a site for the grave of her distinguished husband. His burial at Oakland was temporary and it has been the purpose of Mrs. Crook from the first to have the final interment at Arlington. This cemetery will undoubtedly become the great military burial ground of the country. (Maury Democrat, 23 Oct. 1890.)

CROOK. The widow of General George Crook, the famous Indian fighter, died at Oakland, Maryland, a few days ago. (Maury Democrat, Columbia, TN, 3 Oct. 1895.)

CROSWAIT, Mrs. Mary Johnson, wife of Milton Croswait of Enterprise in Maury County, died May 5; daughter of Mrs. Lottie Johnson. (Maury Democrat, 17 May 1894.)

CROSTWAIT, W. M. Y., died 12 June 1894 in Lawrence County; his wife died May 5; Methodist; buried Pleasant Garden Cemetery; four children have been sent to separate homes. (Maury Democrat, 14 June 1894.) (N.B.--Name spelled two different ways in these accounts.)

CROUCH, Mrs. Dorothy, 88, died at home of son W. H. Crouch in Montgomery County. (Clarksville Weekly Chronicle, 4 March 1859.)

CROW, J. P., has died in Henderson County; he was the largest man in Tennessee at his death, weighed 400 pounds; died of apoplexy; he lived in the same neighborhood as Miles Darden, who died 1858, who once weighed 1040 pounds and was even much larger at his death.

(Nashville Union and American, 10 March 1874.)

CROWDIS, Marion, daughter of Mr. and Mrs. J. T. Crowdis, funeral to be held today in Edgefield. (Nashville Dispatch, 8 May 1863.)

CROWDIS, Edgar, died in Macon, Georgia, on November 8; son of William and Fannie Crowdis of Nashville. (Nashville Republican Banner, 12 Nov. 1869.)

CROWELL, Harvey, committed suicide in Shelby County, Alabama, last week; age 20. (Florence, Ala., Times, 16 July 1892.)

CRUNK, H. C., 35, died 7 Sept. 1895 of flux in Perry County, son-in-law of Col. A. Bowen; buried Rose Hill Cemetery, Columbia; traveling salesman. (Maury Democrat, 12 Sept. 1895.)

CRUTCHER, Parker, 80, died on the 20th; lived near Glenn's Store, Maury County; buried Mt. Carmel Cemetery, Williamson County. (Maury Democrat, 1 March 1889.)

CRUTCHER. Among the marriage licenses issued this week in Maury County will be noted that of R. A. Crutcher to Mrs. Mittie Crutcher and some pathetic circumstances are connected therewith. This couple married seven or eight years ago and lived together for several years, a boy coming to their home during the time, but they could not agree and live happily, so the wife leaving her husband and child returned to her father's home and the husband secured a divorce on the grounds of desertion. For several weeks the wife's health has been sinking gradually lower and lower, and her doctor has told her that it is only a matter of days now till she must face her Creator. Last week she sent for the husband and told him that she knew she did wrong in leaving him and that she was unwilling to die with the cloud of a divorce hanging over her. Yesterday County Clerk Wiley issued the second license authorizing the marriage of this couple and though facing death, the wife is rejoicing in being united once more to her family. (Maury Democrat, 21 Jan. 1897.)

CRUTCHFIELD, Hon. William, member of Congress 1873-1874, noted for his eccentricities, died in Chattanooga last week; uncompromising Union man and was a guide for Federal armies; great friend of Grant, Rose-crans, and Thomas. After war distinguished himself by aiding ex-Confederates in getting their shattered fortunes together. (Maury Democrat, Columbia, TN, 6 Feb. 1890.)

CUDDIHY, Father, of Milford, Mass., has forbidden the Grand Army of the Republic to enter the Catholic Cemetery on Decoration Day. (Erin Review, 3 Jan. 1882.)

CULBERTSON, Captain William, of the 18 Kentucky Volunteers, was wounded in the Battle of Richmond, Kentucky, and died a few days ago. (Nash-ville Dispatch, 7 Oct. 1862.)

CULBUT, William E., son of William and Jane Culbut, age 1 year, died yesterday. (Nashville Republican Banner, 13 Oct. 1869.)

CULL, Lt. F. C., of the __Colored Regiment, committed suicide by over-dose of morphine at the residence 28 Cherry Street, over Thompson's Furnishing Store; had been drinking a great deal of late; fought bravely at Shiloh and Fort Donelson; wounded once; lately was in the fight at Dalton; lately with quartermaster in Nashville; he leaves a wife to mourn. (Nashville Daily Union, 13 Feb. 1865.)

CULLEN, Lt. William, 1st lieutenant, Company K, 3d Kentucky Infantry, died on the 14th in hospital 3 from the effects of gunshot wound in Battle of Stones River; buried on the 16th. (Nashville Daily Union, 19 March 1863.)

CULLWELL, Mrs. David, of Water Valley, Maury County, has died; Baptist. (Maury Democrat, 31 Oct. 1895.)

CULLY. William Philips of District 3 in Bedford County, accidently killed his sister-in-law Miss Cully, aged about 18, on Saturday. He, an
invalid, shot birds in tree out of a window and she passed by and he
shot her in head. (Columbia Herald and Mail, 24 April 1878.)

CULPEPER, Mrs. Elizabeth, 93, died on the 22d ult. in Henry County, TN;
maiden name Swaney; married 1832 near Nashville. (Whig and Tribune,
Jackson, TN, 7 Dec. 1872.)

CUMMINGS, James, son of Mrs. Rachel Cummings of Palmyra, Montgomery Co.,
tribute of respect on his death in paper. (Clarksville Weekly Chronicle, 2 March 1861.)

CUMMINGS, Lt. Commander A. Boyd, was killed in recent attack on Port
Hudson, La., son of Thomas Cummings, Esquire, of Philadelphia; native
of Pennsylvania, age 32; graduate of the Naval Academy; had leg torn
off by shot from the rebels. (Nashville Dispatch, 8 April 1863.)

CUMMIS, William, late county clerk of Williamson County, age 53, died
last Sunday. (Whig and Tribune, Jackson, TN, 4 Nov. 1871.)

CUNNINGHAM, Col. Preston D., 28 Tennessee, killed at Murfreesboro.
(Nashville Dispatch, 8 Jan. 1863.)

CUNNINGHAM, George, 2 years 7 months, son of George W. and A. M. Cunningham, died Sept. 21 at Marietta, Georgia. (Nashville Dispatch,
7 Oct. 1862.)

CUNNINGHAM, J. R., old and esteemed of Hickman County, died 24 Jan. 1872
at Centerville of congestion of brain; age 62. (Columbia Herald,
31 Jan. 1873.)

CURFMAN, Mary, age 83 (?), died on the 26th at Harpeth. (Nashville
Dispatch, 30 Sept. 1862.)

CURL. Sandy Chappell recently visited in Hickman County and saw Mrs.
William Curl on Piney River. She was 105 last November 18 and in
good health and has been living here since 1806; she has been a member of the Baptist Church for 75 years. She has quilt that was her
dress when she was a girl--a yellow silk. She has a teapot she
brought from North Carolina in 1806 when she came; she also has the
old family Bible. She has one son, age 81, Jarrett Curl, who lives
a mile away. He was in the Battle of New Orleans. She remembers
distinctly of seeing General Nathaniel Greene marching at the head
of his army during the Revolution. We trust she may live to the age
of another Hickman woman, Mrs. Trantham, who died years ago at the
age of 130. (Columbia Herald and Mail, 18 Feb. 1877.)(N. B.--Mrs.
Trantham is usually given as being of Maury County.)

Mrs. Kissia Curl, died 9 Sept. 1879, aged 107 years 9 months 23 days,
born in South Carolina; came to Hickman County in 1808; died at home
of her grandson Jarrett Frazier on Pine Creek. (Old Hickman Pioneer
newspaper clipping, Sept. 1879.)

The obituary of her grandson Jarrett Curl Frazier shows that he was
born 27 Jan. 1838, died 19 Jan. 1906 near Vernon in Hickman County;
son of Keziah Curl and Elijah Frazier of Dickson; married 28 Feb.
1860 to Sarah Josephine Jones; served in 48th Tennessee Infantry during Civil War; attended church at Briggs Chapel; he joined the church
in 1863 at camp and his wife joined the same day in Hickman County.

CURREY, Miss Anna Jesse, died of consumption, daughter of John H. Currey.
(Nashville Union and American, 26 June 1873.)

CURREY, Mary Josephine, daughter of J. H. and C. F., died on the 3d.
(Nashville Republican Banner, 4 Nov. 1869.)

CURRIE, Major James, one of the oldest citizens of Haywood County, died
a few weeks ago of heat and exertion in an effort to extinguish a

fire which had caught in his fence. (Nashville Union and American 22 August 1874.)

CURRIN, John, killed in Johnny's Saloon on College Street in Nashville on 5 Sept. 1867 in an affray with John Cochran. (Nashville Republican Banner, 4 Sept. 1867, 5 Sept. 1867.)

CURRIN, Sophronia S., consort of Robert S. Currin, Esquire, 35, died on the 12th in Nashville. (Nashville Dispatch, 24 Aug. 1862.)

CURRIN, Mrs. Elizabeth, relict of Jonathan Currin, age 68, died on the 22d in Murfreesboro; her husband died in autumn of 1843; she had been Presbyterian for 40 years. (Nashville Dispatch, 28 June 1862.)(N.B.--The Currins are buried in the old City Cemetery in Murfreesboro; his stone has no dates on it and the rest of the family stones were down and broken in 1968 and no stone for Elizabeth could be found at that time.)

CURTIN, Andrew G., Pennsylvania's wartime governor, died at his home in Bellefont, Pennsylvania, the other morning. (Maury Democrat, Columbia, TN, 11 Oct. 1894.)

CURTIS, John, 80, died at his home six miles west of Paris, TN, on the 2d. (Whig and Tribune, Jackson, TN, 14 Dec. 1872.)

CURTIS, Maria Louisa Ashley, died 5 March 1871. (Columbia Herald, 7 March 1871.)

CUSHMAN, Charlotte, died at the Parker House, Boston, on the 18th, age 59 years 7 months; afflicted with cancer for a long time; went for a walk, got cold, developed pneumonia. (Columbia Herald and Mail, 3 March 1876.)

CUSTER, George Armstrong, died 25 June 1876.
Described as a "gay and festive youth", some of his letters exposing his various amours were published in Richmond last winter. (Memphis Avalanche, 1 Feb. 1866.)

Colonel Newhall described him: "Custer of the golden locks, his broad sombrero turned up from his hard-bronzed face, the ends of his crimson cravat floating over his shoulders, gold galore spangling his jacket sleeves, a pistol in his boot, jangling spurs on his heels, and a ponderous daymore swinging at his side, a wild dare-devil of a general, and a prince of advance guards, quick to see and act." (Columbia Herald and Mail, 28 July 1876.)

July 6.--Regarding the reported killing of General Custer and the massacre of his forces, neither General Sherman nor General Sheridan will accept it. General Sherman at Philadelphia says, "I don't believe it, and I don't want to believe it."

July 6.--A dispatch confirming the report of the death of General Custer and the terrible disaster has created a profound sensation in Washington. General Custer passed several years of his youth in Monroe, Mich. His wife is daughter of Honorable Daniel L. Bacon of Monroe and the whole town is draped in mourning.

The slaughtered officers included: Custer, Col. Keogh, Col. Yates, Col. Cook, Lt. Smith, Lt. McIntosh, Lt. Calhoun, Lt. Hodgson, Lt. Reilly, Lt. Porter, Lt. Sturgis, and Lt. Harrington is missing. (Columbia Herald and Mail, 14 July 1876.)

Brice W. Custer, brother of the deceased general, has lived in Columbus, Ohio, for years. Bosten Custer, 25, a forage-master, and Thomas Custer, 27, a lieutenant, both unmarried brothers of the general, were killed in the massacre. The brother-in-law who was killed was the husband of the general's only sister. The parents of the general are upwards of 70 and very feeble. Neither the general or his brother-in-law had any children. Mrs. Custer would never leave her husband. She traveled many hundreds of miles with him on a pony, slept

with him in the ambulances, and when duty called him to battle, her grief was inexpressable till he returned. (Columbia Herald and Mail, 28 July 1876.)

One of the most highly prized relics in the possession of General Miles is a plain old style rifle that once belonged to Rain-in-the Face, the slayer of General Custer. (Florence, Ala., Times, 14 Nov. 1890.)

(N.B.--Later accounts tell that Capt. Myles Keogh was so hideously mutilated that he could only be identified by a medallion around his neck. Capt. Keogh's charger, Comanche, was the only survivor. He was found with broken arrows in his flanks (wounded in seven places) and the Indians did not take him because he was so severely injured. He survived to become the mascot of the 7th Cavalry and for years was a proud figure at regimental ceremonies marking the day when 225 soldiers were massacred. No person was ever allowed to ride or work the horse, which was saddled, bridled and paraded at every ceremony of the regiment. Four officers and 14 enlisted men's bodies were never found following the massacre. All bodies were buried in one large grave, top of Custer Hill, except Lt. Crittenden, but in 1931 his body was moved to be buried with the others)

(Custer's body was found naked on the highest part of the ridge, his yellow hair matted with blood and there were bullet holes in his face and chest. Tom Custer had his heart cut out. Custer's nephew Autie Reed was among those killed and Lt. Calhoun was his brother-in-law.)

BONES OF THE BRAVE.--All the graves of both men and officers were discovered without difficulty. The remains were found to be scattered over an area of several hundred acres.

All that evening, in camp, the soldiers were converting cedar boughs into stakes or head-boards, with which to mark the graves. Each stake was cut just three feet long, and was intended to be driven into the ground two-thirds of its length.

On the morning of the 3d a fatigue party was ordered to exhume and re-inter the remains of the soldiers who fell around Custer. There were large and small trenches. Some contained but few remains. Others contained long rows of separate sets of bones, indicating that as many as a dozen had been buried together. Where a little band had fought together, and had fallen side by side, or in a heap, they had received burial in about the same order in which they fell. Only the naked bones remained in the trenches. There was no traces of flesh and corruption, and no odor, except that which was wafted from the shoels of wild flowers blooming in the valley below. In a few hours the thin layer of dirt had been removed from the bones of over two hundred soldiers and the remains re-interred in the same trenches, but rather more decently than before. Three feet of earth, tastefully heaped and packed with spades and mallets was put upon each set of remains, and the head marked by a cedar stake.

The same day the bones of the officers were exhumed. The remains of the following officers were unmistakably identified: Gen. Custer, his brother, Col. Tom Custer, Col. Keogh, Col. Cook, Capt. Yates, and Lts. Smith, Calhoun, Crittenden and Beilly. They had been buried just as they had fallen, with the single exception of Col. Custer, who had received interment alongside his brother.

The grave of the Custers was near the summit of a little knoll, right where the gallant soldier had taken his last stand. The ground for two hundred feet around was filled with remains. Over sixty men had been killed on that little elevation. The surface of the knoll was strewn with dry bones of horses, which were bleached to the whiteness of ivory. From the position of the bones it was evident to the observer that the horses had been shot for the purpose of forming a breastwork. It looked as if the animals had been led into a position describing a half-circle and shot in their tracks.

While the work of exhumation was going on, Col. Sheridan had a party of scouts and interpreters scouring the vicinity for any undiscovered remains. There were eight of these scouts, mostly Crow Indians, including "Curley", who claims to have been the only man who escaped from Custer's command. Col. Sheridan thinks there is great danger that Curley is a liar. He discovered that this red Crow knew very little about the battlefield and probably knew less about the battle.

Another one of the scouts is the celebrated Half-Yellow-Face, who was badly wounded in the Reno fight, and who is a fellow of some veracity. Besides these there were three well known interpreters named Barrett, La Fourge, and Herendeen, the latter having fought under Reno. The country for fifteen miles around was thoroughly searched. They discovered no evidence that any one had escaped and was afterward run down and killed.

Col. Sheridan says that the Indians, after winning a fight, ran away and left a large amount of camp equipage. The bottom where Custer encountered them has been a favorite camping-ground for the Sioux for many years. Every time they broke camp there they abandoned more of less traps. There are not less than ten thousand lodge poles lying around in the tall grass. A search in the vicinity of the battlefield revealed the bones of some twenty or thirty Indians. (Columbia Herald and Mail, 10 August 1877.)

Gen. Custer and five of his officers were insured in the New York Life Insurance Company, of this city, and as their policies were taken out under a special provision made by the company, the claims will be promptly paid and in no way affected by the manner of their deaths. The aggregate insurance of the six officers is $40,000, and is distributed as follows: Gen. Custer, $5000; Capt. Yates, $5000; Capt. Keogh, $10,000; Lieut. Calhoun, $5000; Lieut. Crittenden, $10,000, and Lieut. Porter, $500.--World. (Columbia Herald and Mail, 4 Aug. 1876.)

Gen. Sitting Bull and his Lieut. Rain-in-the-Face, Crazy Horse and the other heroes of the Yellowstone massacre, were armed by the United States with Winchester rifles, that were more effective than the arms of our own troops. They were supplied by the United States with ammunition, stores and horses. The blankets given his command by the Indian agency were freshly supplied and were all new and marked "U. S. Indian Department." While Sitting Bull and his lieutenants were killing Custer's men, the United States was kindly feeding and caring for their squaws and papooses. It now appears that, since Custer's defeat, the Indians are wearing their clothes. Perhaps it would do well now for the United States to keep on with the farce it is playing, pension the Indian widows, and present Sitting Bull with a sword and the freedom of the whole Indian country. (Columbia Herald and Mail, 4 Aug. 1876.)

News from Custer gives the details of the killing of four men near that place on the 24th, while en route to their hay camp, although no names are given. A party pursued the Indians, who numbered by the trail, 22, followed them to the Hay Camp, but the Indians were there in advance, and had taken everything but a grinding stone. The place where these men were ambushed was at the head of a long canyon running eastward; the Indians hiding in the rocks, watched for their approach, although all were not killed at first fire, as the bodies of two men were found in the rocks, whither they had fled. (Columbia Herald and Mail, 15 Sept. 1876.)

N.B.--In 1976 the book KEEP THE LAST BULLET FOR YOURSELF by Thomas B. Marquis was published, which offered a startling theory of what really happened to Custer and his men at Little Bighorn. In the 1920s and 1930s, Dr. Marquis, a Montana physician, investigated the battle and talked in sign language to surviving warriors. His findings were so shocking and contrary to history, that no publisher would touch his book. Only in 1976 was the result of investigation made public.

According to Marquis, the slaughter of Custer and his 213 men was largely self-inflicted as they were panic-stricken by the stampede of their horses, by the scary appearance and chilling war-whoops of Sitting Bull's warriors, and by the fear of the torture awaiting them if they were captured, that they were driven to suicide. Marquis drew the title of his book from an old frontier slogan: "When fighting Indians, keep the last bullet for yourself."

The accepted view of the battle is that Custer and his men were wiped out by a succession of charges by the Sioux and Cheyenne Indians, but some of the Indian survivors told Marquis they had seen some of Custer's soldiers shooting themselves, and one warrior reported that he saw one soldier kill three of his own comrades.

General Custer was reburied at West Point on 10 Oct. 1877.

CUTTEN. Henry Ritter Emma Ritter Denia Ritter Sweet Potato Cream of Gartar Caroline Ostic, 9 year old colored girl, buried at Wetumpka, Alabama. On her slab her parents are given as Bob and Snakey Cutten. (Maury Democrat, 4 April 1895.)

CUTTER, Susan Jane, infant daughter of B. R. and Annie C. Cutter, died on the 22d in Nashville, age 10 months 16 days. (Nashville Dispatch, 25 June 1862.)

CUTTS, James Madison, died on the 11th in Washington, second comptroller of the treasury, father-in-law of late Senator Douglas. (Nashville Dispatch, 14 May 1863.)

D

DABBS, Joseph W., died 4 May 1865 of apoplectic attack near Delia, La., son of Rev. Richard Dabbs, Baptist minister. (Nashville Daily Union 3 June 1865.)

DAHNE, John, 67, died on the 30th ult. in Nashville, lived near the State hospital. (Nashville Dispatch, 1 May 1863.)

DAILEY, John Dailey, one of Dyer County's best men, living a few miles from Trimble, got a package by express, contained $685.

In the early months of 1864 a detachment of 5th Pennsylvania Cavalry were out on a scout, endeavoring to watch the movements of General N. B. Forrest, who was camping near Dr. Dailey's house. Before leaving, one of the Yankees took a horse and Dailey argued, "Turn that horse loose! I wouldn't take $250 for that animal, you confounded Yankee thief."

"Keep your shirt on, pardner," replied the soldier, "my horse turned his toes to the daisies last night and I am compelled to have another. If I do not leave the country at once, Forrest will capture me."

"I wish he had you now," replied Dr. Dailey.

"See here. I'll tell you what I'll do," said the soldier. "You tell me your name and if I ever get through the war alive, and become financially able, I will send you the money for your horse."

"My name is John R. Dailey, damn you, but I'll never hear from you again, you contemptible thief."

"That remains to be proven," smiled the trooper. "Time will tell." and amid the shouts of his comrades he rode away.

Reverses of fortune have repleted the Daily treasury until the home was mortgaged and the future seemed dark and gloomy. On going to the post office Wednesday, Mr. Dailey received the following letter:

Reading, Pa., 3 April 1893
John R. Dailey, Trimble, Tenn.:
Dear Sir--I suppose you remember one April morning in the memorable "64 when a squad of Yanks" as you termed them, came to your home

76

and one of them appropriated your horse which you said was worth $250. The soldier promised to pay for the horse. I am that same Yank.

In the past few years I have received the smiles of fortune and have accumulated considerable property. I am getting advanced in years and look upon the taking of your horse as thieving, I now wish to pay you. I learn through your postmaster that you are still living and in hard luck. I send you by express $685, which is the principal with 6 per cent interest. Probably we may never meet again in this world, but I hope to meet you in the land where sectional hatred is unknown. Trusting you may prosper, I am very truly, Frank K. Waldron. (Maury Democrat 11 May 1893.)

DAIMWOOD, Sammie, 16 months, youngest child of Sam Daimwood, died Sunday in Maury County; oldest son Henry died three months ago. (Maury Democrat, 7 Nov. 1895.)

DAIMWOOD, Mrs. Eliza Jane, 70, wife of H. B. Daimwood, died Friday on Bear Creek, Maury County, buried family burying ground. (The Herald, ___ Jan. 1891.)

DALDWELL, Dr. H. M., one of the founders of Birmingham is dead. (Maury Democrat, 15 Aug. 1895.)

DALE, Miss Jennie, her estate is insolvent in Maury County. (Maury Democrat, 3 Oct. 1889.)

DALE, Mary E., daughter of John P. and Elizabeth Dale, died Tuesday in Nashville. (Nashville Republican Banner, 11 May 1870.)

DALE, Elizabeth. "Mystery of Elizabeth Dale".--A fine stone in Rose Hill Cemetery in Columbia, TN, marks the final resting place of the Reverend Samuel G. Gibbons, who died in 1830, supposedly under mysterious circumstances. How did he die? Was he murdered?

Gibbons was the first husband of Elizabeth Evans Dale, better known in the folklore of North Alabama and Middle Tennessee as the notorious Mrs. Gibbons-Flanagan-Jeffries-High-Brown-Routt.

According to a mountain of legend, Gibbons was poisoned by his wife, and she went on to murder her next five husbands--keeping a top hat of each of her mates as a risly memento. However, according to Gibbons' obituary in a Columbia newspaper, the Western Mercury, he died of yellow fever in Centerville, Hickman County, TN.

The family history compiled by his brother-in-law, Nathan Vaught, also states that Gibbons died of yellow fever. Despite this, his wife remains accused in history. Historians are sharply divided over her guilt or innocence.

Elizabeth Dale was born 28 Oct. 1795, in Worcester County, Maryland, one of the ten children of Adam Dale and his wife Mary Hall. No picture of her has survived (the Tennessee kin destroyed theirs), but she is said to have been most beautiful, well-educated, and always finely dressed.

When she was two years old, the Dale family moved to Tennessee and settled in a rude cabin in what is now DeKalb County where Adam Dale is recognized in that county's history as its first settler.

Dale as a boy of thirteen or fourteen had raised a company of boys to oppose the progress of Lord Cornwallis through Maryland during the Revolution. Later during the Creek War, he organized a company of one hundred men when General Andrew Jackson was fighting the Indians in and around Huntsville. According to his grandson, Dale's company rendezvoused near a big spring at Meridianville about eight miles north of Huntsville--not far from the scene of his daughter's future notoriety.

Elizabeth Dale was only seventeen on 19 Nov. 1812 when she married Samuel Gibbons, a twenty-year old Baptist minister. They were happily
married for 18 years and no scandal was ever attached to the wife. In
the summer of 1830 Gibbons fell victim to yellow fever, commonly called
the black tongue. The manner of his passing was quite horrible, typical
of the course of this dread disease. His swollen, distorted features
and the darkened tongue would be remembered later.

After his death Elizabeth settled in Columbia where her brother Edward
W. Dale was a most prominent citizen and a banker. (He, too, would die
under a cloud--committing suicide after some trouble at his bank.)

At some time between 1830 and 1833, Elizabeth made her second marriage,
to a Mr. Flanagan. No further information is available about him, other
than he soon died.

For the sake of propriety, only three marriages were listed for Elizabeth
in the family history--this was in the day when only three marriages
were considered proper for any lady of decency and quality. The Flanagan marriage is one of those her brother-in-law conveniently omitted in
the family annals.

The family knew of this marriage, certainly, for her name is found as
Elizabeth E. Flanagan when she married Alexander Jeffries in Columbia on
6 Nov. 1833. Jeffries, who originally came from Culpeper County, Va.,
and lived in a log house at Hazel Green, Ala., was the father of Elizabeth's only children--William Jeffries, born 1834, and Mary Elizabeth
Jeffries, born when her mother was almost fifty years old.

It was this marriage that brought Elizabeth to live in Alabama. Jeffries died sometime after 1844 and was buried on his homeplace at Hazel
Green. In short order, Elizabeth married a Mr. High and was soon
widowed.

Her fifth husband was Absalom Brown. He lived long enough to replace
the log house with a larger, more substantial home. When he died, he
was buried immediately, and "in the flickering light of candles."

Both the marriages to High and Brown were left out of the Vaught com-
pilation about the Dale family.

In 1848 she married Willis Routt of near Fayetteville, Tennessee. They
made their home at Elizabeth's house in Alabama, but he did not long
survive his nuptials.

The neighbors had been whispering before Routt's death, but tongues
began to clack audibly when prospective husband number seven appeared on
the scene. He was D. H. Bingham, a school teacher at Meridanville.

At the time Bingham began to court her, Elizabeth was involved in a feud
with a neighbor, Abner Tate, "one of the sharpest tongued among the
Widow's critic". Tate, angered because some of Elizabeth's stock got
into his crops, apparently set out to ruin the widow. He only had to
fan the gossip already smoldering in the community.

The mysterious deaths of the many husbands had caused many eyebrows to
raise. Brown's unexplained funeral after dark were recalled. Jeffries'
death had never been satisfactorily explained--nor had High and Routt's
demises. Someone recalled she had been married briefly to Flanagan.
More gossip. Finally, tales of Samuel Gibbons's ghastly death were
resurrected. Poison! Poison was the only answer to sudden death.

In 1854 one of Tate's own slaves shot and wounded him. Blame was attached to the Widow Routt--supposedly she had hired one of her own
slaves to shoot her antagonist and the slave had in turn paid one of
Tate's slaves to do it.

Matters finally reached the lawsuit stage. Tate, bent on vengeance,
charged that Elizabeth's bridal chamber was a "charnel house" and that
she was a bride "around whose marriage couch six grinning skeletons were

already hung." (There is one tale that Tate's enmity stemmed from the rich widow's rejection of his suit at one time.)

Elizabeth retaliated with a damage suit against her tormentor for $50,000, for defamation of character. According to one writer, "Public opinion was clearly against Elizabeth." She was guilty and Tate became something of a folk hero.

Although Mrs. Routt sold her home in 1855 and moved to Mississippi, the scandal-mongers were not quite through with her. There would be mutterings that she had also killed her own father.

Her father, Adam Dale, had died at her home in Hazel Green in 1851 and had been buried in the Jeffries family cemetery behind the house. His widow Mary returned to Columbia to be with her daughter, Mrs. Vaught, and other children. Elizabeth's troubles and subsequent removal disturbed her aged mother, who was unhappy that her husband was buried in such an unfriendly land.

To appease his distressed mother-in-law, Vaught had Dale's body removed from the little graveyard in Alabama to a new one in Columbia. He had been one of the founders of this new cemetery, Rose Hill, and he chose a lot near his own. (Vaught is remembered chiefly as the "Master-Builder" of Maury County, as many of the fine antebellum homes in that county were his work.)

When Dale's body was exhumed, it was found that it had petrified and turned dark. This unnatural state gave rise to the ill-founded rumor that the father had gone the way of the husbands.

Sometime after her removal to Mississippi, Elizabeth had the body of the beloved husband of her youth removed from Centerville to Columbia. His tombstone is made in the shape of a pulpit with an open Bible on the top.

Careful students of the Elizabeth Dale legend completely discount the stories that she killed Samuel Gibbons and Routt. (Some believe her only crime was being married six times.)

There is certainly documentation that Gibbons died of yellow fever--and some evidence that Elizabeth was not even in Centerville when he took sick and died.

Also, Kate Routt, said to be the daughter of Willis Routt (but at least a close relative) married Elizabeth's own nephew in 1851. It is doubtful that she would have married into Elizabeth's family had there been truth in the rumors.

Was Elizabeth Dale a murderess-or the victim of malicious slander?

She died 7 May 1866 in Marshall County, Mississippi and her secret went with her to the grave.

References:
"Youth and Old Age" by Nathan Vaught (unpublished), copy in the writer's possession.
The Adam Dale Family (unpublished) by Nathan Vaught, copy in writer's possession.
History of DeKalb County, by Will T. Hale.
Maury County Marriage Records, 1833.
Maury County Inquests, 1840.
Western Mercury, Columbia, TN, 20 July 1830.
Letter of C. N. Vaught, 20 March 1906, in Reference Library, Tennessee State Library and Archives, Nashville, TN.
Alabama, A guide to the state, published by the Federal Writers Program, page 329.
Tombstone inscriptions, Rose Hill Cemetery, Columbia, TN.
Tennessee Historical Commission highway marker, located at bridge over Smith's Fork, in DeKalb County, TN.
(This article by Jill Garrett was published originally in the Valley Featurette, Athens, Alabama, 8 January 1971.)

Obituaries of her husbands:

GIBBONS. Died on the 14th inst. in Centreville at the residence of his brother-in-law, Mr. John Philips, the Rev. Saml. G. Gibbons, in his 38th year of age, leaving affectionate wife and large circle of relatives and friends to mourn him. Baptist minister. (Western Mercury, Columbia, TN., 20 July 1830.)

ROUTT. Died in Madison County, Alabama, on the 16th, Colonel Willis Routt, aged about 50...farmer of Lincoln County, TN. (Fayetteville Observer, 16 Dec. 1851.)

DALE, Edward. THE SUICIDE OF MR. DALE.--The Columbia (TN) Observer of the 10th instant, contains two letters left by the late Edward W. Dale--the first bearing date four days before he committed the awful act of self destruction and the last written on Monday evening. Private pecuniary difficulties appear to have led to this shocking catastrophe a minute detail of which is given in his letters, by the deceased. He solemnly protests that he had nothing to do with, and is still ignorant of the author of, the robbery of the bank in 1838. He had his suspicions though not sufficiently strong to authorize the use of names.

Some months since he left the bank in charge of a friend (and director) during a business visit which he made to South Alabama--first counting the funds of the bank to and in the presence of his substitute. When he returned, the acting cashier made known to him the existence of a deficit of $1,960 in the cash account, which they were both unable to trace, and which, we understand has not been discovered.

Of the cause of this deficit, the deceased protests that he was entirely ignorant up to the hour of committing his last words to paper. The Nashville Whig says the details of the letter are mostly of a private nature some of them quite unimportant as to the sums involved, and without public interest, save, perhaps, to the immediate neighbors of the deceased. His concluding conclusion as to the sanguinary act which he contemplated and subsequently carried into final execution will be read with painful emotion. We extract from the letter of July 3:

"As to the robbery of the bank, in 1839, I know nothing about it than it was robbed by some person to me unknown, and who is yet unknown; true, I have suspicions of the person, but not as I conceive sufficient to authorize me to name anyone. It is exceedingly painful to be, driven to the necessity of self-destruction; but such is the inevitable necessity in my case that it cannot be dispensed with-- such flagrant injustice has been done me recently by a body of respectable men, occupying an important trust, is more than I can bear.

"I now have nothing left to live for, no I cannot be of any service to my family. It pains me to leave them in penury; it is also exceedingly painful to me that I leave my friends involved to such an extent on my account--these things have been brought about by a combination of circumstances over which I had only a partial control.

"I went into the bank reluctantly; and I do most sincerely wish that I had never had anything to do with it; regrets do no good now. I wish no funeral solemnities of any description to be had over my poor frail remains--simply consign them to their mother earth; there, there to rest, regardless of the storms, troubles, and ills of this present life. Adieu to all that I hold dear on earth. I have done some good to my fellow men, but I have also done a great deal of harm, though unintentionally."

(Daily National Intelligencer, Washington, D. C., 24 July 1840.)

Edward W. Dale, "being alone on 7 July 1840 did wickedly, unlawfully, and voluntarily kill himself by cutting his throat." (Statement found in box labeled "Inquests Ended 1845-1853" in the basement of the Maury County Courthouse, Columbia, TN.)

E. W. Dale announces he has disposed of his interest in Dale & Phillips
to John Phillips. John Phillips announces that he has purchased the
interest of E. W. Dale in firm of Dale & Phillips and will continue the
business. Notice that firm of A. Dale & Co. is dissolved, signed by
A. Dale, E. W. Dale. (Columbia Observer, 19 July 1838.)

$5,000 Reward--Whereas the Branch of the Bank of Tennessee at Columbia
was entered on the night of the 22d inst. and robbed of a large amount
of their own paper, and also the papers of other banks...reward is
offered for the apprehension and recovery of the money. Signed, E. W.
Dale, Cashier. (Columbia Observer, 24 Oct. 1839.)

N.B.--Mr. Dale was buried in old Greenwood Cemetery in Columbia but his
stone cannot be found in 1978. In 1902 when a listing of the cemetery
was made, the inscription could barely be deciphered and was:
Edward W. Dale, 1790 - ___0.

(For those interested in this particular event, more information may be
found on it in Frank H. Smith's History of Maury County, published in
recent years by the Maury County Historical Society.)

DALLAM, Major, of Paducah, KY, Confederate prisoner, captured at Fort
     Henry, on General Tilghman's staff, died Sunday at Columbus, Ohio.
     (Nashville Dispatch, 28 June 1862.)

DALTON, Bill, notorious outlaw and leader of the Longview, Texas, bank
     robbers, was shot and killed near Elk, Indian Territory, Friday by
     Deputy Marshal Closs Hart; considerable stolen money recovered.
     (Maury Democrat, 14 June 1894.) Bill Dalton was killed at Ardmore,
     Indian Territory. On his person were nearly 200 letters and several
     big rolls of bank bills. His wife was a highly educated and refined
     daughter of respectable people of San Francisco, California. (Maury
     Democrat, 21 June 1894.)

DALY, John, killed on Friday, the 17th, by foul air in water closet;
     was member of the 154th Tennessee, as was Tim Murphy, who tried to
     rescue him. (Memphis Daily Appeal, 19 June 1870.)

DALY, Mrs. Ann W., wife of John N., died Tuesday last in Montgomery
     County. (Clarksville Weekly Chronicle, 4 Dec. 1857.)

DALY, Mrs. Nannie, wife of John N., of Camden, Arkansas, died at the
     home of Samuel Allen in Montgomery County. (Clarksville Jeffer-
     sonian, 1 Dec. 1857.)

DALY, William. William Jenkins arrived Sunday night from his ranch 60
     miles from Colville, Washington, and surrendered. He had killed two
     men, William Daly and Benjamin Shaw, in dispute over horse trade.
     Claimed it was self defense. (Maury Democrat, 14 Aug. 1890.)(N.B.,
     No location given in this account.)

DAMASCUS, Mrs. Walter, died last week and buried at Friendship Church in
     Maury County; niece of Rev. Haywood. (Columbia Herald, 24 July
     1891.)

DAMON, Mrs. Esther S., last widow of Revolutionary War soldier, died 5
     years ago at the age of 91 in Plymouth Rock, Virginia. (Maury
     Democrat, 8 Feb. 1912.)

DANCEY, Miss Mary, died 12 March 1895 in New Orleans; graduate of the
     Columbia Institute. (Maury Democrat, Columbia, TN, 28 Mar. 1895.)

DANCY, Miss Winfield, of LaGrange, TN, died some weeks ago at the Insti-
     tute in Columbia; placed in vault at Rose Hill Cemetery and will be
     removed to Texas this week. (Columbia Herald, 3 Jan. 1873.)

DANEY, Florence, adopted daughter of Mr. and Mrs. Lewis Daney, died on
     the 19th. The child was found abandoned in the Columbia Depot a
     month or so ago. (Columbia Herald, 21 March 1873.)

DANFORTH, James B., Esquire, of Buffalo, New York, died of cholera on the 28th ult.; brother-in-law of D. G. Rumsey of Nashville. (Nashville Daily Gazette, 7 Sept. 1852.)

DANIEL, Abner G., 86, died at Danville, KY, on Jan. 2; he was a soldier of War of 1812 and former member of Kentucky legislature. (Columbia Herald and Mail, 2 Feb. 1877.)

DANIEL, Coleman, 77, old and respected citizen of Louisville, KY, died Friday in Louisville; his history intimately associated with that of Louisville. (Nashville Dispatch, 21 March 1863.)

DANIEL, John, died in Nashville, last Friday. (Maury Democrat, 11 July 1895.)

DANIEL, Jack, most noted distiller, died Oct. 9 in Lynchburg, TN. His estate was worth $250,000. (Maury Democrat, 28 Sept. 1911.)

DANIELS, Samuel T. M., member of 3d Tennessee Cavalry, CSA, died at the hospital in Nashville between May 1 and May 15. (Nashville Daily Union, 25 May 1865.)

DANLEY, Jarrell Jones, age 2 years 1 month 25 days, son of William L. and Lucy, died 1 Nov. in Nashville. (Nashville Union and American, 3 Nov. 1874.)

DANSBY, D., of Mississippi, died of consumption Tuesday at the home of his brother R. C. Dansby in Williamsport, TN; wife and one child survive. (Columbia Herald and Mail, 27 July 1877.)

DARBY, Patrick H., formerly of Nashville, died 18 Dec. 1829 in Brandenburg, Kentucky. (Western Mercury, Columbia, TN, 13 Jan. 1830.)

DARK, Miss Nora, 16, daughter of Mrs. Matilda Dark of South Columbia, died Sunday of typhoid; buried at family burying ground near Rock Springs. (Columbia Herald, 17 April 1891.) Buried at Mrs. Martha J. Jackson's. (Columbia Herald, 24 April 1891.)

DARK, Harris. Executor's notice for Harris Dark, deceased, published in the paper. (Columbia Herald, 24 Oct. 1873.)

DASHIELL, John G., son of Capt. John S. Dashiell, died in Nashville on the 25th. (Nashville Dispatch, 26 June 1863.)

DASHIELL, Stanley P., son of E. H. and M. Hull Dashiell, born 2 January 1841 at Natchez; died of congestion of bowels at Cairo, Ill., on 31 Aug. 1865; buried Elmwood Cemetery in Memphis on 16 Oct. 1865; was in Capt. Wicks Cavalry, CSA; Episcopalian; family moved to Memphis in 1842. (Memphis Avalanche, 14 April 1866.)

DAVANY. The brother of Tom Davany was killed by train on the Nashville and Northwestern Railroad. Tom became demented over this and has disappeared. (Nashville Republican Banner, 29 May 1868.)

DAVENPORT. An old gentleman named Davenport of near Brundidge, Ala., found drowned in creek, Mill Creek near Monticello; he was old and decrepit and was going to visit his daughter at Monticello. It is believed to have been a violent death, but no one as yet has been accused. (Memphis Avalanche, 9 Nov. 1866.)

DAVENPORT. Early on Feb. 16 at Burnsville, Miss., on the M&C railroad, three men lost lives; a band of desperadoes had infested the country around Burnsville for some time, ever since the war under Davenport. The gang had laid a plan to waylay and rob the M&C at Brownsville on Feb. 15 and were betrayed and were attacked. Davenport was shot dead and two of the gang captured. Sheriff started to take them to Jacinto, Miss., and they were overtaken by party of men who took the prisoners from them and put them to death. (Memphis Daily Appeal, 18 Feb. 1869.) Jack Davenport, outlaw, was one of the bravest spirits the late war produced. He once repulsed ten mounted Federal soldiers

82

single-handed and alone near Dickson Depot, Ala., wounding four or five of them and capturing horses, pistols, overcoats. He was from Hardin County, TN, and of respectable parents. He quit the regular army to become guerrilla and since the war has ended has been a professional horse thief. According to the Iuka Gazette the following were killed: Tobe Charlton of Eastport, Miss., R. D. Luter of Pulaski in Tennessee; and George Kinkaid of Moscow, TN. Their bodies are now lying on the platform. (Memphis Daily Appeal, 22 Feb. 1869.)

DAVEZAK, D., dealer in rags and iron, shot himself through the heart on Wednesday night; age 35; born in the South of France. (Nashville Republican Banner, 25 Sept. 1868.) D. Davezoe, a Frenchman, found dead on the 24th in the market house in Nashville; laid down on a bench and shot himself. (Memphis Daily Appeal, 25 Sept. 1868.)

DAVID, Mrs. Marie, died 1 May 1870 in Nashville. (Nashville Republican Banner, 3 May 1870.)

DAVIDSON, Squire Samuel B., killed by train yesterday; born 1802 in Mecklenburg County, N. C., came 1803 to Sumner County and in 1804 to Davidson County and lived in District 12; Seminole War soldier. (Nashville Union and American, 18 July 1873.) Samuel S. Davidson, old and well known citizen of Davidson County, was run over by a passenger train and killed near the Chattanooga Depot in Nashville. (Whig and Tribune, 2 Aug. 1873.)

DAVIDSON, W. H., prominent citizen of District 14 in Davidson County, died Sat. of cholera; Mason and Odd Fellow. (Nashville Union and American, 29 July 1873.)

DAVIDSON, Asa L., funeral to be held today; lived on Gallatin Pike in Edgefield. (Nashville Republican Banner, 14 Dec. 1867.)

DAVIDSON, W. W., was murdered at Pocahontas Station on the M&C Railroad. He was CSA soldier; married Sue Lundy, who was famous throughout the South. Her love for the south caused her to be arrested and incarcerated in the Irving Block and sent thence to Aurora, Illinois. His wife and three children survive. (Memphis Daily Appeal, 13 June 1869.)

DAVIDSON, Colonel, of the 3d Mississippi Regiment, captured at Fort Donelson, died at Fort Warren on the 29th ult; body has been sent to his friends. (Nashville Dispatch, 6 May 1862.)

DAVIDSON, noted guerrilla, was mortally wounded in Kentucky a few days ago. He is at the home of one of his relatives. (Nashville Daily Union, 3 March 1865.)

DAVIES, Mollie Calhoun, age 6, only daughter of F. L. and Mary Ella, died Wednesday. (Nashville Republican Banner, 8 Jan. 1869.)

DAVIES, L. J., a resident of Danville, Pennsylvania, 67, died in Nashville yesterday of heart disease; father of F. J. Davies and was in Nashville on a visit. (Nashville Union and American, 23 Feb. 1873.)

DAVIS, Annie Cora, age 3, only daughter of H. C. and Lucy C. Davis, died 6 March 1866 and buried at Elmwood Cemetery in Memphis. (Memphis Avalanche, 7 March 1866.)

DAVIS, Mrs. Betty, of Mansfield, Mass., celebrated her 101st birthday the other day. (Maury Democrat, Columbia, TN, 17 May 1894.)

DAVIS, Sarah A., 31 years 8 months, died 2 June 1859 in Memphis; she was wife of Col. W. J. Davis. (Clarksville Weekly Chronicle, 17 June 1859.)

DAVIS, Sarah. County court gives widow's dower to Sarah Davis, widow of William L. Davis, deceased, Maury County. (Columbia Herald and Mail, 16 Oct. 1876.)

DAVIS, Mr. and Mrs. Ambrose, Jr., of Montgomery County, married only
two months and on a trip to New Orleans, perished when the steamer
Charmer was burned near Donaldsonville, La. (Clarksville Weekly
Chronicle, 22 Feb. 1861.)

DAVIS, Mrs. Ad, of Culleoka, died; daughter of W. F. McGregor; had
been married 4 years; Methodist. (Columbia Herald, 20 June 1873.)

DAVIS, Perry, inventor of "Pain Killer" which bears his name, died at
his home in Providence, Rhode Island, on the 2d. (Nashville
Dispatch, 10 May 1862.)

DAVIS, John M. G. H. Lander, M. D., in January registered at Louis-
ville Hotel and said he was from Hopkinsville, Ky. He was taken
sick and died Feb. 7. He left will, dated Feb. 2. He left and
the will was signed by George S. Davis of Columbus, Ga. N. B.
Lander of Hopkinsville, Ky, with whom he had stayed visited Florence,
Alabama, and learned that John M. Davis of that place was missing.
May be the same person. He was around 40. His body is now in vault.
(Nashville Dispatch, 7 March 1863.)

DAVIS, William, Jr., son of Mrs. Sarah Davis of Cumberland Street, is
to be buried today. (Nashville Republican Banner, 23 Feb. 1868.)

DAVIS, Lewis Courtney, 9 months 7 days, son of William G. and Jennie
died in Nashville on the 9th. (Nashville Republican Banner, 24
August 1867.)

DAVIS, Sallie, 21, from Indianapolis, Indiana, housekeeper for Mr.
Edwards on Front Street, died yesterday of overdose of opium, in
Nashville. (Nashville Daily Union, 25 June 1865.)

DAVIS, J. C., was shot on Saturday in Davidson County by Mr. Dabbs and
died yesterday; Davis was with the post office at Green Hill.
(Nahsville Daily Gazette, 14 Oct. 1852.)

DAVIS, Thomas B., 52 years 8 months, died in Louisville, Ky., on Jan.
8. (Nashville Republican Banner, 10 Jan. 1869.)

DAVIS, Mary Caroline, infant daughter of Professor M. C. and Mrs. S. B.
Davis died Wednesday night in Paris. (Paris Gazette, 19 Dec. 1877.)

DAVIS, Elizabeth, wife of Henry Davis of 152 Carroll Street, committed
suicide Tuesday night by jumping in cistern, containing 12 feet of
water; for some time she had been out of her mind; once tried to
kill herself by butting her head against a wall. (Nashville
Republican Banner, 23 June 1870.)

DAVIS, Hampe, living on Indian Creek, Tipton County, Tenn. was recently
conscripted by Confederate Army; he made his escape, was pursued and
shot, the ball taking effect in the right side. He asked to send a
letter to his wife, but was refused. They then put gun to his forehead while he was on ground and blew his brains out. They left him
where he was and when body was found it was horribly mutilated by
hogs. Outraged citizens banded together and found group of 60 men
under the noted guerrilla Bob Field and cleaned out the gang.
(Nashville Dispatch, 28 Aug. 1863.)

DAVIS, S. B., rebel spy, formerly keeper of rebel prison of Andersonville, was captured and has been tried at Cincinnati. He is to be
hanged on the 17th. (Nashville Daily Union, 1 Feb. 1865.)

DAVIS, William, of Christian County, Missouri, Union man, was shot from
the brush one day last week whilst plowing and died the next day.
(Nashville Dispatch, 14 June 1862.)

DAVIS, Nelson H., Brigadier General, U. S. Army, died on the 15th; had
just arrived at Governor's Island to visit friends and was in good
health; on entering General Tompkins office stricken by apoplectic

fit and expired. (Houston County News, 23 May 1890.)

DAVIS, Mrs., 75, of Salem, Mass., died Monday night of fright occasioned
by a severe thunder shower. (Memphis Avalanche, 23 May 1867.)

DAVIS, Pumpkin, has gone deranged and tried to kill his wife. (Columbia
Herald and Mail 9 April 1875.) John Daniel "Pumpkin" or "Punkin"
Davis, preacher, was born in Virginia; James O. Davis of Rutherford
Creek is cousin; at this writing Pumpkin was living in Hickman Co.
(Columbia Herald and Mail, 25 Dec. 1874.)

DAVIS, Jefferson.
BATTLE OF BUENA VISTA. - "I was unable to obtain a copy but recollect
among the killed: Capt. Lincoln, Col. Yell of Arkansas cavalry,
Capt. Moore, Adjut. Vaughn, three others of the Kentucky Cavalry,
Colonel McKee, Lt. Col. Clay, Capt. Willis, 2d Kentucky Infantry,
Col. Hardin Major Gorman of the Illinois brigade, many of the
Indiana brigade, several of the Mississippi regiment and two lieu-
tenants of the Texas volunteers. Among the wounded I remember
General Lane, Colonel Jefferson Davis, 1st Mississippi Regiment..."
(Letter published in the Columbia Beacon, 2 April 1847.)

Jefferson Davis's name, which was carved on the arch of the Washington and Potomac Acqueduct has been chiseled out by the order of
Secretary Smith. (Nashville Dispatch, 29 July 1862.)

Jeff Davis continues to grow weaker every day and cannot last much
longer. His failure to take the necessary amount of nourishment is
against him and his stomach is giving way. He is slowly sinking.
(Maury Democrat, 5 Dec. 1889.)

The Dead Chieftain. New Orleans. - This morning at ten o'clock the
doors of the Municipal Building where the body of Jefferson Davis
is exposed were thrown open and thousands of citizens thronged into
the broad passages and were excorted to the council chamber where
they were permitted to look on the features of the illustrious dead.
It was one endless stream of ladies and gentlemen and little
children. Every walk of life was represented. The entire city now
wears a mourning dress. Detachments from the Battalion of Washington Artillery and from the city police are still on duty and the
most perfect order is preserved.

At ten o'clock this morning the Army of Tennessee sent a detachment
of veterans and they will remain on duty the entire day. At midnight last night, Mr. Frazee, a sculptor, reached the city hall and
having obtained permission from Mrs. Davis, commenced to take a
plaster-of-paris cast of Mr. Davis' face. He worked until four
o'clock this morning when he had completed his labors. The cast
will be used for a statue to be erected at Atlanta, Georgia.

Col. D. M. Hollingsworth this morning brought to the hall an old
rifle used by him during the Mexican War which he exposed alongside
his body. The weapon which is in excellent condition, bears the
following inscription: "Buena Vista 23 Feb. 1847. First Sgt. D. M.
Hollingsworth, Co. A First Mississippi Rifles, Colonel Jefferson
Davis."

These rifles were given to the members of the Mississippi Rifles, who
served in the Mexican War by Act of Congress. As Colonel Hollingsworth deposited the weapon near the coffin of his old commander, he
began to weep. The scene was a most affecting one and moved many
of the spectators to tears.

The mayor and all of the city officials were present all morning but
nothing was done as the arrangements for the funeral are now completed,
The program agreed on embraces a funeral procession which will
include all the civic and military organizations of the city.

Floral offers have been pouring in, and the coffin now looks as if

85

placed at the head of a bank of flowers. The Army of Tennessee led
with a design ten feet high, one of the handsomest floral offerings
ever made here.

Jefferson Davis was born 3 June 1808 in that part of Christian County,
Kentucky, which now forms Todd County. His father was Samuel Davis
and he had served in the Georgia cavalry during the Revolution.
When Jefferson was but an infant, the family moved to a place near
Woodville, Mississippi, where young Davis began his education,
later entering Transylvania College, Kentucky. In 1824 he was
appointed by President Monroe to the U. S. Military Academy and
graduated in 1828 and was assigned to the First Infantry.

He served in the Black Hawk War of 1831-32 and on 4 March 1833 was
promoted to be first lieutenant of Dragoons. On 30 June 1835 after
more service against the Indians, he resigned, eloped with the
daughter of Zachary Taylor, then a colonel in the army, and settled
near Vicksburg, Mississippi, as a cotton planter. He remained here
quietly until 1843 when he entered politics and made a reputation as
a popular speaker. In 1845 he was sent to Congress but in June 1846
resigned from the House and accepted a colonelcy of the 1st Mississippi Volunteers and at once moved to reinforce General Taylor on
the Rio Grande. He charged a fort at Monterey without bayonets and
led the command through the streets nearly to Grand Plaza.

He was made a Brigadier General by President Polk but declined the
honor. In August 1847 he went to the Senate where he became a
zealous advocate of States rights. In 1851 after being defeated
for Governor of Mississippi, Franklin Pierce made him Secretary of
War. He increased the standing army, improved the equipment, and
made many changes in the tactics.

In January 1861 he was made commander-in-chief of the Army of
Mississippi and resigned to become President of the Confederate
States.

He was captured near Irwinsville, Georgia, 10 May 1865 and taken to
Fort Monroe. On 8 May 1866 he was indicted for treason but never
brought to trial. In 1879 Mrs. Dorsey of Beauvoir, Mississippi,
bequeathed him her estate and there he has since resided. (Maury
Democrat, 12 Dec. 1889.)

Dec. 11. - The body of Jefferson Davis was laid to rest today...
The city has put on her mourning garb. Along every street the
houses were draped in black and white and purple. Along Canal
Street the drapery reached from the roof on the high business buildings almost to the street. Miles away from the central portion of
the city there were residence bearing the ensign of grief.

The schools all closed. There certainly has been no such demonstration in New Orleans before. All New Orleans was out. Lafayette
Square, stretching out about City Hall, where the body lay in state
was thronged with people.

The pallbearers were: Governor Francis T. Nichols of Louisiana;
Governor Robert Lowry of Mississippi; Governor S. B. Buckner of
Kentucky; Governor John B. Gordon of Georgia; Governor J. S. Richard-
son of South Carolina; Governor D. C. Fowler of North Carolina;
Governor F. P. Fleming of Florida; and Governor James P. Eagle of
Arkansas.

It was 12 o'clock when the lid of the casket was closed forever on
the mortal remains of Jefferson Davis, ex-President of the Confederacy... Obsequies were according to the ritual of the Episcopal
Church and were conducted by Bishop Galleher, assisted by five
clergymen from various denominations. The casket was borne on a
handsome decorated caisson with a canopy... The dome of the canopy
is ornamental and decorated in bronze with furled U. S. flags draped
upon either side and the sides are draped in black. The caisson

was drawn by six black horses, two abreast, caparisoned in artillery harness and plumes and each animal led by a soldier in uniform.

The procession was an hour and a half passing a given point and every church bell in the city tolled as the funeral cortege moved to Metaire Cemetery--"the prettiest cemetery in the South." Within it lie the remains of thousands of Confederate dead veterans. It is this cemetery in a subterranean vault that the Southern Chieftain has been laid to rest... (Maury Democrat, 19 Dec. 1889.)

Mayor Ellison of Richmond, Virginia, has received a letter from Mrs. Jefferson Davis in reply to his request that the body of her husband might be buried here. Mrs. Davis says that so many of the Southern States have put forth claims so strong that she is unable to decide where his remains shall rest and will wait a year before making a selection. (Maury Democrat, 2 Jan. 1890.)

In October, Mrs. Davis will select a site for the burial of her husband in Richmond. Mrs. Davis emphasizes the fact that she desired the remains of all her family to rest beside or near those of the ex-president. (Florence, Ala., Times, 22 August, 1891.)

The remains of President Davis will be removed from New Orleans to Richmond May 30 and receive honors along the way. (Maury Democrat, 16 Feb. 1893.)

The programme for the re-interment of Jefferson Davis' remains in Hollywood Cemetery in Richmond, May 31, has been completed. General John Glinn, Jr., commander of the Louisiana division of the United Confederate Veterans is in charge of all the preparations, at New Orleans. The special train will leave the Crescent City Sunday, May 28. Governor Foster on behalf of the state will give a short address, commit the remains to the escort, which will accompany them to Virginia. The funeral train will reach Montgomery, Alabama, at 6 a.m. Monday. The body will be borne from the car to the capitol building and be placed on the front portico where Mr. Davis took the oath as President of the previsional government.

Leaving Montgomery at 11 o'clock the train will reach Atlanta at 4:30 p.m. and be there 4 hours. The casket will be borne to the capitol of Georgia and there will be some simple ceremonies with a parade and short oration.

There will be a 15 minute stop at Greensville, S. C. to afford the people there the opportunity to testify their affection, and then to Raleigh, N. C., where elaborate preparations are being made for a mammoth demonstration. It will reach Richmond on the night of the 30th.

At Richmond the casket will be placed on caisson and under the escort of troops and veterans organizations and followed by thousands of citizens, the remains will be taken to the Virginia capitol building in the rotunda and will lie in state until the next afternoon.

On the 31st the public school children will visit the capitol in a body, passing through and will place garlands of flowers upon the bier. The reinterment ceremonies will take place in the afternoon.

Mrs. Davis and both of her daughters, Miss Winnie and Mrs. J. A. Hayes, and Mr. Hayes will be there also. Mrs. Davis is in feeble health and will not go to New Orleans but both of her daughters will do so in company with Mayor Ellison and perhaps a few other citizens. (Maury Democrat, 18 May 1893.)

While the body was in the capitol at Montgomery, 10,000 people visited the scene. There were 2000 veterans in the parade at Atlanta. (Maury Democrat, 1 June 1893.)

Miscellaneous items about Jefferson Davis:

Parole granted Jefferson Davis some months ago, giving him the privilege of the grounds of the Fortress, have been extended. (Memphis Avalanche, 4 Nov. 1866.)

Jefferson Davis, now abroad, is engaged in writing a book, a history of the Southern War. He will not return until next spring. (The Monitor, Murfreesboro, 30 Jan. 1869.)

Jefferson Davis, now on a visit to England, was in Alton, Stafforshire, and a large concourse of visitors came to see him at a fair. (Memphis Daily Appeal, 24 Oct. 1868.)

Jefferson Davis has arrived at Liverpool. (Memphis Daily Appeal, 9 Aug. 1868.)

Jefferson Davis accompanied by Mr. Slidell and two old officers of the rebel army went on January 18 to visit the military school at St. Cyr. He was received in state by the authorities and the pupils maneuvered before him. (Memphis Daily Appeal, 15 Feb. 1869.)

Ex-President Davis is in Memphis. (Memphis Daily Appeal, 20 Nov. 1869.) Our beloved ex-President Jefferson Davis will be at the theater this evening. (Memphis Daily Appeal, 1 Dec. 1869.)

Jefferson Davis arrived in Baltimore on steamer from Europe, Oct. 9. (Memphis Daily Appeal, 10 Oct. 1869.) He arrived in New Orleans on Oct. 25. (Memphis Daily Appeal, 26 Oct. 1869.)

Jefferson Davis leaves tomorrow from Memphis to attend Mardi Gras in New Orleans. (Memphis Daily Appeal, 26 Feb. 1870.)

Jefferson Davis is visiting his brother at Vicksburg. (Memphis Daily Appeal, 29 May 1870.)

Jefferson Davis has registered at the Peabody Hotel. (Memphis Daily Appeal, 1 June 1870.)

Jefferson Davis has removed to Baltimore and will make that his home. (Columbia Herald, 17 Nov. 1871.)

The honorable Jefferson Davis reached New York Sunday from Europe on steamer Adriatic and left by rail for Memphis. (Murfreesboro Monitor, 18 June 1874.)

Jefferson Davis has just lost a suit for $70,000 in a court at Vicksburg, Mississippi. He put in a claim for that amount against his brother's estate, but court decided against him. (Columbia Herald and Mail, 4 Feb. 1876.)

Jefferson Davis complains of his precarious state of health which prevents him from attending Southern states fairs. (Houston County News, 7 Oct. 1887.)

General Reuben Davis, cousin of Jefferson Davis, says the latter was worth very near $200,000 when war began and nothing at it close. He thinks Richmond is the place for his burial if the Confederate States unite in the asking. (Maury Democrat, Columbia, 9 Jan. 1890.)

Mrs. Jeff Davis says a New York journal has received 35,000 subscriptions for the life of her husband. (Florence, Ala., Times, 26 Dec. 1890.)

Nashville has contributed over $4000 to the Jefferson Davis monument fund. The entire fund amounts to $30,000. (Florence, Ala., Times, 19 Dec. 1891.)

Mrs. Jefferson Davis is said to be suffering from heart disease, which has reached a critical condition. (Florence, Ala., Times, 28 Feb. 1891.) Mrs. Jefferson Davis has heart disease and has made all her preparations for sudden death. (Florence, Ala., Times, 19 Sept. 1891.)

Mrs. U. S. Grant and Mrs. Jefferson Davis will spend the summer at the same hotel at Cranston's on the Hudson. Editorial comment: "The war is over." (Maury Democrat, 1 June 1893.)

Mrs. Jefferson Davis is said to be about to lease her Beauvoir estate in Mississippi so that by having responsible tenants there she can prevent the decay of the old homestead and preserve its contents intact. It is asserted that furniture, books, silver and china, known to have been the property of the family, appear mysteriously and frequently in the curio and pawn shops of New Orleans, and a stop would be put to these petty larcenies. (Maury Democrat, 16 Aug. 1894.)

Miss Winnie Davis is to unveil the Davis monument erected by Ladies Confederate Monument Association of Mississippi on June 3. U. S. Senator Walthall, formerly major general, is to deliver the address. (Florence, Ala., Times, 15 May 1891.)

Miss Varina Anne Davis, daughter of Jefferson Davis, has her first novel ready for publication. (Maury Democrat, 7 Feb. 1895.)

Mrs. Jefferson Davis and daughter Winnie will spend the summer at Narragansett. (Maury Democrat, 25 July 1895.)

Jefferson Davis' old coachman, the colored man employed by him at the time of his capture and who is now living in Raleigh, N. C., says Mr. Davis was not disguised as a woman when he was captured. He was dressed in his old clothing with cavalry boots and a waterproof over his dresscoat, a shawl thrown over his shoulders, and on his head a broad-brimmed white or drab Texas hat. Mr. Davis went to the tent door and was ordered by soldiers to surrender. He replied that he would not, that he would rather die first. At this Mrs. Davis pressed her husband and put her arms around his neck, begging the soldiers not to kill him, both she and the children crying piteously. (Columbia Herald and Mail, 21 Sept. 1877.)

We have been informed on trustworthy authority that there is a child of Jefferson Davis, the President of the so-called Southern Confederacy, being educated among the Stockbridge Indians at their settlement in Shawnee Country. Davis, it is well known, was stationed at Fort Winnebago some years ago, and there formed the acquaintance of the mother of the child, a Menomonee squaw. Louisville Journal, July 20. Editorial comment in the Nashville Dispatch: "That 'child' of Jeff's must be a very 'old boy' or 'old gal', as the case may be. Jefferson Davis resided in Mississippi several years previous to the breaking out of the Mexican War, which event occurred several years ago." (Nashville Dispatch, 31 July 1863.) (N.B., the Nashville Daily Union published the same account, but without the editorial comment, leaving the impression that there was such a child.)

DAVIS, Sarah Knox, wife of Jefferson Davis, died 15 Sept. 1835, age 21. (Tombstone inscription in the 1930's on a stone in the Smith family cemetery at Locust Grove, West Feliciana Parish, Louisiana, about two miles from Elm Park, Louisiana. The stone was in one corner of the cemetery.)

DAVIS, Winnie, is dead; died at Narragansett Pier, Rhode Island, September 18 of malarial gastritis; born 1863 in Confederate White House at Richmond; called the Daughter of the Confederacy; was her father's constant companion. She was engaged to Mr. Wilkerson but the engagement was broken off in order to maintain her father's name it is said. She is to be buried in Richmond. (Columbia Herald, 23 Sept. 1898.)

DAVIS, Mrs. Margaret, wife of James Davis, died on the 14th, hemorrhage, buried at Pisgah. Isom news. (Columbia Herald and Mail, 21 Dec. 1877.)

DAVIS, youngest child of W. and E. Davis, of Greenfield Bend, died Sunday of general debility. (Columbia Herald, 13 Sept. 1872.)

DAVIS, Mrs. Sarah, 71, esteemed, died near Lawrenceburg last week. (Nashville Union and American, 2 Feb. 1873.)

DAVIS, Hubert, son of Knox Davis of Dickson, was stabbed and fatally wounded in Nashville on Monday by J. G. Cisco, Confederate veteran and consul to Mexico under President Cleveland and one time editor of Memphis Herald. Davis died that night; his father is a wealthy business man. (Columbia Herald, Friday, 19 Aug. 1898.)

DAVIS, Sam. Young Hero Died Game. - Mr. Will P. Taylor of this city tells an interesting story of the execution of Sam Davis, the boy-hero of the Confederacy, which he witnessed when a boy scarce 15 years of age. Mr. Taylor is now a man of 60 years and it was when a boy living with his parents in Pulaski that he heard of the execution of a brave young Southern soldier, at that time confined in the county jail.

"I was just a child," said Mr. Taylor who asked if it was true that he had witnessed the execution: "I was just a child, but even the children of Pulaski had caught the feeling of intense gloom attaching to the tragedy that was just about to be enacted. Our home was just a short distance from East Hill, where the execution took place, and all day we saw the building of the scaffold, and heard the tap, tap, tapping of the hammer driving the nails of the unsightly framework from which was to pass into eternity the brave spirit of Sam Davis. Boylike I followed the sound and hung around the place; sometimes the horror of it would overcome my boy's curiosity and I would rush back home and out into the garden and there kneel down among the lilac and rose bushes and pray aloud for the boy about to be hurled into eternity. The greatness of that tragedy, even then, was plain to my mind, and to the minds of the children of Pulaski generally. All day they cried for him and prayed as their mothers and fathers and sisters were praying."

Do you remember how he looked? asked the reporter.

"Yes, I do, for I was at the jail, too. I remember that to the right of where I was standing there stood a Presbyterian minister, though I do not recollect if he took any part in the service that followed or not. I remember that I heard here, at the jail, that Gen. Dodge had been, or sent, to him, a conditional offer of life, and that his reply was: "Tell him I thank him, but I would die 40 deaths before I would betray a friend."

"I remember how he came out of the jail, hands tied, as I remember, and accompanied by a guard of infantry. He mounted the wagon provided to carry him to the place of execution, head up, body erect, as though he understood in a vague, far-off way that he was not passing to death but through death to a glorious immortal fame.

"I remember following on the East Hill and that passing the court-house, which stood not far from the jail he bowed to some Southern soldiers confined there as prisoners of war. At the hill the wagon drove up into the midst of a regiment or two of infantry and he mounted the scaffold on which he was to die.

"Who was with him? asked the reporter, "had he no friends, no minister of the gospel in this moment of agony?"

"I do not remember anybody but the soldiers and the executioner, Capt. Armstrong, and one other man, Col. Miller of the 18th Missouri Cavalry, who was the official of the day.

"I remember, however, that on the scaffold they brought him another offer of life; and that his reply this time was: 'Tell Gen. Dodge that I thank him, but if I had a thousand lives to give I'd give them all rather than betray a friend.' Then he asked how long he had to live and inquired concerning the news of the day. When told of Bragg's retreat, he smiled in a slow way, and said, 'The boys will have to fight without me, now.'"

Speaking of the story and how he has cherished the memory of it all the years from boyhood to old age, Mr. Taylor said.

"There is a little incident connected with my witnessing the tragedy that my be of some slight interest to you. I was at the railroad station a short time ago and was talking to Mr. Tidwell, a friend of mine, and incidentally the talk drifted around to the Davis tragedy. I remarked to Tidwell, 'I saw that.'

"Immediately two ladies sitting in front of us jumped to their feet and one of them exclaimed: "You mean to say that you saw the execution of Sam Davis?" When I replied in the affirmative one of them said: 'Oh, do tell us about it. I am from Oklahoma, but among the most beautiful treasures of my scrap book I cherish the clippings and stories of that great, grand boy.'

Mr. Taylor will witness the coming unveiling of the monument to the memory of Sam Davis and perhaps he will be the only one of the vast audience which will assemble on this occasion, who saw the execution of this hero, whom the people of the state now honor by the erecting of a monument on capitol hill. (Nashville Banner quoted in Daily Herald, Columbia, TN, 19 April 1909.)

WEARER OF THE BLUE THRILLINGLY DESCRIBES DEATH OF SAM DAVIS. - "He was the bravest man I ever saw." These historic words, spoken by Napoleon Bonaparte while a prisoner on the rock-bound island of St. Helena of the intrepid Marshal Ney, were used Tuesday (Nov. 2) by Capt. T. D. McGillicuddy in describing the death of Sam Davis, the boy hero, whose execution he witnessed nearly half a century ago.

Capt. McGillicuddy was provost marshal at Lynnville during the month of Nov. 1863. He was stationed there at the time that Sam Davis was captured by the 7th Kansas, and the colonel of his regiment was the president of the court martial that sentenced the brave Southerner to an ignominious death. He is therefore in position to speak authoritatively of the occurrences of that trying time.

"In November 1863 I came over with Sherman's Army from Corinth, Miss." he said to a Herald representative in describing the death of Davis. "With our command was the 7th Kansas, commonly referred to as the Kansas Jayhawkers.

"I made my home with the Shields family.

"In some way Sam Davis and his party of scouts ran into the 7th Kansas and was captured. He was tried as a spy and condemned to death by hanging. Thos. W. Gaines, lieutenant colonel of my regiment, the 50th Illinois, was president of the trail commission, the other members being Col. Madison Miller, of the 18th Missouri, and Col. Lathrop. You are familiar with the history of the trial, and know of the offers that General Dodge made to Davis to spare his life if he would betray his friend, and how these offers were spurned.

"The day of execution came. On November 23, 1863, my command was called out to guard and witness the execution. I remember as if it were yesterday how Sam Davis looked as he went by on the wagon. He waved his hand at some friends, and his manner was as calm as if he had been going about the ordinary duties of life. Not once did he show the slightest trace of fear, and it was evident that he had firmly made up his mind to die.

"An aide-de-camp rode up and submitted a proposition from General Dodge offering him his freedom if he would but betray his friend. He declined firmly, and went to his final end with perfect composure. He showed no excitement, offered no resistance. He went to his death with the air of one who was submitting to the inevitable. During all the bloody war I witnessed no other such remarkable exhibition of courage.

"My command was drawn up in the form of a hollow square, as was the custom when a prisoner was to be hung. We were less than 50 paces from the scaffold, and I could see and every movement of the prisoner. He was a hero to the last."

Capt. McGillicuddy is at present spending the winter here with the family of Mr. Will Shields on S. Main Street. During the time that he was stationed at Lynnville he formed an attachement for the family, but after the war lost trace of them. Some years ago he wrote to the postmaster at Lynnville, asking if he could tell him the whereabouts of his old friends.

The postmaster knew nothing of the family, which had moved away many years before. A young lady happened to be present in the office at the time the letter was received, and she knew that the Shields family had moved to Columbia. The letter was forwarded here, and the desired information furnished the Union veteran, whose home is in Cleveland, Ohio.

Capt. McGillicuddy, his mind turning again to the hospitable hosts of the Sixties, concluded to come here for the winter, and is now with the Shields family. Past three score and ten years of age, having been born in Louisville, KY, December 1, 1835, he is still hale and hearty, although badly crippled and slightly deaf. He is now the historian of his regiment, the 50th Illinois, and spends much of his time in writing of the stirring incidents of the Civil War.

Capt. McGillicuddy is an ardent admirer of Sam Davis, and contributed to the fund for the erection of his monument at Nashville, as did General Dodge, who gave ten dollars. Of a literary temperament, he kept a diary of many of the bigger events of the war, and in this diary is a story of Sam Davis' death written shortly after its occurrence. This brief account terminates with a eulogy to the brave Southern soldier.

The flag shown in the cut (i.e., picture in newspaper) now lies in the tomb of General Grant. It's history is as follows:

Made in the spring of 1861 by Mesdames Col. J. T. K. Hayward, Major Josiah Hunt, Capt. G. O. Bishop and Miss Mary Meader at the home of Major Hunt, Lyon Street, Hannibal, Missouri, presented by Geo. H. Shields, July 4th, 1861, to Company B, Marion Battalion, 3d Missouri Service of U. S. Reserve Corps.

At the close of the service, T. D. McGillicuddy, with a number of others, became a part of Co. K, 50th Illinois Infantry. December 26th, 1861, the Regiment then being at St. Joseph, Mo., a delegation of loyal citizens of Hannibal composed of Capt. Robert Tufts, Josiah Young, Joseph E. Streeter and Spencer C. Tible, arrived in camp, and on dress parade in behalf of old Co. B and people interested, presented the same old flag to Co. K.

Strange, but true, the regiment upon leaving Quincy, Illinois, 9
Oct. 1861 had not received its colors from the state, using the flag
of the Quincy Cadets until 21 Jan. 1862, returning it as the regiment passed through Quincy on its way south.

At the request of Col. Moses M. Bane, Capt. T. D. McGillicuddy granted
the use of this flag to the regiment, conditioned that he should
select the color bearer. Selecting Sergt. St. Clair Watts of Co.
K, it was borne through Fort Henry, TN, and was the first flag on
the works of Fort Donelson, TN, at Shiloh, TN, Siege of Corinth,
Miss., at Boonville, Miss., Town Creek and Tuscumbia, Ala., and a
short time before the second battle at Corinth, Miss., was replaced
by its first stand from the State and returned to Capt. T. D.
McGillicuddy, who after keeping it 40 years, on 18 July 1901 brought
it to Hannibal to return it to the donors, and finding that time
had removed them, left it with appropriate ceremonies in the custody
of William T. Sherman Post 43, G.A.R., Dept. of Mo.

October 14, 1903, W. T. Sherman Post, proposed to return this flag
to the Reunion Association of the 50th Illinois Infantry. On November
6, a committee from the Association, Samuel E. Hewes, Quartermaster
Lieut. J. W. Anderson, and Adjt. Chas. F. Hubert with a number of
friends received it with due ceremony from the Post at Hannibal, Mo.

At the Reunion of the Association, Oct. 5-6, 1904, General Greenville
M. Dodge proffered a request for the Association to place this flag
in Gen. Grant's tomb at Riverside, New York, as one of the flags
allotted from Illinois. The request was cheerfully granted by the
Association and interested friends, believing it to be most appropriate as the flag under which General Grant won his first and most
signal victory. (Daily Herald, Columbia, TN, 3 November 1909.)

HUNG FROM THE SAME GALLOWS. - A correspondent to the Pulaski Citizen
says:

Shortly after the execution of Sam Davis, the brave Confederate
scout, whose story is known through the land, I am told that a Federal
soldier was hung from the same gallows.

There is something of a tale in connection with this soldier's fate.
While stationed at Corinth, Miss., he quarreled with a negro servant
of one of the officers and ran the negro into the officer's tent.
The officer took the negro's part and slashed the soldier across the
face with his sword, whereupon the latter drew his pistol and shot
him.

He was court martialed and the papers forwarded for the President's
approval. They were somehow delayed or misplaced. The soldier
served out his time of enlistment, went home on a furlough and
afterwards re-enlisted and was to work on Fort Hill just one year
after the trial, when the papers reached here approved by the
President.

He was hanged the next day. An eyewitness to the execution tells me
that the poor fellow had to be assisted to the gallows by two
comrades and that his only request was for "plenty of whiskey."
I believe he was buried in Maplewood Cemetery. (Columbia Herald,
10 Dec. 1897.) (N.B. Refer to obituary of Col. Florence Cornym.)

DAWSON, Thomas, died Wednesday night. Funeral to be held at the
Cathedral. (Nashville Republican Banner, 1 Sept. 1870.)

DAWSON, N. H. R., brother-in-law of President Lincoln, died at Selma,
Arkansas, recently. He was a South Carolinean by ancestry and birth,
a descendant of Paul Hamilton, who was Secretary of Navy in 1812.
(Maury Democrat, 28 Feb. 1895.)

DEAN, Charles, prominent citizen of Greenwood, Mississippi, was shot
and killed by unknown assassin last week. (Columbia Herald, 3 Nov.
1871.)

DEATH. O. Death lives in Warren County, Ohio. (Memphis Daily Appeal,
21 Jan. 1870.)

DEATHS. The following list of citizens have died in Williamson County
recently: John Nichols, Esquire, aged about 75; John H. Otey, 58;
Thompson Cunningham, 55; Mrs. Thompson Cunningham, 50; Mrs. Claiborn
H. Kinnard, 50; Isaac L. Vaughn, 44; William Vaughn, 20, son of
Isaac L. Vaughn; Capt. Wm. Ewing, 40; Andrew Glass Ewing, 18; Dr.
Hez Oden, 37; John Oden, 33; William Andrews, 45; William D. Andrews
of Hickman County, 40; Mrs. Mary Perkins, 60; Mrs. Polly Vaughn, 65;
and Philip Courtney, 9. (Nashville Dispatch, 18 June 1863.)

DEATON, Capt. Spencer, of 16th Tennessee Infantry has been executed at
Richmond as a spy; he was from East Tennessee; the charges were
false as he was in East Tennessee on recruiting expedition when he
was arrested. (Nashville Daily Union, 20 March 1865, 21 March 1865.)

DeBOW, Miss Clara, stepdaughter of Dr. W. L. Nichols of Nashville was
seriously, if not fatally, burnt by her clothes taking fire from a
blazing match. (Whig and Tribune, Jackson, TN, 9 Sept. 1871.)

DeBOW, John R., late typographer, tribute of respect on his death
published in paper. (Nashville Daily Union, 12 Jan. 1863.)

DeCAMP, Loretta, of St. James Parish, La., raised a cavalry company
for the Confederate Army, donned male attire and fought; she was on
board the Miami (a steamer) when it blew up in February on the
Arkansas River; she was one of the two women saved. (Memphis
Avalanche, 17 March 1866.)

DeCASTRO, Nannie, only daughter of M. and Mme. DeCastro, age 9 1/2
years, died of typhoid on the 25th; was born in Paris , France ;
died in Nashville. (Nashville Republican Banner, 27 Feb.1869.)

DeFOS. The dead body of old man named DeFos was recently found on
road on Egnew's Creek, 5 or 6 miles from Pulaski. (Nashville
Republican Banner, 19 Sept. 1869.)

deGRAFFENREID, Dr. C. L., died in Columbus, Ga., born 1798 in Lunen-
berg Co., Va.; connected by marriage with General Kirkland of
Confederate Army, Chief Justice Ruffin, and Senator Strange of
North Carolina; was lineal descendant of Baron de Graffenreid of
Berne, Switzerland. In 1827 he was commissioned to lay out town
of Columbus, Ga., and has remained there. (Columbia Herald, 26 Jan.
1872.)

DEISS, Mrs. Mary, wife of Gottleib Deiss, funeral to be held on the
22d. (Nashville Daily Union, 24 Jan. 1863.)

DEJEAN, Mrs. Honore, Emile Dejean, Matilda Dejean, Josephn Zeringue and
his child, were all killed when tornado hit Feb. 26 on Bayou Teche
at the Dejean Plantation. (Nashville Dispatch, April 1863.)

DELOZIER, Samuel, was killed in Sevier County on the 7th by D. W.
Lankford over a sheep-killing dog. (Memphis Avalanche, 25 Dec.
1866.)

DEMENT. Caroline, a slave of Mr. Dement of Murfreesboro, was con-
victed in Louisville, KY, of the murder of a small child of Mr.
Levi by poisoning and was to be executed yesterday. (Nashville
Dispatch, 18 Aug. 1863.)

DEMOSS, Delilah, deceased, and administrators for her estate have been
appointed. (Nashville Republican Banner, 21 March 1869.)

DEMOVILLE, Mrs. Mary A., 71, has died. (Nashville Union and American, 10 Oct. 1873; Whig and Tribune, 18 Oct. 1873.)

DENNING, J. W., deceased, his will has been probated. (Nashville Republican Banner, 14 Feb. 1869.)

DENT, John, brother-in-law of General Grant, has been released from being a prisoner of war. (Nashville Daily Union, 8 March 1865.)

DENTON, T. A., died on the 9th at 2 o'clock of typhoid-pneumonia in Nashville; of the house of McClure, Buck and Company; taken to Waverly, TN, for burial. (Nashville Republican Banner, 12 Jan. 1871.)

DESHLER, Major General James was killed at Chickamauga. (Nashville Dispatch, 25 September 1863.) (N. B. Buried Oakwood Cemetery.) Tuscumbia.

DESPAU. DEATH OF CENTENARIAN. - The death of Madame Sophie Despau, nee Carriere Biloxi, at the advanced age of 110 years, has added another feature of interest to what the United States Supreme Court has decided to be the most remarkable suit ever brought to trial in this country.

Madame Despau was born in 1757, when Louisiana was held by France, of an provencial family, and her name will long be remembered in connection with that of her sister Zulime Carriere.

It was while under Madame Despau's care that Zulime, when 13 years of age (1796) and already celebrated in this city for her beauty, was married to Des Grange, a French nobleman, who soon after subsided into a barkeeper or syrup-maker. Some years after Des Grange proved to have been already married, and about the same time an attachment sprung up between her and Daniel Clark, the Congressman, the land speculator, and foremost business man of his time. The attachment result in a marriage, according to Madame Sophie Despau and another sister, and according to all, in the birth of Mrs. Myra Clark Gaines.

Madame Despau, according to evidence in the Gaines case, testified that she was present when the marriage ceremony was performed in Philadelphia--present with a third sister--and it was upon their evidence that the alleged ceremony rested, for the priest who officiated subsequently went to Ireland, the church was burned down and the records destroyed. What added still more the complication of the case was that Zulime Carriere Des Grange Clark was subsequently united to Dr. Gardette and this during the lifetime of Clark.

As Mrs. Gaines' legitimacy depended upon the validity of Clark's marriage, the strain of the whole case turned upon the evidence of Mme. Despau. To test her veracity, the evidence of some 35 witnesses were taken, who had known her while residing in this (New Orleans) city, in Biloxi, Havana, Florida, and Spanish America.

But the answers were in her favor, and in the interpretation given of the bewildering facts of this case by the last decision of the Supreme Court, her statements were taken as correct; and an estate now valued at $15 million was adjudicated to her niece, Mrs. Gaines; adjudicated 50 years after making the will, 30 after the commencement of the suit, after six appeals to the Supreme Court, and when the original suit had been divided into 500 separate actions against subsequent possessors of Clark's estate.

Madame Despau, though living for more than a century, and though involved three-fourths of that period in the troubles of her sister, did not after all live to see the termination of the suit; and save $15,000 of the contested estated yielded by Mr. Slidell during the recent war, none of the contested property has yet been recovered by its lifelong claimant. N. O. Times, 26th ult. (Memphis Avalanche, 18 Oct. 1867.)

DESTIN, Mrs., of New London, Connecticut, died a few days since of dropsy. In the last 18 months her doctor has "tapped" her 24 times and has taken from her 917 pounds of water. (Nashville Dispatch, 1 April 1863.)

DEVELL, Joseph, 38 of Nashville, died at Marietta, Ohio, at the home of his father-in-law A. T. Nye, Esquire. (Nashville Daily Union, 3 June 1865.)

DEVER, Miss Josie, age 11, died Feb. 8; funeral to be held at the Cathedral. (Nashville Union and American, 9 Feb. 1873.)

DeVORE. Warning--"Don't trade with wife Vashtie Devore" as she refuses to be a wife. Signed, Francis P. DeVore. (Murfreesboro Courier, 15 April 1824.)

DEW, William T., died on the 11th from effects of pistol shot in a fracas at Mt. Pleasant. (Memphis Avalanche, 21 Dec. 1866.)

DEWS, Ton Jasper, son of W. W. Dews, age 3 years 5 months, died on the 8th. (Nashville Dispatch, 9 Oct. 1862.)

DEWS, D. L., 63, died July 25, at his home three miles from city. (Nashville Republican Banner, 26 July 1868.)

DIBRELL, Col. Charles L., while suffering from ental aberration, took his own life October 25 at Chattanooga, TN. (Columbia Herald, 1 Nov. 1895.)

DICKENS, Mrs. Augustus N., widow of the brother of Charles Dickens, committed suicide Dec. 25 in Chicago of overdose of morphine. She suffered much from poverty. The acrimonious controversy growing out of the conduct of her brother-in-law towards her on his visit to this country will be remembered by all. (Memphis Avalanche, 27 Dec. 1868.)

DICKEY, Mrs. Fannie H., wife of D. D. Dickey, died May 19. (Nashville Republican Banner, 20 May 1869.)

DICKINSON, Mrs. Anna M., eldest daughter of Jacob and Louise McGavock, wife of Honorable Henry Dickinson of Columbia, died June 25 in Nashville. (Nashville Republican Banner, 26 June 1868.)

DICKINSON, George R., age 2 years 10 months 28 days, died 11 June 1858, son of J. Cole and M. E. Dickinson. (Clarksville Weekly Chronicle, 18 June 1858.)

DICKINSON, ___ (no name given) was killed last week by a gun in Palmer's hand; son of J. C. Dickinson of Todd Co., KY. (Clarksville Weekly Chronicle, 14 Dec. 1860.)

DICKOR, Burk J., age 21 years (age in question), died. (Nashville Republican Banner, 6 Oct. 1870. Name appears to be Deckor in issue of 7 Oct. 1870.)

DICKSON, William, 23, died at his residence near Tuscumbia, Alabama, on Wednesday last. (Tuscumbian, 2 April 1828.)

DIEHL, Colonel William, the oldest native inhabitant and soldier of the War of 1812, died in Pittsburg, Pennsylvania on Friday. (Memphis Daily Appeal, 20 Jan. 1870.)

DIFFENDERFFER, L. A., died on the 15th ultimo in Baltimore; had lived in Clarksville a number of years. (Clarksville Weekly Chronicle, 5 July 1861.)

DIGGS. At the execution of Diggs at Murray, KY, on the 27th ult.
for the murder of Miller, there was a considerable stampede. When
the gallows was reached, it had to be mounted by a ladder, a gun
was heard in the hill and he was launched into eternity. He said
he did not kill Miller but was present. (Memphis Avalanche, 6 Oct.
1867.) (N. B., The papers of the late Raymond Y. McClain of
Florence, Alabama, identifies Diggs as Pud Diggs, a guerrilla from
Tennessee who was accused of calling George Miller of Murray, KY,
to his door one night and shooting him dead. It was predicted that
Diggs' fellow guerrillas would set him free for they boasted that
"Diggs won't never be hanged." At the hanging when the pistol shot
was heard, it was believed that his band had come to free him and
panic ensued, the crowd scattering in every direction. But Diggs
was eventually hanged when it was found his gang was not coming.)

DIGGINS, George, of Nashville, "rebel" soldier was killed in an engagement in Mississippi during the Port Hudson campaign. (Nashville
Daily Union, 30 July 1863.)

DIGGONS, James, 82, died on the 21st; native of England, music teacher
at the Nashville Female Academy and member of Christ Church; had
been in Nashville 30 to 40 years; wife and several children survive.
(Nashville Dispatch, 22 Aug. 1863.) Born 8 Jan. 1783 in York,
England, died 21 Aug. 1863; was in British Army and participated in
the capture of Seringapatam in 1799 and was in India for many years
in service of the East India Company as Master of Band. He was a
muscial genius. In 1822 came to United States and in 1823 to Nashville; left a large family of children. (Nashville Dispatch, 23
Aug. 1863.)

DELBOURNE, John, whose childhood recollection of seeing his father shot
and his mother tomahawked by an Indian has never left him, died at
Piqua, Ohio, on the same farm where the tragedy took place, aged
85. (Columbia Herald, 23 Jan. 1891.)

DILGER, John, Government employee, "at noon yesterday jumped from a
window in the rear of the third story of Hospital No. 19...skull
was shockingly crushed, and his brains scattered around on the
street. His residence was Green Hill, Montgomery County, Missouri."
(Nashville Daily Union, 27 April 1864.)

DILL, Colonel Benjamin F., 56, editor and proprietor of the Memphis
Appeal, native of Georgia, died of pleurisy yesterday at Forest
Hill at 5 o'clock, buried Elmwood Cemetery, interred by J. C. Holst
and Company. (Memphis Avalanche, 4 Jan. 1866.)

DILLAHAY, Marcus Huston, little son of M. L. Dillahay, railroad conductor, is dead. (Columbia, TN, Herald and Mail, 27 July 1877.)

DILLON, Mrs. W. W. (Mary Jones), daughter of S. W. Jones of Santa Fe,
Maury County, TN, died yesterday at Bellbuckle, TN, and buried at
Murfreesboro. (Columbia Herald, 20 March 1891. Also in Maury
Democrat of 2 April 1891.)

DINE, W. C., deceased, letters of administration on his estate given
To L. Wolfstein on 12 Nov. 1864. (Nashville Daily Union, 7 Feb.
1865.)

DISMUKES, Paul, Esquire, 50, of Edgefield died yesterday; he was
baptized just before his death; buried at Spring Hill Cemetery.
(Nashville Republican Banner, 24 March 1869.)

DISMUKES, J. D., of Cheatham County, died on the 20th, age 63; born
in Sumner County; moved to Cheatham in 1854; Methodist; leaves
large family. (Nashville Republican Banner, 13 Feb. 1868.)

DIXON, Robert Emmett, clerk of the Confederate House of Representatives,
who shot dead on Friday by Robert E. Ford, late Journal clerk of

the house. Richmond news. (Nashville Dispatch, 2 May 1863.)

DIXON, Andrew, native of Dumfries, Scotland, died yesterday in Nashville; had lived here 16 years. (Nashville Union and American, 19
Jan. 1873.)

DIXON, Mrs. James, severely burned last Monday, died yesterday morning.
(Nashville Union and American, 19 Aug. 1874.)

DOBSON, Philip, son of W. K. Dobson, of Nashville, drowned in the
Cumberland River, above Nashville, last week; he went bathing and
got beyond his depth. (Whig and Tribune, Jackson, TN, 21 June 1873.)

DODSON, Mrs. Houston, died on Leatherwood in Hickman County of inflammation of the brain produced by an attack of measles. (Columbia
Herald and Mail, 12 Oct. 1877.)

DODSON, Will, of Giles County, died recently. (Nashville Union and
American, 11 March 1873.)

DODSON, Miss Eugenia E., 16 years 17 days, died 27 Sept. 1895, lived
in Knob Creek area of Maury County. (Maury Democrat, Columbia, TN,
3 Oct. 1895.)

DOLE. A monument will be unveiled at Milledgeville, Georgia on July
26 to the memory of Brigadier General George Dole of the Army of
North Virginia. (Maury Democrat, 26 July 1894.)

DONAHO, Dr. Ed, 42, of Lebanon, TN, fell into apoplectic fit on
Thursday and died. (Nashville Republican Banner, 7 July 1868.)

DONELSON, Miss Kate, daughter of Major A. J. Donelson, died 14 Aug.
1868 of inflammation of the brain. (Nashville Republican Banner,
18 Aug. 1868.)

DONELSON, Elizabeth A., widow of Major Andrew J. Donelson, died at her
farm in Bolivar County, Mississippi, on 20 Aug. 1871. (Whig and
Tribune, Jackson, TN, 9 Sept. 1871.)

DONELSON, General Daniel S., of Sumner County, died recently in Knoxville. He had been promoted to Major General a short time before;
brother of Andrew J. Donelson, who was candidate for vice-president on the Fillmore ticket in 1856. (Nashville Dispatch, 28 April
1863.) Buried at Knoxville on the 19th ult. (Nashville Dispatch,
10 May 1863.) (N.B., Daniel Smith Donelson, born 23 June 1801 in
Sumner County, died 17 April 1863, is buried today in Hendersonville, TN.)

DONELSON, W. A., was shot and killed Saturday near Nashville by W. G.
Baker; an old grudge; his father was private secretary to Andrew
Jackson. (Daily Herald, 23 July 1900.)

DONIGAN, G. W., died 15 Jan. 1864; he was shot in arm one night by an
unknown assailant and tetanus developed. (Nashville Daily Union,
16 Jan. 1864.)

DONNELL, Patrick, age 102, died in Toledo, Ohio, Monday; his eldest
son is 80 years old. (Maury Democrat, 31 Jan. 1895.)

DONNELLY, William, noted burglar, recently got 21 years penal servitude;
while in jail seized with diarrhea and died; was commissary sergeant
in 6th Illinois Cavalry, U. S. Army, and after the war remained in
Memphis as a thug and burglar; once made ropeof bed clothing to
escape jail. (Memphis Daily Appeal, 14 Oct. 1868.)

DONOHO, T. J., deceased, tribute of respect to him made by the Clarksville lodge. (Clarksville Weekly Chronicle, 19 Oct. 1860.)

DOOLEY, William A. "Dock", born in Maury County, died in Memphis; brother of P. G. M. and McKinney Dooley; was lieutenant in 48th Tennessee CSA. (Columbia Herald and Mail, 25 Jan. 1878.)

DOOLEY, McKinney, deceased, estate declared insolvent by John L. Beard, administrator. (Columbia Herald, 20 Oct. 1871.)

DORMAN, Florence, infant daughter of Roderick and Fannie, died and funeral to be held 7 June 1870. (Nashville Republican Banner, 7 June 1870.)

DORMAN, May Hays, infant daughter of Roderick and Fannie Dorman, 19 1/2 months, died on the 9th. (Nashville Dispatch, 10 Sept. 1862.)

DORMAN, Jenny, 3 months, died on the 10th, daughter of Roderic and Fanny Dorman. (Nashville Daily Union, 12 April 1863.)

DORRIS, Mrs. Susannah, 76, died 24 Aug. 1870. (Nashville Republican Banner, 25 Aug. 1870.)

DORSEY, J. H., an old Confederate soldier, attracted considerable attention on the streets of Columbia Wednesday. He was on his way from Alabama to Kentucky and was driving a little black mule, 38 years old, that did service in Confederate Army in Duke's Command, 1st Kentucky Cavalry. (Columbia Herald, 3 Sept. 1897.)

DORTCH, Lula McCrory, born 14 July 1867, died 22 June 1868, to be buried today; daughter of Nat F. and Sally A. Dortch. (Nashville Republican Banner, 24 June 1868.)

DORTCH, Bliss, little son of Mr. and Mrs. David E. Dortch of Maury County, died of spinal meningitis and buried Monday. (Columbia Herald, 3 April 1891.)

DORTON, C. H., Sr., funeral to be held today with burial in Elmwood Cemetery. (Memphis Daily Appeal, 9 March 1870.)

DOUBLEDAY, Mrs. Elizabeth, 34 died on the 27th; wife of George Doubleday. (Nashville Dispatch, 28 April 1863.)

DOUGHERTY, Mrs. Catherine, 60, died on the 4th and her funeral to be held at the Cathedral. (Nashville Dispatch, 5 Aug. 1862.)

DOUGLAS, Elizabeth Harding McGavock, wife of Edwin H. Douglas, has died; to be taken to Franklin for burial. (Nashville Republican Banner, 18 Feb. 1871.)

DOUGLAS, Mrs. Nancy Hamilton, wife of Hugh Douglas, died Saturday. (Nashville Republican Banner, 21 Nov. 1869.)

DOUGLAS, William, 37, died yesterday. (Nashville Daily Union, 15 Feb. 1863.)

DOUGLAS. "Uncle Tommy Douglas and wife have our sympathy on the loss of their son Edward...he made a good soldier during the war." (Columbia Herald and Mail, 17 Nov. 1876.)

DOUGLAS, William, 37, died on the 14th in Nashville, of the firm of Douglas & Walsh. (Nashville Dispatch, 15 Feb. 1863.)

DOUGLAS, Major Clint, CSA, of Sumner County, was captured 10 miles from Murfreesboro yesterday; he had received his commission as a colonel about an hour before "he was taken up and done for." (Nashville Dispatch, 4 Feb. 1863.)

DOUGLAS, Stephen A., deceased, his estate in Chicago has been inventoried at $700,000; had no personal property. (Nashville Dispatch, 24 April 1863.)

DOUGLAS, Fred, noted colored orator, died suddenly about 7 on Feb. 20 at his home in Anacostia, suburb of Washington. (Maury Democrat, 28 Feb. 1895.) The will of the late Frederick Douglas leaves all his property to his wife and her children. The document may be declared invalid as it had only two witnesses instead of three as required by law in the District of Columbia. (Maury Democrat, 4 April 1895.) The daughter and widow of Frederick Douglas are about to enter into a contest about his will. (Maury Democrat, 20 June 1895.) Fred Douglas mourns becuase he can never celebrate his birthday, having no idea when it occurs. (Florence, Ala., Times, 18 April 1891.) Fred Douglas has been well paid for his service to the Republican party. Since the war he has drawn from his offices about $170,000. (Florence, Times, 20 Feb. 1891.)

DOWDY, Joe, of Lewis County, died last Monday with typhoid; his mother was also stricken and died soon after. (Maury Democrat, 26 Oct. 1893.)

DOWELL, Miss Addie, 60, died June 1 at Terrell, TN, daughter of Caleb Dowell, formerly lived in Maury County. She was baptized at Smyrna Cumberland Presbyterian Church many years ago. (Columbia Herald, 28 June 1895.)

DOWNING, Mrs. Etta, of Clarksville, took dose of aconite last week, thinking it was dysentary medicine and died 40 minutes later. (Maury Democrat, 7 Aug. 1890.)

DOWNES, Major William P., 52, died on the 23d; native of Nashville. (Nashville Dispatch, 25 June 1863.) The will of W. P. Downs has been admitted to probate. (Nashville Republican Banner, 1 March 1868.) His will is proved to be a forgery. (Nashville Republican Banner, 26 April 1868.) The estate of Major William P. Downes has been in litigation for 7 years. He left $60,000 worth of property and a compromise was reached yesterday. He died 1863 in Nashville and left no heir as he was a bachelor. He had much real estate in Edgefield. In 1867 a will appeared in a mysterious way, leaving everything to Mrs. James C. Allen, whose father was his cousin. The Allens lived in Canton, Miss., at the time and Mr. Allen came to Nashville at once, "but there is no telling when estate will be disposed of." (Nashville Union and American, 23 July 1874.)

DOZIER. The home of Abner Dozier of Cheatham County was burned by the Federals in retaliation for loss of steamer Charter at Harpeth Sholas; the steamer was destroyed by Dick McCann and his band. (Nashville Dispatch, 14 Jan. 1863.)

DOZIER, James J., Esquire, lawyer and father-in-law of General Rousseau, died Wednesday in Louisville, KY. (Nashville Daily Union, 24 Feb. 1865.)

DRAMER. Information wanted on Conrad Dramer, of German descent, by profession a "bonjoist"; last heard of at Cleveland, TN. Signed by W. J. Welch. (Nashville Daily Union, 11 June 1865.)

DRANE, James M., deceased, a tribute of respect on his death on 21 Sept. 1861 published by Company A, 14th Regiment from Valley Mountain, Virginia. (Clarksville Weekly Chronicle, 11 Oct. 1861.)

DRAPER, Mrs. Sarah, has celebrated her 100th birthday in Chesterfield, New Hampshire. Her maternal grandmother lived to be 101. (Nashville Dispatch, 1 Aug. 1862.)

DRAPER, Mrs. Elizabeth, 65, died 4 Oct. 1870, after protracted illness; wife of Thomas L. Draper. (Nashville Republican Banner, 18 Nov. 1870.)

DRAVO, Capt. Wesley, died at St. Louis, Missouri, after six weeks of intense suffering from burns received on steamer Maria at the time of her explosion. (Nashville Daily Union, 26 Feb. 1865.)

DREW, John, the Irish comedian, died in Philadelphia on the 21st instant.
(Nashville Dispatch, 1 June 1862.) The Drew family, a stage family,
has had a sad mortality among its male members. John Drew, the most
correct delineator of Irish character, died May 21 in Philadelphia;
his brother Edward Drew, captain in Berdan's Regiment of Sharp-
shooters, was killed July 22 before Richmond while leading men in
battle; George, the third brother, died on the 17th ult. at Fortress
Monroe while on duty with the 49th New York. The only survivor is
Frank, who was filling an engagement at St. Louis two weeks ago.
(Nashville Dispatch, 4 Sept. 1862.) Frank Drew, brother of John
Drew, is appearing at the theater in Nashville. (Nashville Daily
Union, 7 March 1865.) (N.B., Frank and John Drew were twins;
John Drew was the grandfather of John, Lionel, and Ethel Barrymore.)

DREW, John Owen, 49, died Dec. 22 in Memphis; brother of A. W. Drew.
(Memphis Avalanche, 23 Dec. 1868.)

DREYER, Chris. H., 35, died yesterday of flux; mechanic; wife and
children survive. (Nashville Union and American, 14 Aug. 1874.)

DRISCOLL, Thomas, died on the 7th; several stab wounds on the body and
an inquest held. (Memphis Avalanche, 17 Feb. 1866.)

DROUILLARD, Capt. J. P., prominent citizen and capitalist, died suddenly
Sunday of brief illness; 53 years old; lived in Nashville since the
war; native of Cincinnati; was once prominent iron master in state.
He was a member of General Rosecrans' staff while he commanded the
Army of the Cumberland. (Maury Democrat, Columbia, TN, 20 Oct. 1892.)

DRUMKELLER, Cornelius, fell off the steamer Robert Moore at Lineport
and drowned. (Nashville Republican Banner, 20 Nov. 1868.)

DRUMMOND. Savannah (Ga.) news--the following have died of the pre-
vailing yellow fever: Edward Lee Drummond, 9 years 10 months, on
Aug. 28; Ina Florence Drummond, 13 years 3 months on Sept. 15;
Mary Lillion Drummond, 4 years 9 months on Sept. 19; all beloved
children of Edward W. and Mary A. Drummond; and on Sept. 27 E. W.
Drummond, age 39, died, with wife and one son surviving. (Columbia
Herald and Mail, 27 Oct. 1876.)

DRURY, Captain, chief of artillery of Van Cleve's staff, was shot in
bowels by sharpshooters near Lafayette, Georgia; it is not believed
to be serious. (Nashville Dispatch, 19 Sept. 1863.)

DRYDEN, Thomas, War of 1812 soldier, died recently in Bedford County.
(Nashville Union and American, 3 March 1873.)

DUANE, Mrs. Deborah, died Thursday night in Philadelphia, at the age of
81 years; granddaughter of Dr. Franklin and the eldest of his
living descendants. (Nashville Daily Union, 26 Feb. 1863.)

DUBOIS, Mrs. General Dudley, daughter of the Honorable Robert Toombs
of Georgia, died Monday; the Dubois family have lived in Memphis
for many years. (Memphis Avalanche, 3 Nov. 1866.)

DUBOSE, little daughter of J. J. Dubose of Memphis, died at the home
of her grandfather Col. George W. Polk in Maury County last week.
(Whig and Tribune, Jackson, TN, 9 Dec. 1871.)

DUCKETT, Henry, died in Memphis after weeks of terrible suffering;
he was brutally and horribly assaulted by armed negroes; the editor
called him a "Martyr to negro equality"; was assaulted a month ago
by a gang; was chopped on head with a hoe. (Memphis Daily Appeal,
19 Sept. 1868.) H. A. Duckett, age 55, died of fractured skull.
(Memphis Daily Appeal, 21 Sept. 1868.)

DUCKWORTH, G. A., prominent citizen, took overdose of morphine Thursday
night and died at Savannah, TN; this was his second attempt at

suicide; cause was financial trouble; he often said his family would be better off without him. (Maury Democrat, 10 Sept. 1891.)

DUDLEY, Mrs. Blandina, founder of the Dudley Observatory at Albany, NY died in that city on the 15th. (Nashville Dispatch, 13 March 1863.)

DUDLEY, Mrs. Matilda, died near Port Royal, Montgomery County, last Sunday. (Columbia Herald, 27 March 1891.)

DUFF. Greenwood Cemetery in Brooklyn, NY, has Hill of Graves, nearly 40,000 unfortunates are buried here in rows of 50. The graves are only known by numbers. Public Lot 8999 and Mound 850, is sunken and neglected and the grass is dead; the stone here reads "Mother and Grandmother." This is the grave of beautiful Mary Duff to whom the poet Thomas Moore gave hand and heart, and whose beauty he immortalized in verse. In maturity of her career, she was one of the most gifted of actresses. (Maury Democrat, 1 Aug. 1895.)

DUFFICE, Owen, Esquire, of Ireland, is 122 years old. "He is an orphan." (Memphis Avalanche, 6 Nov. 1866.)

DUGGER, J. A., age 80, died Thursday at Stiversville in Maury County, 10 children survive; buried in cemetery there. (Columbia Herald, 17 Nov. 1899.)

DUGGER, Mrs. Jerry, of Fountain Creek, Maury County, died a few days ago of protracted illness. (Columbia Herald and Mail, 1 May 1874.)

DUGGER, William L., was buried in Oakwood Cemetery at Waco, Giles County. (Columbia Herald, 9 Nov. 1899.)

DUNAWAY, George, who killed his uncle James Dunaway and shot and fearfully wounded his aunt and abused his cousin Miss Malisa Dunaway in April 1889 nine miles from Murfreesboro, was captured las Friday. (Clifton Times, 29 May 1890.)

DUNAWAY, H., refugee from Walker County, Alabama, died in workhouse in Nashville yesterday; said he had wife living with her father at Cedar Plains, Morgan County, Alabama; he came here when Buell's Army retreated from Alabama; had been sick with consumption; died as a pauper. (Nashville Dispatch, 16 Jan. 1863.)

DUNBAR, Ann, 36 years 6 days, died on the 19th; first child born in Montgomery County, was survived by her aged parents. (Tennessee Watchman, 31 Oct. 1823.) (N.B., Her age in question.)

DUNBAR, Daniel, 60, pioneer engineer on western waters, died in Cincinnati of typhoid fever on the 17th; as early as 1827 and 1828 "he stood watch" on the steamers Delaware and Niagara; in modern days was on the J. M. White. (Nashville Dispatch, 21 Feb. 1863.)

DUNCAN, Mrs. S. A., died Mary 24 at Sunrise, Hickman County. (Columbia Herald and Mail, 26 May 1876.)

DUNCAN, Major and Private Davis, of the 7th East Tennessee Infantry were captured by rebels and shot dead in East Tennessee. (Nashville Daily Union, 10 April 1863.)

DUNCAN, Miss Minnie, 17, daughter of the Rev. T. J. Duncan, died in Nashville last week, sudden and unsuspected death. (Maury Democrat, 21 Nov. 1890.)

DUKE of Anhalt-Bernburg is dead, by which his dynasty becomes extinct and the duchy reverts to the elder branch of Anhalt-Dessau, thereby reducing the number of German sovereigns to 34. (Nashville Dispatch, 29 Sept. 1863.)

DUKE, James K., died three weeks ago in Kentucky, one of the most successful breeders of racers in Kentucky. (Nashville Dispatch,

25 Aug. 1863.)

DUKE, William, Sr., citizen of Henry County for many years, died on the
29th ult. in Henry County. (Weekly Register, Henry County, 1 April
1848.)

DUNLAP, Jim, a negro belonging to Dr. B. R. Gaither of Tipton County,
was passing through James Dunlap's farm to go see his wife and was
troublesome. Dunlap told him to quit, and Jim drew knife and
plunged it into Dunlap's stomach almost severing it; he withdrew
the knife and plunged again. Dunlap cannot survive. Jim fled. This
happended at Memphis. (Nashville Dispatch, 30 Sept. 1863.)

DUNLAP, John P., died in Edgefield on January 17; State Attorney for
the Paris circuit. (Whig and Tribune, Jackson, TN, 1 Feb. 1873.)

DUNN, Silas, was shot and killed at Murfreesboro on Saturday by Bob
January. He had previously shot at January and missed. (Memphis
Daily Appeal, 16 Feb. 1869.)

DUNN, Brigadier General William McKee, U. S. Army retired, late Judge
Advocate General, died at Maplewood, Virginia, on the 24th, age 72.
(Houston County News, 28 July 1887.)

DUNN, Delilah, a young girl, "pretty before she yielded to the arts
of tempter," committed suicide Sept. 10 by taking a quantity of
laudanum. (Nashville Dispatch, 12 Sept. 1863.)

DUNN, Leona H., wife of Col. William D. Dunn, died at Mobile, Ala.,
January 8. She was the youngest daughter of Mrs. Sophia W. Horton
of Nashville. (Nashville Republican Banner, 20 Jan. 1871.)

DUNNINGTON, Colonel John W., commander of fort at Arkansas Post at
the time of the surrender is the brother of F. C. Dunnington, one
of the proprietors of the Nashville Union and American; native of
Kentucky; midshipman in U. S. Navy, appoint 10 April 1849; a
lieutenant on 15 Oct. 1856; resigned 1861 to join the Confederates.
(Nashville Dispatch, 29 Jan. 1863.) (N. B., Buried at Rose Hill
Cemetery in Columbia where his stone reads born 8 May 1833, died
10 March 1882.)

DUPREE, Mrs. Amelia, of Memphis, died a few days ago in Memphis;
daughter of Governor Jones; visited Clarksville frequently.
(Clarksville Weekly Chronicle.)

DUTTON, Thomas, now a centenarian, is the only person living who heard
the bell of Independence Hall "proclaim liberty throughout the land."
(Memphis Daily Appeal, 16 Feb.1869.)

DUVAL, Captain George W., of Memphis, died yesterday of his injuries.
(Memphis Daily Appeal, 21 Jan. 1869.)

DWYER, John, 52, died in Nashville on December 7; his funeral to be
at the Cathedral. (Nashville Dispatch, 8 Dec. 1863.)

DYER, Michael, 42, died 3 June 1870; shot himself through the head;
saloon proprietor; known as "a hard case" and treated his family
with great severity. (Nashville Republican Banner, 5 June 1870.)

DYRE, Mrs. Patsey, departed this life on the 17th; buried at Rock
Springs in Maury County; member of Cumberland Presbyterian Church.
(Maury Democrat, 2 May 1889.)

EAGLEHART, Jacob, private, died at Huntsville, Alabama, about 13 April 1864, when caisson of Cogswell 1st Illinois Battery exploded; the bodies of the men were blown to atoms. (Nashville Daily Union, 20 April 1864.)

EAKIN, Mrs. William S., of New York City, formerly of Nashville, died suddenly while traveling in Europe with her son a few days ago. (Nashville Republican Banner, 24 March 1869.)

EAKIN, Argyle, Esquire, of Shelbyville, died in Fayetteville a few day ago. (Nashville Republican Banner, 18 Jan. 1868.)

EAKIN, Rebecca Ewing, infant daughter of Spencer and Milbrey Eakin, and granddaughter of Honorable Andrew Ewing, died on the 31st. (Columbia Herald, 1 Feb. 1870.0

EARLY, Annie, daughter of Mr. and Mrs. William B. Early, age 3 years 9 months 7 days, died on the 17th. (Nashville Daily Union, 18 March 1865.)

EARLY, Willie, infant daughter of W. B. and P. Early, age 3 months 1 day, died on Jan. 6. (Nashville Daily Union, 17 Jan. 1863.)

EARLY, Annie, little daughter of Mr. and Mrs. William B. Early, age 3 years 9 months 7 days, died on the 17th. (Nashville Daily Union, 18 March 1865.)

EARLY, William P., funeral to be held in Nashville today. (Nashville Republican Banner, 2 Oct. 1867.)

EARLY, Mr., murdered by Vaughn's command at Laurel Gap, TN. (Nashville Daily Union, 4 Jan. 1865, quoting the Knoxville Whig.)

EARLY, Jubal, has died. (Maury Democrat, Columbia, TN, 15 March 1894.)

EARTHMAN, Felix Grundy, died yesterday of congestion of the lungs. (Nashville Union and American, 23 Aug. 1873.)

EASLEY, William, killed a few days ago by accidental discharge of a gun in hand of William Webb while they were out hunting in Hickman County. (Nashville Republican Banner, 8 Jan. 1870.)

EAST, Mrs. Celia, mother of Judge Edward H. East, died on the 27th at the age of 78; funeral to be held today. (Nashville Republican Banner, 1 March 1870.)

EAST. Hardin County, chancery court: Joseph East, Sr., complainant, versus Sarah East, Elizabeth Webb, Thomas Webb, Joseph East, Jr., Mariah Abernathy, Sally Bouldin, Richard T. Bouldin, Martha Stanford, ___ Stanford, John Trent, Sarah Jane Trent, Thomas M. East, Thomas H. Maberry, Samuel Ruth, Sarah Ann Ruth, Eli F. Edmiston, Mary Jane Edmiston, Martha Trent, John H. East, Reuben East, Evaline W. Hood, Robert Hood, Edmund W. East, Barclay G. East, all heirs and distributees of Thomas East, Sr., deceased; Thomas Webb and wife Elizabeth, Richard T. Bouldin and wife Sally, Martha Stanford and her husband, and Edward W. East, are all non-residents of Tennessee. (Lawrenceburg Times, 8 July 1847.)

EASTMAN, Edward, 2d lieutenant, of the Nashville Blues, died at Camargo on the 25th of October with the chills and fevers. His death was much lamented by his fellow soldiers. He was a diligent and faithful officer, a grave and gallant soldier. He was a native of New Hampshire and had been a journeyman printer in the office of the Nashville Union for some time before his departure for the war. (The Columbia Beacon, 25 Nov. 1846.)

EASTLAND, Lt. Thomas H., Jr., in his 20th year, died March 21 at the home of his father in White County, TN, of inflammation of the lungs. (Nashville Dispatch, 29 April 1862.)

EASTON, Col. J. D., well known in Maury County, died on his plantation
in Bolivar County, Mississippi, a few days ago. (Columbia Herald
and Mail, 19 April 1878.)

EATON, Edward O., 31, died of pneumonia on the 10th; buried in Elmwood
Cemetery at Memphis; born in Boston; served in the Washington
Artillery, CSA. (Memphis Avalanche, 12 Dec. 1866.)

EATON, Thomas Ryan, little son of Mr. and Mrs. Thomas Eaton, to be
buried today. (Nashville Republican Banner, 9 March 1869.)

ECHOLS, Benjamin, one of the earliest settlers and oldest citizens of
Chattanooga County, Georgia, died a few days ago. (Memphis Daily
Appeal, 1 April 1870.)

EDGARLY, Mrs. Nancy, died at Wolfboro, New York, age 104 years 5 months
28 days. (Maury Democrat, 7 Feb. 1889.)

EDGING, Mrs. Elizabeth, living in Rock Creek township, Carrol County,
Indiana, is 120 years old, enjoying good health and has all her
faculties. (Memphis Daily Appeal, 6 April 1867.)

EDGING, Becky, near 90, of Bear Creek, has been quite ill since
Christmas. (Maury Democrat, 9 Feb. 1893.) Miss Becky Edging, who
died at the home of Volney Cyrus on Bear Creek on Feb. 11 was 96 and
buried in the Beasley graveyard; never married; lived with the
Beasleys a long time. Mr. James Beasley willed her a home for
25 years; she had an atractive face. (Maury Democrat, 16 Feb. 1893.)
Miss Rebecca Edgins died last Friday (the 11th) of extreme old
age at the home of Volney Cyrus on Bear Creek, Maury County; age
98; never married. She had no relatives, near or remote; had lived
5 miles from Columbia but had never been to town, never been in a
store, never seen a railroad. She lived in cabin on the Beasley
farm which was willed to her long ago; buried in the Beasley burying
ground. (Columbia Herald, 16 Feb. 1893.)

EDGINGS. John Rieves, who shot Edgings in Rock Springs a year or so
ago, has been caught and is in jail. Edgins was maimed. (Columbia
Herald, 10 Nov. 1871.)

EDGINS. The following is a tombstone inscription found in a cemetery
east of Centre, Cherokee County, Alabama: "G. J. Edgins, Soldier;
born 24 Oct. 1838, died 24 Jan. 1890; fired the first shot at
Fort Sumter, South Carolina." The nickname "Jeff" is also found
on stone.

EDMONDSON, Mrs. Laura F., wife of the Rev. John A. Edmondson, died at
the home of her father Frank Henderson, five miles south of
Franklin, last week. (Whig and Tribune, Jackson, TN, 6 Sept. 1873.)

EDMONDSON, Mrs. Angeline O'Riley, 72, died January 14; she left an
only child, Fannie Armstrong, with whom she made her home; Methodist;
sister of Mrs. A. O. P. Nicholson; buried Rose Hill Cemetery,
Columbia. (Maury Democrat, 19 Jan. 1893.)

EDMONDSON, John, well known substantial citizen of Williamson County,
has been killed at Owens Cross Roads yesterday by a man named Brown.
(Nashville Union and American, 4 Nov. 1874.) W. A. Brown, who
shot Edmondson, has not been found; Edmondson died Wednesday and
was buried on the 5th. (Nashville Union and American, 6 Nov. 1874.)

EDMONDSON. Lt. Nance, Company H, captured and killed three guerrillas
on Yellow Creek, Dickson County; they were ___ Edmondson, Jim
Rushing, and Frank Warden, notorious men, who have infested this
county too long. (83rd Illinoisan, Clarksville, TN, 12 May 1865.)

EDMUND. The remains of King Edmund the Martyr, the last King of East

Angles from 1855 to 1870, have been returned to England; will be in the private chapel of the Duke of Norfolk until a shrine is ready at Westminster Abbey. (Daily Herald, Columbia, TN, 2 Sept. 1901.)

EDWARDS, S. Walker, born 16 May 1846, died in Nashville Sunday; Confederate veteran; formerly of Maury; died of appendicits. (Maury Democrat, 21 March 1895.)

EDWARDS, Thomas, born March 1820 on Cane Creek in Hickman County, son of Aaron B. Edwards, died on the 8th in Linden; buried in the town cemetery with Masonic honors; circuit court clerk of Perry County; wife and four small children survive. (Linden Times, Perry County, 12 Feb. 1880.)

EDWARDS, Mrs. Fielding, died Saturday while sitting in chair, lived near Whirlpool Island in Maury County. (Columbia Herald, 15 Aug. 1873.)

EDWARDS, Gus, was mortally wounded in the Marbet House yesterday; shot by Charles Hague. (Nashville Republican Banner, 2 March 1869.)

EDWARDS, William, age 108, died a few miles from Union City recently. (Whig and Tribune, 19 April 1873.)

EDWARDS, Melger, took his own life during fit of temporary insanity yesterday; shot himself through the temple; was proprietor of Bell's Exchange for 20 years and later with the Shawnee House; suffered with nervous disorders; wife, one son and four daughters survive. (Nashville Union and American, 3 June 1874.)

EDWARDS, Stella, daughter of Squire Edwards of White Oak, Houston County, died last week of typhoid fever, age 16. (Houston County Times, 7 Dec. 1888.)

EDWARDS, Dr., old and prominent citizen of Bradley County, TN, died in Cleveland a few days ago. (Nashville Dispatch, 27 Jan. 1862.)

EDWARDS, Miss Kate, actress, died at her home in Griffin County, Georgia, on the 13th instant of typhoid fever. (Nashville Dispatch, 19 Sept. 1862.)

EDWARDS, Rebecca, a poor old woman from the Ridge, called asking for information on her son Presley Chamberlain, about 18 years old, who formerly lived at Mr. Wile's near the Buena Vista ferry; anyone with information bring it to the Dispatch. (Nashville Dispatch, 27 March 1863.)

EDWARDS, Capt. C. A., tried as guerrilla at Memphis, TN, and received 5 years in prison at Alton, Illinois. (Huntsville Advocate, 12 Oct. 1865.)

EDYAR, J. E., of Texas,and Miss Martha J. Hadley married after an engagement of 21 years; parents originally objected but now all objections removed; married on Snow Creek, Maury County, November 1873. (Columbia Herald, 12 Dec. 1873.)

EFFINGER, Captain John Ignetius, a veteran of the Revolution, one of the survivors of the distinguished corps of dragoons immediately about the person of Washington, expired at his residence in Woodstock, Virginia, on the 8th inst., at the advanced age of 83, "full of years and full of honor." (Columbia Observer, 24 Oct. 1839.)

EGAN, Mrs. Annette D., wife of Capt. Ben F. Egan, second daughter of the late Capt. Joseph Miller, age 26 years 8 mos. 23 days, died yesterday. (Nashville Republican Banner, 31 Dec. 1870.)

EICHBAUM, William A., 80, died yesterday; born 1787 in Dublin, Ireland, came to the United States in 1820 and settled in Nashville in 1821; a great reader. (Nashville Union and American, 2 Jan. 1873.)

ELAM, Laura McGraw, 41, died August 14, wife of J. J. Elam; buried Rose Hill Cemetery, Columbia; had been married 17 years; daughter of John P. McGraw. (Columbia Herald, 21 August 1891. N.B., her maiden name is really McGaw.)

ELLET, Mrs., wife of Colonel Ellet, died the 29th ult. in Philadelphia. She was present at the death of her husband at Cairo, Illinois. He had been wounded at Memphis. She had accompanied his remains to Philadelphia. (Nashville Dispatch, 7 June 1862.) Wife of Colonel Ellet, who died recently from a wound received in the engagement at Memphis, is also dead. She died of grief. (Nashville Dispatch, 7 June 1862.)

ELLIOT, William, prominent South Carolinian, is dead. (Nashville Dispatch, 26 Feb. 1863.)

ELLIOTT, Thomas, 25, died Friday. (Nashville Republican Banner, 26 Sept. 1869.)

ELLIOTT, William Francis, deceased, tribute of respect to his memory. (Nashville Republican Banner, 12 Jan. 1870.)

ELLIOTT, Samuel, 60, died on the 16th inst. in Lawrence County, Alabama. (Nashville Republican Banner, 19 July 1870.)

ELLIOTT, Mrs. W. F., funeral to be today; widow. (Nashville Republican Banner, 5 Dec. 1869.)

ELLIOTT, Mrs. Ann M., died 24 Nov. 1857, wife of David A. Elliott. (Clarksville Weekly Chronicle, 27 Nov. 1857.)

ELLIOTT, Mrs. Arminda, wife of David, died on the 18th ult., daughter of Robert Davis, Esquire. (Clarksville Jeffersonian, 3 Aug. 1844.)

ELLIOTT, George, 74, died near Gallatin, TN; War of 1812 soldier; was in three campaigns and was at Battle of New Orleans in Capt. John Wallace's Company from Sumner County. (Nashville Republican Banner, 25 March 1871.)

ELLIOTT, Edward, and Charles Eastman of the 14th Connecticut Regiment, on the 18th were shot at the headquarters of the 3d Division of the Army of the Potomac for desertion; Elliott was 21 and a native of Boston; Eastman was 23 and from Cornish, Maine. Eastman was baptized on the spot where he met his fate. Elliott sat on coffin and fell back in it when shot. The firing squad missed Easton and he sprang up. The Provost Marshall took revolver and shot him through the head and then fired another through Elliott's head. (Nashville Dispatch, 1 Oct. 1863.)

ELLIS, Samuel, was killed 8 Jan. 1865; formerly lived in Nashville; was a guerrilla and killed by Lt. Clark, Co. A, 83rd Illinois. (Nashville Daily Union, 10 Jan. 1865.)

ELLIS, Dr. William, of Yellow Creek, died suddenly 16 Nov. 1860. (Clarksville Weekly Chronicle, 21 Nov. 1860.)

ELLIS, R. G., who represented Williamson, Maury and Lewis counties in the last General Assembly, died recently on plantation in Louisiana. (Nasvhille Dispatch, 31 July 1862.)

ELLISON, Harry, was shot and killed last week by Willie Bailey, an old grudge. Near Caney Springs. (Columbia Herald, 29 May 1896.)

ELSOM, James T., funeral to be held today. (Nashville Republican Banner, 30 Oct. 1870.)

ELY, Dr. D. L., First Assistant Physican of the Ohio Lunatic Asylum, died of apoplexy in Columbus on the 21st. (Nashville Daily Union, 29 March 1863.)

ELY, Jesse, an old and well known citizen of Nashville, age 60, died Wednesday; lived in Nashville for 40 years. (Columbia Herald, 17 Sept. 1897.)

EMBRY, Wiley S., 88, died May 5 and buried in Street Cemetery in Maury County. (Maury Democrat, 8 May 1890.)

EMMETT. Old Dan Emmet, author of that famous southern song "Dixie," lives in an old hut in the Koloshing Valley not far from Mt. Vernon, Ohio. In his younger days he was a traveling minstrel. (Maury Democrat, 2 Aug. 1894.) Dan Emmett, 86, composer of "Dixie" died suddenly at Mt. Vernon, Ohio. (Daily Herald, 30 June 1904.)

EMORY, John, and William Emory, men who have been guilty of the foulest crimes as guerrillas, were killed by troops of Lt. Col. J. H. Blackburn, 14th Tennessee Cavalry (Federal) near Liberty, Tennessee, on Thursday, 9 Feb. 1865. (Nashville Daily Union, 11 Feb. 1865.)

ENGELHARDT, William, well known German citizen who has lived here 18 years, died Thursday night of apoplexy. (Nashville Republican Banner, 1 April 1870.)

ENGLISH, Captain Richard P., commercial editor of the Memphis Appeal, died a few days ago. (Columbia Herald, 20 Oct. 1871.)

ENSLEY, Enoch, Esquire, old citizen was attacked yesterday of paralysis in the city, but recovered. (Nashville Daily Union, 7 April 1863.) Colonel Enoch Ensley, one of the wealthiest men in the South, died Wednesday in Memphis; he was worth between 3 and 4 million dollars. (Florence, Ala., Times, 21 Nov. 1891.)

ENSLEY, Capt. Edward L., 25, died May 4 at his brother's plantation near Memphis. (Nashville Dispatch, 4 June 1862.)

ERWIN, Mac, found on sidewalk in insensible condition and taken to the workhouse where he died; was buried yesterday afternoon. (Nashville Dispatch, 29 Nov. 1863.)

ERWIN, Mrs. Elizabeth M., died December 2 in Batesville, Arkansas; sister of Mrs. Curran Frierson. (Columbia Herald and Mail, 21 Dec. 1877.)

ERWIN, Theodoric, died Thursday the 11th inst. near Shady Grove, Hickman County, TN; three score and ten. (Columbia Herald, 26 April 1872.)

ERWIN, W. B., of Shady Grove, Hickman County, received telegram Tuesday that his daughter Miss Mattie was dangerously ill at Manlyville, Henry County. She was dead when he got there. (Columbia Herald and Mail, 8 Dec. 1876.)

ERWIN, Miss Annie, died at the Guest House in Columbia on Monday after a long illness; young lady. (Columbia Herald and Mail, 12 Nov. 1875.)

ERWIN, C. S., died of consumption last Wednesday in Austin, Texas; went to Texas 20 years ago; fourth son of Col. Martin P. Erwin of Maury County. (Maury Democrat, 25 July 1895.)

ESSELMAN, Dr. John M., is to be interred today in Mount Olivet in Nashville. (Nashville Dispatch, 24 Sept. 1862.) Dr. John N. Esselman, tribute of respect on his death. (Nashville Dispatch, 5 Sept. 1862.)

ESTES, Mrs. M. J., 69, widow of Thomas Estes, died Tuesday; to be buried in family burying ground near Ashwood. (Columbia Herald, 17 April 1891.)

ESTES, Ellen, "noted princess of the jungle," died Sunday of overdose of morphine. (Nashville Republican Banner, 21 April 1868.)

ESTES, Mrs. Ellen D., 80, wife of Robert Estes, died Tuesday; buried Rose Hill Cemetery, Columbia. (Columbia Herald, 20 Dec. 1899.)

ESTES, Mrs. Betsy, 84, died last week in Giles County. (Columbia Herald, 18 Oct. 1872.)

ESTEP, Samuel, killed by Vaughn's command at Laurel Gap, TN. (Knoxville Whig, 4 Jan. 1865.)

ESTEVE, Professor A., died Saturday; native of France; Roman Catholic; wife and three children survive; buried Rose Hill, Columbia. (Columbia Herald, 23 June 1871.)

ESTILL, Dr. William, one of the oldest citizens of Franklin County, died on the 28th ult. (Nashville Union and American, 1 May 1874.)

ESTIS, ___, was killed near Athens, Alabama, yesterday by Jack Guichricks, a telegraph operator, who had been discharged from his job. Estis was the son of the superintendent of the Alabama & Chattanooga Railroad. (Nashville Union and American, 25 March 1873.)

EUBANK, Mary Ann, 22, wife of Preston T. Eubank, died September 2; funeral at Trinity Church. (Nashville Dispatch, 3 Sept. 1863.)

EVANS, Charles. John Johnson, colored, was hanged at Mt. Sterling Saturday for the murder of Policeman Charles Evans. It was the first legal hanging in Montgomery County since the war and 4,000 persons turned out to see the job well done. (Maury Democrat, 22 Aug. 1895.)

EVANS, Russ, died yesterday of erysipilas, formerly of Dez Arc, Arkansas. (Memphis Avalanche, 4 Jan. 1866.)

EVANS, Edward F., private in Anderson's troop, died in Nashville Sunday; citizen of Philadelphia; survived by his widowed mother. (Nashville Daily Union, 17 Feb. 1863.)

EVANS, Mrs. Betsy, aged, died recently at Lynnville, Giles County. (Maury Democrat, 30 May 1895.)

EVANS, Charles, deceased, his estate is insolvent. (Columbia Herald and Mail, 19 Feb. 1875.)

EVANS, William, died near Lynnville, Giles County, last Monday. (Columbia Herald, 24 July 1891.)

EVANS, Zebulon, who has been a citizen of Shelbyville for about 45 years, died a few days ago. (Nashville Union and American, 9 Dec. 1874.)

EVANS, Jesse W., stepson of S. H. Timmons, 16, died September 26 of diabetes. (Columbia Herald, 7 Oct. 1870.)

EVANS. "There came very near being a serious difficulty on the square last Monday between Ab Alley and Frank Evans. It originated on account of an old grudge that Frank had against Alley for killing his father during the war." (Columbia Herald and Mail, 29 Sept. 1876. N. B. The tombstone of Jesse E. Evan has the following inscription: "he was willfully murdered 20 Sept. 1862." He was killed by Ab Alley.)

EVANS, Frank, son of W. M. B. and Irene Evans, to be buried today. (Nashville Dispatch, 8 August 1862.)

EVERETT, John B., 74, died Feb. 21 of ulceration of the stomach; he was born 21 Sept. 1822, 7 miles from Nashville on the Murfreesboro Road, one of the 15 children of the Everett and Buchanan families; dry goods merchant; wife and 2 sons survive. (Maury Democrat, Columbia, 28 Feb. 1895.)

EVERETT, George, died July 1, infant of John B. and Elizabeth M. Everett. (Nashville Republican Banner, 2 July 1868.)

EVERETT, William, of Troy, TN, is in Maury County on visit; came here 1831 from Halifax County, Virginia, and kept store at Poplar Top, now Neapolis, until 11 years ago when he moved to West Tennessee. (Columbia Herald, 2 Sept. 1870.)

EVERETT, Elizabeth Buchan, infant of E. F. and Ellen Everett, her funeral to be today at Edgefield. (Nashville Dispatch, 10 May 1863.)

EVES, infant son of Robert and Jane Eves, age 2 years 10 months, died on the 11th inst. (Nashville Dispatch, 13 Dec. 1863.)

EVES, Dr. Paul P., of Nashville, died suddenly Saturday morning; he was born 28 June 1808 near Augusta, Georgia; in 1826 was graduated from the University of Georgia; received M. D. from University of Pennsylvania; was surgeon in the Confederate Army. (Columbia Herald and Mail, 9 Nov. 1877.)

EVINS, Flay, of District 16, Davidson County, accidently shot himself about a month ago, and died of his wounds Wednesday night. (Nashville Republican Banner, 21 March 1871.)

EWELL, Thos. We are permitted to make the following extract from a letter written by Lieut. Thomas Claiborne, descriptive of the last hours of one who is well called "one of the bravest, truest, and most talented of Tennessee's adopted sons": "My poor friend, Tom Ewell, was the hero of the day--the first man inside the works-- and had stabbed two of the enemy with his sabre, when he was mortally wounded in the abdomen. He lived till 1 o'clock that night, and died gently. He behaved with the great courage, and when suffering the greatest agony, would only press firmly his lips together and close his eyes during the paroxysm of pain. He disdained to groan, and refused to mention his misfortunes. One time he said to Major Loring, 'I wish I was dead, I shall be in half an hour.' Gen. Scott came to where he lay, took his hand, and told him 'he was the hero of the battle; that he must not should not die.' He was ready to weep over so gallant an officer. Ewell died calmly, his brother by his side, and lies buried in a rough coffin on the side of Cerro Gordo, near its top, next to the road--the scene at once of his glory and his death. Will not Tennessee claim his remains? He fought for her honor and around the spot, where he lay dying, not only the officers of his regiment, but all who could get there-the commanding general included. His ears were filled with the applause of friends and strangers, but all in vain--nothing could save him." (Columbia Beacon, 28 May 1847.)

EWELL, Richard S. General Ewell, who succeeds Stonewall Jackson, has but one leg, and is said has to be strapped on his horse while on the field. (Nashville Dispatch, 13 June 1863.)

EWING, Edwin H., well known merchant of Nashville, died at his home in Nashville a few days ago; he was the oldest son of Orville Ewing and brother of Major Albert Ewing, who died a few weeks ago in St. Louis. (Whig and Tribune, 2 Aug. 1873.)

EWING, William, who represented Williamson County in the 1859-1860 legislature, died a few days ago at his home in Franklin. (Nashville Dispatch, 30 April 1863.)

EWING, Capt. Orville, son of the Hon. Edwin H. Ewing, was killed in action at Murfreesboro on December 31, he was on General Preston's staff; was twice wounded at Fishing Creek and captured and in hospital at Somerset, KY; he made his escape and rejoined the Confederate Army. (Nashville Dispatch, 9 Jan. 1863.) Major Orville Ewing, rebel soldier, of Nashville, killed at Murfreesboro in battle. (Nashville Daily Union, 8 Jan. 1863.)

EWING, Susan, infant daughter of A. G. and Harriett Ewing, died March 13. (Nashville Republican Banner, 15 March 1870.)

EWING, William H., died yesterday, age 43; brother-in-law of Mr. Perkins of Williamson County; merchant; brother of John H. Ewing. (Nashville Republican Banner, 6 Dec. 1867.)

EWING, Andrew Hynes, was killed at Guthrie, KY, Monday by Thomas Yancey. (Nashville Republican Banner, 12 Jan. 1870.)

EWING, Major Henry, died in St. Louis and buried in Bellefontaine Cemetery there. (Nashville Union and American, 18 June 1873.)

EWING, A. G., of Nashville, committed suicide in hotel in Pulaski by using chloroform on Tuesday of last week; served in Confederate cavalry from Marshall County, wounded at Fort Pillow, which necessitated the amputation of the leg above the ankle. (Columbia Herald, 29 Nov. 1872.)

EZZELL. Miss Ezell of Murfreesboro was outraged by a negro and a mob went after him. (Memphis Daily Appeal, 21 July 1868.) William Gustine brutally outraged Miss Ezzell, 13. He was executed at midnight by the Kuklux. The next day her brother Jeremiah Ezzell was shot and killed on Carters Creek Pike by a band of negroes in ambush. (Memphis Daily Appeal, 23 July 1868.) A Jew, Bierfield, was the leader of the negro assassins who killed Jeremiah Ezzell. (Memphis Daily Appeal, 20 Aug. 1868.)

FAHNESTOCK, B. A., died in Philadelphia Friday. (Nashville Dispatch, 15 July 1862.)

FALL, E. H., well known Nashville business man committed suicide June 24 by shooting himself. (Maury Democrat, 27 June 1895.)

FAIN, Van, brother of James Fain (Nashville and Decatur railroad engineer), died in Memphis on Tuesday of congestive chill and buried in Rose Hill Cemetery at Columbia. (Columbia Herald and Mail, 22 Oct. 1875.)

FAIRCLOTH, Mrs. Melinda, of Mitchell County, Georgia, is 115 years old, is sprightly and in good health. (The News, Murfreesboro, 3 Jan. 1873.)

FAIRES, Mrs. Mary, widow of the Rev. Andrew Faires, of Cloverdale, Ala., died Monday at the age of 78; Methodist; buried at Wesley Chapel Cemetery; born 27 Dec. 1814 in South Carolina; came to Lauderdale County early; married 5 Oct. 1837 to Andrew Faires. (Florence, Ala., Times, 18 June 1892.)

FANNING, Tom, of Franklin County, was fatally wounded by accidental explosion of a gun in his own hands on the 29th ult. (Nashville Union and American, 1 May 1874.)

FANNING, Elder Tolbert, late President of Franklin College, died Sunday at 12:30 of congestion of liver; distinguished member of the Christian denomination. (Nashville Union and American, 3 May 1874.)

FARIS, J. K., of Paris, TN, spy and guide for the United States, was captured and shot on May 21 at Corinth, Mississippi. (Nashville Dispatch, 29 May 1862.)

FARLEY, Miss Zora, 18 of Belleview, 9 miles from Nashville, had fatal
accident last week; her horse became unmanageable, the saddle broke,
she fell to ground and horse fell on top of her. She died soon
after. (Maury Democrat, 18 Sept. 1890.)

FARMER, Mrs. Sarah, about 60, of Rutherford County, froze to death in
woods on way to poorhouse where she was an inmate; she was thinly
clad and barefooted. (Nashville Union and American, 1 Feb. 1873.)

FARRAGUT, David G., Admiral of the American Navy, was a Tennessean,
born on Tennessee soil. His father came from Inorca, an island in
the Mediterranean Sea, east of Spain, and finally settled on the
Tennessee River at the place now known as Lames Ferry, 4 miles east
of Concord, TN. (Columbia Herald, 25 Oct. 1895.)

FARRAR, Thomas James, 30 died at Oak Springs, the old homestead at
Fluvanna County, Virginia, on December 18; son of Garland Farrar;
brother of J. H. and Benjamin J. Farrar of Nashville; this makes
three brothers and one sister who have been lost in the last seven
months. (Nashville Republican Banner, 24 Dec. 1868.)

FARRAR, David S., died May 27 at 42 years in Palmyra, Virginia; brother
of J. B. and T. J. of Nashville. (Nashville Republican Banner,
9 June 1868.)

FARQUHARSON, Elizabeth Smith, 9 years 9 months, died 8 July 1868 at
Heckatoo, Arkansas, oldest daughter of Dr. R. J. Farquharson.
(Nashville Republican Banner, 13 July 1868.)

FARRELL, Austin, 77, War of 1812 soldier, died lately in Scott County,
TN. (Memphis Avalanche, 19 June 1867.)

FARRELL, Mike, of Capt. Unthank's company, Colonel Bayles Regiment, shot
August 6 by Lt. Raplee and died instantly. Raplee had demanded
his sword, Farrell had refused, and Raplee shot him. Raplee is now
under arrest at McMinnville. (Nashville Dispatch, 27 Aug. 1862.)

FARRELL, Ernest Rossier, his funeral to be held at Christ Church today.
(Nashville Republican Banner, 18 Sept. 1870.)

FARRINGTON, Lt. Sam, of Capt. Wade's battery of St. Louis, was among
those killed at Corinth; he fell in the heat of battle. (Nashville
Dispatch, 14 Oct. 1862.)

FARRIS, Miss Sallie, has died and buried in the Cook graveyard near
Campbellsville, TN. (Columbia Herald, 1 Oct. 1897.)

FARROW, Lemeuel, 67, died September 3 on the Hernando Road; born in
Georgia; at an early age moved to Lauderdale County, Ala., where he
grew up; then moved to Marshall County, Mississippi; born 1799;
buried Nonconnah Chapel by side of son who fell at Belmont and a
daughter who had died before. (Memphis Avalanche, 11 Sept. 1866.)

FASK, Mitchell, of Company L, 3rd Ohio Cavalry, shot through the head
on 10 May 1864 near Franklin, TN; was shot off his horse in cold
blood by a band of murderous Rebel guerrillas. (Nashville Daily
Union, 12 May 1864.)

FAULKNER, Col. Sandy, the original Arkansas Traveler, died yesterday
in Little Rock. (Nashville Union and American, 11 Aug. 1874.)

FAULKNER, Jacob, 85, died 1 July 1860 in Stewart County; War of 1812
soldier. (Clarksville Weekly Chronicle, 27 July 1860.)

FEARN, Dr. Thomas, one of Alabama's members of the Provisional Congress
of the Confederacy, died on the 16th ult. at Huntsville, Alabama,
of consumption contracted in jail where he was thrown by General
O. Mitchell when the Federals took that place; born Pittsylvania
County, Virginia; age 74; surgeon in the War of 1812 and dressed

112

the wound of General Andrew Jackson. (Nashville Dispatch, 21 March 1863.)

FEATHERSTON, William, 96, died October 20 in Robertson County. (Whig and Tribune, Jackson, TN, 9 Nov. 1872.)

FEATHERSTONE, General W. S., of Mississippi, prominent citizen and commander of the Confederate veterans of Mississippi, died at his home in Columbus on the 29th. (Florence, Ala., Times, 6 June 1891.)

FELKNER, Jacob, 57, died at Port Royal. (Tennessee Watchman, Clarksville, TN, 23 Feb. 1821.)

FELTS, Charles R., CSA, who had leg amputated made necessary from wound in one of Hood's campaigns against General Thomas, died in Murfreesboro, from a second amputation which was made for the purpose of fitting him with an artificial leg. (Memphis Avalanche, 28 Nov. 1866.)

FELTS, Capt. J. W., of Nashville, died Friday. Some years ago was on the police force as constable; alderman; stonemason. (Nashville Union and American, 26 Jan. 1873.)

FERGUSON, Eleanora H., died on the 21st; wife of Calvin W. Ferguson; daughter of Col. A. W. Johnson. (Nashville Dispatch, 22 Oct. 1862.)

FERGUSON, R. H. C., died on the 28th at Shelbyville; minister of the Gospel for 50 years; age was three score and ten; a year ago had paralytic stroke; buried at home on Thompson Creek where he had lived 15 to 20 years. (Nashville Republican Banner, 1 Aug. 1868.)

FERGUSON, J. F., Esquire, age 73, died a few days ago; he had walked over his place, and failed to come in for dinner. He had died early in the day and his body was cold when found; probably died of apoplexy. (Nashville Republican Banner, 13 Nov. 1870.)

FERGUSON, Lucy, infant daughter of James B., and Elizabeth Ferguson, died in Memphis on the 6th; age 20 months. (Nashville Daily Gazette, 22 Sept. 1852.)

FERGUSON, Champ, is to be hung on the 20th day of October. (Clarksville Weekly Chronicle, 13 Oct. 1865.) Champ Ferguson, noted as a vindictive and merciless guerrilla, was brought yesterday to this city as a prisoner. Colonel Blackburn some days ago sent him an order from General Thomas to surrender with his men. A parley took place between Ferguson, his men, and Colonel Blackburn. The men surrendered but Ferguson declined to do so unless on such conditions as had been granted to the officers of the Confederate Army. He was willing to take the oath. Such terms would not be granted to a name stained and steeped in crime as Ferguson's is. Colonel Blackburn afterwards sent a party after him, to his residence, a cottage on Calfkiller's Creek, 12 miles north of Sparta. He was found to be in the stable. The men got between the stable and the house, cutting him off from his weapons which were in the house, and he was readily taken. He bore his capture with coolness, but his wife showed much vindictiveness and used all an excited woman's eloquence upon the men. Ferguson's only child, a good looking well-mannered, well-educated girl of 14, was wild with grief. He acknowledged to Colonel Blackburn that he knew of 33 persons, white and black, whom he had killed. The neighborhood of Sparta is now clear of guerrillas. (Nashville Daily Union, 30 May 1865.)

NOTORIOUS CHAMP FERGUSON CAPTURED TOGETHER WITH HIS ENTIRE BAND: FERGUSON TO BE HEAVILY IRONED. The notorious Champ Ferguson has been caught, and is in town (Nashville). He and his gang were captured by Col. J. H. Blackburn 4th Tennessee Mounted Infantry) near Sparta, Tennessee. This closes the career of a scoundrel, who for three years, has been the scourge and terror of East Tennessee. Ferguson arrived in the city this morning.

Reports are renewed that the surrendered guerrilla, Duvay McNairy, is
to be arrested and tried for murder.

Just as I close this dispatch, I understand that Gen. Rousseau has ordered Ferguson to be heavily ironed and closely confined. (Louisville Journal, 29 May 1865.)

Champ Ferguson last winter at Emory & Henry College, just after the
Federal raid on the Salt Works, rushed into the hospital and shot
Lt. Smith of Kentucky, then so badly wounded he could not turn
himself on his couch. At the same time Ferguson and his murderous
band, shot several of the negroes belonging to Burbridge's command.
(Nashville Daily Union, 7 June 1865.)

Guerrillas in East Tennessee are led by Champ Ferguson and others.
(Nashville Daily Union, 23 Dec. 1863.)

Larkin Swafford, Esquire, of Bledsoe County, was murdered recently
by Champ Ferguson's gang. Champ said Yanks had stolen two fiddles
from him and he intended to have ten of their scalps for each fiddle.
(Nashville Daily Union, 12 March 1864.)

THE REBEL BARBARITIES IN CLINTON COUNTY, Burksville, Ky., 11 April
1862. Our usually quiet town seems yet deemed to be the theater of
much discord and confusion; it is already being thickly crowded by
refugees from Clinton County, who were driven hither by a lawless
marauding band of ruffians from Tennessee, commanded by the notorious
Champ Ferguson, whose hands were long since dyed in the blood of
more than a half a dozen of an innocent and unoffending citizens
as Kentucky ever produced... They deliberately shot down the
following citizens while attending peaceably to their domestic
affairs, without even assigning any other reason than that of
sympathy for the Union: William Huff, Lewis Pierce, Henry Johnston,
two of the Shellys, John Syms, and several others, besides a promising
little boy, twelve years old, by the name of Zachary, who was taken
out of a sick bed, supported by two of the demons, while a third cut
his abdomen wide open. Col. Woolford went in pursuit of them, but
as usual they fled back into Tennessee... (Nashville Daily Union,
19 April 1862.)

Outrages along the Kentucky border are by Champ Ferguson and O. P.
Hamilton. Soldiers of the 5th Kentucky Cavalry ask for help for
their families living here. (Nashville Daily Union, 19 Feb. 1863.)

FERRELL, Col. Stephen, one of the most gallant officers of the Texas
rangers, died at La Grange, Texas, a few days ago. (Memphis Daily
Appeal, 20 Nov. 1868.)

FERNANCE, Jacob, living near Kansas City, Missouri, is over 118 years
old, still shows considerable activity works in a little garden.
(Memphis Daily Appeal, 1 June 1869.)

FERRIS, William, 31, died 27 Jan. 1863. (Nashville Dispatch, 29 Jan.
1863.)

FERRIS, Capt. W. H., old and successful shipper, died at Norwalk,
Conn., a few days ago. In 1838 when his ship passed the New York
Battery, an anchor caught his great-coat and carried him with it
into 35 feet of water. On touching bottom, he unbuttoned coat and
floated to the surface. (Columbia Herald and Mail, 21 Dec. 1877.)

FERRIS, Aunt Fanny, died Wednesday at the age of 107 years, negress.
She lived 2 miles out on the Charlotte Pike; born 1762 in Virginia
and witnessed the Revolution. She was captured by army of Lord
Cornwallis and retained until the siege of Yorktown when she went
to home of Mr. Ferris' father in Henry County, Va., and lived until
he died 29 years ago. Although set free by his will, she stayed
with Josiah Ferris, Jr., buried in family burying ground on Mr.

Ferris' farm; Baptist. (Nashville Republican Banner, 25 June 1869.)

FETTA, John F., committed suicide on May 17, shot through head. He
had been unwell for some time and addicted to drink. He was native
of Havana, age 34. His parents live in Richmond, Indiana. He lived
in Nashville for 15 years and was a member of the Odd Fellows.
(Nashville Republican Banner, 18 May 1869.)

FETZ, Mrs. Mary, funeral to be held today; age 83; died while sitting
in chair at breakfast Sunday; died of old age and exhaustion; had
daughter Mrs. Theresa Warren. (Nashville Republican Banner, 7 March
1871.)

FIELDING, Jonathan, 14 years, 6 months, son of William Thomas Fielding,
died last night of congestive chill. (Nashville Republican Banner,
13 July 1868.)

FIELD, Joseph, who lives near Red Bank, New Jersey, is 102 years old;
he remained a bachelor until he was 75 when he married Enretto
Headden of Headden's Corner, fifty years his junior. They have
three children: Rebecca, Joseph and Enretta. (Maury Democrat,
11 Oct. 1894.)

FIELDS, Mrs. Matilda, the youngest and only living child of David
Crockett, died at Trenton, TN, last week; she had been married three
times but was a widow at her death. (Maury Democrat, 17 July 1890.)

FIELDS, Mrs. Mary A., 47, died on the 7th; Baptist. (Nashville Republican Banner, 8 Sept. 1868.)

FIELDS, Willie, infant son of Mrs. Lou Fields, 19 months, died 1 August
1863. (Nashville Daily Union, 2 August 1863.)

FIELDS, W. H., died Tuesday; pioneer of Santa Fe in Maury County; he
was related to Jesse H. Fitzgerald, who died last week; Cumberland
Presbyterian. (Columbia Herald, 31 July 1896.)

FILLINGER. BAPTIZED TO DEATH. Last summer William Fillinger and his
wife, who live 3 miles from Perry, Michigan, attended a series of
revivals and became religion mad in a mild way. With them lived
Fillinger's mother, who has long been physically frail. It worried
Fillinger and his wife that the older woman was unbaptized, and
Saturday they decided that the necessary religious rite should be
performed; although the poor woman was confined to her bed, unable
even to rise. Taking water to her room they began the ceremony by
dashing water in her face, and continued it, until from shock and
exhaustion their victim died. Fillinger and his wife were arrested
and taken to jail at Corunna. (Maury Democrat, 23 Oct. 1890.)

FILLMORE, Nathaniel, father of the ex-president, died at East Aurora,
Erie County, N.Y., on the 28th ult, at 92 years. He never drank
intoxicating liquors. He visited his son in Washington in his
80s--the only case when a President of the United States ever
received a visit from father at executive mansion. (Nashville
Dispatch, 8 April 1863.)

FILLMORE, Millard, died at his elegant home in Buffalo, NY, on 8 March
1874 and was buried in Forest Lawn Cemetery. (Maury Democrat,
5 Jan. 1893.) Ex-President Fillmore owns and occupies an elegant
mansion in the City of Buffao. (Columbia Herald, 20 Sept. 1872.)

FINLAN, Larry, native of Ireland, and for more than 40 years a resident
of Harper's Ferry, West Virginia, and at one time an employee of the
United States Army, died there Saturday at 77 years. About 18 years
ago he got the idea of making his own tombstone and procured a piece
of slate, 3 x 5 feet, cut the apex in the form of a cross, chiseled
his name, place of birth, and thinking he would die between the
years 1888 and 1890, cut out the first three figures on face of

115

stone, but not dying at that time, he substituted "9" and set the tombstone in his lot in the Catholic Cemetery. He was buried Sunday, his tombstone being erected after the filling of his grave. (Maury Democrat, 23 Oct. 1890.)

FINLEY, Carroll, son of Luke W. and Cecelia Finley, funeral to be held today. (Memphis Avalanche, 31 Jan. 1866.)

FINLEY, Sgt. James A., Company I, 5th Tennessee Cavalry (Federal) was killed 22 Feb. 1864, on Calf Killer near Sparta, TN. (Nashville Daily Union, 25 Feb. 1864.)

FINLEY, James S., of Stewart County, was executed 8 Jan. 1865 as guerrilla by Lt. Clark, Company A, 83rd Illinois. (Nashville Daily Union 12 Jan. 1865.)

FINN, Henry, rebel soldier in Company C, 1st Tennessee, died of pneumonia at Prison Hospital on the 6th. He was captured at the Battle of Chattanooga and was at the time badly off for shoes. (Nashville Daily Union, 8 Dec. 1863.)

FINN, Daniel, infant son of D. D. Finn, died on the 3d. (Nashville Republican Banner, 5 July 1870.)

FISH, Miss Bettie, died Sunday, 3 miles from Spring Hill. (Columbia Herald, 27 March 1891.)

FISHER, Anson, 75, died on the 9th; buried at the Rock Springs Cemetery. (Columbia Herald and Mail, 17 July 1874.)

FISHER, Margaret Fanny Leonard, 22, died on May 8; wife of J. G. Fisher. (Nashville Dispatch, 10 May 1863.)

FISHER, Cora Eucebia, infant daughter of J. G. and Margaret Fisher, died on the 20th. (Nashville Dispatch, 22 July 1862.)

FISHER, Major W., 65, died November 20 on Poplar Street. (Memphis Avalanche, 22 Nov. 1866.)

FISHER, Elwood, who spent several months in Nashville last winter, died recently in Augusta, Georgia. (Nashville Dispatch, 23 Oct. 1862.)

FISHER, John A., funeral held last Sunday; was member of the Order of Pale Faces. (Nashville Republican Banner, 29 Dec. 1868.) John A. Fisher, Esquire, died yesterday at Madison Station; son-in-law of Captain Mitchell. (Nashville Republican Banner, 26 Nov. 1868.)

FISK, Mrs. Anne, died Sunday a few miles south of Nashville, heart attack. (Nashville Republican Banner, 15 April 1868.)

FISOR, John, 23, is dying; while threshing oats on White's Creek he was caught in the machine and lockjaw has set in. (Nashville Union and American, 8 March 1873.) John Bisor died Friday of lockjaw at Dr. Searcy's on White's Creek. (Nashville Union and American, 9 March 1873.)

FITE, Laura, infant daughter of T. D. and Laura E. Fite, funeral to be held today. (Nashville Republican Banner, 8 July 1870.)

FITE, Dick, son of Elias Fite, was instantly killed on the 11th by Jim Walker, son of G. I. Walker, at Sam Voorhies' in Lewis County; self defense. (Linden Times, 22 April 1880.)

FITZGIBBON, Major T. C., of the 14th Michigan, is dead; died some days ago in Detroit, Michigan, of a wound received through mistake while carrying a flag of truce; son of the Emerald Isle; wrote under the names of Grape Shot and Lance Corporal for the Nashville Daily Union. (Nashville Daily Union, 28 June 1865.)

FITZGERALD, C. P., court paid for inquest over his body. (Columbia
Herald, 11 July 1873.) William Erwin, who killed Fitzgerald, is in
jail. (Columbia Herald, 18 July 1873.)

FITZGERALD, Nathaniel R., 90, War of 1812 soldier, died near Santa Fe,
Maury County, last week. (Whig and Tribune, 8 Feb. 1873.)

FITZGERALD, Bird, 70, died Feb. 15 at his home 7 miles south of Franklin.
(Whig and Tribune, Jackson, TN, 1 March 1873.)

FITZGERALD, George W., died in Maury County on the 2d. (Columbia
Herald and Mail, 29 Oct. 1875.)

FITZPATRICK, Con, of Edgefield, drug his sick wife out of house,
abused her, and kicked her senseless; she died in a few hours; drug
her down the steps. (Nashville Republican Banner, 27 July 1869.)

FITZPATRICK, Miss Polly, 83, died 22 Oct. 1895 in Maury County and
buried at Friendship Cemetery. (Maury Democrat, 31 Oct. 1895.)

FITZPATRICK, ___, 106 years old, is an inmate of the Troy, NY, poorhouse. (Nashville Dispatch, 27 June 1862.)

FITZPATRICK, Miss Sallie, died Monday of bronchial affection; she
was the oldest living member of the Friendship Baptist Church at
Culleoka; her cousin Miss Polly is now sick with same disease and
is quite old. (Columbia Herald, 4 Sept. 1891.)

FITZWILLIAMS, Miss Eliza, died last night at 8 o'clock; Roman Catholic.
(Nashville Union and American, 25 June 1873.)

FLACK, James, died two years ago in Maury County; he came to Maury
County from Pennsylvania and bought land near Spring Hill; land is
now up for sale and the heirs all live out of state. (Columbia
Herald, 24 Jan. 1873. N.B., there was a tombstone for this man at
one time at old Blanton's Chapel in Maury County.)

FLANAGAN, Stephen, old and respected, fell into the cut of the N & C
railroad near Broad Street, Tuesday, and received internal injuries
and died a few hours later. (Nashville Dispatch, 19 March 1863.)

FLANEKEN, George B., of Hurricane has died. (Maury Democrat, 17 Oct.
1895.)

FLANNIGAN, Stephen, died on Tuesday, the 18th; "came to his death by
accidentally falling from a precipice something like 15 feet upon
the Chattanooga railroad near intersection of the Granny White
Pike." He was a blacksmith and survived by wife and three children.
(Nashville Daily Union, 20 March 1863. N.B., see Stephen Flanagan
above.)

FLANNIGAN, John M., age 20 years 15 months 12 days, has died.
(Nashville Union and American, 9 Feb. 1873.)

FLATFORD, Mrs. Cloe, age 118, died recently near Fredericksburg,
Virginia; had chewed and smoked tobacco for 100 years. (Columbia
Herald, 12 Jan. 1872.)

FLATT, Mrs., on the 12th her dead body was found about 8 miles from
Pulaski on Egnew's Creek, supposedly to have died of apoplexy;
described as an old lady. (Nashville Republican Banner, 19 Sept.
1869.)

FLEMING, Mrs. Elizabeth, 43, died May 11 in Nashville; native of
Dumfries, Scotland; emigrated 1842 with her husband; her husband
died of cholera 15 June 1849 the day ex-President Polk died in
Nashville; Presbyterian; two daughter survive. (Nashville Dispatch,
18 May 1862.)

FLEMING, W. H., of Calhoun County, Alabama, who died recently in Atlanta, Georgia, was a subscriber to his county paper for 55 years and alway paid up promptly. (Florence, Ala., Times, 21 Nov. 1891.)

FLEMING, Wilburn, of Roane County, East, TN, has died. (Nashville Daily Union, 6 Feb. 1863.)

FLEMING, Col. John M., leading citizen of Knoxville and well known throughout Tennessee, attempted to commit suicide Sunday afternoon; had been drinking. (Maury Democrat, 7 Nov. 1890.)

FLEMING, James, old and esteemed citizen, died yesterday at 8 a.m. in Edgefield. (Nashville Daily Union, 8 March 1864.)

FLEMING, Eleanor, only daughter of Edward and Anna Fleming, died June 16. (Nashville Republican Banner, 17 June 1870.)

FLEMING, Mrs. W. G., died at Dodson Gap at her father's (Riley Dodson) home. (Columbia Herald and Mail, 8 Oct. 1875.)

FLEMING, Louise, 65, died August 19 of consumption. (Columbia Herald, 28 Aug. 1891.)

FLESHEART, William H., 26 died on the 17th. (Memphis Daily Appeal, 18 Nov. 1866.)

FLETCHER, Mrs. Miriam, age 108, has died at Westford, Mass. She saw the Revolutionary battle at Concord. (Nashville Republican Banner, 11 March 1869.)

FLETCHER, Thomas H., lawyer of Nashville, found dead in his office on Sunday last. (Clarksville Jeffersonian, 18 Jan. 1845.)

FLINT, Dr. Alvin, over 60, of East Hartford, died a week ago on board a transport coming from Aquia Creek to Washington; private in 21st regiment, Captain Marvin's company. His son Alvin was in the 16th regiment and killed at Antietam and as a young boy of 14 had enlisted in the company with his father; a daughter survives. (Nashville Dispatch, 1 Feb. 1863.)

FLINTOFF, Ella, 17, died on the 16th at the home of mother in Cheatham County. (Nashville Dispatch, 21 Sept. 1862.)

FLOURNOY, Capt. Jordan, old and popular steamboat man, died at Paducah, KY, recently. (Nashville Daily Union, 6 Feb. 1863.)

FLOWERS, Eli, died Saturday of congestive chill near Gregory's Mill in Maury County and buried in Timmons Cemetery. (Columbia Herald and Mail, 17 Sept. 1875.)

FLOYD, infant of Henry Floyd, died last week of croup at Hampshire. (Columbia Herald and Mail, 15 June 1877.)

FLOYD, John B., died at Abington, Virginia. (Nashville Dispatch, 1 Sept. 1863.)

FLY, Mrs. James (Annie Baker), died at Nebo in Maury County on 7 March 1891, daughter of Sam G. and N. B. Baker of Shady Grove, Hickman County; born 3 July 1870. (Columbia Herald, 13 March 1891.)

FLY, J. B. H., shot by Green Wells, colored, on Saturday and lived until Monday when he died; buried at Concord in Maury County; wife and two children survive. (Columbia Herald, 29 May 1891.) Green Wells was lynched for killing Fly. (Florence, Ala., Times, 30 May 1891.)

FLYNN, Henry, a Confederate prisoner, died in this city yesterday; member of the Rock City Guards; his relatives live at present in

Philadelphia. (Nashville Dispatch, 8 Dec. 1863.)

FLYNN, Andrew J., former manager of Nashville theater, shot himself with Deringer pistol last week and is in precarious situation; suicide; domestic problems and too much liquor. (Nashville Republican Banner, 5 May 1869.) Mrs. A. J. Flynn died in Huntsville, Ala., Monday. (Nashville Republican Banner, 20 Jan. 1869.) Her husband was the manager of the Adelphi Theater in Nashville from 1864 to 1867. A letter from A. J. Flynn says his wife is not dead. (Nashville Republican Banner, 23 Jan. 1869.)

FLYNN, Mollie Forrest, infant daughter of Andrew and Phoebe Flynn, died on the 1st in Louisville. (Nashville Republican Banner, 3 Jan. 1868.)

FLYNN, infant daughter, 7 months, of Mrs. A. J. Flynn was poisoned negro woman in Louisville; Dr. Yandell was called in and so were others; given an overdose of opiate. (Nashville Republican Banner, 8 Jan. 1868.)

FLYNN, Andrew, attempted suicide April 30; shot himself in heart; died Thursday night finally at Huntsville; suicide; pecuniary embarrassments. (Nashville Republican Banner, 6 June 1868.)

FLYNN, William, son of J. Q. and Mary Flynn, age 30, died on the 2d. (Nashville Republican Banner, 5 May 1868.)

FORD, Miss Antonia, charged with betraying General Stoughton into the hands of the Confederates at Fairfax, Virginia, has been arrested and imprisoned in Washington. (Nashville Dispatch, 24 Sept. 1863.)

FORD, John T., veteran theatrical manager, is dead. He was manager of the theater in which President Lincoln was shot. (Maury emocrat, 22 March 1894.)

FORD, Delaware R., 18, son of Dr. D. J. L. Ford, has died. (Nashville Republican Banner, 7 Nov. 1869.)

FORD, John L., 22, of Nashville, died at Bailey Springs, Alabama, on Thursday, August 19. (Nashville Daily Gazette, 31 Aug. 1852.)

FORD, Mrs. Polly, of Milford near New Haven, Conn., was 100 years old on Sept. 1; had not been to church since 1796, but is member of Congregational denomination; when in the 83rd year she received her second sight and can see better than those of 60 years. (Houston County News, 7 Oct. 1887.)

FOREBECK, Maggie, of Terre Haute, Indiana, committed suicide on May 25 by taking poison; cruelty by her husband was the cause. (Nashville Union and American, 26 May 1874.)

FORGEY, Mrs. Fidelia, 72, died 18 Dec. 1877 of cancer of the breast; lived near Williamsport. (Columbia Herald and Mail, 11 Jan. 1878.)

FORREST, Gen. N. B., died Monday at Memphis after a long and painful illness. (Columbia Herald and Mail, 2 Nov. 1877.) "After the war General Forrest lived on an island in the Mississippi River in order to make money and the malaria got possession of his powerful body. He was the greatest cavalry officer in the war and was one of the two military geniuses developed by the war. He and Stonewall Jackson always whipped the enemy regardless of numbers. In all of his battles he fought superior forces.

"His career commenced at Fort Donelson in Feb. 1862 where he cut his way through Grant's lines after the surrender had taken place. At Shiloh on 7 April 1862 he was severely, aye desperately, wounded in a charge as gallant as any of Marshal Ney's. When he recovered from his wound he crossed the Tennessee River, penetrated the enemy's line. He sabred a Federal soldier there and cut his head off.

"He fought battles at Trenton, Jackson, Humboldt, Spring Creek, Union Town and at Parker's Cross Roads, in all of which he was successful except the last. His greatest victory was at Thompson Station 3 March 1863 where 2000 enemy soldiers were captured.

"Soon after he captured 1000 at Brentwood. The grandest achievement of his life was the capture of Streight. Col. Streight started from Tuscumbia April 1863 with 2500 men for a raid through Alabama and Georgia. General Forrest started after Streight with 600 men, the 9th and 4th Tennessee Regiments. When Streight surrendered near Rome, Ga., with 2200 men and 93 commissioned officers, Forrest had only 360 men--not enough to guard them.

"He was the last general to surrender east of the Mississippi...was always in front of battle and had 29 horses shot from under him. He was the Stonewall Jackson of the west and the Murat of America." (Columbia Herald and Mail, 2 Nov. 1877.)

"General Forrest made a good appearance in society. He attended a party in Columbia during the war, and a brilliant and eloquent talking young lady, now married to C. D., said to him, "General Forrest, why is it that your whiskers are black and your head gray?"

"General Forrest replied, "Because, miss, I work my head more than I do my jaws." No more questions from Miss ___ that evening.

"General Forrest's men say he seemed to always lead. When he crossed Davis Ford on Duck River in front of Hood in 1864, the river was up and swift as a torrent. The enemy was on the other side. Capt. H. P. Pointer and Capt. C. F. Barnes dashed their horses into the turbid stream and started to swim across.

"Hold on, captain," said General Forrest, "I'll go in front." General Forrest rode a fine gray horse which swam so high out of the water that the General never got wet. "Look at Pointer--he is swimming under the water to his shoulders." W. M. Sullivan said he guided Forrest to Davis Ford and wore a new hat." (Columbia Herald and Mail, 16 Nov. 1877.)

Rumors circulate that General Forrest has been shot and killed by a lieutenant in his command at Spring Hill on the 12th. (Nashville Dispatch, 16 June 1863.)

The shooting of General Forrest at Spring Hill on the 12th instant has been confirmed, but the wound was in the left side, instead of the neck, and only a slight flesh one, from which he suffered no inconvenience. It is said that after the Lieutenant fired his pistol, Forrest drew his bowie-knife and stabbed him so severely that he was not expected to recover. (Nashville Dispatch, 17 June 1863.)

We heard it reported yesterday that the guerrilla leader, Forrest, was shot the other day in Spring Hill, by one of his officers or men, in an altercation. We could not trace the story to its origin, and, of course, the rumor is very doubtful. We will have no objections to hearing it verified. (Nashville Daily Union, 16 June 1863.)

THE SHOOTING OF FORREST. A paragraph which we wrote for yesterday's paper giving story No. 2 relative to the shooting of Forrest, was inadvertently omitted. Prisoners brought in Tuesday confirmed the shooting, but not the occasion of it, as stated by others. They say he was shot in the side by Lt. Gould of the artillery service, and that he was alive when they last heard of him. We learn from other sources that the wound is not regarded as dangerous; and that the negro-broker General has yet to get "his rights." Every dog has his day--his is bound to come sooner or later. Let him prepare for it. After he was shot, he stabbed Gould with a bowie knife,

killing him almost instantly. Gould is a Nashville boy, and had
been accused of cowardice by Forrest. (Nashville Daily Union, 18
June 1863.) (N.B., the Forrest-Gould fight took place in Columbia,
not Spring Hill, and Gould was not killed instantly. Refer to
A. W. Gould entry.)

General Forrest was in Memphis on the 4th, looking feeble; his wound
has not entirely healed. (Nashville Daily Union, 25 Oct. 1863.)

Advertisement: N. B. Forrest, Cotton Factor and Commission
Merchant, 272 Front Street, upstairs. (Memphis Daily Appeal,
10 Nov. 1866.)

General N. B. Forrest has joined the Cumberland Presbyterian Church.
(Columbia Herald and Mail, 10 Dec. 1875.)

General N. B. Forrest, the Wizard of the Saddle, was registered at
the St. Nicholas Hotel in New York City on the 31st ult. (Memphis
Daily Appeal, 6 April 1870.)

General Forrest denies saying there were 40,000 Ku Klux Klan members
in Tennessee in August 1868. (Memphis Daily Appeal, 15 April 1870.)

ABOUT GENERAL FORREST. After the confusion and consternation produced by the gunboats shelling the woods where Bell's brigade was
encamped in the cypress woods on the bank of the river the night
before the battle or little fight at Johnsonville, Gen. Bell and
staff, who were encamped a short distance back of the river,
learning of the shelling of his camp by the gunboats were aroused
by the stragglers from his command and hastened to the scene of
confusion.

In passing in the dark down a road leading to the camp, his horse
suddenly stopped and by all sorts of coaxing failed to pass an
object in the road. The staff of the General would move up, their
horses and they would turn and cavort and fail to go by the obstruc-
tion in the road. Gen. Bell ordered some one of his staff, always
ready to undertake anything perilous, dismounted, giving his horse
to someone to hold, groped his way through the dark and soon
spying something in the road approached it and upon passing his
hands on it exclaimed, "General, they have shot a horse wide open."
Upon close inspection with a torch light, it was discovered that a
wagon with a skinned beef in it, rations for the boys, had been
upset in the road by the fleeing cavalry, which proved the obstruc-
tion, and the "horse that had been shot wide open." (Maury
Democrat, 20 Oct. 1894.)

Money is being raised for monument to Forrest; General W. H. Jackson
of Nashville sent $250 toward it. (Florence, Ala., Times, 12
Dec. 1891.)

The John C. Brown Bivouac of Confederate Veterans has set on foot a
movement to erect in Nashville an equestrian statue of Lt. Gen.
Bedford Forrest and is raising a fund as a nucleus to this end.
F. R. Farrar, the "Johnnie Reb" of Virginia, has been engaged for
two lectures Oct. 9 and 10 at the Vendome Theater in Nashville.
An effort will be made to have the unveiling of this statue during
the Centennial Exposition in 1896. (Maury Democrat, 4 Oct. 1894.)

On November 11 the bodies of N. B. Forrest and wife were quietly
removed to Forrest Park. (Daily Herald, 12 Nov. 1904.)

The Forrest statue is in New York, having arrived on the steamer
Consuelo. (Daily Herald, Columbia, TN, 4 Feb. 1905.) The permit
issued to move General Forrest from Elmwood Cemetery to Forrest
Park has been given. (Daily Herald, 17 Sept. 1904.) The Forrest
statue has arrived at Memphis, arriving Feb. 24. C. E. Neihaus
was the sculptor. (Daily Herald, 25 Feb. 1905.)

FORREST, Mrs. Bedford, widow of the lamented, distinguished and once brave ex-Confederate cavalry general, died in Memphis January 22. She was a native of Winchester and was with General Forrest throughout the late war. Her maiden name was Miss Mary Ann Montgomery and she sprang from pioneer stock. She was 66 years old. (Maury Democrat, 26 Jan. 1893.)

FORREST, Captain William, brother of General N. B. Forrest, was killed recently in a personal encounter in Texas. (Columbia Herald, 10 Nov. 1871.)

FORREST, Captain, brother of the general, was mortally wounded in fight near Rome, Georgia. (Nashville Dispatch, 15 May 1863.)

FORREST, Col. Jeff, brother of General Forrest, was killed a few days ago in engagement near Tuscumbia, Alabama. (Nashville Daily Union, 15 Nov. 1863.) Col. Jeff Forrest, brother of the general, has died from wounds received in battle on the 5th. (Nashville Dispatch, 25 Dec. 1863.)

FORREST, Belle, courtesan, killed herself a few days ago in Memphis by taking laudanum. (Nashville Daily Union, 9 Oct. 1863.)

FORREST. The Forrest divorce case in New York "which has attracted so much attention" for the last year has been brought to a close, both suing and both charging adultery. The jury found him guilty and gave her $3000 a year maintenance. The editorial comment: "We have seen and heard enough of Mr. Forrest to believe that the obligations of married life set very light upon his conscience. (Clarksville Jeffersonian, Clarksville, TN, 31 Jan. 1852.)

FORSYTH, Daniel, died Sunday of lockjaw on Little Bigby Creek in Maury County; a shingle nail had pierced his foot, he died on the 26th. (Columbia Herald and Mail, 2 July 1875.)

FORT, Mrs. Martha P., 40, wife of E. P. Fort, died on November 23. (Nashville Dispatch, 25 Dec. 1863.)

FORT, Josiah W., tribute of respect on his death by the Boston, Texas, lodge. (Clarksville Weekly Chronicle, 15 Oct. 1858.)

FORT, Charles M., tribute of respect on his death; was member of the No. 1 Independent Deluge Fire Company. (Clarksville Weekly Chronicle, 15 June 1860.)

FORT, Wiley, Esquire, age 99, was baptised by immersion near Bolivar, Tennessee, a few days ago. Editorial comment at the time: "This is rather late and possibly dangerous to begin to take baths." (Maury Democrat, 25 Jan. 1894.)

FOSTER, Mrs. Mary, 70, died July 17 of pneumonia; buried at Zion Cemetery; husband and four sons survive. (Columbia Herald, 24 July 1891.)

FOSTER, Captain Peter, oldest member of GAR, died at Mt. Pleasant, Iowa, on Thursday at the age of 96 years; served in War of 1812, Mexican War and Civil War. (Maury Democrat, 16 Oct. 1890.)

FOSTER, Mrs., the aged lady who was run over on South Market Street last week, has died of her injuries; sent to Franklin for burial. (Nashville Union and American, 3 March 1873.)

FOSTER, B. F., Jr., died Mary 9; son of Colonel B. F. Foster. (Nashville Republican Banner, 10 March 1870.)

FOSTER, General Robert C., eldest son of Honorable Ephraim H. Foster of Nashville, died December 28 in Nashville. (Whig and Tribune, Jackson, TN, 8 Jan. 1872.)

FOSTER, Mrs. Turner S., who died at Marietta, Georgia, a few days ago, was brought to Nashville for burial. (Nashville Republican Banner, 9 Nov. 1869.)

FOSTER, Miss Rena L., youngest daughter of Robert C. Foster, died December 3, in Haywood County; buried in family cemetery at Franklin, TN. (Nashville Republican Banner, 4 Dec. 1870.)

FOSTER, Mrs. Eleanor, died on the 14th near Nashville; wife of Anthony Foster. (Tennessee Watchman, Clarksville, TN, 21 June 1823.)

FOSTER, Mrs. Agness Temple, 53, wife of B. F. Foster, died yesterday. (Nashville Republican Banner, 6 March 1869.)

FOSTER, Bub, died in Kenton, West Tennessee, two weeks ago of Throat affection; son of late Isaac Foster; married Sallie Porter. (Columbia Herald, 22 May 1891.)

FOSTER, Gertie, infant daughter of William F. and Lizzie N. Foster, to be buried today. (Nashville Republican Banner, 7 Sept. 1870.)

FOSTER, Jonathan, 61, died in Clarksville last week; lived in Dickson County and volunteered last July in a company made up in Hickman County. (Clarksville Weekly Chronicle, 20 Dec. 1861).

FOSTER. Last Wednesday last Lt. Col. Foster of the 1st Tennessee Regiment, U. S. Volunteers, was attending to business in Mt. Pleasant, when three brigands of partisan rangers, CSA, galloped into village and fired upon him. One ball struck back of head, but not dangerous; the other in his back is worse. It is feared the colonel will not recover. (Nashville Dispatch, 9 July 1862.)

ATTEMPTED ASSASSINATION OF LIEUT. COL. FOSTER AT MT. PLEASANT. - THE ROSE WATER LAVENDER FOLLY. On last Wednesday, Lt. Col. Foster, of the 1st Tennessee Volunteers, known as the Governor's Guard, rode into Mt. Pleasant, a little village in Maury County, some 12 miles from Columbia, and took his seat in front of the tavern.

While sitting there the notorious desperado, known as Capt. Williams, commanding a company of cutthroats and robbers, known as the Williams' Avengers, rode up with one of his clan and said to Lt. Foster, "God damn you, surrender!" Lt. Foster being unarmed sprang to the door, when Williams fired at him, hitting him in the shoulder and back of the head. He fell, and made several ineffectual efforts to rise, but was so stunned and blinded with blood that he did not succeed, and at last fell upon a bundle to telegraph wire, in which condition he was found and picked up by his men, who were a considerable distance behind at the time of the firing.

Williams' comrade snapped his gun at him once or twice without effect, and the two rode leisurely away. Williams' troop was at the other end of the street and plundered one of our wagons with a sick soldier in it, of some coats, caps, and a musket. A large crowd of the citizens gathered around Lt. Foster, composed of professed neutral men, and some ostensible Unionists, with a large majority of rebels, not one of whom offered to lift up or assist the wounded officer, who was struggling helplessly at their feet and weltering in his blood. They looked on as those of an ox, or perhaps with secret delight.

No one offered any condolence or sympathy whatever. The soldiers would with difficulty be restrained from retailiating on the rebels immediately, but the officers restrained them. Lt. Foster had several of the rebels arrested, who were evidently cognizant of the whole plot, as their actions indicated too clearly for doubt, but they immediately produced papers of protection from Gen. Negley, and grew highly indignant that they should be molested for enjoying the pleasant pasttime of watching the attempted assassination of a loyal Tennessee officer. Should a man of Southern blood be punished for exulting at an assault on one of "Abe Lincoln's hirelings?"

Mr. Thomas, an old and highly respectable Union merchant of that village, has been greatly annoyed of late by the rebels, who have destroyed his property, entered his garden and cut down and pulled up vegetables and perpetrated all sorts of outrages and annoyances. Mr. T. has also received anonymous letters at various times, warning him that he must leave, that no d__d Union may should stay in that 'place, and that if he did stay, they would ride his wife on a rail! What a pleasant Mount Pleasant that place must be and what brave chivalrous fellows the Mount Pleasant chivalry must be. We are beginning to regard some of our Tennessee towns as dead-falls, into which Federal soldiers are placed, to be butchered on the first opportunity by the rebels. We would inquire too about the propriety of giving letters of protection to any neutral man or rebel, under any circumstances...

Lt. Col. Foster of the 1st Tennessee was in Nashville on Sunday... He had his head bound up but is doing well... He had a very narrow escape...having received a ball in the shoulder and another in the back of his head, which ploughed its way between the scalp and skull for some distance. (Nashville Daily Union, 8 July 1862.. (N.B. Foster was called Lt. Foster all through this account, even though he was a lieutenant colonel.)

FOSTER, infant of Mr. and Mrs. Dock Foster of Dark's Mill, Maury County, is not expected to live. (Maury Democrat, 26 April 1894.)

FOSTER, Carter, killed by guerrillas at Conyersville, Henry County, TN, he was murdered after surrender; the land around here is full of guerrillas. (Nashville Dispatch, 3 Oct. 1863.)

FOSTER, Robert S., son of James H. Foster of Nashville, shot himself while climbing a fence and died. (Columbia Beacon, 18 June 1847, quoting the Nashville Banner of 16 June 1847.)

FOULKES, W. J., old and respected citizen of the neighborhood of Centerville, Hickman County, died a few days ago. (Columbia Herald, 14 Nov. 1873.)

FOWLKES, J. D., and B. Biddle, of the 40th Tennessee, CSA, prisoners of war, died on the passage down the Mississippi to Vicksburg to be exchanged. (Nashville Dispatch, 7 Oct. 1862.)

FOWLKES, Dr. Jeptha, died 2 Jan. 1864 in Memphis; editor of the Daily Avalanche in that city. (Nashville Daily Union, 4 Jan. 1864.)

FOWLER, Mrs. Harriet Campbell, wife of F. L. Fowler, died in Lexington, West Tennessee, on June 20; daughter of Col. Charles I. Love of that place. (Nashville Daily Gazette, 16 July 1852.)

FOWLER, Mrs. Caroline Harris, 98, died at her home near Paris, TN, widow of Capt. J. E. Fowler, CSA; sister of Governor Isham G. Harris; was buried in the same burying ground with father and mother, Isham and Lucy Davidson Harris, who died in the 1840s. (Daily Herald, Columbia, TN, 20 Jan. 1909.)

FOX, Major Nathaniel N., of Forrest's Cavalry, was arrested in St. Louis on the 23d ult., and sent to Camp Chase on the 27th. (Nashville Dispatch, 5 Feb. 1863.)

FOX, Dr. J. E., of Marceline, Missouri, has been sentenced to prison for three years for body snatching. (Maury Democrat, 12 Dec. 1895.) The finding of bodies of well known people in the dissecting room of the Kansas Medical College of Topeka caused a mob to form with the avowed intentions of sacking the building. Governor Morrill ordered out a battery and two infantry companies to protect the college. (Maury Democrat, 19 Dec. 1895.)

FOX, Charles, deceased; widow's allowance made for his widow. (Nashville Republican Banner, 24 Dec. 1867.)

FOX, William H. V., died yesterday near Buena Vista Springs. (Nashville Repbulican Banner, 6 Oct. 1870.)

FOX, Hardin, son of Widow Fox, was killed Wednesday of last week when wagon turned over, mashing him. He lived 10 minutes; wife and one child survive; lived near Leftwich in Maury County. (Maury Democrat, Columbia, TN, 13 Dec. 1888.)

FRALEY. A bushwhacker by name of Fraley, tried and condemned by a military commission was hung yesterday at the Pen. He was from White County. He met his unfortuante death with calm courage and composure. (Nashville Daily Union, 21 May 1864.)

FRALEY. STOP THE MURDERER. $1000 Reward. John Step and Solomon Step murdered Martin Fraley, Sr., on October 8 near Wolf's Ferry, Hardin County, TN. John Step is 26, 5 feet 8 or 9 inches tall, dark complexion, dark eyes; Solomon Step is 23 or 25 years old, 5 feet 11 inches. The Steps formerly lived in Cherokee County, Georgia, and it is thought they will make their way back to Georgia or strike for Texas. Signed, Sally Fraley, Henderson G. Fraley, Jackson Fraley, Samuel Lenox. (West Tennessean, Paris, TN, 20 Nov. 1838.)

FRAME, Joseph, was murdered 25 December 1865 by J. N. Watson. (Nashville Republican Banner, 12 Feb. 1868.)

FRANKLIN, Isaac, 20, died December 24 at Lebanon, TN. (Nashville Republican Banner, 29 December 1867.)

FRANKLIN, Andrew, of Burlington, Kansas, is a genuine veteran, but he only recently got on the pension roll. He fought in the War of 1812 and in the Black Hawk War and Mexican War. During the Civil War, being too old for military service, he served as a teamster. He is now 103 years old. (Maury Democrat, 17 May 1894.)

FRANKLIN, P. D., deceased; his estate is insolvent, signed May 27 by Samuel M. Neelley, administrator. (Columbia Herald, 3 June 1870.)

FRANKLE, Gen. Marcus, died Monday; spent most of life in Shelbyville, TN; age 43; was commissary general on Gov. R. L. Taylor's staff during his last administration; formerly lived at Mt. Pleasant and was one of our enterprising Jewish citizens. (Columbia Herald, 27 Aug. 1897.)

FRANSIOLI, Julia, only daughter of Philip and Mary Fransioli, to be buried today. (Memphis Daily Appeal, 9 May 1870.)

FRASCH, John, well-to-do shoemaker, shot himself in head with revolver; lived in Nashville a number of years; married. He was the third German shoemaker who has killed himself herein last 15 months. (Nashville Republican Banner, 18 Feb. 1871.)

FRASER, Colonel Julian, an aged and respected citizen, died 10th of December after a long and painful illness; served many years as representative in the legislature. (Paris Bee, 18 Dec. 1846.)

FRAZIER. Old Gentleman named Frazier still living in Pennsylvania, who was at Braddock's defeat in 1755 under Washington. Probably the last survivor, about 100 years old. He had two brothers, officers, with him, and Braddock ordered one of them to charge upon a particular dangerous point and he refused. Braddock ran him through with a sword and the other Frazier then leveled a musket at Braddock and shot him dead on the spot. (Columbia Observer, 8 August 1834. The reporter of this story doubted that the old man's story was a true one.)

FRAZIER. At Buffalo, New York, on the 27th ult., the frame dwelling
of the Rev. D. Frazier was destroyed by fire. Mrs. Frazier and four
children perished in the flames. (Nashville Daily Union, 4 March
1863.) The post mortem revealed that Mrs. Frazier and children had
been murdered. The Rev. Mr. Frazier is missing and it is feared
he may have been murdered. (Nashville Dispatch, 8 March 1863.) The
murderer of Mrs. Frazier was Douglas Frazier, husband and father.
He has been heard of wandering about the country in an insane condition, but has not been caught. It is feared he may have been perished
of cold. (Nashville Dispatch, 14 March 1863.) Douglas Frazier has
not been found yet, probably perished in the woods, and has been
covered by the deep snow. He was probably insane. (Nashville
Dispatch, 27 March 1863.) The body of Douglas Frazer has been found,
found on the 21st, about 14 miles from Buffalo on the Aurora plank
road. A knife was found near him, open and bloody. The veins of
his neck on the right side had been severed. It is obvious that he
wandered, became exhausted and took his own life. (Nashville
Dispatch, 30 April 1863.) (N.B., Name spelled both ways in these
accounts.

FRAZIER, Colonel Henry S., 55, died yesterday at his home, 2 1/2 miles
out on the Murfreesboro Pike; father of Mrs. Hart Hillman and
James S. Frazier. (Nashville Union and American, 2 July 1874.)

FREDERICK II, King of Denmark, died on November 15, succeeded by
Christian IX. (Nashville Dispatch, 10 December 1863.)

FREEMAN, Fletcher, enrolling officer in Sullivan County, Indiana, was
shot dead on the 18th while riding along a country road. (Nashville
Dispatch, 21 June 1863.)

FREEMAN, Mrs. Catherine P., 40, died yesterday of pneumonia, buried in
Elmwood Cemetery. (Memphis Avalanche, 17 April 1866.)

FRELINGHUYSEN, Theodore, 75, died in Newark, N.J., in the 12th after
a lingering illness; was candidate for vice president in 1844 on
Whit ticket with Mr. Clay. (Nashville Dispatch, 17 April 1862.)

FREYE, Morgan Johnson, infant son of Robert W. Freye, died suddenly
yesterday. (Nashville Union and American, 23 March 1873.)

FRIEDMAN, S., his mangled remains found in Duck River, Maury County,
and his funeral to be held in Nashville. (Nashville Republican
Banner, 5 April 1870.) He was buried yesterday. (Nashville
Republican Banner, 6 April 1870.) Frank Riddle and D. Griffin are
confessed murderersof Friedman. William Riddle, John Riddle and
John Griffin are being tried for complicity in the Friedman murder.
(Columbia Herald, 1 April 1870.) Frank Riddle and De Griffen
are being kept separate in the penitentiary. Riddle is 19, born
in Williamson County, and during the war lived in Hickman County;
4 years ago he moved to Greenfield Bend in Maury County; powerful
build; illiterate; he had two brothers in the Confederate Army and
one died at Nashville during the war. De Griffin is 22, born in
Maury County; lived on Centerville Road, several miles from Gordon's
Ferry's; his family has moved to Leiper's Creek in Maury. (Columbia
Herald, 6 May 1870.) G. D. Griffin, charged with murder; Frank
Riddle, charged with murder; J. G. Leonard, charged with horse
stealing; Pleasant Madison, charged with horse stealing; and Henry
Love, charged with malicious shooting, are in the Maury County jail.
(Columbia Herald, 14 Oct. 1870.) There was an attempted jail break
in Columbia on Tuesday when Frank Riddle and others attempted to
escape. (Columbia Herald, 9 Dec. 1870.) De Griffin has been
found guilty in the Friedman murder and received 15 years. (Columbia
Herald, 22 Sept. 1871.) George D. Griffin and Morris Griffin
sentenced to two years for murder. (Columbia Herald, 6 Oct. 1871.)
Frank Riddle had son Bug Prewett by Lizzie Prewett of the Williamsport area. (Columbia Herald and Mail, 5 Oct. 1877.)

FRIEDMAN'S BODY FOUND. The people in the northwestern portion of
this county, when they become convinced that a foul and atrocious
murder had been committed in their midst, were as one man fired with
indignation, and determined that no stone should be left unturned
in trying to develop the true facts in the case and bring about a
legal punishment of the murderers. Accordingly, they set to work
last week, and searched every nook and corner, cave, sink-hole, and
the bluff in the Greenfield Bend--everywhere the dead body of Samuel
Friedman, an ex-Confederate soldier, might possibly have been
secreted. No success attended their efforts, however, until Saturday morning, when M. Samuels of Columbia, Mr. Levi, of Nashville
and the following named gentlemen of the Williamsport country got
on the right trail in the Greenfield Bend: Buck Revere, Esq.,
George Stockard, Jesse Taylor, Ben Greer, John Walker, W. Revere,
Dr. J. T. S. Greenfield, G. S. Head, A. Head, R. C. Puckett,
A. Southall, Jesse Brown, Judson Gant, colored.

This party took Esther McAnally, a colored woman of the Greenfield
Bend, along with them, as kind of pilot to the place from whence she
had heard the pistol shots proceed. She led them to an elm tree
near her own spring, about two miles from Williamsport, and about
half a mile from the river. Here they found evident traces of the
life and death struggle. The roots of the tree were sprinkled with
blood and Esther told them that the leaves were also bloody at first,
but those had been removed by the frequent rains and people handling
the leaves.

They then started for the river, and when they had gone about a
quarter of a mile, blood was discovered on some oak leaves; and very
distinct, considering the fact that nine weeks had elapsed since it
was shed. The party continued their march until they reached
the river under an immense perpendicular bluff, where they found
a spool of white thread, and a leather strap. All these things were
taken by the party as "proofs strong as holy writ" that the missing
peddler had been murdered and thrown into the river. (N.B., This
spot is still known in 1979 as Peddler's Bluff from this incident.)

Having this settled and firm conviction, they next proceeded to
discover the place where he had been launched into the cold and angry
waters. A sugar tree was discovered blown down into the river, and
it was suggested immediately, as the murderers were known to have
had no canoe. On Sunday morning they went out on the log and
plunged a long hook which had been brought along for dragging the
river, down into the water among the brushes. The first grab brought
up some rotten clothes.

Finally they hooked the two straps with which the feet and head were
tied to the hugh rocks. They could not bring the body to the surface,
however, so very great was the weights that pressed it to the bottom,
and it was determined to cut the tree loose from the bank, in order
the pull the brush out of the way.

Before the log was severed, however, the axe fell into about eight
feet of water. With hesitating a moment--characteristic of the
impulsive and self-sacrificing Southerner--Esquire R. C. Puckett
plunged into the water and got the axe. The tree could not be
entirely removed, and Judson Gant's canoe was brought into requisition.

The body was in 14 feet water, and could not be lifted by all the
hooks combined. Finally, however, the ligature which bound the feet
gave way, and Ben. Greer and Mr. Levi jumped down into the water
and caught hold of the feet. G. W. Stockard, T. M. Walker, Judson
Gant, colored, and Bill, colored, had hold of the body with their
hooks from the canoes, and with a united pull the waters "gave up
their dead."

Moses Samuels, a merchant of this place, examined and recognized

the body, and was so overcome by fatigue, excitment, emotion, and
the poisonous effluvia from the decayed human flesh, that he had a
slight fainting spell. The bluff was so steep, and the dead body
was in such a state of decomposition, that it was taken to Williamsport in Judson Gant, the ferryman's canoe, where an inquest was
held on the bank of the river by Mr. Stockard, Justice of the Peace.

The following verdict was rendered: "A hole, apparently made by a
bullet was plainly visible in the back of the head, near the left
ear; there is also a hole through one of the legs, evidently
also made by a bullet, said hole near the knee joint; a third hole
likewise supposed to have been made by a bullet was also seen near
the lower extremity of the spine. The head and face were perfectly
bare of both flesh and skin, and the front of the neck was also bare
of most of the flesh and skin, yet from a slit in the wind-pipe
and the smoothness of some of the edges of the remaining skin, we
are of the opinion the throat was cut..."

Several weeks ago a reward of $50 was offered by Henry Zibart, a
merchant of Columbia, doubtless at the instance of all the Israelites
of this vicinity, for the discovery and recovery of the body of
Mr. Friedman. After the body was recovered and identified, Mr.
Samuels asked the crowd to say to whom the reward should be
given. The $50 was claimed and ordered to be given to the bereaved
widow of the murdered man.

During the search a report was circulated that the brothers of
Frank Riddle and De Griffin, the alleged murderers were going to
take up the body of Friedman and burn it. This was doubtless all
purely imaginative, however, as no such thing was discovered.

The body after the inquest was over was brought to Columbia, and
placed in Justice Wood's office (during preaching), where many
people came and looked at it. Monday morning it was uncovered and
a horrible sight revealed. The face was a skelton, and the hands
looked as they had been eaten by fish. The corpse was taken to
Nashville, accompanied by Mr. Samuels, and others who had taken such
great interest in its recovery from its watery grave.

Mr. Friedman, the murdered peddler, was a native of Russia Poland,
but had been living in America a number of years. (Nashville
Republican Banner and Columbia Herald, 8 April 1870.)

Frank Riddle who was sentenced to be hung for the murder of Friedman
is said to be a nephew of the notorious John A. Murrell of bygone
infamy. (Columbia Herald, 14 July 1871.)

The Criminal Court have had a hard time this week in getting a jury
for the Riddle case. Frank Riddle, it will be remembered, is
accused of the murder of Friedman, several years ago, and was
sentenced to be hung, but appealed to the Supreme Court and got a
new trial. The Sheriff and his deputies have swept the eastern
portion of the country--the fartherest removed from the scene of
the murder-- in search of twelve men who had not expressed an
opinion on the subject, and hundreds of people were brought to town.
The people got scared and hid out in briar patches, etc., and many
run over into Marshall county. One of those secured says he was
never in Columbia before, although he is 22 or 23 years old. Among
them are old grey-headedmen, whom our oldest citizens, who ought to
know everybody in the county, do not recognize. As the Sheriff
brought the prisoner, who is a great burly, young fellow, from the
jail the other day, his poor old mother hung to his arm, and shed
such bitter tears as only a grief-stricken mother can shed. The
case will probably consume ten days. (Columbia Herald, 8 November
1872.)

RIDDLE'S SENTENCE COMMUTED - After Twenty-two years in the
Penitentiary for Murder. - Among the last long list of convicts

toward whom Governor Buchanan exercised executive clemency was Frank Riddle of this county. Riddle was confined under a life time sentence for a murder committed about 23 years ago. His sentence was commuted so as to expire now. The crime which he has been expiating was the murder of a Jew peddler near Williamsport.

At that time Riddle was hardly grown, therefore, he is but little past middle age now. Those who saw him only a few years ago, say that he is an exceedingly large, robust man, and was employed in the heaviest manual labor in the molding establishment of the penitentiary. He had been in prison longer than any man there and never gave the prison officials the least trouble.

Those of our people who now recollect the facts, say that the peddler was killed in cold blood for his money, and that there were others implicated with Riddle, but all of them except him and one other escaped punishment. The body of the dead peddler was found in Duck River some distance below Williamsport, and it is still known as the Peddler's hole. (Undated clipping from Maury County newspaper in scrapbook owned by compiler.)

FRIERSON, Sam, son of Judge Frierson, died in Louisville, KY, quite sudden Sunday. (Nashville Daily Union, 3 Feb. 1863.)

FRIZZELL, Hugh, clerk of the Davidson County criminal court, died last Monday in Nashville. (Whig and Tribune, 27 April 1872.)

FRY, Clark, infant son of Mr. and Mrs. Clint Fry of Stiversville, is low and not expected to live. (Columbia Herald, 14 August 1896.)

FRY, David, celebrated East Tennessee bridge burner, has escaped from a Southern prison and arrived in Nashville. (Nashville Daily Union, 3 Feb. 1863.)

FRYER, Mrs. M. M., wife of Robert M. Fryer, died in New York City on the 10th; was formerly of Nashville. (Nashville Union and American, 15 Nov. 1874.)

FULCHER, Mrs. Mary B., wife of John W. Fulcher, age 33, died on the 3d. (Nashville Dispatch, 5 April 1863.)

FULCHER, John R., age 2 years 5 months, son of John W. and Mary B. Fulcher, died on the 23d. (Nashville Dispatch, 24 Sept. 1863.)

FULLER, Captain, Confederate commander of the gunboats Cotton and Queen of the West, died recently in hospital near Sandusky, Ohio. He asked for sisters to come to see him but they refused and would not attend his funeral. They objected to "placing his rebellious bones be side of his loyal father's grave." (Nashville Dispatch, 25 Sept. 1863.)

FULLER, Mrs. C. A., to be buried in Nashville Cemetery today. (Nashville Dispatch, 22 August 1863.)

FULLER, ___, the longtime pilot of Noah's Ark, is dead; died in Charleston, S. C., of yellow fever; he married Mrs. Palmer after he left here (Columbia). "A fine specimen of a carpetbagger." (Columbia Herald, 22 December 1871.)

FULLER, Miss Olive, age 103, is the oldest single lady in the United States; lives at Marston's Mills, Mass. (Nashville Dispatch, 22 April 1862.)

FULLER, Frank Anderson, infant son of S. P. and Olive C. Fuller, died on the 21st (Nashville Republican Banner, 23 June 1868.)

FULLER. The family of the Rev. Arthur B. Fuller of Boston, chaplain to the Massachusetts Regiment, who was killed at Fredericksburg,

Virginia, has had several tragedies. Eugene Fuller, one of his sons was drowned on a voyage from New York to New Orleans in 1859; his wife died 1859; and Margaret Fuller, Countess of Ossoli, perished in shipwreck on Fire Island near New York in 1850; her husband and child also lost with her. (Nashville Dispatch, 14 Jan. 1863.)

FUSON, James H., Company L, 5th Tennessee Cavalry (Federal), was killed 22 Feb. 1864 on Calf Killer near Sparta. (Nashville Daily Union, 24 Feb. 1864.)

FUSSELL, Mrs. Sammella, daughter of Mrs. Dr. James Overton, will be buried on Friday. (Nashville Republican Banner, 19 Feb. 1869.)

FUSSELL, Henry B., died at his home Wednesday morning; born 8 January 1805 in Granville County, NC; came to Maury County in 1812; Cumberland Presbyterian and a charter member of the church. (Columbia Herald and Mail, 17 December 1875.)

GAILOR, Frank M., formerly connected with the Memphis Avalanche, was killed in the Battle of Perryville. (Nashville Daily Union, 16 November 1862.) Frank Gailor, Memphis editor, died when shot pierced his brain 8 October 1862 at Perryville; he and Capt. L. A. McClung of Florence, Alabama, led a charge; McClung fell dangerously wounded and Gailor tried to help McClung from the field. He was buried in a churchyard near the field and a broken wheel of a gun carriage was used as a headstone. (Memphis Avalanche, 9 January 1866.)

GAINES, General F. G., died yesterday morning of paralysis and was buried in the Butler Cemetery. Memphis Appeal, August 13. (Clarksville Jeffersonian, 3 September 1851.)

GAINES, General, his grave is still without a suitable tablet or monument. (Memphis Daily Appeal, 23 December 1869.)

GAINES, Bishop, of the African Methodist Church in Georgia, was once a slave and owned by the brother of Bob Toombs. (Maury Democrat, 21 November 1891.)

GAITHER. The funeral of Mrs. Mary D. Gaither, daughter of the late General Zollicoffer, was a fitting tribute to departed worth. (Columbia Herald, 24 Feb. 1871.)

GALBREATH, Mary Jane, wife of Polk Galbreath, age 37, died Thursday in the Andrews neighborhood and buried in the Hardison Cemetery. (Columbia Herald, 9 December 1899.)

GALLOWAY, infant son of W. T. Galloway, died near Hurricane last Sunday. (Columbia Herald and Mail, 3 September 1875.)

GALLOWAY. Three Forks of Wolf, TN, Fentress County. On the 29th ult. Widow Galloway, two daughters and a small daughter, age 5 or 6, were foully and brutally murdered. The murderer intended to plunder as she had recently received $300 back pay, being her husband's bounty, who died in service. The murderer is believed to be one Grubber, who has escaped. (Memphis Daily Appeal, 7 December 1868.) A man named Longston in Fentress County killed the lady Mrs. Galloway, her daughter, and a two year old child; one child survived. (Memphis Daily Appeal, 20 December 1868.)

GALLOWAY, Mrs. Martha E., consort of Lewis G. Galloway, died at residence of W. L. Murfree Tuesday in Rutherford County; daughter of David Dickenson. (Nashville Daily Gazette, 5 March 1850.)

GALLOWAY, James, age 80, died in Maury County last week. (Whig and Tribune, Jackson, TN, 2 May 1873.)

130

GALT, Alexander, died of small pox in Richmond; noted Virginia sculptor; he was the first Southerner to establish reputation at home and abroad in statuary. The full length figure of Jefferson at the University of Virginia is his work. (Nashville Dispatch, 24 February 1863.)

GAMEWELL, Melville F., 25, died at Water Valley, Mississippi, September 5 of congestion of the brain; only son of late Thomas W. and Mary A. Gamewell of Jackson, Tennessee. (Whig and Tribune, 13 September 1873.)

GANT, Mrs. Martha J., consort of John I. Gant, died at Water Valley, Mississippi, on 8 May 1873; born 17 January 1838. (Columbia Herald, 6 June 1873.)

GANTT, Colonel George, of Memphis, 74, died at Cooper's Well, Mississippi, last Saturday, July 24; one of the foremost members of the bar; had been ill for months and went to health resort as a last effort; formerly lived in Columbia. (Columbia Herald, 30 July 1897.)

GANTT. President Lincoln has signed a petition exempting E. W. Gantt of Arkansas from the penalty of treason, which he incurred for accepting a commission as Brigadier General in the rebel service. He has been reinstated in his rights. He is brother of George Gantt of Maury County. (Nashville Dispatch, 13 December 1863.)

GARCIA, Ignacio Francisco de La Cruz, said to be the oldest man in the United States, died at Los Angeles, California, last week at the age of 117 years. He was a native of Sinaloa, Mexico, and came here when he was 25 years old. He had documents to support his claim. (Maury Democrat, 25 March 1897.)

GARDNER, Mrs. Malinda E., funeral to be held today. (Nashville Republican Banner, 15 March 1870.)

GARESCHE, General, Rosecran's chief of staff, was killed by a solid shot which took off the whole of the head above the mouth. (Nashville Dispatch, 2 January 1863.) Lt. Col. Gareshe, was killed 31 December 1862, at Murfreesboro and Major Garesche was killed 29 December 1862 at Vicksburg. Thus at different points, nearly a thousand miles apart, two brothers have lost their lives within two days of each other. (Nashville Dispatch, 25 January 1863.)

GARFIELD, Brigadier General James A., has reported to Rosecrans for duty. (Nashville Daily Union, 28 January 1863.) (N.B., James Abram Garfield, 20th President of the United States, died 19 September 1881.) A monument to James A. Garfield was unveiled last week at Wilmington, Delaware. (Maury Democrat, 6 June 1895.) Mrs. Garfield is rich, besides having $5000 a year as widow of a president, her daughter, Mrs. Stanley Brown, has purchased fine lot in a Washington suburb upon which she will build a house and where it is believed Mrs. Garfield will make her residence with her. (Florence, Ala., Times, 8 August 1890.)

GARFIELD, Thomas A., only living brother of the president is living on a farm 16 miles from Grand Rapids. He is 70 years old and is lame with rheumatism. In the house opposite lives his son James A. Garfield, also a farmer, who was recently elected justice of the peace. (Maury Democrat, 13 September 1894.)

GARNER, John, the noted horse thief, lately taken by force from an officer of the law in Alabama, was arrested in Nashville Thursday. He will be taken back to Alabama for trial. (Memphis Daily Appeal, 1 February 1869.) John Garner, horse thief, recently captured in Middle Tennessee, has stolen over 500 horses in the last 40 years; arrested 14 times; twice sentenced to be hanged; and once sentenced to be shot. He has served several terms in jail. (Memphis Daily Appeal, 7 February 1869.) The Garner family was outraged at Somerville (Morgan County, Ala.), during the Civil War and the son went

131

on the warpath. (Memphis Daily Appeal, 3 April 1870.) The Garner and Bean clan have been driven from Morgan County, Alabama--they were served notice by 70 citizens. (Memphis Daily Appeal, 12 April 1870.)

GARNET, Mrs. Colonel James, died at home in Albemarle County, Virginia, on May 11 at the age of 60 years; she was sister of late Mrs. Rebecca Gant of Columbia. (Maury Democrat, 11 June 1891.)

GARRETT, Mrs. Elisha, died new Lewisburg, TN, on the 16th of paralysis. (Whig and Tribune, Jackson, TN, 29 March 1873.)

GARRETT, John J., Company F, 156 Illinois Volunteers, while attempting to get upon train at Tullahoma, TN, after it started, fell back on track and was literally cut in two. (Nashville Daily Union, 29 June 1865.)

GARRETT, J. W., 75th Indiana, while on steamboat Liberty was checking to see if his gun was loaded and placed the muzzle in his mouth to blow in it. The weapon fired, the ball went through his head, and killed him instantly. His remains were sent home. He had never married. (Nashville Daily Union, 31 January 1863.)

GARRETT, Alvin D., 59, died yesterday at the hospital of the insane and buried in the family burying ground on White's Creek. (Nashville Republican Banner, 12 August 1870.)

GARRISON, B. P., was wounded in the thigh by a soldier, who was shooting at a negro, and died yesterday; wife and one child survive; buried at Elmwood Cemetery. (Memphis Avalanche, 9 January 1866.)

GARLAND, Dr. Landon C., died at Nashville last week, was President of Alabama State University during the time of the war. (Maury Democrat, 21 February 1895.)

GARLINGTON, Maria, died at Churchville, suburb of Chattanooga, at the age of 110 years; she could remember when George Washington was president. (Maury Democrat, 28 June 1888.)

GARTH, Colonel Lewis, noted rebel partisan, was shot and killed by Captain Wall, CSA, on the 8th at Columbia, TN. (Nashville Dispatch, 11 July 1863.)

GARVIN, Peter, 65, was buried on the 12th at the old Catholic Cemetery in Memphis; he died of yellow fever which he had in 1867. (Memphis Daily Appeal, 13 November 1869.)

GATES, Brigadier General, died this afternoon after short illness in New York, age 80. (Memphis Daily Appeal, 8 October 1868.)

GATEWOOD, well known as a guerrilla in Tennessee during the war, was recently killed in an affray at Waco, Texas. (Nashville Republican Banner, 19 March 1871.) Gatewood is still operating around Chattanooga and on the 28th Colonel Hawkins, 7th Tennessee Cavalry, had brush with guerrillas near Union City. (Nashville Daily Union, 2 May 1865.) (N.B., His name is found in one paper as John Gatewood.)

GATLIN, Lee, infant son of W. D. and Mary Gatlin, age 10 months 29 days, died on October 7. (Nashville Republican Banner, 16 October 1868.)

GATRELL, James, of Memphis, was mortally wounded in Desoto County, Mississippi, on the 20th ult. by Green Blythe of Desoto County. (Murfreesboro News, 8 December 1858.)

GAUT, Mary L., daughter of John C. and Sarah A. Gaut, died June 12 in Nashville at the home of General James Hickman. (Nashville Daily Union, 13 June 1865.)

132

GAVESCHE, Colonel P. Baudney, formerly of Confederate Ordnance Department and leading lawyer of St. Louis for many years, died on Sunday last; married daughter of Louis McLane, Secretary of State in President Jackson's cabinet and sister of the wife of General Joe E. Johnston. (Memphis Daily Appeal, 24 November 1868.)

GAY, Robert, deserter from 71 Indiana Volunteers, was shot at Indianapolis, Indiana, on March 27 by order of court martial; he was taken prisoner at Richmond, Kentucky, paroled, and voluntarily went over to the Confederates, and returned to Federal side as a spy. (Nashville Dispatch, 31 March 1863.) Robert Gay, Company D, 71 Indiana Volunteers, shot as spy March 27; had enlisted in Clay County, Indiana; charged with desertion and for taking oath to South. (Nashville Daily Union, 31 March 1863.)

GAY, Tra, an old gentleman fell into a post hole in Keene, New Hampshire, on the 18th ult., and not discovered until daylight, dead. (Nashville Dispatch, 2 December 1863.)

GAYLORD. Substitutes in war are not new. Elijah Gaylord of New York, who lived to be over 100, engaged one in the Revolutionary War for a cow, one blanket, a few farming utensils, and 12 bushels of wheat per month. (Nashville Dispatch, 25 Sept. 1863.)

GEARY, Mary, deceased; administrator to her estate appointed. (Nashville Republican Banner, 29 August 1869.)

GEE, Miss Rose Porter, died on the 7th ult. in Davidson County; Methodist. (Nashville Dispatch, 5 April 1863.)

GEE. Charles Ward has been arrest at Vaughan's Gap, 12 miles from Nashville, for the murder of George Gee in February 1865. (Memphis Avalanche, 21 December 1866.)

GENTRY, Meredith P., died on November 2 near Nashville. (Memphis Avalanche, 4 November 1866.)

GEBHART, Frank, 24, soldier, was fatally shot in breast at Ash Barracks yesterday by Lt. Andrew Mahoney; the verdict of the inquest was that it was an accident. (Nashville Republican Banner, 24 October 1869.)

GENTRY, David, infant son of Mr. and Mrs. W. B. Gentry, 14 months, died on September 16 after a painful illness. (Nashville Republican Banner, 17 September 1870.)

GERALD, Moses, Texas soldier, drowned Tuesday at Trice Landing, Montgomery County; in Bass' company, Colonel Gregg's Regiment from Harrison County, Texas. (Clarksville Weekly Chronicle, 15 November 1861.)

GERMAN, William, of Livingston, Overton County, was forcibly taken from his home on Wednesday last and hanged; served as member of the 25th Infantry, CSA; his brother Lum German was arrested by Federals just before the close of the war upon the charge of being a bushwhacker and found guilty and paid the penalty. "What do our Radical friends think of this last act by the Ku-Klux, whom they charge to be rebels?" (Memphis Daily Avalanche, 16 January 1869.) Bill German was hung for violating rules of Ku-Klux; his brother Lum was a desperado who infested Overton county during and after the war and was found guilty of murder of a citizen named Hays and hung; no CSA service was known about. (Memphis Daily Avalanche, 17 January 1869.)

GERONIMO is now a gardener at a military station at Mobile where he is held captive and is permitted to act as a tribal justice of the peace. (Florence, Ala., Times, 5 November 1892.)

GERRARD, Dr. R. A., of Chattanooga has been jailed for bigamy in Chattanooga; had 10 wives. (Maury Democrat, 21 November 1889.)

GERRY, Miss Emily L., probably the only surviving child of a signer of the Declaration of Independence, Elbridge Gerry, was 92 years old on April 14 in New Haven, where she has lived half a century. (Maury Democrat, 10 May 1894.)

GHOLSON, John, was buried today in Memphis. (Memphis Daily Appeal, 4 March 1870.)

GIBBONS, Samuel G., died on the 14th inst. in Centreville at the reisdence of his brother-in-law Mr. John Philips, in his 38th year of age, leaving affectionate wife and large circle of relatives and friends to mourn him. Baptist minister. (Western Mercury, Columbia, TN, 20 July 1830.)

GIBSON, Frank, near Chattanooga found a bombshell in field where it has lain since the war. He carried it home to his wife who thoughtlessly placed it on the stove where it exploded. Mrs. Gibson is fatally injured. (Maury Democrat, 1 March 1888.)

GIBSON, Janie Adams, 5 years 8 months, second daughter of Thomas and Lucy Gibson, died 1 January 1878, on Woodlawn farms, Maury County. (Columbia Herald and Mail, 11 January 1878.)

GIBSON, Private James A., Company B, 1st Tennessee Cavalry, received a mortal wound on Monday and died of wounds inflicted by Arthur Morris and William Lavelle, the latter of Company F, 72nd Infantry. Louisville item. (Nashville Daily Union, 11 January 1863.)

GIBSON, Mrs. Fanny, died on Tuesday, wife of William R. Gibson, Esquire. (Tennessee Watchman, Clarksville, TN, 14 June 1823.)

GIBBS, General George W., 82, one of the oldest citizens of West Tennessee, died Wednesday at Union City. (Memphis Daily Appeal, 16 May 1870.)

GIDCOMB, John William, died July 6 in Goshen area of Maury; County Mason. (Columbia Herald, 17 July 1896.)

GIERS, Honorable C. C., one of the best photographists in the South, died in Nashville last week; born on the Rhine in Germany; elected to the Tennessee General Assembly and represented Tennessee at the Vienna Exposition. (Columbia Herald and Mail, 8 June 1877.)

GILBERT, Major Thomas, formerly of Wheeler's Cavalry, was killed by Dr. Pomp Westmoreland, surgeon, 51st Tennessee Infantry, last Thursday near Bethel, Giles County; had been former partners in the mule business. (Nashville Republican Banner, 18 February 1868.)

GILBERT, L. A., to be hanged at Fayetteville on 29 May 1876 for the murder of William Johnson, a blind magic-latern showman; he received his sentence with laughter. (Columbia Herald and Mail, 14 April 1876.)

GILCHRIST, Charles, of Boston, who came to Columbia in January for his health, died at the home of his sister Mrs. W. A. Ruttle Saturday; taken to Boston for burial. (Columbia Herald, 22 May 1891.)

GILL, George Wiley, age 4, died 20 October 1861; infant son of J. M. and E. V. Gill. (Clarksville Weekly Chronicle, 25 October 1861.)

GILLESPIE, Captain R. A., native of Blount County, TN, moved 1831 to Morgan County, Alabama, volunteer in the Florida War, then moved to Texas and was in Captain Jack Hays' Texas Rangers, fell in the battle of Monterey October 1846; was 23 when he was killed; brother of the Rev. James H. Gillespie of Denmark, TN; buried within the fort and upon the eminence which his valor won. (Columbia Beacon, 9 December 1846.)

GILLIAM, America, wife of William G. Gilliam, daughter of J. E. and
B. F. Tarpley, died Wednesday. (Nashville Republican Banner, 9
October 1868.)

GILLIAM, L. P., deceased; in memoriam to his memory in the paper.
(Nashville Republican Banner, 23 January 1870.)

GILLIHAN, Sergeant L. H., Company A, 4th Tennessee Cavalry (Federal),
of Bradley County, TN, killed about 29 February 1864 in a Mississippi
expedition out of Memphis. (Nashville Daily Union, 2 March 1864.)

GILLMORE, William, brakeman on the Nashville railroad, fell from train
Sunday morning at Rocky Hill and was killed. (Nashville Daily
Union, 28 February 1865.)

GIPSON, Mrs. Henry, 82, has been blind several years and is very low.
(Maury Democrat, 28 February 1895.) Mrs. Sarah Gibson died Friday
at Southport in Maury County; nearly blind; aunt of the Rev. J. G.
Gibson. (Maury Democrat, 7 March 1895.)

GIST, Mrs. Hettie, deceased, her noncupative will has been admitted
to probate. (Nashville Republican Banner, 16 October 1874.)

GIVEN, Captain, of the gunboat Benton, died of wounds received in
recent attack on Haynes Bluff. (Nashville Dispatch, 14 January 1863.)

GLADDEN, General, died April 15 of wounds received on the 6th. (Nashville Dispatch, 25 April 1862. N. B., No army identification given.)

GLASCOCK, Thomas Hume, in his 21st year, died 14 January 1870, second
son of E. R. Glascock Esquire. (Nashville Republican Banner, 16
January 1870.)

GLASCOCK, Maggie, 12, died Tuesday, daughter of E. B. Glascock.
(Nashville Republican Banner, 6 January 1870.)

GLASGOW, Mrs. John, murdered by Josiah Cook near Dover, TN, on Saturday
they were neighbors; she had been sent to care for Cook's wife
after the wide had given birth. He took gun and shot her; he is
probably insane and it is thought he might be mobbed. He claims to
be a preacher from Kentucky. (Dickson County Press, 4 June 1884.)

GLASS, David St. Clair, died Saturday in Maury County after a long and
painful illness; wife and infant child survive; buried Clopton
Cemetery. (Daily Herald, Columbia, TN, 24 April 1896.)

GLAZE, Marshal, and John McMullen, of Roane County, West Virginia, were
murdered by 30 guerrillas on Spring Creek. Glaze was a soldier in
ill health, waiting on his discharge papers. Jim Greathouse, Wylie
Dick, and Balus Devers were with the guerrillas. (Nashville
Dispatch, 4 October 1863.)

GLEAVES, Mrs. Carrie D., is to be buried today. (Nashville Republican
Banner, 23 February 1869.)

GLEAVES, Mary Eliza, eldest daughter of H. A. and Eliza Gleaves, granddaughter of late William Tannehill, died 26 December 1862.
(Nashville Daily Union, 8 Jan. 1863.)

GLENN, William, age 106, died, one of the oldest citizens of Williamson
County. (Whig and Tribune, Jackson, TN, 27 January 1872.)

GLENN, child of Nan Glenn, died Monday. (Columbia Herald and Mail,
8 October 1875.)

GLENN, George W., 28, died on the 6th; clerk in city recorder office;
died of disease of the liver; born in Nashville, the youngest son
of the late Simon Glenn. (Nashville Dispatch, 7 April 1863.)

GLOVER, William, died in Edgefield on Tuesday of measles; son of James and Almira E. Glover, age 2. (Nashville Daily Gazette, 27 July 1852.)

GLOVER, Captain Jack R., died at Aylmer, Ontario; his brother Alexander was with him. (Paris Gazette, 20 March 1878.)

GLOVER, Joshua, deceased; his heirs notified that his land is to be sold for taxes. (Weekly Review, 6 May 1848.)

GOAD, White, son of Lewis Goad of Knob Creek, Maury County, died in Nashville on the 17th and buried at father's home. (Columbia Herald, 3 July 1891.)

GOAD, Mrs., died Sunday at Dark's Mill; lived in Williamson County but came to Maury County to be with her daughter, Mrs. Chandler, on her deathbed. She was buried at Lasting Hope Cemetery. (Maury Democrat, 17 October 1895.)

GOAT, William. Dead body found on the banks of Duck River below Columbia in a decomposed condition; papers showed he was a carpetbagger named William Goat, known as Billy. (Columbia Herald, 7 February 1873.)

GODSHALL, Captain Sam C., of Nashville, died in that city on the 5th from cholera; he was a gallant officer in the 11th Tennessee Confederate Infantry during the war. (Memphis Avalanche, 9 October 1866.)

GODWIN, Colonel Aaron S., died at Godwin Station, Maury County, on Wednesday at 5:30 in the afternoon, age 73, and buried in family burying ground; survived by wife; had no children. (Columbia Herald, 11 September 1896.)

GODWIN, Reddick, died on Friday, the 30th, 4 miles from Linden; native of Williamson County and had lived in Perry County a number of years. (Linden Times, 5 February 1880.)

GOE, Louis, a Frenchman of Buena Vista Springs, committed suicide. His wife was insanely jealous and drove him to the rash act. She berated him after he went to bed, and he leaped from bed and sent bullet through brain. (Nashville Republican Banner, 18 December 1868.)

GOFF, Albert, died February 1 of congestion at Vicksburg, Mississippi; brother of Mrs. G. A. Kinzer of Sawdust Valley. (Columbia Herald, 13 February 1891.)

GOFF, Major A. F., 65, died suddenly yesterday at his home Glencliffe, 5 miles from Nashville on the Nashville and Chattanooga Railroad; born in Giles County and had lived in Davidson County 25 years; served in legislature in 1837; and in 1836 he volunteered to fight in the Creek Nation in Florida. (Nashville Union and American, 9 December 1874, 10 December 1874.)

GOFFE, William, died in Boston a few days since; lineal descendant of William Goffe, one of the judges who sentenced Charles I to death; he was the last male descendant of this man. (Nashville Dispatch, 11 June 1863.)

GOLAY, Mrs. Marie died yesterday of injuries received at the stampede at the execution on Friday; she was thrown down and run over by a wagon; age 60. James Galvin and Moody were hanged at a public execution on August 20. (Memphis Daily Appeal, 25 August 1869.)

GOLLADAY, John W., son of J. S. and Elizabeth S. Golladay, died in Logan County, Kentucky, on the 20th. (Nashville Dispatch, 29 April 1863.) James W. Golladay died on 20th at Logan County, KY. (Nashville Daily Union, 29 April 1863.)

GOLDSTON, John H., funeral to be today in Nashville. (Nashville Dispatch, 8 June 1862.)

GOMEZ, John, the veteran Everglades hunter, age 122, the oldest person in the United States, drowned near Fort Myers in Florida. (Daily Herald, Columbia, TN, 25 July 1900.)

GOOCH, Shelby, brakeman on the construction train of the Edgefield and Kentucky Railroad, was crushed to death yesterday at State Line; aged between 40 and 50; lived at Cedar Hill; wife and several children survive. (Nashville Republican Banner, 21 November 1867.)

GOOCH, Claiborne, a very prominent young student at the University of Nashville died suddenly at his home in Smyrna, Rutherford County, last week. (Whig and Tribune, Jackson, TN, 24 February 1872.)

GOOCH, Henry, was killed recently near Smyrna; one Scruggs, colored, is suspected. (Nashville Union and American, 28 May 1874.)

GOOD, Charles, veteran of the Mexican War, of Plattville, Wisconsin, celebrated his 100th birthday a few days ago. One of the guests was his younger brother, only 96, of Missouri. (Maury Democrat, 29 March 1894.)

GOODALE, Lt. W. S., Company H, 4th Maine Volunteers, was killed at Fredericksburg on 13 December 1862. His sword was recently surrendered by an officer of the Louisiana Tigus at an engagement of Rappahannock Station. (Nashville Dispatch, 10 December 1863.)

GOODLET, Sallie D., wife of A. G. Goodlet, daughter of John J. and Mildred R. Hooper of Cheatham County, died on the 22d in Nashville. (Nashville Daily Union, 23 May 1865.)

GOODLET, William A., son of the late Dr. A. G. Goodlet, died on the 2d of a lingering illness. (Nashville Republican Banner, 3 March 1869.)

GOODLETT, Miss Alison, daughter of Dr. A. Goodlett, died in Davidson County. (Tennessee Watchman, Clarksville, TN, 7 Sept. 1821.)

GOODLETT, Mrs. Eliza T., relict of late Rev. A. G. Goodlett, died yesterday. (Nashville Republican Banner, 22 January 1871.)

GOODLOE, James M., esteemed citizen of Maury County, died week before last in Mt. Pleasant. (Whig and Tribune, Jackson, TN, 10 Feb. 1872.)

GOODMAN, Lloyd, son of Henry Goodman of Concord, while walking along with an open knife, stumbled, and the knife blade inflicted stomach wound and he died Tuesday night, Maury County. (Columbia Herald, 1 Jan. 1897.)

GOODRICH, Mrs. Jane H., 54, died on the 10th at the Tennessee Rolling Works, Kentucky, after a short and painful illness. (Nashville Dispatch, 16 August 1862.)

GOODWIN, Asa, oldest man in Alabama, age 108, died March 1; born in Henry County, Georgia, in 1807; lived since 1829 in Alabama and Mississippi; buried at Westover, Alabama. He was formerly a famous wild turkey hunter and killed his last one at the age of 101. (Columbia Herald, 5 March 1915.)

GOODWIN, Amaziah, of Lyman, Maine, was 100 years old on February 16 and died June 16 at Dover; he was going to visit Bunker Hill on the 17th. During the Revolution, he was on guard duty at West Point when the unfortunate Andre was conveyed across the river and took charge of the boat until the return of the officers and soldiers who had charge of that officer. (Nashville Dispatch, 30 June 1863.)

GOODWIN, Grant, notorious guerrilla chief of Trigg County, KY, was
captured by Federal cavalry a few days ago. He was killed as was
his cutthroat crew. "Blessed relief to our friends in the vicinity
where they ravaged so long." (Nashville Dispatch, 8 August 1862.)

GOOSEMAN, Henry, shot himself in head, believed to be a fatal wound,
yesterday. His creditors hounded him for payment of debt. He
recovered. (Nashville Republican Banner, 17 January 1868.)

GORDON, Mrs. Isabella, wife of late William Gordon, mother of William
H. Gordon, to be buried today in Nashville. (Nashville Dispatch,
24 January 1863.)

GORDON. Confederates killed in various skirmishes and fights: Captain
Gordon, E. Niles, and Lt. James A. Smith of Louisville at attack
on stockade at Edgefield Junction; James Hughes, Henry Lewis, David
Moss, James Renfro, Lewis Chandler, and John Waller of Clark County,
KY. (Nashville Dispatch, 29 August 1862.)

GORDON, Mr., who lives 14 miles southeast of Holly Springs, Mississippi,
is one of 27 brothers, all of one father and mother. He is the only
one living and is 70 years old. Most of them lived to maturity and
they were of North Carolina. (Memphis Daily Appeal, 20 April 1870.)

GORDON, Eugene, of Santa Fe, Maury County, died in the penitentiary of
cholera; he was in a jail break not long ago. (Columbia Herald,
25 July 1873.) Eugene Gordon sentenced to 21 years for horse
stealing--"He is a bad man." (Columbia Herald, 14 March 1873.)

GORDON, Mrs. Joseph W., of Nashville, died yesterday after a long
illness; daughter of the late Dr. J. D. Winston; married less than
two years; formerly Jennie Winston. (Nashville Union and American,
16 August 1874.)

GORDON, Mrs. Captain John A., and little daughter of Gayoso, Missouri,
died when a can of lamp oil exploded and burned them recently;
Captain Gordon is a nephew of Bolling and Powhattan Gordon of
Maury County. (Columbia Herald, 1 March 1872.)

GORDON, Senator, says that when he was wounded at the battle of Sharps-
burg, he thought his head had been carried away by a cannon ball.
It then struck him that if his head was gone, he could not think, and
eventually he discovered that the would was not so serious after all.
(Florence, Ala., Times, 13 Feb. 1892.)

GORHAM, Doc, was killed in an affray in Russellville some time since.
Young Murray, who was engaged in the same affray, was shot from his
horse in Adairsville, KY, a few days ago and killed. (Nashville
Dispatch, 27 August 1862.)

GORIN, ___, formerly of Russellville, KY, drowned near Eddyville, KY,
recently while on collecting tour; $40,000 found on his person;
drowned while crossing the backwater. (Clarksville Weekly Chronicle,
15 Feb. 1861.)

GORING, Herr, oldest inhabitant of Hamburg, Germany, died recently at
106 years; was with Napoleon in 1812 at Moscow; watchmaker by trade.
(Maury Democrat, 2 October 1890.)

GORUSH, William K., died yesterday of consumption in Memphis, was orderly
sergeant of the Brown Guards; from Hardin County. (Columbia Herald
and Mail, 30 June 1876.)

GOSNELL, Timothy, was shot five times, and Moody Dryman, shot once
above the left eye, both of Greene County, TN; their bodies found in
Dutch-Ditch, Louisville, KY, on the 28th. They were rebels but tried
to join the Union troops and were being sent to military prison.
They tried to escape and shot. The men who shot them have left:

Capt. Robert C. Carter, David Bush, Burton S. Barket, and James Campbell of the 4th East Tennessee Infantry. (Nashville Dispatch, 5 May 1863.)

GOSS. Udderzook has finally been sentenced for the murder of Winfield Scott Goss; received death sentence. (Nashville Union and American, 3 July 1874.)

GOUAN, Captain A. R., who fell leading his command at Chickamauga, was brought to Holly Springs, Mississippi, for burial Thursday last. (Memphis Avalanche, 21 December 1866.)

GOULD, Aunt Fanny, died in Tuscaloosa, Alabama, in August at the age of 105. (Nashville Dispatch, 4 October 1863.)

GOULD, Lieut., who attempted to shoot General Forrest and was severely stabbed by him, has since died. (Nashville Dispatch, 3 July 1863.) (N.B., Andrew Wills Gould is buried in City Cemetery in Nashville and a few years ago his headstone was broken and illegible and could only be identified by the footstone which had A. W. G. on it. The dates read: A. W. Gould, born 12 July 1840, died 26 June 1863. He was originally buried in Rose Hill Cemetery, Columbia, and was buried in Nashville on 9 February 1866.)

GOWDEY, Thomas, died on the 29th in Nashville, age 67 years 9 months 28 days, (Nashville Dispatch, June 10, 1863.) Jeweler; Mason; lived here for many years. (Nashville Dispatch, 27 June 1863.)

GOWER, Edward H., 27, died 17 August 1867 in Davidson County at the home of Edward H. East. (Nashville Republican Banner, 18 August 1867.)

GOWER, A. C., funeral to be held this morning. (Nashville Republican Banner, 16 November 1869.)

GRADY, Mrs., of Quincey, Indiana, was so badly burned on the 10th by her clothes taking fire from a stove that she died the next day. (Nashville Dispatch, 21 May 1862.)

GRAHAM, Thomas, 53, died 15 March 1863. (Nashville Dispatch, 19 March 1863; Nashville Daily Union, 19 March 1863.)

GRAHAM, Mrs. Thomasella, died August 10 at Pinewood, Hickman County; consort of Samuel L. Graham; husband and two children survive. (Nashville Republican Banner, 12 August 1870.)

GRAHAM, John, once a tailor in Columbia, died in Memphis on the 27th; age 63; paralysis. (Columbia Herald and Mail, 2 April 1875.)

GRANBURY, Hiram B. Carried back Home. Last Monday, Dr. J. N. Doyle, the mayor of Granbury, Texas, reached Columbia, and at once called at The Democrat office, stating that he has been deputised to super-intend the removal of General Granbury's remains, as first suggested by Capt. R. D. Smith and published in The Democrat, to which editorial comment has since been made in these columns on three different occasions...

Maj. Wm. Polk and Capt. R. D. Smith were at once notified and arranged to give Dr. Doyle all needed assistance. Maj. Polk took the distinguished visitor to his hospitable home at Ashwood for the night, and on Tuesday morning they met Col. Yeatman, Capt. Smith and Mr. Frank G. Smith at the Cemetery in St. John's Churchyard, where the gallant soldier had rested since he gave his life's blood for a cause which he believed to be just on the memorable battle-field of Franklin twenty-nine years ago. As was to have been expected, the skeleton only remained, though the casket, which was made of walnut and evidently a handsome piece of work, was in a remarkable state of preservation.

The little group around the open grave were much impressed with the tenderness and care with which Dr. Doyle performed his labor of love; every bone was carefully handled; every lock of hair and bit of clothing was carefully preserved; the wreath with the three stars, wich was the insignia of the office of the Brigadier General was intact; every button was collected, and when one of them was cleaned and shown to the doctor, he remarked that that made the identification of the remains absolutely certain, for upon the button could be distinctly seen "Waco Guards" with the star of Texas in the centre. The doctor agreed that Capt. Smith should take one of these buttons for the Athenaeum museum.

Upon returning to Columbia, the following named gentlemen of the Leonidas Polk Bivouac acted as guard of honor: Maj. Wm. Polk, Capt. D. Smith, Maj. Jno. T. Williamson, Capt. H. L. Hendley, Capt. W. B. Dobbins, Capt. W. J. Whitthorne, Capt. Reece. Also Dr. W. A. Smith, Jas. B. Goodlett, Dr. J. H. Harvey, and Dr. Robt. Pillow.

As the time was limited between the arrival of the remains and the departure of the train, but few of our Confederate Veterans know of this important event, otherwise a much larger delegation would have been present.

The body was sent by express to Fort Worth, Texas, there to remain until the final preparations are completed which we understand will be about as follows:

The memorial exercises and burial are to take place at Granbury, Texas, the town named in honor of this distinguished soldier on the 30th of November, the anniversary of the battle of Franklin, where Gen. Granbury was killed. The funeral train will start from Fort Worth which is about 40 miles east of Granbury on that day and be composed of large delegations from Waco, Dallas, Sherman, and other points in Texas. We have been promised the full program.

The marble headstone which had been placed over the grave at Ashwood by kind friends, was shipped yesterday by freight and will be used in connection with the shaft the patriotic citizens will erect at Granbury... (Maury Democrat, 2 November 1893.)

FALLEN HEROES. Through the kindness of Maj. Will Polk, The Democrat presents this week a list of Confederate soldiers buried in the graveyard at St. John's Church, Ashwood:

Lieut. Harper, Company K, 30th Ala. Regiment, wounded at Columbia, Tenn., Nov. 20, 1864, died at St. John's Church hospital Dec. 6, 1864.

J. A. Seymore, Barber's Co., Forrest's Old Reg't, Fayette Co., Tenn., died Nov. 21st, 1864.

Col. Robert F. Beckham, chief of artillery of Lt. Gen. Stephen D. Lee's corps, born in Culpeper County, Va., May 6, 1837; mortally wounded at Columbia, Tenn., Nov. 29th 1864, died Dec. 5th, 1864.

Joel Dubose wounded in battle at Columbia, Tenn., Nov. 29th, 1864, died Dec. 1864.

Andrew J. Comer, of Capt. Higg's Scouts, Forrest's cavalry, killed near Ashwood on the morning of the 29th Nov. 1864.

Brig. Gen. O. F. Strahl of Confederate artillery, born in Ohio, June 30th, 1834; killed at Franklin, Tenn., Nov. 30th, 1864. (N.B. This grave has been moved since this 1894 article was published.)

Lieut. J. H. Marsh of Hardeman County, Tenn., aid to Gen. Strahl., killed at Franklin, Tenn., Nov. 30th, 1864.

Col. Young of Texas, killed at Franklin, Tenn., Nov. 30th, 1864.

Lieut. Welborn S. McMaury, born in Columbus, Ga., Nov. 24th, 1843, died Feb. 25th, 1864.

Gen. Pat Cleburne, killed at Franklin, Tenn., Nov. 30th, 1864, was buried here after several years was removed to Helena, Ark., his old home.

Gen. Granbury, who was killed at Franklin, Tenn., Nov. 30th 1864, was also removed last year to his old home, Granbury, Texas.

There were also other Confederates buried in private plots:
George S. Martin, born Jan. 3rd, 1840, died Sept. 23rd, 1863.
George M. Pillow, born July 19th, 1839 in Maury Co., Tenn., died Aug. 30th, 1872.
Brig. Gen. L. E. Polk, died Dec. 1st, 1892, age 59 years.
Maj. Campbell Brown, died Aug. 31st, 1893, aged 58.
(Maury Democrat, 18 October 1894.)

GRANGER, General Gordon, so well known in Memphis as a Federal soldier, was united in marriage in Evansville, Indiana, on Wednesday last to Maria Letcher, daughter of Dr. Joseph Letcher of Lexington, Ky. (Memphis Daily Appeal, 8 July 1869.) General Granger has given notice to a large number of women of the town that they must leave Nashville. They are demoralizing the army, and that their removal is a military necessity. They are to be sent north it is said. If so, a fresh importation may be looked for by the return train. (Nashville Dispatch, 8 July 1863.)

GRANNATTA. "The Italians are discussing the advisability of pensioning Mrs. Maddalena Grannatta, a lady of 57, who lives near Nocera, 12 miles from Naples. Her husband has been dead 10 years but during the 19 years they lived together as man and wife they had 62 children born to them, 59 being males. Eleven different times in 9 years triplets were born and on three different occasions, four boys were announced and once there were four boys and a girl." (Columbia Herald, 2 April 1897.)

GRANT, Dr. H. G. W., died at Salem, Franklin County, on the 19th, age 49, of congestion of the lungs and dropsy of the heart. (Nashville Republican Banner, 27 March 1868.)

GRANT, Mrs. Mary, age 68 years 7 months 26 days, died 30 June 1858, wife of Zachariah Grant; born 7 November 1787; on the first Sunday in October 1840 got religion; she was married 27 December 1820. (Clarksville Weekly Chronicle, 23 July 1858.)

GRANT, Ulysses. The remains of General Grant will have been in the temporary tomb built for them ten years next summer. If the contractors fail not, the grand and impressive monument that New York is now slowly building will be finished in December of the same year. It is explained that the work is slow because the quarrying of the great granite blocks is slow and difficult. The subscription fund of over $400,000 has been drawing about $15,000 a year in interest. (Maury Democrat, 8 November 1894.)

On the 27th ground will be broken in New York for the monument to General Grant. (Maury Democrat, 23 April 1891.) General Grant's cottage at Long Branch cost $110,000. (Memphis Daily Appeal, 18 August 1869.) Grant's regiment, the 21st Illinois, will hold a reunion at Effingham on September 19 and 20, and the general has promised to be present. (Erin Review, Houston County, 10 Sept. 1881.)

General Grant and lady stole the plate of Mr. Cox at Holly Springs, no doubt about it or denied that the theft was committed and no restitution has ever been made and there is no likelihood that there will ever be... The law cannot touch him now and conscience never did bother such cattle. (Memphis Daily Appeal, 21 September 1869.)

General Grant has received his legacy from John Minor Botts, a ring, whose signet is made from the filings from the bell of Independance Hall. (Memphis Daily Appeal, 27 April 1869.)

The little cabin in Fairmount Park, Philadelphia, once used by General Grant as headquarters, is going to ruin from neglect. (Maury Democrat, 28 Nov. 1889.)

Around 20,000 people witnessed the memorial exercises at Grant's Tomb on May 31. Governor McKinley delivered the address. (Maury Democrat, 6 June 1895.) The Society of the Army of the Tennessee will ask Congress to appropriate a sum for a statue to General Grant in Washington. Strangely enough there is none to him, Sherman, or Sheridan at the capital. (Maury Democrat, 7 Nov. 1895.)

Mrs. U. S. Grant is seldom seen these days. Since the death of the general, she has been quite a recluse. (Florence, Ala., Times, 15 Aug. 1891.) The highest government pensions being paid out to date are to Mrs. George B. McClellan, $2000, and Mrs. Ulysses S. Grant, $5000. (Florence Times, 31 Jan. 1891.) Mrs. General Grant has an intense love for diamonds. The stones in her ears are as large as gooseberries and very fiery. (Florence Times, 19 Sept. 1891.)

Mrs. U. S. Grant is quoted by Southern papers as having recently given utterance to this remarkable sentiment in Tampa, Florida: "I loved the South, for I was reared in a Southern state, Missouri, and I hardly knew which side to go with. But the general went with the North and I went with him." (Maury Democrat, 7 March 1895.)

Jessie B. Grant, the President's son, is one of the owners of a silver mine in Sonora, Mexico, and there he passes a great portion of his time. He is a quiet, unassuming fellow and quite prominent. (Florence, Ala., Times, 28 March 1891.)

One of the successful cattle raisers of Wyoming is Frank Sartoris, a brother of Nellie Grant's husband. He is a plainsman of thirteen years experience. (Florence, Ala., Times, 9 Jan. 1892.)

Mrs. Nellie Grant Sartoris is engaged to marry H. K. Douglas, adjutant general of Maryland and an ex-Confederate soldier. By her marrying again the fortune left her by her English husband will be forfeited to her children. (Maury Democrat, 21 June 1894.) Nellie Grant Sartoris will forfeit an annual in come of $25,000, and yet the change comes cheap. (Maury Democrat, 19 July 1894.)

GRANT, Jesse, postmaster of Covington, Kentucky, died at his home Sunday last of general debility; nearly 80 years old; father of President Grant. (Whig and Tribune, Jackson, TN, 5 July 1873.)

GRANT, Mrs. Rhoda, 87, died November 11 at home of her daughter Mrs. F. C. Akin. (Nashville Union and American, 12 November 1874.)

GRAVES, George W., of Ascension Parish, Louisiana, 52, died July 18; his estate was worth $156,000. He was native of Clarke County, Virginia, and in 1837 came to Louisiana. Before the war he was worth $1,500,000. His estate is within 15 miles of New Orleans. (Memphis Avalanche, 1 October 1867.)

GRAY, ___, was executed at Murfreesboro December 26 as a traitor and thief. (Nashville Dispatch, 28 January 1863.)

GRAY, Mrs. John, of St. Louis, wife of one of the victims of last week's explosion, is dead. She had only been married a short time and she died virtually of a broken heart. She asked that her husband's funeral be postponed so she could be buried with him.

142

She died April 1 and both were buried in the same grave. (Maury Democrat, 5 April 1888.)

GRAY, Old Man, was shot by his son in his house two miles northwest of old Jefferson in Rutherford County. (Nashville Union and American, 21 Aug. 1874.)

GRAY, Elva More, daughter of J. F. and M. M. Gray, 16 months, died in Nashville; she had been baptized 11 June 1875. (Columbia Herald and Mail, 5 May 1876.)

GRAY, A. T., Esquire, died Sunday of general debility in District 10 of Maury County. (Columbia Herald and Mail, 9 April 1875.)

GREEN, Dr. Myles J., secretary of the Masonic Grand Lodge of Alabama, died on the 27th ult. in Montgomery, Alabama. (Florence, Ala., Times, 9 July 1892.)

GREEN, Virginia, wife of Samuel Green, to be buried today. (Nashville Dispatch, 26 May 1863.)

GREEN, Rev. Lewis W., D. D., President of Center College, Kentucky, age 58, died on the 26th ult. He was one of the ripest scholars in Kentucky. (Nashville Dispatch, 5 June 1863.)

GREEN, James, War of 1812 soldier, died at his home in Bedford County two weeks ago. (Whig and Tribune, 1 June 1872.)

GREEN. After the battle of Newbern, NC, George W. Green, a volunteer from Cooperstown, Oswego County, was sent out with others to bury the dead. Among bodies he and his helpers picked up was Rufus Petty from the same county. The body was placed on stretcher and carried to grave, and as it was being lowered, Green thought he would search body to see if there were anything that might be sent home to his friend. In so doing, he ran his hand up under the vest and discovered that the heart was faintly beating. His helper also felt and heard it. Petty was subsequently carried to hospital and recovered. He returned home as did Green and both men were in Albany last Sunday. (Nashville Dispatch, 12 October 1862.)

GREEN, Harry, author of the catchy song "Mister Johnson, Turn Me Loose" died in Nashville last week. (Columbia Herald, 22 Oct. 1897.)

GREEN, Mrs. Charity, celebrated her 103d birthday in Home of Aged Colored Women at Boston the other day. (Maury Democrat, 14 Feb. 1895.)

GREEN, George W., 25, died in Hopkinsville, KY, a few days ago of typhoid fever; formerly student at Stewart College. (Clarksville Weekly Chronicle, 14 Feb. 1862.)

GREEN, Mrs. J. F., funeral notice published. (Nashville Republican Banner, 31 May 1870.)

GREEN, Mrs. G. B., wife of the clerk and master, died on the 14th of dropsy of the heart at Camden, Benton County. (Nashville Union and American, 18 Jan. 1873.)

GREEN, Colonel Jeremiah George, 82, died May 8, in Nashville; was a purser once in the U. S. Navy; came from Massachusetts in 1839 and established the Nashville Union. (Maury Democrat, 14 May 1891.)

GREEN, W. J., died suddenly Wednesday while being shaved by Stump the barber. (Columbia Herald, 25 Feb. 1870.)

GREEN, Grace, daughter of Mr. and Mrs. W. Jordan Green, died at her home on the Nashville Pike Sunday, age 4; croup; buried Rose Hill Cemetery. (Columbia Herald, 20 Nov. 1899.)

GREENE, Henry, was murdered by Robert Austin in White County, TN.
He had invited Austin to spend the night. After firing the first and
fatal shot, as Greene's body was falling Austin steadied it with one
hand and drove a bullet through the dead man's brain, blood and
brains splattered over both. Still holding the body, Austin sent a
third ball through the heart, then got on his horse and rode away.
(Columbia Herald and Mail, 11 Feb. 1876.)

GREENER, Nicholas, worthy citizen of this place, died Monday night;
fell into a cellar or well that had been left unrepaired in a public
place. (Nashville Daily Union, 12 March 1863.)

GREENFIELD. Departed this life on the 11th November 1826, Capt. Thomas
T. Greenfield, in the 81st year of his age, at the residence of his
son Dr. G. T. Greenfield. He was a native of Maryland, but for
many years a resident of Maury County, Ten. The deceased was one
of the earliest patriots of the revolution; he was never known
though the course of a long life, to lift his hand against his
fellowman except in self-defence, and in defence of his country.
His family have the consolation to know he died a Christian, in full
expectation of enjoying a better and brighter world. (Calvinistic
Magazine, Volume III, page 385.) (N.B. This man is buried in the
Greenfield family cemetery, Greenfield Bend, Maury County, TN.)

GREENFIELD, Rebecca, died on the 3d on the Nolensville turnpike, wife
of Wesley Greenfield, Esquire. (Nashville Daily Union, 5 August
1863.)

GREENFIELD, Miss Carrie M., died 8 March 1869 at home of uncle the
Rev. J. M. Sharp. (Nashville Republican Banner, 9 March 1869.)

GREENFIELD, Gabe, died at his home near Williamsport Sunday of typhoid.
(Maury Democrat, 17 October 1895.)

GREENHALGE, Mrs. Ann, 61, died September 30; her remains were placed
in a vault at the City Cemetery. (Nashville Dispatch, 4 October
1863.)

GREENLAW, Alonso, son of W. B. Greenlaw of Memphis, was wrecked on
an island in the Indian Ocean. He narrowly escaped death and is
now on his way home. (Nashville Republican Banner, 4 March 1871.)

GREENWOOD, A. C., died in Nashville, Company F, 100th Illinois Volunteers,
grave number 2,634. (Nashville Daily Union, 14 June 1863.)

GREENWOOD CEMETERY. Since Greenwood Cemetery in New York was first
laid out as a burying ground in 1840, 89,867 bodies have been
interred within its limits. (Nashville Dispatch, 21 June 1862.)

GREER, James, of Clarksville, died on Thursday last. (Tennessee Watchman, Clarksville, TN, 19 April 1823.)

GREGG, James, of near Screamville, Maury County, was fatally shot by
a desperado named Swan; trouble originated from some Ku-Klux activity
(Nashville Republican Banner, 8 January 1871.)

GREGG, J. H., and John W. Jackson of Tipton County, TN, got into
difficulty, one mile from Covington; Gregg was killed, died with
four pistol balls in him. (Nashville Republican Banner, 28 June
1868.)

GREGORY, Mrs. Anna, age 111 years 8 months, died in Pulaski, Michigan
recently; she was born 1757 in Dutchess County, New York. (Memphis
Daily Appeal, 1 June 1869.)

GREGORY, Levi Pitts, made crazy by a fright during the war, hanged
himself in Dixon Springs, TN, recently. It was an unusual hanging
as he was 63 feet up in the tree and hanging in the forks when

discovered. (Memphis Daily Appeal, 21 October 1868.)

GREGORY, Mrs. L. C., died of consumption at her home near Glenncliff on April 1. (Nashville Republican Banner, 4 April 1868.)

GREGORY, Elise Trudeau, 3 years 6 months, daughter of J. M. and Ella H. Gregory, died August 14; buried Rose Hill Cemetery, Columbia. (Maury Democrat, 22 August 1895.)

GREGORY, Dr. F. H., 89, died on the 18th in Monroe County, TN. (Columbia Herald, 27 Sept. 1872.)

GREGORY, Captain Tom, one of the best known men in Tennessee, died at Winchester last Sunday; he was a gallant Confederate, being in the force at the memorable charge on the stone fence at Gettysburg. (Maury Democrat, 12 Jan. 1893.)

GREIG, Maggie J., died September 9. (Nashville Union and American, 10 Sept. 1874.)

GREIG, George, 52, died on the 31st; had lived here 20 years. (Nashville Dispatch, 1 June 1862.)

GRESHAM, J. A., 73, died of heart disease; lived 3 miles north of Columbia; uncle of Robert G. Irvine; buried Rose Hill. (Daily Herald, Columbia, TN, 24 April 1896.)

GRESHAM, Mrs. Sarah, 60, died on the 25th ult.; widow of Benoni Gresham. (Columbia Herald, 2 May 1873.)

GRESHAM. The remains of Walter Q. Gresham were placed in a vault at Oakwood Cemetery, Chicago, last Thursday. Crowds lined the streets along which the body was borne. (Maury Democrat, 6 June 1895.)

GRIDER, A. J., fell between the cars on 19 September 1867 and died of his injuries. (Nashville Republican Banner, 15 August 1868.)

GRIFFITH, Miss Susan C., 88, died near Mt. Pleasant. (Columbia Herald, 27 Dec. 1899.)

GRIFFITH, Francis E., wife of Benjamin B. Griffith, died 4 June 1878 in Paris, Texas, of pneumonia and paralysis. (Columbia Herald and Mail, 28 June 1878.)

GRIFFITH. Colonel J. G. Griffith of Nashville spent several weeks near Mt. Pleasant with his brother John J. Griffith, who died last Friday in his 65th year. (Columbia Herald and Mail, 31 May 1878.)

GRIFFITH. "A villain of no common stamp." A. F. Griffith, U. S. Army chaplain, was caught taking money from the letters of soldiers. While being taken by guard to the military commission, broke away, jumped into the river, and drowned. He had brother in Chester County, Pennsylvania. (Nashville Daily Union, 8 April 1865.)

GRIFFITH, Colonel Dan F., 32, of the 38th Indiana, died at New Albany Wednesday last of typhoid. (Nashville Daily Union, 21 Feb. 1865.)

GRIFFITH. "An Editor Killed." We learn that Mr. J. O. Griffith, lately of the firm of the Nashville Union and American office, who fled from this city on the arrival of the Union Army, was killed in Decatur, Ala., a few days ago by some of his old party. An attempt was made by the rebels to force him into the service upon which difficulty arose that resulted in his death. He was one of the most active of the secession leaders of this city and has perished by that very power which he helped to create. Nashville Union. (Chattanooga Daily Rebel, 21 June 1863, quoted in the Maury Democrat, 22 March 1897. N.B. The account of Mr. Griffith's death was in error as he was still living when this was published in 1897.)

GRIGS, Burto, an old man, living on the Maury-Giles county line near Ettaton, fell recently, burst his skull, and was killed instantly. (Maury Democrat, 28 June 1894.)

GRIGSBY, Matilda, wife of Ben, died June 27; no children; her only daughter preceded her several years ago; buried Spring Hill Cemetery; age 86; had been a Methodist 54 years. (Columbia Herald, 26 June 1896, 10 July 1896.)

GRIMES, J. L., was shot and killed by his brother-in-law Robert D. Ricketts, former sheriff of Maury County, at Mt. Pleasant. (Whig and Tribune, 16 Nov. 1872.)

CRIMES, Miss Sue, died at the home of her brother-in-law, John N. Meroney on Tuesday; buried at Knob Creek Cemetery. (Columbia Herald and Mail, 26 Oct. 1877.)

GRIMES, infant son of Mr. and Mrs. G. L. Grimes of District 2, Maury County, died last week. (Columbia Herald and Mail, 12 Nov. 1875.)

GRIMMITT, Benjamin, Esquire, old and respected citizen of Hickman County, died on Swan Creek on the 17th. (Columbia Herald and Mail, 27 Feb. 1874.)

GRINDSTAFF, David, sergeant, Company K, 5th Tennessee Cavalry, killed 22 Feb. 1864 on Calf Killer near Sparta. (Nashville Daily Union, 24 Feb. 1864.)

GRINSTEAD, Robert, 91, venerable and esteemed citizen of Lexington, Kentucky, died there on the 18th. (Nashville Dispatch, 24 March 1863.)

GRISHAM, Peter H., corporal, Company F, 2d Kentucky Cavalry, Thomas Corps, at Murfreesboro, left home June 1861 in Washington County, East Tennessee, and went by rail and foot to Liberty, Kentucky, where he enlisted in army of U. S. Volunteers for three years; since when he has neither heard from home, parents, relatives there. He heard recently his brother William Madison Grisham and many others escaped and joined the Union Army in Kentucky. He will greatly appreciate hearing from anyone who can give him information on his family. (Nashville Daily Union 18 Feb. 1863.)

GRIZZARD, James H., committed suicide and his body was recovered yesterday. (Nashville Republican Banner, 29 October 1868.) Henry Grizzard, 26, butcher, committed suicide by jumping off the Suspension Bridge yesterday. (Nashville Republican Banner, 28 October 1868.)

GRIZZARD, James, born 1789 in North Carolina, died 20 Feb. 1868 at Tullahoma; Mason; tribute of respect published by Tullahoma lodge. (Nashville Republican Banner, 11 March 1868.)

GROVER, Mrs. A. P., of Hohenwald, Lewis County, died March 29 at Terre Haute while on a visit. (Maury Democrat, 4 April 1888.)

GROVES, Major Rice, chief of artillery on Breckenridge's staff, died Sunday from wounds received at Chickamauga. (Nashville Dispatch, 7 October 1863.)

GROSKIO (later Gioskios), James, 41, died suddenly yesterday of heart disease; German citizen. (Nashville Republican Banner, 31 December 1870.)

GUENGEL, August, old miser of Dubuque, Iowa, found dead a day or two ago; he died from want of proper food and other comforts of life; had not taken a warm meal for months; leave property estimated at $3000. (Erin Review, 25 March 1882.)

GUILD, Florence, 14 months 5 days, died yesterday; daughter of Walter
  J. and Bettie A. Guild of Gallatin. (Nashville Union and American,
  21 August 1874.)

GUITEAU, Charles J., who shot Garfield, is said to be buried in Shipp's
  Bend in Hickman County; according to legend he was rescued from jail
  by political sympathizers; taught school in Hickman County and buried
  there. (Nashville Tennesseean, 6 October 1968)

GUNN, Dr., CSA, buried at Elmwood Cemetery, Memphis, on Thursday.
  (Memphis Daily Appeal, 15 August 1868.)

GUNNELLS, John R., died June 11 of tuberculosis on Bear Creek in Maury
  County. (Columbia Herald, 13 June 1873.)

GUNNING, James, died in his tinshop last night; addicted to whiskey;
  native of Ireland; aged 50; had three children by his first wife;
  buried Centerville Cemetery. (Columbia Herald and Mail, 10 May
  1878.) Jimmy Gunning died last week in Centerville, good workman.
  (Columbia Herald and Mail, 3 May 1878.)

GUNSOLLIS, John, Sr., 75, died last Friday in St. Louis; native of
  Beaver County, Pennsylvania; first person who piloted steamboat
  from Pittsburg to Cairo. For many years he was in keelboating. His
  brother James was also a steamer captain. He retired 30 years ago
  from the river. St. Louis Democrat, Jan. 12. (Nashville Dispatch,
  16 Jan. 1863.)

GURLEY, John A., died near Cheviot, August 19. Cincinnati dateline.
  (Nashville Dispatch, 20 August 1863.)

GURNEE, Ida May, 4 years 6 months, daughter of S. H. and F. A. Gurnee,
  died on the 6th in Nashville. (Nashville Dispatch, 8 May 1863.)

GUSLER, George, mate, who was murdered on the Clyde last week, was a
  native of Virginia and his parents live in Woolwine, Virginia. His
  sweetheart Miss Birdie Troimer has attempted to commit suicide when
  she heard of his death. (Clifton Mirror, 23 December 1904.)

GUTHRIE, Mrs. Nancy J., wife of Capt. R. A. Guthrie, died on Sunday
  last; daughter of John L. Webb, Esquire. (Linden Times, 5 February
  1880.)

GWALTNEY, Laura Ann Forncrook, the daughter of William D. and Sally
  Forncrook, born 6 July 1841, died 3 December 1899 at Henryville,
  Lawrence County, TN. She was married on 25 November 1865 at
  Oconomowoc, Waukesha County, Wisconsin, to John T. Gwaltney, born
  13 January 1846, in Virginia. Laura Ann Forncrook was first married
  to Julius Rhody, born 1837, died 8 August 1864 while in the Union
  army serving in St. Charles, Arkansas. Laura Ann Forncrook is
  buried in Henryville Cemetery, Henryville, Lawrence County, Tennessee.
  (From pension and family records of Polly C. Warren, Columbia,
  Tennessee.)

GWALTNEY, Rev. Luther, of Edgefield District, South Carolina, has been
  elected pastor of Rome, Georgia, Baptist Church. (Memphis Daily
  Appeal, 6 November 1868.)

GWIN, Berry, 83, died Monday; native of Virginia. (Nashville Republican
  Banner, 13 March 1874.)

HACKLEMAN, Brigadier General, fell mortally wounded at Corinth, Mississippi, on October 3. (Nashville Dispatch, 14 October 1862.)

HACKSTER, Henry, accidently shot himself at Decatur, Alabama, and died
  Monday. (Nashville Republican Banner, 5 November 1868.)

HACKNEY, Nellie, 5, daughter of Ann Hackney, died on the 19th. (Columbia Herald, 21 March 1873.)

HACKNEY, Sarah Emily Catherine, 12, died on the 7th in Nashville, daughter of W. N. and M. E. A. Hackney. (Nashville Dispatch, 8 November 1862.)

HADGEN, Oscar P., of Springfield, Illinois, shot and killed Mrs. Willie Jones, a widow. He then shot and killed himself. (Lincoln County Herald, 13 June 1894.)

HADLEY, Mrs. Kit, her funeral to be at Lockridge on Sunday; only survivor of the family of Robert Lockridge, who founded the Camp Ground and pioneer of the Cumberland Presbyterians of Carter's Creek. (Columbia Herald, 6 June 1873.)

HADLEY, Dr. John L., 83, died on the 26th. (Nashville Republican Banner, 28 December 1870.)

HADLEY, Lucius R., 43, died in Obion County of consumption; half-brother of Henry and Kit Hadley and Mrs. Wash Miller of Maury County; died on the 6th; wife and three daughters survive. (Columbia Herald and Mail, 19 June 1874.)

HADLEY, Julius, servant of Dr. Hadley's, age 35, died on the 9th; suffered greatly with flux; was greatly esteemed by Hadley family. (Nashville Republican Banner, 20 August 1870.)

HAGAN, Anna B., infant daughter of John C. and Margaret Hagan, died on the 19th. (Nashville Dispatch, 20 December 1863.)

HAGAN, James, Jr., editor of the Franklin Review, died at Beach's Hotel, three miles from Franklin on the 25th ult. He was 42. (Clarksville Jeffersonian, 1 October 1851.)

HAGAN, Major W. H., of Davidson County, died December 2 at Col. L. Howe's in Memphis. (Memphis Avalanche, 9 December 1866.)

HAGAN, Thomas, died suddenly in Franklin a short time ago from excessive intoxication. (Columbia Herald, 13 December 1872.)

HAGAN, Annie B., daughter of John C. and Margaret Hagan of Nashville, died May 21 in Huntsville, Alabama; buried in Nashville. (Nashville Dispatch, 24 May 1862.) (N.B. See obituary above for her sister.)

HAGAN, John C., well known engineer, died of cholera yesterday. His engine on the Chattanooga railroad was run by his brother-in-law and draped in mourning. (Nashville Union and American, 19 June 1873.)

HAGEY, Amanda, 24, died on the 7th of consumption; daughter of Mrs. Elizabeth Hagey. (Nashville Dispatch, 19 October 1862.) Miss Amanda A. C. Hagey, daughter of John and Elizabeth Hagey, 24, died 17 October 1862. (Nashville Daily Union, 19 October 1862.)

HAGGARD, Robert, died of congestion Tuesday at the pauper asylum, where he had been an inmate for 20 years. He possessed the esteem of the keeper and his associates. (Nashville Union and American, 15 August 1874.)

HAILE, Mrs. Evaline J., 58 years 24 days, wife of Thomas J. Haile, died on the 6th in Nashville. (Nashville Daily Union, 7 April 1865.)

HAILE, G. M. Dallas, 25 years 10 months, son of Thomas J. Haile of Edgefield, died the 23d of consumption. (Nashville Republican Banner, 24 August 1870.)

HALE, Tom, and Josh Hale, of Giles County, visited Maury County near
New York. (N.B. Today known as Scott's Mill.) Tom became very
drunk and unmanageable and was brandishing a pistol. Josh took
Tom's pistol away and Tom then took a trace chain and tried to kill
his brother. Josh shot him to save his life and was not even tried
as it was a plain case of self defense. Josh took the corpse home
for burial. (Columbia Herald and Mail, 22 December 1876.)

HALE. The venerable widow of the late Nathan Hale, formerly of the
Boston Advertiser, died Sunday in Brooklyn; she was sister of
Honorable Edward Everett. (Memphis Daily Appeal, 21 November 1866.)

HALE, Edward E., was shot and killed last Saturday by Henry Shroeder
at Mackville, Mississippi, on the Sunflower River. (Columbia Herald
and Mail, 28 July 1876.)

HALEY, Jeff, died at Bailey Springs, Alabama, a few days ago of dropsy.
(Columbia Herald and Mail, 3 Dec. 1875.)

HALEY, George Washington, died Thursday of last week after a long
illness; wagonmaker by trade; buried at Rose Hill; his leg was
amputated some time ago. (Maury Democrat, 10 January 1889.)

HALEY, James, was seen crossing railroad bridge when the cars started
across and he was seen trying to get out of the way. He fell into
the river and drowned on the 16th. (Nashville Dispatch, 17 June
1863.)

HALEY, Henderson L., deceased, notice to the creditors signed by A. C.
Pritchett, administrator. (The Republic, Paris, TN, 24 June 1853.)

HALISY, Colonel D. J., 6th Kentucky Cavalry, was murdered Wednesday
near Lebanon by rebel officers. He was shot after he formally
surrendered; shot through the head. His body was recovered.
(Nashville Dispatch, 6 January 1863.)

HALL, F. A., old citizen of Tipton County, committed suicide by hanging.
(Nashville Union and American, 8 July 1873.)

HALL, Maggie Ramsey, age 1 year 9 months 8 days, died at Boscobel family
residence in Edgefield on Sunday, November 1; infant of Dr. F. M. and
Maggie H. Hall. (Nashville Union and American, 3 November 1874.)

HALL, Judge Samuel, one of the oldest residents and most prominent
politicians in Southern Indiana, died at his residence in Princeton
on the 11th. (Nashville Dispatch, 16 May 1862.)

HALL, Addie, daughter of W. C. and C. H. Hall, died December 13 in
Edgefield, age 21. (Nashville Republican Banner, 14 December 1870.)

HALL, E. Taylor is on trial in Murfreesboro for killing William Hall.
(Nashville Union and American, 6 December 1873.)

HALL, Widow of General William, died at her home one mile from Castalian
Springs last Thursday, age 87. (Nashville Union and American, 8
March 1873.)

HALL, John and Burrell Smith (c), were hanged at Murfreesboro on the
20th ult. for the murder of Major H. S. Pugh on 16 May 1879.
(Linden Times, 4 March 1880.)

HALLECK, Jabez, is 103 years old and lives in Waterville, Oneida County,
New York, and is the grandfather of Major General William H. Halleck.
(Nashville Dispatch, 28 August 1863.)

HALLIBURTON, John H., well known citizen of Rutherford County, died last
week. (Whig and Tribune, Jackson, TN, 28 October 1871.)

HALSTEAD, James W. C., 24, died in railroad accident; brakeman with only
7 days experience; cars passed over legs and he lived several hours;
brought to Columbia for burial. (Maury Democrat, 3 Feb. 1887.)

HAM, youngest child of Mr. and Mrs. Henry Ham of Suck Island has died
of whooping cough. (Columbia Herald and Mail, 24 July 1874.)

HAMBLEM, Squire W. H., 75, of District 18, died yesterday at 11 a.m.;
born in Prince Edward County, Virginia; came to Davidson County
in 1808 and settled on Dry Creek; was with General Jackson in the
War of 1812; Methodist; magistrate for many years. (Nashville
Republican Banner, 18 Nov. 1869.)

HAMLET, Mr., Indiana soldier, died at Hospital No. 4 at Nashville two
weeks ago and the body returned to Rochester, Fulton County,
Indiana, and buried. Some Copperheads, 25 in number and armed,
went to his grave, dug up his coffin, and chopped it open with an
axe. They thought it contained fire-arms. Body was reburied by
widow. (Nashville Daily Union, 1 March 1863.) F. C. Hamlet, 29th
Indiana Volunteers, was buried New Castle township, Indiana; the
rumor got out that his body was not brought home but that the coffin
contained arms. His brother Henry protested. The grave robbers
were named Orange Meredyth, George Emmons, B. F. Montgomery, Wash Horn,
Israel Dilley, George Baxter, Alex Barrett, James Coplen, James
Nellens, Robert Coplen, Israel DeBolt, Ellis Strosnyder, Peter
Sanna, Moses Nellens, and Martin Duett. (Nashville Daily Union, 7
March 1863.)

HAMBLIN. Hannibal Hamblin's grandfather had 17 sons, the eldest of whom
were named respectively, Europe, Asia, Africa and America. (Florence,
Ala., Times, 29 August 1891.) (N.B. Hannibal Hamlin was vice
president of the United States from 1860 to 1864.)

HAMLIN, Dr. T. B., of Edgefield Junction, died Sunday morning; born
24 June 1810 Windom, New York and named Theodore Burnam; he was
left orphan at an early age; in 1835 moved to Wytheville, Virginia;
practiced dentistry; Presbyterian; Mason. (Nashville Union and
American, 26 May 1874.) Mary Hamlin was appointed executrix of his
estate. (Nashville Union and American, 29 May 1874.)

HAMILTON, B. S., funeral to be held Sunday with Masonic honors.
(Nashville Republican Banner, 29 May 1869.)

HAMILTON, Alexander, who lived in and around Williamsport, Maury
County, for a long time, died Saturday near Lick Creek and Duck
River in Hickman County. His horse got into quicksand; had trouble
getting out; died all alone during the night of exertion and
cold. (Columbia Herald and Mail, 23 March 1877.)

HAMILTON, Mattie Eason, 19 months, died last night of summer complaint,
second daughter of the Rev. A. L. and Dollie M. Hamilton; buried
City Cemetery. (Clarksville Weekly Chronicle, 17 August 1860.)

HAMILTON, Alcium Eason, infant son of the Rev. A. L. Hamilton, died
in Huntsville, Alabama, within the last three days. (Clarksville
Weekly Chronicle, 24 May 1861.)

HAMILTON, Hardy, was hanged in Rome, Georgia, on June 20 for killing
Joe Lee, a Chinaman, in February. (Maury Democrat, 27 June 1889.)

HAMNED. Freebooters under Captain Rumbaugh in Cocke County, 100 strong,
not subject to any command, are stealing, robbing, setting fire to
homes of Union soldiers. They severed ears from head of a Mr.
Kelley, Methodist minister, then beat him to death with their
guns. They arrested Robert Cody, drove him some 300 or 400 yards
from his house, refused to let him pray, and then shot him. They
shot down in the woods John Benner and Christopher Blazer, 8th
Tennessee Infantry. Two days later went to house of David Hamned,

who has two sons in Union army, robbed him of all his corn, the
house of all furniture, and then outraged his daughters in his
presence. Passing on to his daughter sick upon her bed with an
infant four hours old, they stripped off covering, left her exposed,
until she died. Statement of the Rev. Henry M. Sneed, Parrottsville,
Cocke County, Tennessee, signed General S. P. Carter. (Nashville
Daily Union, 5 January 1864.)

HAMNER, Mrs. Sam, formerly of Columbia, died in Memphis last week, age
82; mother-in-law of Colonel George Gantt. (Columbia Herald and
Mail, 25 May 1877.)

HAMPTON, Abner V., died on the 15th in Eddyville, Kentucky, formerly
of Montgomery County. (Tennessee Watchman, Clarksville, TN, 26
April 1823.)

HAMPTON, Miss Mary F., sister of General Wade Hampton, died at Columbia,
South Carolina, on the 11th. (Memphis Avalanche, 28 December 1866.)

HAMPTON, Rufus N., 9 years 8 months 1 day, died February 26 in Dresden,
Tennessee, eldest son of William F. and Susan S. Hampton. (Weekly
Recorder, Paris, TN, 1 April 1848.)

HAMPTON, The old general, grandfather of the present General Wade
Hampton, a general in the Revolutionary War and the War of 1812, was
one of the wealthiest planters in all the South, having sugar plantations in Louisiana and large cotton ones in South Carolina. He
was a man of intense prejudices. His only surviving son by his
first marriage was Colonel Wade Hampton, who had married a wealthy
lady and was the father of a large family, of which the present
Wade Hampton is one.

A disagreement occurred between the old General Hampton and his second
wife, the mother of three daughters, and in his anger he left them
unprovided for and homeless and went to Louisiana. Colonel Wade
Hampton, not having the fear of his father's wrath before him,
purchased for his stepmother and half-sisters the finest dwelling
in Columbia, and furnished the establishment with servants, equipages,
and every luxury, and through 12 years maintained them in every
comfort.

At his death, he had devised his whole estate, amounting to more than
$1,600,000 to his son alone--but the son divided his inheritance,
share and share alike.

Nor was Mrs. Hampton unmindful of the stepson's devoted sacrifices.
On an occasion in 1838 when Colonel Hampton was in Louisiana, the
notes of a friend for whom he was indorser at the bank, was protested
for $42,000.

When she heard of it, she promptly sent a check to the bank for the
full amount and directed that Colonel Hampton be spared all knowledge of the annoying circumstance. (Columbia Herald and Mail,
24 November 1876.)

Wade Hampton, Frank Blair, and General Preston are cousins.
(Memphis Daily App-al, 11 November 1868.) While hunting birds in
Mississippi Wednesday, Senator Wade Hampton was accidentally
shot in the eye by his son. The shot was small and it is throught
that the sight is not destroyed. (Florence, Ala., Times, 28 November
1890.) General Wade Hampton passed through Pittsburg a few days
ago on his way to the far West. He is now 70 years old, but his
health is good. He told a Pittsburg reporter that he was feeling
better than he had for years past. (Maury Democrat, 4 October 1894.)

HANCOCK. A monument has been erected by Major Bigelow and other
gentlemen on the spot where Hancock fell wounded during Pickett's
charge at Gettysburg. (Houston County News, 24 May 1888.)

HANCOCK, General, is now confined to the house of his mother-in-law
Mrs. Russell, near Carondolet, Missouri, on account of the re-opening
of the wound he received at Gettysburg. (Memphis Daily Appeal,
30 Sept. 1868.)

HANCOCK, Leslie, 70, died near Manlyville, Henry County, recently.
(Whig and Tribune, 26 April 1873.)

HAND, Mrs. Patrick, died at Ashwood September 30, relict of Patrick
Hand. (Columbia Herald, 3 October 1873.)

HANDRICH, Jacob, a proprietor of the Climax Saloon, German citizen,
died yesterday of heart disease. (Nashville Republican Banner,
18 March 1869.)

HANEY, Mrs. Margaret, wife of T. J. Haney, of Cuba Landing, Humphreys
County, died on the 11th of child-bed fever; husband and seven
children survive. (Linden Times, 20 May 1880.) Ann West Haney,
wife of T. J. Haney, born 12 Jan. 1854 in Giles County, daughter of
Spencer and Narcissa Jane Pickard, was buried 11 April 1880; Primitive Baptist; married 5 August 1867. (Linden Times, 20 May 1880.)
T. J. Haney married a Miss Cude on the 13th. (Linden Times, 29 July
1880.)

HANEY, Spence, is dead; for many years proprietor of the Ark.
(Columbia Herald, 19 April 1872.)

HANIFIN, John, age 7, son of Tim Hanifin, compositor of the Union and
American, drowned in the river yesterday opposite the Bucket
Factory; lived in the 6th Ward. (Nashville Union and American,
22 August 1873.)

HANKE, John, who was shot a few days ago by a man named Weeman, died
yesterday of his wounds; the murderer is still at large. (Memphis
Avalanche, 13 Dec. 1866.)

HANKS, Richard K., 73, died in this place on the 2d of bilious fever.
(Nashville Daily Gazette, 18 Sept. 1852.)

HANKS, George W., to be buried today at Edgefield, age 42; died Friday;
published the Russellville, Ky, Herald,then founded the Nashville
Union before the war, which was suspended two years ago; to be
buried in Russellville; wife and one son survive. (Nashville
Republican Banner, 3 October 1868.)

HANKS, James M., on Sunday morning about daylight went out to his wood-
pile and was shot dead by some unknown person; shot in back; lived
on the Waynesboro-Savannah Road 8 miles from Waynesboro; wife and
several children survive; the murder is quite a mystery. (Columbia
Herald, 2 November 1871.)

HANKS, Rev. Elijah, a great Baptist revivalist in Maury County, died
on the 12th. He has been preaching since 1827 and hundreds have
been brought into the church through his influence. (Whig and
Tribune, Jackson, TN, 23 Sept. 1871.)

HANNA, Uncle Joe, of Giles County, has 110 grandchildren, and 31 great-
grandchildren. (Nashville Union and American, 7 Feb. 1873.)

HANNA, Captain John, old and well known steamboat man, died on the
20th in Pittsburg, Pennsylvania, of disease of the heart. (Nashville
Dispatch, 29 March 1863.)

HANSEN, Philip, in 1880 living in Corinth, Mississippi, planter, was
believed to have the longest beard of any man in the world. He
sent to the Washington Anthropological Society single hairs plucked
from his chin, which measured 72 inches in length. (Columbia
Herald, 26 July 1895.)

HANSON, General Roger W., of Kentucky, was wounded at Murfreesboro Friday and died Sunday of his wounds; brought to Nashville and buried in a private vaullt at the City Cemetery. (Nashville Dispatch, 8 January 1863.) Killed at Murfreesboro. (Nashville Daily Union, 7 January 1863.) General Roger W. Hanson, who fell at Murfreesboro, was buried Monday at Lexington, Kentucky, and several thousands attended. (Memphis Daily Appeal, 15 November 1866.)

HANSON, G. A., proposed for mayor of Memphis, declined the honor; former Confederate soldier. (Memphis Daily Appeal, 27 December 1869.)

HANT, Thomas T., aged and respected citizen of Tipton County, died recently. (Nashville Union and American, 11 March 1873.)

HARBERT, Mrs. Agnes H., 29, wife of Dr. R. A. Harbert, died on the 25th. (Nashville Dispatch, 26 June 1862.)

HARBERT, Ellen Jenks, daughter of Mr. and Mrs. E. A. Harbert, age 5, to be buried today. (Nashville Dispatch, 15 July 1862.)

HARBISON, Tom, died June 2 and buried at Dr. Forgey's; one of the stewards of the Akin wheel in Maury County. (Maury Democrat, 20 June 1889.)

HARBOR, Jesse, of Concord township, Champaign County, Ohio, age 76, died Feb. 25; he was twice married and had 31 children, the youngest of whom is 2 years old; he gave all who reached maturity 80 acres of land. (Nashville Dispatch, 20 March 1863.)

HARDCASTLE, Miss Henrietta D., died January 3 at Houston, Texas, sister of P. F. Hardcastle of Nashville. (Nashville Republican Banner, 11 Jan. 1870.)

HARDEMAN, W. D., was shot by Colonel J. S. Prestidge in New Orleans on Saturday night; half-brother of Hardin P. Figuers, who left Monday to get his remains. (Columbia Herald and Mail, 10 March 1876.)

HARDIN, William, 96, died 6 miles south of Paris on the 11th instant. (Whig and Tribune, Jackson, TN, 23 August 1873.)

HARDIN, Charles, Esquire, clerk of court at Illinois for 18 years, died there Friday; brother of Colonel Hardin who was killed at Buena Vista; the last of the children of Martin D. Hardin, an early Kentucky U. S. Senator. (Nashville Daily Union, 6 Feb. 1863.)

HARDING, Marcus, colored, landlord of Hotel D'Afrique and a restaurant frequented by sable mariners, died Monday; formerly belonged to General Harding; claimed to be over 90 years old. (Nashville Republican Banner, 12 Feb. 1868.)

HARDING, Thomas, one of our oldest citizens, age 77, died on the 18th; member of the First Presbyterian Church. (Nashville Republican Banner, 19 March 1869.)

HARDING, Mrs. Rachel, who has just died in Cincinnati at 106 years, was a pioneer of that city and its oldest resident; her parents moved to the present site of Cincinnati when she was three. There were only 4 log cabins in the settlement at the time and the settlers were obliged to wage a constant warfare with the Indians. (Maury Democrat, 14 October 1897.)

HARDISON, infant daughter of Mr. Sherod Hardison of Leftwich, Maury County, died of tonsilitis. (Columbia Herald, 30 January 1891.)

HARDISON, Mrs. Mary, of Andrews, died Tuesday of lagrippe; buried in the old Hardison Cemetery. (Columbia Herald, 6 March 1891.)

HARDISON, Ira, died Thursday of last week in Maury County; born 1806 in North Carolina and came to Maury when he was 16 or 18 years old; until 1855 he lived on Flat Creek in house where Captain Billington lives which he built; wife and 5 children survive, and Mrs. Col. W. J. Sowell, who was his child by his first marriage. (Columbia Herald and Mail, 8 October 1875.)

HARDISON, Mrs. Zack, died at the home of her father David G. Holcomb in District 24 on Sunday; was married only last October 14. (Columbia Herald and Mail, 6 Feb. 1874.)

HARDISON, Seth, little son of Dr. J. T. Hardison, was killed Saturday when he handed gun to his sister; she tripped and the gun went off killing him; buried in the Alexander Cemetery near Beech Grove. (Columbia Herald, 18 Dec. 1899.)

HARDY, Mrs. Christiana C., 50, died May 7; wife of William T. Hardy of Nashville; husband and six children survive; youngest but one of the seven daughters of Rev. William Bell of Scotland. Father was minister of Scotch Kirk at Kirkaldy, County of Fife, where she was born 20 May 1812; came to America 1817 and settled Pattonsburg, Botetourt County, Virginia; married 26 Sept. 1832 William T. Hardy. Her oldest son came to Nashville in 1855 and in Feb. 1861 the family moved here; member of First Baptist Church; nursed sick soldiers in Nashville. (Nashville Dispatch, 1 June 1862.)

HARDY, Hannah, wife of William Hardy, age 62, died in Edgefield and to be buried today. (Nashville Republican Banner, 27 Oct. 1868.)

HARDY, Mattie, daughter of Mrs. Martha M. Hardy, to be buried today. (Nashville Republican Banner, 22 June 1869.)

HARE, August, former private in Company G, 18th Tennessee Infantry, age 33, shot himself yesterday; native of Schatian, Germany. (Nashville Daily Union, 9 July 1865.)

HARFF, Mrs., daughter of Mrs. Turner, funeral to be held today. (Nashville Daily Union, 31 Jan. 1863.)

HARFF, Anna B., granddaughter of Mrs. Turner, funeral to be held today. (Nashville Daily Union, 23 April 1863.) (Also Nashville Dispatch, 23 April 1863.)

HARGROVES, Joe, died March 18. (Columbia Herald, 21 March 1873.)

HARGROVES, John, died Tuesday of Erysipelas near Columbia Mills; an extensive beeraiser. (Columbia Herald, 21 March 1873.)

HARLAN, James, District Attorney of Kentucky, died Feb. 18 of pneumonia. (Nashville Daily Union, 19 Feb. 1863.)

HARLAN, Mrs. Lettie, wife of W. G. Harlan, daughter of D. W. Peeler, died March 26 near Williamsport; born 18 April 1852; married 12 May 1870; buried Zion Cemetery. (Columbia Herald and Mail, 9 April 1875.)

HARMAN, Laura Matilda, age 3 years 11 months 13 days, died September 13, the daughter of Richard and Ann Harman. (Nashville Dispatch, 16 Sept. 1862.)

HARMON, Mary Sheffield, 21 months, daughter of C. C. and Rosa F. Harmon, died Saturday. (Nashville Union and American, 12 July 1874.)

HARNEY, James, of the 1st Mounted Tennessee Infantry, was killed August 26 by a member of the 18th Michigan; he was unarmed at the time; the first shot was fatal and afterwards he was bayoneted in the breast. (Nashville Dispatch, 28 August 1863.)

HARNEY. The body of Frederick Harney, Jr., of Mt. Pleasant, found in the New York bay murdered. He had gone to New York to study art. A heavy stone was attached to his body. (Columbia Herald, 2 November 1899.)

HARPER, Asa, of Williamson County, was 100 years old on March 6 and in good health. (Nashville Union and American, 21 November 1874.)

HARPER, William, prosperous farmer who lived near Hendersonville, was struck and killed by lightning last week. (Maury Democrat, 4 Sept. 1890.)

HARPER, Mr., of Augusta, Georgia, was found dead in bed on the 15th in the Astor House in New York. (Nashville Daily Gazette, 27 Aug. 1852.)

HARPER, Mrs., 92, of Lost Creek, Perry County, died on Friday the 2d; her husband was the educator of Judge Elijah Walker. Judge Walker gave her the farm where she lived at her death. (Linden Times, 15 April 1880.)

HARPER, Mrs. and Miss Ellis Morgan (daughter of Thomas Morgan of New York) were killed in the mill of Smith Harper at Arlington, Pennsylvania, on the 14th. They were in the upper story when one was caught by dress and whirled around the shafting and the other tried to rescue her and was caught. (Nashville Dispatch, 25 April 1863.)

HARPER, William, brakeman on L & N, was run over and horribly mangled Monday at Duck River Station; the railroad sent for his wife and she got there shortly before he died; sent to Nashville for burial; lived South Nashville. (Columbia Herald, 12 June 1896.)

HARPER, Ellis. DEATH OF RAIDER. Captain Ellis Harper was shot and instantly killed yesterday by William Suite in Lebanon at Suite's home. Troubles grew out of letter Suite wrote reflecting on Carmack's local supporters--one of whom was Harper. Harper called Suite out. Harper attacked Suite with heavy cane and was drawing pistol when Suite drew pistol and fired. Three shots in all; one in right breast. During the war Harper was noted partisan ranger and commanded a band of about 25 to 30 men, which operated in the hill country in the northern part of Sumner county and adjoining counties, also often going into southern Kentucky. It was said that a Yankee soldier never wandered into Harper territory and returned to tell the tale.

At that time he was only about 25 years old, but he knew every foot of his stronghold and his capture was impossible. He is said to have killed between 15 and 20 men, most of these during the Civil War. It is claimed that he never found a man of whom he was afraid. Colonel Baxter Smith says: "He was a man of strong likes and dislikes and quick to resent an insult for whoever offended him was sure to bring a fight upon himself. He could never forget an injury, but he was a staunch friend to those so fortunate as to gain his esteem." He was always actively interested in politics. (Nashville Banner, 25 June 1908.)

The noted guerrilla Harper is in vicinity of Gallatin...has received flag of truce under order of General Thomas. (Nashville Dispatch, 5 May 1865.) About 300 guerrillas surrendered last night near Edgefield...said to be Harper's. (Nashville Daily Union, 7 May 1865.)

Notorious guerrillas Harper and Malone have surrendered at Gallatin and at Russellville, KY...they are leaders of desperate bands which have been committing depredations upon peaceable citizens of Tennessee and Kentucky. (Nashville Daily Union, 10 May 1865.)

Harper came into Gallatin recently and was pursued by Judge Barry

and son with double-barrelled shotguns. They ask that military
force be sent to capture Harper. (Memphis Daily Appeal, 15 Nov. 1866.)
Judge Barry and son Raun shot at Harper on the 12th, attempting to
catch Harper. (Memphis Daily Appeal, 16 Nov. 1866.)

HARRINGTON. There is a deed on file in Cambridge, Massachusetts, which
describes a piece of land bounded by "stumps and stones where Daniel
Harrington licked William Smith." (Nashville Dispatch, 31 May
1862.)

HARRINGTON, Seaman Jeremiah, was killed on The Rattler when fired upon
on the Tallahatchie River in Mississippi about March 21. (Nashville
Dispatch, 27 March 1863.)

HARRIS, Mrs. Emily, 74, died on the 22d in Nashville; born Hartford
County, Maryland, lived here for 63 years; widow of William Harris
of Neely's Bend. (Nashville Dispatch, 24 Feb. 1863.)

HARRIS, Mrs. Addie, wife of Pryor N. Harris, daughter of Robert I.
Moore, died on the 24th at Brentwood. (Nashville Dispatch, 25 Feb.
1863.)

HARRIS, Miss Snow, of Texas, formerly of Tennessee, has died. (Maury
Democrat, 9 Aug. 1894.)

HARRIS, Miss Minnie, 14, daughter of Mr. Ed Harris, died Sunday of
pneumonia at Santa Fe, Maury County. (Maury Democrat, 14 June 1894.)

HARRIS, James Peter, 64, born Bedford County, TN, moved to Marshall
County when he was 4 years old, is justice of the peace for District
25 in Maury County; moved to Maury in 1856; served in Company H,
23rd Tennessee Infantry CSA married Mary Orr and had 11 children.
(Maury Democrat, 18 July 1895.)

HARRIS, The Rev. Lundy H., died poor in Nashville the other day.
(Maury Democrat, 19 Jan. 1911.)

HARRIS, infant of Mr. and Mrs. William Harris of Rutherford County,
died recently by choking. (Whig and Tribune, Jackson, TN, 14 Dec.
1872.)

HARRIS, Joseph H., died 24 Feb. 1858, of New Providence, Montgomery
County; was killed with axe by slaves; murdered by one of his own
slaves with an axe last Friday night; slave hanged by group of
citizens. (Clarksville Weekly Chronicle, 26 Feb. 1858.)

HARRIS, William, died lately. (Tennessee Watchman, Clarksville, TN,
14 June 1823.)

HARRIS, Miss Bettie, daughter of T. A. Harris, died Monday, closely
following the death of her father; buried Rose Hill in Columbia.
(Columbia Herald, 19 June 1891.)

HARRIS, Thomas A., leading Republican, died Friday in Mt. Pleasant of
protracted illness; buried Hunter Cemetery. (Columbia Herald, 12
June 1891.) (N.B. Mr. Harris was in Ford's Theater the night
President Lincoln was shot, according to his biographical sketch
in Goodspeed's History of Maury County.)

HARRIS, A. O., died in Memphis a few days ago. Many years ago he edited
the Mobile Advertiser. (Nashville Dispatch, 15 April 1862.)

HARRIS, Mrs. Julia Fillmore, sister of President Fillmore, died in
San Francisco Sunday night of last week, age 79; she was the last
survivor of a family of eight brothers and sisters. (Florence,
Ala., Times, 12 Sept. 1891.)

HARRIS. A man named Harris of Bristol, TN, supposed to have been killed
at Gettysburg and whose "remains" were obtained and buried by his

brother, a few nights ago astonished the latter by walking into
his house. (Memphis Daily Appeal, 15 March 1870.)

HARRIS, Mrs. Mary Adelaid, 23, was buried 5 May 1863. (Nashville
Dispatch, 7 May 1863.)

HARRIS, Elizabeth, widow, who lived 5 miles west of Hampshire, Maury
County, died on Sunday the 29th. (Columbia Herald and Mail, 3 April
1874.)

HARRIS, Sam, Eli Harris' ten year old son drowned at Duck River Station
on Sunday; was swimming near the railroad bridge. His strangled
body was found next morning; got caught in swift water. (Columbia
Herald and Mail, 9 July 1875.)

HARRIS, Mrs. Mary A., daughter of Mrs. R. I. Moore, is to be buried at
City Cemetery today. (Nashville Dispatch, 3 May 1863.) Mrs. Annie
Harris, daughter of Robert I. Moore, wife of Pryor N. Harris, died
at Brentwood on the 24th; to be buried at City Cemetery Nashville.
(Nashville Daily Union, 25 Feb. 1863.) (N..B. See also obituary
for Mrs. Addie Harris.)

HARRIS, Isham G., died July 7 in Washington, D.C., age 79; born on
Blue Creek near Rock Creek in Franklin County, TN, 10 Feb. 1818;
a formal ceremony over his remains held in the U. S. Senate and he
lay in state in Nashville, buried Elmwood Cemetery in Memphis.
(Columbia Herald, 16 July 1897.) A $5000 reward has been offered
by the United States for Governor Harris. (Nashville Union, 4 May
1865.) (N.B. He was Governor of Tennessee at the beginning of the
Civil War.)

HARRIS, Mrs. Martha M., wife of Senator Isham G. Harris, 74, died at
Paris, TN, January 20 after a month's illness and was taken to
Memphis for burial; she was born in Henry County, daughter of Major
Edward Travis; married 6 July 1843 in Paris by the Rev. R. W. Cole;
Methodist; four sons survive. (Columbia Herald, 22 Jan. 1897.)

HARRIS, Mrs. Joe, of Timmonsville, Maury County, died last Tuesday
morning; buried Williams burying ground. (Columbia Herald, 17
April 1896.)

HARRIS, Mrs. K. V., 74, died April 10 of paralysis. (Daily Herald,
Columbia, TN, 17 April 1896.)

HARRIS, Mrs. Will, died Tuesday, member of Philippi Church of Christ;
husband, 3 sons, 1 daughter survive. (Daily Herald, Columbia, TN,
16 April 1896.)

HARRIS, Mrs. Josephine, 56, died April 7. (Columbia Herald, 10 April
1896.) (The Maury Democrat, published in same county, gave her age
as 70.)

HARRIS, Mrs. J. C., 79, died Friday on Fountain Creek; five children
survive; buried family burying ground. (Columbia Herald, 3 April
1891.)

HARRIS, William O., of Sumner County, formerly of Nashville, died
yesterday. Some years ago he was one of proprietors of the Banner;
buried City Cemetery. (Nashville Republican Banner, 28 Aug. 1868.)

HARRIS, Mrs. Unity, 74, died 22 Feb. 1863; born Hartford County, Mary-
land; lived here for 63 years; widow of William Harris of Neeley's
Bend. (Nashville Daily Union 23 Feb. 1863.) (N.B. Her name in
Nashville Dispatch was given as Emily.)

HARRIS, Ransom, for many years pressman of the Banner in Nashville,
died Friday night of pneumonia. (Memphis Avalanche, 8 Nov. 1866.)

HARRIS, Mary J., wife of L. F. Harris, died of consumption 20 Jan. 1871 in Galveston, Texas. (Nashville Republican Banner, 3 Feb. 1871.)

HARRISON, Woodson T., well-known printer of Nashville, died 26 Nov. 1872 of consumption, aged about 45. (Whig and Tribune, Jackson, TN, 21 Dec. 1872.)

HARRISON, Henry, well known river pilot, died Wednesday in Cincinnati. (Nashville Daily Union, 3 March 1863.)

HARRISON. The widow of one of President Harrison's brothers was recently granted a pension, getting $6000 on first payment. Her husband, it is said, died of consumption after the war. (Florence, Ala., Times, 20 June 1891.)

HARRISON, Vessie, 2 years 5 months, daughter of John Elliott and H. M. Harrison died 3 Aug. 1863. (Nashville Dispatch, 4 Aug. 1863.) Vestauli, daughter of John E. and Helen M., died. (Nashville Dispatch, 5 Aug. 1863.)

HARRISON, John Elliott, infant son of Mrs. Helen M. Harrison, is to be buried today. (Nashville Daily Union, 5 April 1865.)

HARRISON, Mrs. Eugenia, wife of Wyatt C. Harrison, died yesterday; cousin of Milton T. Neely. (Columbia Herald and Mail, 22 Feb. 1878.)

HARRISON, Hugh C., Esquire, died Friday night on the Double Branches in Maury County. (Columbia Herald and Mail, 16 July 1875.)

HARRISON, John, 13, drowned in river Saturday at Nashville. (Memphis Avalanche, 6 July 1867.)

HARRISON. Joel Clough, notorious murderer of Mrs. Harrison of Nashville escaped Saturday the 20th in Nashville; he was to have been executed on Friday. (Western Weekly Review, Franklin, TN, 2 Aug. 1833.)

HARRISON, William, died on the 8th at Spring Hill of disease of kidneys; good financier, amassed a fortune; buried family burying ground near Franklin. (Columbia Herald and Mail, 18 Jan. 1878.)

HARRISON, Mrs. Mary, widow of Capt. William Harrison, former sheriff of Williamson County, died at home on Columbia Pike on the 8th in her 58th year. (Whig and Tribune, Jackson, TN, 19 July 1873.)

HARRISON, Eliza, wife of Caleb G. Harrison, is to be buried today. (Nashville Dispatch, 3 June 1863.)

HARRISON, Mr. Benjamin, died 25 Oct. 1892 in Washington at 1:40 o'clock buried in Crown Hill Cemetery, Indianapolis; funeral services were held in the White House. (Maury Democrat, 27 Oct. 1892.)

HARRISTON, Thomas, was mortally wounded by a falling plant from the second story of a warehouse on Broad. (Nashville Republican Banner, 29 Oct. 1868.)

HARRY, Dr. Redmond D., worthy citizen died in Sumner County. (Tennessee Watchman, Clarksville, TN, 9 March 1821.)

HARSH, Dr., died yesterday of injuries; practiced here over 25 years; was thrown from his buggy on Monday; wife and 10 children survive. (Nashville Republican Banner, 28 July 1870.)

HART, W. S., 45, died Monday of typhoid-pneumonia, buried Rose Hill Cemetery. (Columbia Herald, 13 Feb. 1891.)

HART, Colonel Martin D., well-known Unionist, has been hung under the lynch law in East Texas. (Nashville Daily Union, 10 April 1863.)

HART. In an old log house in Russell County, Virginia, near Pat's
    Store lives a remarkable family, comprising five generations.
    Isaac Hart, father, grandfather, great-grandfather, and great-great-
    grandfather is 97 years old. His daughter Julia, 68, her son Isaac,
    45, and his son Charlie, 20, and Charlie's three year old son Dorsey
    live here. (Maury Democrat, 19 April 1894.)

HART, Len K., died in Nashville; was three times county trustee of
    Davidson County; died 14 Feb. 1908 at the age of 55; son of
    Henry Hart; married Lucy Eastman, who with two children survives.
    (Daily Herald, Columbia, TN, 14 Feb. 1908.)

HARTLEY, T. J., an old resident, died in Edgefield yesterday; had been
    a well known ship carpenter. (Nashville Union and American, 8 March
    1873.)

HART, Lt. Commander John E., of the U. S. gunboat Albatross, stationed
    in Bayou Sara, La., on the 11th shot himself in the head. (Nashville
    Dispatch, 11 July 1863.)

HARTUNG, Mary, who murdered her husband in 1858 in Albany, New York,
    has been discharged for double jeopardy. (Nashville Dispatch,
    1 April 1863.)

HARVEY, Governor, of Wisconsin, drowned at Savannah, TN, on the 19th
    where he had gone on a mission of humanity to look after the wounded.
    He fell between two boats. (Nashville Dispatch, 24 April 1862.)
    Ex-Governor Harvey of Wisconsin drowned at Pittsburgh Landing a few
    days after the battle of Shiloh in 1862. (Nashville Daily Union,
    31 May 1865.) Mrs. Cordelia P. Harvey, widow of the lamented
    Governor of Wisconsin, who was drowned in the Tennessee River, while
    attempting to alleviate the wants of the Wisconsin troops last
    spring, is devoting her energies and attentions to the sick and
    wounded soldiers in the hospital at St. Louis. (Nashville Dispatch,
    26 Oct. 1862.)

HARWELL, Thomas S., son of the Rev. William M. Harwell of Athens,
    Alabama, age 22, will be buried tomorrow. (Nashville Republican
    Banner, 7 Nov. 1869.)

HASKELL. Mrs. Rebecca Amis of McCain's, Maury County, has old prayer
    book of the Rev. William T. Haskell, son of Colonel Haskell of
    Memphis, who was wounded during Civil War and carried to the home
    of Thomas Amis at Campbell Station where she nursed him back to
    health. He died at Memphis several years ago. She will give the
    prayer book to anyone in his family. (Daily Herald, Columbia,
    TN, 26 Nov. 1901.)

HASLAM, Mrs. Fanny, wife of Samuel, died Thursday the 25th. (Nashville
    Republican Banner, 27 Nov. 1869.)

HASLAM. The body of Samuel Haslam, 25, stonecutter, has been found
    horribly mulilated. William Gatlin, 45, bricklayer, has been
    arrested for the crime. (Nashville Union and American, 15 Sept.
    1874.)

HASTINGS, Mrs. Mary Ann, of Bedford County, has presented her husband
    with two sets of triplets inside two years. (Whig and Tribune,
    Jackson, TN, 1 Feb. 1873.)

HASTINGS, Pollie, 50, living on Leipers Creek in Maury County, near
    Bethel Church, was found dead; hung herself with rope from rafters
    in bar; was found Monday after being gone all night; she suffered
    with fits of insanity. (Maury Democrat, Columbia, TN, 22 June 1893.)

HATCHER, Clinton, born 1840, died 1861, Company F, 8th Virginia Regi-
    ment, CSA, "Fell bravely defending his native state." (Tombstone
    inscription in Ball's Bluff National Cemetery in Virginia.)

HATTON, Colonel Robert, of Lebanon, was killed in the battle of
Chickahominy near Richmond, Virginia. (Nashville Dispatch, 8 June
1862.) Robert Hatton, killed at Chickahominy, received his
commission as brigadier general only a few days before battle; was
colonel of the 7th Tennessee. (Nashville Dispatch, 14 June 1862.)

HATTON, Captain William S., died at the home of his mother in Lebanon
on the 9th; veteran of the 1st Tennessee Regiment in Mexican War, the
"Bloody First" of the battle of Monterey. (Memphis Avalanche, 18
Oct. 1866.)

HAVEN, Mrs. Alice B., 36, died August 23 in Mamaroneck, New York; her
maiden name was Emily B. Bradley and she was born Hudson, New York;
married first in 1846 to Mr. Neal, and married second Samuel B.
Haven, well known author. She adopted the name Alice at Haven's
request ater the marriage. She wrote under the name of Alice G.
Lee. (Nashville Dispatch, 17 Sept. 1863.)

HAVEN, Professor, D.D., LLD., died in Chicago yesterday. (Nashville
Union and American, 24 May 1874.)

HAVIS, Lt., was firing a double-barreled shotgun a few days since at
Athens, TN. The weapon rebounded, the butt striking him in the face,
literally tearing his head to pieces and killing him instantly.
(Nashville Dispatch, 25 April 1862.)

HAWKINS, Judge Isaac, prominent lawyer and politician, died at his home
in Huntingdon on the 12th. (Linden Times, 19 Aug. 1880.)

HAWKINS, Julia Ella, 8 months 9 days, only child of E. S. and Sue Hawkins,
died August 19. (Nashville Republican Banner, 20 August 1869.)

HAWKINS, Captain James, shot and killed, shot in abdomen at Smithfield,
Virginia, Thursday last week by W. S. Underwood, Esquire, of Surrey
Courthouse; both were in Sothern army. (Memphis Avalanche, 5 Nov.
1866.)

HAWKINS, William, 93, died at home of Dr. J. T. S. Greenfield in Greenfield Bend, Maury County, where he had lived since war; died of old
age on the 13th. (Columbia Herald and Mail, 23 June 1876.)

HAWKINS. Notice to devisees and legatees of William Hawkins, deceased;
Levia Wray and her children of Arkansas; Seletha Erwin and children
of Texas; and Sophronia Winn and her husband O. S. Winn of Mississippi. (Columbia Herald and Mail, 22 Dec. 1876.)

HAWKINS, infant of Mr. and Mrs. John Hawkins, died Wednesday at Theta,
Maury County,buried Alexander Cemetery. (Columbia Herald, 3 Nov.
1899.)

HAWKINS, Elizabeth B., age 40 years 5 months 20 days, died 20 May 1869;
wife of Major James M. Hawkins. (Nashville Republican Banner, 21
May 1869.)

HAWKINS, Benjamin S., of Woodford County, Kentucky, was accidentally
thrownout of his wagon Saturday and instantly killed. (Nashville
Daily Gazette, 14 Sept. 1852.)

HAWKINS, Richard M., died on the 18th in New Orleans of yellow fever;
eldest son of R. M. Hawkins of Nashville. (Nashville Republican
Banner, 30 Oct. 1870.)

HAWKINS, Henry, of Columbia, tried to commit suicide; he had a child
who died a year ago and was buried in Rose Hill Cemetery on someone
else's lot and they recently asked him to move the body. (Columbia
Herald, 18 Feb. 1870.)

HAWTHORNE, Mrs. Agnes, 93, died on the 8th in Memphis of pneumonia;
came here in 1810 and saw the growth of the place out of the

160

wilderness. Buried in Winchester Cemetery. (Memphis Daily Appeal, 9 Nov. 1869.)

HAYES, Ex-President Rutherford B., died suddenly January 17 at Fremont, Ohio, of paralysis of heart; buried in Oakwood Cemetery by his wife. (Mauary Democrat, 19 Jan. 1893.)

HAYES, Marcus L., was killed on the 15th on Lick Creek; a tree fell on him. (Columbia Herald, 25 Nov. 1870.)

HAYES, Mrs. Eunice, 102, died at Milton, New Hampshire, on March 17; left 181 descendants. (Nashville Dispatch, 30 April 1863.)

HAYES, Mrs. David K., 72, died Wednesday near Lasea, Maury County; buried family burying ground. (Columbia Herald, 27 March 1891.)

HAYES. The venerable Dr. John B. Hayes of Columbia is dead. (Nashville Republican Banner, 7 July 1868.) Dr. John Brown Hays was born in Rockbridge County, Virginia, in 1796, and died in Columbia, TN, in 1868, at the age of 72 years. He was educated at the University of Virginia, moved to Nashville, and then to Columbia in 1811. Having read medicine under Dr. Kew of Virginia, he graduated as doctor of medicine at the medical department of the Pennsylvania University. Dr. Hays married Miss Ophelia, sister of President James K. Polk. He practiced medicine successfully in Columbia for 52 years, up to the time of his death, exemplary in his life, he was a learned man in his profession and during the whole of his life he was a close student. (Columbia Herald, 23 May 1873.)

HAYES, Andrew, 18, died May 28 of typhoid fever. (Columbia Herald, 5 June 1896.)

HAYES, Oliver B., died on the 15th near Brentwood. (Nashville Republican Banner, 18 Aug. 1868.)

HAYNES, Hezekiah, found dead in bed at Somerset, Kentucky, on the 17th, died of drunkenness; clever but a hard drinker; age 65; was in the Battle of New Orleans. (Nasvhille Daily Gazette, 27 Oct. 1852.)

HAYNES, Thomas K., of Rutherford County, living 12 miles west of Murfreesboro, hanged himself with a trace chain on the 22d ult. He left a large family. (Whig and Tribune, Jackson, TN, 13 Dec. 1873.)

HAYNES, Mrs. Sarah, died in Lebanon on Wednesday; sister of R. H. Berry of Nashville. (Nashville Republican Banner, 26 April 1869.)

HAYNES, Jack, 103, is a member of the GAR in St. Louis. He was born 1788 in White County, TN; served in War of 1812 and in Mexican War, and was engineer of the gunboat Sumpter during the Civil War. (Maury Democrat, 7 May 1891.)

HAYNES, William Anderson, infant son of James L. and Sarah G. Haynes, one of the proprietors of this newspaper, died in Franklin yesterday. (Nashville Daily Gazette, 7 Aug. 1852.) (William Henry Haynes, age 2, was the name and age given in the Nashville Daily Gazette of 8 August 1852.) William Anderson Haynes, infant son of James L. Haynes of Nashville, died on the 6th. (Home Press, Franklin, TN, 12 Aug. 1852.)

HAYNES, James, old and respected citizen of Cornersville, TN, died Sept. 23. (Whig and Tribune, Jackson, TN, 4 Oct. 1873.)

HAYS, Miss Mary Jane, daughter of General Samuel J. Hays of Jackson, TN, died in Columbia at the home of James Walker on Friday the 17th; a member of the Columbia Female Institute. (West Tennessee Whig, Jackson, TN, 9 March 1849.)

HAYS, General Samuel J., 61, died at Jackson, TN, on the 3d after a protracted indisposition; graduate of West Point but never entered the army; married Miss Middleton of South Carolina. Andrew Jackson was his uncle by marriage and his wife died some years ago. He was Major General of the militia. (Memphis Avalanche, 15 Nov. 1866.)

HAYS, Ira C., died November 13 of heart disease. (Nashville Republican Banner, 16 Nov. 1869.)

HAYS, Thomas, son of Thomas S. Hays of Edgefield, died last Saturday of spotted fever. (Whig and Tribune, Jackson, TN, 9 Dec. 1871.)

HAYS, Colonel Jack, of California, well known as famous Texas Ranger, brother of General Harry T. Hays of New Orleans, is going into extensive purchase of land in California. (Memphis Daily Appeal, 5 Dec. 1868.) (N.B. John Coffee Hays "Jack" was born 1817 in Wilson County, TN.)

HAYS, Bill, a guerrilla, who operated through Salt River County in Kentucky, has sent in to inquire about surrender. (Nashville Dispatch, 7 May 1865.)

HAYWOOD, Mrs. Parthenia, 70, died June 24 on Knob Creek in Maury County. (Columbia Herald and Mail, 29 June 1877.)

HAZED, M., was first person to die of cholera in November 1832 in Nasvhille. (Nashville Union and American, 2 July 1873.)

HEAD, Mrs. Henrietta, wife of G. Spencer Head, died August 31; left a large family. (Columbia Herald and Mail, 3 Sept. 1875.)

HEAD, Honorable John W., died in Sumner County; resolution of respect published. (Nashville Union and American, 10 Nov. 1874.)

HEADRICK, William, of Lincoln County, was severely cut on Monday evening by Harvey W. Johnson and died on Wednesday. Johnson made his escape. (Nashville Daily Gazette, 2 November 1852.)

HEARN, William, well known sign painter, fell from scaffolding in Edgefield last Saturday and died soon after. (Whig and Tribune, Jackson, TN, 17 May 1873.)

HEARN, Mrs. Kate Roberts, died recently in Soochow, China; born and reared in Montgomery County; went to China as missionary with her husband the Rev. Hearn; left an infant son. (Maury Democrat, 3 Sept. 1891.)

HEDBERG, Mrs., the sister of the widow of the captain killed by Capt. Maney, has testified before the court martial at Fort Snelling, Minnesota. (Lincoln County Herald, 13 June 1894.)

HEFFERNAN. Berry, Knight, Craft, and Lysigust are all to hang at Nashville on January 26 for the murder of Mr. Heffernan. (Memphis Avalanche, 27 Jan. 1866.) (N.B. William B. Heffernan, age 46, died 26 Nov. 1865.)

HEFLINE. Information wanted on the following refugees from East Alabama: Hon. R. T. Hefline, Dr. Davis, Wesley V. Thomason, Alfred Wood, M. P. Duncan, D. O. Kelly; they can hear from their families by addressing Dr. J. A. Vaughan, Chattanooga. (Nashville Daily Union, 23 Feb. 1865.)

HEIMARK, Dr. C. B., of Eagleville, Rutherford County, TN, has been arrested for robbing graves in Rutherford County, he has taken several prominent people. (Columbia Herald, 28 Jan. 1898.) Information from the Nashville Banner, 19 March 1940, has the following quotation: "There hasn't been such a country gathering since the day they brought the bodies of Mrs. Corbitt and Steven Bennett back from Vermont. The bodies arrived in Murfreesboro by train and were met by two horse-drawn hearses. Folks crowded to

see them and buggies followed the hearses all the way to the
cemetery at Eagleville. The bodies had been shipped in boxes marked
as books." Dr. Heimark sold cadavers to medical schools and when
the graves of Steve Bennett, Mrs. Corbitt, and Mrs. Pruitt were found
robbed, Gov. Robert Taylor called the state militia out to search
all the state medical schools for the bodies. This incident caused
the General Assembly to tighten the state laws on cemeteries. The
bodies of Steve Bennett and Mrs. Corbitt were found in medical
schools in Burlington, Vermont. Mrs. Pruitt's body was found thrown
over a fence nearby. (Nashville Banner, 19 March 1940; personal
communication with the compiler in 1970.)

HEISKELL, Ferdinand, 68, of Knox County buried today; brother of Judge
C. W. Heiskell of Memphis; he was "first man who crossed the mountains of East Tennessee to enter the Union Army." His brother was
in Confederate Army. (Nashville Banner, 30 May 1908.)

HEISKELL. Surviving members of the 154th (Senior) Regiment of Tennessee
Volunteers will meet this morning to escort the remains of the late
chaplain of the regiment Rev. W. T. Heiskell to depot for departure
for Jackson for burial; son of General W. T. Heiskell. (Memphis
Daily Appeal, 22 Nov. 1868.)

HELTER, Dr. G. F., an old German citizen of Nashville, died on Monday.
(Memphis Daily Appeal, 9 July 1869.)

HELM, Mrs. Emily Todd, aunt of the Honorable Robert Lincoln, a widow
of a Confederate general, has been reappointed for her third term
as postmistress at Elizabethton, KY. (Florence, Ala., Times, 14 Feb.
1891.)

HELM, W. M., of Ripley, TN, has a powder-horn used by his great uncle,
Thomas Helm, in the American Revolution; inscribed: "T.H., 1776,
C.C.C." (Nashville Union and American, 26 May 1874.)

HELM, George, 67, died of pneumonia on the 22d; buried Rose Hill Cemetery
served in Mexican War and Civil War; brother of D. C. Helm; graduate
of Jackson College. (Maury Democrat, 23 March 1893.)

HELM, Ben H., Brigadier General in Confederate Army, was slain in North
Georgia; son of Governor Helm and grandson of famous Benjamin Hardin
of Kentucky; his wife is half-sister to wife of President Lincoln.
(Nashville Dispatch, 1 Oct. 1863.)

HELTON, Daniel, 86, died Wednesday of la grippe; buried at Waynesboro.
(Waynesboro Tribune, 21 Jan. 1897.)

HENDERSON, William Alexander, born 24 Oct. 1841, Lincoln County, TN, son
of James W. Henderson; his father died when he was 7 weeks old and
his mother moved to her father's, Alexander Baldridge, in Giles
County near Lynnville. She died 1855, having lost her second son;
his eldest brother Frank died 1869; served in war in Jones' Company,
CSA. (Maury Democrat, 19 April 1894.)

HENDERSON, Adam, killed yesterday by explosion of soda fountain at
confectionary shop on Union Street in Nashville, cut in bowels and
considerably mangled. (Home Press, 20 May 1852, Franklin, TN.)

HENDERSON, Mrs. Matilda, died on the 11th in Murfreesboro, esteemed
and respected. (Nashville Union and American, 17 Jan. 1874.)

HENDERSON, Mrs. Emeline, born 1 May 1800 in Iredell County, NC, died
27 April 1876, buried Old Ridge, Giles County; widow of John
Henderson; had been a Methodist for 60 years. (Columbia Herald
and Mail, 9 June 1876.)

HENDERSON, Isabella Jane, 12 months, died on the 22d; daughter of David
and Jesse Henderson. (Nashville Dispatch, 23 Aug. 1863.)

163

HENDERSON, A. A., who died recently in Tuskegee, Alabama, was 50 years old and 4 feet high. (Florence, Ala., Times, 30 April 1892.)

HENDERSON, infant son of Matthew and Janette Henderson, died of whooping cough on the 12th. (Nashville Dispatch, 13 May 1862.)

HENDERSON, W. A. C., one of soldiers doing guard duty at the prison, was shot and killed by Joseph Long, another guard; the inquest result declared the act was justified. (Nashville Dispatch, 2 Oct. 1863.)

HENDERSON, Nettie, 6, daughter of Mr. and Mrs. Andrew Henderson, funeral to be held this evening. (Nashville Dispatch, 7 May 1863.)

HENDLEY, Annie Willard, died Monday; daughter of Mayor H. L. Hendley. Buried Rose Hill Cemtery. (Columbia Herald, 10 July 1891.)

HENDRICK, Joseph Thilman, pastor of Edgefield Presbyterian Church, died; resolution of respect on his death published. (Nashville Dispatch, 3 April 1863.)

HENNING, Joseph, old and respected citizen of Nashville, died in New York on 4 May 1862; he had accompanied a young female relative to her home and was not well when he left. His wife survives. He had three sons born and buried--one on verge of manhood. Two sons are buried in Nashville and another in Baltimore. He had intended to visit the grave in Baltimore before coming home to Nashville. He was 65 and was born in Ireland. (Nashville Dispatch, 3 June 1862.) (N.B. He is buried in City Cemetery in Nashville.)

HENNING, Abraham, clothier, was stabbed, murdered, by an unknown Friday in Nashville within a block of the square; Jewish. (Daily Herald, Columbia, 7 Aug. 1909.)

HENRY, Judge, of Madison County, Mississippi, was killed in recent battle before Richmond. He was judge of circuit court before the war came. (Nashville Dispatch, 31 July 1862.)

HENRY, Eli, died on Boon's Creek in East Tennessee a few days ago, age 90. He had the vigor of youth up to his death; soldier under Old Hickory and during General Jackson's memorable Indian campaign it became necessary to run a flatboat to Natchez, Mississippi, laden with supplies for suffering troops. The banks of the Tennessee and Mississippi were at that time lined with murderous hostile savages and not a man could be found who would attempt the hazardous feat of taking the boatload of supplies through until Mr. Henry volunteered and took the boat through. (Memphis Daily Appeal, 25 May 1870.)

HENRY, Lt. John R., of 1st Middle Tennessee Calalry was wounded on train from Murfreesboro on April 10 and died April 12. He was buried in Nashville. (Nashville Daily Union, 15 April 1863.) Lt. Henry of Knoxville in 1st Tennessee Cavalry was killed in attack of rebels on Murfreesboro train Friday. After being shot, he was robbed of $20 and his boots were stolen. (Nashville Daily Union, 14 April 1863.)

HERKE, Mr. and two of his children were murdered on Saturday by two men in Federal uniform near Evansville, Indiana. They entered the house for robbery. Two other children were mortally wounded. (Nashville Dispatch, 2 Sept. 1863.)

HERRERRA, Miss Claudia, a Mexican woman, died in San Francisco the other day at the age of 120 years. Her acquaintances are positive that there is no mistake about her age. (Lincoln County Herald, 13 June 1894.)

HERRICK, Jimmy, little son of T. C. Herrick, was out hunting on Porter Pike; the gun went off and killed him. (Nashville Republican Banner, 14 Nov. 1869.)

HERRINGTON, Mrs. Maria, one of the parties burned by explosion of
    benzie lamp at Vogel's hotel the other day, has died of her injuries.
    (Memphis Avalanche, 4 Jan. 1866.)

HERRON, J. H., long identified with the educational institutions in
    Cincinnati, died there last Wednesday. (Nashville Daily Union,
    29 March 1863.)

HERSTEIN, Buford, 10, son of Jacob Herstein, formerly of Columbia,
    drowned in Cumberland River at Nashville on Saturday evening.
    (Columbia Herald and Mail, 3 Aug. 1877.)

HESLAR, Dr. G. F., an old German citizen, died Monday in Nashville.
    (Nashville Republican Banner, 4 July 1869.)

HESS, Uncle Bill, of Elk Garden, Virginia, was 109 on June 25; has
    32 children, 175 grandchildren, 90 great-grandchildren. Elk Garden
    has two other aged residents; Mrs. Sarah Shelton, 108 and Mrs.
    Dorton, 101. (Maury Democrat, 8 Aug. 1895.)

HETCHCOAT, Maggie Sue, 5 years, died Saturday of dropsy; buried at
    Rose Hill in Columbia. (Columbia Herald, 11 Dec. 1899.)

HEVERIN, Mrs. Mary, died on the 24th. (Nashville Republican Banner, 25
    Aug. 1869.)

HIBBLER, Robert Turnbull, died 10 July 1866 in Tunica County, Mississippi,
    son of Dr. E. B. and Frances G. Hibbler; born Edgefield District,
    South Carolina, at Liberty Hill, on 16 Sept. 1833; Confederate
    soldier; husband and father. (Memphis Avalanche, 6 Nov. 1866.)

HIBBS, James and James Anderson, prisoners who have been committing
    robberies in Humphreys County; William H. Meadows and James E.
    Meadows got them from jail to try them in county. A few hours later
    the bodies of the dead prisoners were found tied to a tree and
    perforated with bullet holes. The men were notoriously bad and
    confirmed horse thieves. (Nashville Dispatch, 1 Dec. 1863.)

HICKEY, William, Company D, 6th Tennessee, died in Louisville, KY,
    during the week ending February 6. (Nashville Dispatch, 8 Feb. 1863.
    Nashville Daily Union, 8 Feb. 1863.)

HICKMAN, Martha, wife of George H. Hickman, died on the 25th. (Nash-
    ville Dispatch, 26 June 1863.)

HICKMAN, Jesse D., of Lawrence County, took overdose of morphine,
    which resulted in his death recently. (Maury Democrat, 2 Oct. 1890.)

HICKMAN, N. S. (Shake), of District 6 in Maury County, died Monday of
    pneumonia at Stiversville; buried New Raymer Cemetery. (Columbia
    Herald, 30 Jan. 1891.)

HICKMAN COUNTY DEATHS. During the last 8 months the following having
    died in Hickman County: James Nelson Bingham; Mrs. Rebecca Clagett;
    Stephen Goodlow Warren; Josiah A. Bizwell; J. L. D. Nunnellee;
    Mrs. M. L. Foster; Mrs. Mattie Dean; Miss S. Veronica Grimmett.
    Captain R. E. Griner is sinking fast with cancer. (Columbia Herald
    and Mail, 1 Dec. 1876.)

HICKNEY, David, age 102, died 9 Nov. 1867 in Lewiston, Missouri; he
    voted for George Washington and remembered Arnold's expedition up
    Kennehech River. (Nashville Republican Banner, 10 Nov. 1867.)

HICKS, Mrs. Charity, died yesterday, age 67; buried at Concord Cemetery.
    (Columbia Herald, 1 Dec. 1899.)

HICKS, Willie, 5, son of Tom, who lives one mile out on White's Creek
    Pike drowned in cistern. (Nashville Dispatch, 15 March 1863.)

HICKS, Willie, 5, son of Tom Hicks, who lives one mile from town on the White's Creek Pike, fell into well and his dog jumped in to save him, but both perished. The fence had been torn down around the well for firewood. (Nashville Dispatch, 14 March 1863.)

HICKS, Mary Margaret, infant daughter of A. H. Hicks, Esquire, about 16 months, died on Sunday the 18th instant. (Nashville Daily Gazette, 20 July 1852.)

HICKS, William D., Esquire, one of the oldest and most esteemed citizens of Murfreesboro, died of heart disease on the 6th. (Nashville Union and American, 9 Jan. 1874.)

HICKS. Governor Hicks' body dug up and mutilated on Wednesday. Some fiends opened the tomb of ex-Governor Hicks in Dorchester County, Maryland; stole his coffin and body; broke tombstone to pieces. The body and coffin are believed to have been sunk in Choptank River. (Nashville Daily Union, 14 May 1865.)

HIDE, John P., Esquire, died yesterday; native of England, near London; born March 1827; was deputy circuit court clerk; Oddfellow; married the daughter of the Rev. John P. Campbell and they had five children. (Nashville Union and American, 22 Jan. 1873.)

HIDE, Mrs. John F., widow, daughter of the late Rev. John P. Campbell, died yesterday; had five children; she was formerly Martha J. Campbell. (Nashville Union and American, 17 April 1873.)

HIDE, Emma M., daughter of John Hide, age 33, died 24 April 1864; her funeral will be held at Christ Church. (Nashville Union and American, 25 April 1864.) (N.B. Her age is in question.)

HIGHTOWNER, Ephis, a former recluse, who has lived since his youth in the Clinch Mounts of Grainger County, TN, died 15 Aug. 1888, age 99 years 10 months. He had had many thrilling adventures with wild animals and Indians and claimed many of them for his victims. (Maury Democrat, 23 Aug. 1888.)

HIGHTOWER, Miss Lou F., daughter of late Dr. R. R. Hightower of Williamson County, died at home of her grandfather Robert C. Foster in Haywood County on the 27th; poisoned milk. (Whig and Tribune, Jackson, TN, 16 Nov. 1872.)

HILDRETH, U. S. Deputy Marshall, died Sunday from effects of wound by Jeff Saunders last month; buried on Monday. (Nashville Union and American, 3 June 1874.)

HILDRETH, Harry, committed suicide by taking overdose of morphine. He came here 3 years ago as a member of Ohio cavalry; married a prostitute named Jennie Nelson; she went home with him and when his parents learned of her past they turned the couple out. He left note asking that his body be sent to Mt. Vernon, Ohio. (Nashville Republican Banner, 14 Aug. 1867.)

HILL, Mrs. Mary, 23, daughter of Ambrose Cayce, died in Davidson County on the 21st; Methodist; left 8-day old infant. (Western Weekly Review, Franklin, TN, 27 Sept. 1833.)

HILL, William Kenan, his funeral to be held Thursday in Memphis; lived at 233 Union Street. (Memphis Daily Appeal, 14 Oct. 1868.)

HILL, Ashley, died 23 Dec. 1872 in Maury County; member of St. James Lodge 105 Free and Accepted Masons; age 50; lived near Concord Church. (Columbia Herald, 3 Jan. 1873.) (N.B. Death also found in same paper as 29 Dec. 1872.)

HILL, J. H., of Williamson County, had his leg torn off below the knee by threashing machine a few days ago. (Nashville Union and American, 17 July 1874.)

HILL, George, 6, son of Joseph Hill, broke neck on South Cherry yesterday when he pulled grocery counter over on him, and he died instantly. (Nashville Republican Banner, 29 May 1868.)

HILL, James S., died August 7 in South Nashville. (Nashville Dispatch, 8 Aug. 1863.)

HILL, Mrs. Nancy C., mother of late William K. Hill, funeral today. (Memphis Daily Appeal, 23 Sept. 1869.)

HILL, William Vilas, manager of Hill Shot Company in Nashville, made an assignment for store last week, left store, went home and shot himself. (Florence, Ala., Times, 30 May 1891.)

HILL, Samuel C., died May 8 in St. Louis; native of Lebanon, Kentucky, and lived several years in Columbia; his beloved friend Dr. Sam Bicknell was near him in his dying hours. (Columbia Herald and Mail, 16 May 1877.)

HILL, Marion, died last week in Greenfield Bend, Maury County, leaving wife and several children destitute; died of typhoid-pneumonia. (Columbia Herald and Mail, 3 March 1876.)

HILL, William H., died in Washington County, Pennsylvania, at the age of 100 years 2 months 22 days; "if he hadn't chewed tobacco for 85 years, he might have lived to a ripe age." (Maury Democrat, 28 Feb. 1895.)

HILL, H. R. W., formerly of Nashville, died at his plantation near New Orleans on the 17th of yellow fever; his property was estimated at $1,500,000, and almost all of it goes to an only son. (Clarksville Weekly Chronicle, 28 Sept. 1853.)

HILL. At the sale of John M. Hill's estate, he left $10,000 fund for distressed ministers and $10,000 for indigent members of his church. (Nashville Republican Banner, 2 June 1870.)

HILLIARD, Hon. Henry W., died Saturday, minister to Berlin under President Tyler; appointed by President Hayes as minister to Brazil; served in U. S. Congress and Confederate Congress; was brigadier general in Confederate Army. (Maury Democrat, 22 Dec. 1892.)

HILLIARD, Mrs. Polk, died yesterday at Bigbyville, Maury County. (Columbia Herald and Mail, 3 Dec. 1875.)

HILLIARD, Mrs. M. M., wife of late Government officer, fell on horns of her saddle and died in a few minutes at her father-in-law's home in Cheatham County. (Nashville Union and American, 20 Aug. 1874.)

HILLMAN, Mrs. Ann J., wife of D. Hillman, Esquire, died 1 April 1862 in Nashville; daughter of the Hon. John H. Marable of Montgomery County; married April 1840; buried in family burying ground at home-stead. (Nashville Dispatch, 24 April 1862.)

HILLMAN, Samuel, of Columbus, Indiana, member of the GAR, has sword captured by him on the battlefield during the late war and he wishes to return it to the owner. It is inscribed: "Lt. Col. Ray, 2d Tennessee Cavalry, CSA." (Houston County News, 7 Oct. 1887.)

HINDMAN, Gen. Tom C., died on the 27th in Helena, Arkansas, murdered; born 1830 in Knox County, East Tennessee, of poor parents; moved to Eipley, Mississippi, and was in Mississippi legislature; was head of a "legion"in Confederate service and rose to brigadier general and major general; after war emigrated to Mexico with other Confederates. He was assassinated by man named Robertson, passenger on the steamer Shreve, who fired through window while Hindman was at supper. He lived only 8 hours. He was a bitter foe of radicals and Republicans. (Memphis Daily Appeal, 29 Sept. 1868.)

HINDMAN, Mrs. Mary B., widow of General Thomas C. Hindman (who was assassinated a number of years ago by Haywood Grant, who was recently hanged in Georgia), died at her residence in Helena, Arkansas, last week. In her young days she was considered the belle of the Mississippi Valley. (Columbia Herald and Mail, 15 Sept. 1876.)

HINES, Barney, died yesterday in District 13; well-known Irish citizen. (Nashville Union and American, 17 Oct. 1873.)

HINES, William, of Edgefield, brakeman on the L & N, fell between two cars at Franklin, Kentucky, and was crushed to death on Monday. His head, arm, and leg were completely severed, and body was horribly mangled; wife and three children survive. (Nashville Republican Banner, 5 May 1869.)

HINES, William, of Totty's Bend, Hickman County, is 84 years old. (Columbia Herald and Mail, 19 Dec. 1873.)

HINSON, James, died April 8; suffered for months with consumption; wife and three children survive. (Columbia Herald, 24 April 1896.)

HINSON, Mrs. Elizabeth, of White Oak, Houston County, will is being probated (Erin Review, 27 May 1882.)

HINSON, E. L., says that only three members of his company are now living; he served in Company H, 18th Cavalry; the three living are Jake Dickson, Isam Walls, and himself. (Perry Coutian, 24 Nov. 1924.)

HINSON, Captain Jack, died 7 Feb. 1873, age 80 years, on White Oak Creek. "It is said he killed about 80 Federal soldiers during the late unpleasantness." (Whig and Tribune, Jackson, TN, 1 March 1873, quoting Nashville Union and American.) The Dover Record of February 27 says death of Capt. Jack Hinson, died on 7th, is mistake and that he is alive. (Nashville Union and American, 3 March 1873.) "Captain Jack is to be tried by a military commission but the peace men propose to get a writ of habeas corpus. Captain Jack is a brave man, a rude untutored hero, a thief and a scoundrel no doubt when viewed through the social ideas we have, but a hero nevertheless. His execution would serve no good purpose, while it would be a crowning act of infamy." (Clarksville Tobacco Leaf, 18 June 1873.)

"It has already been announced that squad of rebel guerrillas, eight in number, belonging to Hinson's command, went to Fort Henry on the 6th inst., at 4 o'clock a.m., and captured the telegraphic operator Mr. C. E. Bush." (Nashville Daily Union, 25 Aug. 1863.)

(N.B. Jack Hinson of Stewart County, for whom Hinson Town was named, had sons put to death by Col. W. W. Lowe, 5th Iowa Cavalry, commander at Fort Henry and Fort Heiman, on the charge of bushwhacking. Jack Hinson swore revenge on the Federals and from then to the end of the war hid in the woods and on the riverbanks killing Federal soldiers.)

HINSON, Ab. "We have heard a great deal of unreliable news about a terrible tragedy that took place at Danville, Tenn. One Ab Hinson was waylaid by two young men named Wiggins and shot and killed. Later, Joe Hinson, a son of the murdered man, killed one of the Wiggins boys with a knife and cut his heart entirely out of his body. We have not heard all the particulars of the double crime except that it originated from an old family feud. We have been very much interested in this affair from the fact that we knew the Wiggins father, when he was our preceptor, and we also knew the father of Ab Hinson, the redoubtable Capt. Jack Hinson." (Bakerville Review, 3 Sept. 1896, abstracted by Marjorie Hood Fischer.)

HINTON, Olivia Jane, wife of James M. Hinton, 39, died 7 July 1870. (Nashville Republican Banner, 8 July 1870.)

HINTON, R. B., aged citizen of Franklin County, died at Winchester on Monday; born and reared in Davidson County and lived here until 1850;

died of heart disease. (Nashville Union and American, 12 Nov. 1874.)

HINTON, Minnie Noel, infant daughter of James M. and Olivia J., died Monday last, age 1 year 16 days. (Nashville Dispatch, 9 April 1863.)

HITE, Abraham, prominent merchant in Louisville, died April 29 of diptheria. (Nashville Dispatch, 30 April 1863.)

HITCHCOCK, Hiram, Company B, 18 Wisconsin Infantry, was killed by an Italian Castello, who lived on Cherry Street, opposite the Maxwell Barracks; said to have insulted Castello's wife; was struck on head and skull broken. (Nashville Daily Union, 16 Jan. 1865.)

HLAZECK, Mrs. Rebecca, 90, hung herself in the basement of her son's home at 169 Hamlin Street, Chicago, last week; despondency because of ill health. (Maury Democrat, 13 June 1894.)

HOAG, John, was hanged at Walkertown, Connecticut, on the 14th; confessed his guilt and advised all young boys to "keep away from whisky, fast women and the United States." (Memphis Avalanche, 27 Dec. 1868.)

HOAG, Fayette, notorious rebel bushwhacker and murderer, was captured in the Sequatchie Valley by detachments of the 14th U. S. Colored Troops. (Nashville Daily Union, 2 April 1864.)

HOBAN, Lawrence, youngest son of James Hoban, Esquire, of Washington City, died on the 29th, age 18 years 1 month, at the home of uncle F. H. French in Nashville; remains taken to Washington City. (Nashville Dispatch, 31 March 1863.)

HOBART, Rev. James, 96, died 16 July 1862 in Vermont; Congregationalist and had preached for 70 years; probably the oldest minister in Vermont or New England. (Nashville Dispatch, 1 August 1862.)

HOBART, James Lewis, 14, died 19 March 1870 of pneumonia in Decatur, Alabama; son of Mr. and Mrs. Lewis Hobart. (Nashville Republican Banner, 26 March 1870.)

HOBSON, Jeremiah, 53, died 30 Sept. 1875 near Williamsport and buried at Pisgah Church; wife and 7 children survive. (Columbia Herald and Mail, 8 Oct. 1875.)

HOBSON, Mrs. Mason, age 104, died 16 Jan. 1873 at Pulaski. (Nashville Union and American, 24 Jan. 1873.)

HOBSON, Nicholas, born 27 Feb. 1796 in Cumberland County, Virginia, died recently; his father was in the Revolutionary War; in 1807 he came to Nashville. (Columbia Herald and Mail, 4 June 1875.) Nicholas Hobson, Esquire, one of the few early settlers of Davidson County now living is seriously ill and not expected to live until this morning. (Nashville Union and American, 10 Nov. 1874.)

HOBSON, Miss Nancy M., age 33 years 5 months 7 days, died on 2d. (Nashville Dispatch, 3 Dec. 1863.)

HODGE, Mrs. Nancy, 83, widow of late James Hodge, died 11 June 1893 of Asthma at her home on Pulaski Pike; she was of an advanced age and very helpless; aunt of J. Mort Hodge, George D. Hodge, and A. A. Hodge; buried Rose Hill Cemetery. (Maury Democrat, 15 June 1893.) James Hodge's residence on the Pulaski Pike was between the Confederate and Federal armies, and a tree in the yard was struck by a Federal cannon ball. (Columbia Herald, 28 Oct. 1870.) James Hodge says he came to Columbia in 1820 and the chimney of John W. Lemaster's blacksmith shop was standing in Kuhn & Turpin's factory yard, half stone and the upper part of brick, at the rear of Felix K. Zollicoffer's printing office. (Columbia Herald and Mail, 15 June 1877.) (N.B. The log home of James Hodge was moved and rebuilt in the rear of the compiler's home in 1976.)

169

HODGE, Richard, deceased; tribute of respect published by I.O.O.F. Lodge 145 of Carenville, KY. (Nashville Dispatch, 5 June 1862.)

HODGE, W. R., his death resulted from overdose of chlora as a bottle was found by his bedside; of Columbia. (Whig & Tribune, Jackson, TN, 23 Sept. 1871.)

HODGE, Mrs. Sarah A., 59, died March 20. (Columbia Herald and Mail, 12 April 1878.)

HODGE, Jack, or Happy Jack or Jack Forrest, was murdered in Jackson, TN, on the 7th; he was well-known orderly of General Forrest and known by everyone in Forrest's cavalry; shot in head by Mr. Pryor. (Memphis Daily Appeal, 9 May 1869.) John Hodges, one of General Forrest's orderlies during the war, was killed near Ganter's Store in Jackson, TN, by John Pryor on Friday; both drunk at the time; known as Happy Jack. (Nashville Republican Banner, 11 May 1869.)

HODGES, Willimina, 5 months 4 days, infant of Samuel and Eveline Hodges; died on 15 May 1863. (Nashville Dispatch, 16 May 1863.)

HODGES, Lewis S., of Giles County, was brought to Nashville under $1000 fine to be worked off at $2 a day for disloyalty and harboring guerrillas. (Nashville Dispatch, 10 May 1865.)

HOEFSTETLER, Christian, has been arrested as a spy. (Nashville Dispatch, 29 March 1863.)

HOFFMAN, merchant of Nashville, was murdered some time ago by James Lysaught, William Dean, George Craft, and Thomas Perry, who are to be hanged 26 Jan. 1866. They were Federal soldiers who robbed and murdered. (Memphis Avalanche, 20 Jan. 1866.) (N.B. Refer to Heffernan entry earlier.)

HOFFMAN, Phil., well-known barkeeper on board the steamer Gem, died on board Monday night; native of Madison, Indiana. (Nashville Dispatch, 4 Feb. 1863.)

HOFFMAN, Jacob, 90, died on the 6th in Henry County. (Whig and Tribune, Jackson, TN, 22 Nov. 1873.)

HOFFMAN, Thomas J., old citizen of Nashville, died yesterday of apoplexy; lived in German town; wife and 5 children survive. (Nashville Republican Banner, 22 June 1870.)

HOGAN, Mrs. Addie, died Saturday near Burns Spring, Columbia, buried at Belfast. (Maury Democrat, 6 Nov. 1899.)

HOGAN, Lizzie H., wife of P. H. Hogan, died yesterday. (Nashville Union and American, 26 June 1873.)

HOGAN, Fannie, and George Estes were married in country church in Marion County, Alabama, on Friday; just as ceremony was over a shot was fired through a window and the bride fell dead at foot of groom, killed by a load of buckshot. A discarded lover told her she would never marry anyone and he is suspected of the crime, although he has not been arrested yet. There is no trace of the assassin. Date line Jasper, Ala., Jan. 13. (Columbia Herald, 16 Jan. 1891.)

HOGE, Mrs. Lucy A., relict of late Hervey Hoge, of Mt. Pleasant, age 56, died on the 20th at "Fonte Nelle," home of John W. Terrass. (Nashville Republican Banner, 21 July 1870.)

HOGG, Col. Harvey, of 2d Illinois Cavalry, was killed in fight at Bolivar, TN, on August 30; was a Tennessean; married a lady of Clarksville, we believe. (Nashville Dispatch, 3 Oct. 1862.)

HOGGATT, Dr. James W., 65, died on 17th at Nashville of protracted illness, old and esteemed citizen. (Nashville Dispatch, 19 March

1863.) Mrs. M. A. Hoggatt, administratrix, published notice in paper about estate. (Nashville Dispatch, 26 Aug. 1863.)

HOGLE, William H. H., of 15th Indiana Volunteers, son of Dr. Hogle, surgeon of Hospital 11 in Nashville, died at Murfreesboro Wednesday from a wound received in engagement of the previous day. (Nashville Daily Union, 9 Jan. 1863.) William Henry Harrison Hogle, died at Murfreesboro, born Feb. 1841 in Coshocton County, Ohio, went to Indiana in 1849; on June 1861 walked 38 miles to get his father's permission to join Union Army. (Nashville Daily Union, 11 Jan. 1863.)

HOLCOMB, Miss L. L., died Thursday of last week of tuberculosis. (Columbia Herald and Mail, 6 March 1874.)

HOLCOMB, Mrs. Patience, 85, died Jan. 19 of paralysis. (Maury Democrat, 26 Jan. 1896.)

HOLCOMB, Tom, formerly of Maury County, was murdered at Forrest City, Arkansas, recently; received two shots in breast and one in head; had $500 on him. (Columbia Herald and Mail, 18 June 1875.)

HOLDEN, Jason S., committed suicide by hanging himself in barn near depot in Columbia on Friday; wife and 5 children survive; tried to kill himself 14 months ago; had suffered bad health; found hanging by his son Charlie Holden; he came here 12 years ago from Marshall County. (Maury Democrat, Columbia, TN, 6 June 1895.)

HOLDER, Mrs. Henry, of Broadview in Maury County, died last Friday week. (Maury Democrat, Columbia, TN, 3 June 1889.)

HOLMAN, W. Boyd, second son of James T. and Clementine H. Holman, age 33, died March 5 at Jacksonville, Florida; buried in Nashville on March 9. (Nashville Republican Banner, 9 March 1870.) Young Holman and James W. McClelland both died in Jacksonville of consumption at the same time and their remains arrived in Nashville together. (Nashville Republican Banner, 9 March 1870.)

HOLMAN, Henry, died Wednesday in Maury County; had a fine mind. (Columbia Herald and Mail, 30 Oct. 1875.)

HOLMAN, Mrs. Susan Harris, died 14 Aug. 1871 in Maury County; born 29 Oct. 1860 in Hanover County, Virginia. (Columbia Herald, 18 Aug. 1871.)

HOLMAN, Lee, Esquire, 69, ex-mayor of Columbia, died last night. (Columbia Herald, 18 Feb. 1870. (N.B. Age also given as 88 in the same paper.)

HOLMAN, notorious guerrilla of Middle Tennessee, has been captured in Decherd, TN, with nine men and four officers; they have been guilty of murder, arson and robbery. (Nashville Daily Union, 26 Sept. 1862.)

HOLLINGSWORTH, Jonathan, died at his home near Sorby, TN, on last Sunday; he was quite old. (Waynesboro Tribune, 23 Sept. 1897.)

HOLLINGSWORTH, Henrietta, 9 years 6 months, youngest daughter of the late Henry Hollingsworth, died on the 6th at Beech Cove of diphtheria. (Nashville Dispatch, 10 Sept. 1863.)

HOLLINS, George White, 15 months, infant son of R. S. and Mary W. Hollins, died on the 24th of scarlet fever; on July 1 their daughter Leila Mary, age 7 years 3 months, died. (Nashville Dispatch, 2 July 1862.)

HOLLINS, Mary W., wife of R. S. Hollins, is to be buried today. (Nashville Republican Banner, 19 Oct. 1869.)

HOLLIS, Will, brakeman, was killed when trains collided just west of the Columbia Milling Company while he was opening the switch of the

Nashville and Florence Railroad; he was "crushed almost to a jelly" and his remains were sent to Nashville for burial; wife and two children survive. (Columbia Herald, 18 Sept. 1896.)

HOLLISTER, James, was killed by a soldier Thursday at the Commercial Hotel in Nashville. (Nashville Daily Union, 15 Nov. 1862.)

HOLLISTER, Henry, "one of the most enterprising and pushing men in Stewart County has died." (Nashville Republican Banner, 13 Jan. 1871.)

HOLLISTER, H. M., whose parents are said to reside near Nashville, died July 20 of measles at Alton Military Prison, Illinois. (Nashville Dispatch, 12 Aug. 1862.)

HOLLYWOOD CEMETERY, once beautiful cemetery at Richmond, Virginia, is said to be overrun with cows, pigs, and goats. (Houston County News, 8 Feb. 1879.)

HOLMES, Sheriff, who was shot through the head at Trinity, Texas, on the 11th ult., while attempting to arrest Capt. McGee of the Indian Territory, died on the 26th ult; McGee is still at large. (Columbia Herald and Mail, 8 June 1877.)

HOLT, Andrew A., noted pirate and smuggler on the Puget Sound for many years, was fatally shot on his sloop near Seattle, Washington, on Thursday while resisting arrest. Dateline March 15. (Maury Democrat, 20 March 1890.)

HOLT, Seth, who lived a hermit life in a rude hut in Sumner County, committed suicide by hanging himself with a slender piece of bark a few days ago--he was found hanging to a tree. (Memphis Daily Appeal, 30 July 1868.)

HOLT, Mrs. Nancy, 86, died on the 26th in Giles County. (Whig and Tribune, Jackson, TN, 9 Nov. 1872.)

HOLT, Mrs. A. K., died on Feb. 27; formerly Sue F. Slayback. (Nashville Republican Banner, 28 Feb. 1869.)

HOLT, Nick, was murdered last week by George Grant. (Nashville Republican Banner, 17 Dec. 1869.)

HOOD, William Calvin, 37, died near Concord in Maury County, buried at Mt. Wesley Cemetery. (Columbia Herald, 15 Nov. 1899.)

HOOD, John Bell. Hennen Tomb, Metaire Cemetery, New Orleans, inscription: Gen. John Bell Hood, C.S.A., born Owensville, Kentucky 21 June 1831; died 30 Aug. 1879. (N.B. He was born correctly 1 June 1831, at Owingsville, Kentucky.)

Major General Hood's leg was shot off in an engagement at Chickamauga. (Nashville Dispatch, 25 Sept. 1863.) General Hood is doing well. (Nashville Dispatch, 6 Oct. 1863.) John B. Hood surrendered at Natchez on the 31st. (Nashville Daily Union, 7 June 1865.)

The Legislature of Texas created a new county called Hood County, but this was vetoed by the Governor. However, it passed by the senate over the veto by 16 to 7. (Memphis Daily Appeal, 16 Nov. 1866.) General Hood is doing good business as commission merchant in New Orleans. (Memphis Daily Appeal, 15 Nov. 1868.)

HOOD'S ROMANCE. I remember to have read somewhere a number of years ago the following story, but I know nothing of its authenticity.

At the time General John B. Hood was given command of the Army of Tennessee, he was engaged to be married to a lady, who for beauty, cleverness and ambition had no superior in the South. She was at the time visiting the family of Jefferson Davis at Richmond, and with all a woman's ambition for her promised husband, she determined, if possible, to help him to a position where his unequalled abilities as a fighter would find a proper sphere.

"I will try to have you given command of the Army of Tennessee," she had written him, and "you must succeed." When he was given the command it was a proud day for the woman he loved, but all the world knows the result. The terrible mistake at Franklin and the great battle of Nashville, which was fought and lost.

Gen. Hood was sent for by the authorities at Richmond. The next day after he arrived in the city he received a note from the lady mentioned, requesting him to call on her at his earliest convenience.

When he went to see her, she met him with a packet in her hand. "Gen. Hood," she said, looking straight into his eyes, "when I became engaged to you I had the fullest faith in your success. I tried to help you and did assist in having the command of the Army of Tennessee given you. You have failed; how or why is now beside the question. I can never bring myself to bear the name of a man who wears the prestige of defeat, and I sent for you to say that our engagement must be at an end. Here are your letters and some things that you gave me. Now, good bye, and let the dead past be forgotten. Good-bye."

While she was speaking, Gen. Hood was standing on his crutches for he had lost a leg and his arm had been shattered in the service of his country. It was hard to bear, for he had done all that mortal could do to win and bowing his stately head, pale and without noticing the hand outstretched to bid him good-bye, he turned and went out from her presence forever. (Hohenwald Chronicle, 19 July 1901.)

LOCAL HISTORY. In an article published in The Times some weeks ago, on the authority of Capt. A. D. Ray, one of the most faithful and gallant soldiers ever sent out by Lauderdale, we stated that Hood's army crossed the river at this point early in the morning. This statement was called in question by the Banner; though Capt. Ray adheres to his opinion nevertheless.

In order to refresh his memory, he wrote to several of his old comrades who crossed with him, and they sustain his view of the interesting local historical point.

Lieut. Nich. D. Malone, of Capt. Wm. Richardson's (Limestone) company says, "I am sure you are right as to our crossing the river about sunrise," and continuing: "Have a vague impression that other forces had crossed elsewhere; whether they had come into Florence or not I don't know."

Lieut. A. S. Ray, of Capt. Ray's company, who lives at Centre Star, says: "I think I recollect very well when Hood's army crossed the river. We crossed on Sunday morning, November 6th, early in the morning. We were among the first that crossed. There were five pontoons crossed near the bridge. Gen. Ed. Johnson, Adj. Wilson and a few men crossed some distance above us and were first on this side. We could see the Yankee pickets when we started to cross, but they were on a hill above us in front of Johnson and Wilson. They fired a few shots and left in confusion. Two Yankees surrendered to Wilson near the courthouse."

Capt. Ray makes a strong case for his side of the question. (Florence, Ala., Times, 4 July 1891.)

EVENING'S REVERIES. I may mention in this connection that it is an historical fact and one often repeated that Gen. Jackson crossed this stream (i.e., the Tennessee River) just above the mouth of Cypress while on his way to defend New Orleans, but there is another

historical fact and one seldom mentioned and that is that General
Hood with 30,000 veterans pontooned the Tennessee at Patton's
Island, just above the bridge, and crossed in one-third of the time
consumed by Jackson, in crossing an army less than one-tenth of
that of the Confederate general. (Florence, Ala., Times, 30 May
1891.)

HOOKER, Dr. Charles, one of the most eminent physicians in Connecticut
died at New Haven on the 19th, age 64. (Nashville Dispatch, 28 March
1863.)

HOOPER, Mrs. Inez, wife of W. F. Hooper, died Sept. 21. (Nashville
Union and American, 23 Sept. 1874.)

HOOPER, John Marion, 11 months 15 days, infant son of W. T. Hooper,
died September 9. (Nashville Union and American, 10 Sept. 1874.)

HOOPER, James Patterson, infant son of J. M. and Mary Hooper, aged
3 months, died on the 17th. (Nashville Republican Banner, 18 Dec.
1868.)

HOOPER, Thomas, oldest Mason in Massachusetts, died; he was the oldest
past master in the country; buried July 26; in 1812 he was Master
of King Solomon Lodge and served on the Charleston Board of
Aldermen in 1847. (Memphis Daily Appeal, 6 Sept. 1868.)

HOPKINS, H. H.,'s infant son died of croup Monday. (Humphreys County
News, 16 Nov. 1877.)

HOPKINS. Lines on the death of Mrs. H. L. Hopkins' infant published.
(Nashville Republican Banner, 31 Jan. 1869.)

HOPKINS, Mr., has been arrested for murder of Mr. Hanson in Washington
County, Missouri. (Clarksville Jeffersonian, 11 Feb. 1857.)

HOPKINS, Stephen A., died 9 Jan. 1900 near Waverly, Tenn. Of a family
of ten children, he was the first one to be gathered Home. There
remains six brothers--William E., Hillsboro, New Mexico; Matthew A.,
Parkman, Ohio; Silas M., Santa Barbara, California; Henry H., Waverly,
Tenn., Edwin J., Thayer, Mo.,; Charles P., of McEwen, Tenn.; and
sisters Mrs. Sarah L. Philleo of Mason, Mich.; Mrs. Lucina R. White
of Waverly, Tenn.; and Mrs. Bettie E. Farrington, of Parkman, Ohio;
and two sons, C. O., of Erin, Tenn.; S. W. (Mott) Hopkins of
Dickson, and Mrs. Lillian Craft, of near Waverly. (Original Clipping
from unknown newspaper in possession of Iris Hopkins McClain,
Columbia, Tennessee.)

HORD, Jante Caswell, died on the 31st ult. of typhoid, daughter of
Thomas Hord of Rutherford County. (Nashville Daily Gazette, 3 Nov.
1852.)

HORN, Nancy B., wife of Richard H. Horn, only sister of John V. Gilbert,
died and funeral to be held today. (Nashville Dispatch, 29 Nov.
1863.)

HORN, Captain W. H., funeral to be held today at Christ Church.
(Nashville Republican Banner, 10 March 1870.)

HORNBEAK, Esther, colored, died last Sunday at Centerville, Hickman
County, age 119 years; the records of her age are unimpeachable.
(Maury Democrat, Columbia, TN, 1 Aug. 1895.)

HORNE, Carl, a German, was hung for murder at Leavenworth on 13th; the
first legal hanging in the state of Kansas. (Nashville Dispatch,
1 March 1863.)

HORSLEY, John Goddard, of the Columbia Herald and Mail, died; he was
the eighth child of the Rev. William Horsley and was born 1838 on

174

Lytles Creek; married 1861 to Mattie Bradshaw; elected Maury County magistrate 1871 and on 1 Jan. 1875 elected county chairman and died before assuming duties; buried Rose Hill. (Columbia Herald and Mail, 29 Jan. 1875.)

HORTON, Mrs. Margaret, age 80, died 1 1/2 miles southwest of Franklin, TN. (Whig and Tribune, Jackson, TN, 31 May 1873.)

HOSEA, L. M., who married the daughter of a prominent doctor of Philadelphia, Pennsylvania, was arrested for forgery and sent to the Pennsylvania peniteniary. (Memphis Avalanche, 22 April 1867.)

HOUGH, A. J., son of the Widow Hough of High Street in Nashville, committed suicide Nov. 21 by shooting himself in eye with a pistol; no cause was assigned for the act. He was not married and had served in the Confederate Army during the war. (Memphis Daily Appeal, 22 Nov. 1868.)

HOUGH, Lewis B., 50, died 7 Nov. 1863 of consumption in Nashville. (Nashville Daily Union, 8 Nov. 1863.)

HOUGH, Joseph H., Esquire, 43 of Nashville, died in New Orleans on January 23; was buried in Nashville last Sunday; Presbyterian. (Tennessee Democrat, 8 Feb. 1844.)

HOUGH, Sarah Frances, 8, died on the 4th; daughter of Mr. and Mrs. T. J. Hough. (Nashville Dispatch, 6 Aug. 1862.)

HOUGH, Lotty, actress, is to appear in the new theater at Nashville on the 21st. (Nashville Dispatch, 20 Sept. 1863.) Lotty Hough, well known actress, has obtained a divorce from her husband. (Nashville Dispatch, 19 Aug. 1863.)

HOUGH, Mrs. Jack, died at home of her son-in-law Robert Scott near Six-Mile Branch on the Huntsville Road Wednesday last, aged about 80 years. (Florence, Ala., Times, 23 Jan. 1892.)

HOUSEN, Mrs., 60, who lived 9 miles from Nashville on the Nolensville Pike, was taken from her home Monday night by unknown persons and hanged in gallows for hogs. When she was found, she was quite dead. (Whig and Tribune, Jackson, TN, 5 April 1873.) Sarah Housen, aged lady, was taken out of her bed and hanged; widow of Dan Housen. She was hanged from cross beam where hogs were slaughtered. She was the step-daughter of Sterling Guy and was the third of the children to meet unnatural death. One drowned in James River, Virginia, and another froze to death. The murder is a mystery. (Nashville Union and American, 26 March 1873.) There is some evidence against two negroes in the murder of Mrs. Housen. William C. Housen has also been accused of murdering his mother. She was buried on the farm. (Nashville Union and American, 30 March 1873.) Mrs. S. J. Housen is in jail as an accessory in the murder of her mother-in-law. (Nashville Union and American, 6 Aug. 1873.) Mrs. William Housen is on trial for the murder of old lady Housen. Sterling Harper, a cousin of Housen's, was implicated in the death. (Nashville Union and American, 16 May 1874.)

HOUSER, Mrs. Brown, died in Hickman County; daughter of W. C. Kennedy. (Columbia Herald, 12 Sept. 1873.)

HOUSER, F. A., of District 17, Maury County, had a twin to die last week, they were born the week before. (Columbia Herald and Mail, 16 July 1875.)

HOUSER, Jonathan, 95, and his nephew William H. French, 72, died of la grippe within four hours of each other near Knoxville last week; they lived on Stock Creek. (Maury Democrat, Columbia, TN, 14 Jan. 1892.)

HOUSTON, Jabez, had leg amputated and died in Houston County. (Erin Review, 6 May 1882.)

HOUSTON, James, was recently murdered in McIntosh County, Ga., and the five negroes who murdered him were tried, found guilty and executed on the 26th. (Nashville Daily Gazette, 12 Aug. 1852.)

HOUSTON, Judge Russell, died of old age in Louisville, KY. He was chief council of the L & N for a quarter of a century and was the only person who ever held that office. In 1868 he became president but declined re-election. (Maury Democrat, 10 Oct. 1895.) Judge Russell Houston, chief attorney for the Louisville and Nashville Railroad Company died 1 Oct. 1895 at 10:15 p.m., principally from the infirmities of old age, superinduced by asthma. Judge Houston, as he was universally known, was born 10 Jan. 1810 in Williamson County, being the son of David and Hannah Houston of a leading Southern family. He was educated at the Nashville University for the law. In October 1862 he was elected director of the Louisville & Nashville Company and until October 1868 he was a director. He was the fourth President of the company in 1868, and in 1867-68 was vice president. In October 1868 he was elected chief attorney of the company, which he held continuously since, though for four or five years his position has been an advisory one. Mr. Houston married Miss Grizelda Polk at Columbia, TN, 4 June 1844. (Columbia Herald, 4 Oct. 1895.)

HOUSTON, Sam, Jr., is among the wounded prisoners taken to St. Louis. He is a nephew, it is said, of the old Texas Sam. (Nashville Dispatch, 20 April 1862.)

HOUSTON, Sam. The Richmond Whig records the death of Gen. Sam Houston, of Texas. His decease has been so often reported, that this present announcement will be received with many doubts. The event is stated to have occurred at his residence, in Texas, on the 25th of July last. It is a little singular that this intelligence was not received long since, still, the report may be correct.

The life of General Houston has been a most eventful one, full of strange and stirring incidents. He was born in Rockbridge County, Va., in 1793. His father, an officer in the war of the revolution, died in 1807, leaving a widow and nine children. Soon after, Mrs. Houston and her children crossed the Alleghany Mountains and took up her residence near the Tennessee river (in Blount county, if we mistake not), then the boundary between the white men and the Cherokee Indians. Sam was soon placed in a country store, but was thus employed only a few weeks, when he ran off and spent several months among the Cherokee Indians.

When 18 years of age, he enlisted as a private in the United States Army, and was soon made an ensign. He distinguished himself at the battle of the Horse Shoe, under Gen. Jackson, in 1814, and was dangerously wounded.

After peace, he was made a lieutenant, but resigned, and studied law in Nashville. He was soon after elected Attorney General and for the judicial district embracing Nashville, and Major General of the State, and in 1823 was sent to Congress. He was re-elected in 1825, and chosen Governor in 1827.

This latter office, in consequence of a domestic affliction, he resigned in 1829, and again made his home among the Cherokee Indians, with whom he remained for three years, and became exceedingly popular with them. Subsequently he was elected a member of the State Convention which met at San Felipe de Austin in 1833, and after adopting a constitution, addressed a memorial to the government of Mexico setting forth the reasons why Texas should be recognized as one of the States of the Mexican Confederacy.

The distinguished part Gen. Houston took in the war that followed this movement is well known. He was the first President of the new Republic in 1836, and was again elected to the same office in 1841. On the admission of Texas into the Union, in 1845, he was elected to the United States Senate, where he served several years, and on his final return to Texas he was again chosen Governor of the State. This office he held at the time of the secession of Texas, and because of his refusal to sanction the act of secession, he was deposed by the State Convention which adopted that act, and the duties of the office were discharged by the Lieutenant Governor. He is reported to have subsequently espoused the Rebel cause. (Nashville Dispatch, 24 Sept. 1863.)

Sam Houston has been elected President of the Texas Republic it is certain. (Tennessee Telegraph, Murfreesboro, TN, 23 Oct. 1841.)

HOWARD, Hattie Bethal, daughter of Tup Howard of Mt. Pleasant, died Friday and buried in family burying ground. (Columbia Herald, 28 Feb. 1891.)

HOWARD, Colonel John K., of Lebanon, died recently in Richmond, Virginia, from wound received in battle at Chickahominy. (Nashville Dispatch, 8 August 1862.)

HOWELL, Mrs. Pattie Card, wife of M. B. Howell, to be buried today. (Nashville Republican Banner, 6 August 1869.) Mrs. Morton B. Howell died 4 August 1869 of congestive chill. (Nashville Republican Banner, 5 August 1869.) M. B. Howell was described as Nashville's fiddle-playing mayor. (Nashville Tennessean, 17 November 1968.)

HOWELL, R. B. C., son of Morton B. and Belle Howell, died September 7 in Edgefield. (Nashville Dispatch, 8 Sept. 1863.)

HOWELL, Mrs. Isabel, died April 13 in Nashville, wife of Morton B. Howell. (Nashville Republican Banner, 14 April 1868.)

HOWELL, Mrs., mother-in-law of Mr. Jefferson Davis, died a few days ago in Montreal. She married a son of General Howell of Revolutionary War fame and was a native of Georgia. (The Minitor, Murfreesboro, TN., 7 Dec. 1867.)

HOWELL, W. H., died yesterday. (Nashville Republican Banner, 25 May 1869.)

HOWELL, Dr. Robert Boyte Crawford, 67, of the First Baptist Church, died Sunday; born Wayne County, NC, on 10 March 1801. (Nashville Republican Banner, 7 April 1868.)

HOWELL, Mrs. Jesse, 70, died on the 29th ult. (Columbia Herald, 2 May 1873.)

HOWELL, Samuel, of Tipton County, was killed instantly with axe by Armstead Randolph (c), while in his own stables; the murderer escaped. (Memphis Avalanche, 4 January 1866.)

HOWERTON, Mrs. M. D., wife of J. T., died yesterday. (Nashville Republican Banner, 27 May 1869.)

HOWERTON, Mrs. Mary A., wife of Captain Robert W. Howerton of Lafayette, Christian County, KY, age 66, died Monday the 17th inst. in Edgefield. (Nashville Republican Banner, 22 Oct. 1870.)

HOWLETT, Lizzie, died Friday in Nashville, buried Wilkes Cemetery in Maury County. (Maury Democrat, 30 Oct. 1899.)

HOWLY, Mrs. Mary, who keeps boarding house on College Street, Nashville, died last night of overdose of morphine; had no family. (Nashville Republican Banner, 7 Sept. 1869.) Mrs. Mary Howly, wife of Richard Howly, died yesterday; funeral to be held at the Cathedral.

(Nashville Republican Banner, 7 Sept. 1869.) Inquest held on Mrs. Mary Howly, who died Monday night, age 42, and who "indulged in excess intoxicating beverages," and the verdict was that she came to her death by overdose of morphine while drinking. (Nashville Republican Banner, 8 Sept. 1869.)

HOWS, Sarah A. M., deceased, and her will has been admitted to probate. (Nashville Republican Banner, 24 Dec. 1867.)

HOWTON, Capt. Van, noted guerrilla, was killed at Wartrace on the 21st. (Nashville Daily Union, 26 Feb. 1865.)

HOYTE, Elizabeth Behren, infant daughter of Eliza B. and J. W. Hoyte, died on the 14th. (Nashville Dispatch, 13 Sept. 1863.)

HOYTE, Mary, young daughter of J. W. and E. B., died 19 May 1864 of scarlet fever. (Nashville Daily Union, 20 May 1864.)

HUBBELL, Mr. and Mrs. Bishop, of Giles County paid a recent visit to their son at Southport. Mr. Hubbell is quite old and served in both the Mexican and Florida wars. (Columbia Herald, 10 May 1895.)

HUCKSTEP, Capt. S. M., Company D, 115 Illinois Volunteer Infantry, died on the 9th in Nashville of wounds received in battle 20 Sept. 1863 at Chickamauga. (Nashville Daily Union, 19 Dec. 1863.)

HUDDLESTON, W. C., well-to-do farmer living near Centerville, Hickman County, met with serious if not fatal accident last Sunday by being kicked by a horse. He was first thrown by the animal, which then wheeled and kicked him, knocked two holes in his head the size of the corks on the shoes. (Columbia Herald, 5 March 1897.) W. C. Huddleston of Centerville is going to Nashville for a trepining operation. (Columbia Herald, 7 May 1897.)

HUDSON, James W., born Mecklenburg Co., NC, 24 Nov. 1808, fell dead 30 Oct. 1893 in San Diego, California; married Mary J. Hill, who died after two years of marriage; moved 1880 to Nashville, and in Feb. 1888 moved to San Diego; one son survives. (Maury Democrat, Columbia, TN, 16 Nov. 1893.)

HUDSON, John, drowned where Rutherford Creek and Carter's Creek come together in Maury County on Sunday; had epileptic fit while fishing. (Maury Democrat, Columbia, TN, 17 April 1890.)

HUDSON, John, while getting off mule, caught foot in trace chain, fell frightened the mule who ran away, drug Hudson and broke his neck; on the J. G. Osborn farm last week; buried at Lasting Hope Cemetery; wife and 10 children survive; his oldest son drowned in Rutherford Creek last year. (Maury Democrat, 10 July 1891.)

HUEY, Mrs. Elizabeth P., wife of James Huey, formerly of Maury County, died August 27 in Collin County, Texas. (Columbia Herald, 10 Oct. 1873.)

HUEY, J. H. The heirs of J. H. Huey are to file a claim for $14,000 for the destruction of property by the Federal Army during the Civil War of the mill five miles north of Columbia. Part of Rose-crans Army camped at the mill and although Huey had taken the oath, Federal soldiers burned $8,000 worth of timber, $2,000 of grain and then asked for a lighted chunk from the fire and deliberately burned the mill down. (Daily Herald, 5 Sept. 1902.) Huey's Mill is five miles east of Columbia. (Columbia Herald, 15 April 1870.)

HUFFMAN, Lewis, and his cousin Mr. Johnson were killed by guerrillas in Brownsville, Texas; were savagely murdered. (Nashville Daily Union, 20 Feb. 1863.)

HUFFMAN. A man named Huffman is on trial in Carroll County, TN; after his sentence he confessed and implicated others as belonging to a band of horse thieves, gamblers, robbers, and counterfeiters, and said they had their headquarters on Reelfoot Lake. (Columbia Herald, 25 Jan. 1871.)

HUGER, Capt. T. B., of the Confederate States Navy, has died; commanded the McRae and was wounded in battle of Fort Jackson. (Nashville Dispatch, 1 June 1862.)

HUGER, General Benjamin, Major General in Confederate Army, died last Friday in Charleston, NC; commanded a division in the Army of Northern Virginia and was censured for his tardiness in the Seven Days Battle before Richmond; age 69. (Columbia Herald and Mail, 14 Dec. 1877.)

HUGGINS, George, died last week at Henryville, Lawrence County, of consumption; had worked at Pump Factory in Columbia. (Maury Democrat, Columbia, TN, 13 July 1893.)

HUGGINS, Miss Tennie, died on the 29th on Col. M. P. Erwin's farm. (Columbia Herald, 9 Dec. 1870.)

HUGGINS, William N., 40, died April 7 of consumption; buried Rose Hill Cemetery in Columbia. (Columbia Herald, 10 April 1896.)

HUGHES, Michael, proprietor of Shamrock Saloon, was halted by two soldiers and shot in breast, believe to be a fatal wound; he was an old and respected man and was going for a doctor for his wife on the eve of her confinement. (Nashville Daily Union, 2 March 1865.)

HUGHES, youngest child of Mr. and Mrs. Monroe Hughes of Greenfield Bend died on the 1st. (Columbia Herald, 15 Sept. 1871.)

HUGHES, Joseph, died of typhoid on August 20 at Godwin. (Columbia Herald, 21 Aug. 1896.)

HUGHES, Miss Missie, died Sunday near Godwin, Maury County, of typhoid; daughter of Mrs. Rebecca Hughes, and was the second child Mrs. Hughes has had to die in last month; buried family burying ground. (Columbia Herald, 18 Sept. 1896.)

HUGHES, John, a very good boy, whose mother resides at corner of Vine Street and Crawford Street, died suddenly Saturday morning and buried this afternoon. (Nashville Dispatch, 7 July 1863.)

HUGHES, Lavinia, daughter of J. W. Hughes of Brownsville, was buried at Rose Hill in Columbia on Friday. (Columbia Herald and Mail, 23 July 1875.)

HUGHES, William, Esquire, age 86, died at his home near Columbia last week. (Whig and Tribune, Jackson, TN, 21 Oct. 1871.)

HUGHES, Col. A. P., 76, was found dead Thursday in front of his residence, his face was in a puddle of water; born in Henry County, Virginia; professed religion 1871 at Hurricane Camp Meeting; had sons Patrick Henry and Dr. James A. Hughes. (Columbia Herald, 18 July 1873.)

HULL, Mrs. Maud, wife of Charles V. Hull, 26, died Tuesday and buried at Rose Hill; sister of Tom Cunningham. (Columbia Herald, 14 Aug. 1891.)

HUMMER, C. W., died yesterday, age 51, funeral at First Baptist Church. (Nashville Republican Banner, 28 Sept. 1870.)

HUMMER, Mrs. Ann, wife of Charles Hummer, died March 1 of consumption; daughter of Mr. and Mrs. B. F. Brown. (Nashville Daily Union, 4 March 1865.)

HUMPHREY, Private William, died at Huntsville, Alabama, about 13 April 1864, when caisson of Cogswell 1st Illinois Battery exploded; body blown to atoms. (Nasvhille Daily Union, 15 April 1864.)

HUMPHREYS, Mrs. Bettie Claibrook, wife of Pillow Humphreys, died on the 7th; was educated at Columbia Female Institute; died in Williamson County. (Columbia Herald, 14 March 1873.)

HUMPHREYS, Mathias, 68, died Saturday in District 1 in Maury County. When he was three years old, he had an attack of fever and became blind. He was born on the farm where he died; twice married and had eight children; shrewd trader. (Columbia Herald, 26 June 1896.)

HUMPHREYS, Judge John Cowan, died recently; born 1 June 1813 in Lexington, Kentucky; cousin of West H. Humphreys. (Memphis Daily Appeal, 6 Oct. 1868.)

HUNT, W. H. H., committed suicide at Memphis on Monday. (Nashville Republican Banner, 2 March 1871.)

HUNT, Mrs., 65, died; buried Elmwood Cemetery in Memphis. (Memphis Avalanche, 4 April 1866.)

HUNT, Mary Eliza, age 7, youngest child of Col. W. R. and Elizabeth Hunt, died on the 11th; called "Minnie." (Memphis Daily Appeal, 12 Nov. 1866.)

HUNT, Miss Pearl, 22, daughter of Mr. and Mrs. Steve Hunt of near Hampshire in Maury County, committed suicide by taking an overdose of morphine; left two letters but contents are not known; pretty, modest, chaste; buried in Pisgah Cemetery. (Columbia Herald, 27 Aug. 1897.)

HUNT, Turner, Esquire, died Wednesday at Culleoka; had been magistrate for many years. (Columbia Herald and Mail, 18 Jan. 1878.)

HUNT, Col. E. F., of Tullahoma, died there on the 12th of consumption. (Memphis Daily Appeal, 20 June 1870.)

HUNT, William Gibbs, Esquire, age 42 years 6 months, died in Nashville on the 13th; editor of the Nashville Banner, native of Boston; wife and three children survive. (Western Weekly Review, Franklin, TN, 17 Aug. 1833.)

HUNT, Jesse M., 14, son of J. W. Hunt, Esquire of Washington County, was thrown from horse recently and injured so badly as to cause his death. (Nashville Dispatch, 23 April 1863.)

HUNTER, Capt. R. P., 43, one of Nashville's prominent business men, died this morning at home of his father-in-law, Rev. A. L. P. Green, on White's Creek; buried Mt. Olivet Cemetery. (Nashville Union and American, 12 July 1874.)

HUNTER, Mr., of Georgetown, Bradley County, was shot by guerrillas a short time ago; he is Union man. (Nashville Daily Union, 18 Feb. 1865.)

HUNTER, W. H., deceased., Non-resident notice for his heirs published in paper and these were Dr. ___ Allen, Henry Hunter, Edwin Hunter, John Hunter, Priscilla Harlan and Mary A. Harlan. William M. Irwin was his administrator. (Maury County Herald, 12 May 1866.)

HUNTINGDON, Rev. Jonathan H., funeral to be held this evening. (Nashville Republican Banner, 26 Sept. 1869.)

HURL, ___, age 12, escaped from an Indian attack on a settlement near Lake Shetck, Minnesota, and he carried and led his two-year old brother 60 miles to New Ulm, the nearest settlement. It took 14 days to make the journey and they lived off wild fruits and roots. His mother has since been rescued. (Nashville Dispatch, 6 Nov. 1862.)

HURLEY, Amos, of Lincoln County, died recently near Nashville.
(Columbia Herald, 21 Feb. 1873.)

HURST, Martha, her body has been found in a cave in Claiborne County,
TN. It is thought her brother Newton Hurst murdered her for $100
which she had saved out of her earnings as a school teacher.
(Daily Herald, Columbia, TN, 9 June 1892.)

HURST, Judge Fielding, has been appointed U. S. Revenue Collector of
Middle Tennessee, and he is being sued by Dr. Wood of Hardeman
County, whom he forced to pay $1000 to prevent the burning of his
house. (Memphis Daily Appeal, 18 Jan. 1870.) In the winter of 1863.
Hurst and his 7th Tennessee came to Bolivar and demanded of Dr.
George Wood $1600 in gold or they would burn the houses of George
Wood, Robert H. Wood, J. H. Bills, R. P. Neely and J. J. Neely.
Hurst pocketed the money. (Memphis Daily Appeal, 20 Jan. 1870.)

HUSHAW, Sol, respected and wealthy citizen of Fountain County,
Indiana, put an end to his existence Thursday. He told some people
in Attica he belonged to a certain secret order and had divulged
some secrets and he was afraid they would kill him. He put a pistol
shot through his brain on the street. Dateline, New Albany, Ind.,
March 28. (Nashville Dispatch, 1 April 1863.)

HUTCHCRAFT, Wiley, died February 15 from blow on head by William
Kizer in Nashville, justifiable homicide. (Memphis Daily Appeal,
16 Feb. 1869.)

HUTCHINGS, David, colored, the oldest man in Lauderdale County, Ala.,
is dead. He was born in Morganton, SC, abut 1788, and was over 100
years of age and up to March of this year was active, industrious
old man. He came to North Alabama in 1817 as foreman for his master,
Colonel John Hutchings and General Jackson, and they settled on a
farm on the south side of the Tennessee River near Melton's Bluff
opposite the mouth of Elk River. Whilst here, General Jackson
took Dave to wait upon him as campman down in the Indian Nation to
hold a treaty. He went also with General John Coffee to run the
treaty line from the mouth of Cane Creek South. Melton's Bluff
being so sickly, Col. Hutchings died, and many of the negroes.
General Jackson moved them in 1819 (the year of the first Florence
land sale) into this county and turned them over to General Coffee
as administrator for Hutchings. Dave continued as foreman until
1833 when his young master Andrew J. Hutchings took charge and made
him gardener and carriage driver. Colonel Hutchings died in 1841.
He had offered Dave his freedom. He worked as foreman again until
the late war broke out and true to his honor, as he had ever been,
and the family was much attached to him. He had looked over the
weaving of the negroes' clothing all those years and his devotion to
the memory of Katie, his wife, who was born in 1792 and died in 1842,
was remarkable. He never married again but went every day to her
grave and prayed. He died a Christian. (Florence, Ala., Times,
18 July 1890.)

The following was taken from a deposition with Dave in 1882; Dave
was known in Rutherford County, TN, and was the personal servant of
Bennett Smith, who was the grandfather of the late Mr. C. M. Burtwell and Mrs. E. B. Weakley of Florence. Bennett Smith married in
Lincolnton, NC, the daughter of General Joseph Dickson of the
Revolutionary War fame. The two families emigrated to Rutherford
County, TN, about 1803. Col. Andrew Hutchings married Mary Smith,
daughter of Bennett Smith and sister of Mrs. Dr. Bedford, nee
Matilda Smith, who was the mother of Mesdames Burtwell and Weakley,
both of whom have reared large families in Florence. Hutchings
emigrated to North Alabama in 1817 and Uncle Dave was given to Mrs.
Hutchings by her father Bennett Smith. At the death of Colonel and
Mrs. Hutchings, David went to the plantation of General Coffee near
Florence. Later Andrew Hutchings, the only child of Col. and Mary
Hutchings, married Mary Coffee, daughter of General Coffee. Their

181

progeny consisted of two sons, Coffee and Andrew, who lived with their grandmother Mrs. Coffee. In this way David became a faithful servant in the Coffee family, being with Capt. A. D. Coffee up until the time of his death. David was born 1783. Bennett Smith was very wealthy and a promient lawyer in North Carolina and lived in princely style. His wife Isabella Dickson brought from her home in North Carolina in a wagon the first piano in the State of Tennessee. This old piano is yet a family relic in the homstead of the late Mrs. Burtwell in Florence. General Dickson was a member of Congress from North Carolina from 1799 to 1803 was was also an elector when Jefferson was made president. (Florence, Ala., Times, 22 Aug. 1890.)

HUTCHINSON, Roney, of Danville, KY, was arrested at Hernando, Mississippi by Confederate troops; he had a belt around his body with $25,000 in counterfeit Confederate money; he was tied up and hanged until dead. (Nashville Daily Union, 22 Feb. 1863, Nashville Dispatch, 20 Feb. 1863.) (N.B. The Union gave his first name as Rorey.)

HUTTON, Mrs. Amelia, of Metcalf, KY, is 103 years old, in good health, and "as lively as a cricket;" reared nine children. (Nashville Union and American, 1 May 1874.)

HYMAN, Jacob, 78, of South Sumner Street, died on the 2d; born in Poland and left there at the age of 13 for political reasons; had lived in Nashville for 10 years and was estimable citizen. (Nashville Republican Banner, 3 June 1868.)

HYRONEMUS, F., Sr., 63, died Sunday; funeral to be held at the Cathedral. (Nashville Union and American, 29 Sept. 1874.)

IMBODEN, General K. D., the noted Confederate cavalryman, died a few days ago at Abingdon, Virginia. (Maury Democrat, Columbia, TN, 22 Aug. 1895.)

INGERSOLL, Loyal C., about 35, of Ashton, Illinois, kills himself with dose of morphine on Tuesday in Nashville; will probably have to be buried by the county; had brother Charles L. Ingersoll of Desoto, Varona County, Illinois, and wife Eliza J. Ingersoll of Ashton, Illinois. (Nashville Union and American, 4 June 1874. N. B. Long letters of suicide published.) Word has been received to have Ingersoll buried and send the bill to his brother; he was buried yesterday at the old city cemetery. (Nashville Union and American, 5 June 1874.)

INGRAM, Francis H., 33, died October 26 in Nashville; was from Amherst, Mass.; merchant here for 10 years; died of consumption; buried City Cemetery. (Nashville Dispatch, 28 Oct. 1862.)

INGRAM, Marion, was shot and killed by John M. Fowler, 4 miles up river Thursday from Columbia; a family quarrel, brewing for a year; killed November 7. (Maury Democrat, Columbia, TN, 14 Nov. 1895.)

INMAN, P. H., was killed in Rutherford County by a negro Wiley Kimbro to whose house Inman had gone in disguise to whip Kimbro. The negro was acquitted. (Columbia Herald, 17 March 1871.)

INTERMENTS at City Cemetery, Nashville, for the month of March 1868:

Frank Vaughn, pneumonia, age 6
Eliza Short, cancer of uterus, age 37
O. G. Miller, old age, age 80
Dr. Waters, unknown cause, age 28
Martha Rundels, childbirth, age 27
Jennie Halsel, consumption, age 31
William W. Halsel, lockjaw, age 6
George Parrish, consumption, age 34

Mrs. Hayes, unknown cause, age 40
F. R. Nickle, hemorrhage, age 36
J. E. Engles, unknown cause, age 20
Sarah F. Jones, congestive chills, age 46
Isaac Hughes, consumption, age 20
Mary E. Allen, cancer, age 47
Capt. E. L. Thompson, wounds, age 28
Elizabeth Jones, consumption, age 28
Catharine Widener, inflammation of bowels, age 39
McKinley infant, pneumonia
James Gleaves, measles, infant
James Moffot, measles, infant

At the Catholic Cemetery for month of March 1868:
Michael Glesson, pneumonia, infant
Jack Supples, run over by cars, age 24

At the County Pauper Cemetery for month of March 1868:
Nancy Swane, measles, white, age 40
Tobe Vaughn, dropsy of heart, age 13
George Jones, consumption, age 16
Caroline Miller, consumption, age 33
Eli Brown, consumption, age 38
Louisa Fisher, age 25
James Rucker, spinal wort, age 32
James Johnson, consumption, age 66
Lucy Thornton, consumption, age 33
Lucy Turner, typhoid fever, age 25
Samuel McCree, white, consumption, age 40
David Payne, spasms, infant
Cameron, lockjaw, infant
Smith, stillborn, infant
Emeline Harris, pneumonia, infant
Annie Smith, scrofula, infant
Vina Roach, measles, infant
Samuel Wickliff, lockjaw, infant
Jennie Booker, measles, infant
Minnie Mitchell, pneumonia, infant
Greene, measles, infant
Larimer, stillborn
Nellie Payne, spasms, infant
Sarah E. Teavill, lockjaw, infant
Georgia S. Shelby, scrofula, infant
Lizzie Amens, catarrh, infant
Fannie Roberts, teething, infant

IRVIN, Mac, of Nashville, was discovered by the watch last night on one
of our streets in an insensible state and taken to workhouse. He
died short time afterwards. (Nashville Daily Union, 28 Nov. 1863.)

IRVINE, James, Esquire, distinguished lawyer of North Alabama, died on
the 16th at Florence, Alabama, after a brief illness. (Memphis
Avalanche, 20 Dec. 1866.)

IRVINE, Judge Caleb E., died Feb. 6 in Anaconda, Montana; he was in
his second term as probate judge; brother of Rev. R. G. Irvine of
Columbia. (Columbia Herald, 13 Feb. 1891.) Judge Caleb Ewing
Irvine, brother of R. G. Irvine, died in Anaconda, Montana, age 65;
in 1847 was in Mexican War while living at Clarksville, TN. General
Harney called for a volunteer to go into the enemy's line and
examine the position of the army. He volunteered and did work so
well that President Polk appointed him second lieutenant. After
the war he stayed in army a number of years. About 25 years ago
went to Montana and married an English woman. He was twice elected
Judge of Probate Court at Butte City; he had not seen his brother
for 43 years. One son and son daughter survive. (Maury Democrat,
12 Feb. 1891.)

IRVINE, Reverend Robert Green, born Golconda, Illinois 7 Dec. 1818;
his parents born and reared in Kentucky and only lived in Illinois
a few years when they moved back to Hickman County, KY. In 1825
his father drowned while crossing a swollen stream; moved to Robertson County, TN, where grandfather lived. On 2 July 1839 he was
converted. Married Oct. 1845 to Fannie E. Chappell of Maury County
and she died 4 Feb. 1880. He died 19 May 1893. He held the great
revival at Pulaski in 1880 at which 250 people were converted.
(Maury Democrat, 25 May 1893.)

IRWIN, Frank A., died yesterday in District 18 of inflammation-rheuma-
tism. He spent his early days on river--his father was a pioneer
on Cumberland and the captain of the first boat that ever went above
Nashville. He was one of the first members of the Knight of Pythias
in Nashville. (Nashville Union and American, 22 June 1873.)

IRWIN, Captain Henry, formerly of Jackson, TN, died recently in
Norfolk, Virginia; during the war he was aide of his brother Gen.
Elzey Irwin, of the Confederate Army. (Memphis Daily Appeal,
11 August 1868.)

ISBELL, Louis, found murdered in cabin near Athens, TN; he was a
decomposed corpse when found; he was single and known to have money.
(Maury Democrat, __ July 1889.) (N. B. This issue was No. 1 for
the year and the date torn from paper.)

IUKA DEAD. The list of Confederate dead obtained from the headboards
of those who lately have been removed and reinterred at Iuka,
Mississippi:

Captain J. W. Fair, Company E, 5th Missouri regiment infant; died
in hospital 5 May 1863.
T. J. Lloyd, Second Missouri Regiment.
C. C. Slay, Company F, 6th Missouri Regiment, killed by a railroad
car on 31 December 1864.
T. J. Reeves, company and regiment unknown.
Captain Daily, Company D, 2d Texas Regiment
S. J. Beaver, Company and regiment unknown
C. D. Hutchinson, private, Company A, 2d Regiment Missouri volunteers
Athulston Johnston, Company A, 2d Regiment Missouri Volunteers,
died in hsopital 21 October 1862.
C. A. White, Company 1, 40th Missouri Regiment
S. Watts, Company F, Stinman's Regiment of Sharpshooters, Arkansas
volunteers.
W. B. Lafave, 20th Arkansas Regiment
W. T. Walton, Company A, 3d Missouri Regiment
W. Malone, Company F, 5th Regiment Missouri Volunteers, died in
hospital 26 October 1862.
___ Knight, company and regiment unknown
T. E. Crook, Company G, 43d Missouri Regiment
M. Langley, Company D, 15th Arkansas Regiment
W. T. Maxwell, Company E, 6th Missouri Regiment
Captain Shelby, Company H, 2d Missouri Regiment, died 18 October 1863
Lt. D. G. Kelley, 26 years, Company K, 2d Regiment Missouri Volunteers,
died 14 October 1863.
S. H. Willis, company and regiment unknown
J. Miller, Company F, 5th Regiment Missouri Volunteers, died in
hospital 12 October 1862
E. D. Simms, Company H, 10th Alabama Regiment
R. Brown, Compnay B, 3rd Arkansas Cavalry
William M. Gort, from Bellville, Rush County, Texas, wounded in the
battle of Iuka, died 4 October 1862
C. Tucker, Company 1, 6th Missouri Regiment
A. G. Smith, Company K, 37th Mississippi Regiment
E. G. Dunham, company and regiment unknown
W. R. Reed, Company E, 4th Missouri Infantry
Corporal M. D. Creasey, Company B, 6th Missouri Regiment, died
28 Oct. 1862
Lt. McGhee, company and regiment unknown

___ Yearger, company and regiment unknown
Lieutenant Wind, from Missouri, company and regiment unknown
Thomas Coffee, from Missouri, company and regiment unknown
___ Westbrook, from Aberdeen, Missouri, company and regiment unknown

There are also 138 others, known to have been from Missouri, but names and companies, etc., have been lost, and the headboards are much defaced. Signed, Dr. William M. Willson. (Memphis Avalanche, 27 June 1867.)

IVY. There is an old lady living on South Street, Memphis, named Mrs. Nancy Ivy, widow of a Methodist minister, and she is in destitute circumstances. She lost two sons in Confederate service at Corinth and has an invalid daughter at home. (Memphis Daily Appeal, 4 August 1869.)

JACKSON, May P., daughter of G. W. and Henrietta Jackson, age 10 years 2 months, died Saturday and buried at Rose Hill Cemetery. (Columbia Herald, 9 January 1891.)

JACKSON. The remains of Brigadier General James S. Jackson were received at Russellville last Monday on the way for burial at Hopkinsville, Ky.; served in 3d Kentucky Cavalry. (Nashville Daily Union, 1 April 1863.)

JACKSON, Bobby, 86, of the upper end of District 24, died Wednesday of last week and found dead the next day; he was quite deaf in his last years. He was a War of 1812 pensioner. At one time he was a very large fleshy man but was greatly reduced in size. Pensioners left in Maury County include Rieves and brother, Poney Little and Arthur Cranford. Mr. Little is now 93 years old. (Columbia Herald and Mail, 11 May 1877.)

JACKSON, Mrs. Nancy, 74, wife of Bobby Jackson, died Saturday in District 24. He is 84 years old. (Columbia Herald, 21 March 1873.)

JACKSON, Elizabeth, of Huntington, West Virginia, widow of Elijah Jackson, War of 1812 soldier, is drawing a pension of $12 per month. She is 104 years old and walks five miles every quarter to receive her vouchers. She is an inveterate smoker and says she will live to be 114. She has three sons who are drawing pensions for wounds received in the late war. (Maury Democrat, Columbia, TN, 2 Jan. 1890.)

JACKSON, John A., died on the 18th ultimo and buried in the new cemetery; he was born in North Carolina but came here as a young man settled in the neighborhood called "Brick Church." (Nashville Republican Banner, 11 Feb. 1869.)

JACKSON, Calvin W., born 19 April 1812 in Chatham County, NC, died 15 April 1862 at Lebanon, TN. (Nashville Dispatch, 1 May 1862.)

JACKSON, Hannah, colored, who has lived for over a century and was a trusted servant of General Andrew Jackson, died one day last week at her home at 1221 South Cherry Street, Nashville. (Maury Democrat, Columbia, TN, 6 Sept. 1894.)

JACKSON, Andrew, 20, late of Edgefield, was killed near Council Grove, Kansas, recently; thrown from hay rake. He was born and reared in Edgefield and was licensed to preach in Methodist Church. (Nashville Union and American, 11 August 1874.)

JACKSON. Curious deed--A tree in Athens, Georgia, is a property holder. Col. W. H. Jackson took great delight in this tree and the thoughts it might be destroyed were repugnant to him. He wrote, "I, W. H. Jackson, of the county of Clarke of the one part and the oak tree

(giving location) of the county of Clarke, in consideration of
great affection he bears said tree and his desire to see it pro-
tected, has conveyed and by these presents does convey to the said
oak entire possession of itself and the land within 8 feet of it on
all sides." (Florence, Ala., Times, 10 Oct. 1890.)

JACKSON, Alex, Harvey Brown, Matt Burns, George Burrows, and ___
Carrigan, have been arrested as spies at Jackson, TN, and were taken
to St. Louis on the 20th to go to the military prison at Alton,
Illinois. (Nashville Republican Banner, 25 July 1862.)

JACKSON, Mr. and Mrs. Dave, lost their oldest child Saturday of a
throat affection; buried at Rock Springs in Maury County. (Maury
Democrat, 21 Nov. 1895.)

JACKSON, William O., 18, died on the 4th in Davidson County of cholera.
(Western Weekly Review, Franklin, TN, 8 Feb. 1833.)

JACKSON, James, newsboy on the Nashville and Chattanooga railroad,
was crushed to death by a train Thursday; cut off one leg and
mangled the other, and he died soon afterward. His father is Sherwood Jackson of Shelbyville, TN. (Nashville Republican Banner, 11
Jan. 1868.)

JACKSON, Capt. Samuel, killed in battle of Chickamauga; his remains
are to be buried at Hermitage today. (Nashville Republican Banner,
17 April 1868.)

JACKSON, William, drunk, in a stupor, fell into a muddy ditch and was
killed. When found he had been half devoured by hogs. He lived
at Galloway Station on the L & N, about 28 miles from Memphis.
(Maury Democrat, Columbia, TN, 5 Dec. 1889.)

JACKSON, Mary Elizabeth, infant daughter of General William H. and
Selene Jackson, died October 11 at Belle Meade. (Nashville
Republican Banner, 12 Oct. 1869.)

JACKSON, Alfred, 96, long-time servant of Andrew Jackson, died at the
Hermitage. He will lie in state in front hall of the mansion from
which he will be buried according to his wishes just north of the
President's grave. (Nashville paper, clipping dated 4 Sept. 1901.)

JACKSON, Andrew. A historic trunk was sent to the Atlanta Exposition
last week from Leighton, Alabama. It was once the property of
General Andrew Jackson, now owned by Mrs. Lucy King of Leighton.
General Jackson had trunk with him during the time of the military
survey from Nashville to Florence in 1814 when he was on his way
to New Orleans. He presented the trunk to Edward Thomas, Esquire
an ancestor of Mrs. King as a testimonial of friendship. Since
1873, it has been in the possession of Mrs. King, who prizes it very
highly. (Columbia Herald, 25 Oct. 1895.)

When Westbrook, the Polk home in Maury County, burned, 100 pieces of
china belonging to Andrew Jackson burned. (Maury Democrat, 16
Feb. 1893.)

FIRE. Yesterday evening at 4 o'clock the roof of the Hermitage
was discovered to be on fire, and all attempts to stop flames were
useless. Entire edifice consumed. Furniture on lower floor was
saved. Second story furniture all gone. Thought the fire caught
from a spark from the chimney. (Columbia Observer, 20 October 1834.)

Movement to purchase Andrew Jackson's home under way. The Hermitage
Association is being organized. (Maury Democrat, 14 Feb. 1889.)

JACKSON, Rachel, wife of Andrew Jackson, died 23 Dec. 1828; caught
cold and pleuretic symptoms supervened upon her constitutional
nervous affections; thousands attended her funeral and the coffin

was borne to grave dug in the garden. General Jackson went to her
grave with his left hand in the arm of Governor Carroll. An old
servant of Mrs. Jackson's burst through the group around the pit
and tried to get into the grave with the coffin. She was about
60, robust and strong, and falling near the brink she was able to
get both feet over the edge of the grave. General Jackson told the
others to leave the servant alone as "Her grief is sweet to me."
However, she was drug away by the sexton and others, and she hindered
the burial until some friends persuaded her to leave. She cried
out during the burial "My mistress, my best friend is gone, my life
is gone--I will go with her." After the funeral Jackson met friends
in the northeast room of the house and made a short speech, saying,
"I can forgive all who have wronged me but will have fervently to
pray that I may have grace to enable me to forget or forgive any
enemy who has ever maligned that blessed one..." (Columbia Herald,
2 Feb. 1872, quoting article by Henry A. Wise.)

JACKSON, Stonewall. Suffold Observer: R. E. Whitehead, our townsman,
has an acorn neatly carved out of wood, which he received from
Dr. Lafferty who gave it to him. "In 1864 a gentleman in Cincinnati
sent through the lines a twig of paulonia imperialis to Col. J. T. L.
Preston of T. J. Jackson's staff with the request that it be planted
by the tomb of the Confederate warrior in the cemetery at Lexington,
Virginia. It made rapid growth and in years disturbed the modest
mound. In 1884 Mrs. Jackson directed its removal. The sexton opened
the earth and the company present found the roots had gone directly
to the coffin and embraced by curious curves and bendings the body
of the dead champion of the south. My friend, the sexton, handed
me a section of the tree, and these little objects are made from
wood nourished by the mighty dead and holding in its fibers the dust
of the matchless hero. They are presented to me who honor the
memory of the great captain and Christian soldier." (Florence, Ala.,
Times, 26 Dec. 1890.)

The death of General Stonewall Jackson from amputation and subsequent pneumonia is announced. (Nashville Dispatch, 14 May 1863.)

General Stonewall Jackson died on Sunday afternoon, the 10th. He
was shot by accident in an engagement at Chancellorsville by his
own men. (Nashville Dispatch, 15 May 1863.)

General Jackson was shot in left arm and through the right hand. He
has been known as Stonewall since the first battle of Manassus.
"Look at Jackson, his men stand like a stone wall," uttered by
General Bartow of Georgia, and he stood until he received his death
wound. (Nashville Dispatch, 16 May 1863.)

With deep grief, the commanding general announces to the army the
death of Lt. Gen. T. J. Jackson, who expired on the 10th instant at
a quarter past 3 p.m. Signed, R. E. Lee, general. (Nashville
Dispatch, 19 May 1863.)

Mrs. Stonewall Jackson, after a week of unavoidable detention,
reached her husband's deathbed. She returned to her father's with
her baby. Her daughter married Mr. Christian of Richmond and moved
to California. Mrs. Jackson went with them and they returned
together to Charlotte, NC. Mrs. Christian got protracting fever
and died. (Maury Democrat, Columbia, TN, 17 Aug. 1893.)

Mrs. M. A. Jackson, widow of Stonewall Jackson, who now lives in
Charlotte, NC, has recently undertaken the editorship of a promi-
nent monthly magazine published at Richmond, Virginia. (Maury
Democrat, Columbia, TN, 28 March 1895.)

General Jackson's left arm was skillfully amputated below the
shoulder by Dr. McGwynn of Winchester. The general has been removed
to his country house 15 miles from Richmond and is doing well.
(Nashville Dispatch, 13 May 1863.)

It is said that Stonewall Jackson's dying words were that General A. P. Hill might be assigned to command of his troops. (Nashville Dispatch, 19 May 1863.)

Clay Whitely of Indianapolis has sent to the widow of General Stonewall Jackson the general's Bible, which Whitley took from the Confederate leader's house at Lexington, Virginia, while it was burning in June 1864. Whitley was a corporal at the time the detachment of General Sigel's troops were sent to burn the house. Mrs. Jackson is now living at Charlotte, NC, where the Bible was sent her by express. (Maury Democrat, 22 March 1894.)

Mrs. Stonewall Jackson says that whenever she visited the general in camp he "spent all of his leisure time playing with their baby." (Florence, Ala., Times, 23 Jan. 1892.)

Mrs. Stonewall Jackson is in the prime of life, her black hair still unmixed with gray, and she possesses a most attractive face. Her eyes are large and dark. (Florence, Ala., Times, 5 Sept. 1891.)

A bronze statue of heroic size is to be placed over the grave of Stonewall Jackson at Lexington, Virginia. (Maury Democrat, 20 Dec. 1888.)

A memorial window to Stonewall Jackson is to be placed in the Presbyterian Church at Lexington, Virginia, of which he was a member. (Maury Democrat, Columiba, TN, 19 April 1894.)

JACKSON. A slab of wood marks the grave of Stonewall Jackson's mother, who was buried on an eminence 700 feet above the river at Hawk's Next, Virginia. (Houston County Review, 3 April 1880.)

JACOB, Mrs. Sarah Benton, wife of Col. Richard S. Jacob, of the Kentucky Volunteer Cavalry, died at the National Hotel in Louisville on the 4th; daughter of the Honorable Thomas Hart Benton. (Nashville Dispatch, 22 Jan. 1863.)

JACOBS, William, 98, died in poorhouse in Bracken County, KY. He was a soldier of the Pennsylvania Whiskey Rebellion. (Memphis Daily Appeal, 5 April 1870.)

JAMES, Nancy, age 113, has died in Nashville; born a slave in Georgia and came here after the Civil War; buried Mt. Arrarat. (Nashville Banner, 3 May 1913.)

JAMES, Miss Betsy, celebrated her 93d birthday at the Maxwell House on the 31st ult; lived in home of Col. John Overton. (Nashville Union and American, 2 April 1873.)

JAMES, Mary, little girl, was hit by a rail thrown by a little boy and died Saturday. (Nashville Republican Banner, 23 March 1869.)

JAMES, Charles T., was killed recently at Sag Harbor while experimenting with one of his guns; born 1804 in West Greenwich, Rhode Island; in 1851 was sent to Congress from Rhode Island and served six years in the Senate. (Nashville Dispatch, 1 Nov. 1862.)

JAMES, T. C., inventor of James's projectile, was wounded by explosion of shell at Sag Harbor, Long Island, and died Oct. 17; age 58. (Nashville Dispatch, 22 Oct. 1862. See also one above.)

JAMISON, Marshal, 84, died on the 14th instant in Adamsville, KY, the father of Dr. S. M. Jamison of Edgefield. (Nashville Union and American, 17 Nov. 1874.)

JAMISON, John F., died Sunday of tuberculosis. (Nashville Republican Banner, 22 Oct. 1869.)

JAMISON, Clarence, 11, of Carters Creek, Maury County, shot himself in head Wednesday night while handling pistol; accident; died that night; son of R. C. Jamison. (Columbia Herald, 9 Jan. 1891.)

JARNIGAN, Alexander, 60, of Coffee County, was taken to the woods recently and unmercifully whipped by the Kuklux. (Memphis Daily Appeal, 14 Jan. 1869.)

JASPER, Mathew, who lived near Columbia, committed suicide on the 8th inst. (Whig and Tribune, Jackson, TN, 16 Nov. 1872.)

JASPER, Louis, who lived in Southern Virginia at about the time of the Revolutionary War, had a beard 9 1/2 feet long. He could take his mustache between his fingers and extend his arms to their full length and still the ends of the beards were over a foot beyond his finger tips. (Columbia Herald, 26 July 1895.)

JEFFERSON, Isham Randolph, nephew and adopted son of Thomas Jefferson, age 71, died on July 6 in Todd County, Kentucky. (Nashville Dispatch, 12 Aug. 1862.)

JEFFERSON, Alexander, of Henry Station, Henry County, was killed by a sawmill a few days ago. (Nashville Union and American, 6 March 1873.)

JEHL, infant, of Mr. and Mrs. Jehle, who had survived the loss of its parents at the burning of Specht's restaurant in Memphis, died yesterday while the parents were being followed to the grave. (Memphis Avalanche, 21 Dec. 1866.)

JENKINS, I. K., assistant jailor, died of cholera yesterday; he was sergeant of the Metropolitan police at one time. (Nashville Union and American, 21 June 1873.)

JENKINS, George and Daisy Jenkins, two beautiful children of George W. Jenkins, died Sunday of cholera. (Nashville Union and American, 23 June 1873.)

JETER, Mrs. R. L., died at Reynolds Station, Giles County, on the 11th. (Columbia Herald, 17 April 1891.)

JETTON, Rufus B., old citizen of Murfreesboro, dropped dead of apoplexy on the public square one day last week. (Whig and Tribune, Jackson, TN, 23 November 1872.)

JOHNS, Glover, formerly of Davidson County, died near Clinton, Mi. (Central Monitor, Murfreesboro, 19 July 1834.)

JOHNS. Three ghouls made an unsuccessful attempt to rob grave of Eli Johns (c), near Nashville on Tuesday but were foiled by relatives who were watching the grave. They fired upon the robbers and one robber (c) was found dead the next morning. The other two were Vanderbilt University medical students but sufficient evidence against them has not been gathered. (Columbia Herald, 28 Feb. 1897.)

JOHNSON. B. W. Ferguson of Columbia received information this week of the whereabouts of his sister Armindy Jane Johnson of Pierce County, Missouri, whom he has not seen or heard from in 36 years. She is 69 years old and wrote the postmaster at Pulaski and the letter was brought to Mr. Ferguson's notice. They were separated during the war and neither knew of the whereabouts of the other until this week. (Columbia Herald, 24 Dec. 1897.)

JOHNSON, John, 29, native of Belfast, Ireland, died in South Florence in this county Thursday the 24th inst. (Tuscumbian, Tuscumbia, Ala., 28 March 1825.)

JOHNSON, Miss Nettie, attempted to kill herself on the Allen Harlan farm last Monday by shooting herself near the heart with a pistol.

A love affair it is said was the cause. (Maury Democrat, Columbia, TN, 1 August 1895.)

JOHNSON, Dr. Alfred, son of Governor Johnson, died yesterday; was riding a horse which became unruly and threw him, inflicting fatal head injuries; wife is in Cincinnati. (Nashville Dispatch, 5 April 1863.)

JOHNSON, James, 66, died Tuesday in Edgefield, buried in the Nashville Cemetery. (Nashville Dispatch, 29 April 1863.)

JOHNSON, Mrs. James, of Porters Chapel in Maury County, died a few days ago and buried in Hunters Cemetery; husband and several children survive. (Maury Democrat, 7 June 1894.)

JOHNSON, W. M., died July 14 in Phoenix, Arizona; wife and 11 children survive; born in Maury County; went to Kansas City early in life; age 58. (Maury Democrat, Columbia, TN, 26 July 1894.)

JOHNSON, Robert, infant son of B. M. Johnson, 8 months, died September 21 at Santa Fe in Maury County. (Maury Democrat, 19 Sept. 1895.)

JOHNSON, Jane, 35, semi-lunatic, committed suicide near Nashville on Thursday by hanging. When found, her pipe was firmly clenched between her teeth. (Memphis Daily Appeal, 23 Sept. 1868.)

JOHNSON, Col. Thomas B., was buried Sunday; funeral took place at his father's place, Walnut Hill, 3 1/2 miles from Nashville near the Nolensville Pike; born in Kentucky; lived 42 years in Davidson County; age 67. (Nashville Union and American, 28 July 1874.) Died on 25th. (Nashville Union and American, 26 July 1874.)

JOHNSON, Charles, 83, of District 6 in Davidson County has lived here since 1800; he served in War of 1812 under General Jackson; he is son of a Revolutionary War hero. (Nashville Union and American, 24 Oct. 1874.)

JOHNSON. On Thursday the bright little nephew of W. S. Johnson of Franklin fell into scalding tub while family was killing hogs and died at 11 the following night. (Nashville Union and American, 21 Nov. 1874.)

JOHNSON, Alfred, was killed December 1876 by J. V. Brown, who has been bound guilty of murder and given 15 years. (Paris, TN, Gazette, 13 Feb. 1878.)

JOHNSON, N. H., died 20 June 1870; was member of old 154th Regiment. (Memphis Daily Appeal, 21 June 1870.)

JOHNSON, Robert, son of the ex-President, died April 22 in Greenville, TN. (Memphis Daily Appeal, 24 April 1869.)

JOHNSON, T. B., his funeral to be held today, son of Mrs. M. B. Johnson, and member of the 154th Tennessee Regiment. (Memphis Daily Appeal, 4 April 1870.)

JOHNSON. The first execution for desertion in the Department of Tennessee took place at Corinth on the 23d ult., and was A. J. Johnson of the 1st Alabama (Federal) Cavalry. (Nashville Daily Union, 1 Aug. 1863.)

JOHNSON, Bart, of Santa Fe, who married Mrs. Sallie Lamar on October 17, was one of the few men in Maury County that when the war ended was carrying a musket with his original command at Greensboro, NC, April 1865. (Maury Democrat, Columbia, TN, 25 October 1894.)

JOHNSON, Ida, infant daughter of Henry and Sarah Johnson, age 9 months 14 days, is to be buried today. (Nashville Dispatch, 12 July 1862.)

JOHNSON, Henry, is in North Carolina jail and is from Maury County, son
of esteemed and aged couple of Columbia. At the age of 15 or 16
he married Miss Mary Roane in 1857. In 1860 he was indicted for
three different cases of malicious shooting and sentenced to the pen
for 5 to 8 years. In 1861 he was pardoned to go into the Confederate
Army and made a good soldier. In 1867 he was heard from and said he
wanted to come home. In April 1870 a young woman came to Columbia,
saying she was his wife. In the meantime he had married a third time
in North Carolina. His first wife thought he was dead and is living
near Columbia. He married the second time in 1862 in Charleston and
the third time in McDowell County, NC. (Columbia Herald, 15 July
1870.)

JOHNSON, Dr. Charles, son of Governor Johnson, died on the 4th, a surgeon
in the 1st Mounted Tennessee Infantry; his horse fell on him, fatally
injuring him, and he died in a few hours in a Nashville camp.
(Nashville Daily Union, 5 April 1863.) (N. B. See another obituary
before this.)

JOHNSON, Miss Nona, 12, daughter of John Johnson, died in Williamsport.
(Columbia Herald, 1 Dec. 1899.)

JOHNSON, W. T., 53, died of pneumonia. (Maury Democrat, Columbia,
TN, 20 May 1886.)

JOHNSON, Robert, 6, died Wednesday and buried in Mt. Pleasant.
(Columbia Herald, 21 Dec. 1899.)

JOHNSON, Mrs. James, of Leipers Creek, Maury County, died on the 12th
of pneumonia. (Columbia Herald and Mail, 24 Dec. 1875.)

JOHNSON, John, who lives in West Tennessee, died Tuesday morning and
buried at Rock Springs in Maury County; father of S. S. Johnson.
(Columbia Herald, 23 Jan. 1896.)

JOHNSON, Benjamin, recently appointed postmaster at Vicksburg, Mississippi, died there a few days ago; was from New York. (Nashville
Dispatch, 2 Sept. 1863.)

JOHNSON, Mrs. Andrew, widow of the late ex-President, is dead; a good
woman, highly esteemed. She possessed a better education than her
husband and assisted him greatly in the beginning of his political
career. (Columbia Herald and Mail, 21 Jan. 1876.)

JOHNSON, Alexander, infant son of John B. and Eliza A. Johnson, age
2 months died yesterday. (Nashville Daily Gazette, 22 Oct. 1852.)

JOHNSON, Col. John B., died last night; born in Rockingham County, NC,
20 Oct. 1808; married 1835 to Miss Baird of Nashville; lived in
Columbia, TN, until 1844, moved to Nashville; had son killed in the
Confederate Army; died of heart diease. (Nashville Republican
Banner, 25 Aug. 1868.)

JOHNSON, J. Randall, of Nashville, was found in the Cumberland River
Sunday; he had been subject to violent headaches. (Maury Democrat,
14 Aug. 1913.)

JOHNSON, Colonel Thomas B., will bury his wife today. (Nashville
Republican Banner, 2 March 1871.)

JOHNSON, Mollie, fined $5 in Nashville for keeping a house of ill fame.
(Nashville Republican Banner, 12 Sept. 1869.)

JOHNSON, Bushrod, Major General in Confederate Army, died 1880 and
was buried in the Methodist Church Cemetery at Miles Station,
Illinois. On 23 August 1975 his body was returned to Nashville and
he was reburied with honors in the City Cemetery beside his wife
Mary. His tombstone was also brought from Illinois. (Nashville
Tennessean, 17 August 1975.)

191

JOHNSON. There seems to be no doubt that George W. Johnson, the
Provisional Governor of Kentucky, was killed at the Battle of
Pittsburg Landing. (Nashville Dispatch, 15 April 1862.)

JOHNSON, Honorable Cave, the postmaster general under President Polk,
died Friday at Clarksville, age 72; served 14 years in Congress.
(Memphis Avalanche, 1 Dec. 1866.) Cave Johnson has a son among the
prisoners at Camp Douglas in Illinois and he visited the camp on
the 14th. (Nashville Dispatch, 23 April 1862.)

JOHNSTON, General Albert Sidney, who was killed in the Battle of
Pittsburg Landing Sunday the 6th, was the senior general in the
Confederate service and regarded by President Davis as the best
general in the whole service; he was born 1803 in Mason County, KY;
educated at West Point; served in the Black Hawk War; was 6 feet
1 inch tall, had large, bony sinewy frame. His brother Stoddart
Johnston was blown up several years ago on a steamboat on Red
River, Louisiana, and was at that time U. S. Senator from Louisiana
and had acted as second for Mr. Clay in his duel with Mr. Randolph.
(Nashville Dispatch, 16 April 1862.)

General A. S. Johnston was certainly killed. Huntsville Advocate,
April 9. (Nashville Dispatch, 14 April 1862.)

General Johnston lay in state two days at the City Hall on the 14th,
and his remains were placed in a vault in the St. Louis Cemetery.
(Nashville Dispatch, 25 April 1862.)

Charles M. McGhee of Knoxville has made $500 donation for the benefit
of the family of General A. S. Johnston and the hope is that others
will do the same. (Nashville Dispatch, 3 May 1862.)

When Albert S. Johnston lay dead on the battlefield of Shiloh in
1862, a Federal soldier went through his clothes and took his gold
watch. After the war he sold it to a man in Ohio for $100. This
man was in Richmond, Virginia, recently and happened to see General
Johnston's portrait. "Why, I have that man's watch." General
Fitzhugh Lee was instrumental in having the watch returned to the
General's family. (Maury Democrat, 11 April 1895.)

Only a rough board with his name inscribed marks the grave of
General Albert Sydney Johnson in the cemetery near Austin, Texas.
Further honors to the dead were forbidden by the Federal authorities
at the time of his burial and the matter has been neglected since.
(Columbia Herald, 31 March 1871.)

JOHNSTON, Allen, of Franklin County, TN, was murdered by rebels, shot
on 12 March 1863, died 14 March 1863. (No date on paper.)

JOHNSTON, H. H., died in Columbia yesterday and is to be buried in
Nashville; son of Jack Johnston of Nashville. (Nashville
Republican Banner, 10 April 1868.)

JOHNSTON, John, one of the oldest businessmen, died here yesterday
afternoon; had consumption for two years; born in Scotland and had
lived here for 20 years. (Nashville Dispatch, 28 Nov. 1863.)

JOHNSTON, Colonel Thomas J., late President of Macon College, Danville,
Virginia, was killed at Mattoon, Illinois, Saturday last. Train
ran over him; said to be brother of General Joseph E. Johnston.
(Memphis Daily Appeal, 14 Aug. 1868.)

JONES, Alonzo, 88, of McConnellsville, Ohio, is dead; grandson of
Benedict Arnold. (Daily Herald, Columbia, TN, 15 Jan. 1900.)

JONES, Andrew, 80, died May 2 of pneumonia. (Maury Democrat, Columbia,
TN, 8 May 1890.)

JONES, A. S., formerly a well known Chicago electrical contractor, was placed in Asylum today by Nashville Humane Commission, age 66; clothed in rags, graduate of Oxford, once managed hotel in Louisville; destitute and had lived alone five years. He tried to support himself through his efforts to discover the secret of perpetual motion. (Maury Democrat, Columbia, TN, 25 Jan. 1912.)

JONES, Charlie, died Sunday from wound received on Cedar Street in Nashville; was shot by William Walsh. (Nashville Daily Union, 23 Dec. 1862.)

JONES, C. C., of Stewart County, died as prisoner of war at Alton, Illinois; died since the opening of the prison. (Nashville Dispatch, 28 May 1862.)

JONES, Charles, Company B, 33d Kentucky Volunteer Infantry, is to be shot 4 Sept. 1863 at Mumfordville, KY, for desertion. (Nashville Daily Union, ___ August 1863.)

JONES, Colonel, and Colonel Nicholas are the two Dromios of St. Louis. They each weigh about 200 pounds and attend the same theatre, eat the same restaurant, bet on the same horses, and otherwise daily pool their separate fortunes. (Florence Times, Ala., 21 Nov. 1891.)

JONES, Mrs. Deborah, aged 118, has a daughter, 84 years old, living with her in the family homestead in Toronto. (Maury Democrat, Columbia, TN, 13 Dec. 1894.)

JONES, Colonel Edward P., prominent resident of Canton, Mississippi, committed suicide by taking hydrate of chlorine. Business trouble and excessive drinking was the cause. (Columbia Herald and Mail, 14 April 1876.)

JONES. The grave of Eli Jones, colored, was watched by three of his friends; men began to dig and were fired on and the next day the dead body of Nathan Huggins, colored, was found; he was one of the grave robbers. (Maury Democrat, 4 March 1897. Refer to Eli Johns entry also.)

JONES, Ellis, is now 79 years old and he has a sister Mrs. Mary McDaniel who is 90 years old. They are the children of Captain Charles G. Jones of the Revolutionary War and his wife Elizabeth. Ellis married 1819 to Lucy Lavender, daughter of George and Nancy Lavender; she died 6 May 1847. Both families came to Maury County in 1820 and cleared land here. (Columbia Herald and Mail, 5 Nov. 1875.)

JONES, Felix, of District 17 had one of his twins to die last week. (Columbia Herald and Mail, 16 July 1875.)

JONES, Fannie E., consort of Thomas Jones, died in Nashville on the 13th. (Nashville Dispatch, 14 April 1863.)

JONES, Frank, well known merchant on South Market Street bled to death Sunday from a nosebleed; nose kept bleeding until he died. (Nashville Republican Banner, 2 Nov. 1869.)

JONES, George W., died last Monday; got overheated while working on the new iron bridge. (Columbia Herald, 21 Nov. 1873.)

JONES, Henry L, resolution of respect on his death published in the paper. (Nashville Republican Banner, 8 Nov. 1868.)

JONES, Henry, and his 17 year old daughter were murdered by Alexander Henderson, colored, in Bainbridge, Georgia; Henderson was hanged June 17 and confessed his guilt on scaffold. (Maury Democrat, Columbia, TN, 20 June 1889.)

JONES, James H., merchant of Edgefield, died last night after a long
and painful illness; originally from Jonesboro. (Nashville Union
and American, 7 Feb. 1873.)

JONES, daughter of James (Shug) Jones drowned in river near Hardison's
Mill Monday. (Columbia Herald and Mail, 4 June 1875.)

JONES, James, 72, died Friday; built school and brick church in his
neighborhood; was first a Baptist and then a Methodist. (Columbia
Herald, 1 Dec. 1871.) Jones Academy is a first class male school;
the ground was donated and the buildings erected by James Jones.
(Columbia Herald, 14 Jan. 1870.) In Feb. 1888, the bones of a
soldier were found at Jones Academy by workmen, digging a cellar.
They have now found a second one. In 1864 Hood's advance guard
arrived at the old Rock House, 4 miles south of Columbia, and
surprised Federal pickets; they killed one and wounded another, who
died. The pickets fell back--one to Thomas Woods. These were
hurriedly buried by roadside. The fences were burned and later
the graves could not be located. Jones Academy was built over the
graves. The property is now owned by John M. Gray, who have having
a cellar dug under the old academy. (Maury Democrat, Columbia,
TN, 12 April 1888.) Old pupils at Jones Academy, located on the Mt.
Pleasant Pike on the John M. Gray farm, want to hold a reunion.
Those who attended this school were: George P. Martin, Josephus
Borum, Seth Warfield, Will Thomas, Matt Armstrong, Jim Shepard,
Drake Stanfill, Walter Estes and Clarence Embry. Among the teachers
at the old school were Miss Laura Peacock, Professor Paul Dodson,
Professor George Elliot, Professor O. H. P. Bennett, and E. F.
Everett. (Daily Herald, Columbia, TN, 30 May 1921.) Advertisement
for Jones Academy: new pianos received; faculty: Professor Herz,
music; Annie E. Tavel, artiste P. W. Dodson, principal. (Columbia
Herald, 15 Sept. 1871.)

JONES, Dr. Gustavus V., 53, died; lived in Union County, KY; only
brother of Honorable John W. Jones. (Nashville Daily Gazette,
7 Nov. 1852.)

JONES, Miss Jennie, 27, died on Spruce Street of consumption.
(Nashville Republican Banner, 19 Dec. 1867.)

JONES, Joel J., of Fayetteville, TN, Captain of the 44th Regiment
Tennessee (Confederate) and a member of the Tennessee Senate of
1861-1862, was killed in the battle of Perryville on October 8.
(Nashville Daily Union, 28 Nov. 1862.)

JONES, Colonel John A., gallant colonel of the 20th Georgia regiment,
his remains went down November 10 with steamship Kingfisher. His
son had exhumed his remains on the battlefield at Gettysburg and
was returning with them to Georgia when the ship wrecked. The
passengers were all picked up at sea in boats by the U. S. S.
Susquehanna. (Memphis Avalanche, 9 Dec. 1866.)

JONES, Jonathan, private, Company K, 5th Tennessee Cavalry, was killed
on 22 Feb. 1864 at Calf Killer near Sparta, TN. (Nashville Daily
Union, ___ Feb. 1864.)

JONES, Lewis, age 56 years 8 months 1 day, died at his home, Spring
Place in Davidson County on the 19th; native of Rutherford County;
staunch Union man. (Nashville Daily Union, 23 April 1865.)

JONES. A tomb in a western New York cemetery has the following
inscription: "The last remains of Mary Jones/Are buried beneath
these stones/Her name was Brown, the name of Jones/Used because it
rhymes with stones." (Maury Democrat, Columbia, TN, 17 October
1895.)

JONES, Mrs. Mary, 90, died 18 October 1874 near Carters Creek Station.
(Columbia Herald and Mail, 30 October 1874.)

JONES, Miss Mollie A., died on the 22d in Nashville, (Nashville
    Dispatch, 24 Jan. 1863.)

JONES, Mrs., wife of Captain Richard W. Jones, died November 25 in
    Yalobusha County, Mississippi; daughter of late E. G. Clouston of
    Franklin. (Columbia Herald, 11 Dec. 1870.)

JONES, Mrs. Nancy, widow of Shadrach Jones, died Tuesday at the age of
    106 years in Galveston, Texas; she was familiar with the scenes
    of the Revolution. (Maury Democrat, Columbia, TN, 30 Aug. 1888.)
    Mrs. Nancy Jones, widow of Shadrack Jones, mother of Mrs. Barney
    Tiernan of Galveston, Texas, died Tuesday night. "Though her age
    was fixed at 100 years, it is possible that it exceeded that by
    several years, as her familiarity with scenes and incidents dated
    back to the first year of the Revolutionary War." She remembered
    when her father took his flint lock from the walls of the old cabin
    and went away to battle. (Maury Democrat, 6 Sept. 1888, 13 Sept.
    1888.)

JONES, Patrick, convict, was killed trying to escape from prison on
    Thursday, age 35. (Nashville Republican Banner, 17 July 1869.)

JONES, Peter, almost 100, died at Bristol, TN, last week, one of the
    old original inhabitants of Bristol. (Maury Democrat, Columbia,
    TN, 17 Dec. 1891.)

JONES, Captain R. N., of Giles, died Friday of consumption; was
    captain in Company H, 1st Tennessee Infantry, CSA, at the surrender.
    (Nashville Republican Banner, 16 Dec. 1868.)

JONES, Ross, 16 months, died Feb. 26 on Cathey's Creek in Maury
    County. (Columbia Herald, 6 March 1891.)

JONES, Rufus R., deceased; an insolvency notice about his estate
    published in paper. (Maury County Herald, 12 May 1866.)

JONES, Mrs. wife of Col. Sam Jones, died in Shelby County and buried
    at Mt. Nebo in Maury County. (Columbia Herald and Mail, 9 Jan. 1874.)

JONES, Seborn, lived on Lincoln Alley, near Wilson's Spring, age 60,
    about three years ago married a widow with two daughters, ages 8
    and 10. His wife died February 4 and the night after the funeral
    he took the 13 year old girl in his room for three months and forced
    her to share his couch. He has relatives in Maury County and the
    girls have an uncle in White Bluff. (Nashville Republican Banner,
    16 May 1868.)

JONES, daughter, 9 months, of Mr. and Mrs, Silas Jones, died Friday
    night in the Iron Bridge neighborhood; buried at Rose Hill.
    (Columbia Herald, 18 Nov. 1899.)

JONES, Thomas, died at La Platta, Charles County, (state not given)
    on Monday, age 74. He was the man who helped John Wilkes Booth
    to escape into Virginia after the assassination of Lincoln and
    refused a large sum of money to betray Booth. (Columbia Herald,
    8 March 1895.)

JONES, Professor T. D., of Mulberry Institute, died on the 20th
    instant. (Nashville Union and American, 23 August 1873.)

JONES, Walter T., of Pegram's Station, died April 7 at 1 p.m.; had
    only married last November. (Nashville Union and American, 9 April
    1873.)

JONES, William, of Selina, Kansas, drowned at the upper landing day
    before yesterday in Nashville, intoxicated; aged about 22.
    (Nashville Republican Banner, 13 June 1869.)

JONES, Dr. William P., one of Nashville's oldest and most distinguished citizens, died last Saturday; was postmaster at Nashville for over 9 years. (Columbia Herald, 1 October 1897.)

JORDAN, Joseph, was murdered near Nashville on Thursday last by K. Ryan, a notorious desperado, who resides in Williamson County. (Murfreesboro Monitor, 7 Dec. 1867.) ___ Jordan, about 20, was accused by Carey Ryan of coming with the Federals during the war and taking his father's horse. Jordan admitted it and Ryan shot and killed Jordan, who was son-in-law of John McCandless, and lived 5 miles east of Nolensville. Ryan's brother killed a Mr. Walton at Triune not long ago. (Nashville Republican Banner, 6 Dec. 1867.)

JORDAN, General Thomas, a classmate of General Sherman at West Point and chief of staff of General Beauregard, is dying. He served all through the Seminole, Mexican and Civil Wars. (Columbia Herald, 15 Nov. 1895, Maury Democrat, 14 Nov. 1895.)

JORDAN, Warren W., 85, died at poorhouse 13 Feb. 1876; born in North Carolina. (Columbia Herald and Mail, 25 Feb. 1876.)

JORDAN, Mary A., deceased, insolvency notice about her estate published in newspaper. (Maury County Herald, 12 May 1866.)

JORDAN, Mrs. Kate, her corpse was exhumed at Elmwood Cemetery in Memphis and found to be petrified. It had only been in the ground but three years. (Maury Democrat, Columbia, TN, 13 April 1893.)

JORDAN, Johnson, of Murfreesboro, 86, died on the 5th. (Nashville Union and American, 17 Jan. 1874.)

JORDAN, Lillie, 14 months, daughter of Stephen Jordan, died June 17 on Carter's Creek; buried family burying ground. (Columbia Herald, 20 June 1873.)

JOSEY, Colonel J. E., died October 31 at Osceola, Arkansas; former Confederate soldier; graduate of Nashville Medical College. (Memphis Daily Appeal, 12 Nov. 1866.)

JOSSEY, Mrs. Mary, 89, died in Williamsport yesterday; sister of Mrs. Powhattan Gordon. (Columbia Herald, 17 Jan. 1873.)

JOYCE, Mrs. Hannah, wife of John Joyce, 25, died on the 21st. (Columbia Herald, 23 Feb. 1870.)

JOYCE, Mrs. Nancy Lethgo, died September 4; married about a year; buried Rose Hill Cemetery. (Maury Democrat, Columbia, TN, 17 Sept. 1891.)

JOYCE, Mrs. Mary, widow of Pat Joyce, private, Company B, 1st Middle Tennessee Infantry, who died in camp near Nashville 10 August 1863, should write a Louisville bank about a matter that will be of interest to her. (Nashville Daily Union, 4 Feb. 1865.)

JOYNT, Robert, died last evening of disease of heart and will be buried at Mt. Olivet. (Nashville Dispatch, 30 June 1863.) Robert Joynt, 31, died on the 29th, was a native of Ireland and was of the firm of Joynt & Treanor; had no relatives here. (Nashville Dispatch, 2 July 1863.)

JUDD, Mrs., of Nashville, was recently sent to Alton, Illinois, military prison. She represented herself as wife of an Episcopal minister and attempted to smuggle medicine to Atlanta. She made several trips in this regard. (Nashville Dispatch, 6 Feb. 1863.)

JULIAN, Captain, 1st Tennessee Cavalry (Federal) while on a scouting expedition to Franklin in Williamson County, got separated from his command and was shot by a rebel cavalryman. He was a native of

Maury County and leaves wife and three children. (Nashville Daily
Union, 20 March 1863.) Captain Armine T. Julian was buried in the
Nashville City Cemetery; leaves six children. (Nashville Daily
Union, 22 March 1863.) Captain Julian of the 1st Middle Tennessee
Cavalry was killed Tuesday while charging some Confederates near
Franklin; brought to Nashville for burial. (Nashville Dispatch,
20 March 1863.) Martin Redman has been arrested for robbing Mrs.
Julian. (Nashville Dispatch, 25 Feb. 1863.)

A house owned by the late General Heiman and occupied at the present
by Capt. A. T. Julian of the 1st Middle Tennessee Cavalry, his wife
and five small children--one Henry had been employed by Capt.
Julian as a servant, but was discharged some time ago for dishonesty;
yet while the captain was away on duty, the negro frequently intruded
himself into the house as slaves are accustomed to do, although he
had been told to stay away...he depredated on Julian and his
neighbors. Henry and others broke into the stable and then rocked
the house; Henry ran into Mrs. Julian's room where she was lying
sick and took the captain's sword and double-barreled gun. All this
took place while the captain was on duty with his regiment in the
neighborhood of Harpeth. (Nashville Dispatch, 18 Jan. 1863.)

Family of A. T. Julian entered and robbed by three whites. (Nashville
Dispatch, 21 Feb. 1863.)

KALEER, David, died on the 1st on Buena Vista Place near Ash Barracks.
     (Nashville Republican Banner, 2 Feb. 1870.) Dave Kaleer flourished
     in a grocery store on the upper wharf; married the widow of Smith
     Criddle, who had plenty, and he quit the grocery business. His wife
     died and left everything to him. He left his estate to R. M. Brien,
     widow of Judge John C. Brien, $5000; to Mary Ann Horn, $10,000, who
     took care of him in his last illness; Thomas Horn his lands and what
     they sell for; to Thomas Newell, $10,000; and John Costello, $1000,
     and $1000 to each of his servants. He wrote "I have not given any-
     thing to my wife's relatives because they did not visit my wife
     during her sickness nor after she was dead and my wife's sister
     desired me to send a carriage for her while her sister was dying."
     (Nashville Republican Banner, 9 Feb. 1870.)

KARL, Mrs. Clara, died October in New York City and her remains have
     been scattered from the torch of the Statue of Liberty. (Daily
     Herald, Columbia, TN, 16 Dec. 1899.)

KARNES, Jacob, colored, 1st North Carolina, CSA, died at a hospital
     in Nashville between May 1 and May 15. (Nashville Daily Union,
     25 May 1865.)

KEAN, Georgie Young, wife of M. Kean, died at the Maxwell House on
     Sunday evening. (Nashville Republican Banner, 31 Jan. 1871.)

KEARNEY, J., young married man, shot himself yesterday with a pistol;
     frightful wound near heart; he died about 4 hours later; domestic
     trouble was the cause. (Nashville Daily Union, 5 May 1865.)

KEARNEY, Martin, 18, fell into a boiling vat of sour mash at Manning's
     Distillery Saturday and died at 11:30 that night; he was scalded
     from knees to neck and suffered intense agonies; buried today.
     (Nashville Republican Banner, 7 Dec. 1869.)

KEARNEY. The following officers fallen in battle received appointments
     to higher grade in service: to Major General, Brig. Gen. Phillip
     Kearney, killed in battle of Chantilly; Brig. Gen. Israel B.
     Richardson, died of wounds received at Antietam; Brig. Gen. Jesse L.
     Reno, killed in battle of South Mountain; Brig. Gen. Joseph K. F.
     Mansfield, died of wounds received in battle at Antietam, and
     Brig. Gen. Isaac J. Stewart, killed in battle of Chantilly. Promoted

197

to Brigadier General, Capt. W. R. Terrell, killed at battle of
Perryville. The promotions were a token of the Government's
approbation of their merits. (Nashville Dispatch, 20 March 1863.)
General Philip Kearney was killed in battle on the 30th ult., and his
remains arrived in Newark, New Jersey on the 4th. (Nashville
Dispatch, 7 Sept. 1862.) Philip Kearney killed on the 1st was the
grandson of Hon. John Watts, founder of Lake and Watts orphanage.
He was nephew of Stephen Watts Kearney, conqueror of New Mexico
and California, who died 1849 at Vera Cruz. His great-great-grand-
father settled 1716 at Monmouth County, New Jersey. General Philip
Kearney was an officer in the old army and served with gallantry
in Mexico, where he lost an arm, "subsequently he made himself
notorious by deserting his own and running away with the wife of
another man in New York City." (Nashville Dispatch, 23 Sept. 1862.)

KEATING, Mrs. Fanny, committed suicide in the cellar of her home by
throwing herself in the "back water" from the river at Covington,
KY, on the 13th; age 35; husband and two children survive.
(Nashville Dispatch, 21 May 1862.)

KEEBLE, Edwin A., died August 26 in Murfreesboro; lawyer. (Nashville
Republican Banner, 28 August 1868.)

KEEBLE, Harriet A., wife of Sampson W. Keeble, 30, died on the 16th.
(Nashville Republican Banner, 17 June 1870.)

KEEF, Mrs. Nancy, 70, died 6 September 1871, born 1801 in North Carolina;
buried Greenwood Cemetery; one of first settlers of Maury County.
(Columbia Herald, 8 Sept. 1871.)

KEENER, Michael La Voi, alias Keener, age 23, native of Alsace, France,
enlisted in DeKalb Rifleman 11 January 1862; on 22 January 1863 he
attempted to desert with a comrade. The comrade committed suicide.
La Voi shot at officer trying to arrest him and was executed on the
10th on the common east of Laurel Grove Cemetery. Four of the six
bullets took effect, killing him instantly. From Savannah Republican.
(Nashville Dispatch, 2 May 1863.)

KEESEE, Mrs. Elvira, widow of T. W. Keesee, died December 11; buried
Rose Hill Cemetery. (Columbia Herald, 13 Dec. 1895.)

KELLEY, Alice, died last week near the bridge at Williamsport; died of
fever. (Columbia Herald and Mail, 17 August 1877.)

KELLEY, Miss Ellen, her funeral to be preached this evening at 2 p.m.
(Nashville Daily Union, 7 March 1863.)

KELLEY, Mrs. M., 52, died on the 17th. (Nashville Republican Banner,
18 June 1870.)

KELLEY, son of Mrs. Joe Kelley, accidently shot and killed himself last
week on Cedar Creek in Perry County. (Linden Times, 1 April 1880.)

KELLOGG, Spencer, was hanged on the 28th ult. at Richmond as a spy;
was really named Spencer Kellogg Brown, son of O. C. Brown and
grandson of Levi Cozzens, both Esquires of Utica, New York; he had
been a scout under Fremont in Missouri and had been in prison for
many months; he was of great service to the Union. (Nashville
Dispatch, 7 October 1863.)

KELLY, John, deck hand, was lost overboard from the Rose Hite near Fort
Donelson night before last. He suffered from mania potu and jumped
overboard in his wild ravings. Every effort was made to save him but
swift current carried him under; has wife and three children in
Louisville. (Nashville Daily Union, 2 March 1865.)

KELLY, A. J. A citizen of Wayne County has brought us the story that
Capt. A. J. Kelly, or as he was familiarly called, "Hick Kelly,"
of Dunc Cooper's guerrillas, was killed near Bainbridge, eight miles

above Florence (Ala.), a few days since. Kelly had crossed from the south bank of the Tennessee River with a detachment of ten men, when seeing three Federal soldiers standing near the door of an adjacent house, he charged upon them, but instead of only three being there, twenty soon emerged, and firing upon Kelly's squad, mortally wounded him and killed all but one of his party.

Kelly was about 21 years of age, was born and raised in this city, and before Cooper induced him to join his thieving band, he bore an unsullied reputation. His parents, who are now dead, were highly respectable, and gave him a liberal education. Indeed, he was the brains of the "Cooper Battalion" and never countenanced his chief's mode of warfare. It is sad that such noble but misguided young men as he should be cut down on the very threshold of manhood.

But thus will it continue while this accursed rebellion lasts, or, rather while foolish and heartless mothers and girls consider it dishonorable to desert a hopeless and wicked cause. They would rather see the souls and bodies of these deluded youths perish than that they should abandon their mythical Dixie's land. Columbia Sentinel. (Nashville Daily Union, 17 Feb. 1864.)

DEATH OF CAPTAIN KELLY CONFIRMED. The nobly gallant and unselfish youth, Captain A. J. Kelly, whose demise we announced in our last, met his death as was then stated. The influence of Dunc Cooper and vicious virageos of this neighborhood induced the brave boy to take the unwilling step that cost him his life and brought mourning and tears to his family. He was shot through the heart, never uttered a word afterwards, and was buried where he fell. Peace to his ashes. (Nashville Daily Union, 20 Feb. 1864.)

CAPT. KELLY. The body of the late Captain A. J. Kelly has been brought to this city for interment. He will be buried today (Saturday) at 10 o'clock. The funeral starting from the residence of his bereaved mother. Services by Rev. Mr. Leftwick. (Columbia Sentinel, 27 Feb. 1864.)

Cap Hardeman, colored, died Tuesday of pneumonia and his funeral was at the Missionary Baptist Church near Burns Springs; he had belonged to Thomas Kelly and was sold to a Hardeman. He was a friend of Don and Hick Kelly--one was killed and the other died. He was 55. (Columbia Herald and Mail, 21 Dec. 1877.)

KELLY, B. F., the late general, received the first wound of the war at the Battle of Philippi. His blood-stained vest, with the rent in it made by the bullet, is preserved by a Washington officer. (Florence, Ala., Times, 29 August 1891.)

KELLY. Two deaths at Castle Thunder recently were for John Kelly, Company E, 1st Tennessee Regiment, in prison since Feb. 16 for disloyalty, and William Fitzgerald, a citizen of Nelson County, in prison since May 25 for disloyalty. (Nashville Dispatch, 4 August 1863.)

KELLY, John D., his funeral to be held this morning. (Nashville Republican Banner, 21 November 1869.)

KELLY, John T., son of Timothy and Margaret Kelly, funeral to be held today from his home near Fort Gillem. (Nashville Republican Banner, 1 August 1869.)

KELLY, Margaret E., 2 years 1 month, daughter of Timothy and Margaret Kelly, died on the 4th inst. (Nashville Republican Banner, 5 May 1868.)

KELLY, Mrs. Sarah J., died Friday of consumption, of Columbia, widow of Thomas J. Kelly; leaves a host of friends to mourn. (Nashville Republican Banner, 15 March 1868.)

KELLY, Mr. and Mrs. William, are accused of disorderly conduct toward their brother, John Kelly, who is appointed administrator of deceased sister's estate; quarrel is one of a family characteristic; William Kelly was fined $10 and costs. (Nashville Dispatch, 21 May 1863.)

KELSEY, Thomas, Esquire, of Henryville, Lawrence County, died suddenly last week; age 60. (Whig and Tribune, Jackson, TN, 16 March 1872.)

KENDALL, George, and Reuben Kendall, brothers, were drowned last week while bathing in Sandy River near Paris; neither could swim. (Whig and Tribune, Jackson, TN, 9 August 1873.)

KENDRICK, Dr., Archbishop of Baltimore died on the 8th in Baltimore. (Nashville Dispatch, 11 July 1863.)

KENNAN, Tom, notorious guerrilla and boat-burner, better known as Wild Irishman, was killed 22 April 1864, while attacking steamer Curlew, which was aground on Johnson's Island near Memphis. (Nashville Daily Union, 29 April 1864.)

KENNEDY, David, was "hanged to death," old and loyal citizen of Marion County, Alabama, by the Alabama Cavalry. From statement of Wesley Williams made 24 Jan. 1863. (Nashville Daily Union, 4 March 1863.)

KENNEDY, George A., died last Saturday in District 2 of advanced age; grandfather of Mrs. W. A. Howard. (Maury Democrat, 27 Feb. 1890.)

KENNEDY, Michael, was killed at Johnsonville on Tuesday; walking near the railroad not far from the hotel; shot fired and he was heard to say, "that was well done," then another shot and he fell hit in the breast. (Nashville Republican Banner, 10 October 1869.)

KENNEDY, W. C., died January 4, near Kettle Mills in Maury County; buried in family burying ground. (Columbia Herald, 9 Jan. 1891, 16 Jan. 1891.)

KENNEDY, William E. Sometime in 1840's Judge William E. Kennedy of Maury County concluded to manumit his slaves and send them by installment to Liberia.

He arranged with a colonization society to send thirty of them, among them was Cyrus, a blacksmith who hesitated and had some misgivings. He would not consent to go until his master agreed that he might return in case he did not like his African home and returned to being a slave for life.

He remained perhaps a year in Liberia and revolting savagery, and then began to sigh "for fierce blood hounds, the cruel lash, and falling chains." He returned to this country and went to Ohio, but did not like it and returned to Tennessee. Cyrus is still living here. (Columbia Herald and Mail, 10 Dec. 1875.)

KENNEDY, W. H., of Culleoka area, died on the 17th of congestive chill; elder in the Evergreen Cumberland Presbyterian Church; wife and four children survive. (Columbia Herald and Mail, 21 Sept. 1877.)

KENNISON, David, last survivor of the Boston Tea Party, died 24 Feb. 1852 at the age of 117 years. (Daily Herald, Columbia, TN, 24 Feb. 1906.)

KENNY, Martin, who has figured frequently in our police proceedings during the past year, died in the workhouse yesterday of fit of apoplexy, age 60. He was a stone cutter and spent time drinking whiskey. (Nashville Dispatch, 19 Nov. 1863.)

KERL, Joel, will be 100 years old in a few days; he lives in Hickman County near Duck River and is one of the pioneers. His conversation about early times in this country is very interesting. (Columbia

Herald, 12 July 1895.) (N.B. This surname possibly should be correctly Curl.)

KERLEY, James F., 48, died June 13 at his home on West Gay Street, Nashville; buried in family cemetery in Smith County. (Nashville Dispatch, 14 June 1863.)

KERR, Andrew, who is buried in Greenwood Cemetery in Columbia, lived in what is now a barber shop over Helm Branch, near the northwest corner of Ninth and South Main Street. (Maury Democrat, 2 August 1894.) (N.B. This was not an obituary, but an old person remembering places that others had lived and where buried.)

KERR, Convict, elderly, died in Nashville of cholera. (Western Weekly Review, Franklin, TN, 21 June 1833.)

KERR, John, 39, soldier at the Arsenal in Columbia, died Wednesday of ulceration of the larynx; from Indiana. (Columbia Herald, 17 July 1891.)

KERR, John, infant son of William and Bridget Kerr, died on the 26th. (Nashville Republican Banner, 27 June 1869.)

KERR, Mrs. Joseph B., died on the 23rd; Baptist; buried at McCain's. (Columbia Herald and Mail, 30 Oct. 1874.) Jar of money unearthed at Campbell Station on the J. B. Kerr farm by Lee McKelvey, who was recently plowing and dug it up in a fence row. It was a stone jar and in it was $5, four pearl-handled knives, one pair scissors, some brass buttons, and a daguerrotype of J. B. Kerr, name and dated 1861. It was thought that Polly Kerr, J. B. Kerr's mother, put it there during the war. (Daily Herald, 12 March 1917; Maury Democrat, 15 March 1917.)

KERR, Mrs. Mary, 76, died on the 13th; had been a widow for 22 years. (Columbia Herald and Mail, 20 August 1875.)

KERR, Robert M., 60, of Mallard in Maury County, died August 19, and was buried in family burying ground near Port Royal. (Columbia Herald, 28 August 1891.)

KERR, Ross, old and esteemed citizen of Campbell Station in Maury County, died Thursday of last week. (Columbia Herald and Mail, 8 Oct. 1875.)

KESLEY, Bert, of Loretto, TN, while clearning a rifle which he did not know was loaded, was shot through the heart, killing him instantly. (Maury Democrat, Columbia, TN, 24 Sept. 1891.)

KETCHUM, Charles, alias Charles Hardin, wanted by Wells Fargo for robbing express of $35,000 was captured at Alma, Arkansas, last week. He had $19,000 on him. (Maury Democrat, Columbia, TN, 5 April 1894.)

KETCHUM, Levy, of Fayette County, TN, died Sunday last at the Overton Hotel in Memphis, age 69; had been afflicted with paralysis lately; born in Maury County. (Memphis Avalanche, 13 June 1867.) The plantation of Levi Ketchum is for sale in Sommerville, 600 acres and a new brick residence. (Memphis Avalanche, 13 June 1867.)

KETCHUM, Mrs. T. J., died August 4 at Cornersville, TN. (Columbia Herald, 13 August 1897.)

KEZER, Mary Isabella, 9 years 8 months, only daughter of T. Kezer, deceased, died on the 2d of typhoid. (Nashville Daily Gazette, 7 Oct. 1852.)

KIDD, Richard, age 115, is the oldest voter in the United States; lives in Texas. (Maury Democrat, 27 Sept. 1888.)

KIDDELL, James, died on August 16; son of James and Clara Kiddell,
of England, recent residents of Nashville. (Nashville Dispatch,
21 Aug. 1863.)

KIEISER, George, proprietor of the Battle House Bar in Nashville, died
on the 16th of heart disease. (Whig and Tribune, 1 Feb. 1873.)

KIKER, Emory, charged by state with murder of Lewis Bird in 1862 was
found not guilty in Greenville, TN. Kiker was a rebel soldier,
private in Company H, 5th Tennessee Calvalry. The deceased was a
Federal soldier and killed while making his way to Federal lines.
(Murfreesboro Monitor, 21 Nov. 1868.)

KILLICK, Sister Lou, died April 21; resolution passed by Lasting Hope
Lodge. (Columbia Herald and Mail, 10 May 1878.)

KILPATRICK, W. A., has testified that his age is 105 years and he has
applied for a pension under the Indigent Pension act. His home is
in Bartow, Georgia. Physicians confirm his claim of age. (Maury
Democrat, Columbia, TN, 8 August 1895.)

KILPATRICK, General, died 4 Dec. 1881. The marriage of General
Kilpatrick to a Chilean lady has been announced. (Memphis
Avalanche, 13 Dec. 1866.)

General Kilpatrick, late minister to Chile, has returned and will
report to Secretary Seward. He was recalled by the President.
(Memphis Daily Appeal, 20 Sept. 1868.)

General Kilpatrick on Saturday night was presented with $2000 worth
of silverware by Connecticut soldiers in Hartford, Conn. (Memphis
Daily Appeal, 12 Jan. 1869.)

General Judson Kilpatrick, the imbecile libertine, who has disgraced his uniform by cowardice, society by indecency, and mankind
by his existence, has been basely misrepresenting General Forrest
in speeches in the East. Forrest denounces him in a letter as a
liar and poltroon. (Murfreesboro Monitor, 21 Nov. 1868.)

KIMBROUGH, Elder Bradley, one of the oldest ministers in Middle
Tennessee, died at his home in Mulberry, Lincoln County, on the
30th ult. (Nashville Union and American, 4 July 1874.)

KINCAID, Sarah Jane Scales, wife of James Kincaid, died 5 May 1868 at
Pine Creek, Red River County, Texas. (Nashville Republican Banner,
21 June 1868.)

KING, little child of David King, near Clifton, TN, recently fell out
of the door and into a kettle of water and was killed, or drowned.
(Columbia Herald, 26 April 1872.)

KING, Mrs. Frank, of Quality Creek in Maury County, died and left
several children; she was buried June 1 at Reese's Church.
(Columbia Herald, 5 June 1896.)

KING, George, of District 1, Giles County, was killed when his coat
tails caught in the gearing at Sam Merrill's mill which he was
tending. (Whig and Tribune, 9 Dec. 1871.)

KING, Colonel Henry, native of North Carolina, who fought as a private
at New Orleans and was on the electoral ticket of Alabama in
President Andrew Jackson's first presidential campaign, died on the
13th ult. in Montgomery County, Alabama. (Clarksville Jeffersonian,
1 Sept. 1858.)

KING, Henry, 60, and "old enough to have known better, drank a quart
of whiskey to win a bet of one dollar." He was found dead soon
after. He lived at Courtland, Alabama. (Maury Democrat, 12 Sept.
1895.)

KING, Mrs. Jane, wife of B. M. King, one of lower Green River's oldest citizens, died this week; Primitive Baptist. Her husband and two children survive. (Waynesboro Tribune, 4 Feb. 1897.)

KING, J. G., son of Levi King, is ill at Eureka Springs with meningitis and his recovery is doubtful. (Maury Democrat, Columbia, TN, 19 April 1888.) Mr. Gentry King, formerly of Williamsport, is exceedingly ill with meningitis in Arkansas and his father Levi King has gone to him. (Maury Democrat, 12 April 1888.) J. G. King died April 18, in Arkansas; lawyer; buried at Concord in Maury County. (Maury Democrat, 26 April 1888.)

KING, Jeff, colored, died on the 19th at Nannie, Georgia, age 128 years; he was born a slave in Virginia. (Maury Democrat, 25 Oct. 1888.)

KING, Mrs. John, died of inflammation of the brain Saturday last in District 17 in Maury County. (Columbia Herald, 15 Aug. 1873.)

KING, Michael, 1st Tennessee Infantry (U.S.), had words at breakfast with Comrade Naughton, who took a club and struck King over the head. He died that night and was buried yesterday. (Nashville Dispatch, 3 June 1863.)

KING, Mollie B., 30, died May 31, of heart disease. (Columbia Herald, 5 June 1896.)

KING, ___, was killed Saturday on the Frank Craige farm near Williamsport; was shot by Mr. Ham while they were rabbit hunting. (Columbia Herald, 9 Feb. 1872.)

KING, Mr., of Culleoka, died yesterday of consumption; had infant child to die last week; buried Wilkes Cemetery. (Maury Democrat, Columbia, TN, 20 June 1889.)

KING, Mrs., "who aspires to be queen of the liquor traffic," found guilty of tippling and fined $10 and given 20 days to reflect. (Nashville Daily Union, 1 Feb. 1863.)

KING, West, a prominent citizen of Benton County, died a few days ago. (Nashville Union and American, 22 May 1874.)

KING, William B., Esquire, 53, died May 21 of paralysis near Triune. (Whig and Tribune, Jackson, Tn., 1 June 1872.)

KINGSBURY, Colonel, of the 11th Connecticut Regiment, killed in the battle of Antietam, Maryland, was brother of the wife of General Buckner. (Nashville Dispatch, 25 Oct. 1862.)

KINLEY, John, died December 15; funeral to be held at the Cathedral. (Nashville Republican Banner, 18 Dec. 1870.)

KINZER, Abram, died recently at Water Valley. (Columbia Herald, 10 April 1891.)

KINZER, Mrs. Brown, of Concord died. (Columbia Herald, 9 Jan. 1891.)

KINZER, the youngest child of Mr. and Mrs. Frank Kinzer of Sawdust died of whooping cough. (Columbia Herald and Mail, 24 July 1874.)

KINZER, Mrs. William Brown, who had been charged with the murder of Mrs. Kinzer, has been found not guilty. (Columbia Herald, 6 Dec. 1872.)

KINZER, Henry, old and esteemed citizen of Sawdust Valley, died Saturday at the age of 75; born Petersburg, Virginia, came to Maury County in a wagon at the age of 10; first settled on the Lunn Place near Kinderhook; 40 years ago moved to place he died. (Columbia Herald, 12 Jan. 1872.)

KIRBY, James Graves, 8, died April 13 near Antioch Depot; eldest child of Rebecca J. and Elias R. Kirby. (Nashville Dispatch, 27 April 1862.)

KIRBY, Mrs. Nancy, died at the home of F. A. Polk on the 14th; buried at Lasting Hope. (Columbia Herald and Mail, 22 Feb. 1878.)

KIRK, J. S., of Maury became a millionaire in Chicago in the soap field; ran away from home before he was 10 years old and not heard of for many years. (Maury Democrat, 29 March 1894.)

KIRK, Mrs., aged woman of 78, died at home of her daughter Mrs. H. Craig on 9th Street on April 28; buried Rose Hill Cemetery; formerly of Giles County and Mt. Pleasant. (Maury Democrat, Columbia, TN, 2 May 1895.)

KIRK, William P., Esquire, died six miles south of Mt. Pleasant last Friday; native of Lawrence County, father of Capt. Lewis Kirk of Biffle's. (Columbia Herald and Mail, 26 Oct. 1877.)

KIRK, Lewis. A Guerrilla Brute. Refugees from Maury County report that a most deplorable state of affairs exist in that county. A band of rebel cavalry is scouring the country led by one Capt. Lewis Kirk of Lawrence County. He has forced numbers of gray-headed Union men, 50 and 60 years of age, into the rebel army, and now hold in confinement several of the oldest and most estimable citizens of the county, because they refuse to take up arms. One brave man told him that if he would give him a chance, he would take up arms for the Federal Government. This Kirk was formerly a blacksmith, we are informed, and a noted bully in Lawrence County. He was in jail at Columbia for nearly three years for murdering Mr. Westmoreland of Giles County, without provocation, and in cold blood. When the rebellion broke out, he sent word to Governor Harris that if he would get him out of jail, he would join the rebel army, and he was let loose. (Nashville Daily Union, 20 Feb. 1863.)

A Base Scoundrel. Some days ago we mentioned that a guerrilla chief Capt. Kirk was perpetrating numberless outrages in Maury County. Kirk murdered a man some three years ago under circumstances which made it an aggravated offense. He was a hired political bully and probably murdered his victim for pay. Kirk was tried in Maury County circuit court and received 15 years sentence, appealed to the supreme court. He was let out on the application of A. J. Polk and W. V. Thompson to enter the Rebel army. Now holds captain's commission in Forrest's troops. (Nashville Daily Union, 5 March 1863.)

Infamous Guerrilla Killed. Capt. Lewis Kirk, who preyed on Maury County Union men, was killed in a recent fight at Spring Hill. He was buried there a few days ago. Kirk was one of the most degraded and blood thirsty wretches, who ever persecuted the loyal citizens of the State. (Nashville Daily Union, 17 March 1863. N.B. This report of his death was not true. According to contemporary diary accounts Lewis Kirk was shot 26 July 1865 at Pulaski following a court martial.)

A Strange Story of the Old Days, by Payton A. Sowell. In my youth, the story of Washington and of the struggle in the 1700's for American and human liberty, did not seem far in the past. On every side were living discharged soldiers of the Seminole, the Second British, the Creek and the Mexican Wars. Then came the dark cloud that settled over our fair land, in the War Between the States.

First, as a volunteer in Capt. B. F. Mathews' company, called the Lawrence County Invincibles, afterwards as the Captain of a cavalry company, made up through his personal influence, by the authority of military headquarters, Lewis Kirk, a citizen of Lawrence County served gallantly in the Confederate Cause.

KIRK, Lewis - Continued
He was honorably paroled and returned to his home and family in
May 1865. I remember to have seen him at least once. He was not
allowed to enjoy long the freedom and safety of a paroled soldier.
In the summer, perhaps early part of the summer of 1865 he was
arrested by military authority and carried to Pulaski and after a
brief incarceration, was, without any warning to him, or notice to
his family, taken out on the (perhaps) Columbia pike and shot dead
as a beast. No one to this day knows the charges against him; it
is only surmise.

Last week I was in Mount Pleasant, and as I always try to do before
I leave there, I spent an hour with Lt. John Hildreth, a Confederate
veteran of 80 years. He was lieutenant in Capt. Mathews' company
and served loyally the Confederacy until the end.

We were talking of those dark days of the 60's and actors from
Lawrence County. The name of Capt. Lewis Kirk was mentioned and
Lt. Hildreth recited the following incidents.

He said, "Several of us, a short time after getting home, went deer
hunting south of Lawrenceburg, going afoot. A number were placed
on 'stands' while the dogs searched for deer. Lewis Kirk and I
happened to be on stands not a great distance apart.

"While the dogs were sniffing, Lewis Kirk left his stand and came
to me. I said: 'Lewis, why have you left your stand; the deer may
come out by you.'

"He said: 'I can't remain. Last night I had the strangest dream.
I dreamed a beautiful spotted bird came to me. It had a beak more
than two inches long, and pushing its beak far down into my ear,
it whispered something I dare not tell you, and I can't stay there
by myself.'

"We closed our hunt and walked home. I lived at the little brick
near Mr. J. T. Dunn's. Kirk lived south of the creek. After dinner
we came up to the square, and a squadron of Federal Cavalry came
about the same time from Pulaski. We all stood about and talked
to them. Lewis Kirk being one of us. After a time they rode away,
as if gone, but out about Wm. Parke's place, they galloped back.
Lewis Kirk was standing in front of Tom Dunn's and William Dustin's
store (now the Racket) and the Federals surrounded Kirk, and the
officer said, 'Kirk, get on this horse. We are going to take you
with us.'

"They rode away and no friend of his ever saw him again. In a
few days, Mr. Tom Dunn went to Pulaski and called on the authorities
seeking to do something for Kirk.

"The officer said: 'If you have come to do anything for Lewis Kirk,
you may as well go home. In a few days, so far as anyone knows,
without trial, he was taken out on a pike a few miles and shot like
a beast.'

Those were days of uncertainty and darkness. Others perished as
Capt. Lewis Kirk did. (Lawrenceburg Democrat, no date; clipping
sent to compiler by late John F. Morrison, Jr., Lawrenceburg, Tenn.
Many of the historical articles by Payton Sowell were published in
the 1920's in the Lawrenceburg Democrat.)

KIRKPATRICK, R. L., old merchant and prominent citizen, died in
Nashville last week. (Columbia Herald, 20 Oct. 1871.)

KIRKPATRICK. The "late Kirkpatrick to be buried today." (Nashville
Daily Union, 8 June 1865. N.B. No better identification published
in paper.)

KIRKPATRICK, Moses, 42, died May 24, in Davidson County; born Monroe County, Kentucky. (Nashville Daily Union, 27 May 1865.)

KIRKPATRICK, Miss Emma, died Wednesday. (Nashville Union and American, 24 Sept. 1874.)

KIRKSEY, William H., of Lawrenceburg, recently died. (Columbia Beacon, 4 Feb. 1848.)

KISER, Florence, infant daughter of W. M. and Nancy Kiser, 18 months 4 days, has died. (Nashville Republican Banner, 11 July 1868.)

KISSANE, William, major in the rebel army, was killed in desperate battle of Fort Craig, New Mexico; from Cincinnati. He was notoriously implicated in the burning of the steamer Martha Washington five years ago. (Nashville Dispatch, 17 April 1862.)

KITTRELL, Captain R. W., Confederate soldier, has been arrested as a spy in Nashville. (Nashville Dispatch, 16 April 1863.)

KITTRELL, Mrs. Thomas M., has brought suit against O. C. Owen for killing her husband a year or so ago; she lost the suit. (Columbia Herald and Mail, 1 Feb. 1878.)

KLEIN, Burl, deceased, his will admitted to probate. (Nashville Republican Banner, 24 July 1870.)

KLEPFEL. Romantic and Practical. Jacob Klepfel, 20 years ago married Miss Kate Schmidt in Germany, and two or three years later Jacob came to America and settled in Auglaze County, Ohio. He neglected to inform his wife of his whereabouts, and she, believing him dead, married again.

Twelve years ago she came across the seas with her second husband and located in the same county, not more than ten miles from her former lord. Strangely enough, though living so near, they had never met until last Thursday, when Jacob, visiting the county fair at Wapakonetta, was rather surprised to meet his deserted frau "swinging around the circle mit anoder man," and half a dozen children. He made himself known and the two sat down and had a long talk about the old times in Germany. She advised him, that under the circumstances, he had better retire for another 16 years, as her second husband suited her best, and she intended to stick to him. Dayton, Ohio, Empire. (Memphis Avalanche, 3 Nov. 1866.)

KLINE, Adam, deceased; administrators to his estate appointed. (Nashville Republican Banner, 28 March 1869.)

KLING, two young daughters of S. W. Kling of Birmingham, Alabama were drowned the other day in the Tennessee River at Hobb's Island, Alabama, while attempting to cross in a skiff. (Lincoln County Herald, 13 June 1894.)

KLINK, Captain Hayne, was killed at the Battle of Franklin in 1864 and was a member of the 154th Senior Tennessee Regiment; buried at Elmwood Cemetery in Memphis 7 Feb. 1866. (Memphis Avalanche, 7 Feb. 1866.)

KNIGHT, Bolivar W., Esquire, died at Pulaski yesterday. (Columbia Daily Herald, 18 April 1892.)

KNIGHT, Charles T., a gallant soldier of the Mexican War and the Civil War, died on the 21st at Jackson, Tenn. (Nashville Republican Banner, 1 July 1868.)

KNIGHT, E. H., private, Company B, 7th Tennessee Volunteers, was shot in lungs severely at Fredricksburg, Virginia, on 13 Dec. 1862. (Nashville Daily Union, 11 Jan. 1863.)

KNIGHT, G. W., released from paying poll tax for 1886 in Houston
County. (Houston County News, 8 Jan. 1887. N.B. George Wade Knight,
born 2 Feb. 1839, died 17 Sept. 1893, buried Brown Cemetery, Houston
County.)

KNIGHT, James L., of Davidson County, died on the 16th ult. of small
pox in prison at Alton military prison. (Nashville Dispatch, 16
Sept. 1863.) James L. Knight and Martin Harrington have been
arrested as guerrillas and horse thieves. (Nashville Dispatch,
19 Feb. 1863.) James L. Knight, robber and spy, is one of the
prisoners being sent to Alton, Ill. (Nashville Daily Union, 4 June
1863.)

KNIGHT, J. F., deceased; year's allowance for widow and family being
allowed. (Nashville Republican Banner, 5 April 1868.)

KNIGHT, ___, of Lafayette, Christian County, Ky., has killed a negro
for insulting his sister. (Memphis Avalanche, 20 Nov. 1866.)

KNIGHT, Mrs. Mary, of Indiana, has died. (Columbia Herald, 15 Sept.
1871.)

KNIGHT, T. J., the old gentleman who was riddled with buckshot near
Decatur, Alabama, died of his wounds at St. Vincent Hospital Sunday.
He was shot by Alexander Tarver and Polk Mackner. Tarver's first
wife was Knight's daughter and Tarver wanted Knight's property.
He was 65 years old and was brought to Nashville to prevent further
attempts on his life. His assassins left him for dead. (Nashville
Republican Banner, 8 Feb. 1870.)

Judge Charlton of Alabama, who was recently killed, was said to be
the leader of the faction now headed by one Bob Garner. They have
burned houses, killed and driven off several persons. Another is
the Robinson party. Each has 50 men. They are camped near Falkville,
Ala., and seem to be carrying on a guerrilla mode of warfare in this
section. A one-legged man, Tarver, was killed by young Knight,
whose father was wounded in the mountains and died in Nashville.
(Memphis Daily Appeal, 28 March 1870.)

KNIGHT, W. H., deceased; inventory of his estate returned 2 May 1866
by John H. Knight, administrator; final settlement was made 29 Nov.
1875; one of the items was for payment of a jury of inquest.
(Humphreys County, Tenn., Will and Inventory Book K, pages 536-538;
this was Wade H. Knight, War of 1812 soldier, who died in Humphreys
County. He was knocked from his horse by a tree limb and killed.)

KNODE, Sarah Agnes, died 7 Oct. 1868 in Memphis; born in Kentucky;
wife of Dr. O. B. Knode. On the breaking out of the war in Missouri
she left home to encounter all the hardships of Confederate life and
was ardently devoted to the cause of the South. (Memphis Daily
Appeal, 18 Oct. 1868.)

KNOX, infant daughter of George A. and Geneva S. Knox, is to be buried
today. (Nashville Republican Banner, 4 June 1869.)

KOONCE, Mrs. Salena "Lena", died near Cloverdale, Alabama, 28 May
1891; daughter of George and Lavina Roach; born 24 June 1820;
professed religion 1833; married 1837 to William R. Koonce; became
ill with paralysis six weeks ago; buried Wesley Chapel Cemetery.
(Florence, Ala., Times, 6 June 1891.)

KOONTZ, John, age 102, first white settler in Miami County, Indiana,
died at Peru, Indiana. (Daily Herald, Columbia, Tenn., 6 May 1892.)

KOPP, Christian, of Newport, Kentucky, was killed by explosion of a
bomb shell which was carelessly thrown to ground by a soldier, who
was handling it. Mr. Kopp and five soldiers were wounded. A
large piece struck Mr. Kopp on thigh and passed through the other
thigh causing his death. Mrs. Kopp was struck on neck and severely

KOPP, Christian - Continued
wounded, probably mortally. The soldier who let the shell fall
was frightfully cut to pieces though still alive at last accounts.
(Nashville Dispatch, 28 Oct. 1862.)

KRAUSE, George C., of Hartford, Connecticut, has become insane through
fear of lightning. (Maury Democrat, Columbia, Tenn., 3 Oct. 1895.)

KUHL, Henry, and Hamilton W. Wondon citizens of West Virginia, are to
be hanged May 9 at Suttonville, Virginia, for the murder in cold
blood of a Federal soldier. (Nashville Dispatch, 8 May 1862.)

KUHN, Ferdinand, 51, died on the 7th instant. (Nashville Union and
American, 10 June 1874.)

KUSKOVY. Descendants of Chief Kuskovy, Cherokee Indian, twenty in all,
are on their way to Gadsden, Alabama, to visit and to make known the
locality of lead and silver mines said to be within one mile of
Double Springs. Old citizens remember that Indians use to get lead
less than one hour from the time they left Double Springs, Alabama.
(Memphis Daily Appeal, 18 June 1870.)

KYLE, Honorable Gale H., 63, died on the 16th at Arkadelphia, Arkansas;
born in Giles County, Tenn.; in 1855 moved to Dallas County, Arkansas
was Union man during the war. (Memphis Daily Appeal, 6 April 1870.)

LACWERTZ, Fred, was fatally shot by W. F. Keltner at Mrs. Holden's
boarding house near the depot in Columbia; made remarks about Mrs.
Keltner; died Sunday, buried Rose Hill; son of Mack Lacwertz of
Ottenheim near Crab Orchard, Ky. (Maury Democrat, 12 Sept. 1895.)

LACY, Miss Abigail, 75, died on the 15th at Carter Station, Carters
Creek, Maury County; much esteemed. (Columbia Herald, 27 Sept.
1872.)

LADD, William Meredith, 19 months, died Friday at Mt. Pleasant, buried
Zion Cemetery, son of Mr. and Mrs. H. B. Ladd. (Columbia Herald,
11 Dec. 1899.)

LADD, Mrs., age 108, died March 11 at Hartford, Connecticut. (Memphis
Daily Appeal, 13 March 1869.)

LAFAYETTE. Anastasie, youngest child of General Lafayette and last
member of his family, has died; married Count de la Tour Manburg
and died in Turin, Italy, surrounded by children and grandchildren.
(Nashville Dispatch, 14 April 1863.)

The anniversary of the battle of Brandywine was recently celebrated.
The citizens of Chester County, Pa., unveiled a memorial shaft to
Gen. Lafayette. The shaft is located on the highest point of the
battlefield, and on the spot where it is supposed Lafayette stood
when he was wounded 118 years ago. (Columbia Herald, 11 Oct. 1895.)

LAMB, Isham, formerly of Spring Hill and Columbia, has died at
Beauregard, Mississippi. (Columbia Herald and Mail, 16 Oct. 1874.)

LAMB, Joseph, age 110, of Hawkins County, Tenn., died October 10.
(Whig and Tribune, Jackson, Tenn., 16 Nov. 1872.)

LAMBERT, Aaron, living near Lee & Gordon's Mill, 13 miles from
Chattanooga, hung himself recently with a bridle halter to a beam
of a shed. (Memphis Avalanche, 4 Oct. 1866.)

LANDLIN, Lucy, keeper of a house in Nashville, took morphine and died
within two hours last Wednesday evening; jealousy; she prepared
her shroud, purchased a lot of crape for use at her funeral; then
went to drug store for the poison. "Suicide is becoming epidemic

among prostitutes. (Memphis Avalanche, 7 Nov. 1866.)

LANE, J. H., of Lynnville, Giles County, was shot and killed by his son Joseph Lane, age 16 or 17; the elder Lane came home drunk and was offering some violence to his wife. (Memphis Avalanche, 19 Oct. 1866.)

LANE, Martin M., living near Brick Church, Giles County, had his finger so badly crushed in a cider mill Wednesday that amputation was necessary. In a short time he took lockjaw and died. (Nashville Republican Banner, 5 Dec. 1869.)

LANGLEY, Mary, daughter of Rev. J. M. Sharp, funeral to be held today. (Nashville Republican Banner, 3 Nov. 1870.)

LANIER, Mrs. Fredonia, wife of B. H. Lanier, died on the 9th. (Nashville Dispatch, 11 Oct. 1862.)

LANIEVE, Isaac T., deceased, insolvency notice on his estate published in paper by J. H. Dugger, administrator. (Maury County Herald, 12 May 1866.)

LANKFORD, Thomas, old gentleman living in the southern part of Henry County, died; he fell backward from a long ladder while gathering cherries. (Whig and Tribune, 6 July 1872.)

LANKFORD, Elizabeth, died onthe 1st in Williamson County; daughter of Rev. T. N. and P. G. Lankford; age 6 1/2 years. (Nashville Dispatch, 4 Sept. 1863.)

LAPSLEY, Louisa, 25, colored, wife of Daniel Lapsley, died yesterday. (Nashville Republican Banner, 8 May 1869.)

LARESHE, Paul, Esquire, was shot and killed by J. S. Bossier, Esquire, 25, at the back of the barracks in a duel at New Orleans. (Memphis Daily Appeal, 30 July 1868.) Two young Frenchmen fought duel Saturday of last week; both served in the Washington Artillery, Confederate Army. (Memphis Daily Appeal, 1 August 1868.)

LARUE, Mrs. Hannah, age 103, widow of Richard Larue, soldier of the War of 1812, died in Jefferson County, Virginia. (Memphis Daily Appeal, 8 July 1870.)

LATHROP. Information wanted: William Lathrop, son of Lyons Lathrop and Hannah Lathrop, who lived in New London, Conn., at Norwich Landing in 1793; William Lathrop was captured 25 Aug. 1800 by Algerian frigate and sold as slave and was slave until 1817 when he was released. "I have tried in vain to find my parents who are said to have removed to Cincinnati, Ohio, thence to Kentucky, and from thence to Tennessee, where it is supposed they now reside." William Lathrop wants information on them; He was at Nashville when the advertisement was published and signed 15 Jan. 1820. (Clarksville Gazette, 29 Jan. 1820.)

LATIMER, Mrs. Jane, 69, was buried at the City Cemetery in Nashville yesterday; known for her activity and benevolence. (Nashville Union and American, 2 June 1874.)

LATTA, A. B., died in Cincinnati Saturday; inventor of steam-fire engine. (Nashville Daily Union, 2 May 1865.)

LATTA, Mr. Jon, 77, father of Capt. S. R. Latta of Dyersburg, died December 2. (Whig and Tribune, 14 Dec. 1872.)

LATTA, Moses, froze to death 27 Dec. 1872 near his house; he left Santa Fe in Maury County on the 26th under the influence of Whiskey; he was found by his wife; uncle of Sheriff Sims Latta; age 50. (Columbia Herald, 3 Jan. 1873.)

LATTA, William, 80, died; War of 1812 soldier; had lived on his present farm for 60 years. (Columbia Herald and Mail, 16 Oct. 1874.)

LATTA, William A., born 30 Dec. 1838 in Maury County, died Feb. 1877 in Columbia, Tenn., married 15 July 1863 to Mary S. Braden of Giles County; buried Rose Hill Cemetery. (Columbia Herald and Mail, 13 April 1877.)

LATTENBERGER, Mr., did not die of cholera. (Nashville Union and American, 23 June 1873. N.B. He died of something else but newspaper was blurred and could not be deciphered.)

LAUDERDALE, James, died in Washington County, Texas, at the age of 96 years; was with General Jackson at New Orleans. (Memphis Avalanche, 28 Dec. 1866.) Colonel Lauderdale who died Dec. 9 in Washington Co., Texas, was long a citizen of Sumner County, Tenn., was an officer in the Creek War; his life covered the political revolutions from 1776 to 1866. (Memphis Avalanche, 14 Dec. 1866.)

LAW, Stephen W., private, Company F, 5th Tennessee Cavalry, found murdered and lying in the water near Mill Creek bridge, Nolensville Pike; brought to camp and buried; he left on 21st to go to Shelbyville to get married; shot passed through his head; severe stab in throad; some notorious bushwhackers who live about a mile from here are under suspicion. (Nashville Daily Union, 25 Feb. 1864.)

LAWRENCE, D. V., was murdered in Edgefield; age 22; leaves wife; shot by William H. Cox; justifiable homicide; .buried on the 26th. (Nashville Republican Banner, 27 July 1869.)

LAWREY, David. Eight persons died of cholera at his residence near Hendersonville, Ky. last week. (Nashville Daily Gazette, 14 Sept. 1852.)

LAWSON, Mrs. Ellen, wife of the Rev. T. D. Lawson, died October 21 after a long and painful illness. (Nashville Union and American, 22 Oct. 1874.)

LAWSON, Mrs. John, died of congestion in Greenfield Bend, Maury County, last week. (Columbia Herald, 26 April 1872.)

LEACH, Double murder at Coldwater, Michigan, Saturday night--Mrs. Ebenezer Leach and George Brown, a young lawyer, were shot dead while walking together on the streets; her husband is the murderer and jealousy was the cause. (Memphis Avalanche, 7 Nov. 1866.)

LEADBETTER, Danville, late brigadier general in the Confederate Army; his remains have reached Mobile to find a resting place among those who knew and loved him well and around whose homes he had thrown those ramparts which were to protect them against invasion. (Memphis Avalanche, 18 Oct. 1866.)

LEATH, Ferrell, 2, son of the Rev. and Mrs. W. A. Leath, died Saturday; buried Rose Hill Cemetery. (Columbia Herald, 3 April 1891.)

LEBAM, John, a Missouri man, has been sentenced to the State Prison for life for a heinous crime and given an additional 8 years for horse stealing. (Nashville Daily Union, 15 Jan. 1863.)

LECKEY, Fanny, infant daughter of John and Clara Regina Leckey, died 8 March 1863 in Brooklyn, New York, granddaughter of E. E. Jones of Nashville. (Nashville Daily Union, 18 March 1863; Nashville Dispatch, 18 March 1863.)

LEDBETTER, John of Perry County, was killed last week by Charles Young, they were first cousins and Ledbetter shot Young a year ago. (Columbia Herald and Mail, 16 Feb. 1877.)

LEE, Major A. M., engineer in the Confederate service, had a son who
was a lieutenant in Federal Navy and was on board the Harriet Lane.
He was mortally wounded and only lived long enough to recognize his
father, against whom he was fighting, before he died. (Nashville
Daily Union, 22 Feb. 1863.)

LEE, A. Murton, Buford's escort, Confederate Army, died at hospital in
Nashville between the 1st and 15th. (Nashville Daily Union, 25
May 1865.)

LEE, Absalom, died Friday and was buried at Lasting Hope; two of his
sons fell at Perryville; Cumberland Presbyterian. (Columbia Herald
and Mail, 15 Feb. 1878.)

LEE, Thomas Charles, 1 year 8 months, son of Thomas G. and A. Lee,
died yesterday. (Nashville Union and American, 30 Oct. 1874.)

LEE, Winifred, 7 years 8 months 20 days, daughter of Thomas and
Annie Lee, funeral to be held today. (Nashville Dispatch, 10 Oct.
1863.)

LEE, Commodore S. S., brother of General R. E. Lee, died at his home
in Stafford County, Virginia, on Thursday. (Memphis Daily Appeal,
25 July 1869.)

LEE, Robert E. Mrs. Robert E. Lee, who with two of her daughters, were
captured two weeks ago, have been released. They are now in Richmond. (Nashville Dispatch, 21 June 1862.)

General Lee has not been arrested; he was in church last Sunday
at Richmond and responded audibly to the prayer for the President
of the United States. (Nashville Daily Union, 16 June 1865.)

General Lee's application for pardon was forwarded to Washington
by General Grant with a letter favoring granting the pardon.
(Murfreesboro Monitor, 7 Oct. 1865. N.B. Lee's citizenship was
not restored to him until 1975.)

General Lee has a Bible class of 105 members in his college in
Virginia. (Memphis Daily Appeal, 5 Nov. 1868.)

General Robert E. Lee will attend funeral of Mr. Peabody at
Peabody, Mass., on invitation. (Memphis Daily Appeal, 20 Jan. 1870.)

General Lee left Savannah on the 12th to visit the grave of his
father General Henry Lee at Dungeness, Cumberland Island, where he
died March 1818 and was buried. This is now the property of William
Nightingale, grandson of General Greene, whose guest Lee was then.
(Memphis Daily Appeal, 20 April 1870.)

General Fitzhugh Lee will deliver an address before the Virginia
Society of Atlanta, Georgia, on the anniversary of General Lee's
birthday, January 19, which is a legal holiday in Georgia. (Maury
Democrat, 27 Dec. 1894.)

The telegraph brings us the sad news that General R. E. Lee is
dead. A shadow of gloom and sorrow will be spread over the entire
South... (Columbia Herald, 14 Oct. 1870.)

The telegraph announces the death of General Robert E. Lee... We
shall not look upon his like again. On Wednesday, Sept. 28, he was
at Washington College and about the streets diligently attending to
the duties of the Presidency. During the afternoon he presided at
a meeting of the vestry of the church in which he was a communicant.
Thence he went home, partook of a light tea, and while sitting
surrounded by his family he was attacked with stupor, becoming
speechless, and so continued during the night.

Monday found the General worse and though his sudden demise was not

LEE, Robert E. - Continued

anticipated, it was thought best to telegraph for his sons, General
Fitzhugh, General Custis, and Captain Robert to come to his bedside.
Before the message reached them their father was dead. He died at
half-past 9 o'clock on Monday morning. The physicians who attended
him in the last moments say that the remote cause of his death was
long-continued depressing influences incident to responsibilities
resting upon him during the last year of the war, the disastrous
termination of the struggle in which all his energies were enlisted
and the afflictions of the South since the surrender of the Confederate armies.

Citizens of Maury County will meet Oct. 22 to pass resolutions of
respect for General R. E. Lee. All business houses and residences
are requested to be draped in mourning by the owners. Business
will be suspended. Church bells will toll during the procession
which will begin at 10 o'clock. (Columbia Herald, 21 Oct. 1870.)

Lee's Coffin - Lexington, Va., 15 Dec. 1906 - Mrs. Hunter Marshall,
Lynchburg, Pa. - Dear Mrs. Marshall: Your letter of the 13th
inst., came to hand last night. The story to which you allude is
literally true. At the time of Gen. Lee's death in 1870 there was
a great freshet in North River at Lexington. There was no suitable
casket for Gen. Lee's burial in our town, and we were cut off from
the rest of the world. Some caskets had been ordered from Richmond
by our town undertaker, and they had arrived a few days before the
freshet at A. Alexander's commission house on North River. This
house, with contents, including the caskets, was washed away. One
of these caskets was reported as lodged on an island a few miles
below our town. It was brought up, and Gen. Lee was buried in it.
The casket needed only a little cleaning, and it suited the purpose
in every way except that it was rather small at the foot, so that
Gen. Lee could not be buried in shoes or boots. These are the facts
as I distinctly remember them. Yours truly, A. L. Nelson.
Philadelphia Press. (Nashville Banner, 15 May 1927.)

Mrs. Lee's Premature Burial - Gen. Lee's mother was by no means an
entirely healthy woman, and the physician at Stratford, Va., the
home of Henry Lee (Light Horse Harry) was kept in constant attendance. Mrs. Lee suffered from catalepsy and during a prolonged
trance she was pronounced dead. The body was prepared for interment and the morning of the third day after her supposed death the
remains were laid to rest in the family vault in the graveyard of
that pretty little Virginia village.

While the sexton was cleaning up and arranging some fresh flowers
to be placed on the casket he heard a faint voice as though someone calling for assistance.

Of course, the old man was somewhat alarmed, but as he had seen
many years of service in the "city of the dead," he did not leave
the vault. He listened closely and the voice was distinctly heard
again.

Becoming satisfied that the voice came from within the casket, he
at once set to work and opened it, discovering that Mrs. Lee was
alive. He then summoned assistance and within a short time she
was safe in her bed in her own home.

Mrs. Lee's recovery was slow, but she did regain good health, and
a little more than a year after she was buried alive, her youngest
son Robert E., was born, and thus came into the world one of her
bravest and greatest generals." Philadelphia Press. (Nashville
Banner, 15 May 1927.)

LEEPER, Mrs. Caroline, wife of B. F. Leeper, died on the 11th; had not
been able to get out of her yard for nine years; lived in Lobelville,
Perry County. (Linden Times, 1 April 1880.)

LEFEVER, ___, drowned from the steamer Luminary at White River Landing
on Sunday evening. (Memphis Avalanche, 21 Dec. 1866.)

LEFTWICH, Hon. J. W., goes to Hampshire, Tenn., to make a speech; he
was raised near Hampshire. (Memphis Avalanche, 11 Dec. 1866.)
John W. Leftwich is mayor of Memphis. (Memphis Daily Appeal, 16
June 1869.) Mayor Leftwich has died. (Memphis Daily Appeal, 8
March 1870.) Honorable John W. Leftwich, mayor, was buried at
Elmwood Cemetery, Memphis. (Memphis Daily Appeal, 11 March 1870.)

LEFTWICH, Mrs. Victoria, died on Bear Creek, Maury County on 27 Feb.
1871; wife of H. P. Leftwich. (Columbia Herald, 4 March 1871.)

LEFTWICH, Thomas A. The kitchen of Major Thomas A. Leftwich was discovered on fire last Monday and was destroyed; fears were entertained that the dwelling would be consumed but it was saved. Major
Leftwich's kitchen burned about a year ago, accidental. The last
burning may have been the work of an incendiary. Voting on Bear
Creek was for many years held under a tree near the old Leftwich
gin. Major Leftwich and two sons, Captain Jim and Dick Leftwich.
bought a splendid Steam Threshing machine and have had it steadily
going ever since, so far have threshed about 15,000 bushels. These
gentlemen deserve credit for introducing such expensive machinery
into our county. (Columbia Herald, 20 Aug. 1869.)

Bear Creek is noted for its Sulphur Spring, its big Sycamore tree,
its rocky road, its hospitable people, its gallant beaux, lack of
old maids, its forlorn old bachelors, and its pretty black-eyed
girls. (Columbia Herald, 17 Sept. 1869.)

The Rev. W. M. Leftwich of Missouri, distinguished Methodist
minister, is with his father Major Thomas A. Leftwich, who is
"lying dangerously ill." (Columbia Herald, 20 Jan. 1871.)

Thomas A. Leftwich was "a poor man when he came here, but by fine
business qualifications amassed a good estate," which was injured
during the war. He was very fond of fine stock and during his life
owned many splendid horses. (Columbia Herald, 17 Feb. 1871.)

Major Thomas Leftwich, of Bear Creek, died 10 Feb. 1871, at 3:30
p.m., of a long and painful illness; born 10 Dec. 1800 in Bedford
Co., Va.; came to Maury in 1830; one of his last requests was that
his riding horse "Gunboat" was to be kept in the family. Gunboat
was tied behind the hearse and followed his master to the grave.
(Columbia Herald, 17 Feb. 1871.)

Challenge to Fight a Duel. William C. Reynolds of Maury County
charged with challenge to fight a duel, Thomas Leftwich was the
prosecutor; the grand jury found this to be a true bill.
Challenge sent on 30 May 1861: Mr. Thomas A. Leftwich--I understand
you that you say I am a coward why do you say so because you took
the advantage of me when I have no arms all I ask of you is to meet
me at Farmville, Ky., there is where our regiment will rendezvous
at, meet me there is all I ask of you we will settle it in any way
that is honorable, I cannot challenge you in this state and I do
not challenge you in this state but meet at the above named place
on the 10th of June or fill a coward's grave. Signed: W. C.
Reynolds. (Original challenge in box labeled State Causes May
Term 1856, Civil Causes May Term 1834. The box is mislabeled.
Spelling and punctuation are as found in the challenge.)

LEFTWICK, ___, was shot by James Adkins four times in back, face,
shoulder, and arm at Waverly a few days since while Leftwick was
trying to force his way into a store which Adkins had. Adkins left
for parts unknown. (Nashville Republican Banner, 11 June 1870.)

LEGG, Jim, notorious East Tennessee horse thief, was arrested in
Athens, Ala., the scene of many of his depredations; but before
reaching town, he managed to make his escape by jumping from the
train. (Memphis Daily Appeal, 30 Dec. 1868.)

LEIPER, Captain, the first man married in Nashville in 1780, was killed 2 May 1781 in the famous Battle of the Bluffs on the ground just south of Broad Street; was killed by the Cherokees. (Nashville Dispatch, 2 May 1863.)

LENNON, Mary Jane, wife of Edward Lennon, died yesterday. (Nashville Republican Banner, 23 Nov. 1869.)

LEONARD, W., was killed in spring of 1865; Watt Little accused and is to be tried. (Memphis Avalanche, 23 Jan. 1866.)

LEONARD, Mr. Linus, of Stockbridge, Mass., committed suicide on the 12th ult. by hanging himself by a rope from a beam in the upper part of a shed behind his barn. He committed the deed from fear that he would be drafted into the army. (Nashville Dispatch, 4 Sept. 1862.)

LEOPER, Leopold, a German, was found in dying condition night before last on Cherry Street; it was thought he was drunk and he was taken to the stationhouse where he died. His discharge from the Confederate Army was found on him. He had been shot in hip and the shot had penetrated the cavity of his stomach. (Nashville Dispatch, 10 July 1862.)

LESHLEY, Mrs. Thomas, mother of Mrs. W. C. Ingram and Mrs. Charles Regenold, died Monday in Mt. Pleasant and buried at the family burying ground near Sandy Hook. (Maury Democrat, 24 July 1891. N.B. The surname is believed to be correctly Lasley.)

LESTER, Napoleon R., 60, was hanged April 20 at Lebanon, Tenn. for a crime last July. He made a speech on the scaffold, saying he had done right in killing Lane because Lane had ruined the happiness of his home and made a wanton of his wife. (Maury Democrat, 26 April 1888.)

LESTER, Henry, well-to-do farmer of Franklin, committed suicide Oct. 9 by hanging himself on his corn crib. (Columbia Herald, 18 Oct. 1895.)

LESTER, Hiram, of Henry County, Georgia, is 122 years old. (Florence, Ala., Times, 15 Aug. 1891.)

LESUEUR, Margaret E., died on the 24th in Edgefield, wife of O. B. Lesueur; born 9 Dec. 1832. (Nashville Republican Banner, 25 Aug. 1870.)

LETSINGER, Mrs. George, died on the 17th of rheumatism, near Williamsport. (Columbia Herald and Mail, 5 Feb. 1875.)

LETSINGER, Mrs. William, nee Ida Finch, died of consumption on the 8th in District 17. (Columbia Herald and Mail, 17 Aug. 1877.) One of the beauties of District 17, Miss Ida Finch, was married Thursday evening to William Letsinger. (Columbia Herald, 16 Sept. 1870.)

LEVY, Charlie, was killed at Hot Springs, Ark., by Lem Bowen on May 4, he was a sporting man by avocation, formerly a dealer at McCarthy's on Deaderick Street, Nashville; brought to Nashville for burial. He was a member of the Pale Faces, who conducted his funeral. (Nashville Republican Banner, 7 May 1869, 11 May 1869.)

LEWIS, Asa, of Captain Page's Company, 6th Kentucky, CSA, was hanged 26 Dec. 1862 at Murfreesboro by order of General Bragg. He had distinguished himself at Shiloh, but deserted. His comrades refused to let him be executed and General Breckenridge said he would not be executed, but Bragg ordered the execution. Jefferson Davis was there. (Nashville Dispatch, 25 April 1863.)

LEWIS, Charles, was hung on the 3d on scaffold at Trenton, New Jersey, for the murder of James Rowan in Princeton on 13 Nov. 1862; died in about 3 minutes. It is believed that he also killed Dr. Burdell

214

in Jan. 1857. The people in Trenton refused to have him buried
even in their Potter's Field. He was coarse, brutal, vulgar,
devilish to the last moment. His real name is said to be Simonds.
(Nashville Daily Union, 12 April 1863.)

LEWIS, Mrs. General, died last week in Gray's Bend, Hickman County.
(Columbia Herald and Mail, 25 August 1876.)

LEWIS, Harry Flournoy, 2 months 17 days, infant son of G. F. and S. A.
Lewis of Augusta, Georgia, died June 21 in Nashville and was
buried in Nashville. (Nashville Republican Banner, 22 June 1870.)

LEWIS, Loui, 67, old and respected, died on the 11th at home near the
first toll gate on the Murfreesboro Pike. (Nashville Daily Union,
13 March 1863.)

LEWIS. The first baby born in Oklahoma was born April 25, in a wagon
and named Oklahoma Lewis. Her parents are from Texas. (Maury
Democrat, 18 April 1889.)

LEWIS, Mr. and Mrs. Quienna, of Summit, Miss., on September 25
celebrated their 50th wedding anniversary. (Memphis Avalanche,
13 Oct. 1866.)

LEWIS, Stephen, of Sylvania, Georgia, came back to life Tuesday. His
son went to attend his burial and detected a quiver in his father's
eyelid and asked him if he wanted water. The corpse nodded its
head. Doctors were called and he was soon brought back to
consciousness. (Maury Democrat, 16 Oct. 1890.)

LEWIS, Tobe, in the Hamilton County, Tenn., workhouse claims to be 137
years old. He has proof to show he is over 100. (Maury Democrat,
12 March 1891.)

LEWIS, Major William B., 82, of Nashville, died Monday of catarrh
fever; was personal friend of Andrew Jackson. (Memphis Avalanche,
16 Nov. 1866.) He was on his staff in battle of New Orleans. He
was one of the commissioners who adjusted line between Kentucky
and Tennessee. (Memphis Avalanche, 16 Nov. 1866.) The estate of
William B. Lewis is to be sold at auction. (Nashville Republican
Banner, 10 Dec. 1867.)

Weddings at the White House - Two that occurred in Jackson's Time -
Both the brides from Tennessee. Under Jackson, two weddings took
place at the White House, the precise dates of which oddly enough,
no one can now fix. The bride in the first instance was Mary Lewis,
the daughter of an intimate friend and companion-in-arms of Jackson,
William B. Lewis, and the groom, M. Alphonse Joseph Yver Pageot, a
native Martinique, Secretary of Legation at Washington from France
in 1836 and again in 1840, and Minister from 1842 to 1848. Louis
Philippe appointed him, the gossips said, that he might look after
his wife's property in Tennessee. Mme. Pageot is still fondly
remembered here. She died at Montpelier, in France, about 15 years
ago. Jackson gave the lovely bride away. He was always emphatic
and impressive on such occasions, as witnesseth the way in which,
when he and Van Buren were standing sponsors for Mrs. Donelson's
baby, he replied, "I do. I do; I renounce them all."

The other marriage was that of Miss Eastin of Tennessee, Gen.
Jackson's niece, to Mr. Polk of the same State, a kinsman of
President Polk. The lady was to have married Lieut. Bolton Finch,
of the navy, an Englishman by birth, who in 1833 had his name
changed by Congress to Bolton, and in 1849 as Commodore Wm. Compton
Bolton. He was one of the beaus of time, of whom one story runs
that he was an heir to large estates in England.

Captain Finch has been engaged to marry several women before Miss
Eastin accepted him. The day was fixed and the guests were invited,
when suddenly Miss Eastin dropped him and married Mr. Polk, who had

LEWIS, Major William B. - Continued
posted from Tennessee with his coach and four in the stateliest
Southern style to make a last appeal.

Tradition lays the change to Gen. Jackson's advice: "Take care, my
dear; with love marriage is heaven, without it hell." Capt. Bolton
then consoled himself with Miss Lynch of New York, daughter of the
well-known Dominich Lynch and niece of Mrs. Admiral Wilkes.

Andrew Jackson, Jr., the President's adopted son, married Miss
Yorke, daughter of Peter Yorke, of Philadelphia, at her father's home,
though the wedding reception took place at the White House. (Original clipping in compiler's possession; no date; no name of paper
on clipping. N.B. Hamilton Place between Columbia and Mt. Pleasant
still stands and this was the home Lucius Polk built for his bride
Mary Eastin.)

Andrew Jackson Pageot, 32, died 9 Jan. 1865 in Nashville, of acute
attack of heart; grandson of Major William B. Lewis, son of Hon.
A. Pageot of France and Mary Ann Lewis. (Nashville Daily Union,
10 Jan. 1865.)

LEWIS, Meriwether. In 1848 at the exhumation of his remains, only a
few bones were found and even the skull was in an abandoned state of
decay. (Daily Herald, Columbia, TN, 2 Oct. 1905.)

Cooper Frierson Statement. Mr. Bruce Cooper and his brother Alfred
told me before the Park was dedicated that their father, Mr. Robert
Cooper, said that Meriwether Lewis was murdered by the man, who ran
the house, where he stopped to spend the night. The brothers told
me they played, when boys, with a boy about their age, named
Whitesides, who said his father was on the Jury of Inquest and had
told him that they had all the proof they needed to convict him but
were afraid to do it, for they said the murderer was one half
Indian and would kill them. He said they were cowards and did not.
The jury was satisfied that it was not suicide. They also said
Mr. Robert O. Smith was mail carrier and came along the Natchez
Trace about sunup and found the body lying with the feet in the
road. Mr. Smith was connected with the Coopers and told the Cooper
brothers and their father, Robert M., told them. Mr. Robert Cooper
was a blacksmith, living eight or ten miles from where Lewis was
killed and they sent to him to make some spikes or nails and he went
to the burial. In those days, they made coffins with wooden pins.
They could not find any lumber to make a coffin, so they found a
tree that would split easy and they hewed and split it in thick
slabs, and made a coffin. Mr. Robert M. Cooper helped to bury him.
When the Legislature ordered a Monument erected, the parties in
charge of the work, came to Mr. Robert M. Cooper to locate the grave.
His son Thomas told me he was a boy, half grown, and he asked his
father to let him ride behind him and he was there. The remains
were dug up and they found a few coins, a brass button or two, and
a medal or insignia, and a piece of his uniform. They went to the
Spring and found a flat rock, and scraped a hole in it and put
everything in it, and put another rock on top, and put those rocks
in the grave. Mr. Thomas Cooper told me all about the remains and
finding the grave. Signed, Cooper Frierson. (Copy of Cooper
Frierson statement found in the papers of the late Judge W. B.
Turner, Columbia, Tenn., no date.)

Letter of Frank H. Smith - The advocates of the suicide theory
generally accept President Jefferson's dictum in support of that
view, but after a careful study of this question for more than 25
years, and numberless conversations with people of Lewis, Hickman
and Maury counties, descendants of those who knew the circumstances,
I am fully convinced that Lewis was murdered. And I believe that
this is the tradition and opinion of most of the people of Lewis
County. Signed, Frank H. Smith, Columbia, Tenn., 28 June 1904.
(Nashville American, 1904 clipping in scrapbook owned by Jill
Garrett.)

LEWIS, Meriwether - Continued
Cunningham Rebuttal to a Webster Letter. Mr. Webster says: "It
is a fact that the husband of Mrs. Grinder was arrested and accused
of the murder of Lewis." I apprehend he means Robert O. Smith's
chimney corner tradition, because I am sure it is not history. Capt.
Joel P. Morrison, who is now 81 years old, was born and raised in
Hickman County, and lives near the Lewis County line and was well
acquainted with the people of Lewis County long before Mr. Webster
was born.

Capt. Morrison is now present as I write and authorizes me to say
on his authority, that Mr. Grinder was not arrested for the murder
of Gov. Lewis. He has known the Grinder family all his life and
feels morally certain that he would have heard of the arrest of Mr.
Grinder years ago if it had ever occurred. He says all this talk
of murder and the arrest of Grinder has originated within the last
35 or 40 years.

Capt. Morrison is one of the most conservative, truthful and well-
informed men in our county. He was a soldier in the Mexican War
and a Captain in the Confederate army. He is one of the best
preserved men mentally I ever saw of his age. He has within the
last 12 months written for publication in the Hickman County Progress
a number of papers on the Mexican War, all of which show wonderful
memory.

Horatio Clagett, who is now 85 years old, is President of the First
National Bank of Centreville. He has lived in Centreville 67 years,
and during this time was well acquainted with the people of Lewis
County, a part of the time part of Lewis' territory belonged to
Hickman County. He says: He is sure Grinder was never arrested
for the murder of Lewis. Only a few years after the death of Lewis,
Grinder moved from the Grinder Stand to Centreville, and lived
within sight of the town till his death. His son, Robert Grinder,
lived at the same place until his death. His grandson W. P. Grinder
now lives at the same place, and all of these people have been known
as honorable men and no breath of suspicion has ever been whispered
against them.

Mr. Clagett says he had repeated talks with Pete, a negro who was
owned by Grinder and was present at the time of Lewis' death. His
version was substantially the same as that given by Alexander
Wilson in his letter of 1811. He tells of Lewis' stopping and Mr.
Grinder not being at home; of his refusing to sleep on a bed, but
using his buffalo robes; of his strange conduct; of Mrs. Grinder
being afraid of him, and barring herself up in the kitchen with her
little children, the boy Pete and a negro girl Malinda; of hearing
the pistol and seeing Lewis after he was shot.

The negro girl who was present lived to be very old. She told
substantially the same story up to the time of her death, about 20
years ago. A short time before the death of this negro, she was
visited by the Hon. W. P. Clark, of Centreville, and Col. J. H.
Moore, now of Dolanega, Ga., who took her statement which was
published in the Hickman Pioneer, which is a substantial corrobora-
tion of the story as given by Wilson and Jefferson.

Maj. James H. Akin, of Williamson County, says his mother was living
in the Hampshire neighborhood and was 14 years old at the time of
Lewis' death. She lived to a ripe old age, retaining her mental
faculties to a remarkable degree and always said she understood it
was suicide. It will be remembered that she lived in the nearest
white neighborhood to the place of his death.

But Mr. Webster tells us that all sources of information of suicide
evidently emanated from Grinder's Stand. In this I am sure he is
correct. It was at Grinder's Stand on that night in October that
Mrs. Grinder, who with her little children and the negro boy and

girl, listened from her log kitchen to the incoherent utterances
of Gov. Lewis as he paced the floor of his room. It was there she
heard the pistol. It was there that he said, "Oh, madam! give
me some water and heal my wounds." It was there the negro boy
Pete and girl Malinda witnessed one of the most melancholy and
lamentable deaths ever recorded in the annals of American history.
It was there that his attendants and the attendants of Neely, some
of whom were intelligent white men, together with Mr. Neely, examined
the body, and knowing all the circumstances leading up to his death,
knew it was suicide.

Yes, this is the place from which all our information originated,
and the only place from which a true version could come. We know
the tradition that had its origin elsewhere is not true. We know
Mr. Grinder was not arrested for his murder, and we know Grinder
did not go to Texas, Arkansas, or West Tennessee soon after Lewis'
death and buy a large farm and many negroes, as has been reported
and believed by those who are ever ready to accept chimney corner
tradition for truth. In the first place, there were no farmers or
settlers in Texas, Arkansas, or West Tennessee for many years after
his (Lewis') death, and as a matter of fact, Grinder never moved
from the county in which Lewis died, Hickman. He moved from the
place, going to Centreville but not from the county. His bones
and Gov. Lewis both lie at what at that time was Hickman County.
Signed, J. A. Cunningham, Centreville, Tn., 22 July 1904.
(Nashville American, 25 July 1904.)

In the year 1809, Meriwether Lewis committed suicide at Grinder's
Stand in the southwest corner of Maury County. Settlers were
scarce, and they came to Cathey's Creek for two of the jury, James
Fariss, Robert Whiteside, and Samuel Whiteside, an officer.
(Maury Democrat, 2 April 1908.)

Mrs. F. M. Watson lives in Columbia; her father, Mr. Robert O.
Smith, was for many years the surveyor of Lewis county, Tennessee,
and his father, Mr. Robert Smith, was a mail carrier from Nashville
to Natchez, along the Natchez Trace, which was opened about 1800.
The hostile Indians were conciliated by permitting them to work on
the Trace. Mr. Robert Smith was carrying mail when Governor Meriwether Lewis killed himself. On one of his return trips, Mr.
Robert Smith, Mrs. Watson's grandfather, saw Lewis' corpse, shot
in the head, a single hole by an unknown weapon. And 39 years
afterwards, in 1848, the corpse was identified by the bullet hole
in the skull. The nails in Lewis' coffin were made by Mr. Robert
Melville Cooper, the father of Captain Cooper of Mount Pleasant
Tennessee; Mr. Robert Melville Cooper had a blacksmith shop some
ten miles away from the place where Lewis is buried. The shop was
on the west prong of Big Bigby Creek. For some years the Natchez
Trace was the boundary between the United States and the Cherokee
Nation, from the south bank of Duck River to the ridge dividing
Buffalo from Duck river. It was the western boundary of civiliza-
tion, the resort of thieves and cutthroats.

Mrs. Watson tells us that her grandfather did see Meriwether Lewis
after he was shot. Mr. Robert Smith was also there when Lewis'
remains were taken up, and he identified Lewis' body by the bullet
hole in the skull. Workmen opened three graves to find the right
one, in 1848, and the monument is over Meriwether Lewis' grave.

Mr. Robert Smith is buried near the same grave. Tradition says
that Mr. Cooper made the iron nails for all the coffins that were
buried there about the time of Lewis' death. Some people long
supposed that Grinder killed Lewis, or that it was done by one of
his servants. It is said that Whiteside and Faris in that neighborhood have the coroner's inquest papers about Meriwether Lewis. A
famous deer stand for hunters was near the monument. At present
the Trace bends away from it. The monument is about three miles
southeast of Newburg, Lewis County, Tennessee. The said county is

named in honor of Meriwether Lewis. As there are no fences, the
roads have been changed. The Natchez Trace ran on top of the ridge,
but people have found a nearer way...Major James H. Akin has
introduced a bill into the Tennessee legislature at its present
session, calling for an appropriation of $500 to repair Meriwether
Lewis' monument. One of our old citizens tells us that Mr.
(Ethelburt) Kirby quarried the present limestone shaft of the
monument from near a spring 3 1/2 miles north of Colubmia and just
west of the Nashville turnpike road. (Maury Democrat, 11 April 1895.)

Peter Grinder, a colored man, was the property of Robert Grinder,
Sen., and was at an early day our village (Centerville) blacksmith.
He came from what is now Lewis county, and with his master then
lived at the Grinder Stand on the Natchez Trace, where the monument
is erected over the grave of Gov'r. Lewis, and was the boy of all
work at the hotel; was with Gov'r. Lewis during his stay at the
hotel, and the first one that saw him after he had commited the rash
act of self-destruction. He was, like most of his race, superstitious, and did not like to talk of the event. Uncle Peter was
a man of great muscular power, a favorite amongst the white people
and lived to a good old age, having died since the war. (Hickman
Pioneer, Centerville, Tn., 5 April 1878.)

Descendants of Robert and Priscilla Knight Griner of Hickman
County will be shocked to learn of the vandalism and almost total
destruction of the old Griner Cemetery in Shipp's Bend in March
of this year. Vandals overturned all stones, broke most of the
stones into many pieces, and threw the stones across a field, so
that it will be impossible to put the stones back at the proper
grave. (The River Counties Quarterly, July 1979; the family name
was spelled Griner on the stones; Robert and Priscilla Knight Griner
were the owners of Grinder's Stand at the time of Lewis' death.)

Tombstone inscription in the Meriwether Lewis National Park;
Meriwether Lewis, born near Charlottesville, Virginia, 18 Aug.
1774, and died 11 Oct. 1809, aged 35 years. Inscription on the
monument placed by the Legislature of Tennessee A.D., 1848: In
the language of Mr. Jefferson: His courage was undaunted, his
firmness and perseverance yielded to nothing but impossiblities;
a rigid disciplinarian, yet tender as a father to those committed
to his charge; honest, disinterested, liberal with a sound under-
standing and a scrupulous fidelity to truth. An officer of the
Regular Army, Pvt. Sec'y to Pres. Jefferson, Commander of the
Expedition to the Oregon in 1803-1806; Governor of the Territory
of Louisiana. His melancholy death occurred where this monument
now stands and under which rest his mortal remains.

LEYTON, Christopher Columbus, of Arizona, is 74 years old, has had
    12 wives; has 54 sons who vote and 10 girls. (Columbia Herald,
    17 Sept. 1897.)

LICK, James, San Francisco millionaire, has died. He has become famous
    for his magnificent public donations and bequests amounting to 5
    or 6 million dollars. (Columbia Herald and Mail, 20 Oct. 1876.)

LIGON, Mary, infant daughter of Mr. and Mrs. W. H. F. Ligon, age 7
    months 20 days, died in South Nashville on August 25. Clarksville
    Papers please copy. (Nashville Daily Gazette, 26 Aug. 1852.)

LILES, daughter of Washington Liles, who lives east of Hampshire,
    Maury County, died Thursday of consumption. (Columbia Herald and
    Mail, 24 Aug. 1874.)

LILES, David H., 45, was instantly killed by falling tree while cutting
    timber near his home on Wolf Creek, 3 miles from Iron City, Tn.,
    wife and 5 children survive. (Daily Herald, Columbia, Tn., 7 Dec.
    1899.)

LILLY, Patrick, son of Owen Lilly, Esquire, died on the 2d.
(Memphis Avalanche, 3 March 1866.)

LINCOLN, Abraham, died this morning at 22 minutes past 7 o'clock.
Signed 15 April 1865, E. M. Stanton, Secretary of War. (Nashville
Daily Union, 16 April 1865.)

The funeral cortege of President Lincoln has reached Michigan City.
(Nashville Daily Union, 2 May 1865.)

J. H. Fagherty has been arrested in Nashville for asserting
vehemently that President Lincoln ought to have been killed 4
years ago and that the man who killed him was better and more
worthy of the gratitude of the people than his victim. (Nashville
Daily Union, 30 April 1865.)

The Honorable David Davis, administrator of Abraham Lincoln, made
final settlment of estate at Springfield on the 14th. There remains
$110,294.62 to be divided. The widow got $36,765.30. (Murfreesboro
Minitor, 23 Nov. 1867.)

An attempt has been made to steal Lincoln's bones. (Columbia
Herald and Mail, 17 Nov. 1876.)

The old walnut bedsteadon which Lincoln was laid after Booth shot
him, together with mattresses of the bed, have come into the
possession of a Chicago relic-hunter. (Maury Democrat, 16 March
1893.)

Mrs. Abraham Lincoln gets a Federal pension of $3000 a year.
(Linden Times, 9 Dec. 1880.)

The Lincoln family now has six members buried in the Lincoln
monument at Springfield, Illinois: Mr. and Mrs. Abraham Lincoln,
their sons Edward, William and Thomas (called Tad), and a grandson
Abraham Lincoln. (Florence, Ala., Times, 27 June 1891.)

Republicans in Fox Lake, Wisconsin, are rejoicing over the recovery
of a cannon which was unearthed Oct. 30 by Joseph Good, while
digging a trench. It was stolen and buried by the local Democrats
in 1860 to prevent the Republicans celebrating the election of
Abraham Lincoln. (Columbia Herald, 15 Nov. 1895.)

The body of Abraham Lincoln, son of Robert T. Lincoln, will be
brought from London to Springfield, Ill., and placed in a crypt
in the Lincoln monument. (Florence, Ala., Times, 7 Nov. 1890.)

The Lincoln monument at Springfield, Ill., completed 1876, will
have to be torn down. It cost $206,500 and was found to have
crumbled away too much to be repaired. (Maury Democrat, 7 Nov.
1895.)

Lincoln's body has been moved after 24 years to a temporary vault.
(Daily Herald, Columbia, Tn., 12 March 1900.) The reburial of
Lincoln is completed. Six feet of cement was put over him. (Daily
Herald, 30 Sept. 1901.)

It is reported that Mary Lincoln, daughter of Minister Robert
Lincoln, is engaged to marry her father's secretary. (Florence,
Ala., Times, 15 Aug. 1891.)

Andrew J. Russell, corporal, has been reduced in rank and dis-
honorably discharged for expressing joy at the President's death.
(Nashville Daily Union, 10 May 1865.)

All the bodies of the assassination conspirators, except Haynes,
have been given up and it is thought his will be soon by his
friends. The remains of the Andersonville victim, Wirz, will then

be left alone in the arsenal ground, but only because nobody has applied for them. (Murfreesboro Monitor, 30 Jan. 1869.)

Non-Resident Notice: Elias Rumbo vs Abraham Lincoln: "It appearing to me from complainant's bill that Abraham Lincoln, President of the United States, is non-resident of the State of Tennessee, so that the ordinary process of law cannot be served on him; the said Lincoln is ordered to appear and plead, answer, or demur...signed 20 Jan. 1862, A. M. Wingfield, C & M, Maury County. (Seventh Brigade Journal, Columbia, Tn, 8 April 1862.) (N.B. The original papers for this lawsuit have never been located in Maury County, so the reason for the lawsuit remains unknown.)

LINCOLN, Mrs. Anthony, died Sunday, of Columbia. (Columbia Herald and Mail, 13 March 1874.)

LINDSEY, A. D., 35, died on the 16th; member of the Memphis Light Guards, 154 Tennessee Regiment; his old regiment will attend. (Memphis Daily Appeal, 17 Nov. 1869.)

LINDSEY, Dolph, died yesterday at Danville, Houston County. (Houston County Times, 14 Oct. 1887.)

LINDSEY, Miss Maria Ann, died on the 29th in New York City; sister of John W. Lindsey of Nashville, native of Tennessee; left 8 years ago and went to California to live with her uncle Samuel Miller; to be buried in Tennessee. (Nashville Republican Banner, 3 July 1868.)

LINDSEY, Mrs., wife of Col. Joachim Lindsey of Maury County, died July 28 near Elkton, Giles County, of pistol wound fired by her husband. (Augusta Constitutionalist, Augusta, Ga., 16 Aug. 1825.)

Stop the Murderer. Joachim D. Lindsay, late of Maury Co., has murdered his wife Elenor B. Lindsey and has escaped justice; reward if returned to jailor in Giles Co.; reward offered by governor and Elizabeth Phillips, Elkton, Tn. He will probably head of New Orleans and then to Liverpool where he has an uncle of his own named. (Nashville Whig, 17 Oct. 1825.)

LINDSEY, William Alexander, born March 1853 at Sandy Hook; married 8 Jan. 1894 to Rhoda Neeley, justice of the peace in Maury County. (Maury Democrat, 30 May 1895. N.B. - This paper was torn.)

LINDSEY, W. D., Company E, 19th Alabama, CSA, Confederate prisoner of war, was killed instantly by the falling of the stairs at the Convalescent Barracks on Tuesday. (Nashville Daily Union, 1 Oct. 1863.)

LINDSEY, Zemira C., wife of Robert L. Lindsey of Putnam County died on the 21st; age 46. (Nashville Republican Banner, 26 Nov. 1868.)

LINCH, Mrs. John, of Greenplains farm, Maury County, died on the 5th of congestive chill and buried at Williamsport; leaves 4 month old baby. (Columbia Herald and Mail, 11 June 1875.)

LINCK, Mrs. Julia C., died on the 20th ult. at Madison, Indiana, wife of John W. Linck, 3d daughter of Isaac and Christiana LeCroix of Nashville; funeral in Nashville; was an excellent artist. (Nashville Republican Banner, 2 Aug. 1870.)

LINKER, Mattie, wife of William Linker, died suddenly on the 16th. (Nashville Republican Banner, 17 June 1870.)

LINLY (or LINEY), John, was shot and wounded on the Charlotte turnpike by guerrillas on Sunday the 28th ult; he came on to Nashville and was taken by Federal pickets; nothing has been heard of him since; information is wanted by his son Leroy Liney. (Nashville Daily Union, 2 Jan. 1863.)

LINZEY. Information wanted on John Linzy, shot and wounded on
Charlotte Pike, 17 miles from Nashville by guerrillas last 28th.
He came on to Nashville on Sunday night and was taken by Federal
pickets and nothing heard from him since. Information would be
gladly received by son Leroy Linzy at McDennets a short distance
from the penitentiary. (Nashville Daily Union, 7 Jan. 1863. See
also one above.)

LIPPINCOTT, George A., prominent nurseryman of Huntsville, Ala., died
last week. (Florence, Ala., Times, 15 Aug. 1891.)

LIPSCOMB, Mrs. Mattie B., wife of H. B., daughter of General G. W.
Gordon, died in Columbia on the 17th. (West Tennessee Whig, 26
Oct. 1860.)

LIPSKI, Joseph, brother of Meyer Lipski, was murdered in South America;
a dealer in fine watches, diamonds, etc. He had jewels worth
$30,000 with him; murdered by Major D. Carlos Verea, nephew of
Don Balta, President of Peruvian Republic. (Nashville Republican
Banner, 19 Jan. 1871.)

LISENBY, ___, member of the Volunteer Company from Stewart County,
died of pneumonia in the hospital at Clarksville Monday of last
week; taken to Stewart County for burial. (Clarksville Weekly
Chronicle, 14 June 1861.)

LISENBY, Mrs. Rufus, died near Lasea, Maury County, Monday of consumption; buried Hardison Cemetery. (Columbia Herald, 20 March
1891.)

LISLE, ___, was shot and killed by Mr. Hughes in Carter County, Tn,
on Saturday last; family matters. (Memphis Avalanche, 25 Dec.
1866.)

LITTLE, General, CSA, was killed in the fight at Iuka, Mississippi.
(Nashville Dispatch, 2 Oct. 1862.)

LITTLE CROW, his son was captured on the 29th and confirms the death
of his father, Little Crow. (Nashville Dispatch, 15 Aug. 1863.)

LITTLEFIELD, William, of Columbia, has in his possession the pay
chest that his grandfather used for carrying money to pay the
soldiers in the Revolutionary War. (Columbia Herald, 7 June 1895.
N.B. His grandfather was General Nathaniel Greene.)

LITTON, William, 18, was accidently killed July 1 on Leiper's Creek;
fell off mule, the trace chain wrapped around leg of mule and he
was drug for 250 yards, died in one hour; right arm and leg
were torn loose. (Columbia Herald and Mail, 10 July 1874.)

LITTON, Mrs. Louise M., 49, consort of Benjamin Litton, died on the 10th.
(Nashville Daily Gazette, 21 Aug. 1852.)

LIVINGSTON, James, 59, died on the 25th. (Nashville Daily Union,
26 May 1865.)

LIVINGSTON, Andrew, died in Lawrenceburg. (Columbia Herald, 1 April
1897.)

LIVINGSTON, William Oswell, 3d and last surviving son of famous
African traveller, died recently at St. Albans, England. (Maury
Democrat, 30 Jan. 1890.)

The wife of Dr. Livingston, the African explorer, joined him at
the Zambesi last spring and died on the Shire April 27 last from
African fever. She was attended night and day by her husband.
His brother writes: "A grave was dug the next day under the large
Baobab, mentioned by the officers of Capt. Owens' expedition and

about 150 yards from Shupanga house and there we buried her."
(Nashville Dispatch, 23 Oct. 1862.)

LIZENBY, Rufus, found dead on the bank of Duck River, frozen; he had
been drinking. (Maury Democrat, 17 Jan. 1895. N.B. - see Lisenby
also.)

LOCK. The First Shot in the Revolution - The first American who discharged his gun on the day of the battle of Lexington was Ebenezer
Lock, who died at Deering, New Hampshire, about 50 years ago. He
resided in Lexington in 1775. The British regulars, at the order
of Major Pitcairn, having fired on a few "Rebels" on the green in
front of the meetinghouse, killed some and wounded others, it was
a signal for war. The citizens, writes one, "might be seen coming
from all directions, in the roads, over fields, and through the
woods, each with his rifle in his hand, his powder horn hung to
his side, and his pockets provided with bullets. Among the number
was Ebenezer Lock."

The British had posted a reserve of infantry a mile in the rear in
the direction of Boston. This was in the neighborhood of Mr. Lock
who instead of hastening to join the party at the green, posted
himself in an open cellar at a convenient distance for doing
execution. A portion of the reserve was standing on a bridge, and
Mr. Lock commenced firing at them. There was no other American
in sight. He worked valiantly for some minutes, bringing down one
of the enemy at nearly every shot. Up to this time not a gun
had been fired by the rebels. The British, greatly disturbed at
losing so many men by the random firing of the unseen enemy, were
not long in discovering the man in the cellar, and discharged a
volley of balls, which lodged in the wall opposite.

Mr. Lock remaining unhurt, continued to load and fire with the
precision of a finished marksman. He was driven to such close
quarters, however, by the British on his right and left that he was
compelled to retreat. He had just one bullet left, and there was
now but one way to escape, and that was through an orchard, and not
one movement was to be lost. He leveled his gun at the man near by,
dropped the weapon, and the man was shot through the breast. Lock
reached the brink of a steep hill, throwing himself upon the ground,
tumbled downward, rolling as if mortally wounded. In this way he
escaped unurt. At the close of the war he moved to New Hampshire
where he resided till his death, twenty years after. He lived in
seclusion and died in peace. (Nashville Daily Union, 3 June 1864.)

LOCKE, Capt. J. Bowdoin, native of Memphis, died in Louisville, Ky. on
Monday the 23d; educated at West Point; captain in 9th Tennessee
Infantry, CSA; shot through left lung at Battle of Franklin and
never entirely recovered; buried Elmwood Cemetery, Memphis. (Memphis
Daily Appeal, 25 Nov. 1869.)

LOCKE, Andrew J., was killed in Tipton County, Tn, by S. P. Driver,
a justice of the peace, for intimacy with Driver's wife; both
respectable and quiet citizens. (Hickman Pioneer, 28 March 1844.)

LOCKEN, James, died on the 5th, age 19. (Nashville Republican
Banner, 6 Feb. 1869.)

LOCKRIDGE, Pattie Odil, shot herself and her three children Sunday.
(Columbia Herald, 24 July 1891.)

Murder and Suicide. - Mrs. Pattie Lochridge, wife of Tom Lochridge,
shot her three children and herself about 1 o'clock Sunday afternoon
at her home, three miles southeast of Spring Hill, Tn. Mrs.
Lochridge was 30 years of age, her eldest child 4 years old, the
second 3 years old, and the third 4 months.

The awful deed was done with a double-barreled breech-loading
shotgun. After dinner Tom Lochridge went to church, leaving his

223

LOCKRIDGE, Pattie Odil - Continued
home in its usual state of quietness. His wife had been complaining
for some time past, but on that particular afternoon she was no
worse than she had been during the week past. The children were
playing around as usual, and there was not the slightest hint of
the frightful tragedy so soon to be enacted.

About 3 o'clock he returned to the pleasant little house he had
left, and found the front door locked. This seemed strange to him,
but concluding his wife had gone off on a visit he went around the
house intending to enter by the back door. This, too, was locked,
and he was compelled to force a window sash in order to gain an
entrance.

He had never known his wife to so securely fasten the house, and as
he climbed through the window a strange feeling of impending evil
came over him. Not, however, until he had gone into the living
room, the place where he had spent so many happy hours, did the full
meaning of the sealed doors and windows burst upon him.

There upon a pallet, nicely arranged, lay his three darling children
dead. And across the room with her feet turned to theirs was his
wife, their mother, cold in the grasp of the grim destroyer. A
double-barreled breech-loading shotgun, his companion on many a
jolly hunt lay between them.

As near as can be learned from the surroundings, Mrs. Lochridge
had drawn up her children's clothes, one by one, placed the gun
against their hearts, and fired. Then she placed them side by side
on a pallet which she had made for the purpose, and arranged their
dresses neatly about them.

Standing at their feet, and probably gazing down upon them, the
distracted mother placed the muzzle of the gun at her own heart and
sent her own soul to follow her children.

After killing the first two, she must have reloaded the gun, and
that she did it shows that she was at least partly calm. How she
pulled the trigger when the gun was against her own breast is a
mystery, unless she did it with a stick held in her hand or with
her feet.

The burials took place at the family burying ground Monday, the
services being conducted by the Rev. Mr. Sullivan, owing to the
unavoidable absence of the Rev. Mr. Thompson, who had been requested
by Mrs. Lochridge before her death by letter of officiate. The
sad burial of these four victims was largely attended.

The report which gained circulation that her husband, Thos. Lochridge
had taught a negro Sunday School, is we are informed, unfounded.
Some of his kin and intimate friends emphatically deny this, saying
Mr. L. is and always has been a clean, straight Democrat. He was
at Port Royal teaching a Sunday School composed of some of the
children of the best citizens of that community when the rash act
was committed. My the sod rest lightly upon the bosoms of the
slain.

The following letter was found in the room with the murdered and
the suicide:
19 July 1891
Dear Tom:

I know you will be shocked when you get back and find what I have
done. This is not my first attempt. I took 40 drops of laudanum
at one time and 60 at another, before I was married, and failed to
accomplish my purpose, but think I will succeed this time.

If Eunice had been at home last Sunday evening, this deed would
have been committed then, but she had gone to church. I could not

bear to leave her behind. I do wish you could go with us. But
for you I would gladly, gladly, give up all and go home to heaven.
I sometimes feel that I am a terrible sinner, but now I feel that
the good Lord is waiting with the doors open to welcome me and our
little ones in.

And what a relief it would be to know before I go that you could go
with us. Tom, you have been too good to me. You have kept your
marriage vows so much more perfect than I have, but you know my
health is bad now. I have been in a bad state of mind some time.
I feel that I am tired of life and must go.

You will find all your receipts and deeds and papers of all kinds
relating to your business in a wooden box in the west room at the
head of the bed. I want you to have the ring. It will cause you to
think of me. My last request is for Mr. Thompson to preach my
funeral; he knows me better than Mr. Sullivan. My side hurts so
bad I will have to quit writing. Good-bye, Pattie.

P.S. You will find our burial clothes in the west room on the bed.
Let Berda and Rose divide my clothes and the children between ma
and Matthew and Mrs. Chumney, Minnie, Berda, Rose, and Parilee, just
as they think best. You will have no use for them now. Berda and
Rose may have all my jewelry except the ring you gave me. Pattie.
(Maury Democrat, 23 July 1891.)

LOCKRIDGE, Robert D., justice of the peace for District 19, next to
J. T. S. Greenfield, is one of the wealthiest men on the county
court; he was born 24 July 1849; married 1871 to Florence Potter,
who died 1889; and married secondly to Christie Polk. (Maury
Democrat, 4 July 1895.)

LOCKRIDGE, Mrs. W. T., died August 19 near Spring Hill; daughter of
F. K. and S. E. Odil. (Maury Democrat, 21 August 1891.)

LOFTIN, Mrs. Eliza, died January 31 of congestion of the brain; age
63; died in Marshall County, but lived in Maury County. (Columbia
Herald and Mail, 26 Feb. 1875.)

LOFTIN, Shade, 90, died Sunday evening. (Columbia Herald and Mail,
1 June 1877.)

LOFTON, Colonel Walton C., died September 12 after a lingering illness;
died in Nashville; wife and several children survive. (Nashville
Dispatch, 13 Sept. 1863.)

LOGAN, Andrew, 17, burned to death May 6; his mother's house caught
on fire while he was asleep. (Maury Democrat, 10 May 1888.)

LOGAN, General, his remains have been removed from the vault where they
have been deposited for the past two years to a new chapel in the
Soldiers Home Cemetery in Washington, D.C. (Maury Democrat, 3 Jan.
1889.)

LOMANNEY, P., died yesterday; funeral to be held at the Cathedral.
(Nashville Union and American, 25 March 1873.)

LOMAX, Honorable Judge John Taylor, 81, died on the 1st at Fredericksburg Virginia; was member of the bar in 1825 when he was called to
be a law professor at the University of Virginia. (Nashville
Dispatch, 18 Oct. 1862.)

LOMAX, Thomas, 74, has lived in Perry County for 66 years and has been
register for 34 years. (Linden Times, 8 April 1880.)

LONG, ___, Company I, 14th Tennessee Regiment, from Montgomery County,
was killed in battle near Washington. (Nashville Dispatch, 2 Oct.
1862.)

LONG, Patrick, ex-Confederate soldier, private in Early's brigade, and on sentry near the tent of Stonewall Jackson the night that great general met his tragic death, died in Baltimore on October 7. (Columbia Herald, 18 Oct. 1895.)

LONG. Information Wanted - Of Thomas Long, formerly of the Parish of Mayora and Templetooky, County of Tipperary, Ireland, but who has been for about 20 years past in this country. It is supposed that he resides somewhere in Tennessee. Any information respecting him and his present residence will be gratefully received and may be communicated by mail to his brother James Long, residing in Worcester, Mass. (The Columbia Beacon, 2 Dec. 1846.)

LONGEVITY. Thomas Cam of England lived to be 207 according to the Parish Register of St. Leonard's, Shoreditch, England.

Henry Jenkins of Yorkshire lived to be 169 according to his tombstone.

William Edwards, lived to be 168, according to a slab at Caerey Church in Cardiff, Glamorgan, and died 1668.

Betsy Trantham of Tennessee is said to have died 1834 aged 154 years.

Thomas Parr lived to be 142.

Peter Czart or Rotin, Belgian patriarch died at 150 or 180 years.

The Countess of Eccleston died in Ireland at 143.

The Countess of Desmone, died 1694 at 140 years, 70 years after the death of her husband and renewed her teeth twice.

Dr. William Mead of Ware, County of Hertsford, has stone which says he lived to be 141 years.

Farmer Khalisa died at 141 years at Korte in the government of Kotais.

Margaret Scott of Dalwelth, Scotland, died 1738 at the age of 125 according to her tombstone.

Mark (Marcus) Jordan, died at 107, and was a Westphalian patriarch.

Jean Frederick Waldech died 1876 at 109 years.

The woman soldier Phoebe Hessel, born 1713 at Stephancy, died at 108 years at Brighton. (Maury Democrat, 14 Aug. 1913.)

LONGINETTE, James, 82, old resident of Nashville and native of Italy, died yesterday. (Nashville Union and American, 14 March 1873.)

LONGSTREET, General James, famous Confederate commander, and Miss Ellen Dortch, assistant state librarian of Georgia, were married in Atlanta Wednesday. The bride is a young lady while the groom is growing ripe in years. (Columbia Herald, 10 Sept. 1897.) General Longstreet and his family are boarding in Huntsville, Alabama. (Memphis Daily Appeal, 24 Sept. 1868.) General Longstreet is still hard at work on his history of the war and hopes to have it published some time in 1891. (Florence, Ala., Times, 28 Feb. 1891.)

LONGWORTH, Nicholas, of Cincinnati died February 10. (Nashville Daily Union, 12 Feb. 1863.)

LONGWORTH, William, has been naturalized in Nashville. (Nashville Daily Union, 14 June 1865.)

LOONEY, Mrs. Mariah Ann, 29, consort of William B. Looney, died in this county on the 29th ult. at the home of her father. (Weekly Patriot, Paris, Tn, 4 Sept. 1856.)

LOONEY, Sarah, murderess, from Coffee County, Tn, has been pardoned; she was sent to prison for 20 years at the age of 16 and sent to prison in 1889. (Daily Herald, Columbia, Tn, 25 Aug. 1900.)

LORING, General W. W., pasha, formerly of the U. S. Army and also in the Confederate Army, later commander of Loring's Corps in the Egyptian Army, died of pneumonia at New York on the 30th. (Erin Review, 8 Jan. 1887.)

LOUCKS, Jacob, the largest man in York County, Pa., died in Manchester on the 12th of apoplexy; weighed 500 pounds; his coffin was 35 inches abroad and 23 inches deep. (Memphis Avalanche, 28 Dec. 1866.)

LOVE, Samuel J., 27th Tennessee, CSA, prisoner of war, died between April 12 and April 19 in the general hospital at Paducah. (Nashville Dispatch, 7 Aug. 1862.)

LOVE, Lucius, of Love's Branch, Maury County, went to Kentucky on a visit and had hemorrhage and died; brought back for burial. (Columbia Herald, 12 Dec. 1873.)

LOVELL, Mrs. R. A., died; funeral to be held this evening. (Nashville Union and American, 4 June 1874.)

LOVET, General Charles S., died 3 Jan. 1871 in Louisville; commanded Nashville after the war; contracted disease in California while commanding Fort Yuma; aged about 58 years; married 1845 to daughter of General Armstrong; brother-in-law of Joseph Vaulx of Nashville; native of Massachusetts; served in Mexican War. (Nashville Republican Banner, 4 Jan. 1871.)

LOVETT, Mrs. Josie, 17, wife of William Lovett, died Wednesday at the home of her grandfather Mr. Hardison in Lasea; had been married only a short time; buried Hardison Cemetery. (Columbia Herald, 15 Dec. 1899.)

LOVETTE, Mrs. Josie, 22, died November 7 of consumption; youngest daughter of W. R. Sharp; husband and three children survive. (Columbia Herald and Mail, 30 Nov. 1877.)

LOWE, Major Wash, has died of cholera in Robertson County; eminent lawyer. (Memphis Avalanche, 8 Nov. 1866.)

LOWE, Captain William E., of General Donelson's staff, accidentally killed on the 15th ult. some 8 or 10 miles north of Munfordville, Ky. (Nashville Dispatch, 2 Oct. 1862.)

LOWELL, James Russell, famous poet, author, lecturer, and statesman, died at Cambridge, Mass., Wednesday. (Florence, Ala. Times, 15 Aug. 1891.)

LOWRY, M. W., John N. Hicks, James Jones, and ten others are buried near Lake Station, Miss. They were killed in railroad accident here early in 1862. They were members of the 5th Tennessee Infantry, CSA. (Nashville Republican Banner, 28 May 1869.)

LOWRY, Levi, died in DeKalb County, Ala., last week at 100 years. (Florence, Ala., Times, 4 June 1892.)

LOWRY, Emma, convicted of keeping house of ill fame in Memphis in June 1869 and received 120 days; has been pardoned by the governor. (Memphis Daily Appeal, 10 Sept. 1869.) Emma Lowry is in jail again for keeping house of ill fame; Fannie Woods is one of the inmates there. (Memphis Daily Appeal, 6 Dec. 1869.) Emma Lowry sues Fannie Woods for stealing a watch chain. (Memphis Daily Appeal, 23 Dec. 1869.)

LUCAS, George, died August 26; lived in Chappell Church neighborhood in Maury County. (Columbia Herald, 12 Sept. 1873.)

LUCAS, H. C., born 2 August 1831, died at Donelson November 30; buried at old Mill Creek Church. (Nashville Union and American, 1 Dec. 1874.) Major H. C. Lucas' lifeless body was found Monday near Donelson Station on the Tennessee and Pacific Railroad; body discovered by lady in a field 1/4 mile from road; it is supposed he fell asleep in the field and froze to death. (Nashville Union and American, 2 Dec. 1874.)

LUCAS. There are anxious hearts interested in the recovery of Mrs. Martha Lucas, who is now struggling in the last stages of consumption. All hopes of restoration are given up by loving ones. Mr. Phate Lucas, her son, of Little Rock is expected on any passenger train coming in. (Columbia Herald, 3 June 1897.)

LUCAS, Nimrod, of Humphreys County, died last week; old pioneer and prominent Mason. (Maury Democrat, 21 Aug. 1890.)

LUCAS, W. R., died yesterday from his injuries. $250 reward has been offered for his murderer. (Nashville Republican Banner, 8 Jan. 1868.)

LUCK, John, of Milawukee, enlisted some months ago. His wife was most broken-hearted at his departure for the war and just as she began to recover their little boy drowned. He got a furlough and just as he arrived at home he found she had lost her reason and had been sent to almshouse and would not recover. He reported back to headquarters but very soon afterward committed suicide with a pistol. (Nashville Dispatch, 13 Sept. 1862.)

LUCKETT, William C., War of 1812 soldier, died near Santa Fe, Maury County, last week. (Whig & Tribune, Jackson, Tn, 8 Feb. 1873.)

LUCKETT, Thruston S., Esquire, native and for many years resident of Nashville, died November 16 at Uniontown, Alabama. He was editor of the Alabama Herald. (Memphis Avalanche, 5 Dec. 1866.)

LUCKEY, George, 2 months 21 days, son of John A. and Clara A. Luckey, died November 16. (Nashville Union and American, 17 Nov. 1874.)

LUNA, James, of Marshall County is 84 years old; has 12 children, 120 grandchildren, 125 great-grandchildren, and 50 great-great-grand-children. (Memphis Daily Appeal, 1 Nov. 1868.)

LUNN, Mrs. Eli, died a few days ago; buried Ragan Cemetery; Cumberland Presbyterian. (Maury Democrat, 29 Aug. 1895.)

LURATT, J. L., of McNairy County, John Briggins of Decatur County, and E. H. Sharp of Gibson County, guerrillas, have been captured in lower Kentucky and sent to Nashville. (Nashville Daily Union, 9 May 1865.)

LURINGTON. Brownsville, Ala. - Near the west end of the Eagle and Phoenix Dam, the skeleton of Henry Lurington was unearthed; he was killed by Wilson's raiders on 15 April 1865. He was buried near a China tree on the bank, which has long since been washed away by the river. It was unearthed in 1874 and reburied again. J. A. Allen has assisted at all three burials. (Maury Democrat, 1 March 1888.)

LUSK, J. W., died Tuesday in South Columbia of typhoid fever. (Maury Democrat, 13 June 1889.)

LUSTY, Marianna, daughter of Thomas K. and Mary Lusty, to be buried today. (Nashville Republican Banner, 22 Feb. 1870.)

LYMAN, Charles C., died at the St. Cloud Hotel; native of Canada and
sent there for burial. (Nashville Daily Union, 24 Dec. 1862.)

LYON, Colonel, of an Arkansas regiment, was killed at the Tennessee
River by fall of his horse over the embankment of the M. C. and L.
railroad near the bridge. (Clarksville Jeffersonian, 16 Oct. 1861.)

LYONS, Paul, oldest man in Mobile County, Alabama, died recently at the
age of nearly 111 years. (Columbia Herald, 2 Feb. 1872.)

LYONS, William, of the 3d Cavalry, CSA, has been charged with being a
bushwhacker, belonging to Witherspoon's command, is now a prisoner
of war. (Nashville Daily Union, 28 March 1865.)

LYONS, Grandma, died on the 3d at McMinnville, almost 100 years. "One
of the most remarkable women that ever lived in Tennessee."
(Nashville Republican Banner, 12 Jan. 1869.)

LYTLE, Lutie A., colored, age 23, of Memphis has been licensed to
practice law in Tennessee; she is the first of her sex of any color
admitted to the bar and the only colored woman in the South to
practice law. (Columbia Herald, 10 Sept. 1897.)

LYTLE, William, 77, died 14 Jan. 1878 at his ranch in Medina, Texas;
born 1801 in Maryland; 1834 moved to Columbia, Tn; 1838 went to
Washington County, Texas; 1845 to San Antonio where he established
a ranch; married Mary G. Gullett, daughter of Sammy Gullett; he was
a blacksmith in Columbia and built a brick shop occupied by Kuhn
and Turpin. (Columbia Herald and Mail, 8 Feb. 1878.)

LYTLE, General, U. S. Army, was killed while gallantly leading his
command at Chickamauga on September 20. (Nashville Dispatch, 1
Oct. 1863.)

MACK, Mary F., 31 wife of W. R. C. Mack, died 13 Feb. 1875 in McKinney,
Texas, of consumption; buried Hack Berry Cemetery on Sunday in Maury
County. (Columbia Herald and Mail, 9 April 1875.)

MACK, Mrs. Sarah M., was buried Tuesday at Rose Hill, Columbia, widow
of Judge Robert Mack; died in Franklin; sister of ex-Governor Aaron
V. Brown. (Columbia Herald and Mail, 11 May 1877.)

MADDIN, Annie Pillow Gray, 25, died in Nashville; wife of J. W. Maddin,
Jr., daughter of John M. Gray; married Dr. Maddin 18 April 1894;
an infant daughter survives. (Maury Democrat, 14 Nov. 1895.)

MAGASI, Mrs. Alphonse, died on the 10th ult. in St. Louis; husband is
known as one of the Antonio Brothers in the Theatrical world.
(Memphis Daily Appeal, 9 Dec. 1869.)

MAGEE, Mrs., of Rowena, Wells County, Indiana, had 12 children in 3
years 7 months and 13 days, all alive. On 24 June 1858 she had 1;
on 30 June 1859 she had 2; on 29 May 1860 she had 2; on 29 March
1861 she had 3; on 13 Feb. 1862 she had 4. (Nashville Dispatch,
13 Feb. 1863.)

MAGEVNY, Nellie, daughter of Colonel Michael Magevny, died yesterday.
Buried Elmwood Cemetery. (Memphis Avalanche, 11 Jan. 1866.)

MAGOFFIN, Col. James, brother of ex-Governor of Kentucky, died in San
Antonio, Texas, recently at 71 years of age. (Memphis Daily Appeal,
6 Nov. 1868.)

MAGRUDER, Bill. A gang of guerrillas under Bill Magruder attacked a
company of negro soldiers near Rolling Fork and three soldiers were
killed. They met and robbed a lot of passengers who were walking

229

from Lebanon Junction to Colesburgh to get on the train; one man lost $600. (Nashville Daily Union, 21 Feb. 1865.)

MAHON, A., Company I, 7th Tennessee, died in Louisville, Ky. during the week ending Feb. 6. (Nashville Dispatch, 8 Feb. 1863.) A. Mahon, Company K, 1st Tennessee Cavalry, William Hickey, Company D, 6th Tennessee, and Isaac Prissnella, 1st Tennessee Cavalry, were among those who died in Louisville the week ending Feb. 6. (Nashville Daily Union, 8 Feb. 1863.)

MAHON, John, was hung by guerrillas 12 Jan. 1865; lived 4 1/2 miles from Memphis; guerrillas were after his money which was in a bank and not at his home. (Nashville Daily Union, 15 Jan. 1865.)

MAHON, little girl, daughter of George Mahon, was accidently shot by a gun some time ago and died yesterday. (Columbia Herald, 7 March 1873.)

MAHONE, General, the remarkable Virginian, is doubtless on his deathbed and his death may be expected at any time. (Maury Democrat, 10 Oct. 1895.) General William Mahone died in Washington on the 8th instant. He was widely known and at one time a most active and successful politician in Virginia. (Maury Democrat, 10 Oct. 1895.) General William Mahone of Norfolk, late Confederate general, is richest man in Virginia. (Memphis Daily Appeal, 30 Sept. 1868.)

MAHONEY, Mrs. Johanna, funeral to be held at the Cathedral this morning; mother of T. T., P. T., and Jeremiah Mahoney. (Nashville Republican Banner, 17 Dec. 1870.)

MAHONEY, Nath., Sergeant, Company B, 4th Tennessee Cavalry was killed about 29 Feb. 1864 in Mississippi expedition out of Memphis. (Nashville Daily Union, 2 March 1864.)

MALATESTA, James, was killed two years ago in Memphis by Antonio Marre. Marre has been found not guilty. (Memphis Daily Appeal, 21 Oct. 1869; 23 Oct. 1869.)

MALONE, Mrs. Anna, died at Claiborne, Michigan, on October 2; was one of the four settlers of Monroe County in 1818; was over 100 years old at her death. (Memphis Daily Appeal, 8 Dec. 1868.)

MALONE, Miss Annie, recently died in Claiborne County, Mississippi, over 100 years. (Memphis Avalanche, 17 Dec. 1868. N.B. Note the obituary before also, and the difference in information.)

MAJORS, A., died yesterday. (Nashville Republican Banner, 26 Aug. 1870.)

MAJORS, George, of Knox County, was murdered for his money on Saturday last, and partly for political reasons; he was loyal Union man. Dateline May 31. (Nashville Daily Union, 6 June 1865.)

MANEY, Dr. James, old citizen of Murfreesboro, died at the home of his son Major Lewis Maney on the 11th inst. (Whig and Tribune, Jackson, Tn, 23 Nov. 1872.)

MANLOVE, Dr. J. F., died August 17 and buried at W. H. Hyde's on White's Creek. (Nashville Republican Banner, 17 Aug. 1870.) Name given as Joseph E. Manlove. (Nashville Republican Banner, 18 Aug. 1870.)

MANNING, Charles J., died at his home in Sparta on Saturday last from effects of poison administered by doctor through mistake. (Nashville Daily Gazette, 19 Feb. 1850.)

MANNING, John, took out naturalization papers in Nashville. (Nashville Daily Union, 9 April 1865.)

MANSFIELD, Nathan, found dead 4 miles north of Lebanon, Tn, on Thursday; an idiot and had run away from home; died of sunstroke possibly. (Nashville Republican Banner, 25 July 1869.)

MAPES, Ida, 5 years 5 months 3 days, youngest daughter of A. R. and E. P. Mapes, died 6 Jan. 1865 of typhoid. (Nashville Republican Banner, 7 Jan. 1865.)

MARABLE, ___, found hanging to a tree on the Murfreesboro Pike with a note on him warning others that the use and name of Kuklux for evil purpose. He and some others had posed as Kuklux and committed outrages on negro family. (Memphis Daily Appeal, 21 Jan. 1870.) Marable was hanged near Lavergne. The note read: "Here is your man who plays Ku-Klux and ravishes negro women." (Memphis Daily Appeal, 1 Feb. 1870.)

MARCH, Irene, 11 months 2 days, infant daughter of H. C. and Elizabeth March, died on the 7th. (Nashville Republican Banner, 9 March 1869.)

MARONEY, P. T., died on the 8th; funeral to be held at Cathedral; brother of T. T. and Jere Maroney. (Nashville Union and American, 10 Sept. 1874. Refer also to Mahoney, Johanna.)

MARR, James, of Marshall County, Miss., was found dead at steamboat landing at Memphis on the 4th in the morning; had $400 to $500 on him; it is presumed he was murdered and robbed. (Nashville Daily Gazette, 15 Jan. 1850.)

MARR, Miss Sarah, of Lake County, was burned to death by her clothing taking fire from ignited coal oil from a broken lamp. (Nashville Union and American, 5 Feb. 1873.)

MARSHALL, Fred., oldest policeman in Nashville, died Wednesday and will be buried this morning. (Nashville Dispatch, 2 April 1863.) Fred. Marshall, 56, died on the 1st. (Nashville Daily Union, 2 April 1863.)

MARSHALL, George, Esquire, formerly of Nashville, died on the 21st of apoplexy in St. Louis; mother lives in Nashville; age 40; lawyer; unmarried; lived in St. Louis for 21 years. (Nashville Republican Banner, 24 July 1868.)

MARSHALL, Judge John, of Williamson County, died on the 3d of congestive chills, aged about 60; man of giant intellect; lawyer. (Nashville Dispatch, 6 Oct. 1863.)

MARSHALL, Minnie Pearl, age 2, died July 14, daughter of J. R. and Minnie A. Marshall of Bear Creek; buried Butler graveyard. (Columbia Herald, 17 July 1896, 24 July 1896.)

MARSHALL, William, died Wednesday of dropsy, native of England, part owner of Columbia Foundry; Mason; Rose Hill. (Columbia Herald, 16 Feb. 1872.)

MARSTON, Squire, citizen of Chattanooga, prisoner of war in Nashville, was killed instantly by the falling of the stairs and floors at the Convalescent Barracks on Tuesday. (Nashville Daily Union, 1 Oct. 1863.)

MARTIN, Anna H., wife of Andrew J. Martin, age 25, died 20 July 1868. (Nashville Republican Banner, 21 July 1868.) Administrator appointed for estate of Anna R. M. Martin. (Nashville Republican Banner, 21 March 1869.)

MARTIN, Miss Bettie, and other young girls are under arrest; charged with smuggling out under their capricious crinoline, gray cloth and making it up into uniforms. (Nashville Daily Union, 1 Dec. 1863.)

MARTIN, Charles C., son of Dr. Charles and Fannie H. Martin, was
killed in fight at Minton several weeks ago; was in first cavalry
company raised for Confederate Army in Nashville. (Nashville
Dispatch, 22 May 1863.)

MARTIN, Charles, of Giles County received 20 years hard labor by
military commission at Pulaski for being a guerrilla and a thief.
(Nashville Daily Union, 25 May 1865.)

MARTIN, Mrs. George, of LaGrange, Stewart County, fell during the sleet
last winter and received injuries that necessitated amputation of
her foot, from which she died on Wednesday; maiden name was Fowler;
widow of James Martin. (Dover Courier, 13 May 1892)

MARTIN, George M., age 88, died in Columbia two weeks ago; now his
widow is dead, age 73. (Whig & Tribune, Jackson, Tn, 7 June 1873.)
Mary Hamilton Thomas Martin, born 26 Sept. 1806 in Bedford County,
Va., died Monday at the age of 72 years 8 months. She married 23
May 1816 to Reese Porter, who died 1823; they were the parents of
Mrs. W. H. Pillow, W. B. Porter, and Reese Porter, who was killed
in the Mexican War. She married 11 May 1852 to George M. Martin.
(Columbia Herald, 30 May 1873.)

MARTIN, George S., bookbinder, died yesterday of paralysis; age 67;
born Manchester, England; came 1839 to the United States.
(Nashville Union and American, 7 April 1874.)

MARTIN, John, "sole survivor of Custer massacre," rode at the head of
Battery I at Grover Cleveland's inaugural. (Maury Democrat, 9 March
1893.)

MARTIN, Assistant Surgeon, J. D., 14th Tennessee Regiment of Clarksville, was killed in the Battle of Seven Pines near Richmond.
(Nashville Dispatch, 14 June 1862.)

MARTIN, Gen. John D., killed in battle of Corinth was from Memphis.
(Nashville Dispatch, 16 Oct. 1862.)

MARTIN, Miss Lillie Y., a sweet and lovely girl, died Monday of painful
illness, daughter of Mrs. Sarah Martin. (Columbia Herald and Mail,
7 Dec.1877, 14 Dec. 1877.)

MARTIN, Lizzie Williams, young daughter of James J. and Mary H. Martin,
died on the 11th. (Nashville Republican Banner, 16 April 1870.)

MARTIN, Nancy, sues Philip C. Martin for divorce; non-resident notice
published for him. (Nashville Dispatch, 51 July 1862.)

MARTIN, Martha A., widow of G. F. Martin, who died intestate; dower
set apart for Martha A. Martin. (Nashville Republican Banner,
15 Dec. 1867.)

MARTIN, Patrick, native of Ireland, received his naturalization papers
in circuit court yesterday. (Nashville Union and American, 26
Sept. 1874.)

MARTIN, Mrs. Priscilla W., died on 21st of cancer, age 74; buried
beside her husband who has been dead many years. (Columbia Herald,
24 May 1872.)

MARTIN, Robert C. K., born August 1806 in Davidson County at the Mansfield Place, has died; brother of Mrs. Gideon Pillow; his father
George Martin moved to Maury County in 1815; married Priscilla
Douglas, daughter of Harry L, Douglas. (Nashville Republican Banner,
15 Feb. 1871.) Dr. R. C. K. Martin, age 65, died yesterday; funeral
at Christ Church; lived on Cherry Street; practiced medicine here
for many years; universally loved. (Nashville Republican Banner,
20 Feb. 1871.)

MARTIN, Thomas of Giles County; in memoriam published in paper.
(Nashville Republican Banner, 25 Jan. 1870.)

MARTIN, Thomas, rebel guerrilla, hung May 11 in Cincinnati; others
named Bowles, Milligan and Horney to be hung on the 19th. (Nashville
Daily Union, 13 May 1865.)

MARTIN, William, died near Sawdust Valley on the 15th instant.
(Columbia Herald and Mail, 26 June 1874.)

MARTIN, Col. Wilson Y., died near Dixon Springs, Smith County, 25 March
1868. (Nashville Republican Banner, 4 April 1868.)

MARTINSTIN, John Henry, was almost buried alive; he was in a trance
and believed dead. On the way to the cemetery the horses ran away
and threw the coffin out. Undertaker has sued him for payment.
(Memphis Daily Appeal, 17 Nov. 1868.)

MASON, Aleck, colored, burglar, was lynched at Pulaski; man of bad
character; some say he was shot in jail. (Memphis Avalanche, 24
Dec. 1868.)

MASON, Mrs. Isaac, daughter of Maj. General Richard Butler, one of
Washington's trusted commanders, is living in Uniontown, Pa., age
95. (Columbia Herald and Mail, 21 Dec. 1877.)

MASON, Peyton H., 2 years 6 months 27 days, son of L. T. and M. M.
Mason, died on the 18th at Lavergne, Tn. (Nashville Republican
Banner, 22 Nov. 1868.)

MASON, Mrs., sister of the late Major St. George Harney, who was
murdered by loyal militia of Arkansas, arrived in Memphis yesterday,
stopping at the Peabody. She will remove his body to Washington.
(Memphis Daily Appeal, 15 Feb. 1869.)

MASON, Samuel, colored, the oldest man in Tennessee, died last week
in Nashville, was 106 years old at Christmas; purchased by the city
of Nashville in 1827 from John Y. Mason of Southampton County, Va.,
for $900; served Nashville for 73 years and was receiving a pension
of $10 a month; plumber and grader of streets. (Hohenwald Chronicle,
5 Jan. 1900.)

MASSY, Sally, has left her husband Drewry Massy, and he advertises
warning against trading with her. (Central Monitor, Murfreesboro,
Tn, 11 Oct. 1834.)

MATHERELL, Joseph, Esquire, 82, died recently in Williamson County.
(Whig and Tribune, Jackson, Tn, 5 Oct. 1872.)

MATHEW, Captain, noted guerrilla, along with 40 men, was captured on
the 23d near Germantown in Memphis and is in Irving prison.
(Nashville Dispatch, 30 Sept. 1863.)

MATHEWS, J. P., died on the 28th at Edgefield. (Nashville Republican
Banner, 29 Nov. 1868.)

MATHIS, H. T., married his niece Miss L. E. Mathis at Dresden, Tn.,
one day last week. The magistrate was unaware of the relationship.
Her father advised his brother to leave county and the marriage
would be passed over as the girl is non-compos mentis. The penalty
for such is not less than 5 years nor more than 20 years in prison.
(Columbia Herald, 19 Nov. 1897.)

MATHIS, L., of Henry County, old and respected, was killed by his
grandson John L. Mathis, son of Dr. John L. Mathis, who recently
moved to Texas and left his son. The son was drinking and quarreled
with his grandfather about some stove wood. He shot him three times
and made his escape. (Linden Times, 26 Aug. 1880.)

MATHIS, Thomas, 77, died in the northern part of Henry County. (Whig and Tribune, Jackson, Tn, 6 Sept. 1873.)

MATLERER, Andrew, young man, found frozen to death on the commons near Nashville Monday. (Memphis Avalanche, 15 Feb. 1867.)

MATTIL, ___, German citizen of Chattanooga, fell from wagon in Nashville and was killed; buried by the German citizens of Chattanooga. (Nashville Republican Banner, 10 March 1869.)

MATTHEWS, Mrs. Annie M., wife of S. S. Matthews, died this morning of cancer; member of Hopewell Church; buried in family cemetery at Bigbyville. (Colubmia Herald, 14 Dec. 1899.)

MATTHEWS, Stanford B., 63rd Indiana Regiment, was court martialed at Indianapolis, Indiana, for theft and found guilty; sentenced to one year with ball and chain to leg and to work on the Bowling Green fortifications. Deserters, Richard Johnson, Thomas Willams, George Morgan, and William D. Finck were found guilty of desertion and branded "D" on hip and other punishments. (Nashville Dispatch, 19 Feb. 1863.)

MATTHEWS, Col. Stanley, has been assigned by General Rosecrans to be in charge of the removal South of the Federal lines all disloyal persons and supporters of Rebels, is in the city today. (Nashville Dispatch, 28 March 1863.)

MATTHEWS, Thomas M., was found dead and inquest held 28 Nov. 1862; apoplexy. (Nashville Daily Union, 28 Nov. 1862.)

MATTHEWS, The Rev. William D., died 21 Sept. 1869; tribute of respect published by the Bigbyville lodge. (Maury County Herald, 22 Oct. 1869.)

MAUBEC, Mrs., granddaughter of John Sevier, one of the rear guard of the Revolution, is in New York penniless. Her second husband has squandered her entire fortune of nearly a million dollars and then decamped. (Maury Democrat, 7 March 1895.)

MAURER, Mary, died in Chattanooga on the 23d. (Nashville Republican Banner, 31 March 1870.)

MAURY, Lt. Gen. Dabney H., of the Confederate Army, has been appointed to a position in the war records office of the War Department. (Florence, Ala., Times, 5 Sept. 1891.)

MAURY, Colonel Henry, of Mobile, Alabama, has been wounded. (Nashville Dispatch, 30 July 1863.)

MAURY, Brigadier General Z. M. P., of Warren County, Tn, died on the 29th ult. at Johnson Island military prison in Lake Erie; he was taken prisoner at Fort Donelson. (Nashville Dispatch, 5 June 1862.)

MAXEY, General B., died Friday at Eureka Springs, Arkansas, native of Todd County, Ky, veteran of the Mexican and Civil Wars. (Maury Democrat, 22 Aug. 1895.)

MAXEY, Dr. John, 83, died Thursday, the 13th inst., 8 miles from Nashville on the Gallatin Pike. (Nashville Republican Banner, 15 Oct. 1870.)

MAXEY, William O., son of P. W. and J. A. Maxey, funeral to be held today. (Nashville Dispatch, 6 July 1862.)

MAXIMILIAN has accepted the Mexican throne. (Nashville Dispatch, 23 Sept. 1863.) Maximilian, Emperor of Mexico, was shot on the 4th. (Memphis Avalanche, 19 June 1867.)

MAXWELL, Mrs. A., died Thursday, formerly Carrie Well of Huntsville, Ala., and taken there for burial. (Columbia Herald, 14 Aug. 1896.)

MAXWELL, Colonel Cicero, late commander of the 26th Kentucky, died Friday last at Bowling Green. (Nashville Daily Union, 21 Feb. 1865.)

MAXWELL, Jesse, patriot of the Revolution, died on the 23d. (Tennessee Watchman, Clarksville, Tn., 26 Oct. 1821.)

MAXWELL. Lexington, Ky. - The old Maxwell burying ground is being excavated for a tobacco warehouse and bones being unearthed and dumped into the fill. Bones of many of the early settlers are here. Despite protests, the work goes on. (Columbia Herald, 4 Nov. 1899.)

MAXWELL, Col. W. L., died May 19 of pneumonia at Bigbyville. (Columbia Herald and Mail, 24 May 1878.)

MAY, Mary Jane, sues George May for divorce in Davidson County chancery court. (Nashville Daily Union, 5 May 1865.)

MAY, William, of Egnew's Creek, Giles County, is 103 years old. (Memphis Daily Appeal, 1 Nov. 1869.)

MAYBERRY, Daniel, over 100 years of Rutherford County, received his pension in the mail yesterday. (Nashville Union and American, 11 June 1874.) Daniel Mayberry, 101, went to the polls in Rutherford County and voted the entire Democratic ticket. (Nashville Union and American, 5 Dec. 1874.) Daniel Mabury of Rutherford County was 100 years old on the 12th instant; born 12 August 1773 in Virginia and at an early age moved to Lincoln County, NC; came 1805 to Rutherford County. (Nashville Union and American, 16 Aug. 1873.)

MAYES, S. M., dropped dead in Columbia on Monday. (Memphis Daily Appeal, 22 April 1870.)

MAYO, Captain William A., died at the residence of his sister in Monroe County on the 10th; at the beginning of the war was living in Nashville and entered the Confederate service in Col. Maney's regiment and served gallantly until the close. (Memphis Daily Appeal, 19 Sept. 1869.)

MAYS. Laurel Gap between Hawkins and Greene County, rebels murdered here were Jesse Mays, Henry Hokely, Samuel Estep, Pleasant Morris, ___ Early, all murdered by a portion of Vaughn's command. Lt. John Rogers was in command, but the deed was done by Thomas Rogers, Ab Crabtree, Lorenzo Potter, and ___ Smith. (Nashville Daily Union, 8 Jan. 1865.)

MAYS, The Reverend William, of Perryville, Ky, has preached the gospel for 60 years and has never accepted a dollar for his services. (Maury Democrat, 14 June 1894.)

MEACHAM, Mrs. Lucy K., wife of James M. Meacham, died at Pinewood, Hickman County, Monday the 3d; age 25; daughter of Mrs. Mary Cameron; left two children, one an infant. (Nashville Republican Banner, 7 Oct. 1870.)

MEADORS, Mrs. Amanda E., wife of John A. Meadors, died March 31. (Nashville Republican Banner, 1 April 1870.)

MEADOWS, Josephus, 18, son of Moses of Macon County, was shot Friday. (Nashville Republican Banner, 25 Dec. 1868.)

MEADOWS, Capt. Daniel, 4th East Tennessee Cavalry, was drowned; body found and buried on the 10th with military honors; from Campbell County. (Nashville Dispatch, 11 August 1863.) Capt. Meddill, 4th East Tennessee Cavalry, was drowned yesterday near the upper wharf while trying to swim a horse across the river; the body had not been found by dusk. (Nashville Dispatch, 9 Aug. 1863. His name was first reported as Meddill and corrected in later editions.)

MEECE, Richard, old and respected citizen of Swan Creek, Hickman County, died last week of pneumonia. (Columbia Herald and Mail, 26 Oct. 1877.)

MEEK, Maxmilian B., 20 years 9 months, died in Pulaski on the 7th after 14 days illness with typhoid. (Middle Tennessean, Pulaski, 21 March 1851.)

MELE, H., shoemaker, committed suicide at Edgefield. (Nashville Republican Banner, 28 Oct. 1868.)

MELROSE, Richard, shot and mortally wounded by Edward J. Foley at the Chattanooga car shops in Nashville yesterday; quarrel over a newspaper; there are some hopes entertained for his recovery. (Nashville Republican Banner, 9 August 1868.)

MELROSE, Robert, 18, of Nashville poisoned his three sisters and they died; he also died without confessing to his crime; gave them arsenic. Katie, 18, Mattie, 17, and the other not named, were children of Mrs. R. Melrose and were poisoned on March 17. (Maury Democrat, 24 March 1892.)

MELVILLE, Robert R., son of the late John Melville, plumber and founder died on the 1st. (Nashville Republican Banner, 23 July 1870.)

MEMPHIS - Old Folks at Home - The group met yesterday and Col. John H. McMahon delivered the address. The following was taken from his talk: Those who have gone from among us since our last meeting are:
Nathaniel Anderson, president, died 8 March 1867, came to Memphis 1822.
W. D. Ferguson, vice president, died 1866, came here 1819.
Thomas B. Crenshaw, died Aug. 1866, came here in 1836.
Wm. R. Smith, died 12 June 1867, came here 1837.
Samuel T. Morgan, died 3 July 1867, came in 1844.
John Wildberger, died 12 July 1867, came to Memphis in 1838.
Wm. K. Poston, died 7 July 1866, came 1839.
W. C. Bryan, died 1866, came in 1842.
Wm. M. Folwell, died 16 March 1867, came in 1845.
James E. Felts, died July 1866, came 1835
Daniel Bogart, died 22 Jan. 1867, came in 1842.

The first newspaper published in Memphis was by Thomas Phoebus in 1826 and called the Memphis Advocate, followed by the Memphis Gazette by Gaines and Murray. In 1836 the Memphis Enquirer was started by F. S. Latham, who had previously established at Randolph, then a rival of Memphis, the Randolph Recorder. In 1838 he disposed of half interest to J. H. McMahon.

Memphis was the first place in Tennessee at which Lafayette landed in 1824. There was not sufficient population to make a formal reception. A salute was fired, however, by the few citizens and his boat remained long enough at Memphis landing to take on wood.

The first postmaster at Memphis was Captain James Stewart, formerly a officer of the U. S. Army. He died in office and was buried on the lot at the corner of Third and Poplar Streets, on which the Presbyterian Church now stands.

The first white child born in Shelby County, now the wife of William Pittman near Bray's Station, was Miss Mary Bettis, fifth child out of the 17 children of Tilman and Sally Bettis. (Memphis Avalanche, 26 July 1867.)

MEMPHIS DEATHS, ending the week of 17 Feb. 1866:

Mrs. Anne Davis, 35, died of metritis.
R. W. Tiensch, 2, pneumonia.
Nathan Rysdale, 6 months, spasms.
Richard Hannon, 78, phehesis.
E. O. Adkins, 47, scrofula.
Infant of W. Bailey, 10 days, spasms.
Lelilia Ruay, 2, croup.
Thomas E. Willis, 13, measles.
Charles Atwood, 58, pneumonia.
Mary E. Brawn, 9 croup.
Mrs. Davis, 34, unknown cause.
Honora Connelly, 34, died by hanging.
Child of Thomas Carter, stillborn.
Andrew Ryan, 23, railroad accident.
James Irwin, 40, pneumonia.
Mrs. A. Green, 75, effects of a fall.
John Hogan, 76, hydropericardiam.
Catherine McCarty, 100, old age.
Mary A. Sheffield, 52, pneumonia.
                              (Memphis Avalanche, 17 Feb. 1866.)

MENEES, Mrs. Elizabeth, wife of B. W. Menees, died in Robertson County
    on August 19; born 9 Feb. 1796 in Davidson County. (Nashville
    Dispatch, 2 Oct. 1862.)

MENIFEE, Jonas, old and respected citizen, died in Davidson County.
    (Tennessee Watchman, Clarksville, Tn, 26 Oct. 1821.)

MERCER, Robert F., 21, one of the proprietors of the Nashville Press
    and Times, died Tuesday in Nashville (Memphis Avalanche, 16 June
    1867.)

MEREDITH, Washington, formerly of Columbia, died January 14 in Howard
    County, Missouri, of paralysis. (Columbia Herald and Mail, 26
    Jan. 1877.)

MEREDITH, Frederick, in 1816 settled on Buffalo River at the mouth of
    Moccassin Creek in Wayne County. He came originally from North
    Carolina. This country was then a dense wilderness, heavily timbered,
    and covered in many places with canebrakes and infested with wild
    animals. (Clifton Mirror, 6 April 1906.)

MEREDITH, Miss Lela, sister of the Hon. T. H. Meredith, died in
    Pulaski on Saturday and buried Sunday; had been low for some time
    with consumption. (Lawrenceburg Democrat, 13 Feb. 1891)

MERONEY, Lily, daughter of John N. Meroney of Knob Creek died November
    7; age 4. (Columbia Herald and Mail, 12 Nov. 1875.)

MERRELL. Fairview, Tn. - A few days ago the body of Mrs. Samuel
    Merrell, wife of a prominent planter, was found in Cane Creek; she
    had been mentally affected and thought to be a suicide. (Houston
    County News, 7 Aug. 1886.)

MERRITT, Henry J., old and honored citizen of Williamson County, age
    70, died six miles south of Franklin last week. (Whig and Tribune,
    Jackson, Tn, 8 Feb. 1873.)

MESTER, George, died at Lawrenceburg; three have been arrested for
    his murder. (Florence, Ala., Times, 23 July 1892.)

METCALF, Mrs., the oldest proprietress of a house of ill repute in
    Cincinnati, Ohio, died Saturday evening. On Wednesday last she
    married Mr. Brodericks, a brother of the late Senator Brodericks,
    then joined the Episcopal Church, took the sacraments, stopped her
    nefarious business, and died; very wealthy. (Memphis Avalanche,
    1 Feb. 1866.)

METCALF, Henry A., son of Charles Metcalf, who lived one mile from Edgefield Junction, funeral to be held today. (Nashville Republican Banner, 8 May 1869.)

METCALF, Joseph, Esquire, age 94, oldest Mason in the United States, died at Erie, Pa., recently. (Memphis Daily Appeal, 9 Feb. 1869.)

MEXICAN WAR DEAD - We learn from the Nashville papers of yesterday that the remains of Capt. W. B. Allen, Peter H. Martin, Robert W. Green, Julius C. Elliot and Inman Elliott, who fell at Monterey reached that place on the 9th of this month. On yesterday they were taken to the First Presbyterian Church, Nashville, where a funeral discourse was delivered by the Rev. Dr. Edgar. (Columbia Beacon, 12 March 1847.)

MIACO, William, who fell during a performance on trapeze at the Great Eastern Circus in Nashville Friday, died from the effects of the injuries at Bowling Green, Ky. (Nashville Union and American, 9 March 1873.) Miaco is not dead, but in U. S. hospital in Louisville and is rapidly recovering. (Nashville Union and American, 11 March 1873.)

MILAM, A. J., deceased, his will has been admitted to probate. (Nashville Republican Banner, 1 Jan. 1871.)

MILAM, Dick, colored, of near Indian Mound, Stewart County, is 104 or 105 years old; still drives a team of oxen. (Houston County News, 7 Oct. 1887.)

MILIKA, Private Julius, of Company E, 10th Michigan Infantry, is to be shot on Friday for desertion in Nashville; deserted September 16 and on November 16 enlisted in Company K, 1st Tennessee Infantry and deserted. This will be the second soldier who had paid the death penalty in Nashville. (Nashville Dispatch, 13 May 1863.) Julius Milika is now in his grave, shot at noon yesterday; brigade under General Morgan shot him; he was seated on his coffin and his body was pierced by 5 balls. (Nashville Dispatch, 16 May 1863.) (The Nashville Daily Union also reported this, but his name appeared to be Julius Meliea and the editor noted "first capital punishment since Nashville occupied.")

MILLER, Amos, colored, was hanged at Franklin on August 10 for the outrage on Mrs. Scott in Williamson County on June 15. He was hanged on the railing of the front porch of the courthouse by an unmasked mob. (Maury Democrat, 16 Aug. 1888.)

MILLER, Dave. "Captain Dave Miller of Hickman County, whose name was once a terror to Federal soldiers in Hickman County was in Columbia last week." (Columbia Herald, 11 July 1873.) "Dave Miller of Hickman County, whom the Yankees did not quite succeed in hanging during the war was in town Wednesday. He was a terror to the blue coats during the late unpleasantness." (Columbia Herald and Mail, 14 July 1876.) "Excitement in Town was this man Miller that killed Willie J. Briggs last year; he was in custody of the civil authorities for robbery and was released from the civil authorities and let at liberty." (Diary entry for 15 Oct. 1865, diary of Nimrod Porter, unpublished.) "The Federal soldiers went to Hickman county and caught Dave Miller and he got away." (Diary entry for 1 Nov. 1865, diary of Nimrod Porter, unpublished.)

Tombstone inscription in Rose Hill Cemetery, Columbia: William J. Briggs - born 27 Oct. 1838, died 3 July 1864, "He was killed by the guerrillas. He fought bled and died for his country. He leaves a wife and one child."

Tombstone inscription in Anderson Cemetery, Hickman County; D.C. Miller, born 18 April 1838, died 23 August 1916.

MILLER, Dave - Continued
Duel at Night - Very few are the Maury countains 50 years of age
that do not remember Dave Miller, Pate Sowell and Newt Vaughn, and
others who were hot-blooded southerners, game as men as ever made...
They used to ride into Columbia right up to the courthouse and fire
several volleys at the Federal soldiers inside, then ride as swift
as the swiftest wind out of harm's way for they were always splendid-
ly mounted and pursuit was utterly useless.

Dave Miller was perhaps the best known of all the southerners in
that day who fought the northern enemy not in the ranks of the
Confederate armies, but on the outside; "guerrillas" they were
called. At last accounts Dave Miller was still living near Shady
Grove in Hickman County.

It was Miller, it was said, that killed Jay Briggs, the famous
Federal scout and guide, who was perhaps the most noted of all the
men in the northern secret service in Middle Tennessee during the
Civil War. Briggs was a "home-made" Yankee and not only by reputation, but by sight and name was well known in this and adjoining
counties.

One bright moonlit night two horsemen, both superbly mounted, booted
spurred and armed to the teeth, met in the pike near Spring Hill.
As they approached each other they instinctively drew rein.

"What is your name," demanded one of the other.
"Jay Briggs," was the intrepid reply.
"Dave Miller, you cur" was almost shouted back.

Quick as a flash both men drew their guns and fired. Miller
galloped away with a hole in his hat. Briggs fell from his horse
and died upon the highway. His body was brought to Columbia and
buried in Rose Hill Cemetery. The shooting provoked intense excitement and all the countryside was greatly disturbed for several days.

Briggs' wife had a very bitter inscription placed on the tombstone
and erected over her husband's grave and it is there yet for the
curious to read. (Daily Herald, Columbia, Tn, 24 Jan. 1903.)

MILLER, Mrs. Frances M., died 23 September 1895 at Shady Grove, Hickman
County; born Mary J. Kinzer, 1828 in Maury County; married 1849;
buried in Miller Cemetery, Hickman County; daughter of Michael
Kinzer. (Columbia Herald, 27 Sept. 1895, 4 Oct. 1895.)

MILLER, Frank, a well-known German citizen, died of heart disease
yesterday; in 1861 was first lieutenant in 1st Tennessee Regiment
in the German company; son-in-law of Officer Frazier of the police
force; lived in Giles County after the war for a time. (Nashville
Union and American, 19 Nov. 1874.)

MILLER, Henry, of Murfreesboro, was shot through the bowels and it is
thought he is dangerously wounded. (Nashville Union and American,
26 June 1873.)

MILLER, Henry W., committed suicide in Edgefield on Monday; shot near
the heart; brother of William Miller; age 25. (Nashville Union and
American, 8 July 1874.)

MILLER, James, 18, was killed yesterday, by being struck on head with
rope which was attached to a raft which broke loose from its
moorings. (Nashville Union and American, 8 April 1874.)

MILLER, John, Esquire, of District 10, Maury County, died on the 10th,
buried Mt. Nebo. (Columbia Herald and Mail, 20 Aug. 1875.)

MILLER, Mrs. John, died April 20 near Pleasant Ridge; daughter of the
late Joseph and Mary Wells. (Columbia Herald and Mail, 3 May 1878.)

MILLER, John F., 37, died in Raleigh, NC on March 4, after a long illness. (Nashville Republican Banner, 10 March 1870.)

MILLER, John F., of Henry County, a dentist, formerly of New York, was found dead March 8, near Paris; died of debility and exposure. (Nashville Republican Banner, 10 March 1869.)

MILLER, Mrs. Martha, 87, widow of War of 1812 soldier, got a pension of $1600 recently; she is feeble and needy; lives 2 miles north of Vernon in Lamar County, Ala. (Florence, Ala., Times, 30 April 1892.)

MILLER, Mrs. Nancy E., wife of John Miller, age 28, died on the 4th. (Nashville Republican Banner, 4 March 1870.)

MILLER, S. H., well known citizen of Murfreesboro, was assassinated on the streets of Murfreesboro last week; he was shot in the bowels by an unknown person. (Whig and Tribune, Jackson, Tn, 5 July 1873.)

MILLER, Willie B., 15 months 20 days, son of James and Esther Miller, died on the 29th ult. (Nashville Dispatch, 1 May 1863.)

MILNER, Cooper, 19, jumped into the Cumberland River Saturday from the Woodland Street Bridge in Nashville; buried Zion Cemetery, Maury County; son of late George Cooper of Columbia; nephew of Colonel D. B. Cooper. (Maury Democrat, 10 May 1894.)

MILLS, Abner, 6th Mississippi, CSA, died at hospital in Nashville between the 1st and 15th. (Nashville Daily Union, 25 May 1865.)

MILLS, William, one of the last three or four survivors of Waterloo in Canada, died in Blanshard township on the 3d, age 80. (Memphis Daily Appeal, 26 March 1870.)

MILSOM, Mary Louise, age 2 years 9 months 7 days, young daughter of J. O. and Mattie Milsom, died July 20. (Nashville Republican Banner, 21 July 1870.)

MINGE, Dr., a Virginian, just died; had not shaved since Henry Clay's defeat in 1844, according to a vow he made. (Memphis Daily Appeal, 19 Nov. 1868.)

MITCHEL, Robert, a desperate character, was shot and killed by William Hammonds, age 19, on Richland Creek in Giles County. (Nashville Republican Banner, 19 April 1868.)

MITCHELL, Abijah Davis, born 25 May 1797, came to Maury County when he was 13 years old, lived here many years and then moved to Marshall County where he died; joined Friendship Baptist Church at 90; great Mason; broke rib two weeks ago and died July 25. (Columbia Herald, 31 July 1891.)

MITCHELL, Alice, died April 1 in the insane asylum; murdered Freda Ward in Memphis. (Columbia Herald, 8 April 1898.)

MITCHELL, Charles, 78, and Mrs. Margaret Crump, age 83, died recently in Lincoln County. (Nashville Union and American, 7 Feb. 1873.)

MITCHELL, Mrs. E. A., 86, died on the 12th ultimo in Morgan County, Ala. (Florence, Ala., Times, 9 July 1892.)

MITCHELL, General G. M., of Charleston, Ill., dropped dead in his garden Saturday morning, and his wife was so overcome with grief she died four hours later. (Maury Democrat, 6 June 1895.)

MITCHELL, infant son of Thomas and Annie Mitchell, died of brain fever. (Nashville Union and American, 26 Aug. 1874.)

MITCHELL, John Newton, born 24 March 1804 in North Carolina, died

MITCHELL, John Newton - Continued
1 January 1889 at Woodbury, Cannon County, Tn; married Sarah
Hutcheson, born 19 April 1804, died at Woodbury, 15 January 1867.
(Family records of Polly C. Warren, Columbia, Tn.)

MITCHELL, Leroy E., 52, died August 5; funeral held at the Sewanee
Hotel. (Nashville Dispatch, 6 Aug. 1863.)

MITCHELL, Mr., of Wayne County, Tn, hanged himself Wednesday of last
week in an old unused house on his farm; age 62; had been justice
of the peace for many years. (Florence, Ala., Times, 19 Nov. 1892.)

MITCHELL, Major General O. M., died 30 Oct. 1862 at Beaufort, South
Carolina, of yellow fever, which is prevailing there. (Nashville
Dispatch, 8 Nov. 1862.)

MITCHELL, William, youngest son of John Mitchell, Esquire, editor of
the Enquirer, is believed to have been killed in the battle of
Gettysburg; age 18; has two brothers in Confederate Army. Richmond
Sentinel. (Nashville Dispatch, 20 Sept. 1863.)

MITCHELL, William Terry, justice of the peace of District 21 in Maury
County, was born 8 Oct. 1837 in Maury County and at the age of one
year his family moved to Giles County; served in 3d Tennessee
Infantry and taken prisoner of war at Fort Donelson; married 1880
to Ellen Davis and they are the parents of four children. (Maury
Democrat, 11 July 1895.)

MITCHELL, Rev. Dr., has arrived at Alton Prison on 22d; from Florence,
Alabama. (Nashville Dispatch, 2 Sept. 1862.)

Traitor Clergyman Arrested - On Sunday the 26th ult., a large
number of Union officers attended Old School Presbyterian Church
of the Rev. Dr. W. H. Mitchell at Florence, Alabama. So many of
them were present that they constituted a majority of the congregation. After the usual opening hymn, the minister asked the
congregation to unite in prayer, when, to their utter astonishment
the reverend traitor prayed for Jeff. Davis, for the success of the
Confederate arms, and for the attainment of the independence of the
Confederate people. The Union men were greatly indignant at this
gross insult, but remained standing until the prayer was concluded,
when they all left the church. After he had commenced his sermon,
Col. Harlan returned to the church, walked up to the pulpit, arrested
the preacher and delivered him, in compliance with the orders of
General Thomas to a detachment of cavalry, which immediately con-
veyed him as a prisoner to Tuscumbia. (Nashville Daily Union, 8
August 1862.)

MOFFETT, Dr. R. C., formerly of Kentucky, attached to Capt. Shaw's
Texas Rangers, drowned at San Antonio on the 15th while bathing in
the river. (Nashville Daily Gazette, 14 Sept. 1852.)

MOFFATT, King William, in an interment vault at Elmwood Cemetery, is
to be removed and buried; son of J. G. and E. M. Moffatt. (Memphis
Daily Appeal, 21 Aug. 1868.)

MOFFATT, Dr. William B., inventor of several patent medicines, died
suddenly the 11th in New York; had accumulated a handsome fortune.
(Nashville Dispatch, 17 April 1862.)

MOGGIANA, Antonio, one of the early settlers of Edgefield, died
Wednesday of asthma; native of Italy. (Nashville Union and
American, 6 Dec. 1873.)

MOLLOY, D. E., member of Capt. Yeatman's company of 2d Tennessee, fell
mortally wounded in a charge made by Gen. Cleburne's division before
Murfreesboro. (Nashville Dispatch, 17 Jan. 1863.)

MOLLOY, Mrs. Margaret Jane, died November 9. (Maury Democrat, 14 Nov. 1859.)

MOMOLU MASSAQUOI has been called home to Vey, which adjoins Liberia in Africa; he has been in Nashville being educated at Central Tennessee College; age 20. His father King Balah was killed in battle and his mother died of starvation. His 16 year old niece is now in charge of the nation and he will return home to become king. (Florence, Ala., Times, 1 Oct. 1892.)

MONROE, Josephine, wife of James Monroe, age 21, died on the 2d. (Nashville Dispatch, 3 Dec. 1863.)

MONROE, General Nelson, of Boston, is nephew of President Monroe. He is otherwise distinguished as the next-to-the-oldest member of the Sons of Veterans and is a champion of the "eight-dollar pension law." His father is living at the age of 96. (Florence Times, 21 Nov. 1891.)

MONROE, T. B., CSA, "killed 6 April 1862" is found carved in a tree at Shiloh. (Maury Democrat, 10 July 1891.) Thomas B. Monroe, Jr., was killed in battle of Pittsburg Landing; he resigned as Secretary of State under Governor Magoffin and joined the Confederates. (Nashville Dispatch, 18 April 1862.)

MONTGOMERY, Mrs. Agnes, died on the 5th; formerly of Gallatin. (Nashville Republican Banner, 9 Feb. 1871.)

MONTGOMERY, Edmund, died at Nick Jordan's place near the county line of Schley, Georgia, a few days ago, age 102. He was an African chief of the Askari tribe and taken to Virginia from Africa in 1807 when a stalwart young man. He had a large family in Virginia and was survived by his third wife and 25 children in Georgia; had remarkable eyesight; never took a dose of medicine in his life; had teeth like ivory and had every one at his death. (Houston County News, 7 Oct. 1887.)

MONTGOMERY, John, Esquire, one of the oldest citizens of Hickman County, died at his home on Pine River Thursday last. As a boy was in the War of 1812 under General Carroll and was wounded at Battle of Talladega; was member of the Constitutional Convention in 1834; lawyer; age 77. (Nashville Republican Banner, 11 Nov. 1869.)

MONTGOMERY, Father Samuel L., born 1788 in Maryland, then moved to Kentucky; 1807 entered the Dominican convent, Washington County, Ky and ordained 1829; died on the 26th of severe stroke, age 76; a man, who made no enemies; funeral at the Cathedral in Nashville; (Nashville Dispatch, 27 Nov. 1863, 28 Nov. 1863.) Father Montgomery's remains to be sent to cemetery of St. Rose in Kentucky. (Nashville Dispatch, 9 Dec. 1863.)

MOODY, Mrs., living near Smyrna, sister-in-law of John S. Trigg, Esquire, had pneumonia for 10 weeks; was given morphine instead of quinine and died Tuesday afternoon. (Nashville Union and American, 29 May 1874.)

MOONEY, Z. P., deceased; his estate is insolvent. (Columbia Herald, 20 May 1870.)

MOORE, Alfred, one of the earliest settlers of McNairy County, died on the 25th. (Memphis Daily Appeal, 31 Aug. 1869.)

MOORE, Infant of Mr. and Mrs. Ben Moore of Columbia, died Wednesday. (Columbia Herald, 21 Aug. 1896.)

MOORE, Mrs. D. J., 61, died Friday of the Concord area. (Columbia Herald, 24 April 1891.)

MOORE, Mrs. Emily, died yesterday. (Nashville Republican Banner, 2 March 1871.)

MOORE, James, well known in Nashville as a billard player, was killed by a negro in Decatur, Alabama, yesterday. (Nashville Republican Banner, 13 Nov. 1868.)

MOORE, Major James T., born 30 Jan. 1809, died 11 June 1896, lived 4 miles out of Mooresville Pike; married three times; buried Rose Hill. (Columbia Herald, 19 June 1896.)

MOORE, J. M., 45th Tennessee and J. E. Carson, 47th Tennessee Regiment, prisoners of war at Camp Douglas, died there between 1st and the 12th; 27 have died from Texas, 24 from Arkansas, 18 from other places, during this same period. (Nashville Dispatch, 15 March 1863; Nashville Daily Union, 17 March 1863.)

MOORE, Colonel Joseph, who died at Indianapolis recently, planned and constructed all the pontoon bridges used by General Sherman in his march to the sea. (Maury Democrat, 7 June 1894.)

MOORE, Mrs. J. Tip, died on the 5th. (Columbia Herald, 13 Feb. 1891.)

MOORE, Lucy, 18, daughter of T. M. and Ann J. Moore, died at the home of grandfather James Wilkins on Monday of consumption; she was the last of her family; parents had eight children, and parents and one by one the children died of consumption. (Columbia Herald and Mail, 15 Jan. 1875.)

MOORE, Mrs., passenger on the Rose Miller from Pine Bluff, fell overboard 35 miles below Little Rock last week and drowned. (Columbia Herald and Mail, 3 March 1876.)

MOORE, Lt. Michael, who was born 4 July 1800 and lives in Brooklyn is probably the oldest soldier in the world. (Maury Democrat, 14 March 1895.)

MOORE. Death of R. B. Moore - The people of Maury County will be pained to learn that Richard Buster Moore died at his residence in Columbia on Monday the 18th day of June 1877. Mr. Moore was born on the 20th day of December, 1801, in Albermarle County, Va., near Charlottesville. He moved to Franklin County, Tennessee, near Winchester in 1818, where he resides until 1835. There he was married to Miss Mary Gillespie. Being a brick mason by trade, he was employed by the Trustees of the Columbia Female Institute to Columbia to erect that building, which he did in the year 1835. He resided here from then up to his death, with the exception of when he went to Lewisburg to build the old courthouse there and the Richland Factory near Pulaski.

He was twice elected Trustee of Maury County, first in 1844 and again in 1846. He was also twice elected Sheriff of Maury County, first in 1852. He was Postmaster at Columbia under Buchanan's administration, and held that position up to the beginning of the war, when he resigned because of his Southern proclivities.

Such were the historical events of his life. He was known to all men in the county, as a regular apostle of Democracy. Born within the shadow of Monticello, the home of Thomas Jefferson, he seemed to breathe the atmosphere that prevaded that sacred hill until his last day. He never countenanced fraud or wrong, and was one of the most upright men in his dealing that ever lived in our county. In every political contest since the "Log Cabin" days, he was an active worker in the ranks of the Democrats and was probably the best man in Maury County.

He was an oracle, being nearly always able to tell how many votes a man would get long before others had arrived at a conclusion. His

MOORE, R. B. - Continued
text book was the Union and American, having been a subscriber to
that paper, under its different names from the time it was first
issued.

He had six children, all of whom are dead except one daughter, the
wife of J. M. Cabler of our city. He had in his charge several
orphan grandchildren, who together with his venerable wife, his
daughter, and the entire community will long mourn his loss.

His handy work is exhibited in many of the oldest buildings in our
city, but in none so beautifully as the Columbia Female Institute,
which shows a workmanship long in advance of the age in which it
was constructed, and will, as long as it stands, be a monument to
the perfection of his mechanical skill.

He was a member of the Methodist Church, and in his younger days
an active class leader. His funeral was preached on Tuesday at
4 p.m. at his residence by the venerable Green Irvine. There is
something peculiar in the fact on Monday, General J. B. Clements of
Nashville died. He and R. B. Moore were the patriarchs of the
Democracy in Tennessee.

He was buried at Rose Hill Cemetery on Tuesday evening, his remains
being followed to their resting place by a large concourse of
citizens, all of whom will miss him. Thus has passed away one of the
oldest, strongest links that binds us to the past and its golden
memories. (From original clipping, no date, in possession of Annie
Elizabeth Barrack Graham, Columbia, Tn.)

MOORE, Mrs. Robert L., widow, died suddenly of heart disease at Brentwood on Saturday; buried Sunday. (Nashville Union and American,
2 June 1874.)

MOORE, Dr. S. B., of Hickman County, died there on the 14th. (Memphis
Daily Appeal, 22 Dec. 1869.)

MOORE, Mrs. Samuel B., died 1856; Dr. Samuel B. Moore died 14 Dec.
1869. (Hickman Pioneer, Centerville, Tn, 15 March 1878.)

MOORE, William H. We are informed that on Saturday, the 7th inst.,
Lt. Clarke, Company A, 83d Illinois, crossed the Cumberland at
Clarksville with thirty men, went to Yellow Creek, Montgomery County.
He divided his force, placing part under Sgt. Brady. They took
different routes. Clarke discovered, pursued, and killed Samuel
Ellis, formerly of Montgomery County, a guerrilla. Sgt. Brady
captured James Jacob Sly, formerly of Montgomery, James S. Finley
and William H. Moore of Stewart County, noted guerrillas. Jake
Sly had the reputation of being one of the most murderous of the
breed in Tennessee. He had gone so far as to offer a reward for
Lt. Clarke's head. These three scoundrels were executed by the
Lieutenant on the 8th. G. H. McCauley, also of Stewart County,
was captured but the evidence of his being a guerrilla not being
satisfactory, he was carried to Clarksville and is held for further
investigation. (Nashville Daily Union, 10 Jan. 1865.) Gustavus H.
McCauley, citizen, was sentenced to seven years in penitentiary
for being a guerrilla, but was released as evidence was not enough.
(Nashville Daily Union, 11 June 1865.)

MOORE, Willie, 5 years 11 months, son of George and Mary Moore of
Division Street, Nashville, funeral to be held today. (Nashville
Republican Banner, 19 Oct. 1870.)

MORAN, Thomas, 51, died. (Nashville Republican Banner, 29 Dec. 1870.
This paper quite faded, surname could be Martin.)

MORAN, Mrs. Annie, late consort of Morris Moran, died yesterday; funeral
to be held today. (Nashville Republican Banner, 15 March 1871.)

MOREY, Rev. Ira, formerly of Franklin, Tn, died in Bennington, NH, on
26 Nov. 1864. (Nashville Daily Union, 7 Feb. 1865.)

MORGAN, Ben., killed 5 years ago in Obion County by S. T. Morgan
with W. R. Smith being implicated; both were honorably acquitted.
(Memphis Avalanche, 29 Nov. 1866.)

MORGAN, General George Washington, the only surviving general of the
Mexican War, died at Fortress Monroe last week. (Maury Democrat,
3 August 1893.)

MORGAN, Mrs. Henrietta, 86, died in Lexington, Ky, on the 14th; mother
of the Confederate general John H. Morgan; she had six sons in the
Confederate Army; one daughter married General A. P. Hill and one
married General Basil Duke. (Florence, Ala., Times, 26 Sept. 1891.)

MORGAN, Dr. F. B., funeral to be held today. (Nashville Republican
Banner, 7 Oct. 1869.) Will of Frank H. Morgan has been brought
to court for probate; Calvin Morgan, administrator. (Nashville
Republican Banner, 7 Nov. 1869.)

MORGAN, Colonel John F., of Columbia, died recently, rupturing a blood
vessel. (Whig and Tribune, 7 Dec. 1872.)

MORGAN, John, shot and instantly killed by a man named James Wyles, six
miles out on the Lebanon Pike on the 13th. Morgan was not quite
21 years old and his widowed mother and three sisters survive; he
was their main support. (Nashville Dispatch, 16 Sept. 1862.)

MORGAN, Mrs., sister of famous General Morgan of Tennessee, committed
suicide in New Yrok last week by taking laudanum. The cause is
attributed to excessive grief over the loss of a daughter some time
ago. (Columbia Herald and Mail, 28 April 1876.)

MORGAN, Samuel D., 21, youngest son of Samuel D. Morgan of Nashville,
died 26 Oct. 1862 at Augusta, Ky; cousin of John H. Morgan and a
private in John H. Morgan's regiment. (Nashville Daily Union, 1
Nov. 1862.)

MORGAN, Major Sam was supposed to have been killed in a fight at
Augusta, Ky., captain of CSA company. (Nashville Dispatch, 1
Nov. 1862.)

MORGAN, Major Wash, cousin of John Hunt Morgan, is lying wounded at the
home of John Hunt Morgan's mother in Lexington, Ky; dangerously
wounded. (Nashville Dispatch, 1 Nov. 1862.)

MORGAN, General John H., and six of his captains escaped from the Ohio
Penitentiary this morning, Nov. 27, by digging through their cell
floor to the sewer leading to the river. $1000 reward has been
offered for Morgan. (Nashville Dispatch, 29 Nov. 1863.) (He was
killed near Knoxville, 4 September 1864.) A monument over the
remains of Gen. John H. Morgan is suggested. (Memphis Daily Appeal,
26 March 1870.)

Mr. William Miller says that after General John H. Morgan was killed
in Greenville, East Tennessee, his body was buried in Sinking
Springs Cemetery at Abingdon, Va., on the lot owned by General John
B. Floyd. The grave was first occupied by the corpse of Capt.
Castleman of Kentucky, and secondly by General Morgan, and finally
by General John B. Floyd. The three burials took place in a very
short time of each other. Captain Castleman's remains were disinterred and carried to Kentucky. General Morgan's body was
removed so far as we know. (Maury Democrat, 21 March 1895.)

MORGAN, Little son of Thomas W. Morgan of Decatur County, age 2, fell
into a spring near the house and drowned a short time ago.
(Nashville Union and American, 7 July 1874.)

MORGAN, ___, age 76, father of Dr. W. H. Morgan, died yesterday in Russellville, Ky. (Nashville Republican Banner, 4 Jan. 1870.)

MORRIS, George Trabue, 10 months, son of John B. and T. P. Morris, died August 19. (Nashville Republican Banner, 21 Aug. 1868.)

MORRIS, Mrs. Elizabeth, 72, died in Williamson County on the 19th. (Whig and Tribune, 5 Oct. 1872.)

MORRIS, Commodore Henry W., died on August 14. (Nashville Dispatch, 15 Aug. 1863.)

MORRIS, Captain James H. of 2d East Tennessee Cavalry, was killed in the Battle of Stones River. (Nashville Daily Union, 27 March 1863.)

MORRIS, Peter, residing near Jellico, Tn, attempted Wednesday to kill an old man named Higdon near Cumberland Gap. Higdon's daughter Martha interferred and fatally shot Morris. December 28 dateline. (Maury Democrat, 3 Jan. 1889.)

MORRIS, Gen. Pitcairn, USA retired, died in Baltimore recently age 82; appointed to army in 1820. (Houston County News, 7 Oct. 1887.)

MORRIS, Major Robert, 6th Pennsylvania Cavalry, grandson of Robert Morris of Revolutionary memory, died on the 13th at Libby Prison; buried Oakwood Cemetery. (Nashville Dispatch, 23 Aug. 1863.)

MORRIS, Thomas, colored, of Stuart, Virginia, claims to be 110 years old; father of 48 children and married five times, but all his wives are dead. (Florence, Ala., Times, 19 Sept. 1891.)

MORRIS, W. F., Wayne County, brought in a Civil War relic, an army canteen left in front of his father's house April 1862 by General Buell's command while en route to Shiloh from Fort Donelson. (Clifton Mirror, 27 July 1906.)

MORRIS, W. S., freight conductor on the L & N, was crushed to death June 20 in freight yards at Birmingham, Alabama; was from Atlanta and had been married two weeks. (Maury Democrat, 27 June 1889.)

MORRISON, Jim, Bibb County, Alabama, most celebrated outlaw, was killed recently by officers attempting to arrest him. (Florence, Ala., Times, 16 July 1892.)

MORRISON, Joel, son of J. P. Morrison, Esquire, of Brushy Fork in Hickman County, died Sunday last. (Columbia Herald and Mail, 25 Aug. 1876.)

MORTON, Dr. John M., Jr. of Nashville, gallant chief of artillery on General Forrest's staff, was married on Wednesday last to Miss Annie P., daughter of Judge West H. Humphreys. (Memphis Daily Appeal, 18 Sept. 1869.)

MOSELEY. Dr. J. L. Wooden, surgeon of the 68th Indiana Volunteers, who was captured in the battle of Chickamauga, called to see us Saturday night, and left us some memoranda relative to Tennesseans captured by the rebels.

In the military prison at Atlanta, he saw Major B. F. Moseley, formerly quartermaster of the 1st Middle Tennessee Infantry. He learned that after Moseley's capture he was placed in a damp dungeon at Chattanooga without any bedding and with an 80-pound ball and chain attached to his leg. After remaining in this situation for six weeks, he was transferred to the prison at Atlanta. When Dr. Wooden saw him there, he was much reduced by chronic diarrhea, but the keepers of the prison refused to remove the ball and chain. Dr. W. was subsequently informed by Dr. Fithian, of the 18th Kentucky, who remained at Atlanta several weeks with our sick, that Moseley had died in a week after Dr. W. saw him, and

MOSELEY - Continued
that the ball and chain were not removed till about 12 hours before
his death.

Capt. Levi L. Carter, of the 9th East Tennessee Cavalry, formerly a
citizen of Georgia, was also in confinement at Atlanta with a ball
and chain. He was charged with arson and treason, and was to be
tried at the next session of the Confederate Court at Atlanta. He,
however, made his escape after the doctor left.

On the 25th of September about 350 of Patterson's 5th Alabama
Cavalry made a dash upon Hunt's saw mill, 18 miles below Stevenson,
Ala., captured the men in charge of the mill, the guard, and a few
recuits for the 1st Alabama (Federal) Cavalry. The rebels lost six
killed; the Federals, two. An hour after the capture, the rebel
Adjutant May ride along the line, and one of his men pointing to a
prisoner said, "There is the man that killed your brother!" The
Adjutant drew his pistol and fired at John Laddington of the 4th
Indiana, inflicting a mortal wound. He then said to Zachariah Isbel,
Company A, 1st Alabama (Federal) Cavalry, "Damn you, I will shoot
you!" Isbell replied, "Don't shoot me; I am a prisoner." May
responded, "Follow that man" and when Isbel turned to obey, May
fired at him twice, inflicting a slight wound in both shoulders.

The Alabama and Tennessee prisoners were marched, with their hands
tied behind them to Gadsden, Ga., where they were handcuffed and
sent to Rome. The military commandant at Rome removed the irons
and sent the prisoners to Atlanta, where Dr. W. saw them.

Peter F. Ryerson, of 73 University Place, New York City, and John
Walter, engineer, of Springfield, Ohio, were running Hunt's saw
mill for the Government. From them and Sergt. Maj. Myram Whitthorn,
44th Illinois, and Z. Isbell, 1st Alabama Cavalry, Dr. W. obtained
these facts. (Nashville Daily Union, 12 Jan. 1864.)

MOSS. P. W. Moss, now of Paragould, Ark., and his brother of this
State during the war fought for Southern rights in the same regiment-
the 20th Tennessee. After peace had been restored, they separated
and in some manner lost trace of each other. Both of them went to
the reunion last week, and the Tennessee brother registered his
name at headquarters and procured the badge of his regiment.

The Arkansas brother happened to see the Tennessee man, and, noticing
his badge, engaged in conversation with him, hoping to gain some
information concerning his brother. The Arkansas man, never dream-
ing that the person whom he was addressing was his brother, told
the Tennessee man that he had a brother in the 20th Tennessee regiment, whom he had not seen for many years.

He asked him what company he belonged to, and, finding that he
belonged to, the same company, inquired as to his name. Then
imagine the surprise of both when the happy fact was revealed that
they were the brothers who had been looking for each other for so
long, and had come together unawares. Two more happy persons could
not have been found in all Nashville. They laughed with each other,
and talked of the happy days, and sad days of by-gone years; and
they declared that as brothers, they would never be separated or
lost to each other again until death came and separated them.
(Columbia Herald, 2 July 1897.)

MOSS, Mrs. John T., of Mt. Pleasant, died on the 14th; husband survives;
old and highly esteemed. (Columbia Herald and Mail, 18 Jan. 1878.)

MOTT, Mrs. Marcy, 80 years 8 months, died September 18; and her husband
Stephen Mott, 86 years 8 months, died on September 19; they had been
married 63 years and lived in Scituate, Mass. Husband survived
her only a few hours and when he had been told that his wife could
not survive, he said, "Marcy is going and I guess I shall go, too."
They were buried in one grave. (Nashville Dispatch, 1 June 1862.)

MOULTON, Col. Thomas J., 58, of Williamson County, died July 30.
(Whig and Tribune, 9 August 1873.)

MOULTON, Thomas J., young body was found three weeks after he disappeared in a clover field north of Franklin; he had fallen by
accident and his gun had discharged. He had been missing from home
since Christmas. (Whig and Tribune, 27 Jan. 1872.)

MUDD, Dr., has recalled nearly all his former practice. His innocence
of complicity with the late John Wilkes Boothe is conceded, and his
neighbors love him the more for the injustice which he has undergone.
His health is much impaired. (Memphis Daily Appeal, 4 Aug. 1869.)

MUELLER, Mrs., died in a fit of apoplexy. (Nashville Dispatch, 23
May 1862.)

MUELLER, Charles H., deceased; estate is insolvent, John Longhurst,
administrator. (Nashville Dispatch, 9 Jan. 1863.)

MULLEN, John, of Oxford, Maine, is 133 years old, and has led a wandering life; he runs a 43-acre farm, eats a plain diet, and wears
woolens. (Maury Democrat, 26 Sept. 1889.)

MULLEN, Mrs. T. A., wife of Wilson Mullen, funeral to be held today
at the First Baptist Church. (Nashville Daily Union, 30 Nov. 1862.)

MULLENS, Betsy, famous East Tennessee mountain giantess, is 82 years
old, weighs 500 pounds, and has never been a dozen miles away from
her birthplace near Sneedville. (Columbia Herald, 18 Dec. 1895.)

MULLINS, Mahala, famous fat woman of Hancock County, Tn, has died.
(Columbia Herald, 23 Sept. 1898.)

MULLINS, George, died on the 23d. (Nashville Republican Banner,
24 Nov. 1867.)

MULLINS, Colonel James, of Shelbyville, died of cholera recently.
(Whig and Tribune, 5 July 1873.)

MULLINS, Alexander, was shot by John Engle near Humboldt a few days
ago. (Paris Gazette, 30 May 1878.)

MULLINS, Mrs. Jane, died recently in Lincoln County at the age of 105.
(Nashville Union and American, 6 Feb. 1874.)

MULLOY, Mrs. Mary, wife of John Mulloy, who was supposed to have been
killed in battle, died in Nashville on Saturday in great destitution;
it is believe she has relatives in Pittsburgh, Pa. She left three
children. (Nashville Dispatch, 10 March 1863.)

MULLOY, Patrick, 65, died March 24, of pneumonia. (Nashville Republican
Banner, 25 March 1871.)

MURDOCK, Joseph, of Scott County, Virginia, who was supposed to have
been murdered 25 years ago and for which crime Bud Lindsey served
21 years in the Virginia penitentiary, has returned to his former
home. Lindsey died recently. (Columbia Herald, 26 Feb. 1897.)

MURDOCK, Captain of Van Cleve's staff, was killed at Chickamauga; son
of James E. Murdock, the tragedian, who went for his body.
(Nashville Daily Union, 29 Sept. 1863.)

MURPHY, Guy, little adopted son of Mr. and Mrs. James Hamilton of
Spring Hill, died Saturday and taken to Elora to be buried by
mother who died a few weeks ago. (Maury Democrat, 17 May 1894.)

MURPHY, Captain James B., formerly of Columbia, died on the 7th in
Ithaca, Texas, born and reared in Maury County; 8 years ago went
to Texas; lawyer; married Lizzie Looney, daughter of A. M. Looney.
(Columbia Herald, 15 May 1891.)

MURPHY, Sgt. John, Company D, 4th Tennessee Cavalry, of Ducktown, Blount County, was killed about 29 Feb. 1864 in the Mississippi expedition out of Memphis. (Nashville Daily Union, 4 March 1864.)

MURPHY, John W., will is being probated. (Nashville Republican Banner, 22 August 1869.)

MURPHY, Joseph Cleveland, died October 13; son of Mr. and Mrs. John Murphy of Godwin. (Maury Democrat, 24 Oct. 1895.)

MURPHY, Mrs. Margaret E., died; wife of Capt. J. B. Murphy of McCain's Academy; native of Marshall County and daughter of Dr. W. J. Anderson. (Columbia Herald, 3 June 1870.)

MURPHY, Michael, found lying dead on floor last night in his bedroom in the boarding house of William Flannigan's; died from apoplexy; single man; had relatives in Richmond, Va.; spent four years in Confederate Army. (Nashville Union and American, 10 June 1874.)

MURPHY, Octavine, wife of W. L. Murphy, age 21 years 6 months 11 days, died on the 2d of consumption at the home of G. B. Polk. (Columbia Herald, 10 June 1870.)

MURPHY, Capt. P. E., died near Mobile, Alabama, last week of apoplexy while taking a bath. When war began, he was commanding the ship Pennsylvania at Norfolk, but resigned to enter Confederate service. He commanded the Selma in the battle of Mobile where he was wounded and captured. (Columbia Herald and Mail, 13 Oct. 1876.)

MURPHY, Sallie A., daughter of W. I. and Alice L. Murphy, died in Nashville June 11, age 8 months, 2 days; granddaughter of the Rev. William Doss of the Tennessee Conference; buried City Cemetery, Nashville. (Columbia Herald and Mail, 14 July 1876.)

MURRAY, Mrs. Austria Sanders, 68, died October 23 in McMinnville; born in Smith County, eldest daughter of Col. George Matlock. (Nashville Union and American, 8 Nov. 1874.)

MURRAY, child of James Murray of Lobelville, Perry County, died on the 23d. (Linden Times, 1 April 1880.)

MURRELL, Mrs. Mary Jane, 72, died and removed to Bowling Green for burial. (Nashville Republican Banner, 18 May 1870.)

MURRELL, John A., was discharged last week after 10 years in prison. (Tennessee Democrat, Columbia, Tn, 18 April 1844.) John A. Murrell died in Pikeville, Bledsoe County, of pulmonary consumption, on Sunday the first instant; on his deathbed he acknowledged he had been guilty of almost every crime charged against him except murder and of this charge he declared himself "guiltless." (Tennessee Democrat, 23 Nov. 1844.)

The Sparta (Tn) Index says of John A. Murrell: It is a fact not generally known, that Murrell reformed before his death and lived for several years a member of the Methodist Church in good standing.

He was a carpenter by trade and worked mostly in Bledsoe County, boarding usually at the house of John M. Billingsley, Esquire, 5 miles above Pikeville, who now resides on Cane Creek in Van Buren County. Murrell was a man of uncommonly good education and intelligence and had one of the best libraries in the neighborhood.

Several of his books are now in the Library of Preisdent Carnes of Burritt College.

Murrell acknowledged his former crimes, and with his intimates he talked freely but regretfully of them, but he denied to the last that he had ever committed murder. This declaration was repeated

MURRELL, John A. - Continued
on his deathbed. Those who knew him best believed that he was
sincere. He died at old Squire Billingsley's and was buried in a
graveyard near old Smyrna Church.

A few nights after, the grave was violated and the head taken away,
by whom was never known. The body was reinterred and has since
remained undisturbed.

To distinguish it the grave was dug at an angle of 45 degree to
the usual east and west line. It is still pointed out to curious
strangers who visit the spot. (Columbia Herald and Mail, 4 Feb.
1876.)

Birthplace of John A. Murrell - In the adjoining 11th district of
Williamson County, but little over a mile east from the Ridge meeting house, a Prebysterian Church, on the Franklin and Lewisburg
pike, there is a noted and historic hill. We stood, recently, on
its bare and lonely summit. Tall, precipitous and wooded hills
bound it on the east; on the north the same range of hills, with
their bare southern slopes, seamed with gullies and ravines and
dotted with patches of sedge, and interpersed with thickets of
briers and thorns, presents a bare and uninviting prospect.

South, lies the basins of Rutherford Creek. Looking west and south,
spreads out a lovely smiling valley, on which rich and fruitful
bosom repose the neighboring villages of Thompson Station and
Spring Hill. The hill on which we stood for half a century has
borne the name of the celebrated freebooter. A few scattered
hearthstones and wild rose vines now alone mark the birthplace of
John A. Murrell. The place where the celebrated bandit chief was
born, and played around these scattered hearthstones, in boyish
innocence (and prattled by his father's side, and bowed his curly
head upon a fond mother's knee) looks dreary and desolate. It is a
hill of broom sedge and thorny thickets, a covert and walk for foxes;
like the birthplace of other great criminals, it seems to be avoided;
as a habitation by man, and blighted by the hand of Prividence, and
made desolate.

Murrell was a great robber and chief of banditi, and he was not
believed by those who had known him long and well to be the red-
handed murderer as painted by Virgil A. Stewart, betrayed for money,
and by many believed to be a member of the clan. A highly colored
life of Murrell was written to make money. It was a success, and
made Murrell famous in the annals of vice and crime, and his
betrayer has left behind the heritage of a dubious name and doubtful
fame.

The Murrells were said by old citizens, who knew them well, to be
a very handsome family. John A., especially, was remarkable for
his manly beauty, curling auburn hair, worn long generally, decorated a classic head, and a prepossessing face, that would, said an
observer, have drawn attention and been noticed among a thousand
people.

His sister, Leanna Murrell, was remarkable for her beauty, and was
the most skillful and graceful dancer of her day. She possessed
a face of exquisite beauty and sweetness; a form of queenly grace,
and an eye of melting softness. None that looked on her in her
youthful bloom ever forgot her wonderful beauty. (Columbia
Herald and Mail, 13 April 1877.)

Not Murrell's Birthplace - In rebuttal to the above article, a
writer wrote that Murrell was not born in District 11, but was born
in Virginia and that the above article was written to cast reflec-
tion on the neighborhood. (Columbia Herald and Mail, 8 June 1877.)

Prison Record - "John A. Murrell was received in the Penitentiary
August seventeenth one thousand eight hundred and thirty four; he

MURRELL, John A. - Continued
is five feet ten inches and a half in height and weighs from
one hundred and fifty eight to one hundred and seventy pounds; dark
hair; blue eyes; long nose and much pitted with small pox; tolerably
fair complexion; twenty-eight years of age. Born in Lunenburgh
County, Virginia and brought up in Williamson County, Tennessee;
his mother, wife and two children reside in the neighborhood of
Denmark about nine miles from Jackson, Madison County, Tennessee.
His wife's maiden name was Mangham; her connexion reside on the
waters of South Harpeth, Williamson Co., Tenn. His brother Wm. S.
Murrell, a Druggist, resides in Cincinnatti, Ohio; he has another
brother living in Sumpter County, S. Carolina; he has a scar on the
middle joint of the finger next to the little finger of his left
hand and one on the middle finger of the same hand; a scar on the
inside of the end of the finger next the little finger of the right
hand; has generally followed farming; was found guilty of Negro
stealing at the Circuit Court of Madison County and sentenced to
Ten Years confinement in the jail and penitentiary House of the
State of Tennessee." (From 1831-1842 Prison Record Book, Tennessee
State Library and Archives, Nashville, Tn.)

Marriage Bond: John A. Murrell to Elizabeth Mangham, dated ___
March 1829; bondsman: Patton Churchwell. (This original marriage
bond was found in the basement of the Maury County, Tn, courthouse
in 1963 by Jill Garrett and Virginia Wood Alexander.)

MURRELL, William. Suicide of William Murrell in Hickman County. Lily
Swamp, Tenn., Oct. 21 - The citizens of this community were shocked
yesterday evening by the intelligence that young William Murrell
had committed suicide, about 1 1/2 miles from this place, by placing
a revolver to his head and blowing out his brains. Murrell was
returning from Nashville in company with his young wife (having been
married but two weeks) and Mr. Sylvester Booker. When near Mr. R. D.
Lyell's house, on the Nashville and Pinewood Road, he and his wife
separated, she going to her mother's and young Murrell proceeded
homeward with Mr. Booker. His wife had gone but a short distance
from the wagon, in which Mr. Booker and Murrell were driving, when
Murrell stepped a few rods from the road and drawing his pistol,
placed it to his forehead and pulled the trigger, the ball entering
a little above the base of the brain, killing him instantly.
Justice Jones summond a jury, and held an inquest over the remains,
and returned a verdict in accordance with the facts as stated above.
Domestic troubles are supposed to have been the cause of the young
man's rash act. He was a man noted for his amiable temper, steady
habits and sterling industry, and leaves many sympathizing friends.
(Columbia Herald and Mail, 26 Oct. 1877.)

MURRY, Mrs. Mary Jane, relict of Henry Murry, died Monday in Nashville;
daughter of Benjamin Cabler, one of the pioneers of Davidson County,
and Wife Rebecca Moss; buried Nashville. (Daily Herald, Columbia,
Tn, 21 Feb. 1905.)

OLD MURRY, an old colored man living at Rocky Hill, Conn., will be
117 years this month. (Nashville Dispatch, 6 May 1862.)

MUSGROVE, Edward F., 47, died in Columbus, Mississippi, on the 28th
ult., born near Lexington, Ky; early in life settled in Nashville
and in 1836 moved to Columbus, Mississippi. (Nashville Daily
Gazette, 8 Sept. 1852.)

MYERS, David, 85, died on the 24th in Jackson County; soldier in the
War of 1812. (Nashville Union and American, 31 Dec. 1872.)

MYERS, D. E., of Morgan's Cavalry, was killed in a skirmish near
Readyville on the 26th. (Nashville Dispatch, 31 May 1863.)

MYERS, Henry, of New Orleans, was killed there on the 13th by lightning.
Funeral preparations made, body coffined, and about to be closed,
when the corpse was observed to move and soon set bolt upright and

looked around and asked why the gloomy preparations. (Nashville Dispatch, 2 Sept. 1863.)

MYERS, Col. L. D., funeral held and largely attended and only about half of the people could get in his house; he was admitted to the bar on 5 Jan. 1848. (Columbia Herald and Mail, 29 April 1876.)

MYERS, Small child of Ten Myers of Hunt's Mill, Houston County, died Sunday. (Houston County News, 7 Aug. 1866.)

MYERS, Mrs. William, of Danville, Ky, died recently and while she lay in her coffin she was fitted with a new set of teeth by her family dentist. (Maury Democrat, 16 May 1895.)

MYERS, Sgt., of the 7th Illinois Infantry, who, in a difficulty, shot and killed his captain in Corinth, Mississippi, was hung in Pulaski on Thursday last. He was tried by court-martial immediately after the crime but by some means the sentence was never brought to light until recently. He had been, we believe, released from arrest and had re-enlisted as a veteran. Athens Volunteer, April 30. (Nashville Daily Union, 6 May 1864.) (Refer to sketch on Sam Davis gallows under Sam Davis.)

McANDREWS, Andrew, funeral to be held at the Cathedral this afternoon. (Nashville Republican Banner, 10 Sept. 1870.)

M'ALISTER, John, Esquire, late of Frederick County, Virginia, in the 74th year of his age, died at Cabin Row, Montgomery County, Tn. (Tuscumbian, Tuscumbia, Ala., 13 Feb. 1826.)

MACALPIN. A man named Halfpenny lived in Dublin, Ireland, at the end of the last century. Having been very successful in business, his children persuaded him to change his name to a more dignified one, which he did by dropping the last letter.

In the course of time the orthography was also changed and when the man died he was buried as Mr. Halpen. The fortunes of the family increased still further and the son soon dropped the H.

The next transition was an equally easy one, and he had run the streets as little Kenny Halfpenny came out as Kenneth MacAlpin, the descendant of a hundred kings. (Columbia Herald, 4 Oct. 1895.)

McANALLY, Mr., of Pulaski was assaulted by a party of masked men; tried to escape and he was shot; he was a wife-whipper and guilty of abusing his wife. Some of her friends took the law into their own hands. (Nashville Republican Banner, 22 Jan. 1870.)

McANALLY, R. P., is the oldest native of Birmingham; was born a few hours after the town was incorporated, 11 Nov. 1871. (Florence, Ala., Times, 30 July 1892.)

McARLEY, Mrs. Catherine, her will is being probated. (Nashville Republican Banner, 31 Jan. 1869.)

McBRIDE, Charles Winston, infant son of Thomas H. and Elizabeth McBride, died at Mt. Vernon, Illinois, on June 26, age 11 months 25 days; formerly of Nashville. (Nashville Daily Union, 30 June 1865.)

McCABE, Patrick, infant son of Barney McCabe, 9 days, died on the 11th. (Nashville Union and American, 12 Nov. 1874.)

McCABE, Mr. Sosthenes, one of the oldest citizens of Fairfield County, Ohio, died on Thursday last, age 82. (Memphis Avalanche, 11 Dec. 1866.)

McCAFFREY, John T. C., 73, is in St. Louis; he was reared in Knoxville, Tn; has 15 sons and 3 daughters; 11 sons are in Union Army until the siege of Vicksburg where four were killed. The old man himself enlisted in the 10th Illinois at Fayetteville, Ark., a year ago but lately discharged; he served 8 months in Florida War, 12 months under General Jackson, 32 months in the Mexican War, and 12 months in Civil War; he has three brothers and three stepsons in Union Army. (Nashville Dispatch, 1 Sept. 1863; Nashville Daily Union, 23 Sept. 1863.)

McCALL, Bob, was shot and killed by Rufe Kittrell last Thursday; Kittrell lived just over the line in Wayne County and was acquitted. (Linden Times, 19 Aug. 1880.)

McCALL, Thomas A., about 45, fell into the Chattanooga railroad cut and was mangled mortally; lived on Granny White Pike; he could not be identified for a time as the body was so terribly mangled; lived near the old Magazine; brother-in-law of James M. Hawkins and Hugh McCrea; had been in mercantile business for 20 years. (Nashville Republican Banner, 14 Jan. 1871, 15 Jan. 1871.)

McCAMPBELL, James, died on the 1st instant at home of Thomas C. McCampbell; formerly of East Tennessee. (Nashville Daily Gazette, 6 Oct. 1852.)

McCANDLESS, Mrs. Laura, died February 9 in the Bigbyville area. (Maury Democrat, 1 March 1889.)

McCANDLESS, James, son of Carroll McCandless of Triune, burned to death Monday; drunk, lay down on some hay and was cremated alive. (Columbia Herald, 20 March 1891.)

McCann, Mrs. Ann, died yesterday. (Nashville Republican Banner, 23 Feb. 1868.)

McCANN, Mrs. Ben W., Sr. of Nashville, met a horrible death on August 18; her clothing caught on fire by lamp, she had dropped the lamp which exploded. Her residence was also destroyed. She was alone at the time. (Columbia Herald, 20 Aug. 1897.)

McCANN, Dick, has been captured at Weems Spring, Hickman County. (Nashville Dispatch, 21 Aug. 1863, 25 Aug. 1863.)

Capt. Dick McCann is at Nashville, 16 miles from here, with some 100 boys and worthless vagabonds under him, where he is carrying things with a high hand, writing passes, administering oaths, etc. Frank McNairy of the "Bloodhound" notoriety was at the head of the band which destroyed 11 of our forage wagons and captured some 40 cavalry yesterday, some 10 miles out on the Franklin road, at a villainous lowflung little settlement, known by the soldiers as Secesh-town. He prowls around there, and when a chance offers, he sends his runners out through the neighborhood and the citizens gather in. (Nashville Daily Union, 21 Sept. 1862.)

Dick McCann robbed the stages of Mr. J. LeAble. Dr. Patterson, an old physician of this vicinity, about 60 years old, was among the guerrillas holding the rank of lieutenant. He was conspicuous by his violent and furious denunciations of the Yankees. He said that all Federals ought to be killed, and said that he was not in favor of taking any prisoners. The guerrillas were all exceedingly ragged and dirty and were very drunk and smelt badly. (Nashville Daily Union, 2 Nov. 1862.)

Dick McCann, guerrilla captain and perambulating pickpocket, General of the great Butternut Confederacy, made an attack on one of our forage trains on Saturday. Several of his men were badly wounded. He was greeted warmly and fled. (Nashville Daily Union, 2 Dec. 1862.)

McCANN, Mrs. Margaret Dunaway, wife of Major J. R. (Dick) McCann, died
Sunday night at Antioch, Davidson County. (Whig and Tribune, 26
August 1871.) The property of Richard McCann and Thomas Kilkirk,
leading a gang of guerrillas, will be destroyed by fire--all houses,
barns, and fences. (Nashville Dispatch, 11 Jan. 1863. Also same
paper reports that it was "done last evening.")

McCARROLL, Israel, died 10 Jan. 1873; when he was young came to Williamson County and in 1830 to Maury County; married Mrs. Giddens; was
born 1800 in either NC or Tn. (Columbia Herald, 24 Jan. 1873.)
Colonel Israel McCarroll, an old and honored citizen of Maury, died
at Spring Hill about two weeks ago. (Whig and Tribune, Jackson, Tn,
1 Feb. 1873.)

McCARTHY, Henry J., infant son of R. J. and Anna E., to be buried today.
(Nashville Republican Banner, 2 Feb. 1871.)

McCARTHY, son of Martin McCarthy, age 12, of Edgefield, drowned in the
back water near Spring Street last evening. (Nashville Union and
American, 15 April 1874.)

McCARTY, Margaret, died yesterday, age 3, youngest daughter of Daniel
and Ellen McCarty. (Nashville Republican Banner, 28 May 1870.)

McCAULEY, Daniel, deceased, his estate is insolvent. (Erin Review,
10 Sept. 1881.)

McCAULEY, Missouri U., daughter of David and Louisa McCauley, age 22,
of Stewart County, died 21 Aug. 1860. (Clarksville Weekly Chronicle,
___ August 1860.)

McCAULEY, Dony, sues Henry McCauley for divorce in Dickson County; he
is non-resident of Tennessee. (Dickson County Press, 12 Oct. 1882.)

McCLAIN, William P., 44, died on the 3d at his residence in Lebanon,
Tn. (Nashville Daily Gazette, 11 Sept. 1852.)

McCLANT, R. N., of Bedford County, was found dead drunk in N&C Depot
last night. (Nashville Republican Banner, 16 Feb. 1868.)

McCLANAHAN, Ditter, his home near Hampshire, Maury County, burned
Wednesday and his daughter Cattie, age 12, burned to death; burned
to a crisp. Her screams were heartrendering to hear. Candles
set fire to bed. (Columbia Herald and Mail, 1 May 1874.)

McCLANAHAN, Mary Eva, daughter of Mr. and Mrs. W. T. McClanahan of
Embargo Street, Columbia, died October 2 and buried Rose Hill
Cemetery. (Maury Democrat, 10 Oct. 1895.)

McCLANAHAN, Robert, Sr., tanner at McClanahan's Mill, died near Centerville the other day, survived by wife and several children; poor
but respectable man. (Columbia Herald and Mail, 16 July 1875.)

McCLELLAN, Mrs., 81, of East Greenwich, Rhode Island, died March 19;
grandmother of General McClellan. (Nashville Dispatch, 28 March
1863.)

McCLELLAN, William, Company F, 58th Alabama, CSA, prisoner of war
confined in the Maxwell House, was shot by guard yesterday and
died instantly. He had his head out of an upper story window and
refused guard's order to put it in. (Nashville Dispatch, 5 Dec.
1863.) William McClellan, 58th Alabama "rebel prisoner," was shot
and killed at Convalescent Barracks on the 4th by guard; he was at
one of the windows on 4th story and kept calling out to passers-by.
Guard told him to stop; he was shot near the mouth. (Nashville
Daily Union, 5 Dec. 1863.)

McCLELLAN. A sister of General McClellan resides in Alabama and a
nephew of his was in the Battle of Shiloh fighting for the

Confederates. (Nashville Dispatch, 9 May 1862.) The highest
government pensions are being paid out to Mrs. George B. McClellan,
$2000, and Mrs. Ulysses S. Grant, $5000. (Florence, Ala., Times,
31 Jan. 1891.) An equestrian statue of Major General George B.
McClellan was unveiled at Philadelphia a few days since. (Maury
Democrat, 1 Nov. 1894.)

McClung, "Captain" was killed at Knoxville recently. (Nashville Dispatch, 7 July 1863.)

McClung, Maggie Gardner, 18 months 13 days, died August 24 at Atlanta,
Georgia; daughter of Matthew and Julia F. McClung. (Nashville
Dispatch, 30 Sept. 1862.)

McCLURE, Mrs. Jennie L., age 33 (or 23), died February 14, wife of
James A. McClure, protracted illness. (Nashville Republican
Banner, 16 Feb. 1869.)

McCLURE, John, who lived 3 miles from Lawrenceburg, on January 8
became too drunk to go home, took lodging in courthouse for the
night; found next day froze to death. (Murfreesboro News, 2 Feb.
1859.)

McCLURE, Miss Margaret, of District 7, gave birth to a child last week
and died of childbed fever. (Columbia Herald, 12 Sept. 1873.)

McCONNELL, William Kennedy, prominent citizen of Talladega, Alabama,
died last week; married 7 May 1868 to Ellen Smith of Columbia,
Tn, whom he met here during Civil War; four children survive; died
January 16. (Columbia Herald, 30 Jan. 1891, 6 Feb. 1891.)

McCONNER, Aunt Albcany, colored, died in Nashville Sunday. (Nashville
Union and American, 11 March 1873.)

McCOOK. Major McCook's youngest son, Charles, was killed in battle of
Bull Run on 21 July 1861; his son Colonel Robert McCook was killed
on 21 July 1862; and the father himself was killed on 21 July 1863.
(Nashville Dispatch, 29 July 1863.)

McCOOK. Frank Gurley, charged with the murder of Brigadier General
Robert L. McCook is now in custody and is ordered to stand trial
before a military commission. (Nashville Daily Union, 2 Dec. 1863.)

McCORD, Mrs. Sarah, widow of John McCord, of Urbana, Ohio; daughter
of famous pioneer settler of Champaign County, Simon Kenton, died
at West Liberty on the 12th inst., age 70. Her husband was once
jailor of Champaign County and a prisoner attempted to escape while
her husband was gone and she caught the prisoner by collar and held
in iron grasp until assistance came. (Nashville Dispatch, 24 April
1862.)

McCORKLE, W. A., of Charleston, West Virginia, slapped the face of
U. S. Marshall White for some remark about Jeff. Davis and Saturday
whipped the editor Robert of the Tribune for an uncomplimentary
criticism. He was presented with a gold-headed cane last evening
by his admirers. (Maury Democrat, 19 Dec. 1889.)

McCORMACK, Mrs. Ann, of Carters Creek Station, died of consumption;
sister of W. J. Adkisson of Texas; buried Blanton's Chapel Cemetery.
(Columbia Herald and Mail, 21 June 1878.)

McCORMACK, Peter, age 6 months 4 days, son of Michael and Mary
McCormack died 24 Dec. 1862. (Nashville Daily Union, 26 Dec. 1862.)

McCORMACK, Mrs. Wallace, died suddenly Thursday; left a large family;
buried by her deceased children at Spring Hill Cemetery. (Columbia
Herald and Mail, 11 May 1877.)

McCOY, David, oldest white man in California, died near San Bernardino, California, recently at the age of 104 years; if he had lived until May 2 he would have been 105; born 1790 in North Carolina; a Democrat. (Maury Democrat, 16 May 1895.)

McCOY, Captain J. N., paymaster of L&N railroad died near Evansville, Indiana, last week. (Columbia Herald, 29 May 1896.)

McCOY. Hatfield-McCoy Feud - Information was brought in by courier from Hamilton, Lincoln County, West Virginia, that about midnight October 25, a mob surrounded the Lincoln County jail and forced an entrance after a short resistance by the authorities and took two of the prisoners, Green McCoy and Milton Haley, and hung them to a tree a short distance from the jail building. Haley and McCoy, natives of Kentucky, and are allied to the McCoy faction of outlaws whose murderous feud with the Hatfields is generally familiar to the public. McCoy was engaged in a shooting scrape with Paris Brumfield about a year ago and about a month ago he, in company with Haley, ambushed and attempted to murder Brumfield and his wife. The shooting occurred on Sunday night and both victims were badly wounded. Mrs. Brumfield was shot in the breast and her husband in the leg. For a time it was thought that the woman would die, but she finally recovered. McCoy and Hatfield escaped to Kentucky but not before they had made two more attempts at assassination in the county, in one of which a man named Adkins was wounded.

The two would-be murderers were arrested at Ben post office, Martin County, Ky, and were confined in jail there. Friday they were locked up in the Lincoln County, West Virginia, jail and in the absence of definite information it is supposed they were lynched by some of the Hatfield sympathizers. (Maury Democrat, 31 Oct. 1889.)

McCOY. Two weeks ago four guerrillas, who have been stealing and doing acts of violence in Maury County, had a quarrel among themselves at Mt. Pleasant about the division of some stolen property. The quarrel ended in a fight in which three of them were killed and the fourth mortally wounded. Two of them were brothers named McCoy from Lewis County. The gratified citizens petitioned Col. McCoy stationed there to fire joy guns on the result. (Nashville Daily Union, 22 April 1865.)

McCRAY, Dick, was killed on the 7th, 8 miles from Lebanon; run over by wagon and instantly killed. (Memphis Avalanche, 19 Dec. 1866.)

McCRAY, Samuel, who came here as a member of a Minnesota regiment, ran a candy store, took opium and died. (Nashville Republican Banner, 21 March 1868.)

McCREA, Mrs. Sallie, wife of Hugh McCrea, commission merchant of Nashville, died in Nashville on the 17th. (Whig and Tribune, 27 Jan. 1872.)

McCREADY, William C., the actor, died recently; born 3 March 1793 in London and made his debut in 1810 as Romeo. (Nashville Dispatch, 26 July 1863.) William Macready, the painter, and not the actor, died recently. (Nashville Dispatch, 29 July 1863.)

McCRORY, Mrs. Elizabeth Mahaley, born 28 Oct. 1801 in Davidson County, died 15 May 1886 in Columbia, Tennessee; married at 15 to Abner Potts and they had 10 children, four of whom survive; she married secondly to Thomas McCrory and they had no children. She was a pioneer in Mississippi and Tennessee; 40 years ago joined church in Mississippi. (Maury Democrat, 20 May 1886.)

McCRORY, Martha Douglas, 5 years 3 months, daughter of J. C. and Emma J. McCrory, died yesterday. (Nashville Daily Union, 11 Nov. 1862.)

256

McCUE, ___, rebel prisoner in jail at St. Joseph, Missouri, was killed by a guard on the 4th. The prisoner fired a pistol at the guard, who returned fireby blowing out his brains. (Nashville Dispatch, 12 Aug. 1862.)

McCullough, John, 3rd East Tennessee Cavalry, fell off his horse and drowned in the Cumberland River. (Nashville Daily Union, 23 June 1863.)

McCULLOCH, Ben, his body has arrived at Austin, Texas, where it was interred. (Nashville Dispatch, 11 May 1862.)

McCURDY, Macy, who had taken oath, was shot in throat and left a naked corpse in road by guerrillas under Captains Witherspoon and Davenport on the 18th at Stevenson, Alabama. (Nashville Daily Union, 21 Feb. 1865.)

McDANIEL, George, well known to Company A, 2d Tennessee Volunteers, CSA, died Tuesday of flux at his home in Rutherford County. (Memphis Daily Appeal, 24 Jan. 1870.)

McDANIEL, Captain James M., about 50, veteran printer and writer, died in Nashville on the 12th inst. (Whig and Tribune, 21 Oct. 1871.)

McDANIEL, J. W., old citizen of Rutherford County, died of heart disease last week. (Whig and Tribune, 14 Dec. 1872.)

McDANIELS, an old convict at the Nashville prison, had his head smashed in by fellow convict and died a few days ago. (Erin Review, 17 Dec. 1881.)

McDONALD, A. W., died yesterday of consumption, age 70; for 15 years had been keeper of the suspension bridge. (Nashville Republican Banner, 25 June 1870.)

McDONALD, F. H., Company C, 23d Tennessee, prisoner of war, died at the general hospital in Paducah between April 12 and April 19. (Nashville Dispatch, 7 Aug. 1862.)

McDONALD, James, 60, died yesterday, funeral to be held at Cathedral. (Nashville Union and American, 23 August 1874.)

McDONALD, Mrs. Mary O., funeral to be held 15 Jan. 1864; lived on Fatherland Street at Edgefield. (Nashville Daily Union, 15 Jan. 1864.)

McDONOUGH, J. P., formerly city marshall, was killed by William Scruggs of near Beech Grove, Coffee County, during a drinking session in Murfreesboro, he had fired the first shot at Scruggs. (Whig and Tribune, Jackson, Tn, 14 Dec. 1872.)

McDOUGAL, George, the man who killed Col. Faulkner of the 12th Kentucky in 1865 at Dresden, was killed at Pierce's Station, Weakley County, a few days ago. (Memphis Daily Appeal, 25 March 1869.)

McDOUGLASS, Joseph, 47, of Jasper, Pike County, Ohio, was killed by Morgan's Raiders. He was in a canoe facing Capt. Mitchell and his two men, and they fired at him, one shot hit below the right eye, and the other in the left breast near the heart; he died immediately; wife and five children survive; happened in July. (Nashville Daily Union, 22 Aug. 1863.)

McDOWELL, Dr. Joseph N., one of the distinguished surgeons of the west, who lived in St. Louis for 28 years, died on the 26th inst. of congestive chill, age 63; Dr. M. will be remembered by all the survivors of the Army of Tennessee, as he was identified with it from the commencement till the close of the war. (Memphis Daily Appeal, 28 Sept. 1868.)

McELROY, Mr., 85, had stroke Wednesday, paralyzed all over, and died; had boarded several years with N. J. Vaughan. (Columbia Herald and Mail, 16 Nov. 1877.)

McEWEN, Major John L., has been living at his present house near Franklin, Tn, since the 16th day of March 1798, more than 78 years, and he is now in his 80th year. (Nashville Union and American, 5 Juen 1874.)

McFADDEN, James, 96, died October 6, in District 9, Marshall County; born in South Carolina in 1780 and came here 50 years ago. (Columbia Herald and Mail, 27 Oct. 1876.)

McFADDEN, Miss Peggy, 80, District 14, Maury County, died last week. Columbia Herald, 18 Aug. 1871.)

McFADDEN, Sidney E., sues Robert McFadden for divorce in Henry County. (The Sentinel, Paris, Tn, 20 Aug. 1858.)

McFALL, James of Gallatin, died recently of pneumonia; aggravated from wound received in the war. (Nashville Union and American, 3 March 1873.)

McFARLAND, Mrs. Winny, 69 years 6 months, died April 30 in Nashville. (Nashville Dispatch, 1 May 1863.)

McFARLAND, Lon. There was an attempt to assassinate Lon McFarland, legislative candidate from Wilson County. Two bullets were fired at him as he was mounting his horse. One shot hit his watch, which saved him. The assassin escaped. (Daily Herald, Columbia, Tn, 5 Aug. 1900.)

McFERRIN, James W., Company C, 2d Tennessee Infantry, was killed in a railroad accident near Birmingham on the 16th; body sent to Nashville for burial. (Free Press, Murfreesboro, 19 Nov. 1880.)

McFERRIN, William, son of John C. McFerrin, formerly of Nashville, was killed in Louisville last Saturday night by William Buck Newton. (Nashville Daily Union, 3 March 1864.)

McGAUGHRAN, James, died on the 8th. (Nashville Dispatch, 9 Sept. 1863.)

McGAUN, A., of Alexandria, Tn, a dangerous guerrilla, was killed at Snow Hill near Liberty, Tn. (Nashville Dispatch, 16 June 1863.)

McGAVOCK, Caroline Eliza, wife of Dr. D. T. McGavock, funeral to be held today. (Nashville Daily Union, 8 Dec. 1863.)

Heirs of Mrs. Caroline R. McGavock versus Miss Louisa A. Pugsley: in 1862 Dr. Pugsley made a will leaving all the remainder of his estate to his wife Eliza to be used during her lifetime and for support of two daughters, Caroline E. (who married Dr. David T. McGavock) and Louisa and at his wife's death the estate was to be divided equally. Mrs. Pugsley made a will in 1867 and left every-thing to Louisa. (Nashville Republican Banner, 3 Dec. 1869.)

McGAVOCK, Colonel Frank, died on the 23d at his residence near Nash-ville on the Harding Pike. (Memphis Avalanche, 28 Dec. 1866.)

McGAVOCK, Mrs. Frank, 66, died yesterday; lived in District 12; sister of General W. G. Harding. (Nashville Union and American, 25 Oct. 1873.)

McGAVOCK, James L., between 18 and 20, was killed by Jeff M. DeGraf-fenreid Sunday in a fight; DeGraffenreid fled. (Nashville Republican Banner, 1 June 1869.)

McGAVOCK, Mary Mengam, wife of Dr. F. Grundy McGavock, died June 8
at the Gayoso House in Memphis; was of Shawnee Village, Mississippi
County, Arkansas. (Nashville Dispatch, 26 June 1862.) Mary Manoah
McGavock, died in Memphis, wife of F. Grundy McGavock. (Nashville
Dispatch, 27 June 1862.)

McGAVOCK, Colonel Randall W., of the 10th Tennessee, CSA, was killed
in the fight at or near Raymond, Mississippi, on the 14th. (Nashville
Dispatch, 18 May 1863.) Randall W. M. McGavock was killed as reported; the fatal shot is said to have passed through his heart. (Nashville Dispatch, 20 June 1863.)

McGAW, Miss Margarette Eliza, 57, died 15 June 1891 of cancer; born
17 Jan. 1835 near Zion, buried Rose Hill Cemetery in Columbia; sister
of James C. McGaw. (Columbia Herald, 19 June 1891)

McGEE, John, died of hemorrhage of lungs at the depot yesterday; native
of Canada. (Nashville Republican Banner, 22 June 1869.)

McGee, John, private, Company I, 5th Tennessee Cavalry was killed 22
Feb. 1864 on Calf Killer near Sparta, Tn. (Nashville Daily Union,
24 Feb. 1864.)

McGEE, Mrs. Mary, 86, died of consumption yesterday at home on South
College Street. (Nashville Republican Banner, 23 Nov. 1867.)

McGILL, ___, age 35, lived at Carter's Creek on the Nashville & Decatur
Railroad, smothered to death Tuesday night; was drunk; covered head
with a blanket and shortly smothered to death; finely educated;
taught school. (Nashville Republican Banner, 29 Oct. 1869.)

McGILL, John D., died suddenly last Thursday; before the war taught
school on Bear Creek near the Sulphur Spring and after the war on
Carter's Creek; served in 48th Tennessee Infantry, CSA. Native
of Chambersburg, Pa. (Columbia Herald, 29 Oct. 1869.) (See entry
before.

McGILL, R. P. Miles, infant son of Mr. and Mrs. J. H. McGill, died
on the 9th. (Nashville Dispatch, 10 Oct. 1862.)

McGIMSEY, Dr. J. W. P., died 24 Dec. 1874 near Baton Rouge, La.,
formerly of Columbia. (Columbia Herald and Mail, 22 Jan. 1875.)

McGINNIS, George W., arrested May 1869 at Bush Arbor Church, DeSoto
County, Mississippi, and not heard from since; arrested by Dr. F. T.
Payne, who said he stole hogs; carried to Short Creek Swamp and not
heard of any more. (Memphis Daily Appeal, 2 Feb. 1870.)

McGLAUGHERTY, George, of Nashville, while under the influence, was
run over by the switch engine in Nashville Sunday and killed.
(Whig and Tribune, 8 Nov. 1873.)

McGREW, William G., of Giles Cointy, violated the laws of war by
robbery and sentenced to 25 years in prison by military commission
at Pulaski. (Nashville Daily Union, 25 May 1865.)

McGREW, Mrs., of Pulaski, died Monday of injuries received by a fall
during the cold weather some weeks ago. (Nashville Union and
American, 11 Feb. 1873.)

McGuire, child of Mr. and Mrs. R. J. McGuire died recently in Newark,
New Jersey, and brought to Columbia for burial; mother was formerly
Miss Mary Ruttle. (Maury Democrat, 4 July 1895.)

McGUIRE, Dr., of Fayetteville, cut a bullet from the right arm of
Dr. G. D. Buckner that he had carried 33 years. He was shot in a
cavalry engagement at Morristown, Tn, October 1864. The bullet went
in near shoulder and worked down to the elbow where it rested on a

nerve. It was a large bullet weighing an ounce and considerably flattened by hitting the bone. (Columbia Herald, 15 June 1897.)

McINTOSH, Lt., and Lt. Hogden, both killed in Custer fight with Indians, were both young and promising Georgians and recent grad-uates of West Point, and were both still beardless boys. (Columbia Herald and Mail, 28 July 1876.)

McINTOSH. Thirty-three years ago James McIntosh and Samuel Johnson, members of Company A, Second Regiment, stood side by side, in the beginning of one of the hottest engagements of the Civil War.

In the thickest of the fight, when thousands of bullets whistled through the air and clouds of smoke curled over the Blue and Gray, Johnson dropped his gun and took to the woods. McIntosh kept up a fire at the enemy, 'till a stray ball shattered his right arm, and a cannon ball took off his left leg below the knee. He was carried off the field apparently dying, but he finally recovered and at the close of the war he returned home.

He never saw or heard of Johnson, the deserter, until yesterday when they met on Church Street in Nashville near the Nicholson Hotel. McIntosh at once recognized the deserter. They both wore Confederate badges.

"Is your name Johnson?"
"Yes."
"Thought so. Thirty-three years ago we were members of Company A Second regiment. In the thickest of that famous battle, you dropped your gun and deserted your post. You have no right to wear that badge. No more right than the Yankee across the street there."

McIntosh snatched the badge from the lapel of Johnson's coat and put it in his pocket and hobbled off on his crutches to the dis-comfiture of Johnson. (Columbia Herald, 2 July 1897.)

McKAE, William, W. B. Sloon, and Pat Lynch, three old citizens of Vicksburg, Mississippi, died recently. (Memphis Daily Appeal, 3 Aug. 1869.)

McKAY, Alexander, 94, of Carter's Creek, Maury County, died on the 22d; born in South Carolina; came here 60 years ago; lived on Carter's Creek for 45 years. (Columbia Herald, 29 July 1870.)

McKAY, Mary Jane, 3 years 9 months 10 days, died on 16th; daughter of Felix G. and Jane W. McKay. (Nashville Daily Gazette, 18 Sept. 1852.)

McKEE, Ed, Williamson County horse thief, was killed and another one named Benjamin Knight is in jail at Athens, Alabama. (Whig and Tribune, Jackson, Tn, 2 Sept. 1871.)

McKEE, Miss Lizzie, and an infant of Mr. and Mrs. Whit Harris were buried May 19 at cemetery on Carter's Creek. (Columbia Herald, 5 June 1891.)

McKEE, Patrick, well known Irish citizen of Nashville, died Monday last. (Nashville Union and American, 1 April 1873.)

McKELVEY, Dr. P. B., of New Orleans, late medical director of General Dick Taylor's staff, CSA, died at his home on the 8th instant; about 63 years; native of Albany, New York. (Memphis Daily Appeal, 21 Dec. 1869.)

McKENNON, infant son of Mr. and Mrs. Ed McKennon, died near Sawdust Valley, Maury County, Sunday night. (Columbia Herald and Mail, 17 Aug. 1877.)

McKENNY, Aaron, died in Saco, Maine, on the 6th at the age of 102 years 1 month 16 days; had always lived at his birthplace; had never needed a doctor until he was 100. (Free Press, Murfreesboro, 23 April 1880.)

McKENZIE, Alexander, formerly a large slave dealer in Nashville, died in that city last week. (Whig and Tribune, 20 July 1872.)

McKENZIE, Isabella Gay, 11 months, died September 18; daughter of John T. and Josephine McKenzie. (Nashville Dispatch, 19 Sept. 1863.)

MacKENZIE, Robert J., died May 4, youngest son of Robert and Mary V. MacKenzie. (Nashville Republican Banner, 5 May 1870.)

McKENZIE, ___, who perished in the flames of the burning of the Rainbow Hotel in New York, three or four weeks ago, was for many years in the early part of this century the secretary to the Duke of Wellington. (Nashville Dispatch, 4 Sept. 1862.)

McKEON, James, funeral to be today at the Cathedral. (Nashville Union and American, 10 Dec. 1874.)

McKEY, Washington, Esquire, died last week near Roberts Bend. (Columbia Herald and Mail, 8 Oct. 1875.) (N.B. The surname is possibly correctly McKee.)

McKINLEY, Mrs. Elizabeth, wife of Justice John McKinley of the U. S. Supreme Court, died 11 Feb. 1891 in Louisville on her 91st birthday; she was a long time resident of Florence, Alabama; her husband was licensed to practice law here in 1818; they lived in a large house south of Wallace's School and lower down is the family burying ground, a substantial vault. (Florence, Ala., Times, 21 Feb. 1891.)

McKINLEY, Mrs., mother of the President, was stricken with paralysis the first of the week and has been slowly but surely sinking into an eternal rest. Her death may occur at any moment. The President is with her. (Columbia Herald, 10 Dec. 1897.)

McKINLEY, Mrs. Mary, 40, wife of William McKinley, died on 14 Nov. 1874. (Nashville Union and American, 15 Nov. 1874.)

McKINNEY, Smith, his condition grows grave; he was hit on head by Major Crane, colored, a few days ago and was delirious yesterday. (Nashville Republican Banner, 30 Dec. 1870.) Died yesterday. (Nashville Republican Banner, 31 Dec. 1870.)

McKINNIE, Lucretia, 70, wife of Caleb McKinnie, died on the 6th. (Nashville Republican Banner, 8 Sept. 1870.)

McKINNIE, Martin, died in workhouse yesterday; was put there for stealing some months ago. (Nashville Dispatch, 19 Nov. 1863.)

McKISSACK, Alexander C., 68, buried 28 Sept. 1898 on George B. Peters lot at Elmwood Cemetery, Memphis; brother of Jessie Helen McKissack Peters. (Elmwood Cemetery records has him listed as J. H. McKissack in their records.) Alexander C. McKissick of Holly Springs, Miss., died at the home of his sister, Mrs. Peters, at Gill's Station at 11 o'clock Tuesday night. The funeral took place yesterday at 4 o'clock by Rev. Frederick P. Davenport. The interment was in Elmwood Cemetery; was 69 years of age. (Memphis Commerical Appeal, 29 Sept. 1898.) Alex McKissack, Esquire, of Pulaski, "a gentleman of fine intellect and the ripest scholarship" is spending several days with his brother-in-law Major N. F. Cheairs. (Columbia Herald and Mail, 8 Sept. 1876.)

McKISSACK, Mrs. Eliza B., died at Woodlawn Farm near Spring Hill on August 23, consort of the late Dr. Spivey McKissack, buried Rose Hill, Columbia. (Columbia Herald, 30 Aug. 1872.)

261

McKISSACK, James, becoming suddenly insane attempted to kill his own
child. His mother prevented him, and he struck her on the head and
split her skull, she cannot possibly live. His sister, Miss Tee,
interferred, and he struck her on the head, and penetrated the
brain. Another sister, Mrs. Robert I. Moore, ran in and he made
at her; she caught the hatchet, and it made a terrible wound in her
face. He then took a razor out of his picket and cut his own throat,
severing the windpipe. The McKissack family is well known all over
the county. The terrible tragedy happened yesterday. (Columbia
Herald, 1 Dec. 1871.)

Is He Insane? Tuesday last, James McKissack, a young man of about
28 years of age living at or near Spring Hill in this state went
to the depot accompanied by his father for the purpose of taking
the train for New Orleans. Young McKissack's trunk was put aboard
the train and arrangements for his departure was made, when he
suddenly changed his mind just as the train started and had his
trunk removed.

His father inquired the cause of his strange action, when the son
replied that he had not been furnished with enough money. The old
gentleman said he had quite enough for all his wants when the young
man at once turned upon him and stabbed him, severely inflicting
three wounds in chest and three in the back, one of the cuts barely
missing the heart. The father fell to the ground unable to defend
himself when in answer to the shouts of a negro standing near, a
gentleman ran to the assistance of the wounded man. The son then
started off crying, "Oh, I've killed him, I've killed him."

He had gone but a short distance when he was intercepted by a
brother and taken into custody. He has since been lodged in the
jail at Columbia. Our readers will doubtless recall that young
McKissack made an attempt last summer to kill his mother and sister.
The only explanation which he offered for his strange and unnatural
conduct is that he suffers under temporary fits of derangement.
(Nashville Union and American, 11 April 1873.)

McKISSACK, Booth (Bud), son of O. W. McKissack of Spring Hill, age 18,
died Saturday of dropsy of the brain. (Nashville Union and American
19 Sept. 1873.)

McKISSACK, Robert, 76, died May 30. (Columbia Herald, 6 June 1873.)

McKISSIC, Mrs. Eauris Murphy, died on May 30; husband and child survive.
(Maury Democrat, 13 June 1889.)

McKNIGHT, Major George, known as "Asa Hartz," died in New Orleans on
Feb. 10 on consumption. (Memphis Daily Appeal, 11 Feb. 1869.)

McLAIN, Alice, 23, died May 23. (Nashville Republican Banner, 26 May
1870.)

McLANAHAN, Minnie, sues for divorce from J. Craig McLanahan for inhuman
treatment; has created a sensation in Lawrenceburg as he denies that
they were ever married; he is son of J. K. McLanahan, wealthy iron
man, who lives in Pinkney in Lawrence County. (Florence, Ala.,
Times, 10 Oct. 1891.)

McLAUGHLIN, James, 80, has died in Williamson County; born in North
Carolina; had broken his hip previously. (Nashville Union and
American, 15 Aug. 1873.)

McLAUGHLIN, John, died Sunday morning of congestive chill; funeral at
the Cathedral. (Nashville Union and American, 7 Oct. 1873.)

McLAUGHLIN, Mathew, of Nashville, died Dec. 3 at Hot Springs, Arkansas;
native of County Sligo Ireland. (Nashville Union and American,
4 Dec. 1874.)

McLAUGHLIN, Willie, 3 years 3 months, only child of Thomas and Sarah
McLaughlin, died September 5. (Nashville Union and American, 6
Sept. 1874.)

McLAWS, General Lafayette, oldest surviving Confederate major general,
died in Savannah, Georgia, last Saturday; born 15 Jan. 1821; fought
in Mexican War and was an Indian fighter; assisted in opposing
Sherman's march through Georgia. (Columbia Herald, 30 July 1897.)

McLEAN. We are pained to learn that Mr. Frank McClean, a prominent
and popular lawyer of Columbia, and son-in-law of Granville Pillow,
Esquire, was found last Saturday morning lying on the floor of his
room with his neck broken. It is supposed that he fell from the
bed while asleep. The announcement of the sad event which appeared
in the Press & Times of yesterday was incorrect in every particular
and altogether heartless. (Nashville Republican Banner, 6 August
1867.)

Sue Martin is in town; one of our leading belles and said to look
like Mary Queen of Scots. She was loved by Frank McLean of Kentucky
but married Mr. Martin, and then divorced him. Major McLean had
always remained true to his first love and they were married.
McLean was accidentally killed 1867 and she remarried Martin.
(Columbia Herald, 7 Feb. 1873.)

Romantic Marriage in Maury County. Yesterday at Columbia: the
bride, who belonged to one of the most aristocratic families of
Maury County, married not long before the war broke out, a gentleman,
who was, it is said, more the choice of her family and friends than
her own. Two years afterward she procured a divorce and was united
to a gentleman who was spoken of as her "first love." Then a year
ago the second husband met with an accident which caused his death.
Yesterday she was again married to her first husband after a legal
separation of 7 or 8 years. (Nashville Republican Banner, 11 Dec.
1868.)

Maury County marriage records: 1. 7 Sept. 1853 Hugh Martin married
Susan Amanda Pillow; 2. Frank Jay McLean married 27 Aug. 1860 to
Susan Amanda Martin; 3. Hugh Martin married 10 Dec. 1868 to Mrs.
Sue A. McLean.

McLEMORE, John C., born 1 January 1790 in Orange County, North Carolina
died 20 Feb. 1846 in Memphis; one of the original founders of City
of Memphis and founder of town of Fort Pickering. He purchased
Andrew Jackson's part in the Rice grant on which Memphis now stands.
"John C. McLemore came from North Carolina, was a clerk in the office
of the Land Register and succeeded Robert Searcy as Register. He
was the largest dealer in lands in the State of Tennessee. He was
exeedingly popular throughout the Middle and West Tennessee. After
an eventful career, he finally died in poverty in Memphis, only two
or three years since." (Nashville Republican Banner, 2 July 1869,
quoting an early article by Anson Nelson.) The heirs of John C.
McLemore have filed suit, laying claim to land in most of Memphis.
In 1840 McLemore deeded land to the LaGrange and Memphis Railroad
for a rightaway and the company went insolvent; they claim that
Broadway is not a legal highway. (Maury Democrat, 19 Dec. 1889.)

McLEMORE, Wilbur W., noted character of Memphis, died Thursday at the
home of his guardian Charles McLean in Memphis; he was formerly
wealthy and the son of John C. McLemore, whose property enabled him
to drink himself to death. (Columbia Herald, 17 Jan. 1873.)

McLEMORE, R. A., died Saturday and buried in Rose Hill in Columbia;
brother of W. S. McLemore; his second wife was Rebecca Frierson.
(Columbia Herald, 8 May 1891.)

McLIN, Alexander, 18, son of J. D. McLin, of the Nashville American,
fell through an elevator shaft a distance of 70 feet at the Baxter

Court on the 29th and died on December 30. He was one time reporter on the Nashville Democrat. (Maury Democrat, 2 Jan. 1890.)

McMAHAN, Mrs. Catherine, 103, died October 12 in Greencastle, Indiana; native of County Clare Parish of Kilformey, Ireland; born 11 Nov. 1785; maiden name Flanigan; came to America in 1853 and settled first at New Albany, Indiana, then Dubuque, Iowa, then Bedford, Indiana, and has been in Greencastle since 1863. (Maury Democrat, 18 Oct. 1888.)

McMAHAN, Thomas, city constable, accidentally shot with a revolver and died yesterday morning. (Memphis Avalanche, 3 Jan. 1866.)

McMAHON, Col. Jesse H., will be buried at Calvary Cemetery in Memphis. (Memphis Daily Appeal, 1 Feb. 1869.)

McMAHON, Col. John H., long connected with the press in Tennessee, died recently in Meridian, Mississippi; native of Williamson County and in 1836 was in Florida War. (Nashville Daily Union, 11 April 1863.)

McMAHON, Robert, 16, died last week in Williamson County. (Whig and Tribune, Jackson, Tn, 9 March 1872.)

McMEEN, infant son of W. F. and B. L. McMeen, died March 2; buried at Lasting Hope Cemetery. (Columbia Herald and Mail, 8 March 1878.)

McMINN, Robert, brakeman on Nashville and Decatur Railroad, fell from the top of the train near Harris Station and died of his injuries Monday. (Nashville Republican Banner, 14 June 1870.)

McMURRAY, Mrs., who died of cholera during its prevalence here, did not use the water out of Hackberry Spring. (Nashville Union and American, 19 Aug. 1873.)

McMULLEN. A few days ago a human skull was found near Milboro, Virginia, with a bullet hole in center of the forehead and near the skull was an old pair of shoes and the barrel of a rifle; the stock of the rifle had rotten away. It is believed to be the remains of John McMullen, who left his home in 1857 or 1858, and had never been heard of since. He was supposed to have committed suicide. (Memphis Avalanche, 17 Dec. 1868.)

McNAIRY, Alexander Duval. A Ghost by Daylight - The residents in and around Burn's Post Office in the county of Dickson, are greatly wrought up over the appearance in broad daylight of a mysterious visitor or apparition. The following is a statement made by a Mr. Terrell, who saw the strange spector, and it is reliably vouched for.

"I have visited the haunted spot and seen the ghost. The place where the apparition is most frequently seen is in a sag just beyond the noted McNairy Cut, about a mile east of Burn's Station on the Nashville, Chattanooga & St. Louis Railroad. It was in the forenoon when I approached the spot, walking quietly, and concealed myself where I could have a good view of the headless mystery, should it materialize.

"I had not long to wait until the apparition made its debut to my vision, and I know I was not the least excited when I saw the ghost moving along the railroad tract about 200 yards distant. It did not seem to move with any object in view, nor did it apparently make any progress in its travel, yet it looked to be moving all the time. It was in the form of a large, chuffy man, and it was plainly visible that the object had no head; aside from this it appeared a perfect man.

"Taking my tourist's glasses from my pocket, the headless monster was apparently brought within ten feet of me, as I beheld it moving

McNAIRY, Alexander Duval - Continued
aimlessly about--a man without a head. The bleeding neck appeared
as if it had been severed with a sword, while the arteries and
veins constantly blubbered and spurted blood-stained foam. I
removed the glasses and the ghost was where I first saw it. I
turned to flee, but hesitated, and then determined to go to it.

"As I approached, it neither came forward nor retreated, it
vanished completely. I returned to my first place and saw it as
before. Then several men came up the track, and I heard their
story, unmixed with my own, and it corresponded with mine. They
had seen the object also.

"I do not believe that any living mortal can explain the presence
of the mysterious human body. McNairy Cut has been haunted for
years. It was here that, during the late war, the noted bushwhacker, McNairy, committed many bloody deeds. Two trains collided
here and the engineer, named Johnson, was caught between the
engines and his body scalded and cut from his lower limbs, and
lifted from the roasting pyre, only in time to die, by Dr. Anderson.
It was here, also, that an unknown negro was murdered a short while
ago.

"I confess I do not believe in ghosts, but it may be that away
down in the silent depths of nature where mortality ceases and
immortality begins there is a power that reflects back to mother
earth the image of deeds that have angered and defied the just-
loving God of the universe." (Columbia Herald, 8 Dec. 1893.)

(N.B. Alexander Duval McNairy of Nashville commanded a company of
independent scouts which operated between the Cumberland and
Tennessee rivers from 1862 until 1865, and he was considered the
terror of the Federal Army. His gang specialized, or so it seems,
in harrarssment of the railroad workers. On 18 Oct. 1864, the
track repairers were captured by McNairy and his men somewhere on
the railroad between White Bluff and Sneedsville (now Dickson).
Three days later the bushwhackers burned nearly all the dwellings
and workers' huts along the railroad near here.)

McNAIRY, Colonel Frank, was killed at Fort Donelson. (Nashville
Dispatch, 6 Feb. 1863.) It was pretty generally believed in the
city yesterday that Col. Frank McNairy was killed in the attack on
Fort Donelson on the 3d. It is reported that Colonel Coffee was
also killed. (Nashville Dispatch, 8 Feb. 1863.)

McNAIRY, Henry Clay, 32, was accidentally killed at Guntersville,
Alabama, on the 28th; he was returning home from New Orleans with
his aged mother and a young lady friend. (Nashville Dispatch, 8
Aug. 1862.) Henry Clay McNairy went to visit his sister Mrs.
Goodrich in New Orleans; a shell exploded in the hotel at Guntersville where they were staying, during a skirmish. His body was so
mangled he only lived 25 minutes. (Nashville Dispatch, 14 Aug.
1862.) H. C. McNairy was the youngest son of Dr. Boyd and Ann
McNairy; born 9 Nov. 1828 in Nashville; also killed on July 25 with
him was Mrs. Rayburn, wife of the hotel keeper. (Nashville Dispatch,
23 Aug. 1862.)

McNAIRY, Mrs., widow of late Nat. McNairy, mother of Col. H. C. McNairy,
died in Nashville suddenly a few days ago. (Whig and Tribune, 8 Feb.
1873.)

McNAIRY, Mary Frank, daughter of Colonel R. C. McNairy, died of
cholera yesterday. (Nashville Union and American, 22 June 1873.)

McNAIRY, W. H., 59, died in Nashville on the 14th of paralysis;
formerly a druggist. (Whig and Tribune, 22 Feb. 1873.) W. H.
McNairy died in West Nashville yesterday; stricken with paralysis
Tuesday last; was long a druggist here. (Nashville Union and
American, 15 Feb. 1873.)

M'NEAL, Lt., CSA, was shot and killed a few days since near Savannah by one of his own pickets who mistook him for a Federal officer. (Nashville Dispatch, 25 April 1862.)

McNEWSON, John, blacksmith, and an old respected citizen of Nashville, died Tuesday morning in the workhouse and was buried the same day. He was admitted as a pauper in December and rheumatism had caused the loss of the use of his limbs. His wife is living in Cincinnati. (Nashville Dispatch, 2 April 1863.)

McNISH, Thomas, was buried yesterday. (Nashville Republican Banner, 3 Jan. 1869.)

McNISH. A negro woman belonging to Mrs. McNish of Davidson County died 9 March 1863, age 109 years; born in Fauquier County, Va.; had always served in the McNish family and had nursed four or five generations; could recall events of the Revolution. (Nashville Dispatch, 12 March 1863.)

McNUTT, James, committed suicide last Saturday; remains taken to Franklin for burial; aged about 50; wife and four children survive; for last three weeks had been in a state of depression; shot himself through back of the head; was one of nine brothers, eight of whom died of tuberculosis; recently inherited considerable property. (Nashville Union and American, 30 June 1874.)

McNUTT, Rev. Samuel H., deceased, sale of his property to be held by executor. (Nashville Republican Banner, 13 Jan. 1870.)

McPHAIL, Dr., surgeon of 1st Regiment of Tennessee Volunteers, died 6 July 1846 at encampment on Rio Grande. (Tennessee Democrat, Columbia, Tn, 23 July 1846.)

McPHERSON, Richard, son of Wiley, was recently killed by a log he was cutting on a hillside rolling on him; lived on South Harpeth in Williamson County. (Whig and Tribune, 5 Oct. 1872.)

McQUIDDY, Mrs. Ida, who died in Visala, California, a few days ago, was married a year ago to W. R. McQuiddy, son of Thomas J. McQuiddy and had recently moved from near Normandy, Bedford County, to California. She was daughter of Mrs. E. C. Putnam of Manchester and granddaughter of Col. A. W. Putnam, deceased, of Nashville. (Nashville Union and American, 9 May 1874.)

McQUIDDY, G. W., died 14 May 1864, lived No. 8 Spruce Street. (Nashville Daily Union, 15 May 1864.)

McRAE, James Nelson, died on the 3d, son of D. McRae and Morgiana Nelson, age 1 year 11 months. (Nashville Republican Banner, 4 July 1868.)

McRADY, Ephraim W., 72, died at his home in Columbia on August 13. (Whig and Tribune, 24 Aug. 1872.) Ephraim McRady, oldest and most worthy citizen of Columbia, died one mile from Columbia; age 72; lived here over 50 years; Presbyterian; one son and one daughter survive; daughter lived in Texas and son Joseph A. McRady lives in Marshall County; on city council; buried Greenwood Cemetery. (Columbia Herald, 16 Aug. 1872.) J. A. McRady, a prominent citizen of Marshall County, is dangerously ill. He is a brother-in-law of Mr. F. J. Ewing, who, with Mr. Robert Ewing, are at his bedside. (Columbia Herald, 9 August 1895.)

McRADY, Miss Mabel, only child of Mr. and Mrs. J. E. McRady of Lewisburg, age 16, died at Belmont College in Nashville after a few days illness on October 7. (Columbia Herald, 18 Oct. 1895.)

McRADY, Bill, and Margaret Dunnington, colored, have been living together several years and have seven children, the oldest a girl

McRADY, Bill - Continued
of 17 or 18. Bill became blind and Margaret strayed. She listened
to the "serpentine pleadings" of Israel Franklin, at one time a
lieutenant of the negro Loyal League Military company. She and
Israel rented a house and began to live together until one night last
week they were visited by negroes in disguise, who told her to go
back to her husband. Israel escaped out of a window. The next day
Israel and the woman were at the depot with their clothes ready to
leave. The blind husband swore out a warrant for Israel, but
Israel escaped. Margaret did not go back to her husband and vows
she will get out of town soon. Bill has a little son, the only one
of his children that adheres to him in adversity. (Columbia Herald,
7 July 1871.)

McRUNNELLS, William, 1st Regiment Texas Rangers, was murdered in
Richmond on the 15th ult. (Nashville Dispatch, 3 May 1862.)

McSPADEN, Daniel, colored, blacksmith of Huntingdon, fell out of bed
and was found dead recently. (Nashville Union and American, 24 Aug.
1873.)

McSWINE, ___, was murdered some time ago in Coffeeville, Mississippi.
A "masked cavalry" hanged the two negro murderers in Coffeeville.
The Loyal Leaguers had threatened to rescue the murderers so masked
men went to jail at midnight and got them out and hanged them.
(Memphis Daily Appeal, 5 Aug. 1868.) A deaf and dumb negro, an
important witness in the McSwine murder case, was murdered on the
3d by Loyal Leaguers. A few nights later a band of men in masks
took McSwine murderers out of jail at Coffeeville and hanged them.
(Memphis Daily Appeal, 18 Aug. 1868.)

McWHINNEY, Helena, daughter of William Jenkins and Wife of William
McWhinney, age 26, died 28 June 1865; lived on the Porter Pike.
(Nashville Daily Union, 29 June 1865.)

McWHIRTER, Eddie, 6, youngest son of Capt. A. J. and Lizzie McWhirter,
died 13 Dec. 1862 of brain fever. (Nashville Daily Union, 14 Dec.
1862.)

NAGLE, General, committed suicide recently in New York; notorious
for his espousal of Ireland's liberation; born Niagara County, New
York, 21 Sept. 1828; enlisted as a private in 88th New York Regiment
of Irish Brigade and commanded it. (Memphis Daily Appeal, 20 Aug.
1869.)

NAIRY, Thomas, sentenced to be hanged in June for the murder of Pat
Carney. (Nashville Dispatch, 19 April 1863.)

NANCE, Mrs. Fannie, died Saturday at Sandy Hook, Maury County; husband
and two children survive; buried at Hunters. (Maury Democrat,
5 April 1894.)

NANCE, Thomas V., died Thursday at Santa Fe, Maury County; cut the end
of his finger while dressing a rabbit, got blood poisoning.
(Columbia Herald, 30 Jan. 1891.)

NAPIER, Colonel, next in command to Forrest has been killed. (Nashville
Dispatch, 8 Jan. 1863.) The rebel Colonel Napier was killed.
(Nashville Dispatch, 4 Jan. 1863.)

From the Tennessee River - A quartermaster the other day in traveling alone from Fort Donelson to Fort Henry in turning a short
curve in the road, was suddenly confronted by three of Napier's
guerrillas, with shot guns cocked, and ordered to surrender, and
seeing that it was, probably, the best thing he could do, he complied
and was taken some 40 miles to the rebel camp, where they took his
horse, equipments, and all the money he had, except three five

NAPIER, Colonel - Continued
   dollar treasury notes, which they pronounced worthless; and then,
   after relieving him of his overcoat, and other clothing that they
   judged he could do without, they allowed him to depart.

   The camps are overrun with negroes of all sorts, size, and ages,
   and this is the case at Forts Henry, Heiman, and Donelson. Almost
   without an exception, they have left good homes, where they had
   food, rainment and shelter, only to find that liberty to them is
   nothing at present, but destitution of all three of these, and
   worse degredation than they ever experienced in bondage. And the
   officers are so trameled by the orders now in force, that they
   cannot restore these poor, deluded and suffering creatures to their
   owners, where they would be made more comfortable, and the service
   be relieved of a burden. (Nashville Dispatch, 25 Nov. 1862.)

   Tombstone inscription, Wyly Cemetery, Waverly, Tn; Colonel T. A.
   Napier, 10th Tennessee Cavalry, born 2 October 1837, killed at
   Franklin Cross Roads, 31 December 1862. (N.B. The stone is in
   error, he was killed at Parker Cross Roads instead. His full name
   was Thomas Alonzo Napier.)

NAPIER, Mrs. R. S., of Johnsonville, was among those who died in the
   past 24 hours in Nashville of cholera. (Nashville Union and
   American, 28 June 1873.)

NAPIER, E. T. of Union Springs, Alabama, was killed recently while
   riding with a brother, and they stopped at a roadside; the horse ran
   out from under him, fell against a tree and he was killed.
   (Memphis Avalanche, 15 Nov. 1866.)

NAPIER, infant of Mr. E. W. Napier, died Friday at home of aunt Mrs.
   T. C. Sowell; buried in Rose Hill Cemetery by its mother. (Columbia
   Herald, 3 July 1891.) Dr. W. J. Bunch of Arkansas came to attend
   the burial of his sister Mrs. Napier in Columbia last week.
   (Columbia Herald, 8 May 1891.)

NAPIER, William. The library of the late William Napier is being sold;
   there are several hundred of the finest bound English standard
   works in this library, which is valued at $7,000. (Nashville
   Republican Banner, 9 Sept. 1868.) The Honorable William Napier's
   library was sold for $2,500. (Nashville Republican Banner,
   11 Sept. 1868.)

NAPIER, W. C., who died of paralysis at Napier's Furnace, Lewis County,
   was brought to Rose Hill Cemetery, Columbia, for burial; age 78,
   "had been helpless" for some time; made his home with son Elias
   Napier. (Maury Democrat, 7 August 1890.) Mr. Napier, father of
   Willis Napier, died 30 July 1890 at Napier's Furnace at the age of
   78. (Maury Democrat, 31 July 1890.) Napier's Furnace was completed
   1860 and in full operation before the war. Since the war, it has
   been idle in consequence of Col. W. C. Napier's lack of funds.
   (Columbia Herald, 12 July 1872.)

NAPIER, Mrs. E. W., 29, died 25 April 1891 of heart disease. (Maury
   Democrat, _ May 1893.) E. W. Napier has offered to donate land
   at Napier for a courthouse if the Lewis County Courthouse is moved
   from Newburgh. (Maury Democrat, 28 May 1891.)

NAPIER, Mrs. Leroy, died recently in Lewis County. Mrs. Napier like
   her lamented husband was a staunch advocate of the Southern Confederacy and during the trying days of the unhappy war her home was
   often the resort of Rebel soldier boys who always met with a warm
   welcome and open-hearted hospitality. She is survived by four
   children. (Maury Democrat, 29 May 1890.) On November 30, 1863,
   the Federals captured James Dale and Ed Frierson, soldiers of
   Columbia, William Martin, and ex-sheriff Dick Monroe and Leroy
   Napier of Lewis County; they were in jail in Pulaski for ten days.
   (Confederate Veteran Magazine, Volume 5, page 215.)

NAPIER. Runaway - in jail on the first put in Williamson County jail,
George, 40, very dark, stout, belonging to R. C. Napier. (Western
Weekly Review, Franklin, Tn, 20 Sept. 1833.)

Col. Richard Napier was an officer in the Revolutionary army, having
himself raised and equipped a regiment which he commanded. In
return for his services rendered their country, he and his two
brothers, Patrick and Thomas, received each 1,000 acres of land in
Georgia or Kentucky. They preferred the former, but Col. Napier
caring not for the sandhills around Augusta, Ga., where his entry
was made, later came to the Cumberland country, bringing with him
his wife and children, 100 negroes, carriage and wagons. He arrived
in Nashville and settled "across the Cumberland" in 1791, but
moved to Dickson County on Barton's Creek soon after and here built
the first brick house erected in Middle Tennessee. The old structure remains standing and is in fair state of preservation, being
occupied by Allen Elliott, a substantial farmer of Barton's creek
and his family.

Col. Napier was born in Washington, NC, in 1747, and his death
occurred in this state in 1823. He was the father of Richard C.
Napier II, whose exploits in the early history of the iron industry
for this county is outstanding. Richard C. II owned and operated
the Carroll Furnace on Barton's Creek, the properties being located
almost directly in front of what is now the farm residence of James
Jackson. Plain marks of the furnace grounds are yet visible.
Carroll Furnace ceased operations several years prior to the Civil
War. Richard C., the iron industrialist, was buried in the old city
cemetery in Nashville, the tomb being near that of Gen. James
Robertson. Col. Richard Napier was distinguished from his son in
legal procedure by omitting the initial C., which was invariably
added to the signature of the iron manufacturer, Richard C. Napier.
(Dickson County Herald, 16 Oct. 1931.)

NASH, Anne Hawkins, implores the public for information on her mother
Mrs. Arabella Nash, who formerly lived in Florida not far from
Thomasville, Georgia. After the surrender of Atlanta, her mother
and four sisters went north and she heard that they were seen in
Nashville. (Nashville Daily Union, 23 April 1865.)

NATHURST, John Theophilus, infant son of Mr. and Mrs. E. O. Nathurst,
died on the 26th. (Nashville Dispatch, 27 May 1863.)

NATHURST, Eliza Sophie, daughter of Mr. and Mrs. E. O. Nathurst, 3
years 3 months, died on the 26th. (Nashville Dispatch, 28 May
1863.)

NEAL, John T., of Tennessee, late counsul of the United States to
Kingston, Jamaica, died at that place. (Nashville Daily Union,
24 Feb. 1863.)

NEAL, Josephine B., wife of W. Z. Neal, died 31 March 1865 in Lebanon.
(Nashville Daily Union, 5 April 1865.)

NEALIS, The Rev. John Thomas, former Catholic Archbishop, of Ohio for
the last year or so pastor of a church at Chattanooga, has just
died in that place from the effects of wounds inflicted on him by
party of three ruffians who waylaid him on the public highway and
cruelly beat him, then shot him with a revolver. He lingered a
month in great agony when death ended his sufferings. (Nashville
Daily Union, 5 Feb. 1863.)

NEALIS, Rev. John Thomas, 34, fell from window of bedroom accidentally
on 19 March 1864; born in New York; ordained 8 years ago in Perry
County, Ohio; funeral to be held at the Cathedral in Nashville
on Summer Street. (Nashville Daily Union, 20 March 1864. N.B.
See the obituary before; although the names are the same and they
were both Catholic priests, there must have been two men by the
same name or one of the obituaries was in error.)

NEATHERY, James M., deceased, his estate is insolvent. (Columbia Herald and Mail, 15 June 1877.)

NEBLETT, S. M., 40, died 15 Dec. 1859 at his home in Humphreys County of consumption; formerly of Montgomery County. (Clarksville Weekly Chronicle, Dec. 1859.)

NEBLETT, Sterling N., 3 months 19 days, son of George P. and Mary B. Neblett, died 11 Oct. 1861 in Humphreys County. (Clarksville Weekly Chronicle, __ Oct. 1861.)

NEELAN, Mr., well known over Maury County, as a peddler of fine linen goods, died in his store house at Bailey Switch on one of the coldest nights of the cold spell. He was a kind-hearted man. (Columbia Herald and Mail, 19 Jan. 1877.)

NEELY, Mrs. Elizabeth, died in Columbia on Thursday. (Columbia Herald and Mail, 16 April 1875.)

NEELY. In the spring of 1865, a son of Mrs. Neely, who resides near Okolona, Miss., was accidently drowned in the Tallahatchie River. A few days subsequent his body was recovered from the water and buried. His mother being desirous of removing his remains, proceeded a short time since to bring them home. Upon opening the grave the coffin was discovered to be in a decayed condition, and the body seemed to be in a perfect state of preservation. The features were perfectly natural, and the mother was permitted once more to look upon the features of her son.

The remains were placed in a new coffin, prepared for the occasion, and brought over the dirt road. On their arrival, and, before reinterment, a wish was expressed on the part of relatives and friends of the deceased, to have the coffin re-opened.

The mother objected on the ground that the manner of transporting the remains doubtless had a tendency to disfigure them, but she finally yielded her consent that the friends of the deceased might open the coffin.

When this was done, the face of the corpse presented a bare skeleton-the flesh being dry as dust had fallen off. (Memphis Avalanche, 12 Dec. 1866.)

NEELY, Mr. and Mrs. A. E., celebrated their 50th wedding anniversary yesterday on South Garden Street; they were married 2 Sept. 1851 near Williamsport. He is 71, and she will be 71 on September 17. They had seven children; Mrs. J. F. Kerr, deceased; Thomas S. Neely; Mary E. Neely; Mrs. W. R. Craig; John S. Neely; Mrs. Thomas A. Dugger; Mrs. John W. Wilson. John B. Wilkins is a brother of Mrs. Neely. (Daily Herald, 3 Sept. 1901.) The home of Elijah Neely on South Garden Street was burglarized last night. (Daily Herald, Columbia, Tn, 22 Nov. 1901.)

Coffins, Common and Fine - Mr. Boyd of Lamb & Boyd being in the army as Ordnance Sergeant of the 2nd Tennessee, the factory was run by Mr. Lamb as opportunity offered and as material could be obtained. Much of the work done on the coffins for the soldiers who had died here in hospitals or who were killed in the various skirmishes about Columbia. These coffins were generally made by Mr. Elijah Neely, who tells me that when lumber was scarce he often made them of old house partitions and even weatherboarding plank; and finally made them all of one size, 6 feet long, with plain swell sides and a top. Of course, there were many fine coffins made, as the old account book now in my possession will show, notably those for General Van Dorn, Lieut. Wills Gould, Generals Pat Cleburne, Granberry, Strahl and many other officers and citizens. (Columbia Herald, 26 Sept. 1904.)

NEELY, Mr. and Mrs. A. E. - Continued
At the January 1908 meeting of the Maury County Historical Society,
Capt. R. D. Smith read the paper for the evening, concluding his
biography of Gen. P. B. Cleburne. The article dealt with the
search for the general's body on the battlefield of Franklin and
how from the mistaken information of an escaped Confederate prisoner
the search had been stopped; the finding of the body and laying
it out on the back porch of the McGavock house, every room being
filled with wounded soldiers; the bringing of the remains to Columbia
to Mrs. Dr. Polk's (where the Elks home is now), the walnut casket
made by Elijah Neelley, who is yet a cabinetmaker here; the funeral
services by Rev. C. T. Quintard, afterwards Bishop of Tennessee; the
mistake in burying among the Federal soldiers at Rose Hill and the
second burial a few days later at Ashwood with so many other
Confederate officers who had fallen at Franklin; the removal of
the remains to Helena, Arkansas, in April 1870, and the honors paid
here and at Memphis; the dedication of the monument at Helena in
1891, these and other facts and incidents were all told in graphic
detail by the author. (Daily Herald, Columbia, Tn, 15 Jan. 1908.)

NEELY, Dr. Phil P., died about the 10th in Mobile, Ala.; Methodist
    minister. (Memphis Daily Appeal, 14 Nov. 1868.) Mrs. Henrietta
    Neeley, wife of the Rev. P. P. Neeley, died in Columbia, Tn, on
    the 6th instant. (The Christian Record, 20 March 1847.)

NEGLEY, General, arrested A. O. P. Nicholson and Colonel Joseph
    Branch, avowed Confederate sympathizers, on the 29th ult. (Nashville
    Dispatch, 13 Aug. 1862.)

General Negley Dead - The Florence Herald says; After an illness
of four days, Major General James S. Negley died last Friday at
his home in Plainfield, New Jersey, at the age of 75 years. Death
was due to complication of diseases.

General Negley was born at East Liberty, Pa., on 22 Dec. 1826. He
was graduated from the Western University of Pennsylvania, and at
the age of 19 ran away from home and, in spite of the protests of
his family, enlisted in the Mexican War, serving under General
Winfield Scott in the battles of Cerro Gordo, La Porta, Las Vegas,
and Puebla.

At the breaking out of the Civil War he organized a brigade and
joined the command of Major General Robert Patterson, being placed
in command of a military camp. At the battle of Stones River he
was rewarded for his distinguished services by being made a major
general. He was honorably discharged from the army 19 Jan. 1865.

General Negley then returned to Pittsburg and entered politics
as a Republican. He was subsequently elected to the 41st and 42nd
Congress from the 22d Congressional District of Pennsylvania.

General Negley was the first Union general that entered Florence,
Ala., and is remembered by many of the older citizens for his kind
and considerate treatment of our people. General Negley was a
cousin of Major A. G. Negley of this city. Florence Herald.

General Negley will be well remembered by the older citizens of
Columbia. During the Civil War he held Columbia for several months
he fortified Mt. Parnassus. He was here at the time Jackson
College was burned and was to have been a witness for the Masons
in their claim before Congress to recover $50,000 from the Govern-
ment for the burning of the school, it being alleged that it was
set afire by the troops under him, although without his knowledge
or consent. (Columbia Herald, 23 Aug. 1901.)

Everyone who lived in Maury County during the Civil War recollects
General James Negley and his acts of oppression. (Columbia Herald
and Mail, 12 Oct. 1877.)

271

NEIL, Mary, Irish woman, living in New York was arrested on the 17th for the death of her three year old child by seating it on a hot shovel. This was a rest to see if it were her child or not. She said fairies were in her house and that meant a fairy child had been changed for it in the cradle. She set it on the red hot shovel because a fairy child would fly away. The child was burned so bad it died in a week. Her husband Mathias Neil did not know about it. He thinks she is insane. (Nashville Dispatch, 26 March 1863.)

NELLINS, Mrs., has been granted a divorce from her husband by the Pennsylvania legislature. She claimed her husband was drunk when they married and stuck out his tongue during the ceremony and never lived with his wife. Cause enough. (Nashville Daily Union, 12 March 1863.)

NELSON, J. E., of Memphis was brutally murdered 28 Oct. 1866. (Memphis Avalanche, 3 Nov. 1866.)

NELSON, James John, infant son of Adolph and Elvina Nelson died yesterday in Nashville. (Nashville Daily Union, 9 June 1865.)

NELSON, Brigadier General Jeff C. Davis will be brought before court-martial for killing Major General William Nelson in Louisville. (Nashville Dispatch, 9 Oct. 1862.) General Nelson's remains are to be interred at Camp Dick Robinson. (Nashville Dispatch, 10 Oct. 1862.) Jeff C. Davis has been indicted for manslaughter for killing General Nelson. (Nashville Dispatch, 4 Nov. 1862.) The 17th is the day fixed by the Kentucky General Assembly for the burial of the late General Nelson at Camp Dick Robinson. His remains will be moved from Louisville on June 14 and thence to the camp. (Nashville Dispatch, 5 June 1863.)

How Nelson's men crossed Duck River on the way to Shiloh. General William Nelson commanded the Fourth Division of Buell's Army. He had been a naval officer, and his tyranny and harshness caused his men to dislike him at first. But as the march southward took the troops into the enemy's country, the soldierly perceptions and instincts of the old general as well as his stern sense of duty and pride in his command, won for him respect, and a strange sort of feeling that was almost affection.

Nelson was a strict disciplinarian, and always moved, or went into camp, or left camp, as if in the presence of the enemy. He super-intended early every morning the formation of line of battle, was on his horse at the first bugle-blast, and rode down the line like a hurricane, expecting every man, officer as well as private, to be in his place, and ready for duty. Men under this training, became unconsciously alert, and emphatic in action. It was a standing joke that Nelson's division could "tumble out" quicker than any other. Nelson was particular and exacting as to little things which seemed trifling until the men realized in their first battle that all had constituted a part of their training for battle.

The realization that their commander had seen with clearer vision than they, and that he had compelled them to do what was best, caused the men to turn with rare trust to the Old Stormer, and to become rather proud of his oddities and his obtrusive individuality. He was a thorough soldier, and was terribly in earnest, and they knew it.

On the march southward from Nashville, Buell's advance was delayed by the destruction of the bridge across Duck River. Nelson fretted under the delay, protested against it, and finally volunteered to put his division across without a bridge, if he were allowed the advance. Permission was given for him to cross, and he issued one of the queerest military orders on record.

This was read to the troops in the morning, and was in substance like this: The men will march to the river, fix bayonets and stack

NELSON, Brigadier General - Continued
arms. They will then take off their pants, blouses and accoutre-
ments, putting all in a bundle which will be placed on the bayonets
and will then take arms, and with bundles on bayonets as ordered,
will wade the river in their shirts and drawers. Officers will
see that there is no confusion, and that on reaching the farther
bank, the men dress quickly and march rapidly forward to restore
the circulation.

Imagine the looks of 8,000 or 10,000 men as this order was read
to them on a cool bright spring morning. They marched down to the
river; they undressed to their shirts; and in view of the entire
population of Columbia, men, women and children, they with cheers
and shouts and jokes, and laughs, plunged into the cold water. The
scene was ludicrous in the extreme; but in not very many hours the
entire division was marching southward. It kept the advance during
the interval between that date and the battle of Shiloh...Had his
men not waded Duck River in their shirts, Buell's Army would not
have been within call to turn the tide at Shiloh. (Columbia Herald
and Mail, 21 April 1876.)

NELSON, Lizzie Grady, infant daughter of Mr. and Mrs. H. A. Nelson,
9 months, died yesterday. (Nashville Republican Banner, 22 July
1870.)

NELSON, Marie, 68, died. (Nashville Republican Banner, 30 May 1868.)

NELSON, Mrs. E. A., has died on consumption at her brother's in Albany,
Athens County, Ohio. (Nashville Union and American, 29 July 1874.)

NELSON, W. Oscar, son of P. H. Nelson of Columbia, died July 27 of
typhoid in Corsicana, Texas. (Columbia Herald and Mail, 13 Aug.
1875.)

NESBITT, Robert N., 42, Esquire, one of the oldest born citizens of
Somerville, Tn, died on the 15th at Somerville; his father Nathan
Nesbitt was one of the first settlers and kept the first hotel
here. He was born 26 Sept. 1826 and his father died when he was
an infant and his mother died a few years later. He is survived
by wife and two children. (Memphis Avalanche, 25 Oct. 1867.)

NEWCOMB, Dr. T. A., died early Sunday of inflammation of the lungs
and heart; last male of his name in Hickman County; lived on
Leatherwood Creek. (Columbia Herald and Mail, 10 Sept. 1875.)

NEWCOMB, William, died June 24 of cholera in Hickman County; caught
the disease in Nashville; several in his family are ill. Business
has suspended at Shady Grove. (Columbia Herald and Mail, 4 July
1873.)

NEWMAN, E. W., died at the Confederate Soldiers Home from wound
received in the war; enlisted in the 10th Tennessee Irish Regiment
and transferred to Wright's Artillery; age 66 at his death; born
in London, England. (Maury Democrat, 13 April 1893.)

NEWMAN, J. C., M.D. died 9 Sept. 1870; member of the Pale Faces.
(Nashville Republican Banner, 11 Sept. 1870.)
NEWMAN, John E., deceased; year's support for wife made. (Nashville
Republican Banner, 15 Dec. 1867.)

NEWMAN, Miss Leah, funeral to be held today (Nashville Republican
Banner, 13 Jan. 1871.)

NEWMAN, Price, rebel from Louisville, was killed in battle April 6 at
Shiloh. (Nashville Dispatch, 15 April 1862.)

NEWMAN, Tazewell W., died on the 2d at Winchester, Tn, from protracted
illness; was Speaker of the Tennessee Senate from 1860 to 1861,

273

colonel of 17th Confederate Regiment during the war; eldest son of
Jacob Newman; born in Knoxville. (Memphis Daily Appeal, 9 Oct. 1868.)

NEWSOM, A. B., died at Gallatin, Tn, August 6 of pneumonia, lived in
Hartsville; born 1838; Confederate soldier; had served in both
houses of the General Assembly. (Maury Democrat, Columbia, Tn,
15 Aug. 1895.)

NEWSOM, Dr. Bellefield C., 21, died on the 16th. (Nashville Republican
Banner, 19 May 1868.) Dr. Belafield Carter Newsom, only son of
late Colonel James E. Newsom, nephew of Dr. W. J. Carter, practiced
at Belleview Station, was murdered by one Phipps. (Nashville
Republican Banner, 24 May 1868.)

NEWSOM, Colonel James E., died near Big Harpeth, Williamson County;
he was born within a mile of his residence; age 59; was manufacturer
of the famous Newsom whiskey; died of inflammation of the brain;
wife and four children survive; had brother Joseph M. Newsom.
(Nashville Dispatch, 5 August 1863.) Colonel James Newsom died on
2 August 1863 on Harpeth in Davidson County of inflammation of the
brain. (Nashville Dispatch, 1 Sept. 1863.)

NEWSOME, Dr. B. C., was murdered on the 16th by Bob Phipps; Governor
Brownlow has offered $250 reward for Phipps. (Nashville Republican
Banner, 29 May 1868.)

NEWTON. A Confederate soldier died near the residence of E. Clower
near Raymond, Mississippi, on 6 Dec. 1863 and was buried by his
comrades in arms on Mr. Clower's plantation. The grave still stands
with this inscription: Died, A. L. Newton, Company C, 28th
Mississippi, 6 Dec. 1863. (Memphis Daily Appeal, 24 May 1870.)

NEWTON, Eliza, infant daughter of N. A. and Hannah C. Newton, 3 months
3 days, died 20 Feb. 1865 in Nashville. Binghampton, NY, paper
please copy. (Nashville Daily Union, 21 Feb. 1865.)

NEYLAN, the only child, a son of D. N. Neylan, died yesterday.
(Nashville Union and American, 23 Feb. 1873.)

NICHOL, Alexander, son of Mr. and Mrs. F. R. Nichol, funeral to be
held this morning. (Nashville Daily Union, 14 March 1863.)

NICHOL, Eva Bradford, infant, died yesterday; daughter of B. F. and
Maggie Nichol. (Nashville Republican Banner, 5 Oct. 1867.)

NICHOL, Ellen Lewis, little daughter of C. A. and Nannie W. Nichol,
died August 1. (Nashville Union and American, 5 Aug. 1874.)

NICHOL, James B., funeral was held last Sunday. (Nashville Republican
Banner, 29 Dec. 1868.)

NICHOL, William, died yesterday from the effects of having his leg
amputated 23 July 1864; was captain in 11th Tennessee Regiment.
(Nashville Republican Banner, 3 July 1869.) W. C. Nichol, funeral
to be held today. (Nashville Republican Banner, 3 July 1869.)

NICHOLS, Benjamin, of Guilford, Massachusetts, committed suicide a
few days ago by cutting his throat; had made two attempts previously;
he believed he was coming to want although he was in good pecuniary
circumstances. (Nashville Dispatch, 25 May 1862.)

NICHOLS, Governor Francis T., of Louisiana, lost a leg and arm and
an eye; he lost the leg at Chancellorsville; and the arm was
carried away by a cannon ball at Winchester. (Maury Democrat, 20
Nov. 1890.)

NICHOLS, John, of Missouri, was tried and found guilty at Jefferson
City of being a guerrilla and sentenced to be hanged. (Nashville
Dispatch, 1 Oct. 1863.)

NICHOLS, Theo, of Greenfield Bend, Hickman County, drowned on the 10th in Duck River, his mule became frightened; body was found near Gordon's Ferry; one hundred people had hunted his body for three days; age 20. (Maury Democrat, 25 May 1893.)

NICHOLSON, C. H., 73, died last Sunday at Lawrenceburg; brother of A. O. P. Nicholson; buried in cemetery at Lawrenceburg. (Columbia Herald and Mail, 30 Nov. 1877.)

NICHOLSON, Mrs., venerable widow of Cordy Nicholson, aunt of the Chief Justice, died at her home in Williamson County last week from a fall from a buggy; was 80 years old. (Whig and Tribune, Jackson, Tn, 9 Sept. 1871.) Mrs. Cordy Nicholson, 80, fell and broke hip or three weeks ago and is in great suffering; her husband was one of the early settlers of Williamson County; mother of Isaac Nicholson of the Nicholson House in Nashville. (Columbia Herald, 18 Aug. 1871.)

NICHOLSON, George G., funeral to be held today. (Nashville Republican Banner, 13 Dec. 1868.) Will of George G. Nicholson is being probated. (Nashville Republican Banner, 21 March 1869.)

NICHOLSON, infant daughter of H. M. and Emma Nicholson is to be buried this morning. (Nashville Republican Banner, 1 April 1870.)

NICHOLSON, J. M., justice of the peace in District 24 of Maury County was born 24 Jan. 1841; served in Company B, 24th Infantry, CSA, and later in the cavalry; married Henrietta Hardison. (Maury Democrat, 18 July 1895.)

NICHOLSON, Joseph P., 2, died June 9. (Columbia Herald, 12 June 1891.)

NICHOLSON, Osborn, died at his home in West End on Thursday at an advanced age; son of the late A. O. P. Nicholson; had lived in Texas for several years; buried Rose Hill Cemetery. (Maury Democrat, 25 Oct. 1894.)

NICHOLSON, Patrick, 45, Irishman, found dead last night; "end of a career of dissipation;" "On a drunk for two months;" unmarried. (Nashville Republican Banner, 14 Nov. 1867.)

NICHOLSON, Samuel, 32, died. (Nashville Republican Banner, 31 May 1868.)

NICKS, Colonel A. T., died suddenly 4 miles south of Fayetteville last Friday; before the war was postmaster at Fayetteville; register of the county since the war. (Nashville Union and American, 24 Aug. 1873.)

NINDE, Miss Clarinda G., youngest daughter of late James and Catherine Ninde of Baltimore, died in Nashville; to be buried in family vault in St. Paul's Cemetery, Baltimore. (Nashville Republican Banner, 12 May 1869.)

NIXON, Colonel J. O., of the New Orleans Crescent, has suffered a number of afflictions lately. His sister Mrs. Parks died on steamer at Davenport, Iowa, and he took her remains to New Orleans. On arriving there, he learned that an uncle, aunt, and two cousins on the way home from New York, went down on the ill-fated steamer the Evening Star and another cousin died of congestion of the brain. (Memphis Avalanche, 9 Nov. 1866.)

NIXON, Travis Henry, chairman pro tem for the county court in 1894, was born 19 Nov. 1841 near Mt. Pleasant, married 1880 Mildred Akin; served in Barnes Company, 9th Tennessee Regiment; member of Maury County court. (Maury Democrat, 6 June 1895.)

NOAH, Major J. J., of St. Paul, after serving in Federal Army more than one year was arrested and sent to the penitentiary at Jeffersonville,

Indiana, and confined with convicts and felons. Then he was
released if he would go to New York and stay; was discharged.
(Nashville Dispatch, 11 Jan. 1863.) J. J. Noah has been appointed
Supervisor for Tennessee; was opposed by Arnell, Brownlow, Stokes
and Company. (Memphis Daily Appeal, 15 Nov. 1868.)

NOAH, J. J.,Esquire, request to the military authorities at Columbia,
Tn, that they vacate the courthouse building at said place and
deliver the same to the civil authorities for the transaction of
public business and the preservation of the public records of Maury
County. (Maury County Circuit Court Minutes, 1862-Jan. 1866, entry
dated 5 Sept. 1865, page 205. Noah was head of the radicals in
Maury County after the Civil War; had been sent here as he was
supposed to be a personal friend of General Grant.)

NOBLES, Mrs. Ellen, of Washington, D.C., widow has died, age 120 years;
born in Maryland; died of apoplexy. (Maury Democrat, 30 Aug. 1888.)

NOLAN, Honorable James N., a prominent Tennessean, died at his home
in Waverly last Saturday. (Columbia Herald, 3 Sept. 1897.)

NOLAN, John T., was murdered 30 Sept. 1887 at Shiloh, Montgomery County.
(Houston County News, 7 Oct. 1887.)

NOLAN, Mrs. Katherine, of Hillsboro, Illinois, who is just now in
bed with a broken leg, was born of Wickslow, Ireland, on Christmas
morning, 112 years ago, before the Treaty of Paris had been signed
or Washington elected President of the United States. (Maury
Democrat, 9 Aug. 1894.)

NOONAN, Peter, died of sunstroke at Memphis on the 20th. (Erin Review,
7 Aug. 1886.)

NORMAN, A. J., who lived 9 miles from Franklin on the Hillsboro Pike,
was killed on the 19th by guerrillas. (Nashville Daily Union, 21
June 1865.) J. Norman of Williamson County was killed by guerrillas
a few days ago when at work in a field. (Nashville Daily Union, 27
June 1865.)

NORMAN, James is dead at Augusta, Houston County, Texas; he claimed
to have been born 1783, and remembered the Battle of New Orleans.
(Daily Herald, Columbia, Tn, 17 Jan. 1900.)

NORMAN, Mrs. Martha, deceased; estate insolvent. (Maury Democrat,
13 Sept. 1894.)

NORRIS, ___, fatally stabbed Sunday near the brewery on Stones River
Pike by W. F. Morris; both had been drinking; he was disemboweled;
Morris, about 25, was from Georgia; Norris, an old man, was from
Wilson County. (Nashville Republican Banner, 7 July 1868.) Norris
stabbed near Spring Water Brewery, still survives, but only expected
to live a few more days. (Nashville Republican Banner, 9 July 1868.)

NORTH, Jennie Bell, daughter of Lyman C. and Susan A. North, age 6
years 8 months 3 days, died July 13. (Nashville Republican Banner,
14 July 1870.)

NORTHERN, Samuel, 81, died in Williamson County on the 15th on the
Hillsboro Pike a few months ago; he and his aged wife celebrated
their golden wedding in the same house and same room in which they
were married 50 years ago. (Whig and Tribune, 25 Nov. 1871.)

NORVELL, Henry L., old and respected citizen, 57, died on the 11th;
lived on Franklin Pike; son of Moses Norvell and was born 28 Feb.
1818 in Nashville. (Nashville Union and American, 12 Sept. 1874,
13 Sept. 1874.)

NORVELL, infant daughter of G. F. and N. J. Norvell, died 26 Dec. 1863
at farm home 2 1/2 miles out on Murfreesboro Pike. (Nashville
Daily Union, 28 Dec. 1863.)

NORVELL. A Dastardly Deed - On Thursday night last, some guerrillas
came to Thomas Norvell's at dark, a good Union citizen of Simpson
County, Ky, and reported that they belonged to the command of Major
Cropsey of the Federals at Richland Station, Sumner County, Tn, and
entered the house and said, "You are the man that shoots at Southern
soldiers," and shot him through the right arm, above the elbow, and
seized him violently and carried him about 13 miles into Robertson
County, Tn, just below Price's Mill, and killed him by stabbing
him 11 times in the breast, and belly, and four times through and
through; then cut his neck from ear to ear through the bone and left
a little to hold the head on the body, and split down the right ear
with a great gash, and cut the skin on top of the head across and
pulled it down, and broke the skull to get a trophy, and took out
some, if not all the brains, and dragged him down a rocky cliff
and put a rock on the waist of his pantaloons and threw him into
Red River, where he was found Friday last by some fishermen and
soon identified to be Mr. Norvell. The word soon came, and the
Federal soldiers at Richland went and brought him home, and he was
buried on Monday. He leaves a good wife and two children--one
smart little girl and the other a baby--to mourn his untimely end.
The country is robbed of one of her best friends. Oh! humanity;
say how long shall these thieves and prowling villians be tolerated.
No family is safe at home. Oh! God, rid the country of them
speedily. (Signed) A Citizen. (Nashville Daily Union, 30 April
1863.)

NOTGRASS, baby, 16 months of Mr. and Mrs. H. Notgrass died at Godwin
of meningitis. (Maury Democrat, 24 Oct. 1895.)

NUETZEL, Lorenz, 51, died 18 April 1870. (Memphis Daily Appeal, 19
April 1870.)

NUNNELLEE, Mrs. Mary A., of Centerville, Hickman County, is drawing
a pension as a widow of a Revolutionary War soldier. (Columbia
Herald and Mail, 16 Jan. 1874.)

NUNNELLEE, Dr. J. A., died near Centerville the other day. (Columbia
Herald and Mail, 28 Aug. 1874.)

NUNNELLY, Dr. T. J., formerly of Williamsport, died recently in
Missouri. (Columbia Herald and Mail, 29 Jan. 1875.)

OAKES, David T., was suddenly killed at Ferguson & Griffith's planing
mill last Tuesday and was buried yesterday at the City Cemetery
by the Odd Fellows; nothing was known about his family. (Nashville
Union and American, 22 May 1874.)

OAKES, John F., Company L, 5th Tennessee Cavalry, was killed 22 Feb.
1864 on Calf Killer near Sparta, Tn. (Nashville Daily Union,
24 Feb. 1864.)

OAKLEY, Mrs. Elizabeth Oliver, has celebrated her 82d birthday.
(Maury Democrat, 23 April 1896.)

OATHS. The Provost Marshal at Murfreesboro has administered the
amnesty oath to: James M. King, Mary A. Burton, John S. Fletcher,
James M. Brown, William Lane, R. D. Jamison, Charles H. King,
James M. King, Jr., Mordecai Lillard, John W. Acuff, Hardy Murfree,
Thomas M. King, Elisha R. Vaughn, Joseph G. Putnam, Rufus L. Vaughn,
John E. Dromgoole, John Putnam, Caleb A. Robinson.
(Murfreesboro Monitor, 9 Sept. 1865.)

OBANNION. On the evening of 24 December 1862, near Cuba in Shelby
County, James Obannion was mortally wounded by gunshot wound in the
left breast. Previous to this time Obannion had made violent
threats to take the life of Edward Bartlett on sight. His reason
being that Bartlett was a G_d d_n Union man. Bartlett was arrested
for the crime after the war and his trial was held at the January
term in 1867.

At this time it was brought out that on one occasion prior to the
shooting, Obannion had gone to Barlett's home, accompanied by one
of his comrades in arms, and his avowed purpose for the visit was
to kill Bartlett. Bartlett greatly feared his life would be taken
and fled from his home, seeking refuge in a canebrake.

Obannion at the age of 18 or 19 had joined the Confederate army in
1861, but later deserted and returned within the Federal lines of
occupation and became a guerilla, going armed, and subsisting "on
the peaceable, unoffending citizens of the country." He was
considered a dangerous man. At the time he received his fatal
wound, he and one of his cohorts were on horseback in the public
highway. A gunshot was heard and a short time afterwards Obannion
was found in a dying condition. A person, carrying a gun, was seen
in the distance leaving the scene. Obannion made a dying statement
that Bartlett shot him.

Obannion's companion at the time of the fatal shooting died before
Bartlett's trial for murder, as did another witness, the man who
had delivered Obannion's threats. There were many proofs submitted
to the court, however, which established that Obannion had belonged
to an armed band of guerrillas.

Bartlett's lawyer pleaded self-defense for his client and vowed
that Obannion "was an enemy to mankind and consequently not the
object of murder in any of the degrees recognized by law."

Piracy and robbery at this time were defined as an offense against
the universal law of society and punishable by death. The terms
pirate and robber being convertible and used to denote the same
class of offenders. They were enemies to mankind, and should be
exterminated. (Pamphlet entitled "Argument for Bartlett" in possession of Jill Garrett; privately distributed.)

OBAR, George, killed in railroad accident last week and buried in
Houston County. (Erin Review, 19 Oct. 1878.)

O'BRANNON, Willis, of Columbus, Georgia, died at the home of his son-
in-law Dr. Tuggle Sunday after a fall; age 94 years; as a boy he
had seen and spoken to General Washington. (Memphis Daily Appeal,
11 Nov. 1869.)

O'BRIAN. Negro belonging to General Overton in Davidson County,
sentenced to be hanged on the 20th for murder of his overseer
O'Brian. His wife is also on trial as accessory. (Town Gazette
and Farmers Register, Clarksville, Tn, 21 Nov. 1819.)

O'BRIEN, Fitzjames, late of General Landers' staff, died on the 6th
of lockjaw from wound received in skirmish two months ago; native
of Ireland; came to New York 10 years ago; popular contributor to
eastern magazines and papers. (Nashville Dispatch, 14 April 1862.)

O'BRIEN. One of the queer documents in the office of county judges
is a will on a piece of unpainted plank, 5 feet long, 1 foot wide.
The plank was sawed out of a house of Mrs. Arnold and was part of
wall. On the bed by the wall, a man named John M. O'Brien, whom
Mrs. Arnold befriended, died; but before he died he wrote on the
plank, in pencil, these words: "Mrs. Arnold, God bless her! shall
have all I leave." He left $500. The will is probably the most
unhandy document to file in all Duval County. (Maury Democrat,
6 Dec. 1894. Note - No state given.)

O'BRYAN, James, old and respected resident of Bardstown, Ky, died
Sunday of cholera. (Nashville Daily Gazette, 3 Oct. 1852.)

CHIEF OE-CON-OS-TO-TA, Cherokee chief, lies buried on Major Morgan's
farm at Citico, Morgan County; Major Morgan serves in the 3d
Tennessee. The Indians named their camp for him. (Nashville
Dispatch, 13 May 1862.)

ODEL, Mrs. Minnie, died Sunday at Mt. Pleasant and buried at Thompson
Station. (Columbia Herald, 11 Dec. 1899.)

ODIN, Richard, died 6 April 1867 near Kemper Springs, Mississippi, at
the age of 112 years; born August 1755 in North Carolina; at 19
moved to South Alabama and lived there until he was 90 years old.
His wife, age 107, survives. (Memphis Avalanche, 30 June 1867.)

OFFUTT, Clarence L., born 2 Dec. 1891, died near Lane, Dyer County on
August 3; only child of Paris and Bettie Offutt. (Columbia Herald,
28 Aug. 1896.)

OGDEN, Mrs. Eliza, died of suffocation from excessive corpulence near
Philadelphia, Georgia, on Tuesday; weighed 600 pounds; in her dying
she fell to floor and it took 6 men all they could do to raise her
by the carpet; took 8 or 10 men to get her to first floor; her coffin
was 3 feet wide. (Memphis Daily Appeal, 21 June 1869.)

OGLIVIE, Harry, age 16 youngest son of R. H. Oglivie, died Tuesday;
Methodist. (Columbia Herald and Mail, 25 Jan. 1878.)

O'KANE, Margaret Howard, 30, died 30 Jan. 1864, wife of Andrew A.
O'Kane; lived 103 North College Street. (Nashville Daily Union,
1 Feb. 1864.)

O'KANE, Mary Elizabeth, 20 months, died Wednesday; daughter of Andrew
A. and Margaret O'Kane. (Nashville Daily Union, 20 Feb. 1863.)

OLD BLACK JOE. The original of the song "Old Black Joe" was a native
of Virginia and died this summer at his home in Mt. Holly, New
Jersey, at the age of 112 years. (Maury Democrat, 27 Nov. 1890.)

O'LEARY, Mrs. Catherine, who owned the cow that kicked over the lamp
that caused the fire in Chicago that caused $190 million damage,
died Wednesday, June 30, of pneumonia. (Maury Democrat, 11 July
1895.)

OLEVILL, Philip T., 2 years 9 months, died yesterday; son of Laurence
and Theresa Olevill in Edgefield. (Nashville Republican Banner,
4 Oct. 1868.)

OLIPHANT, Sgt. William C., Company D, 12th Tennessee, prisoner of war,
died at general hospital at Paducah, Ky, between April 12 and April
19. (Nashville Dispatch, 7 Aug. 1862.)

OLIVER, of Hickman County, was going West and sold everything he had.
His mother persuaded him to stay another year and he set out to
buy a horse and he disappeared. A week ago a woman living on a
small branch below Lick Creek, while hunting ginseng, found a
skeleton which has been identified as Oliver. (Columbia Herald, 24
June 1870.)

OLIVETTI, Rev. Michael, Catholic priest, at Port Henry, Essex County,
NY, was murdered on the 10th ultimate near that place; his body
was thrown into Lake Champlain. (Nashville Dispatch, 4 Oct. 1863.)

OLSTON, John, a Confederate soldier, supposed to have been killed at
Murfreesboro, turned up in Nashville last week and found wife wedded
to a Federal soldier and with a new Yankee baby. He threatened her
and has been placed under bond. (Memphis Avalanche, 19 Oct. 1866.)

OLWILL, Mrs. Philip, of Edgefield, died after protracted illness. (Nashville Union and American, 13 June 1873.) Mrs. Olwill's funeral at the Cathedral had one of the largest funeral processions seen in a long time. (Nashville Union and American, 15 June 1873.)

OMO, Mrs. Clara, a woman cowboy, who claimed to have killed five men in her career, is dead at Perry, Oklahoma. (Maury Democrat, 18 March 1897.)

O'NEAL, Isaam, 91, died in Bedford County last month; had six sons living, the youngest being over 40; had been a resident where he died since 1807; Missionary Baptist for 60 years. (Nashville Union and American, 15 Dec. 1872.)

O'NEAL, James, tramp, died Sunday, suddenly in the office of the freight house; said to be of Newburg, New York; buried at the county's expense. (Paris Gazette, 13 Feb. 1878.)

O'NEAL, Michael, 35, died suddenly yesterday; Government employee; native of Cork, Ireland. (Nashville Daily Union, 28 July 1865.)

ORMAN, William, killed at Rally Hill; was shot by Robert Cunningham who fled; about 20 and unmarried; had been drinking. (Columbia Herald and Mail, 9 Jan. 1874.)

ORNE, Edward J., 26, died on the 29th ultimo in New Orleans at the home of D. Galbreath; buried Elmwood Cemetery, Memphis. (Memphis Avalanche, 2 May 1867.)

ORR, James of Marshall County, died on the 13th at the age of 90; lived 4 miles east of Campbell Station. (Columbia Herald and Mail, 20 Oct. 1876.)

ORR, John and Sam Orr, came from Nashville on Thursday and had bodies moved to Nashville for interment; their father, John, died 1860 or 1861; mother; sister Mary, died 1867; and sister Lizzie, died 1868. (Maury Democrat, 2 May 1895.)

ORR, Miss Lizzie, died last Thursday; Dr. Beckett preached her funeral in St. Peter's; buried Rose Hill. (Columbia Herald and Mail, 28 July 1876.)

ORR, Mary, eldest daughter of late John Orr, Esquire, died on December 1. (Columbia Herald, 4 Dec. 1869.)

ORR, William T., one of the publishers of the Nashville Union died on the 28th ultimo in Nashville. (Clarksville Weekly Chronicle, 3 Nov. 1865.)

OSBORNE, Ada, colored, died last week in Williamsport. (Columbia Herald and Mail, 17 Aug. 1877.)

OSBORNE, Henry T., died 11 Jan. 1875 of consumption; born 24 Dec. 1833; was shot in back in 1835 by John P. Campbell and the effects followed him to the grave; sick 8 years; had served in the General Assembly; once read law. (Columbia Herald and Mail, 15 Jan. 1875.)

OSLIN, Capt. John W., formerly of Murfreesboro, in 18th Tennessee Regiment, died at his home in Friendship, Crockett County. (Free Press, Murfreesboro, 3 Feb. 1882.)

OTEY, The Right Reverend James Hervey, D.D., L.L.D., venerable Bishop of Tennessee, died at his home in Memphis April 23; consecrated 1834; his piety, eloquence and learning caused him to occupy a high and honored position in the church. (Nashville Dispatch, 5 May 1863.) St. John's Episcopal Church at Ashwood, Maury County: "The Right Reverend James Hervey Otey lies here. We are told he and Bishop Leonidas Polk made a promise to each other to be buried here."

OTEY - Continued
(Maury Democrat, 21 Sept. 1893) Pilgrimage to St. John's drew large
crowd. - Bishop Maxon told of Bishop Otey who rode away from his
home with his saddle bags swung across his horse, and his wife
called to him that there was no corn meal in the barrel. "The Lord
will provide." he said and rode on his way to establish the Episcopal
Church in Tennessee. (Daily Herald, Columbia, Tn, 27 May 1929.)

OTIS, Dora L., wife of Capt. E. A. Otis, died on t he 29th of congestion in Nashville, age 21 years 3 months; had been here only four
weeks. (Nashville Daily Union, 30 April 1865.)

OTT, William T., 32, died October 28; one of the proprietors of the
Nashville Union in 1862; survived by two sisters in Murfreesboro;
one of the proprietors of the Murfreesboro Monitor; his mother died
near Murfreesboro some months since. (Murfreesboro Monitor, 4 Nov.
1865.)

OTTENVILLE, Alice Idell, 11 years, daughter of F. and S. Ottenville,
died December 2. (Nashville Republican Banner, 4 Dec. 1868.)

OUTLAW, William, Jr., shot and instantly killed last Monday by Henry
W. McNeill near the Stewart County line; McNeill's daughter became
enciente and Outlaw was charged with seduction. (Clarksville
Weekly Chronicle, 20 July 1860.)

OVERALL. "Somehwere in the margin of Columbia rests what is left of
the stalwart body of Rev. Lorenzo Dow Overall. He as a lad walked
20 miles to Windrow Camp Meeting to hear that remarkable preacher,
Rev. Sterling C. Brown, preach; born and reared in Giles County.
He was converted--he himself became a marvelous preacher. In the
summer of 1834 he conducted a far famed revival at Wilkes Camp
Ground near what is now Culleoka. In August 1834 on the 29th he
died of a fever and was buried on the margin of Duck River. He
fell asleep and his body was carried to the grave from the home of
Mr. P. Nelson and no one knows where his grave is." (Maury
Democrat, Columbia, Tn, 9 Feb. 1928.) Died--of Bilious fever on
August 28, Rev. Lorenzo Dow Overall, age 32, in 12th year of his
ministry. On Tuesday morning preached sermon at Wilkes Camp Ground.
Buried at public burying ground. The Rev. Thomas Maddin delivered
the funeral sermon. (Columbia Observer, 19 Sept. 1834.) Tombstone
inscription in Greenwood Cemetery, Columbia, Tn: Rev. Lorenzo
Dow Overall, son of Nathaniel & ___, born Davidson County, Tenn.,
8 Jan. 1805. Born of the spirit 1820, died 28 Aug. 1834. He
devoted 11 years to the itinerant ministry of the Meth. E. Church.
Amiability, firmness, intellectual tenderness and so ___ piety
adorned his character. He was beloved in life, honored in death
but his triumph and his reward glorious.

OVERTON, infant of Mr. and Mrs. W. I. Overton, was buried Sunday at
Thompson Station. (Maury Democrat, 10 Oct. 1895.)

OWEN, Mrs. Catherine, wife of James C. Owen, Esquire, died on the 24th
instant, age 72, near Franklin, had no children of her own.
(Nashville Union and American, 26 Sept. 1874.)

OWEN, Mrs. Elizabeth, 61, died on the 19th at the home of son W. W.
Owen in South Nashville; lived many years in Neely's Bend.
(Nashville Dispatch, 20 May 1862.)

OWEN, Infant of Mr. and Mrs. George Owen, died Wednesday; buried Rose
Hill Cemetery. (Columbia Herald, 28 Dec. 1899.)

OWEN, H. B., clerk of the Metropolitan Police, died yesterday while at
work of hemorrhage of the lung. (Nashville Republican Banner, 2
July 1868. The issue of 3 July 1868 gives his name as H. H. Owen.)

OWENS, John, who lives two miles west of Fulton, Tn, will be 111 years
old on October 15; has son Dr. W. A. Owens. (Memphis Daily Appeal,

19 May 1870.) John Owens of Fulton, Mississippi, is 111 years old. (Memphis Daily Appeal, 12 June 1870.)

OWEN, John E., was shot and killed by his neighbor Mr. Fly in Williamson County. (Nashville Union and American, 4 Nov. 1874.)

OWEN, Mrs. Robert Dale, and Mrs. Richardson, wife of Captain Richardson of the 53d Ohio, were lost on the steamer Acacia. (Nashville Dispatch, 29 Aug. 1862.)

OWEN, Sue, 5 years 6 months, daughter of James E. and Mary V. Owen, died on the 7th. (Nashville Union and American, 8 Nov. 1874.)

OWSLEY, Captain, rebel captain was arrested July 30 in Bowling Green. (Nashville Daily Union, 1 August 1862.)

PAGE, John W., 77, died on the 27th in Cheatham County. (Nashville Republican Banner, 28 Oct. 1868.)

PAGE, Mattie, little daughter of R. H. and Sallie C. Page, died and funeral to be held today. (Nashville Union and American, 14 Aug. 1874.)

PAGE, Minnie, age 3, daughter of N. H. and L. C. Page, died on the 19th at home of grandfather, 12 miles from Nashville. (Nashville Union and American, 21 June 1874.)

PAGE, Mrs. P. T., wife of John J. Page, age 28, died yesterday; daughter of Thomas Hamlet. (Nashville Republican Banner, 4 Nov. 1868.)

PAGEOT, Mrs., died November 18 of pneumonia in the south of France; only daughter and child of late William B. Lewis of Nashville; her husband was formerly French Minister to the United States; her father died a few days before. (Memphis Avalanche, 28 Dec. 1866.)

PALMER, General J. B., last commander of Brown's old Brigade (the 3d, 13th, 33d, 43d Tennessee, CSA), was married in Pulaski on Friday to Mrs. Margaret Mason. (Memphis Daily Appeal, 16 June 1869.)

PALMETER. The last pensioner of the Revolution has been removed from the roll by death and was Mrs. Phoebe M. Palmeter of Brooklyn, New York, daughter of Jonathan Worley. (Maury Democrat, 8 Feb. 1912.)

PASCHALL, Edwin, 70, died Sunday near Triune; native of North Carolina; established academy in Nashville; in 1845 was elected to be the Williamson County representative to the General Assembly; in 1863 was the editor of the Nashville Press. (Nashville Republican Banner, 9 June 1869.)

PASCHAL, Edwin, Jr., committed suicide Tuesday at Kingston Springs by taking morphine; was a teacher at Kingston Springs. (Nashville Republican Banner, 27 Aug. 1868.)

PASTEUR, Professor Louis, eminent bacteriologist, died in Paris Saturday afternoon. (Maury Democrat, 3 Oct. 1895.)

PATRICK, Elijah was killed on his way home to Arkansas at Bolivar. (Central Monitor, Murfreesboro, Tn, 6 Sept. 1834.)

PATRICK, Lorenzo D., 43, died on the 17th at Logansport, Indiana, of erysipelas; formerly of Murfreesboro. (Nashville Daily Union, 24 Nov. 1863.)

PATTEN, Sam, of the 8th Indiana Artillery, died March 6, at the home of Mrs. Davis, 12 miles from Nashville on the Nashville and

Chattanooga Railroad. There had been a railroad accident there on the 4th and Miss Alice Davis requested the wounded be brought in the house--there were 5 wounded in all. He was buried in the Davis family burying ground. (Nashville Daily Union, 10 March 1863.)

PATTERSON, ___, four year old son of man who lived on Rutherford Creek in Maury County, was killed by a wagon wheel on Wednesday; they were going to Bunch's Mill, the wagon became uncoupled and the wheel crushed his head. (Columbia Herald, 17 Dec. 1869.)

PARHAM, F. A., founder and for many years editor of the Chattanooga Gazette, died recently. (Nashville Dispatch, 25 April 1862.)

PARK, Alonza, rural mail carrier, was murdered in Carroll County about two weeks ago. (Clifton Mirror, 8 June 1906.)

PARK, Mrs. Elizabeth, of Columbia, died of lockjaw a few days since; stuck nail in her foot. (Whig and Tribune, 16 Nov. 1872.)

PARK, Mary Ann, wife of Dr. J. S. Park, died on the 21st of inflammation of the stomach at Franklin, Tn. (Nashville Dispatch, 23 Aug. 1863.)

PARK, Samuel, died August 18; died at family residence on Hampshire Pike; of retiring disposition and studious habits and not widely known; taken to Franklin for burial; born 2 August 1839. (Columbia Herald, 21 Aug. 1896.)

PARKER, E. B., private, 5th Kansas, was captured by Morgan near Gallatin and was charged with being a deserter from Bennett's Battalion of Cavalry, found guilty, and sentenced to be executed on the 23d. (Nashville Dispatch, 29 Aug. 1863.)

PARKER, General Ely Samuel, a full-blooded Indian, who was General Grant's secretary at Appomattox, died at Fairfield, Conn., Friday night. He engrossed the first copy of the terms of Lee's surrender. (Maury Democrat, 5 Sept. 1895.)

PARKER, Isham A., Esquire, died in Davidson County. (Tennessee Watchman, Clarksville, Tn, 9 March 1821.)

PARKER, Perry H., 1 year 11 months, infant son of W. D. and Sallie Parker, died on the 13th. (Nashville Republican Banner, 15 Dec. 1867.)

PARKER, Susan, a frail girl, was shot in the back at New Orleans, two months ago by a soldier George White. He said she had insulted him by using disloyal language. She has since died and he is charged with manslaughter. She was a native of Louisville, Ky, young, handsome and respectably connected but of bad character. (Nashville Dispatch, 30 June 1863.)

PARKS, George B., colored, of Atlanta, Georgia, who accompanied by his family went to Liberia last May to try his fortune, has returned; he reports the condition of slavery in Liberia is worse than in Georgia before the war. (Florence, Ala., Times, 19 Sept. 1891.)

PARKS, Thomas, age 108, died Feb. 15 in Marshall County. (Whig and Tribune, Jackson, Tn, 1 March 1873.)

PARR. The remains of Colonel James Parr, gallant Confederate, have arrived in Jackson, arrived on the 10th instant. He was a Northern man by birth, but was killed during the Georgia compaign, fighting on the side of his adopted South. (Memphis Avalanche, 18 Oct. 1866.)

PARRISH, James, accidently drowned Saturday while driving a team across Brown's Creek, wagon upset and his body was caught under it. (Nashville Dispatch, 10 March 1863.)

PARRISH, Mrs. Jane R., wife of W. C. Parrish, age 47, died 6 Jan. 1871 and put in a vault yesterday. (Nashville Republican Banner, 8 Jan. 1871.)

PARROW, William, 42, was killed by Colbert, an Indian student at the Cumberland University. Colbert found guilty of second degree murder, aged about 17 or 18, and 1/8 Indian; lives at Colbert's Ferry on Red River in the Indian Territory. He has been a student for some time. Parrow was well known in Lebanon. (Nashville Republican Banner, 1 Dec. 1870, 2 Dec. 1870.)

PARSONS, J. H., found murdered on April 20 at Turkey Creek, Alabama, about 15 miles west of Birmingham. (Maury Democrat, 24 April 1890.)

PARSTON, Sam, and Cordelia Peirier, will be hanged at Montreal for murder of woman's husband. They will be hanged back to back with only a black curtain between them. (Hohenwald Chronicle, 17 March 1899.)

PARTIAN, Archibald, in the Confederate Soldiers Home, was born 15 Jan. 1803 in Montgomery County, North Carolina; in 1825 came to Wilson County and was postmaster at Lagardo in 1861; enlisted in the 17th Tennessee Regiment; shoemaker. During General Andrew Jackson's time he had a shoe shop at Green Hill, two miles from Hermitage and made for a number of years the shoes and boots the General wore and the boots placed on Jackson's feet when he was buried were made by Partain. He is 6 feet high and weighs 210 pounds. His father died in Wilson County in 1873 at the age of 110 years. (Maury Democrat, 13 April 1893.)

PARTEE, Mrs. J. D., daughter of Mrs. William B. Partee, died on Monday last at her mother's. (Columbia Herald, 19 Aug. 1870.)

PARTINGTON, Thomas, foreman, moulder, died yesterday at City Hospital after a protracted illness; native of Manchester, England; 65 years; buried in the city graveyard. (Nashville Union and American, 22 Aug. 1874.)

PATTERSON, General Bernard M., 79, one of the oldest settlers of Fayette County, died on Friday; was in War of 1812. (Memphis Daily Appeal, 9 May 1870.)

PATTERSON, Dr., an old citizen of Davidson County, was killed in skirmish in an attack on wagon train near the Lunatic Asylum Saturday; he had joined the Confderate Cavalry a few months ago. (Nashville Dispatch, 6 Jan. 1863.)

PATTERSON, Elijah, of Bedford County, was killed by a runaway team he was driving. (Nashville Union and American, 24 Oct. 1874.)

PATTERSON, Hugh K., age 90 years 3 months 13 days, War of 1812 soldier, died in Arkansas; brought back to Hartsville, Trousdale County for burial. (Nashville Union and American, 3 March 1873.)

PATTERSON, Mrs. Isabella, wife of A. Patterson, died April 28. (Nashville Dispatch, 29 April 1863.)

PATTERSON, Mrs. T. M., died near Hartsville, Tn; funeral today in Nashville. (Nashville Republican Banner, 16 March 1871.)

PATTERSON, Martha T., wife of R. S. Patterson, age 36, died on the 20th. (Nashville Dispatch, 21 Nov. 1863.)

PATTERSON, Mrs. Mattie, of Murfreesboro, arrested for treasonable correspondence with the enemy and sentenced to life imprisonment at Jeffersonville, Indiana; her sentence was commuted to three years. (Nashville Dispatch, 12 June 1863.)

PATTERSON, Thomas, deceased; estate is insolvent. (Erin Review, 8 Feb. 1879.)

PATTERSON, William N., died on the 4th of consumption, age 33; brother of Capt. Robert Patterson, chief of the night police. (Nashville Republican Banner, 8 July 1868.)

PATTI, Adelina. Patti's good looks are disappearing. (Memphis Daily Appeal, 8 Dec. 1868.)

Adeline Patti to be in Nashville on January 8. (Maury Democrat, 28 Dec. 1893.)

Adelina Patti has just celebrated her 51st birthday. (Maury Democrat, 15 March 1894.)

Mme. Patti's annual income for some years has not been less than $200,000. (Maury Democrat, 23 Aug. 1894.)

Usually Patti sleeps with a silk scarf around her neck. (Maury Democrat, 7 March 1895.)

Adelina Patti is presenting a farewell concert, gets standing ovation at Tabernacle in Nashville before a large audience. (Daily Herald, 1 Feb. 1904.)

Adelina Patti really made her first appearance before audience at the old Avon Beach hotel at the Beach, Long Island; she was in village with her guardian when Archibald Young arranged a concert for a local charity. The ruins of the old hotel still stand, though sadly injured by fire. (Maury Democrat, 14 Feb. 1895.)

Columbia Discovered Patti. Few are aware of the fact that the great songstress, Adeline Patti, at one time lived in Columbia and sang in concert here in her girlhood at the old Hamner Hall in days long gone by. She had also a brother here at that time by the name of Carlo Patti, who himself too was a musician of much talent. Carlo Patti went out from Columbia into the Confederate army, joining Company B, 2nd Tennessee Regiment--this being the same company in which Mr. Robert L. Farris, present foreman of the Democrat, belonged. Mr. Farris says he has often heard Patti sing here.

Carlo Patti's name appears plainly at this time on the roster of Company B, now posted on the wall in the Democrat office. People can now account for Adeline's "extraordinaryness"--she having been discovered by Columbia, making her entree upon the lyric stage on South Main Street, the hall at that time being situated about where Angie Samuels' business house now stands. It will also be discovered by carefully reading the announcement elsewhere in this issue of her appearance in Nashville, that it will be necessary for the Columbia young man to discover $12.00 to pay for a pair of select seats for himself and sweetheart, in order that he and she may hear the melodious voice of the now world famed songstress on January 8th. (Maury Democrat, 28 Dec. 1893.)

The Carlo Patti Troupe will perform at Hamners Hall tomorrow evening at 7 o'clock...Carlo Patti is a brother of the celebrated contatrice Mlle Patti. (Maury Press, Columbia, Tn, 4 April 1861. Note, there is a similar advertisement in the issue of 21 Nov. 1860.)

Carlo Patti, brother of the great Prima Donna, Adelina Patti, was a member of the Maury Rifles. (Columbia Herald and Mail, 13 August 1875.)

285

PATTI, Adelina - Continued
Carlo Patti is in concert in Montgomery, Alabama. (Memphis Avalanche,
26 May 1867.)

Patti's brother plays the violin in an ice cream saloon in New
Orleans for $15 a week, a very ignoble position for the brother of
a marchioness. (Memphis Daily Appeal, 16 Sept. 1868.)

J. Herstein, photographer of Nashville, was living in Columbia in
1860 and 1861 when Adelina Patti came here with a troupe and
appeared in concert. Barilli and Gottschalk were in the troupe and
Gottschalk was her brother-in-law, having married Carlotta Patti.
Adelina was 16 or 17 and her singing made little impression.

Soon after Carlo Patti came here from New Orleans where he had been
leader of an orchestra, gave a concert, had no money, and stayed
several months at the Franklin Hotel at Mr. Herstein's expense;
Carlo was for some time a member of the 2d Tennessee Regiment
which he joined in Columbia. (Maury Democrat, 8 Feb. 1894.)

Carlo Patti's remains are to be removed from St. Louis to Paris,
France, to be interred in the family mausoleum in Perela-Chaise.
He led the Grand Opera House orchestra, was in Columbia when the
Civil War broke out, and joined the Maury Rifles, commanded by
Capt. John G. Anderson and remained with the company until after
Shiloh when he was detailed by Beauregard as a member of the Signal
Corps. (Columbia Herald, 3 April 1874.)

PATTISON, Reuben K., died December 24 from injuries received in an
accident and frightful shock to the nervous system by an explosion
of a rocket and long exposure of the body to the bitter cold
weather and great loss of blood. (Memphis Avalanche, 27 Dec.
1868.) Reuben Pattison, son of Col. George Pattison, was wounded
on Thursday and died on Friday, was shot and mangled by a sky
rocket; instead of the rocket going up, it went across the street
and up in air; members of the 154 Confederates turned out en masse
for his funeral. (Memphis Daily Appeal, 28 Dec. 1868.)

PATTON, George, an old citizen of Columbia, dropped down suddenly and
clasped both hands to his head and died before the doctor reached
him a day or two ago. (Nashville Republican Banner, 27 March 1870.)

PATTON, Jason T., deceased, of Williamson County, left legacies of
land and $12,000 to the Methodist Church. (Nashville Union and
American, 21 Nov. 1874.)

PATTON, Martha Jane, 2 months, one of twins, died July 28 of cholera
infantum; daughter of N. A. and N. A. V. Patton of Mt. Pleasant.
(Columbia Herald and Mail, 6 Aug. 1875.)

PATTON, R. M., died on Friday morning. (Nashville Republican Banner,
17 Sept. 1870.) R. H. Patton, funeral to be held Sunday. (Nashville
Republican Banner, 18 Sept. 1870.)

PATTON. Bennet Dooly of Abbeville District, supposed murderer of
William Patton, was found not guilty; self defense; trial was held
in Marion County, Tn. (Western Weekly Review, Franklin, Tn, 29
Nov. 1833.)

PAUL, Brigadier General, killed in fight near Gettysburg. (Nashville
Dispatch, 4 July 1863.)

PAYNE, Anna, daughter of Mrs. Olivia Payne, died on the 7th at Bellevue.
(Nashville Dispatch, 8 Aug. 1862.)

PAYNE, Dr. J. B., died recently in Tipton County; gallant soldier;
gave his whole time and fortune to the Confederacy. (Maury
Democrat, 13 Aug. 1891.)

PAYNE, Mr., an old Texan, died recently in Denton County, Texas, at the age of 115 years. (Columbia Herald, 17 March 1871.)

PAYNE, Solomon, one of the oldest citizens of Robertson County, died recently. (Nashville Republican Banner, 20 March 1869.)

PEACH, Emerson Etheridge, 4, died Tuesday of diptheria; son of H. S. and Mary Peach. (Nashville Dispatch, 21 Aug. 1862.)

PEACH, Houston, 5 years 1 month, son of H. S. and Mary Peach of Edge-field died on the 25th. (Nashville Dispatch, 27 Aug. 1862.)

PEARCY, Alice, wife of William Pearcy, a brass founder, was found dead yesterday of intemperance and exposure. (Nashville Union and American, 18 June 1873.)

PEARL, Thomas, 23, died Wednesday. (Nashville Republican Banner, 31 March 1870.)

PEARMAN, William, of Goshen, Indiana, recently eloped with a young woman, leaving a wife and three children to discourse the event at their leisure. (Memphis Avalanche, 31 Dec. 1868.)

PEARSEL, Miss L., died on the 1st in Wilson County, daughter of W. and M. Pearsel. (Nashville Republican Banner, 6 June 1869.)

PEARSON, Mrs. Kate, died August 8 at Macon, Georgia; wife of W. L. Pearson of Nashville. (Nashville Republican Banner, 12 Aug. 1870.)

PEARSON, ___, 8 years, son of Mrs. Sam Pearson, was frozen to death on the 17th ult. in Madison County, Ala. (Nashville Republican Banner, 6 March 1870.)

PEAY, Tommy, of Rally Hill, Maury County, died March 1; Methodist. (Columbia Herald, 21 March 1873.)

PECK, George P., Esquire, of Shelbyville, Ky, fell overboard from the steamer Imperial at Helena, Ark., a few days ago and drowned; his body was recovered and buried. (Nashville Daily Union, 8 March 1863.)

PECK, Mrs. Louisa, age 100 years 8 months 6 days, widow of the late Amos Peck of Hamden, Conn., died lately. (Nashville Daily Gazette, 29 Oct. 1852.)

PEDEN, Mrs. Dorinda, 74, died in Paris, Tn, on the 9th. (Whig and Tribune, Jackson, Tn, 24 Aug. 1872.)

PEEBLES, Thomas, about 80, died last week in Maury County. (Whig and Tribune, Jackson, Tn, 21 Oct. 1871.)

PEEBLES, ___, one of twin infants of Rev. W. R. Peebles, died one day last week. (Columbia Herald and Mail, 17 Sept. 1875.)

PEEL, William, Company K, 1st Tennessee Cavalry, died in Louisville, Ky, the week ending on the 6th. (Nashville Dispatch, 8 Feb. 1863.)

PERRY, Miss Mary, 16, of Shady Grove, Hickman County, died Feb. 4 while talking to her mother, fell dead at mother's feet. (Columbia Herald and Mail, 16 March 1877.)

PELHAM. An effort is being made to raise funds for a monument over the grave of the gallant John Pelham at Jacksonville, Alabama. (Florence, Ala., Times, 20 June 1891.)

PEMBERTON, General, was killed at Selma, Alabama, by a Texas soldier. (Nashville Dispatch, 25 Aug. 1863.) Pemberton's death has been denied; he has been taken to Richmond under strong guard. His officers and men have sworn to kill him. (Nashville Dispatch, 4 Sept. 1863.) (N.B. General Pemberton did not die until 1881.)

PENDER, an old gentleman, living 3/4 miles north of Bigbyville in Maury County, hung himself in his buggy house on Monday. For some time he had symptoms of insanity. (Nashville Republican Banner, 28 Nov. 1869.)

PENNEBAKER, Samuel Pearse, 33, died on the 11th in McMinnville. (Nashville Republican Banner, 13 Aug. 1869.)

PENNINGTON, German, of Lawrence County, was killed December 11 by a horse which he was riding falling on him. (Columbia Herald, 17 Dec. 1897.)

PENNINGTON, Mrs., 75, died on the 18th in Monroe County, Tn. (Columbia Herald, 27 Sept. 1872.)

PENNINGTON, John B., resolution of respect on his death published by the St. James Lodge, No. 223, Free and Accepted Masons. (Lawrenceburg Democrat, 12 Sept. 1890.)

PENTECOST, George Hampton, 1 year 7 months, youngest son of James A. and Lizzie S. Pentecost, died of scarlet fever and will be buried today. (Nashville Republican Banner, 15 Dec. 1868.)

PENTECOST, Maggie Alison, youngest daughter of J. F. and E. N. Pentecost, died on the 21st of whooping cough. (Nashville Republican Banner, 22 July 1870.)

PENSIONS granted last week to the following persons:
Henry J. Gossett, Boyd's Creek, Tn.
James J. White, Trump, Tn.
Joseph Chauncey, Ducktown, Tn.
Daniel Carlock, Coghill, Tn.
Elisha Starnes, Brownsborough, Tn.
James Bowman, Cane Creek, Tn.
James R. Kesterson, Sunbright, Tn.
William M. Murry, Morgantown, Tn.
William T. Coleman, Greenville
James Ashby, Fayetteville, Tn. (Mexican War survivor)
James McBroom, deceased, Cookeville, Tn.
John Fanone, Cedar Creek, Tn.
Alfred T. Tidrow, Otto, Tn.
Alvin H. Morrow, Red Boiling Springs, Tn.
James McNew, Forkvale, Tn.
David Hogan, Memphis, Tn.
Thomas J. Miller, Kingston
John N. Dolen, Butterfly, Tn.
Henry Sims, Gap Run, Tn.
Andrew J. Bright, Church Grove, Tn.
Mary E. McBroom, widow of James McBroom, Cookeville
(Maury Democrat, 23 Jan. 1890.)

PERCIVAL, Commodore John, died recently at his home in Boston, age 84, born Barnstable, Cape Cod; entered Navy as Sailing Master in 1809; his last command was the Constitution from 1843 to 1847; infirm health and put on retired list. (Nashville Dispatch, 10 Oct. 1862.)

PERDUE, James, an old soldier residing at Monroe, Michigan, was severely afflicted with rheumatism, but received prompt relief from his pain by using Chamberlain's Pain Balm. (Maury Democrat, 20 June 1895.)

PERES, H., of Memphis, and brother-in-law L. Wolf were 9 miles from Helena, Ark., on business last week and stayed with a Judge Anderson. Guerillas surrounded house, battered down door, dragged them from the house, robbed them of their money and told them to prepare for their deaths. They shot Mr. Peres in the heart and Wolf got three

shots in the back. The body of Mr. Peres was returned to Memphis.
Mr. Wolf is critical and his life is hanging on a mere thread.
(Nashville Dispatch, 1 Dec. 1863.)

PERKINS, a notorious guerrilla and bandit, who has been for months
past committing murder and robberies in Robertson, Cheatham, and
Davidson counties, was killed on Wednesday at the hands of a citizen
whom he had just robbed. (Nashville Daily Union, 28 Nov. 1863.)

PERKINS, C., deceased; administratrix notice published in Maury County
on 11 March 1865 by Nancy R. Perkins. (Nashville Daily Union,
12 March 1865.)

PERKINS, John, ex-Federal soldier, from Massachusetts, who came to
Virginia in the 2d New Hampshire Regiment, will be hanged on the
9th for rape on Miss Ford. Ben Benjamin, colored, was his accomplice.
(Memphis Daily Appeal, 9 Oct. 1868.)

PERKINS, Nicholas Tate, old citizen of Brownsville, died there on Feb.
25. (Whig and Tribune, Jackson, Tn., 9 March 1872.)

PERKINS, William M., of New Orleans, died in Chicago on September 15;
he had formerly lived in Nashville and had lived here for 30 years;
prosperous merchant in New Orleans. (Nashville Union and American,
16 Sept. 1874.)

PERRY, Miss Ella, died yesterday in West Tennessee on a visit; lived
at Bigbyville in Maury County, was visiting at Rosville; daughter of
John S. Perry, deceased. (Columbia Herald and Mail, 20 July 1877.)

PERRY. Maury Confederate - John M. Witt, Clerk of the Chancery Court
of Lee County, Mississippi, of which Tupelo is the county seat
has written the Herald as follows: "As you know, after the battle
of Shiloh the Confederate army fell back to Tupelo and camped for
several months and a great many of the soldiers died here. The
other day I ran upon a monument in an old field with this inscription on it: Isiah S. Perry, born Maury County, Tennessee, 18 Dec.
1823, died Tupelo, Miss., 8 July 1862. He was a Confederate
soldier and a Mason and I thought perhaps some of his relatives
might still be living in Maury County and would like to know this."
(Daily Herald, Columbia, 14 April 1926.)

PERRY, John R., was shot in Griffith's saloon Friday by Pat Murphy
(alias James Moore) of Maury County and died yesterday. (Nashville
Republican Banner, 28 March 1869.) James R. Perry, born 31 April
1845, died 27 March 1869. (Nashville Republican Banner, 31 March
1869) (N.B. In one account his name was John and in the other
James was given.)

PERRY, John, of Coffee County, died of smallpox on the 19th. (Nashville
Union and American, 27 May 1873.)

PERRY, Old Man, murdered in Butler County, Alabama, by a woman named
Martha Ann Petty. His son had succeeded in breaking off an
intimacy between them and she waylaid him at the spring and cut
his throat. (Memphis Daily Aypeal, 27 July 1868.)

PERRY, W. B., who went to Texas from Tennessee in 1839, died at
Colorado, Texas, on the 7th of consumption. (Memphis Daily Appeal,
20 June 1870.)

PETERS, George Boddie. (Refer also to Earl Van Dorn entry.)
Reported Killing of Van Dorn - A gentleman brought us intelligence
yesterday, derived from a source in which he has implicit confidence,
that General Van Dorn, the notorious commander of the rebel cavalry
was killed last Thursday at Spring Hill, by Dr. Peters of that
place.

It is stated that in prosecuting his reconnoissances, General Van

PETERS, George Boddie - Continued
Dorn found it necessary to occupy the bed of Dr. Peters, in flagrant
violation of the Seventh Commandment. Dr. Peters coming on the
guilty couple in flagrant delicto, pulled out a pistol and shot Van
Dorn, killing him almost instantly. Van Dorn's private character
was infamous. Some years ago he deserted a beautiful and devoted
wife, and took up with a filthy, drunken, degraded harlot. Like
John Morgan, he has had a great number of featherbed adventures with
the "she adders" of the Sodom and Gomorroh Confederacy.
(Nashville Daily Union, 10 May 1863.)

Killing of Van Dorn - The announcement of the killing of Van Dorn
made by us some days ago is now fully confirmed. Some doubted it
at the time, but as we had given a similar report about Bragg a
short time before, we felt sure that we had not missed fired twice
in succession. We shall be happy to announce the death of
Breckenridge, Isham Harris, or Jeff Davis, in the same manner. The
dispatch of yesterday morning gives the following particulars of
Van Dorn's death:

The reported killing of General Van Dorn by Dr. Peters has been
confirmed. It occurred in his quarters at Spring Hill, on the
morning of the 7th inst. Dr. Peters has arrived in this city, and
from him we learn that the cause of the difficulty which resulted
in the death of Van Dorn, was an interview, held 30 hours previous
to the killing, in which the latter agreed, on his honor, to give
Dr. Peters a written statement the next day, setting forth four
distinct facts. Dr. Peters said to him that upon the fulfillment
of this promise, he would spare his life to his wife and children,
although Van Dorn had said he cared nothing for his own wife.

The next day Dr. Peters was sick and did not call on Van Dorn, until
the second day, Thursday morning about eight, when he demanded of
Van Dorn a compliance with his promise which he seemed not inclined
to do.

Dr. Peters then said that he would give him half an hour in which
to comply, and distinctly notified him that, in case of failure,
his life should be the forfeit. He then walked up to the village.
On his return Van Dorn read to him what he had written. The first
clause fully complied with his promise; the second was an entire
misrepresentation; and the other two acknowledgements he refused to
make. Dr. Peters then denounced him for his bad faith, when Van
Dorn cursed him for a "cowardly dog," and ordered him to leave the
room, or he would kick him out. Dr. Peters then drew his pistol
and fired, the ball taking effect in the left side of the head, and
producing instant death.

Dr. Peters picked up the statement Van Dorn had prepared, and has
preserved it as circumstantial evidence of preceding events, and
mounting his horse, rode off. Avoiding the pickets at Hurt's he
crossed Duck River and arrived at Shelbyville, when he learned that
Gen. Polk, to whom he had intended surrendering himself, had issued
an order for his arrest. The next morning he left for Winchester,
disguised and passing through Gainsboro and Gallatin arrived at
this place Monday morning.

Dr. Peters says it is not true that he detected Van Dorn in a
criminal act with his wife. He refused to reveal the history of
the thirty hours previous to the tragedy, and will only do so in a
court of justice, in justification of the course he felt it his
duty to pursue.

Dr. Peters was for a number of years a distinguished practitioner
of medicine in West Tennessee and was a member of the Senate of
this State one or two sessions. His present residence is in
Mississippi where he is regarded as a wealthy planter. (Nashville
Daily Union, 14 May 1863.)

PETERS, George Boddie - Continued
Dr. George B. Peters has been arrested and taken to Meridian, Miss. and subsequently brought before William Kilpatrick at Okalona on November 25 and discharged. There was nothing against him to justify his detention. (Nashville Dispatch, 13 Dec. 1863.)

Voluntary Statement of Dr. George B. Peters - Report given to army police in Nashville. "I was born in the State of North Carolina, and raised in Murray County, Tennessee, where I now reside. I have practiced medicine 23 years in Bolivar, Hardeman county, Tennessee. I was State Senator from the 21st Senatorial District of Tennessee in the years 1859-61. For some years past I have been planting in Philips county, Arkansas, where I have been constantly during the past twelve months.

"After the Federal troops reached Helena, Arkansas, and had possession of the Mississippi River to that point, I went to Memphis and took the oath of allegiance to the United States Government. This was in the summer of 1862. After that time I dealt in cotton and carried supplies to my neighbors by consent of the military authorities there commanding, and never went beyond the Federal lines until recently. I have in my possession safeguards from Rear-Admiral Porter, commanding the gunboat flotilla, and Major-General U. S. Grant, commanding Department of Mississippi, for the protection of my property.

"About the 4th day of April 1863 I came to Memphis and obtained a pass to go to Bolivar, Tennessee, at which place I received a pass from General Brannan, commanding post, to pass out of the Federal lines, my intention being to go to Spring Hill, Murray county, where my wife and family were staying.

"I arrived at home on the 12th of April, and was alarmed at the distressing rumors which prevailed in the neighborhood in relation to the attentions paid by General Van Dorn to my wife. I was soon convinced of his intentional guilt--although a doubt still lingered on my mind as to the guilt of my wife. After witnessing many incidents too numerous and unpleasant to relate, and which confirmed the guilt of General Van Dorn, on one occasion, when a servant brought a note to my house, I distinctly told him I would blow his brains out if he ever entered the premises again, and to tell his whiskey-headed master, General Van Dorn, that I would blow his brains out, or any of his staff that stepped their foot inside of the lawn, and I wanted them to distinctly understand it. My wife did not hear this order.

"Notwithstanding all this, I came to Nashville on the 22d of April, and was exceedingly mortified on my return home to hear that Van Dorn had visited my house every night by himself during my absence, my wife having no company but her little children. I was then determined to catch the villain at his tricks; so I feigned a trip to Shelbyville, but really did not leave the premises. The second night after my supposed and pretended absence, I came upon the creature, about half-past two o'clock at night, where I expected to find him...

"(On his visit to Van Dorn's headquarters 7 May 1863)...I immediately drew my pistol, aiming to shoot him in the forehead, when by a convulsive movement of his head, he received the shot in the left side of his head just above the ear, killing him instantly. I picked up the scroll he had written for evidence. I then went to Shelbyville to surrender myself to General Polk, believing they would not arrest me. Finding out, however, that they intended arresting and incarcerating me, I came around by McMinnville, thence by Gallatin to Nashville, within the Federal lines. I shot him about eight o'clock in the morning. Van Dorn was seated at his desk. When I arrived at Spring Hill first, Van Dorn immediately had me paroled. When I reached Nashville, having left my certificate

PETERS, George Boddie - Continued
of having taken the oath of allegiance at Memphis, I renewed the
oath and gave security. (Signed) George B. Peters." (Full statement
published 1864 in "Annals of the Army of the Cumberland," pages
618 through 620.)

Dr. Peters, who killed Van Dorn, has been captured by rebels at his
plantation in Mississippi; said he had been desirous of getting
back to Dixie and stand trial. (Nashville Daily Union, 2 Dec.
1863.)

We learn that a difficulty occurred yesterday evening near Marion,
Arkansas, in which a man named Lusby had his throat cut by a knife
in the hands of Dr. Peters. It is said that Lusby first approached
Peters, and, drawing a Derringer pistol, fired, the ball passing
through the sleeve of the Doctor. The Doctor held in his hand a
pen-knife and immediately attacked Lusby with the result above
given. It is said that he cannot survive his wound. The difficulty
grew out of a misunderstanding, which has existed for years. Dr.
Peters is the same who shot and killed General Van Dorn during the
war. (Memphis Avalanche, 13 Nov. 1866.)

Dr. Peters, widely known as the man who shot and killed General
Van Dorn of the Confederate Army, during the war, for alleged
intimacy with Mrs. Peters, was in this city one day this week in
company with the quondam Mrs. P. The long estranged couple are
now said to be on the best of terms, and it is reported that the
broken marriage vows are soon to be renewed. (Nashville Republican
Banner, 9 July 1868.)

George B. Peters, Jr., of Bolivar, son of Dr. George B. Peters, who
killed General Van Dorn, received five gold medals at the recent
commencement of Washington College. (Memphis Daily Appeal, 15
Aug. 1869.)

Dr. Peters, one of the largest planters of Arkansas, is spending
the summer at his home near Spring Hill. (Columbia Herald, 15 Aug.
1873.)

Dr. Peters and his wife have sold their residence near this place
(Spring Hill) or exchanged it for an Arkansas plantation near
Memphis and intend making their future home there. Mrs. Wilson
has bought their place. (Columbia Herald, 10 Oct. 1873.)

Only a Woman's Heart - The most startling and tragic occurrence
of the late war, not even excepting the wholesale slaughter of
human beings in battle, was the killing of Gen. Van Dorn, of the
cavalry department in the Confederate Army, by Dr. Peters at one
time a Senator in the Tennessee Legislature. The tragedy occurred
at Spring Hill, a short time previous to the battle of Murfreesboro.

The sad details of that affair and circumstances which led to it
are too familiar to our readers to render repetition of them
necessary here. The recollection of the sad story is revived by
a paragraph going the rounds of the press to the effect that a
daughter of Dr. Peters, young, accomplished, and beautiful, had
arrived in St. Louis where she was about to enter a convent and
take the veil.

The St. Louis Times of the 21st alluding to the arrival in that
city and the contemplated devotion of herself to the church, says
feelingly, that "every calamity that war may beget has befallen her
family, kindred, fortune, and home. The residence in which she
dwelt from childhood was in the path of the destroying army that
swept wide districts with unsparing desolation. Every species of
property was destroyed, and she and an only brother beggared, and
fated to encounter even great calamities, wandering among strangers.

PETERS, George Boddie - Continued
The mother, a weaker woman than the daughter, accustomed to ease, flattery, and every pleasure that wealth could buy, yielded, never criminally, to the flattery of an army officer, and overstepped rules of decorum prescribed by the social habits of the South.

The father wreaked terrible vengeance upon him who destroyed the delights of his proverty-stricken home, and while the people approved the deed there was bitterness insufferable in the cup of grief pressed to the lips of the faultless daughter.

The brother bore accumulated misfortunes unsustained by that divine faith which never fails to give consolation and strength. His sorrows made him insane, and in moody madness he dragged out a miserable existence. Life at length became insufferable, and in an evil hour he put a period to his own existence.

The sister lived to soothe a father's sorrows and lighten anguish that almost dethroned his reason. She was divinely inspired. Her soft, sweet voice never lost its tenderness, and its very tones were silvery with hope that beamed from her lustrous eyes... Time sped. The father's grief became melancholy and the church his resource.

The daughter, who reached St. Louis a few days since from a Southern city, has sought repose in the bosom of the holy Catholic Church. During the week, she will assume vows of a sisterhood famed the world over for those charities which this daughter of the South has learned so well how to practice within the precincts of her own unfortunate household. We are induced to write this simple recital of her misfortunes that a sad chapter of personal history might find a place in the memories of men. (Nashville Republican Banner, 25 June 1868.)

Senator George B. Peters of Bolivar was Senator from the district formed out of the counties of Hardeman and Hardin. He had been a leading physician of Hardeman County for several years and was a wealthy and popular man. He was then a widower, but married before the close of the session. Two or three years afterwards, he gained much notoriety by killing Maj. Gen. Van Dorn near Columbia, Tenn.

I only saw Dr. Peters once after the Legislature adjourned. On my way to Oxford, Miss., during the fall or winter of 1865, I came up with a man who had been riding in front of me, mounted on a poor mule, with an old army saddle and a large roll tied behind the saddle. He wore a slouch white hat, a very much worn suit of clothes, looking as if he were a returning soldier. On looking closely, I was surprised to recognize Dr. Peters, and during our ride of several hours together he told me that he was making his way to his plantation on the Mississippi River, and that he had come through the mountains of Alabama and the hills of northeast Mississippi to avoid publicity as much as possible, as it had been reported to him from various sources that some of Van Dorn's staff officers had declared their intention of killing him, should they ever see him. (Nashville Banner, 1 April 1913, from letter published in paper of G. L. Morphis, Cleveland, Oklahoma.)

Elmwood Cemetery Records, Memphis, Tennessee. Lot 36 was purchased by George B. Peters, 8 Oct. 1887. No stones on lot, but buried here are:

Lucy Peters, buried 24 Oct. 1887, age 12.
W. M. Peters, buried 6 April 1885, age 25.
Dr. George B. Peters, buried 30 April 1889, age 74 years.
Mrs. Jessee H. Peters, buried 18 July 1921, age 83 years.
Medora Peters Lenow, buried 28 Oct. 193 , age 62.
Mrs. Kate Peters Holden, buried 27 March 1943, age 70 years.
Also listed as being buried here: Mrs. J. H. Peters, buried 28 Sept. 1898, age 68 years. This is correctly the burial for

PETERS, George Boddie - Continued
A. C. McKissack, brother of Mrs. J. H. Peters.

Died - G. B. Peters, age 75, died 29 April 1889, funeral to be
held at home of Henry J. Lenow, No. 18 Walker Ave., Memphis, Tuesday
at 10 a.m. (Memphis Appeal, 30 April 1889.)

PETERS, George B., Jr. General Peters passes away. Conscious to the
End - Distinguished lawyer died yesterday afternoon at Colorado
Springs, Colo. Death caused by an abscess of the liver. Able as
a Pleader and a Practitioner, quiet in Demeanor, modest and
courteous at all times, Gen. Peters was admired both as a Lawyer
and as a man - General George B. Peters of Memphis, Tenn., a member
of the law firm of Wright, Peters & Wright died this afternoon at
Glockner Sanitarium in this City. (Colorado Springs, Colo., Dec. 8)
General Peters was conscious to the end and was surrounded by his
eldest daughter, Mrs. Evelyn Peters Estes, and a son, Arthur, who
arrived here a few days ago. George B. Peters, Jr., was en route,
but telegrams have been sent advising of death of father.

General Peters was born at Bolivar, Tenn., 23 Jan. 1850. His father
George B. Peters removed to Memphis a few years afterwards and
Gen. Peters lived here practically all of his life. He married
Miss Kate Bell Greenlaw, daughter of Oliver Greenlaw in Sept. 1874.
Mrs. George B. Peters died some ten years ago. Received early
education in this City afterwards attended Washington & Lee
University. Elected Nov. 1874 to lower house of General Assembly
serving on Judiciary and Finance Committees. Returned to Memphis
and in 1875 formed law partnership with Luke W. Finney. Lasted nine
years. Served as Attorney General of Shelby County 1883-1884.
Considered one of the greatest criminal lawyers. Noted for his
trial expertness. (Memphis Commercial Appeal, 9 Dec. 1906.)

Gen. George B. Peters. Interment Elmwood Cemetery. (Memphis
Commercial Appeal, 10 Nov. 1906.)

Hon. G. B. Peters delivered a great speech before the legislators
on the Governor's message; son of Dr. Peters and grandson of Capt.
James Peters, deceased, and has host of kinfolks in this county;
is one of the foremost senators in the state. (Columbia Herald and
Mail, 1 Feb. 1878.)

PETERS, Mrs. Jessie H., 83, died 16 July 1921 of chorea morbus; lived
1533 McLemore, Memphis. (Memphis Commercial Appeal, 19 July 1921)
Mrs. Jesse H. Peters funeral to be held at home 1533 McLemore Ave.,
Memphis; had lived here 42 years; her home offered as a site for
a park but offer not yet accepted; was unusually attractive young
girl; survived by two daughters, Mrs. Henry Lenow and Mrs. Kate
Peters Holden, and son Robert L. Peters. (Memphis Commercial
Appeal, 18 July 1921.)

Jessie Peters' Letter - My father William McKissack had three
girls and two sons. I am the youngest and only living one of the
children. My oldest sister Susan Peters McKissack married Nathaniel
Cheairs; Lucy Hutson McKissack married William Parham; Jessie Helen
McKissack married Dr. George B. Peters; James Thomson McKissack
married a woman from Maine, Miss Rowe; Alexander Cogel McKissack
married Miss Aykrod of North Carolina.

Uncle Spivey McKissack married my grandmother, Mrs. Jeffries. My
father married the daughter and my uncle, a younger brother,
married the mother. My uncle's children by this marriage were
William and John.

My grandmother's name was Susan Peters. She married Colonel
Jeffries of North Carolina, said to have been the wealthiest man
in the State at the time--had a coach and four and outriders--
my grandmother travelled in silk velvet. Her second husband was

PETERS, Mrs. Jessie H. - Continued
my grandfather from Edinburgh Scotland, Dr. James Thomson. Dr.
Peters told me that he was one of the most learned men in the world.

My mother's name was Janet Susan Cople Buckstan Thomson. Her only
brother's name was Thomas.

I have heard that one McKissack did marry a widow Edwards. When I
was 12 years old, my father carried my sister and me all over the
U.S., travelling and we went through North Carolina and visited a
widow Edwards who lived in Person Co., Roxboro, N.C. She probably
was his sister-in-law or aunt. I was not concerned about family
affairs at that time.

I think Thomas McKissack was a private and was shot through the
body and fell by the side of Lafayette on the field of battle at
Brandywine.

Cousin Orville (Uncle Archie's son) raw away with my half-sister
and they were married at Cousin Melena's home. My father never
forgave her.

The McKissacks were all devoted to their wives. At one time letters
came from Scotland saying there were lands, a title, castle, etc.,
for the oldest McKissack. I asked Cousin Orve why he did not go
and attend to it, and he said, "I wouldn't leave Ell for the whole
of Europe." (N.B. Ell was Eleanor, his wife.)

A few years ago there was a notice about the same in a New York
paper, and some girls who were working in a factory proved they
were entitled to the property, and as no one else put in a claim
they got it. (From letter in possession of Jill Garrett.)

Maury County Marriage Records - Jessie Helen McKissack married
George B. Peters, 1 June 1858.

PETERS, Thomas. Distressing Case of Suicide. Yesterday afternoon
Thomas Peters, son of Dr. Peters of this State committed suicide
by shooting himself through the head with a pistol. The circumstances connected with this unfortunate and sad affair are as
follows.

Mr. Peters passed through our city, a week ago, on his way to his
father's plantation below the city. His friends state that he
looked unusually well while in Memphis and no signs were discovered
of any intention to commit an act that heaps distress upon a doting
father, and deprives society of one of its bright ornaments. On
his return from the plantation Sunday night, he seemed cheerful
as usual and still presented no indication of anything unusual in
his feelings.

A few hours before his death, he was in the store of Pitzer Miller
on Second Street where he slept the night before, and gentlemen
who were with him, say that he was in a pleasant humor, and his
mood was as agreeable as was the habit of this companionable young
gentleman. A short while previous to the shooting, he went upstairs
into the sleeping room, placed his shawl carefully on the floor,
arranged a pillow, polished his boots carefully, combed his hair,
dressed himself complete in an artillery uniform of the late C.S.A.
in whose ranks he was a commissioned officer, buttoned the coat
to the chin, laid himself down, and deliberately placing a pistol
with the muzzle behind the ear, fired.

His appearance after death, warrants us in these statements. He
must have died without a struggle, as after the report of the
pistol, some gentlemen rushed upstairs and the flesh was still
quivering. There was very little blood upon the pillow, and the
shawl was not disturbed.

PETERS, Thomas - Continued
He had written three letters, two to his parents, and the other to
some one whose name we did not learn. Thos. Peters was a promising
young man. Previous to his death he was studying law with General
Walthall of Coffeville, Miss., and bid fair to take an honorable
position in the social world; but with an organization to sensitive
to combat the cruel decree of fate--it seems so in this case; too
keenly alive to the woes of others, the gallant and the true, the
talented and generous has, by his own hand, deprived himself of an
existence whose burdens were too heavy for his sensitive nature to
bear. Every heart knoweth its own sorrow and what the lacerated
heart of this noble fellow was called up to bear, is known only to
his God. (Memphis Avalanche, 10 April 1866.)

Burial of Thomas Peters. - The remains of the lamented (Thomas
Peters) unfortunate were escorted to this place by his family,
Bishop Quintard, and numerous friends where they arrived on last
Wednesday at 12 M. The corpse was taken to St. James Church, and
an opportunity given to the immense concourse of mourning relatives
and friends to once more behold the features of him they so much
esteemed. After the imposing ceremonies were over at the church,
the coffin and all that remained of Thos. Peters, was followed to
the Polk Cemetery, where it was deposited near the sacred ashes of
his sainted mother. Bishop Quintard officiated and caused many an
eye to grow dim as he performed the last sad rite that man pays to
man. The afflicted family of the deceased have the heartfelt
sympathy of this community in their bereavement. (Bolivar Bulletin,
14 April 1866.)

(The following statement came from the book A SOLDIER'S HONOR,
page 250, in regard to the assassination of General Earl Van Dorn
by Dr. George B. Peters: "The dastardly crime led to a series of
tragedies in the family of the murderer, his daughter taking the
black veil for life and a son committed suicide after receiving a
letter from the staff officers of Gen. Van Dorn in reply to one he
had written asking if it were true that they had resolved to take
the life of his father on sight, to which they replied they were
not assassin.")

PETTIGREW, Mrs. Cordelia, wife of T. J. Pettigrew, died Saturday at
Oak Grove, Decatur County. (Linden Times, 12 Feb. 1880.)

PETTIGREW, Major J. L., of Charleston is dead. (Nashville Dispatch,
22 March 1863.)

PETTIGREW, Rudolp, young man recently in employ of the Illinois Central
Railroad as a telegraph operator, fell dead last week while walking
to church at Adamsville, McNairy County. (Columbia Herald, 11 Oct.
1895.)

PETTUS, Dr. T. S., prominent physician of Swan Creek in Hickman County,
died recently. (Columbia Herald and Mail, 22 May 1874.)

PETTY, William, son of Hardy Petty, lived near Pinewood, Hickman
County, died suddenly Thursday night; had worked all day in fodder
field and was dead by 10 p.m. (Columbia Herald and Mail, 24 Sept.
1875.)

PETWAY, Elizabeth N., wife of Rev. Dr. F. S. Petway, died on the 31st
in Memphis, to be buried in Nashville. (Nashville Republican
Banner, 6 June 1869.)

PEYTON, Major James T., died 20 July 1869 at Red Sulphur Springs,
Virginia. (Memphis Daily Appeal, 13 Aug. 1869.)

PEYTON, Honorable R. L. Y., Confederate senator from Missouri, died
September 3 at Bladen Springs, Alabama. (Nashville Dispatch,
2 Oct. 1863.)

PHEIFER, Captain, stationed at Fort McRae, went to Hot Springs some
distance from the fort for his rheumatism; took wife, servant, and
four sick soldiers. While he was in the water, Navjoe Indians
fired on them, wounding him and killing the soldiers. They carried
off the women, who were recovered the next day, but both died.
He succeeded in escaping to the fort, though badly wounded.
(Nashville Dispatch, 6 August 1863.)

PHELPS, Major, of the 5th Virginia Federal forces, was killed near
Millersport, Ohio, on the 18th by Major Dayton of the 4th Virginia
Volunteers, whose parents live in the vicinity of New Creek,
Virginia. Phelps introduced himself into the family as single and
as a preacher and induced Dayton's sister to elope with him. Phelps
had wife and two children in Burlington, Ohio. (Nashville Dispatch,
1 Nov. 1862.) Dayton shot him four times at Point Pleasant, and
has been told to report to his regiment. (Nashville Dispatch, 1 Nov.
1862.)

PHILLIPS, Andrew Hooper, born 5 Dec. 1865, died yesterday; son of
Captain William and Sallie K. Phillips; lived four miles from the
city on the Dickerson Pike. (Nashville Republican Banner, 5 Oct.
1870.)

PHILLIPS, Bettie, age 10 or 11 years, daughter of Captain William
Phillips, was thrown from a carriage and instantly killed. (Nashville Republican Banner, 15 Nov. 1868.)

PHILLIPS, Bud, team ran away with him, crushed his skull and killed
him. (Columbia Herald, 31 May 1872.)

PHILLIPS, Mrs. Elizabeth, 75 years 11 months, died at Shelbyville on
Monday. (Nashville Republican Banner, 28 Nov. 1869.)

PHILLIPS, Uncle Elisha, died in Western North Carolina on Wednesday
at the advanced age of 107 years. (Florence, Ala., Times, 30 May
1891.)

PHILLIPS, James H., of Nashville died on the 13th inst.; survived by
wife and several children. (Nashville Daily Gazette, 17 Oct. 1852.)

PHILLIPS. Shooting affray in Nashville on Wednesday between Patterson
and Connell, resulted in the fatally wounding of a bystander, James
Phillips. (Memphis Daily Appeal, 20 Feb. 1869.)

PHILLIPS, James, was baptized at Memphis and less than three minutes
later fell into the river and was drowned. (Daily Herald, 6 June
1900.)

PHILLIPS, Jared, of Leavenworth, Kansas, on his way to California
overland a month or two ago, was captured by Indians and put to
death by torture, being unjointed limb by limb. It is said that
many emigrants have been found murdered and scalped at the instance,
it is said, of the Mormons. (Nashville Dispatch, 20 March 1863.)

PHILLIPS, Joel, old and well known, a member of the police force for
a long time, died yesterday. (Nashville Union and American, 16 June
1873.)

PHILLIPS, John, age 14, died 22 Nov. 1864, was killed by Ira Morton,
also 14 years; son of Joel Phillips. (Nashville Daily Union, 23
Nov. 1864.)

PHILLIPS, Mary J., native of Ulster County, New York, who has been for
the past 10 years a captive among the Indians of Colorado, has
excaped and is now on her way to Ulster where some of her mother's
relatives live. (Columbia Herald, 7 July 1871.)

PHILLIPS, Samuel; the funeral of Samuel Phillips and wife Anna will be preached 18 May 1864 at the residence in Bedford County by George W. Phillips; this notice is given in hopes the absent children and their friends will be present. (Nashville Daily Union, 1 May 1864.)

PHILLIPS, William, accidentally shot and killed a Miss Calley of Wartrace a few days ago. (Paris Gazette, 30 May 1878.)

PHILLIPS, William D., Jr., youngest son of W. D. and Eliza Phillips, died July 12. (Nashville Dispatch, 18 July 1862.)

PHILPOTT, Miss Asenath, of Gainesville, Texas, has the longest hair in the country, measuring 10 feet 7 inches. (Maury Democrat, 25 July 1895.)

PHIPPS, Robert, murderer of Dr. B. C. Newsom, has drowned according to rumor. The river has been drug for four days. (Nashville Republican Banner, 31 May 1868.)

PICARD, Mrs. Susan, 55, relict of late Jerome Picard, died Thursday. (Nashville Republican Banner, 18 Sept. 1868.)

PICKETT, Major General George E., CSA hero of Gettysburg, was married yesterday, Sept. 15 at St. Paul's Church, Petersburg, to Sallie Corbell, daughter of John D. Corbell, Esquire of Nansemond; salute of 20 guns fired in honor of the event. (Nashville Dispatch, 2 Oct. 1863.)

PICKETTO, Francesco, applies as administratrix of the estate of late Pietro and Paulo Picketto. (Memphis Daily Appeal, 12 Feb. 1870.)

PIERCE, Franklin, ex-president, was in Boston on the 2d inst., looking remarkably well. (Nashville Dispatch, 8 July 1862.) Ex-President Pierce died this morning, Oct. 8. (Memphis Daily Appeal, 9 Oct. 1869.)

PIERCE, J. W., 35, brother of D. C. Pierce, died on the 10th; formerly of Harrison, Ohio. (Nashville Republican Banner, 12 Aug. 1870.)

PIERCE, Captain Joseph, died in Cincinnati a few days ago, was an eccentric on the subject of his coffin and shroud. Twelve years ago had coffin made of solid mahogany and had a stone sarcophagus made and purchased an American flag to be used as his shroud. (Nashville Dispatch, 20 March 1863.)

PIERCE, Mrs. Jane M., wife of ex-president Franklin Pierce, died on the 2d at Andover, Mass; had been in feeble health for several years. (Nashville Dispatch, 4 Dec. 1863.)

PIGG, Dan, 71, died on the 12th. (Maury Democrat, Columbia, Tn., 21 June 1894.)

PIGG, James, of Snow Creek, died last week of chronic case of paralysis. (Columbia Herald, 10 Oct. 1873.)

PIKE, General Albert, has retired from editorship of Memphis Appeal and has gone to Washington to practice law. (Memphis Daily Appeal, 4 Sept. 1868.) General Albert Pike, deceased, owned 150 pet birds which he kept in cages hung in all parts of his house. (Maury Democrat, 7 May 1891.)

The Nelson House (in Columbia) was then the principal, if not the only hotel in the town. This is where Albert Pike boarded, who it was said by his political enemies, stole old man Nelson's canoe and ran away down Duck River it was said he went down Duck River to the Tennessee, down the Tennessee, to the Ohio, down the Ohio to the Mississippi and to the mouth of the Arkansas, and up the Arkansas to Little Rock where he located and where he made a

PIKE, General Albert - Continued
national reputation as lawyer, statesman, poet, and soldier.

I remember he went back of Columbia in 1844 during the red hot
compaign between Polk and Clay over the annexation of Texas and
made a speech at old Ashwood near Columbia at the Whig barbecue
advocating Clay against Polk for president. The Democrats got up
a song about his running away from Columbia, two lines of which:
"He eat old Nelson's meat and bread, and stole his old canoe."
(Columbia Herald, 11 Oct. 1895.)

PIKE, Isadore, age 27 years 5 months 6 days, daughter of General
Albert Pike, died on the 6th in Memphis by accidental chloroform;
sent to Little Rock for burial. (Memphis Daily Appeal, 8 July
1869.)

PIKE, James M., 43, died in Nashville on Saturday last; Lottery manager.
(Western Weekly Review, 23 Dec. 1831.)

PILLOW, Captain George, son of General G. J. Pillow, has been appointed
aide-de-camp in his father's brigade, formerly held by General
Palmer. (Nashville Dispatch, 17 Jan. 1863.) Died - In this county
on the 26th of August, Captain George M. Pillow, son of Gen. G. J.
Pillow. Capt. Pillow was a man of powerful intellect and much
learning, and he might have made his name even more famous than his
illustrious father, but for a total lack of ambition. Peace to his
ashes. (Columbia Herald, 30 Aug. 1872.)

PILLOW, Gideon Johnson. General Pillow states his losses during the
war at 409 negroes, 4 gin houses, valued at $10,000, each; 10,000
pounds of bacon; 2,000 hogs; 500 head of cattle; 2,100 bales of
cotton burned by his own Government beside the destruction of his
houses and desolation of his plantations by Federals.
(Nashville Dispatch, 26 March 1863.)

General Pillow spent $300,000 of his private funds in equipping
troops for the field. He owned plantations and slaves in three or
four different states and was reduced to comparative poverty by
the results of the war. (Columbia Herald, 31 March 1871.)

One hundred fifty of General Pillow's negroes, freed by General
Curtis, arrived at Cairo on the 28th. (Nashville Dispatch, 6 Sept.
1862.)

Gen. Pillow is in seclusion at Grenada, Mississippi. July 21.
(Nashville Dispatch, 9 Aug. 1862.)

Blue Lick Water is highly recommended by Gen. G. J. Pillow.
(Columbia Herald, 10 Sept. 1869.)

Gen. G. J. Pillow has moved to Memphis. (Columbia Herald, 28 April
1871.)

A Memphis correspondent says that the law firm of Pillow and
Harris (i.e. Isham G. Harris) do big business at Memphis and that
there are 300 lawyers there. (Nashville Republican Banner, 25 Feb.
1871.)

Married in New Orleans on Nov. 27, Gideon J. Pillow and Mrs. P. D.
Trigg of New Orleans. Married in Memphis last Wednesday, Daniel
P. Farguson and Miss Alice Pillow, youngest daughter of Gideon J.
Pillow. (Columbia Herald, 6 Dec. 1872.)

Gen. Gideon J. Pillow and his handsome young bride came to Maury
County one day last week. The general never looked handsomer or
in better health. (Columbia Herald, 24 Jan. 1873.)

General Pillow is in town, stayed at the Nelson House. (Columbia
Herald and Mail, 3 Sept. 1875.) General Gid Pillow of Memphis

PILLOW, Gideon Johnson - Continued
attended chancery court in Columbia this week. (Columbia Herald
and Mail, 27 Oct. 1876.)

Gen. Gideon Pillow's property was sold at bankrupt sale in Memphis
and purchased by a gentleman, who promptly presented it to Mrs.
Pillow. (Columbia Herald and Mail, 31 March 1876.)

March 10, Memphis - Henry Clay King, brilliant lawyer, is in jail
for killing another lawyer because of a woman: Mary J. Pillow,
widow of General Gideon J. Pillow, who is about 45, looks 30, has
queenly presence, the daring of Bernhardt, the wit and polish of a
Recamier. She is known to be a "risky woman and women of her social
rank gradually drew away from her after her husband's death."

Mr. King was captivated by her; deserted wife and children for her;
it was a notorious scandal; he took her to Lee County, Arkansas,
where they lived together; her daughter, age 12 went with them. He
gave her $10,000 to furnish the place, but she put everything in her
name. They had a falling out and she ordered him off the place.
He brought suit to recover his property and sued the newspaper when
they wrote about it. Her lawyer was David H. Poston, who had
brother Frank Poston. King got mad at Poston, shot him in the
stomach, cutting intestines. For a while there was talk of lynching
King as the city was "boiling with indignation." King is now in
jail; he was a Confederate soldier. (Columbia Herald, 13 March
1891.)

King was convicted of murder in the first degree; has appealed.
(Columbia Herald, 10 July 1891.)

Henry Clay King is to hang August 12. (Florence, Ala., Times,
16 July 1892.)

King died in prison of stomach cancer and is buried in Calvary
Cemetery, Nashville. (The Commercial Appeal, Memphis, 5 June 1977,
from article on Poston Murder by James Cole.)

Mrs. Pillow still lives near Memphis; is poor and forsaken.
(Florence, Ala., Times, 27 Aug. 1892.)

General Pillow is to rest at Arlington Cemetery; the Masons plan
to move him. (Daily Herald, Columbia, Tn, 27 April 1915.) (N.B.
This was never done.)

In Elmwood Cemetery is a grave known as lot 217 Evergreen division.
The lot is scarcely as large as an ordinary room, and the low
concrete wall makes it look even smaller. At the right of the
entrance, a plain mound rises. It has no marker of any kind, not
even a plain headstone. The footplate at the entrance bears one
word: Pillow. That is the only marker to the resting place of
Gen. Gideon J. Pillow, hero of the Mexican War, defender of Memphis
during the early stages of the Civil War--a gallant fighter of
whose outspoken citicism of his superiors kept him in hot water. The
only other remembrance of General Pillow is a simple bronze plate
in Confederate park, almost hidden in the shrubbery. It reads:
"These bluffs were fortified by General Pillow, May 1862."

...When an old man, Pillow took up farming in Arkansas and was there
when the yellow fever broke out. He died of the disease on Mound
plantation in Phillips County, 8 Oct. 1878. He was 72 years old.
Six years later the body was moved to Memphis and buried in Elmwood
Cemetery. One of his sons paid $72 for the upkeep of the grave
in 1885. Since that day nothing has ever been done. There is no
statue honoring him, no park named in his memory, nothing for
Gen. Gideon J. Pillow, but an unmarked grave and a half-hidden
bronze tablet. (Memphis Press-Scimitar, __ March 1927, quoting
article by Don L. Hogan.)

PILLOW, Gideon Johnson - Continued
Tombstone inscription, Elmwood Cemetery, Memphis: General Gideon
Johnson Pillow, born Columbia, Tenn., 8 June 1806. Here beneath
this peaceful earth, hallowed by the heroic Confederate dead, rests
a great man, who in peace and in war sought to serve beyond the
call of duty.

A major general 1847 in the Mexican War. Second in command to
General Winfield Scott. He fought at Vera Cruz, Cerro Gordo,
Contreras and Chapultepec. He was wounded twice in the Mexican
campaign and was shot out of the saddle by grape-shot while leading a charge against the heights of Chapultepec, the decisive
battle that ended the war.

He was an unsuccessful aspirant to the vice-president of the United
States in 1852 and 1856.

Upon secession, he was appointed senior major general of Tennessee's
provisional army, 1861. When his troops were transferred to the
Confederate service, he accept a brigadier generalship. Later
troops under his command defeated General Grant's forces at Belmont,
Missouri. He served as major general, second in command to General
Floyd at Fort Donelson. Here, hard pressed Confederate forces
under General Pillow's command, with the help of Forrest's cavalry
sliced through Union lines, and laid open an escape route to
Nashville, but General Floyd was not equal to the critical moment.
He lost his nerve and ordered the defenders back to their trenches.
Surrender to General Grant followed.

At the war's end, Pillow returned to his law practice in Memphis.
Died Helena, Ark., 8 Oct. 1878. This memorial was erected by his
great-grandson Alston Boyd Wade, 1976.

PILLOW, Major Granville A., died in Maury County. (Memphis Daily
Appeal, 1 Sept. 1868.) Major Granville Pillow died at Clifton,
Tenn., a few days ago, buried Columbia, Tn. (Nashville Republican
Banner, 28 Aug. 1868.)

PILLOW. Murder of Granville and William Pillow - Just before going to
press we have learned from a trustworthy gentleman, who lives in
the neighborhood of Leighton, Ala., a true statement of the facts
connected with the murder of Granville and William Pillow. Granville was in his own house, alone, when he was first shot. He went
to a neighbor's, Horn's, and after sending for a doctor, he told
Horn that his murderers had given their names before the shooting
as Hugh Phillips and Granville Spangler.

Young Horn, on his way for the doctor, met some disguised men, to
whom he told all that Granville had said. The maskers asked if
Mr. Pillow had given any names, and receiving an affirmative
answer, they went immediately to old Mr. Horn, or Horner's, and
waited about an hour for Mr. Pillow to die.

They then went in and drove everybody out of the house, and though
Mr. Pillow was unconscious and probably dying, they shot him in the
breast, killing him instantly.

Granville talked to Mr. Horn about the shooting until he could not
speak and then wrote down the balance. This paper the murderers
destroyed. Young Phillips was engaged to be married to a young
lady near Lagrange to whom he acknowledged he had helped to murder
Granville, but that he had been urged and instigated to it by
influential parties in the neighborhood. The young lady went to
Pillow's funeral next day and told on her love.

Spangler was also at the funeral, and getting alarmed, he and
Phillips fled the country. One of the murderers came back after
daylight, and stayed with the corpse. It was he that carried the

PILLOW - Continued
dispatch to Leighton and sent it to Mrs. Pillow at Columbia,
telling her that her sons had been killed.

William Pillow was doubtless killed on the same night and by the
same party that murdered Granville, but nothing positive is known,
except that he was found in a sink-hole, shot all to pieces, and
with the throat-latch of a bridle around his neck. Everything goes
to show that Mr. William Pillow must have reached home just as his
brother Granville was shot, and recognizing the murderers, they
left their first victim and pursued him. He was shot in the back,
and must have made a desperate struggle for his life. Public
sentiment is very strong against one or two persons in the neighborhood, and some fear is felt that there will be some lynching done.
(Columbia Herald, 21 Jan. 1870.)

These young men were sons of the late Major Granville A. Pillow of
this county; and Gen. Gideon J. Pillow's nephews. Young Granville
married in North Alabama, and had been living there several years.
He was a Confederate soldier and received a wound in the Streight
raid on Sand Mountain. Willie went to Alabama a year or so ago.
It is a sad commentary on the evil days upon which we have fallen,
that two such young men should be murdered in cold blood. There
is another rumor to the effect that Granville had received that
day in town $800 for the rent of his farm, and he was robbed as
well as murdered. (Columbia Herald, 14 Jan. 1870.)

Hugh Phillips and Granville Spangler are believed to be the murderers
of the Pillow brothers. They have fled the country. (Memphis
Daily Appeal, 22 Jan. 1870.)

Huntsville Democrat says the Pillow boys were murdered for the ill
treatment of one of their wives. They had been warned to cease
the abuse and the husband became enraged, beating his wife even
more. This is not true. (Memphis Daily Appeal, 20 Jan. 1870.)

PILLOW, James C., youngest son of Dr. A. L. Pillow, died Wednesday;
had been confined to his room for several months. (Columbia
Herald and Mail, 14 Dec. 1877.)

PILLOW, John C., age 84, of Henry County, married Miss Georgie Raines,
age 25, in a buggy at the north gate of the courthouse yard on
August 3. (Columbia Herald, 9 Aug. 1901.)

PILLOW, Mrs. Mary, wife of Gen. G. J. Pillow, of this county, went to
St. John's Chapel last Sunday morning, after service returned home
in her usual health, and while at dinner took suddenly ill, and
continued to sink under the disease, which proved to be apoplexy,
until night, when she died. Gen. Pillow was in Memphis, and did
not get home until the next evening. Mrs. Pillow was a model good
woman, a devout Christian, and though her death gives unmingled
pain in the sphereof her labors, it will bring joy in the land of
her rewards. (Columbia Herald, 8 Oct. 1869.)

PILLOW, Marcus. Suicide of Colonel Marcus L. Pillow at Nashville -
The community in the neighborhood of Sandy Carter's saloon, Union
Street, was startled about 7 o'clock last evening by the sudden
report of a pistol. A crowd immediately rushed to the saloon to
ascertain the cause and beheld in amazement the stark dead body
of Col. Marcus L. Pillow, of Maury County. He had shot himself in
the right temple with a Derringer pistol, which still remained in
his hand, which had fallen to his lap.

At the time of the suicide he was sitting in a chair, out of which
he never moved. For the past two months he had been suffering
intensely from chronic disease of the kidneys of 20 years standing
and which at last drove him to his self-destruction. Only the
night previous he had told friends in a mysterious manner that
"it would only last 24 hours longer," that he had reached his

PILLOW, Marcus. - Continued
   65th year, and he now had no immediate kin and he felt lonely. He
   had told often that he intended to put an end to his sufferings
   which were no longer tolerable. When he went into Carter's saloon,
   he complained of extreme debility.

   Justice Creighton held an inquest over the remains of the deceased
   and the verdict was self-destruction. They were then removed to
   Combs' undertaking establishment at the instance of friends and
   neatly encoffined.

   A dispatch was sent to Dr. Anthony Pillow, cousin of the deceased,
   at Columbia, and he responded that his son would arrive in Nashville
   this morning to take charge of the body.

   Col. Pillow was the son of Col. William Pillow, who died seven or
   eight years ago at the age of 101 years. Col. William Pillow was
   an aid-de-camp to General Jackson at the battle of New Orleans and
   also served with distinction in the Indian wars.

   Col. Marcus L. Pillow was for many years previous to the war one of
   the leading bureau citizens of Washington. Upon the breaking out
   of the late war, he resigned his office at Washington and went to
   Richmond, where he was tendered by President Davis the same position
   in the Confederate service, which he occupied in the United States
   service. He remained in that position, discharging its duties with
   remarkable fidelity and ability, until the Confederacy fell.

   Since then he has lived in Maury County and was for some time clerk
   in the Circuit Court of that county, the county of his nativity.
   He was subsequently appointed one of the deputies of Major Childress,
   clerk of the Tenn. Supreme Court. He was ever retiring and true
   man, esteemed by all with whom he had acquaintance and deeply
   beloved by all who knew him. For many years he had been prey to
   disease as stated; yet, until the last moment he bore it with
   heroic fortitude. His death will be regretted by those who knew
   him, North and South, as a chivalrous and courtly gentleman.
   Nashville American. (Columbia Herald and Mail, 21 Sept. 1877.)

   The Remains of Col. Marcus L. Pillow - Eugene Pillow, W. J. Whit-
   thorne, and A. S. Horsley arrived here yesterday morning from
   Columbia and escorted the remains of the late Marcus L. Pillow
   to that point in the afternoon. Capt. J. W. S. Ridley and Col.
   W. D. Bethel, Col. Pillow's kinsmen also accompanied the remains.
   They were here Thursday night, but knew nothing of the sad affair
   until they read it in the American of yesterday morning. Col.
   Pillow's remains will be interred in Rose Hill Cemetery, Columbia.

   Co. William Pillow, father of the deceased, while in the Indian War,
   was wounded at the battle of Talladega, the ball passing through
   his body. A silk handkerchief was drawn through the wound, and it
   was believed his death was certain. But himself and troops had
   for days been on short rations and the lack of food in this
   instance proved very beneficial to him. He recovered. He was at
   one time one of the wealthiest men in Maury County and left a large
   fortune to his son.

   Col. Marcus L. Pillow was one of the most elegant gentlemen of his
   day, and no social entertainment was given in Maury County in which
   he was not the leading spirit. Nashville American. (Columbia
   Herald and Mail, 21 Sept. 1877.)

   On Thursday night last, a squad dressed in Federal soldiers'
   uniform robbed Mrs. A. O. P. Nicholson of three gold watches and
   all the money she had; Mrs. Constantine Perkins of one gold watch
   and her money; after which they paid Mrs. Gen. Pillow a call but
   upon being told they could come in the house, but not go out, by
   Mr. Mark Pillow, they thought best to vamose. Columbia Chronicle.
   (Nashville Daily Union, 14 April 1864.)

PILLOW, William - Wouldn't Fall Back - Very few of the young men of
this generation know much about the late Col. William Pillow.
Although he has been dead but little more than a year, and passed
a life having more remarkable events crowded into it than any other
man in the county. He was 100 years old when he died, having been
born before Humboldt and the real Napoleon. During all his early
manhood, his was a soldier's life, fighting Indians and enduring
the hardships of frontier life. There are enough incidents of a
historical nature to fill a huge book, and yet so quiet and unpre-
tentious was his life near Bigbyville, that no one knew when they
met him in the road, that they were passing one who was in many
respects a "grand man." He had the fine sensitive instincts of a
woman united to a lionic courage, and the purity of honor of a young
girl. He possessed sinews of iron, and even up to his death, he
walked as martially upright as old Hickory himself.

The 8th day of November, last Sunday, recalls to mind one of the
incidents of his life. A number of years ago Nimrod Porter, Esquire,
probably then a candidate for some office, met Col. Pillow on the
square one day, and in a smiling way said, "Col. Pillow, do you
remember the 8th of November, 1813?" "Yes, very well, the day of
the battle of Talladega."

The circumstances thus recalled by these two old warriors are these:
On the 7th of November 1813 Col. Pillow commanded a regiment of
Tennessee troops under old Hickory. Gen. Jackson's aid-de-camp,
Capt. Sinclair, rode up to Col. P. and ordered him to go up a
certain ravine, while the main army under the General would take a
different route.

"If you meet the enemy," said Capt. S., "fall back immediately."
The Colonel replied emphatically, "I'll do no such thing--I will
not fall back." Away went the Captain and promptly Gen. Jackson
rode up furiously and demanded in a stern tone, "Col. Pillow, what
is this I hear--do you refuse to obey my orders?" "Yes, sir, I will
not fall back in retreat after I once become engaged in a fight--
I will not leave my wounded men on the field to be scalped by the
demons. But, General, I will 'hold them off' till you come up."

The face of Jackson melted in an instant from inflexible rigidity
into a bland smile of pleasure, and his porcupine hair smoothed
down, as he said quickly, "All right, Colonel, all right, just
fight 'em till I come up. All right." They met the Indians the
next day and the world knows the result.

Some time after this event, on a certain occasion, Gen. Jackson
became very violent at some reports and said he would cowhide any
many who started the reports in question. "No, you won't," said
Gen. Roberts of Rutherford Creek, "you will do no such thing. You
will not cowhide this man, he is not to be cowhided by mortal man.
"It's Col. Pillow." It is hardly necessary to say, no more was
heard of cowhiding. (Columbia Herald, 12 Nov. 1869.)

PINION, Dovey, who is considered insane has been placed in jail for
safekeeping. (Columbia Herald, 12 June 1872, 26 July 1872.)

PINKARD, Matt J., of Nashville, sergeant in Harding's Artillery, was
killed at Vicksburg a few days before the surrender; being very
tall, his head frequently loomed up above the breastworks and shot
was frequently aimed at him. One shot struck him in head and
killed him. (Nashville Dispatch, 5 Aug. 1863.)

PINKERTON, Jos., of Williamson County, was killed at his sawmill by
a falling limb which lodged in a tree ten days ago. (Whig and
Tribune, Jackson, Tn, 21 Oct. 1871.)

PINKNEY, Henry L., founder of the Charleston Mercury, died there on
the 3d; formerly a U. S. Congressman. (Nashville Dispatch, 26 Feb.
1863.)

PINKSTON, Turner, an old citizen of District 4 in Maury County, is very low and not expected to live. (Columbia Herald and Mail, 25 Aug. 1876.) Died a few days, oldest man in this end of the county. (Columbia Herald and Mail, 1 Sept. 1876.)

PINKSTON, Mrs. William, of Brush Creek, District 4, Maury County, horse ran away, ran under a tree, her head was struck crushed her skull and killed her instantly. (Memphis Daily Appeal, 28 March 1870.)

PIPER, David C., ord. sgt., Company F, 18th Ohio, was drowned Saturday in Elk River near Fayetteville, Tn., from Frankfort, Ross County, Ohio, age 22; only relative is a sister in Pennsylvania. He was buried in a church cemetery at Fayetteville. He was swimming in deep water and got the cramps. (Nashville Dispatch, 20 June 1862.)

PISE, Rev. Dr., died in Ohio a few days ago. (Maury Democrat, 6 Sept. 1894.) Memorial window to David Pise will be placed in Episcopal Church in Glendale, Ohio; he was born 1815 at Northampton, Mass.; died 19 Aug. 1895 at Glendale where he had been rector 19 years; once served St. Peter's in Columbia. (Columbia Herald, 11 Oct. 1895.)

PISTOLE, Thomas, Company K, 5th Tennessee Cavalry, was killed 22 Feb. 1864 on Calf Killer near Sparta, Tn. (Nashville Daily Union, 24 Feb. 1864.)

PITT, Jacob, was killed in Springfield by Presley Pollock on Monday the 2d; difficulty about a horse. (Nashville Daily Union, 8 Feb. 1863.)

PITTMAN, Major John B., died on August 25. (Nashville Dispatch, 27 Aug. 1863.)

PITTS, Rev. Fountain Elliott, of West End Church, died of pneumonia on Friday, 12 miles from Louisville; was colonel in 61 Tennessee Regiment and fought at Vicksburg; buried in Mt. Olivet, Nashville; Methodist. (Nashville Union and American, 24 May 1874.)

PLAXTON, John, well known printer, born in England, died Sunday morning of dropsy of the heart. (Nashville Union and American, 11 Aug. 1874.)

PLOWMAN, Mrs. Joshua, died of cholera; lived on Granny White Pike. (Nashville Union and American, 22 June 1873.)

PLUMMER. There are seven living widows of Revolutionary War soldiers. The oldest is Nancy Aldrich, relict of Caleb Aldrich; she is 98 year old and a long time resident of Michigan, but now of San Francisco. She applied for a pension in 1894 in Williamson County, TN. Husband was a private in Capt. Yoult's company of Tennessee militia for 182 days. She was Nancy Plummer before her marriage. (Columbia Herald, 12 Aug. 1898.)

POCAHONTAS. The grave of Pocahontas was opened on 30 May 1923 and found to be empty. She married John Rolfe, an Englishman, and lived in London. She died 1617 of smallpox just as she was about to return to the colonies. According to records, she was buried under the chancel of the church at Gravesend 300 years ago. A movement had recently been started to have her buried at Arlington Cemetery. (Daily Herald, Columbia, Tn, 30 May 1923.)

PODESTA, Tony, 24, shot himself through the head in an alley at the Gayoso Hotel in Memphis; he had quarreled with quadroon Mary Hinson in a fit of jealousy; will die. (Memphis Daily Appeal, 5 Jan. 1868.)

POE, L. M., Company A, 28th Alabama Infantry, CSA, Confederate prisoner of war, died of injuries received from the falling of the stairs and floors at the Convalescent Barracks on Tuesday. (Nashvill Daily Union, 1 Oct. 1863.)

POGUE, Conner, infant son of Alexander and Addie Pogue, died Wednesday last at Hampshire. (Columbia Herald and Mail, 24 Aug. 1874.)

POHLMAN, Sue Holt, infant daughter of W. H. and Georgie Pohlman, will be buried Saturday. (Nashville Republican Banner, 24 April 1869.)

POINDEXTER, notorious rebel guerrilla leader in Missouri, was caught on the 1st, 12 miles from Hudson and was condemned as a spy and will suffer death. (Nashville Dispatch, 6 Sept. 1862.)

POINTER, Col. William H., formerly of Williamson County, died on his plantation near Helena, Ark., last week; brought back to family burying ground near Thompson Station. (Whig and Tribune, 5 July 1873.)

POINTER, E. H. Camp Gillem, Tn. - An article appeared in the columns of last Saturday's paper under the head of Daring Deed; and as it needs correction, I now propose giving you the particulars of the occasion. The scout was sent out under the command of Capt. Russ B. Davis, 10th Tennessee Volunteer Cavalry, instead of Col. Spalding, as stated in your article. The command was subsequently divided and Lt. Crecy, 12th Tennessee Cavalry, was sent by Capt. D. with a detachment of twenty men up Duck River with instructions to scout the country thoroughly. He, instead of meeting a company of guerrillas, merely struck the trail of two, and after a brief pursuit, he came upon them while they were dismounted, resting at a house.

Lt. Crecy perceiving this, dashed upon them and killed both ere they had time to escape. The names of the killed were Capt. E. H. Pointer of Gen. Forrest's command, and Edward Beaufort, of the same command. Much credit is due the Lieutenant for his gallantry in this single contest.

During the same scout Capt. Davis captured and brought to camp several prisoners among whom were Capt. Geo. H. King, Thos. Fitzgerald, and Henry Love, all deserters from the Federal prisons. The former Geo. H. King was once a captain in the 102 Illinois Volunteer Infantry and more recently captain of a band of guerrillas.

This section of the country is greatly infested by these bands and much trouble is apprehended during the summer from these villians, yet I trust during the summer they may be wiped out from our midst. Signed, John Rodgers. (Nashville Daily Union, 18 May 1864.)

Private Edward H. Pointer, 11th Tennessee Cavalry, was killed on Lick Creek, Hickman County, Tn. He was killed after he had surrendered on 7 May 1864. The Federals took his pistol and shot him. He was on detached service as a scout and was captured at or near the house of Mr. Bradford on Lick Creek. The company who murdered him is said to have been commanded by a captain or lieutenant Creecy. (J. B. Lindsley's Military Annals, pages 708-709.)

Edward Pointer, son of W. H. Pointer of Maury and Joseph Buford, eldest son of E. W. Buford of Williamson county, were murdered in cold blood in Hickman County by orders and perhaps by the hands of Capt. Cressy, commanding some Tennessee Federal troops; Cressy himself was a deserter from the Confederate army. (Columbia Herald, 4 July 1873.)

Edward Pointer and Joseph Buford are buried in the same grave in Spring Hill, they were foully murdered in Hickman County by men wearing uniforms of U. S. soldiers. (Columbia Herald and Mail, 1 Nov. 1875.)

Tombstone inscription in Pointer Cemetery, Williamson County, out
from Spring Hill; Edward H. Pointer and Joseph W. Buford, died
7 May 1864, fell in Confederate cause.

POLK, Alexander Hamilton, son of Colonel William Polk died in jail at
Raleigh, North Carolina on September 9. (National Intelligencer,
Washington, 21 Sept. 1830.)

POLK, Mrs., mother of the Baroness de Charette, is dead in Cannes,
France ; descendant of William Penn, founder of Pennsylvania and
widow of Andrew Polk, CSA. (Daily Herald, 6 June 1904.) Andrew J.
Polk of Maury County married on the 14th by the Rt. Rev. James H.
Otey to Miss Rebecca Vanleer, daughter of A. W. Vanleer, Esquire, of
Nashville. (Nashville Whig, 17 Jan. 1846.)

POLK, Antoinette. Antoinette Polk's Ride. Miss Antoinette Polk is a
native of this county and a daughter of Colonel Andrew J. Polk,
before the war the princely owner of the Ashwood palatial residence
and magnificent farm. Soon after the war, Col. Polk and his family
went to Europe, and remained there until his death, which took
place in Switzerland in 1867. The family remained only a short time
at their beautiful home in this county, before they returned to
Europe to give the younger children an education which only Europe
can afford. Miss Polk has always been a fine horseback rider, and
during her visit to her home several years ago, she horrified her
city gallant, one day when they riding together in the woods, by
clearing a fence at a leap, while he had to get down and let down the
fence in order to keep up with her.

When Columbia was first occupied by the Federal forces, all the roads
were picketed by cavalry, who halted everybody and appropriated
such horses as they thought fit for service. Miss Polk had been in
town, and was on her return home to Ashwood, when she was stopped
by a picket, but was finally allowed to proceed. She had gone but
a short distance, however, before the Federals noticed that she was
riding a very fine animal and called for her to halt. She had no
idea of turning her horse over to the enemy, and accordingly set off
at full speed for home, followed by half a score of the boys in
blue. The chase was an exciting one and last for some five or six
miles, after which the pursuers drew rein and the daring girl was
soon safe under the shelter of her own roof. (Columbia Herald,
29 March 1872.)

Antoinette Polk's Ride. She was visiting me when I saw in front of
my house, on the Hampshire pike, Maj. Hunter Nicholson dashing down
the pike, pursued by cavalry in blue coats. I knew at once that
Columbia had been taken possession of by the Federals and I called
to Antoinette Polk. She came down the steps, the gauntlets in her
hand, and her hat with its long ostrich plume in the other, ran for
the horses in the stable, dashed through the woods, to reach the
Mount Pleasant pike, where Ashwood Hall, and the homes of her two
uncles, each a mile apart, were situated. They were filled with
soldiers who would be taken by surprise and captured, unless she
reached them in time.

She gained the gate which opened upon the pike, and as she did so,
she saw approaching her three Federal soldiers, fast riders, thrown
out to capture prisoners, and then commenced a wonderful race. The
horse was a young thoroughbred, and seemed to realize her peril.
The last she saw of the cavalrymen they were riding their spurs into
their horses sides with her head almost on a level with those of
their horses. She gained the woods and was lost to their sight.
On reaching Ashwood, she roused the Confederate soldiers, and was
taken almost fainting from her horse; the horse's mouth covered with
blood and foam from its bit. The soldiers picked up a trophy,
her long ostrich plume, which dropped from her hat, and returned
showing it to the colonel, who said, "Why did you not shoot her in
the back?" (Memoirs of a Southern Woman, by Mary Polk Branch;
Mrs. Branch was first cousin to Antoinette Polk.)

POLK, Antoinette - Continued
Antoinette Polk's Ride - The ride of Miss Antoinette Polk is
historical. When Wilder's cavalry on a raid into Columbia one
morning, some of them started to Ashwood, six miles away, to surprise and capture some Confederates recuperating there. Miss Polk,
a beautiful young woman, heard it, and quietly slipped out to the
stable and put the bridle and saddle on her through-bred mare.
(The Polks were among the first to introduce the thoroughbreds into
this country.)

She mounted and started across the lawn for the gate to the pike.
A countryman seeing her coming through opened the gate just as a
squad of cavalry thundered down on her to intercept her. But the
girl, carrying the good blood of a long line of nervy ancestors in
her veins, and the mare the blood a "a hundred kings of the desert"
in hers, and striking her spirited animal with her ostrich-plumed
riding hat, she left the cavalrymen as if they were hitched to the
fence, and flew down the pike like a winged angel on a beam of sun-
light! No prisoners were taken at Ashwood that day. Columbia
Daily Herald. (Florence, Ala., Times, 16 July 1892.)

Baroness Charette, Patroness of U. S. Soldiers in Dead. Baronesse
de Charette, formerly Miss Antoinette Polk of Maury County, belle and
beauty of antebellum days and heroine of the Confederacy, wife of a
member of the old French nobility and recently the hostess and angel
of good cheer to Tennessee soldiers in France, passed away on
February 3.

Recent articles in the press of the country told of Baroness
Charette's interest in the soldiers from her native state and how
whenever she met a group of them she would say, "I am going to kiss
every one of you."

Although she was 76 years of age, the Baroness entertained lavishly
for the soldiers at her beautiful chateau, working hand-in-hand with
the Y.M.C.A. to help make the men happy and contented so far from
their homes and loved ones.

She felt, no doubt, as was told a few days ago in the Herald, that
in ministering to these men she was but performing another chapter
in that romantic career that begun more than half a century ago
when she outrode a squad of Federal troops from Columbia to Ashwood
and prevented the capture of Confederate soldiers billeted in the
palatial home of her father, Ashwood Hall, which was later destroyed
by the invaders. (N.B. Ashwood Hall did not burn until after the
Civil War; the editor was mistaken here.)

Baroness Charette was a daughter of the late Col. Andrew J. Polk
and went with her parents to Europe soon after the close of the
Civil War. There she married General de Charette of the French
nobility. Her husband is said to have commanded at one time the
papal Zouaves. Her son, Marquis Antoine de Charette, played a
gallant part in the war, fighting with the French army. With her
at the time of her death in addition to her son was her nephew
from America, Lieut. William Dudley Gale, Jr., of Nashville, an
officer in the 18th Field Artillery, who had gone for a visit to
the Brittany chateau when the beloved woman succumbed to a brief
illness.

Baroness Charette had a number of relatives in Maury County and in
Nashville. She was a cousin of Mrs. Campbell Brown of Spring Hill
and Mrs. Mary E. Branch of Nashville. (Daily Herald, 27 Feb. 1919.)

General Baron de Charette died at his home in Brittany France;
married Miss Antoinette Polk of Maury County while she was visiting
in France. She was daughter of Andrew Polk and sister of Van Leer
Polk; they had one son; he was one of the best known Royalists in
France and was closely related to the royal family; grandson of the

POLK, Antoinette - Continued
Duke de Berry; was one time commander of Papal Zouaves; met Miss
Polk in Rome. She visited Nashville two years ago. (Maury
Democrat, 26 Oct. 1911.)

Baroness de Charette of France, who is visiting her relatives the
Polks and Van Leer Kirkmans of Nashville, was before her marriage
to the Baron, Miss Antoinette Polk, daughter of Capt. Andrew J.
Polk of Ashwood, Maury County, Tn. (Columbia Herald, 15 Nov. 1895.)

POLK, Leonidas. Buried in Christ Church, 2900 St. Charles Ave., New
Orleans at the right of the altar; marble slab in floor reading:
Leonidas Polk, 1806-1864, First Bishop of Louisiana, and his wife
Frances Ann Devereux, 1807-1875. (Inscription on marble slab in
church.)

At the battle in which General Leonidas Polk was killed, General
Sherman espying a group of rebel officers upon a neighboring
eminence engaged in scanning our lines through their field glasses,
called an artillery officer and pointed toward this group and
ordered a few shells to be thrown in that direction. A few were
fired into the group, one of which seems to have burst and struck
one of the number. It appeared that General Polk was the victim of
his own temerity by venturing within the range of our artillery.
(Nashville Daily Union, 22 Jan. 1865.)

The Bishops of Vermont and Mississippi have arrived in New Orleans
and will consecrate J. P. Wilmer as Bishop ofLouisiana in place of
Bishop Polk, killed at Lost Mountain during the war. (Memphis
Avalanche, 7 Nov. 1866.)

Bishop Polk's wife and daughter are about to open a school in New
Orleans. (Memphis Daily Appeal, 24 Oct. 1868.)

Captain William M. Polk, son of the late Bishop, and Miss Ada Lyon,
daughter of the Hon. F. S. Lyon of Demopolis, Ala., were married
there on the 14th by Bishop Wilmer. (Memphis Daily Appeal, 21 Nov.
1866.)

General Polk's Widow. After the war, General Forrest went all the
way from Memphis to Columbia to offer his home to the widow of Gen.
Polk as long as he had a crust of bread to divide. Mrs. Polk's
daughter, in telling the incident to Dr. Cowan, said she loved
Forrest next to her own father, whose memory Forrest so greatly
revered. She said when he came to Columbia and sent up his card,
her mother did not wish her to go down to see him for fear the
daughter might notice some of the General's bad grammar or rough
ways. But the daughter begged till she was allowed to go down
with her mother.

She said a magnificent specimen of a man arose with all the grace
of a Chesterfield, free from any ungrammatical language in his
conversation, and after talking with her mother and learning of
her strained circumstances, told her with great tact and gentle-
ness how he had talked it all over with his wife, and had come from
Memphis to Columbia to offer their home to the "widow and daughter
of one of the greatest soldiers I ever knew, a man I loved as my
brothers," and adding, "and as long as I have a crust of bread,
madam, you and your daughters shall share it if you will."
(Maury Democrat, 20 Oct. 1894.)

POLK, General Lucius E., died on December 1 at 6 a.m.; was taken ill
four weeks ago returning from Pennsylvania where he attended the
marriage of his son Rufus; died of typhoid-dysentary; buried
December 2 at St. John's Church. (Maury Democrat, 8 Dec. 1892.)

POLK, James K. Death of Ex-President Polk - Intelligence of the death
of Ex-President Polk having reaching Columbia by telegraphic dispatch on Friday night, a number of our citizens met at the Court
House on Saturday afternoon to testify the interest which they
felt in this melancholy result. Bishop Otey was requested to act
as chairman and T. J. Kelly as secretary. (The Maury Intelligencer,
21 June 1849.) Ex-President Polk, who has been prostrated by one
of those attacks of diarrhea to which he is subject is still very
low and the prospect of his recovery doubtful. (Maury Intelligencer,
14 June 1849.)

A. L. Pillow is beginning to build a house in front of his present
residence, which many years ago was the home of President James K.
Polk. (Columbia Herald, 16 Feb. 1872.)

Many changes are taking place in Columbia. The famous cottage in
which James K. Polk resided at the time he was elected president
and for a great many years before has disappeared and in its
stead an elegant tactful residence in the modern style has been
erected. (Columbia Herald, 12 July 1872, quoting the Memphis
Appeal.)

Dr. A. L. Pillow is gong to pull down the house he now lives in and
build a new one. The one he is going to raze was the resident of
James K. Polk when he was made president. Mr. Sims Latta is about
to build a residence on the vacant lot adjoining the old Polk lot.
(Columbia Herald, 22 March 1872.)

The remains of James K. Polk are to be moved to the Capitol grounds
in Nashville. (Maury Democrat, 21 Sept. 1893.)

The contractor who was to remove the tomb of ex-President James K.
Polk from Polk Place to the Capitol grounds quit work. On taking
the tomb down, some of the parts so disintegrated that they fell
to dust and others lost their symentery, so the remains of President
and Mrs. Polk will lay in the vault unmarked until other arrangements
can be made. (Maury Democrat, 11 Jan. 1894.)

Polk's Election. W. C. (Carol) Sellers recalled a memorable
incident recently. He was in town in 1844 the night Polk's election
to the presidency came to Columbia, which was six weeks after the
election.

News came by relays through the country from Washington and when it
reached Columbia a crowd of several hundred enthusiastic Democrats
began to jubilate. They secured every old musket, anvil, and one
or two old cannons that could be found and kept up a continual
firing for several hours. Finally, they marched in a body to Polk's
home on West 7th Street and demanded a speech. The President
responded in a ringing address. The celebration went on for several
days.

Only two other men now living who were in the crowd that night:
Capt. St. Ledger White and E. C. Overton. (Daily Herald, Columbia,
Tn., 3 Jan. 1903.)

McFerrin Letter. To the editor: I read your paper with interest.
I know of no paper in the interior that excels it as a newspaper.
Your local intelligence is very interesting to Tennesseans
especially. I always like to hear of the prosperity of Maury
County, and especially of Columbia. Columbia has long been a
favorite place with me. I first preached in your city in 1832. I
was then a young man and a young preacher. In 1833 I was at Nebo
Camp-meeting at Peak's near Columbia. All those were seasons of
refreshing. I also attended a camp-meeting at Mt. Pleasant the
same year. Of all the preachers at those meetings only a few are
left. The Rev. Dr. McMahon was one of the Presiding Elders; my
honored father, the Rev. James McFerrin, Rev. Dr. Maddin, and many

POLK, James K. - Continued
others were there; but they "rest from their labors and their works
do follow them."

It was at Peak's camp ground that Mr. Polk and his excellent wife
were present when a sermon I delivered made a deep impression on
his heart, and which formed the ground of our friendship. I baptized
him, gave him the Lord's Supper, and took him into the Methodist
Church, closed his eyes in death, and preached his funeral sermon.
All this, not because we were political friends, but because we were
friends by the power of the gospel.

No marvel then, that I favor a window in the Columbia church as a
memorial of Mr. Polk. He was a Christian, not from momentary
impulses, nor only from fear of approaching dissolution, but from
a settled conviction that the religion of Christ was true, and that
he was personally interested in it, and that without faith in Christ
there was no salvation. Nearly 20 years had elapsed, but still his
purpose to be a Christian remained, and he finally consummated
that purpose of his heart.

Let no one say we want a memorial window because of political con-
siderations, but because Mr. Polk was a Christian and highly
esteemed citizen of Maury County and Columbia. The whole of Maury
should help the Methodists to re-build their house. Let every man
give a little, and the work will be done, and no one be hurt.
Signed, J. B. McFerrin. (Columbia Herald and Mail, 4 Feb. 1876.)

The Rose Window in the Methodist Church in Columbia is in memory
of ex-President James K. Polk. It is very large and is in several
departments. In the centre is a striking likeness of Mr. Polk and
these words, "James Knox Polk, 10th president of the United States."
Immediately over the centre piece is a beautiful white dove des-
cending. On the right is a sword and scales of justice, on the left
a compass and square. Below, supporting and sustaining the whole is
an open Bible. (Columbia Herald and Mail, 20 Oct. 1876.)

Days of the 40's - In 1844 when the Democrats had their big barbecue
in Columbia, an old gentleman who resided in this vicinity at that
time, concluded that he would take the "Ole 'oman" and "the gals"
and go to the barbecue. He went in true primitive style in the ox
cart. After seeing all the sights that were to be seen during
the day, he concluded to stay over night. Being a great admirer
of Mr. Polk, he put his family in the ox cart, and drove to the
residence of the candidate for President to spend the night and
bid him farewell before he left for Washington. Some of the old
gentlemen's neighbors found it out just in time to save Mr. Polk
from a very unpleasant dilemma.

They persuaded him not to go to Mr. Polk's to stay all night. He
took their advice, but he must go and tell him goodbye. Accordingly,
he, the "ole 'oman" and the "gals" went to the house and told Mr.
Polk they came to tell him goodbye before he went to Washington.
Mr. Polk shook hands with them very cordially. In the parting
interview the old gentleman and his family took a big cry and said
they were very sorry to part with him. (Columbia Herald and Mail,
10 Nov. 1876.)

Probably the best time ever made over the turnpike from Columbia
to Nashville was made by Uncle Tommy, many years ago, in the good
old slow days. President J. K. Polk was sick and sent for his
brother-in-law, Dr. Hayes, and Uncle Tommy took him in a buggy
behind two of Keesee's fine bays. He made it in four hours exactly.
It is forty-two miles from Columbia to Nashville by turnpike.
(Columbia Herald and Daily, 4 July 1874.)

POLK, Mrs. James K. (Sarah Childress) Mrs. James K. Polk is visiting her niece Mrs. I. N. Barnett and other relatives in Columbia. (Columbia Herald, 16 Aug. 1872.)

The widow of President Polk is in her 87th year. She is feeble and rather forgetful, but she maintains her cheerfulness and her interest in the world about her. (Maury Democrat, 27 Sept. 1888.)

Mrs. Jas. K. Polk, wife of Ex-President Polk, the 10th president of the United States, died at her home Polk Place in Nashville last Friday morning at the advanced age of 88 years. (Maury Democrat, 20 Aug. 1891.)
Mrs. Polk had been in perfect health until last Wednesday evening when on returning from a short drive, she was taken suddenly ill, from which she never rallied. The cause of her death was simply exhaustion, resulting from old age. Mrs. Polk, who was Sarah E. Childress before her union with James K. Polk, was born near Murfrees-boro, Tennessee, 4 Sept. 1803.

President Polk's Peculiar Will - Nashville, Aug. 15 - President Polk left one of the queerest wills that was ever left to be probated by an intelligence man. Everything was given to his wife and at her death it was to be turned over "to the most deserving member of the family bearing the name Polk." The decision was to be made by the State Legislature. The nearest relative until recently was State Treasurer Polk of Tennessee, to whom it was supposed the estate would come. It will be remembered that a few weeks ago, he became a defaulter to a large amount and fled the country, finally dying in Texas. His dishonesty cut him and his family off and just how the estate will be settled is a mystery. There are no other deserving members of the family bearing the Polk name and now that Mrs. Polk is dead the courts will have to decide the matter. It is not believed that the document will stand a legal test. (Florence, Ala., Times, 16 July 1892.) (N.B. The will was set aside.)

POLK, Joseph, deceased; his estate is insolvent. (Columbia Herald, 2 Sept. 1870.)

POLK, William H., died suddenly at the St. Cloud Hotel in Nashville on Monday night. Col. King was with him when he expired. (Nashville Daily Union, 17 Dec. 1862.)

The honorable William H. Polk passed through Cincinnati on the 28th ult. with dispatches from Governor Johnson to President Lincoln. (Nashville Dispatch, 7 Oct. 1862.)

William Polk, Esquire, who has for nearly three years resided at the Court of Naples, Italy, arrived at Boston by the last British steamer. He will probably meet with his distinguished brother, the President, in New York, from thence proceed with him to the Capital, and lastly pay a visit to his relatives in this county. (Columbia Beacon, 2 July 1847.)

Maury County Circuit Court Records; On 30 Nov. 1838 William H. Polk did "beat, bruise, and wound" Richard H. Hayes. Polk was later charged with murder. Hayes had called William Polk a "drunken fellow" and Polk horsewhipped him. Hayes threatened to kill Polk and later when the two men met on a downtown Columbia street, Polk fatally shot Hayes. His family tried to prevent an indictment for murder. The grand jury finally by a split vote said that William Polk had acted in self-defense and he was tried for assault, received a sentence of 6 weeks in jail, and $750 fine. His wife was allowed to move into the jail with him during the term of his sentence.

POLK, Mrs. William H., died on the 26th at her father's Dr. Dickinson's in Nashville after a protracted illness. (Tennessee Democrat, 28 March 1844.)

POLK, Col. William, died at his residence, Walnut Bend, Arkansas, on the 19th ult. His negroes, some 300 in number, are reported as in open rebellion. They allege that their master promised them liberty at his death, if they served him faithfully while he lived, and they are consequently committing all sorts of depredations. (Maury Intelligencer, 7 Dec. 1848.)

POLK, Capt. W. H., nephew of the ex-president, is among the wounded from Pittsburg Landing; received a severe leg wound and leg was amputated. (Nashville Dispatch, 22 April 1862.)

POLK, Frank, colored, of Maury County, is 105 years old; was born 12 July 1765. (Memphis Daily Appeal, 9 May 1870.)

POLLARD, Hugh, of Nashville, lost his life by being horribly mangled by an electric car near the Vanderbilt University on May 1. A. A. Hobbs, the motorman of the car, was put under arrest. (Columbia Herald, 7 May 1897.)

POLLARD, William, formerly of Wayne County, died in Mississippi on Jan. 12. (Wayne County Citizen, 10 Feb. 1876.)

POLLARD, W. S., a guerrilla, was committed to military prison yesterday. (Nashville Daily Union, 26 March 1865.)

POLLOCK, Miss, of Bedford County, was murdered by a negro boy, age 16, who belongs to Mr. Couch on the 23d, five miles from Shelbyville; the deed was done with a rock and she was dreadfully mangled. (Academist, Lawrenceburg, Tn., 1 July 1846.)

POMAR. St. Augustine, Florida, 27 Feb. 1894. No one could peep into the churches Sunday, and after witnessing the well-filled pews, go away doubting the devoutness of the people. All the churches were well filled. This resort has the reputation of being the rendezvous of members of society who feel a hesitancy in continuing social festivities at home, but who feel that they can keep right along here. Be that as it may, there is no difference in the number that attend, the hopes given during Lent from that held before. Society considers nothing but the qualification of its own sweet will.

There has been quite a commotion here among the native population by the spirit rapping and antics which occur at the house of the 14-year-old Rosalie Pomar. The local papers have an article every day about the visits of the Spirit, which chokes, scratches, and generally ill treats this child. A lady visitor who is a mediumistic spiritualist and claims to possess the power of communicating with the spirit-land by writing, called to see the child. She says that while she was seated there, she heard the rapping very distinctly and it came from a different part of the room from where the girl was standing. She also says that her chair was disturbed and that she knew that evil spirits were about. Questions were asked and the "spirit" wrote the answers. The information was that it was the tormented spirit of a man named Canova, who had been dead 100 years, but when on earth he had killed an Indian girl with whom he was in love in the house now occupied by the Pomar family. When asked by he tormented this child, he answered because it afforded him amusement. This, in the 19th century! (Maury Democrat, 1 March 1894.)

POOL, Mrs. Jestin, of Fallville, Missouri, is 100 years old and has been a church member of 90 years and still walks one mile to church. Some of her children are nearly 80 years old. (Maury Democrat, 17 May 1894.)

POPE, Miss Ann, died in Williamson County recently. (Whig and Tribune, 5 Oct. 1872.)

POPE, Mrs. Elethea, 105, died April 10 in Dyer, Tn; born 1796 in Sampson Co., N.C.; in 1824 her parents emigrated to West Tennessee and settled within two miles of where she died; there were three children in her family. (Columbia Herald, 19 April 1901.)

POPE, Jack, died a few days ago in Lewis County; had a hard life. (Columbia Herald, 13 May 1881.)

POPE, Mitchell, well known in Nashville, committed suicide in Chattanooga on Tuesday. (Nashville Republican Banner, 9 Sept. 1869.)

POPE, Thad, was killed by Martin L. McLean in Madison County on April 25; shot without provocation; the murderer had been arrested. (Nashville Union and American, 1 May 1874.)

PORCH. The oldest woman in America is Mrs. Porch, who lives in the mountains of East Tennessee at the age of 121 years; blind; hearty; walks without assistance; memory is unimpaired and she can recount many events of the Revolution. (Memphis Avalanche, 18 Oct. 1866.)

PORTER. The late Admiral Porter for 50 years swore off from the smoking habit every night and began again the next morning at 10 o'clock. (Florence, Ala., Times, 14 March 1891.)

PORTER, David, was killed at Nashville last week on the square by a painter throwing pieces of planks from a fifth story and killing him. (Whig and Tribune, 5 April 1873.)

PORTER, Francis, Eld. died of cholera in Nashville. (Western Weekly Review, Franklin, Tn, 7 June 1833.) (Possibly should be Porterfield.)

PORTER, Kenney, Son of the venerable ex-Governor James D. Porter, shot and seriously wounded Charley Thomason, respected young lawyer of Paris, last week. (Maury Democrat, 30 Jan. 1890.)

PORTER, Richard, colored, was 107 on July 4. (Columbia Herald, 12 July 1895.) "Uncle" Richard Porter died March 26 age 120 years; died in Macedonia; came to Maury County from Smith County in 1833 with Peg Legged Billy Porter, his master; in 1843 the estate of Porter was divided with Dick became the property of Marsh Mayes and valued at $250 at the age of 60 years. Four years ago his youngest son Stump Porter died at an advanced age. (Daily Herald, Columbia, Tn, 28 March 1906.)

PORTER, Mrs. Sarah M., 25, wife of Professor John L. Porter of Winchester, died; daughter of Dr. Samuel D. Whitsett of near Nashville. (Rutherford Telegraph, 6 Dec. 1856.)

PORTER, Willie, second son of W. T. and M. I. Porter, 6 years 11 months, died on congestion on the 12th inst. at Williamsport. (Columbia Herald and Mail, 18 Aug. 1876.)

PORTER, Capt. William N., formerly of Paris and lately of Memphis, has died and was buried in the South Memphis Cemetery; served in Col. Thompson's regiment of Tennessee Cavalry. (Paris Bee, 18 Dec. 1846.)

PORTER - Williamson Murder. Shocking Outrage - On Saturday the 1st inst. there occurred in this town, the most frightful scene we have ever witnessed.

It consequence of some previous mis-understanding between Mr. Isaac N. Porter and Augustine B. Hardin, a recontre ensued on the evening of that day, in which Mr. Porter and Mr. Wm. Williamson were mortally wounded by the discharge of pistols. Mr. Porter died in a few minutes, and Mr. Williamson in a few hours.

The former was shot by A. B. Hardin and the latter by his brother Benjamin F. Hardin--both of whom immediately fled and have not since

314

been heard of with certainty. The father of the fugitives, Swan Hardin together with Wm. Hardin and Watson Hardin, his other two sons, have been apprehended and committed to jail on the charge of being connected in this daring outrage.

But as a public trial awaits them, justice and humanity seem to forbid that any circumstantial detail of the affair should be offered at this time with a view to anticipate their conviction or to prejudice their trial by turning the current of public feeling against them. (Nashville Whig, 24 Oct. 1825, quoting the Columbia Telegraph.)

Isaac Newton Porter, who fell by the hands of an assassin in the early days of his manhood, was the handsomest man in the county. (Columbia Herald and Mail, 27 Nov. 1874.)

Tombstone inscription: Isaac Newton Porter was born 1802 and died 1825. He was civil and courteous in his manners, honorable in his views. Industrious in his habits and correct in his actions, in life beloved and respected; in death resigned and lamented. Thus humanity weeps over the flowers of youth, the life of Society cut down and crushed by hand of an assassin. (Columbia Herald and Mail, 2 July 1875.)

William Hardin was editor of the "Columbia Reporter" at the time he and his brother killed Porter and Williamson. (Columbia Herald, 12 May 1866.)

One of the most tragic events in Columbia's history was the deaths of Newton Porter and Bill Williamson on the same day. A feud between the Hardins and Porters culminated in the killing of these two popular young men. An hour before his death, I saw young Williamson from our window ride by. It was one Saturday afternoon. I recall the very pace of his horse. These Hardins who lived at the Robert Allen place all left the county soon after this fatal affair, in which Williamson was only endeavoring to make peace between his mutual friends. (Maury Democrat, 25 Jan. 1894.)

POSEY, E. M., died last week. (Linden Times, 8 April 1880.)

POSEY, Honorable Sidney C., 67, died on the 22d in Florence, Alabama; legislator; husband; judge. (Memphis Daily Appeal, 17 Dec. 1868.)

POSTON, William K., 47, died Saturday of congestion buried Elmwood Cemetery, Memphis. (Clarksville Weekly Chronicle, 27 July 1866.)

POTTS. Messrs Travis and Brown, law firm in Crawfordville, Indiana, wrote the courthouse asking about a Mrs. Potts, widow, who lived 15 miles from Columbia in May 1862. She had a son who owned or operated a blacksmith shop near her house at the time and she took in and nursed through a long spell of sickness, a Federal soldier. That soldier is very anxious to learn if she, or any of her family, are now living...I expect the soldier wishes to remunerate her or them in some way. (Maury Democrat, 1 June 1893.)

POTTER, Byron, 32, died recently in Chicago; last survivor of Dr. Kane's Arctic Expedition; was a seaman of the Rescue then. (Nashville Dispatch, 18 April 1862.)

POWELL; Columbus Powell's son was accidently killed while hunting recently. (Columbia Herald, 10 Nov. 1871.)

POWELL, Isaac M., Jr., age 17, died 17 May 1886 in South Columbia of consumption of the bowels; buried Rose Hill Cemetery; (Columbia Herald, 20 May 1886.)

POWELL, Mrs., 105, is the oldest person in Nashville; she was married 3 times, (1) Tibbetts, (2) Powell, (3) Dennis; had 10 children. (Nashville Union and American, 21 Dec. 1873.)

POWELL, Sam, died June 28 in Snyder, Texas; has many friends here. (Maury Democrat, 7 July 1892.)

POWERS, Albert, is confined in jail on the charge of killing Maurice Egan. He has received a telegram that his mother and brother will arrive today from New York. (Nashville Union and American, 30 July 1874.) Powers found not guilty of the murder of Egan. (Nashville Union and American, 11 June 1874.)

POWERS, Ora, daughter of S. B. and Mary Powers, died 19 Sept. 1887 of flux and her brother Fred, age 2, died Thursday of flux-pneumonia. (Houston County Times, 7 Oct. 1887.)

POWERS, Samuel H., 48, died on the 15th in West Nashville. (Nashville Dispatch, 16 June 1863.)

POYNER, Mrs. Elender, 90, member of Methodist Church for 62 years, died a few days ago. (Nashville Republican Banner, 13 July 1868.)

PRATT, C. H., of State Line City, Indiana, committed suicide at the Commercial Hotel with a knife. (Nashville Republican Banner, 28 Jan. 1868.)

PRATT, Henry H., 27, married his own niece, age 17, and when an attempt was made to separate them, he cut her throat and attempted to committ suicide. He has been convicted of murder in Lenox, Mass. (Nashville Dispatch, 12 June 1862.)

PRATT, Capt. H. P., formerly adjutant general on the staff of General Kirby Smith, fell from the veranda of hotel in Eufaula, Ala., and was killed. (Memphis Daily Appeal, 15 Nov. 1866.)

PRATT, J. P., merchant of Memphis, died of overdose of chloral on the 9th. (Nashville Republican Banner, 12 Jan. 1871.)

PRENTICE, Capt. Clarence, CSA, was wounded in fight at Augusta, Ky, and died on the 30th ult; son of George D. Prentice of the Louisville Journal. (Nashville Dispatch, 7 Oct. 1862.)

PRESLEY, John, was caught in band of a sawmill at Jackson, Tn, the other day and instantly drawn over large wheel; horribly mangled and died the next day. (Columbia Herald, 28 June 1872.)

PRESTON, Mrs. Hattie McMeens, formerly of Spring Hill, Tn, died on May 15 in Dewit County, Texas. (Maury Democrat, 20 June 1895.)

PREWETT, Lily V., daughter of C. L. Prewett, died August 20 at Beaver Dam Springs and was buried 7 miles from Culleoka. (Columbia Herald and Mail, 27 Aug. 1875.)

PREWETT, ___, 5 months, child of Mr. and Mrs. J. Prewett died. (Maury Democrat, 9 Aug. 1894.)

PRICE, Mrs. Ann, wife of A. Price, to be buried today. (Nashville Republican Banner, 31 May 1868.)

PRICE, Edwin, 18, died. (Nashville Republican Banner, 30 Jan. 1870.)

PRICE, Fillis, colored woman, who lives in District 20 of Bedford County is 120 years old. (Nashville Union and American, 28 March 1874.)

PRICE, James, his son and nephew, were hung by Lynch Law in Jefferson, Ashe County, N.C., a few days ago. (Nashville Dispatch, 29 May 1863.)

PRICE, Mrs. Joana J., wife of John Price, died on 7th in Nashville. (Tennessee Watchman, Clarksville, Tn, 15 Feb. 1822.)

PRICE, John, was killed in Columbia before the war by Capt. Wiley
George. At a recent difficulty in Columbia, George shot James Fain
in left hand and George was cut 11 times with a dirk. (Whig and
Tribune, 23 Sept. 1871.)

PRICE, Lemuel, deceased, estate is insolvent. (Nashville Dispatch,
5 Sept. 1862.)

PRICHARD, little son of Jesse Prichard of South Nashville, fell down
stairs Saturday night and so severely hurt that he will hardly
recover. (Nashville Republican Banner, 21 Sept. 1869.)

PRIDE, Capt. J. F., oldest man in Tennessee Valley, died Monday,
suddenly at Pride's Station. He would have been 100 in August;
born Wake County, N.C.; came to Tuscumbia, Alabama, 1818; four
children survive. (Florence, Ala., Times, 20 June 1891.)

PRIEST, ___, was killed on Cedar Creek, Perry County, last week by
one Blanchett; Priest had given Blanchett 10 days to leave the
county and Blanchett shot him on the 9th day. (Columbia Herald,
26 July 1872.)

PRIESTLEY, Dr. James, president of Cumberland College, died in Nashville. (Tennessee Watchman, Clarksville, Tn, 2 Feb. 1821.)

PRIGMIRE, Captain Thomas, 85, died September 24, died in Athens, Tn,
served in War of 1812. (Whig and Tribune, 12 Oct. 1872.)

PRIM, Dr. A. M., of Hardin County, died last week. (Whig and Tribune,
27 April 1872.)

PRIMM, Thomas Nathan, justice of the peace in District 24 of Maury
County, was born 20 April 1858; married at 19 to Miss Mattie Gray.
(Maury Democrat, 18 July 1895.)

PRINCE ALBERT. Queen Victoria has prepared the following inscription
for the memorial for Prince Albert at the Bath United Hospital in
England: "His life sprung from a deep inner sympathy with God's
will; and therefore, with all that was true, beautiful and right."
He left an estate of five million dollars. (Nashville Dispatch,
15 March 1863.)

PRISONERS OF WAR - The following Union prisoners have been released
from rebel prisons:

    Capt. F. M. McCall, 8th Tennessee Cavalry
    Maj. J. E. Deakers, 8th Tennessee Cavalry
    Major Charles Inman, 2d Tennessee Cavalry
    Lt. P. Aikens, 2d Tennessee Cavalry
    Lt. E. W. Robbs, 1st Tennessee
    Lt. Q. Fortz, 11th Tennessee Cavalry
    Lt. W. L. Brown, 17th Tennessee Cavalry
    Lt. J. J. Douglas, 10th Tennessee Cavalry
    Lt. J. W. Lentz, 8th Tennessee Cavalry
    (Nashville Daily Union, 4 March 1865)

PRISSNELLS, Isaac, 1st Tennessee Cavalry, died in Louisville the week
ending on the 6th of Feb. (Nashville Dispatch, 8 Feb. 1863.)

PRITCHARD, William H., telegraphic agent of the Southern Associated
Press, died at Richmond on the 31st. (Nashville Dispatch, 14
April 1862.)

PRITCHARD, W. M., 34, of Maryland, married his 5th wife last week.
(The Monitor, Murfreesboro, 7 Dec. 1867.)

PRITCHETT, Van, 23, killed his father Clark Pritchett; shot him twice
with pistol in the presence of his mother, four miles from

Nashville; had been drinking; Clark Pritchett was the son of the late Samuel Pritchett, a wealthy man; Van was a free liver and a high liver; married Katherine Kirkman. (Maury Democrat, 5 July 1894.)

PROFIT, Alvina, an aged woman, fell off the steps and broke her neck and died; she had son who was blown up in steamboat several years ago and she became insane; she was a habitee of the court because of her drinking. (Nashville Republican Banner, 23 Aug. 1868.)

PRYOR, Mr. Samuel, died on Monday last near Nashville of a lingering illness. (Western Chronicle, Columbia, Tn, 17 Nov. 1810.)

PUCKETT, little son of Mr. and Mrs. Gus Puckett of Shady Grove, Hickman County, died Monday, age 5, died of brain fever. (Columbia Herald and Mail, 12 Oct. 1877.)

PUCKETT, John H., infant son of John H. and Septima F. Puckett, died May 8, age 4 months 17 days. (Nashville Dispatch, 9 May 1863.)

PUCKETT, Mary F., versus William P. Puckett, divorce case filed in Nashville. (Nashville Daily Union, 2 Feb. 1865.)

PUCKETT, Perry M., private, Company I, 5th Tennessee Cavalry, was killed 22 Feb. 1864 on Calf Killer near Sparta, Tn. (Nashville Daily Union, __ Feb. 1864.)

PUCKETT, Rufus Coleman, born 1832, of Williamsport, served in Gant's Cavalry and was taken prisoner of war at Fort Donelson; he was in prison for 7 months 16 days. (Maury Democrat, 27 June 1895.)

PUCKETT, William, of District 17, Maury County, died Sunday of pneumonia on his way home to Williamsport. (Columbia Herald, 14 March 1873.)

PUGH, Emmet Anderson, 9 months, son of Mr. and Mrs. Sam Pugh, died Saturday, buried Mt. Pleasant. (Columbia Herald, 20 Nov. 1899.)

PUGH, James, died yesterday near Terry of old age. (Maury Democrat, 3 Oct. 1895.)

PUGH, John, age 24 years 10 months 27 days, died of consumption on the 13th in Franklin at the home of his mother. (Nashville Republican Banner, 14 April 1868.)

PUGSLEY, Mrs. Eliza, relict of Dr. Charles Pugsley, of London, died August 29 in Nashville; her husband came to the United States in 1819; resided 7 years in Indiana and founded the town of Albion, county seat of Noble County; he came 1825 to Nashville and died 1832, his wife and two daughters survived him; she was born Dartmouth, Devonshire, England in 1793 and married 1841: Episcopalian. (Nashville Dispatch, 9 Sept. 1862.)

PULLEN, Ellen, daughter of Mrs. J. C. Pullen, died 22 July 1869 at Wales Station, Giles County; attended Ward's Seminary. (Nashville Republican Banner, 22 Aug. 1869.)

PULLEN, John C., was accidently shot to death a few days ago. (Nashville Republican Banner, 28 March 1868.)

PULLEN (or PULLEM), John, was drowned in Elk River, Lincoln County recently; he was subject to fits and must have had an attack it is believed. (Nashville Daily Gazette, 19 April 1852.)

PULLEN, Mrs. Sarah, died last Tuesday, aged about 80 years; wife of Thomas Pullen; sister of the late Jeremy Gilmer; funeral at McCain's. (Columbia Herald, 29 Nov. 1895.)

PULLEN, W. A., blacksmith, Wayland Springs, Lawrence County, in shoeing a wild horse on the 2d instant, was thrown to the ground and his leg broken; he died that night. (Nashville Union and American, 17 March 1874.)

PUNDI, Henry, the first man to operate a store in Nebraska, died Sunday in Berlin. (Maury Democrat, 29 Aug. 1895.)

PURVIS, John, Esquire, of Monroe, La., had his home consumed by fire four or five days ago; he was badly burned and died; four children were burned to death; Mrs. Purvis escaped out of a second story window. (Nashville Dispatch, 7 Jan. 1863.)

PURVIS, Mrs. Sophia S., wife of George W. Purvis, has died. (Nashville Union and American, 19 April 1873.)

PUTNAM. Some of the spoons which General Israel Putnam had made of silver he received for his services in the Revolutionary War have come into the possession of Col. J. Ware Butterfield of Concord, New Hampshire. He has four tablespoons, 8 inches long, and on the handle is engraved I.P.B.D., the later initials for his wife Betsey Dana. (Columbia Herald, 3 Nov. 1871.)

QUAITS, Samuel B., died in this city on the 12th; former conductor of Nashville and Decatur Railroad; born in Virginia; belonged to Biffle's regiment and contracted disease that left him in feeble health; taken to Owen Station for burial. (Columbia Herald, 14 Oct. 1870.)

QUANTRILL, William Clarke. Monument in Lawrence County, Kansas: Dedicated to the memory of the 150 citizens who defenseless fell victims to the inhuman ferocity of border guerrillas led by the infamous Quantrell in his raid upon Larence on 21 Aug. 1863. Erected 30 May 1896.

Quantrell, Kansas guerrilla and murderer, was captured in Kentucky last week; brought to Louisville, badly wounded. (Nashville Daily Union, 16 May 1865.) (N.B. He signed his name Quantrill; he was born 31 July 1837 at Canal Dover, Ohio, died 6 June 1865 in Louisville; was buried in hidden grave at St. John's Catholic Cemetery; in Dec. 1887 his remains were moved to Canal Dover, Ohio.)

Man known as T. G. Henderson died one day last week at the home of Mrs. Parnell in Birmingham, Alabama. Before he died he confessed to her that he was Charles William Quantrell, the famous Missouri outlaw, who was supposed to have been killed in a fight with Federal soldiers in Kentucky near the close of the war. (Florence, Ala., Times, 17 Oct. 1890.)

The Lawrence Massacre. Up to this morning 128 bodies have been buried but it is still utterly impossible to obtain a complete list of their names, as so many are so much disfigured as to prevent recognition, while others are still missing, and are supposed to be concealed in the woods nearby or, they may be in the ruins of the buildings, besides many left with Lane in pursuit of Marmaduke and not yet returned.

Fifty of Quantrell's gang who are citizens of Jackson County, Missouri, and are all well known here and have been considered Union men; many of them are paroled prisoners from Pemberton's army, and some of them are from Price's command, from the fact that they are much sunburnt and have the appearance of having been long in the service.

After they had accomplished the destruction of Lawrence, some of them became much intoxicated, but being strapped to their horses, there were none left behind to give information as to who they were or where they were from.

QUANTRILL, William Clarke - Continued
Aug. 22 - The citizens of Lawrence, shot by Quantrell's band,
number 108, including the Major and his son. The inhabitants fled
into ravines and bushes, where they were fired into by the guerrillas. Twenty-five negro recruits were shot. The guerrillas took
all the money in the pockets of citizens and in houses. They stole
ladies jewelry even the rings from their fingers.

Jim Lane escaped on horseback, rallied about 200 men and followed
Quantrell about 12 miles south of Lawrence, where a fight occurred,
the result of which is unknown. Quantrell is now retreating toward
Missouri, burning everything on his route. No resistance was made
at Lawrence, the people being shot down as they ran through the
streets in their night clothes, and their bodies thrown into wells
and cisterns. The citizens had been expecting this raid and had
organized into companied for defence, but from assurances that
Quantrell would not invade Kansas, their organizations were abandoned and the guerrillas found them entirely defenceless. (Nashville
Daily Union, 22 Aug. 1863.)

Quantrell's force reached the headwaters of Grand River, Cass
County, Missouri, about noon on August 25, after burning Lawrence,
and then divided into squads of from 40 to 50, and scattered in
various directions.

Quantrell's men told many persons before reaching Lawrence that
they were going to destroy the town, but by some strange fatality,
the people along the route, who might easily have gotten word to
Lawrence, did not try. A messenger was sent by Capt. Coleman to
notify the people of Lawrence of Quantrell's approach, but failed to
get through. (Nashville Daily Union, 25 Aug. 1865.)

Quantrell's raid made 85 widows and 250 orphans. (Nashville
Dispatch, 28 Aug. 1863.)

Aug. 20 - Guerrillas under Quantrell with 800 men crossed into
Kansas near Gardner, 4 miles below Leavenworth, and started for
Lawrence and pillaged stores, shot citizens and fired houses.
(Nashville Dispatch, 22 Aug. 1863.)

Quantrell's band is now retreating toward Missouri, burning everything on the route. His force consists of guerrillas who have been
robbing and murdering along the border for months. (Nashville
Dispatch, 23 Aug. 1863.)

As of the 24th, 128 bodies have been buried at Lawrence, Kansas;
others are missing and are probably in the ruins. (Nashville
Dispatch, 26 Aug. 1863.)

At Lawrence, Kansas, 183 bodies have been buried and there are 182
buildings burned. (Nashville Dispatch, 27 Aug. 1863.)

QUATES, Samuel B., resolution of respect on his death passed by the
Nashville and Decatur Railroad conductors. (Nashville Republican
Banner, 16 Oct. 1870. Refer also to Quaits listing.)

QUEEN OF COREA, who died last June, is still salted down and according
to the custom of the country, will remain in her brine bath until
cool weather. (Maury Democrat, 18 Sept. 1890.)

QUINN, Mrs. Ann T., 91, died March 5 at Columbus, Mississippi at the
home of her son Major James H. Turner. (Nashville Repubulican
Banner, 10 March 1870.)

QUINN, Mrs., an aged Irish lady, died suddenly yesterday at her home
on corner of Spruce and Cedar Streets. (Nashville Dispatch, 13
June 1863.)

RADCLIFF, Joan, versus Thomas Radcliff, divorce suit filed in chancery court in Davidson County. (Nashville Daily Union, 5 May 1865.)

RADFORD, Henry, was killed by a train at Guthrie, Ky, recently. (Paris Gazette, 19 Dec. 1878.)

RAINES, Rufus P., 23, died of consumption on the 30th; son of F. R. Raines. (Nashville Dispatch, 1 Feb. 1863.)

RAINES, Dr. William N., died yesterday of pneumonia in Shelby County. (Memphis Avalanche, 31 Jan. 1866.)

RAINEY, Walter, son of W. S. Rainey, died in Nashville December 27, student at East Tennessee University, brought to Columbia for burial. (Columbia Herald, 3 Jan. 1873.)

RAINS. The family of General James E. Rains in Nashville have received word that he was killed in battle last week at Murfreesboro. (Nashville Dispatch, 6 Jan. 1863.)

The body of General James E. Rains brought to Nashville from Murfreesboro last night. (Nashville Dispatch, 7 Jan. 1863.)

General James E. Rains, commanding the 3d Georgia, 9th Georgia, 11th Tennessee and 20th North Carolina, minie ball struck him in breast and he fell near the colors uttering, "Forward, my brave boys, forward." (Nashville Dispatch, 8 Jan. 1863.)

The body of late General James E. Rains brought to city Tuesday and conveyed to Currin vault at City Cemetery yesterday. (Nashville Daily Union, 8 Jan. 1863.)

RAINS. Mrs. Ida Rains has been appointed administratrix of estate of James E. Rains of Davidson County. (Nashville Republican Banner, 18 Dec. 1870.)

RAINS, Mr., died recently near Hampshire, Maury County, of sunstroke; he had recently returned from Texas where he was bitten by a mad dog. (Columbia Herald and Mail, 13 July 1877.)

RAINS, Nancie, versus George P. Rains, divorce suit filed in Cannon County. (Monitor, Murfreesboro, 9 Sept. 1865.)

RALPH, Mr., was murdered near Covington, Tn, a few days ago. The sheriff of Tipton County is after the murderers. (Memphis Daily Appeal, 8 Feb. 1870.)

RALSTON, Rev. William, died. (Nashville Republican Banner, 7 April 1870. N.B. This paper quite faded and hard to read.)

RAMBO, Ellis, age 105, died last week in Pulaski, had been resident of Tennessee since 1807. (Whig and Tribune, Jackson, Tn, 27 Jan. 1872.)

RAMSEY, Major Jack, well known citizen of Davidson County, died at home on Nolensville Pike several days ago. (Nashville Union and American, 22 Jan. 1873.)

RAMSEY. Anderson of the 11th Kentucky convicted of having burned the house of Dr. J. G. M. Ramsey in Knoxville, was driven through the files of soldiers to the tune of the Rogues March with his head shaved and a placard of disgrace on his breast as being unworthy to be in the Union Army. (Nashville Dispatch, 6 Oct. 1863.)

RAMSEY, Mrs. M. J., 81, died near Blanton's Chapel. (Columbia Herald and Mail, 29 June 1877.)

RAMSEY, Jane, daughter of the late Robert Ramsey, died on the 6th at home of brother-in-law in Marshall County. (Columbia Herald and Mail, 12 Feb. 1875.)

RANDOLPH, Frank, a onetime Probate Judge and prominent politican, has been sentenced to death for murder in the United States of Columbia. (Columbia Herald, 23 July 1897.)

RANKIN, Roma May, daughter of D. P. and L. J. Rankin, 3 years, died in Edgefield on the 10th. (Nashville Union and American, 10 Nov. 1874.)

RANKIN, W. T., of Bellbuckle advertises that his wife Tabitha B., has left him and he will not be responsible for her debts. (Columbia Herald, 20 Sept. 1872.)

RANNIE, Katey, died Thursday, age 2 years 2 months 14 days, daughter of William and Mary Rannie. (Nashville Republican Banner, 13 Nov. 1868.)

RASBURY. In 1816 Lovic Rasbury came from North Carolina originally and made a brush pile and hung up some article as a saddle or bridle. This gave notice that the land (i.e. in Wayne County) had been occupied and no one else would attempt to settle there. This was what the writer was told was laying off an occupant claim of perhaps 160 acres. Most of the farms along the Buffalo River were originally occupant claims. Mr. Rasbury afterwards built a house and reared a large family on the site he marked out, all of whom are now dead.

One of the daughters was the writer's mother and he has heard her relate that bears, panthers, and other wild animals were plentiful in the woods, and some Indians roamed through the country.

The land was heavily timbered and covered with dense thickets of cane called canebrakes. The land was cleared with great labor. All the settlers for miles would assemble to help pile the logs in heaps so that they could be burned and great feats of manhood were displayed. The best dinners that could be had were prepared, and the day was wound up by an old fashioned dance at night.

This land now is the most valuable or among the most valuable land in the country. It is still in the possession of the first settler's descendants, being owned at present by his grandson John C. Rasbury.

Here the first settlers built, or had built, one of the first, if not the first, church in the county. It was constructed of hewn logs and was called Salem. The congregation was of the Primitive, or Hard-Shell, Baptist faith and the members of this demomination still worship there. A church house of more modern style has been built of late years. A large, well-kept cemetery is near the church and deed for same has been made by the original settlers. Signed, "Here and There." (Clifton Mirror, 9 March 1906.)

RASCAL. Notice the Rascal - Runaway from this place a man named John Boyd, or at least that is what he called himself. He is trying to impose on the public as a shoe and book maker, but is by no means a workman. He is 5 feet high, spare made, large eyes, strait black hair, and the fingers of the left hand are cut off. He is always making a fuss when by himself by grunting. Signed, W. P. Stewart. (The Academist, Lawrence County, 15 July 1846.)

RASMUS. A man named Rasmus, who came here from Lawrenceburg or Summertown a few weeks ago, died at Harbison House Wednesday. (Columbia Herald, 17 April 1891.)

RASOR, Edwin, who grew up at Williamsport, died in Bastrop County, Texas, of consumption; married only a year; went to Texas five or six years ago. (Columbia Herald, 6 Oct. 1876.)

RASOR, Mrs. H. H., formerly of Williamsport, died in Texas of congestion a short time ago; sister of Capt. James Forgey, daughter of Mrs. Fidelia Forgey. (Columbia Herald and Mail, 6 July 1877.)

RASSINE, James, of Blairsville, Pennsylvania, fell 40 feet down an embankment, his foot caught in a bush or fallen tree top which held him head downward. He remained there until the next day and when found he died in a few hours from inflammation of the brain. (Nashville Dispatch, 3 May 1863.)

RATCLIFF, Jesse, 27, inquest held on his body; he died 7:30 a.m. from acute inflammation of the heart. (Nashville Republican Banner, 14 Sept. 1869.)

RAWLINGS, Edward G., died November 30 in Ecleto, Texas. (Nashville Republican Banner, 14 Dec. 1867.)

RAY, Albert W., "Prince of Murderers," a few days ago passed through Nashville on his way home to Kingston Springs on parole; he boasted he had killed 17 men during the war. He no sooner got home than he was killed by a relative of a murdered man. (Nashville Dispatch, 31 May 1865.)

RAY, Alexander, Esquire, formerly of Shady Grove, Hickman County, died recently in Arkansas. (Columbia Herald, 7 Feb. 1873.)

RAY, Mrs. E. A., wife of Kindred Ray, died 16 Dec. 1867 after a long illness. (Nashville Republican Banner, 17 Dec. 1867.)

RAY, J. C., formerly of Nashville, committed suicide at St. Charles hotel Monday night; he was unemployed and out of funds. He will be sent to Murfreesboro for burial. (Nashville Republican Banner, 1 July 1868.)

RAY, John, of Theta, committed suicide Friday night by shooting himself in the head; he said he was going to kill rats. (Columbia Herald, 31 July 1891.)

RAY, Mrs. Lou Keyes, born 12 Feb. 1821 in Limestone County, Alabama, died 29 Jan. 1892 at Florence, Alabama, at her daughter's, Mrs. A. F. Wilkinson; widow of John M. Ray, who died 30 years ago; sister of George R. Cowan of Fayetteville, Tn; buried Florence Cemetery. (Florence Times, 13 Feb. 1892.)

RAYMER, William Riley, murdered at the Ridge, 17 miles from Nashville on Sunday by Thomas Coolan in some dispute. (Nashville Dispatch, 24 Aug. 1862.)

REA, W. W., of Pulaski, murderer, was executed on May 19 at Pulaski. (Erin Review, 27 May 1882.)

REAGAN, Mrs., 80, died on the 18th in Monroe County, Tn. (Columbia Herald, 27 Sept. 1872.)

REAGS, Mrs. Elizabeth, widow living near Flat Creek in Bedford County, fell dead from her horse last week while on her way to debate between a Methodist and a "Christian" preacher at Flat Creek Meeting House. (Whig and Tribune, 1 Feb. 1873.)

REAK, John W., Company C, 1st Alabama; a solitary stone placed in Oakwoods Cemetery at Chicago, Illinois, by the writer "Canny Scot." (Maury Democrat, 7 June 1894.)

REAMS, Henry, died a few days ago and buried in cemetery near Spring Hill; he served in Confederate Army and married the daughter of old Jerry Crafton, no children. (Columbia Herald and Mail, 22 May 1874.)

REAVES, Mrs. James, over 80, is very ill; her husband is 84 and blind. (Columbia Herald, 20 March 1891.)

REAVES, Mrs. Elizabeth, 92, died in Bedford County last week. (Whig and Tribune, Jackson, Tn. 20 July 1872.)

REDDING, T. J., formerly of Fountain Creek, Maury County, died Feb. 23 in Wayne County; had been sick for six months. (Columbia Herald and Mail, 3 April 1874.)

REDDICK, Julia E., wife of Charles P. Reddick, to be buried today. (Nashville Dispatch, 20 Nov. 1863.)

REDDICK, J. W., murdered his wife on Tuesday of last week at Campbellsville, Giles County, while she was asleep; arrested Thursday by James Brown in Wayne County, who met up with him and arrested him on suspicion. (Columbia Herald Mail, 21 Sept. 1877.)

REDDICK, George W., funeral to be held today at Elmwood Cemetery in Memphis. (Memphis Avalanche, 6 May 1866.)

REDDIN, The Rev. T. W., died at the home of the Rev. W. M. Neelley of malarial fever, age 27; his home was Iredell, Texas; was student at Cumberland University. (Lawrenceburg Democrat, 25 July 1890.)

REDFORD, W. H., funeral to be today. (Nashville Republican Banner, 15 July 1869.)

REDMAN, Colonel, well known citizen of Crittenden Co., Ark., was murdered in cold blood August 2 by three negroes who ran away from him about a year ago. (Nashville Dispatch, 20 Aug. 1863.) Colonel George Redman of Arkansas, upward of 70 years, died August 2, left large family; owned plantation 30 years at Redman's Landing, ten miles above Memphis. (Nashville Dispatch, 22 Aug. 1863.)

REED, Col. W. P., died about 9 May 1864 at Jackson, Mississippi, of wounds received at Fort Pillow; former pastor of Cumberland Presbyterian Church on Sumner Street in Nashville; in 1861 he became infantry colonel; transferred to cavalry under Forrest; he was wounded in three places during engagement. (Nashville Daily Union, __ May 1864.)

REED, James F., one of the survivors of the ill-fated Donner Party to California in 1848, died at Santa Cruz, California, age 61, native of Illinois. (Daily Herald, 20 Sept. 1901.)

REED, Charles, a circus actor, belonging to Madigan and Carrol's circus, was instantly killed on the 17th at Greenpoint by falling on his head from the top of the center pole while helping to put up the tent. (Nashville Dispatch, 30 May 1862.)

REEDER, John Morton, 47, died on the 31st ult; principal engineer of the City Waterworks; member of the Odd Fellows. (Nashville Dispatch, 7 Aug. 1863.)

REESE, Patrick, died 1865, left $60,000 and his will was contested, being broken by the widow. The case was finally decided at Franklin and the will sustained. (Nashville Republican Banner, 3 Aug. 1869.)

REESE, Capt. W. A., of Mt. Pleasant, has in his possession a very handsome sword that was taken from the body of a Lt. Colonel of the 22d Ohio Regiment at the Battle of Kennesaw Mountain on 27 June 1864. It was taken by Adam Clark Kinzer of Sawdust Valley, Maury County, and given to Capt. Reese. It was in this same battle our good friend Capt. J. C. Cooper of Mt. Pleasant was so severely wounded in the head by grape shot. (Columbia Herald, 5 March 1897.)

REID, Ava Georgia, died on the 14th inst. in Sumner County, youngest daughter of George H. and Carrie V. Reid; funeral in Nashville. (Nashville Republican Banner, 16 July 1869.)

REID, Reverend Carson P., 73, father of Rev. W. P. Reid, died at home of W. H. Long near Pulaski, Giles County; died on the 2d; minister in Cumberland Presbyterian Church for 50 years. (Whig and Tribune, 21 Dec. 1872; Columbia Herald, 13 Dec. 1872.)

REID, David, esteemed citizen, died at Macon, Georgia, on the 19th nearly 70 years old; had traded with Indians in vicinity of Macon when it was a settlement of just a few houses. (Memphis Avalanche, 2 Dec. 1866.)

REID, Dr. George H., funeral to be held today. (Nashville Republican Banner, 20 Oct. 1869.)

REID, Mary Litton, 19 years 6 months, died May 16 at home of father in New York. (Nashville Dispatch, 11 June 1862.)

REGION, William, Esquire, of Hen Island Bend, Hickman County, died. (Columbia Herald and Mail, 29 Oct. 1875.) (N.B. Some question in wording in paper about whether he died or not.)

REGISTER, Vernandia H., age 2 years 1 month 7 days, daughter of A. J. and Z. A. Register, died 4 March 1864. (Nashville Daily Union, 5 March 1864.)

RENFRO, Mrs. Bryant, burned to death near Culleoka, 1 mile east, last Wednesday; face and breast burned to a crisp; her face was in the fireplace; no children. (Columbia Herald, 17 April 1891.)

RENNER, Lilly, daughter of Alexander Renner, committed suicide 18 Sept. 1869 in Memphis by taking a phial of laudanum. (Nashville Republican Banner, 21 Sept. 1869.)

RENO, General, was killed in battle on the 14th inst. (Nashville Dispatch, 26 Sept. 1862.) The body of General Reno, who was killed in one of the Maryland fights, arrived in Baltimore on the 16th. It has been embalmed. (Nashville Dispatch, 25 Sept. 1862.) The citizens of Boston have raised $11,000 for widow and children of the brave and lamented General Reno, who was killed in the battle of South Mountain. (Nashville Dispatch, 24 May 1863.)

RESURRECTIONS. The bodies of Sioux Indians recently executed at Mankato, Minnesota, have been resurrected by doctors for scientific purposes. (Nashville Daily Union, 28 Jan. 1863.)

REVERE, Joseph Warren, formerly a well known merchant of Boston, died yesterday in Canton, Mass., age 92, son of Paul Revere of Revolutionary War fame. (Memphis Daily Appeal, 16 Oct. 1868.)

REXFORD, Capt. J. P., died in Nashville two or three weeks ago; left $3,300 to Baptist Theological Seminary in North Nashville. (Whig and Tribune, Jackson, Tn, 30 Aug. 1873.)

REYER. The funeral of the late George Reyer was attended yesterday by the German Relief Society of which he was a member; a portion of the 16th Infantry band joined the procession. (Nashville Union and American, 2 May 1874.)

REYNOLDS, Captain, Sutler of the 78th Pennsylvania and a wagon-master of an Ohio Regiment, while en route to Columbia on the 10th, was fired upon by bushwhackers; Captain Reynolds was pierced by 10 balls and instantly killed; the wagon-master was shot several times and cannot recover. (Nashville Dispatch, 11 July 1862.)

REYNOLDS, David T., of Pulaski, died Tuesday; prominent citizen and member of Vanderbilt University of Trust. (Columbia Herald, 26 June 1891.)

REYNOLDS (or RUNNELS), James, 5th Cavalry, Company B, got his brains beaten out at "Flat Top," which is "inhabited by the lowest class of prostitutes;" he was killed by Bonner and Gilmore, members of Company A, 45th Infantry. (Nashville Republican Banner, 14 Jan. 1868.)

REYNOLDS, Major, was killed at Franklin; a subscription is being raised in Hernando, Miss., to erect a monument over his grave. (Memphis Daily Appeal, 21 May 1870.)

REYNOLDS, Major General, mortally wounded at the fight near Gettysburg, has since died. (Nashville Dispatch, 3 July 1863.)

REYNOLDS, Mrs., wife of Lt. Reynolds of Company A, 17th Regiment, resident of Peoria, Illinois, accompanied her husband through the greater part of the campaign and at the battle of Pittsburg Landing she attended to the wounded and the dying. Governor Yates has given her a commission of major in the army, an unprecedented honor. She leaves to join her regiment in a few days. (Nashville Dispatch, 1 May 1862.)

REYNOLDS, Private Hiram, 35, of Company H, 82d Indiana Volunteers, was executed on the 17th in yard at penitentiary for the wilful murder in May of Washington Losier of the same company; had wife and two children in Indiana; he made a statement from the gallows. (Nashville Dispatch, 18 Aug. 1863.)

REYNOLDS, Samuel, Esquire, father of Mrs. A. G. Negley, age 85, died in Cynthiana, Kentucky on April 2, and buried at Covington, Kentucky. (Florence, Ala., Times, 9 April 1892.)

RHEA, Robert H., shot and killed his wife and accidently killed himself on Sunday last in Blountsville, Sullivan County, Tn. (Memphis Daily Appeal, 21 Nov. 1868.)

RHEA, Matthew, old citizen of Fayette County, died last week. (Memphis Daily Appeal, 23 April 1870.)

RHEA, Sheriff, of Monroe County was killed by moonshiners last week. (Maury Democrat, 21 April 1892. N.B. Later correctly given as the deputy sheriff.)

RHODES, Mansfield, has been arrested as a guerrilla. (Nashville Dispatch, 21 May 1863.)

RHODES, notorious guerrilla, was shot near Racine, Ohio; he had been in the rebel army and was one of a gange of Mocassin Rangers, who infest Western Virginia and was probably acting as a spy in Ohio. He was captured and was shot in an attempt to escape. (Nashville Dispatch, 26 Aug. 1862.)

RICE, Dr., of Marshall County, died 2 years after a dog licked a wound; died of hydrophobia. (Columbia Herald, 9 May 1873.)

RICE, Dan, famous clown, was captured on the 30th by Col. Grierson's cavalry east of Vicksburg. (Nashville Dispatch, 13 May 1863.)

RICE, Maggie, infant daughter of Capt. James E. Rice, died on the 28th. (Nashville Republican Banner, 31 July 1869.)

RICH, J. B., shot and killed his wife in East Nashville Saturday; then killed his brother-in-law; and then shot himself. He is expected to die. (Columbia Herald, 26 Aug. 1897.) Robert Blum Rich, the man who killed his wife and brother-in-law and then turned the pistol on himself, died last Sunday in Nashville. (Columbia Herald, 15 Oct. 1897.)

RICHARD III. On the east wall of a building in Leicester, England, the following inscription may be seen: "Near this spot lies the remains of Richard III, the last of the Plantagenets," fell at Bosworth 1485. (Memphis Avalanche, 7 Dec. 1866.)

RICHARDS, Ollie, little daughter of Joseph and Leona Richardson, age 2 years 11 months 17 days, died in Nashville, 13 Jan. 1887. (Maury Democrat, 3 Feb. 1887.)

RICHARDS, R. D., 63, died 31 Dec. 1867. (Nashville Republican Banner, 1 Jan. 1868.)

RICHARDS. James Hagan killed R. M. Richards, proprietor of Academy of Music on Monday for seducing his sister, in Nashville. (Columbia Herald, 17 Oct. 1873.)

RICHARDS, Walter, was buried at Elmwood Cemetery, Memphis, today. (Memphis Daily Appeal, 2 Aug. 1868.)

RICHARDSON, William, President of Northern Bank of Kentucky, died in Louisville on the 23d. (Nashville Dispatch, 27 Jan. 1862.)

RICHARDSON, Dr. Joseph W., 63, of Rutherford County, died at his home near Smyrna on November 19. (Whig and Tribune, 30 Nov. 1872.)

RICHARDSON, Riley, private, Company I, 5th Tennessee Cavalry was killed 22 Feb. 1864 on Calf Killer near Sparta, Tn. (Nashville Daily Union, __ Feb. 1864.)

RICHARDSON, John C., sergeant, Company I, 5th Tennessee Cavalry, was killed 22 Feb. 1864 on Calf Killer near Sparta, Tn. (Nashville Daily Union, __ Feb. 1864.)

RICHARDSON, W. W., radical of Coosa County, Alabama, hung himself on the 11th; justice of the peace; left letter of remorse for the manner in which he had treated the white people of his neighborhood. (Memphis Daily Appeal, 20 Nov. 1868.)

RICHARDSON, William, of Perry County is in his 100th year. (Columbia Herald and Mail, 18 Feb. 1876.)

RICHARDSON, Benjamin, 70, died last Friday. (Houston County Times, 7 Oct. 1887.)

RICHARDSON, W. L., of Tennessee, was among the wounded John Hunt Morgan left at Cynthiana, Ky. (Nashville Dispatch, 1 Aug. 1862.)

RICHARDSON, John, in Richmond, has been sentenced to death for stealing, forging and passing counterfeit notes; will hang May 9. (Nashville Dispatch, 26 April 1862.)

RICHELIEU. Richelieu's skull has been put back in the tomb in the church of the Sorbonne whence it was stolen during the French Revolution. The tomb was sealed up with great celebration the other day. (Maury Democrat, 18 July 1895.)

RICHET, C., of Pinckneyville, Perry County, Illinois, while in a meadow near Beaucoup Creek, was killed by some animal of the cat species; body was torn to pieces and devoured; only his leg, or the large bones from the legs, were found lying neat together. (Nashville Dispatch, 3 Sept. 1863. The surname could be Ricket.)

RICHMAN, Mrs. James, died on the 11th and her infant on the 12th of typhoid-pneumonia; husband and four children survive; lived at South Petersburg, Perry County. (Linden Times, 22 July 1880.)

RICHMOND, Major, of Polk's staff was killed at Chickamauga. (Nashville Dispatch, 26 Sept. 1863.)

RICKETTS, Robert Daniel, born 26 Dec. 1826 in Orange County, North Carolina, came to Mt. Pleasant as an infant; led reckless career until 1875 when he joined Mt. Joy Cumberland Presbyterian Church and in 1877 was licensed to preach; was vested at Fiducia in Giles County; married (1) Mary Smith and (2) Ruth Stewart, sister of his first wife; he was a miller during the war and was exempt from service; served as High Sheriff of Maury County one term 1868; was elected justice of the peace in 1849. (Maury Democrat, 30 May 1895.)

RICKETTS, Ruth Cox, wife of R. D. Ricketts, died 7 April 1895; born
5 May 1827 in Meigs County; came to Maury County at the age of 11;
married (1) Will Stewart and joined the church at Stewart's Spring,
8 miles from Mt. Pleasant. (Maury Democrat, 18 April 1895.)

RIDDLE, Frank. After Twenty-two Years in the Penitentiary for Murder -
Among the last long list of convicts toward whom Governor Buchanan
exercised executive clemency was Frank Riddle of Maury County.
Riddle was confined under a lifetime sentence for a murder committed
about 23 years ago. His sentence was commuted so as to expire now.
The crime which he has been expiating was the murder of a Jew
peddler new Williamsport.

At that time Riddle was hardly grown, therefore, he is but little
past middle age now. Those who saw him only a few years ago, say
that he is an exceedingly large, robust man, and was employed in
the heaviest manual labor in the molding establishment of the
penitentiary. He had been in prison longer than any man there and
never gave the prison officials the least trouble.

Thoseof our people who now recollect the facts, say that the peddler
was killed in cold blood for his money, and that there were others
implicated with Riddle, but all of them except him and one other
escaped punishment. The body of the dead peddler was found in Duck
River some distance below Williamsport and it is still known as the
Peddler's hole. (Undated clipping in scrapbook owned by Miss Emma
Porter Armstrong of Columbia, possibly dating in the 1890's as
Riddle was sentenced in 1871 and again in 1872 for this murder.
Refer also to the Friedman entry in this book.)

RIDDLEBURGER, famous restaurant man of Nashville, died there last
Monday; at one time weighed 545 pounds, but only weighed 375 pounds
at his death. (Columbia Herald and Mail, 12 Jan. 1877.)

RIDINGS, Dr. G. W., estate being settled 21 July 1886. (Houston County
Times, __ July 1886.)

RIEVES, John, son of Joseph Rieves, was mortally wounded at Aspen
Hill, Giles County, on Friday by one Read. (Columbia Herald,
11 Nov. 1870.) __ Reeves, of Giles County, was mortally wounded
Friday night at midnight near Aspen Hill by one Read, son of the
representative from Giles County; both had been drinking; Read
shot Reeves in the stomach and Reeves stabbed Read in the side.
(Nashville Republican Banner, 6 Nov. 1870.)

RIEVES, Elijah, 81, died in Maury County on May 6. (Whig and Tribune,
18 May 1872.)

RIGGINS, John, one of the oldest men in the neighborhood of Spring
Hill, has lived 20 years or more on Rutherford Creek not far from
John Glenn; known for his slowness, honesty, and strength; he never
rode faster than a walk even when going for a doctor. Mr. Isbell,
his son-in-law, was going to the cotton patch to pick cotton and
found him in the field insensible; he was one of the oldest native
born in the county. (Columbia Herald and Mail, 7 Dec. 1877.)

RILEY, __, of the Tennessee Volunteers, confined at Camp Douglas near
Chicago was shot and killed by guard on the 14th while attempting
to pass through the lines. (Nashville Dispatch, 23 April 1862.)

RILEY, Colonel James, was killed on the second day of battle on the
Teche in Louisiana; brother-in-law of the Hon. L. D. Campbell of
Camp Chase, Ohio, and by marriage a nephew of Henry Clay. His wife
and daughter accompanied the troops from the beginning of the war.
(Nashville Dispatch, 8 May 1863.)

RIPLEY, General James W., of the U. S. Army, died at his home in
Hartford, Conn., Tuesday; born Windham, Conn., 10 Dec. 1794; had

been in feeble health; commissioned 1 June 1814. (Memphis Daily Appeal, 23 March 1870.)

RIVARI, Rosia, wife of Thomas Rivari, age 26, died April 9. (Memphis Daily Appeal, 10 April 1870.)

ROACH, Benjamin, was shot through the head by his brother David on the 26th at Good Hope Plantation on Wolf Lake, Yazoo County, Miss. Benjamin was the executor of the father's will; David had been drinking and Benjamin had tried to straighten David out. (Memphis Daily Appeal, 3 Feb. 1870.)

ROACH, James, was accidently killed at Denmark, Tn, last week by Neil Smith, who fired at a dog but hit Roach. (Nashville Republican Banner, 30 Nov. 1869.)

ROACH, Mrs. John, Jr., died Friday near Goshen in Maury County. (Maury Democrat, 7 June 1894.)

ROANE, Dr. James, died Feb. 1833 of cholera in Nashville. (Nashville Union and American, 2 July 1873.)

ROANE, Daniel, 90, died on the 10th near Neapolis, Maury County. (Whig and Tribune, 26 April 1873.)

ROBARDS, Julia C., young daughter of Col. Nathaniel Robards, died on Dec. 26 after long illness. (Lawrence Journal, 11 Dec. 1858. Note the deathdate and date of paper.)

ROBB, William, Sr., nearly 80, died January 1 in Sumner County. (Western Mercury, Columbia, Tn, 13 Jan. 1830.)

ROBB, Fountain Pitts, was killed at picnic in Williamson County two or three weeks ago by Litterl Gwinn; the governor has offered a reward for Gwinn. (Whig and Tribune, Jackson, Tn, 2 Sept. 1871.)

ROBERSON, Capt. Andrew, died in Morgan County, Ala., on the 17th. (Florence, Ala., Times, 29 Aug. 1891.)

ROBERTS, Daniel, has been arrested for having two wives. (Nashville Daily Union, 17 March 1865.)

ROBERTS, Ellen, little daughter of William Roberts of Green Plains farm, died on the 4th. (Columbia Herald, 19 April 1872.)

ROBERTS, Emily, of Cave Spring place, near Williamsport, had twins last week; one of them has died. (Columbia Herald and Mail, 28 May 1875.)

ROBERTS. The comptroller of the treasury has passed favorably on a claim for $65 in favor of George P. Roberts of Tennessee, which was filed nearly 30 years ago. Mr. Roberts was a member of Captain David Beaty's company of independent scouts, which had never been regularly mustered into service. Congress recognized their service in 1870 and Mr. Roberts was originally allowed $1034. Mr. Roberts actually had served compulsively in Confederate service and did not join Capt. Beaty's scouts until 1 Aug. 1864. He returned the check and asked to be paid for his actual time in service. That was 6 Dec. 1871, and now the matter has been settled. Mr. Roberts' honesty resulted in his waiting 30 years and the government made a big saving. (Hohenwald Chronicle, 19 July 1901.) (N.B. David Beattie or Beaty, known as "Tinker Dave," was a Union guerrilla and lived in a cove in Fentress County. He was considered an outlaw by some and organized his band in 1862.)

ROBERTS, John, Senior proprietor of the Nashville Republican Banner, died last Monday at his home in Edgefield Junction; born 30 June 1809 in London, England, came 1834 to Nashville; Episcopalian. (Columbia Herald, 15 Sept. 1871.)

329

ROBERTS, wife of Capt. John W. Roberts of the Burd Levi, died at her
husband's home in this city last night. (Nashville Daily Union,
26 Feb. 1865.)

ROBERTS, Capt. John K., died 2 Jan. 1927 in Nashville; if he had lived
until January 3 he would have been 91 years old; he was the next-
to-the-last living man who knew Old Hickory and in 1845 shook his
hand at the gate of the Hermitage; born 3 Jan. 1837 in Sumner
County; served in the 6th Tennessee Regiment, CSA, and was in 27
battles. (Confederate Veteran Magazine, Feb. 1927, page 68.)

ROBERTS, Mrs. Martha, 83, died October 31; had lived in Maury County
since 1849; her husband died 1863; she was born 1813 in North
Carolina and had lived in her home for 46 years; she had 11 children.
(Maury Democrat, Columbia, Tn, 7 Nov. 1895.)

ROBERTS, Capt. Matthew W., old and respected citizen of Athens,
Alabama, died with congestive chill last Saturday. (Memphis
Avalanche, 9 Nov. 1866.)

ROBERTS, Sarah I., wife of William Roberts, funeral to be held today.
(Nashville Dispatch, 3 March 1863.) Funeral to be held today from
the Sewanee House, age 53, buried City Cemetery. (Nashville Daily
Union, 3 March 1863.)

ROBERTSON, Mrs. Cordelia, died on the 25th. (Nashville Republican
Banner, 28 Dec. 1870.)

ROBERTSON, Duncan, bookseller, died Wednesday in Nashville, May 1;
lived on the corner of Market Street and Wood's Alley. (Western
Weekly Review, Franklin, TN, 3 May 1833.)

ROBERTSON, Eddy, was struck by a 6-pound ball passing through a
steamer and hit in the left breast; died instantly on the steamer
on the Mississippi; was from Kentucky. (Nashville Dispatch, 1
July 1863.)

ROBERTSON, Miss Gertrude, of Dickson County, funeral to be held at
the Cumberland Presbyterian Church today. (Nashville Republican
Banner, 9 Feb. 1869.)

ROBERTSON, Miss Lizzie, funeral to be held today on Charlotte Pike.
(Nashville Republican Banner, 10 June 1870.)

ROBERTSON, Mrs. Matilda G., died near Williamsport on the 26th;
daughter of William P. Pool, one of the pioneers of the county;
she was almost an octogenarian. (Columbia Herald and Mail, 3 Dec.
1875.)

ROBERTSON, Nancy, widow of Elijah Robertson, funeral to be held today
on the Charlotte Pike. (Nashville Republican Banner, 15 Oct. 1869.)

ROBERTSON, Lt. Patton, son of A. B. Robertson, was killed in fight
before the surrender of Harper's Ferry several months ago; was a
graduate of the University of Nashville. (Nashville Dispatch, 13
Feb. 1863.)

ROBINS, H. A., Company E, 38th Tennessee Confederate Regiment, died in
general hospital in Louisville last week. (Nashville Dispatch,
27 July 1862.)

ROBINSON, Rev. Edward, Professor of Biblical Literature at the Union
Theological Seminary in New York, died on the 27th ult. at the age
of 69. (Nashville Dispatch, 4 Feb. 1863.)

ROBINSON, Emeline Maria, appointed administratrix of the estate of
Daniel E. J. Robinson, deceased. (Nashville Republican Banner,
29 Aug. 1869.)

ROBINSON, Caroline Howard, wife of Harry Robinson, died in Nashville on the 26th; native of Bootle in the vicinity of Liverpool, England. (Nashville Daily Gazette, 29 Sept. 1852.)

ROBINSON, James C., Esquire, of Williamson County, died on the 13th at his home; age 58. (Nashville Daily Gazette, 16 Oct. 1852.)

ROBINSON, James A., William Baldwin and Franklin Bratcher, privates, 5th Kentucky Infantry, were shot on Friday near Nashville for quitting post to plunder and pillage, for robbery, for disorderly conduct, and for straggling. (Nashville Dispatch, 17 Nov. 1863.)

ROBINSON, John A., a wealthy gentleman of Norwich, Connecticut, died recently and in his will directed that his remains should be kept for three days before they were placed in the grave, where the lid to the coffin was to be removed, and the coffin so closed that a person could readily get out. It was provided that food and water be placed in the coffin. A hammer, too, was to lie near his right hand, while a lamp was to burn in his sepulcher for three days and three nights. Every one of the provisions was rigidly enforced. (Maury Democrat, 3 May 1888.)

ROBINSON, Capt. Joseph W., died on the 7th in Nashville, age 38, native of Bangor, Maine; resolution of respect to his widow is to be made. (Nashville Daily Union, 8 April 1863.) Capt. Joseph W. Robinson, commissary of subsistence, 38, died on the 7th; survived by widow. (Nashville Dispatch, 9 April 1863.)

ROCHE. A daughter of Mr. Roche of Nashville was mortally wounded in the late bombardment of Chattanooga. (Nashville Dispatch, 1 Sept. 1863.)

ROCHE, Amanda, wife of F. G. Roche, was among the deaths Sunday of yellow fever in Memphis; a little daughter also died. (Democratic Herald, 27 Oct. 1855.)

ROCHE, F. G., formerly of Columbia, died in Nashville; remains returned and buried at St. John's. (Maury Democrat, 20 Oct. 1892.)

ROCKWELL, Eugene B., telegraph operator at Nashville, died Tuesday of cholera; his wife died of the same a few days before as did S. Adams, music professor at Ward's Female School. (Memphis Avalanche, 22 Sept. 1866.)

RODDY, infant child of A. J. Roddy, died Sunday and buried at Ebenezer Church at Ettaton, Maury County. (Maury Democrat, 20 June 1895.)

RODDY, Captain, of Washington County, Tn, recently arrested and charged with being a member of the Haun court martial. (Monitor, Murfreesboro, 9 Sept. 1865.)

RODDY, or RODDEY, Philip Dale. Roddy was to come in at Decatur, Ala., yesterday and surrender. (Nashville Dispatch, 14 May 1865.)

General Roddy, Confederate cavalry officer, now in New York and a businessman, is stopping at the Overton Hotel. (Memphis Daily Appeal, 23 Dec. 1868.) General Roddy, the distinguished cavalryman, is at the Peabody Hotel. Gen. S. B. Buckner left Memphis last evening for Louisville. (Memphis Daily Appeal, 7 May 1869.)

General P. D. Roddy says he met Fanny E. Shotwell in 1867 and contracted an intimacy which lasted several years; the infatuation has cost him a great deal of money. She calls herself Carlotta F. Roddy and she is charged with larceny and is on trial. (Nashville Union and American, 21 July 1874.) (N.B. He died in London, England, 20 July 1897 and is buried Tuscaloosa, Ala.)

RODDY, Miss Lizzie Henrietta, of Kedron died. (Columbia Herald, 14 Aug. 1896.)

RODGERS, Jacob, of Henry County, Iowa, died 30 Aug. 1889 at the age of
112; born 1 Jan. 1777 near Pittsburgh; fought at Lunday's Lane, as
did Capt. Peter Foster and J. Chandler in the War of 1812. (Maury
Democrat, 1 Sept. 1889.)

RODMAN, Brigadier General, died 29th ult. near Hagerstown of wounds
received in battle of Antietam. (Nashville Dispatch, 7 Oct. 1862.)

ROGAN, Bud, of Gallatin, Tn, is perhaps the tallest person in the world;
colored; 8 feet tall; each arm is 96 inches long, hands 13 1/2
inches long, and feet 18 inches long; for the past 10 years he has
been unable to walk and rides in a homemade wagon drawn by two
full grown billy goats; he only weighs 156 pounds. (Columbia
Herald, 17 Dec. 1897.)

ROGERS, Barney, of Sumner County, of 109 years old. (Nashville
Republican Banner, 2 March 1871.)

ROGERS, Edmund, died on the 28th at the age of 82; born 5 May 1762 in
Caroline County, Virginia, died in Barren County, Ky; was a soldier
in the campaign of 1781 when Cornwallis surrendered; came to
Kentucky in 1783, and made military surveys; another Revolutionary
patriot gone. (Murfreesboro News, 18 Sept. 1843.)

ROGERS, Aunt Haley, colored, pure-blooded Ethiopian negress, died on
the farm of Drew Mays, 4 miles west of Milan, at the age of 116
years; oldest person in Tennessee; brought to North Georgia from
Africa in 1810 and to Gibson County 60 years ago; was an original
Voodoo worshipper. (Maury Democrat, 12 Feb. 1891.)

ROGERS, James K., married Miss Mary Ann Oakley of Paris on the 22nd.
(Gazeteer, Paris, Tn, 23 Feb. 1849.)

ROGERS, Dr. James, well known physician of Knox County, Tn, dropped a
pistol and the ball went through both legs; the wound is dangerous.
(Nashville Dispatch, 4 Feb. 1863.)

ROHR, George, 30, died on the 7th, CSA, served in Liberty Guards, 5th
Confederate Regiment until the end of the war. (Memphis Daily
Appeal, 8 Oct. 1868.)

ROKE, Aunt Susan, colored, died Sunday, four score years and past.
(Nashville Republican Banner, 22 June 1869.)

ROLER, Wiley, old and valuable citizen, died last Monday; came here
in 1847 or 1848 and went to work for Cross and Kuhn and made buggy
wheels. (Columbia Herald and Mail, 4 May 1877.)

ROLLS, J. Stanley, 75, died a few days ago of heart failure; Mason;
deputy sheriff of Stewart County under Taylor Bogard. (Stewart
Courier, 6 May 1892.)

RONEX, Thomas, of Decatur, Ala., was sent to military prison yesterday
for bushwhacking. (Nashville Daily Union, 31 May 1865.)

ROOKS, T. S., a Baptist minister, was tarred and feathered at Westmoreland, Kansas. He was accused of an attempted assault on a
young woman. (Maury Democrat, 1 August 1895.)

ROOKS. Infant son of Joe Rooks died in District 2. (Columbia Herald,
12 Sept. 1873.)

ROOKS, Jacob. Several years ago one of the strangest human creatures
we have ever heard of lived in the vicinity of the old Hammer Mill
now owned by the hospitable and excellent Colonel Sowell. His
name is that of a tribe of birds, cousins to the crows, and very
inappropriately named, because the birds in question always go in
immense droves and the old gentleman was so misanthropic he lived

alone and died alone. His little grandson went to see him as usual, one cold winter day, and found him stark and cold in death. The old man was very unfortunately constituted and one of his children could live with him. He would sometimes take his rifle and start off through the woods and be gone for months, and years. Not a word would his family hear of him until some day he would quietly and unexpectedly return with as little concern as if he had only been gone on a day's hunt. Not a word as to his travels would ever escape his lips. (Columbia Herald, 29 April 1870.)

ROONEY, Frank, old and respected citizen of Nashville and lately a constant visitor to the workhouse and jail, died there on the 7th of sea-scurvy. (Nashville Dispatch, 8 Feb. 1863.)

ROOP, Joseph C., was found dead in his store at Flat Rock, Davidson County, Sunday morning with two bullet holes in his head; murdered and robbed on Saturday. (Murfreesboro News, 29 Sept. 1876.)

ROPER, Mr. William, of this town died Saturday. (Nashville Whig, 2 March 1814.)

ROOSEVELT, James H., who died in New York last week, left an estate of nearly a million dollars. (Nashville Dispatch, 15 Dec. 1863.)

ROSBOROUGH, A. M., now living in Oakland, California, was in the Florida War 1836-7. (Maury Democrat, 25 July 1895. N.B. Formerly of Maury County.)

ROSE. Joel A. Battle, Jr., wounded in the Battle of Mill Springs and killed at Pittsburg Landing, was an adjutant in his father's regiment, the 20th Tennessee; married near Chillocthi, Ohio. His body was found by Lt. Cliff W. Rose of the 31st Indiana and there was a letter from his wife on his body. Three former students at Oxford, Lt. Rose, Lt. Jack Lewis of the 41st Illinois, and Sgt. Major John R. Chamberlin, 81st Ohio, decently composed his limbs and buried his body in his native soil. Battle's father is a prisoner. (Nashville Dispatch, 20 April 1862.)

ROSECRANS, William Starke. General Rosecrans is paralyzed and not expected to live. (Florence, Ala., Times, 3 Dec. 1892.)

General Rosecrans has ordered the name of Stones River to be inscribed on the national colors of each regiment and the guidon of each battery that was engaged in the recent battle before this city. (Nashville Dispatch, 21 Feb. 1863.)

Mrs. General Rosecrans and daughter arrived in Nashville from Murfreesboro and are guests of Surgeon Swift. (Nashville Dispatch, 2 April 1863.)

W. S. Rosecrans is in Nashville, stopping at the St. Cloud Hotel. (Nashville Daily Union, 15 July 1863.)

A daughter of General Rosecrans is an Ursuline nun, who until recently was assigned to the convent of Santa Rosa, California. Fifteen years ago she was one of the most charming and most popular of the society ladies of Cincinnati. (Florence, Ala., Times, 7 Nov. 1890.)

The body of Gen. William S. Rosecrans has been reinterred at Arlington. (Daily Herald, Columbia, Tn, 19 May 1902.)

ROSECRANS, Charlotte Josephine, 13 months died November 11 at Yellow Springs, daughter of General W. S. and A. E. Rosecrans. (Nashville Daily Union, 18 Nov. 1863.)

ROSIN. The ashes of Rudolph Rosin were cast into Mississippi River on May 23 at St. Louis from the center of the Eads bridge, where he

had spent most of his life. About a year ago he visited his birthplace in North Germany and died. His will provided for cremation
and for his ashes to be returned to relative in Cincinnati and on
23 May 1897, his birthday, to be thrown in Mississippi at St. Louis
from the center of the Eads bridge. (Columbia Herald, 4 June 1897.)

ROSS, Christian K., father of Charley Ross, died in Philadelphia this
week. Up to the last, Mr. Ross never gave up the search for his
missing boy whose abduction startled Philadelphia 1 July 1874 and
became an unsolved mystery of the world over. (Columbia Herald,
15 June 1897.)

ROSS, Capt. James, died Thursday in Neville, Ohio, age 68; pilot on the
river for 40 years and with his neighbor John McFall was pilot on
the Duke of Orleans in May 1844 when she made her celebrated run
from New Orleans to Cincinnati in five days 18 hours, the quickest
trip on record. (Memphis Daily Appeal, 16 Oct. 1868.)

ROSS, Sir James C., explorer, died at Aylesbury, England, April 3, age
62; discoverer of the North Magnetic Pole and in 1839-1843 reached
78 degrees 10 seconds, south, the nearest approach to the South
Pole every made. (Nashville Dispatch, 3 May 1862.)

ROSS, Sgt. William, quartermaster sergeant of the 5th regiment of
Artillery, committed suicide on the morning of the 30th at Fort
Hamilton by cutting his throat. (Nashville Dispatch, 6 July 1862.)

ROSS, Roberta Alice, died on the 28th, youngest daughter of Dr. J. C.
and L. J. Ross. (Nashville Dispatch, 29 Oct. 1862.)

ROSSELL, Peter, of Oswego, New York, was 110 on April 22; he was born
1753 in Brooklyn and was full grown at the time of the Revolution;
he remembers the time when New York was under allegiance to the
British Crown; has been bedridden several years and of late has
been quite childish. (Nashville Dispatch, 7 May 1863.)

ROSSER, Mrs. Isaac, of Memphis was burnt to death while turning down
a lamp, age 32; remains were taken to Columbia yesterday; daughter
of Col. P. Gordon, and sister of Jo Gordon; married 1870 and
leaves two months old son. (Nashville Union and American, 18 Aug.
1874.)

ROST, Judge Pierre A., of Louisiana, one of the most eminent jurists
of the state, died in New Orleans recently. He was Confederate
Commissioner to the court of Spain during the war. (Memphis Daily
Appeal, 14 Sept. 1868.)

ROTH, Mrs. postmistress at Mt. Pleasant, committed suicide. (Maury
Democrat, 21 Oct. 1894.)

ROTHROCK, Mrs. Mildred, died on the 18th in Giles County; granddaughter
of Dr. Hunt of Culleoka; married George Rothrock. (Columbia
Herald and Mail, 29 Jan. 1875.)

ROTHROCK, Noah, of Muhlenberg County, Kentucky, adjutant of Col.
Howard's Alabama Cavalry, was shot and died December 30 near
Murfreesboro. (Nashville Dispatch, 25 Jan. 1863.)

ROUNTREE, Mack, is gradually wasting away under the fell destroyer
consumption. (Columbia Herald and Mail, 12 Jan. 1877.)

ROUNDTREE, Mr., well known proprietor of the Memphis race course, was
recently killed in a skirmish in Middle Tennessee; was in cavalry
under Bragg. (Nashville Daily Union, 1 Feb. 1863.)

ROUNDY, George F., Boston salesman, died on the 17th ult.; had a tooth
extracted two weeks ago and an artery was severed, blood flowed
constantly up until time of his death, which was caused by
exhaustion. (Nashville Dispatch, 9 Oct. 1862.)

ROURKE, Mrs. B., died April 17, wife of Michael Rourke and sister of
M. McCormack. (Nashville Dispatch, 19 April 1863; also Nashville
Daily Union, 19 April 1863.)

ROURKE, Malachy, nephew of Michael and Malachy McCormack, age 10, died
of protracted illness; funeral to be held Tuesday. (Nashville
Repbulican Banner, 7 Feb. 1871.)

ROUSSEAU, Mrs. Annie W., of Clarksville, died on the 8th. (Nashville
Union and American, 16 Dec. 1873.)

ROUSSEAU, Major General Lovell Harrison, is ill of inflammation of the
bowels, and is almost beyond recovery at New Orleans. (Memphis
Daily Appeal, 8 Jan. 1869.) Major General L. H. Rousseau died at
11 p.m. on January 7, buried at New Orleans on the 10th. (Memphis
Daily Appeal, 9 Jan. 1869.) He was born in Lincoln County, Ky, in
1820; his father was first cousin of President Harrison; served as
captain of Indiana volunteers in the Mexican War in 1846; in
Kentucky Senate in 1860; at Shiloh was a division commander under
Buell; buried at New Orleans; funeral at Christ Church by the
Bishop of Louisiana. His pallbearers were Generals Hatch, Mower,
Bickwith, Babcock, Porter, Tompkins, McClem, Steedman, Herron, Lee,
McMillan, Bussey and Gurney. (Memphis Daily Appeal, 10 Jan. 1869.)
General Rousseau died poor; his horses are being raffled off by his
staff to aid his widow. (Memphis Daily Appeal, 16 Jan. 1869.)

ROUSSEAU, Col. N. G., born 1816 on Bear Creek in Maury County, died
2 Sept. 1875; early in life he went to Mississippi; he was connected
with the Voorhies, O'Reilly and Herndon families. Methodist.
(Columbia Herald and Mail, 10 Sept. 1875.)

ROWLAND, John, 78, died on the 13th at Spring Hill; Cumberland
Presbyterian; married daughter of J. L. Dunlap. (Columbia Herald,
17 March 1871.)

ROWLAND, Major Thomas, who has been dead some years, had estate in
Detroit, Michigan, now the property of Confederates, belonging to
his grandchildren in Virginia; the property has been seized under
the Confiscation Act. (Nashville Dispatch, 2 June 1863.)

ROWLAND, William, private in Colonel Fowler's 54th Tennessee Regiment
Volunteers, who deserted and was captured on Shiloh battlefield on
the 6th in Federal ranks and in a Federal unit, was subsequently
shot in presence of all the Tennessee Regiments. (Nashville
Dispatch, 6 May 1862.)

A Sad Memory of the Civil War - Many of the good people of Tennessee
loved the stars and stripes and the Union with the warmest forces
of their lives. There went out in the Confederate army many men
who opposed secession and through the four years they trudged with
knapsack and musket on their shoulders...they loved the Southland.
Many a man volunteered because the South was dearer to their
spirits than all else, and because Tennesseans felt the stigma of
being drafted.

Some--many of these were poor men--without slaves or homes.

There lived on the Grandaddy Road, perhaps six miles west of
Lawrenceburg, in the wooded wilderness, in a log cabin, maybe of
two rooms, with a passage or entry between them a poor illiterate
man.

As I now remember, he could not read or write. He was a lonely
settler by the side of the road. His name was Carroll Rowland, or
Roland. He was what was then called a Union man. But in the heat
and passion of the time, he felt, for personal safety, and the
added fact that he was in the South, that it was the obligation of
the hour to volunteer. Perhaps, beyond a reasonable doubt, he
joined Captain W. B. Moore's company, in the 23rd Tennessee.

335

ROWLAND, William - Continued
I remember hearing him say--or it might have been my father
repeating what Carroll Rowland said--after he enlisted, "Take care
of my family," to the citizens who were remaining at home. There
were no resources in the Southern Confederacy, to give an allotment
to the poor wives and children, not to arrange for a ten thousand
dollar life insurance.

When Carroll Rowland lived with his family in that log house, he
knew no way to ease that white clay to eke out other than a bare
living of coarse bread and meat. And that illiterate and poor
woman was left to battle against poverty without him.

I am not prepared to say when, but perhaps after the army had
retreated into Mississippi, following the fall of Fort Donelson,
that Carroll deserted. He also joined the Federal army, and thereby became a traitor.

No one knows the struggles and temptations that came to the heart
of this illiterate Unionist wearing the gray. At any rate, he
became a traitor to the Confederate cause!

In some way he was captured, either before or after the battle of
Shiloh; recognized; tried and shot.

In that section when the waterline was so near the surface, shallow
wells yielded the water supply. I am impressed with the memory
that in his grave, which was dug for his burial the next day, the
water rose overnight, and when he sat on his coffin, awaiting the
final command to be fired, and as they were dipping water from his
grave, he asked for and was handed a drink out of his own grave.

After I had been a Presiding Elder for perhaps five years, I was
preaching one night in Cross Plains, Robertson County, on "A Good
Soldier of Jesus Christ," and alluded, without name, to the
incident of Rowland's desertion and death. A gentleman said at the
close of the services: "I saw Rowland shot."

It may be that he was one of the detail. I have often thought of
this poor man and his sad fate. I had lost the memory of what
company he joined and today a letter from a dear old friend in
Texas, Mr. G. K. Welch, told me that he belonged to Capt. Wm. B.
Moore's Company.

The wild and soill ess wood in the midst of which he existed in
1861, is now gone, and fertile fields are spread out for miles, and
today they are covered with crops of corn and white as snow with
cotton, worth in the market at or near forty cents per pound.

This poor man perished and the Confederacy he first volunteered to
defend, failed. His early comrades are with him in that Land
beyond the roar of cannons. Signed, Payton A. Sowell. (Undated
clipping from Lawrenceburg newspapers sent to the compiler by the
late John F. Morrison, Jr., county historian of Lawrence County.)

"This morning all the Tenn. troops at this place were ordered to
attend a military execution - Wm. Rowland, a private in Capt.
Fowler's Co., 54th Regiment Tenn. Vols - deserted and joined the
enemy-he was taken prisoner at the battle of Shiloh last Sunday -
he was recognized by some of his company and arrested and tried by
order of Genl. Beauregard - yesterday he was found guilty on two
charges - 1st a deserter - 2nd a spy - the court ordered him to
be shot this evening at 4 o'clock - 24 men were detailed to shoot
him - the troops were formed on three sides of a square - the
prisoner on the right side and placed between his grave and coffin;
then the charges were read, after which he was allowed to speak -
I could not hear what he said, he was then blindfolded and made to
kneel behind his coffin; the guards advanced in line, they were

ROWLAND, William - Continued
halted 30 paces in front of him, then the command Ready-aim-fire!
was given, and he fell backward, dead, having been pierced by six
balls. The prisoner appeared to be very cool and self-possessed
all the time and showed no signs of fear until he was blindfolded,
when he suddenly became very pale, he shook hands with his body
guard, and the chaplain before they left him, and conversed very
freely up to the time he was shot." (12 April 1862 entry in the
Confederate Dairy of Robert D. Smith, published 1975 by the Capt.
James Madison Sparkman Chapter, United Daughters of the Confederacy.)

ROYCE, Rev. Dr., formerly minister of Episcopal Church in Franklin and
afterwards with Confederate army, was captured two months ago as
guerrilla and is to be tried by a military commission. (Nashville
Dispatch, 27 Sept. 1863.)

ROZELLE, Peter, is the oldest man in the United States, and is of
French descent; born Brooklyn, New York, 22 April 1753, and is 110
years old and three months; has had two wives, one living at 82;
has never used glasses; last summer his legs began to fail him;
chewed tobacco since he was 12 years old; father of 25 children,
mostly boys, and the oldest died at the age of 82 years. (Nashville
Dispatch, 29 July 1863.) Peter Rozelle, died in Oswego, New York,
on September 17, age 110 years 4 months 26 days; he retained
consciousness until the last; of French descent; born 22 April 1753
in Brooklyn, New York; his second wife is now living at the age of
82 years; a poor but happy man; old veteran. (Nashville Dispatch,
1 Oct. 1863.) (Also refer to Peter Rossell entry in this book.)

RUCKER, Joshua, was shot and mortally wounded at the Academy of Music
last night by Hat Macey. (Nashville Republican Banner, 31 July
1868.)

RUFF, Gus, was killed in South Memphis by George Gibbs with a pistol.
(Memphis Avalanche, 30 Jan. 1866.)

RUFF, Colonel, of Georgia, was killed during the siego of Knoxville.
(Nashville Daily Union, 13 Dec. 1863.)

RUFFIN, Edmund, committed suicide Saturday near Richmond by blowing
his head off with a gun; fired the first gun on Fort Sumter.
(Nashville Daily Union, 24 June 1865.)

RUGAR, Capt. J. M., AQM, died Wednesday of congestion of brain and his
remains were sent to Galesburg, Illinois. (Nashville Daily Union,
29 June 1865.)

RUMMAGE, Asal, deceased; his estate is insolvent. (Columbia Herald and
Mail, 27 Nov. 1874.)

RUNNEBAUM, Henry, has not improved. The doctors believe his arm will
have to be amputated at an early day. (Lawrenceburg Democrat, 16
Jan. 1891.) Dr. Bader of Giles County assisted by Drs. McClain
andHarvey amputated the right arm of Henry Runnebaum last Monday.
It is believed he will recover. This was the result of a gunshot
wound he received in late war when he was a Federal soldier. He is
a carpenter. (Lawrenceburg Democrat, 23 Jan. 1891.)

RUPPRECHT, Mrs. Elizabeth, 91, died in Owensboro, Ky, recently; born
1796 in Pegintz, Bavaria; had lived in Owensboro 30 years. (Houston
County News, 7 Oct. 1887.)

RUSHING, Bob was shot and killed in Paris, Tn, last week by one Swaim.
(Houston County Times, 19 Oct. 1886.)

RUSHING, Joel, esquire, one of the pioneer settlers of West Tennessee
died in Jackson yesterday. (Columbia Herald, 1 July 1892.)

337

RUSHTON, Mrs. Ella, wife of Jesse L. Rushton, daughter of the Rev.
J. P. Sebastian, had been married one year and one week, and she
died with her little babe at her side in Santa Fe, Maury County.
In two weeks at Santa Fe, Mr. William Lewis and Mr. James Fitzgerald
have also died. (Columbia Herald, 14 March 1873.)

RUSSELL, Burrell, colored, died in District 2 of Maury County last week;
industrious, honest old man. (Columbia Herald and Mail, 17 Aug.
1877.)

RUSSELL, Captain, of the 11th regulars, died at Cincinnati on Saturday
of cholera. (Memphis Avalanche, 7 Nov. 1866.)

RUSSELL, Mrs. F. B., Hickman County, who has been confined to bed for
some time is not expected to live. Five deaths occurred on January
25: J. S. Rogers, Mr. Wilkes, Mary Aydelotte, daughter of Alexander
George, Mrs. Bill Akers, and Mr. D. Hines, age 87 (in Mexican War),
all of the grippe. (Columbia Herald, 24 Jan. 1897.)

RUSSELL, Haley, aged between 65 and 70, died Sunday near Culleoka; was
drummer for Brown's 3d Tennessee in Capt. George W. Jones' company;
his wife died several weeks ago. (Columbia Herald and Mail, 13
Aug. 1875. At one point his name was also given as Russell Haley.)

RUSSELL, Mrs. Mary, wife of A. W. Russell, daughter of Leslie Hancock,
died in Henry County on the 9th. (Whig and Tribune, 22 Nov. 1873.)

RUSSELL, Captain, adjutant to General Granger, was killed at Chickamauga after he had been in the fight for only 10 minutes. (Nashville
Daily Union, 23 Sept. 1863.)

RUSSELL, Osiah; his body was recovered at the lower wharf in Nashville
yesterday. (Nashville Republican Banner, 7 June 1870.)

RUSSELL, William, was murdered recently at a church near Indian Mound
in Stewart County. J. M. Ferguson is raising a subscription for a
reward and is asking governor to give a reward for his murderer.
(Houston County News, 17 Aug. 1886.)

RUSSELL, James, well known and much respected citizen of Giles County,
who lived on Bradshaw Creek near the Lincoln County line, died
Sunday; hanged himself; an aged mother survives; he left a splendid
estate. (Nashville Union and American, 24 July 1874.)

RUSSEL, Major William, aged about 63, an officer in late Creek and
Seminole War, died at his residence in this county on the 16th inst.
(Tuscumbian, Tuscumbia, Ala., 28 March 1825. N.B. Russellville,
Ala., was named for this man.)

RUTLAND, Dr. W. C., of Stewart County, is to be tried this week for
murdering his wife; charged with gross negligence for leaving her
entirely alone while she was in childbed. (Clarksville Weekly
Chronicle, 28 May 1858.) He received 9 years in state prison.
(Clarksville Weekly Chronicle, 4 Feb. 1859.)

RUTLEDGE, Colonel Arthur Middleton, died at Sewanee, Tn, a week or
two ago; descended from two signers of the Declaration of Independence; his funeral was preached by George Beckett, a thorough
Englishman. (Columbia Herald and Mail, 30 June 1876.)

RUTLEDGE, Lee, of Marshall County, received three years at hard labor
for theft by the military commission at Pulaski. (Nashville Daily
Union, 25 May 1865.)

RYAN, Col. John, who fought with Sam Houston for Texas Independence
died as a pauper in the city hospital at Kansas City. (Maury
Democrat, Columbia, Tn, 15 Dec. 1892.)

RYAN. Monument has been erected over the remains of Father Ryan, poet and priest, in Mobile, Ala. (Florence, Ala., Times, 12 Dec. 1891.)

RYAN, Major Moses, old and respected citizen, died April 8 at the home of his daughter Mrs. M. E. Payne. (Nashville Dispatch, 1 May 1862.)

RYAN, Patrick, was murdered by one Flannery of the 1st Tennessee Infantry. (Nashville Dispatch, 7 Aug. 1863.)

RYMAN, John, 47, died 15 Jan. 1864 of pneumonia. (Nashville Daily Union, 17 Jan. 1864.)

SAFFARANS, Davis, esteemed citizen of Nashville, died on Tuesday; his health had been bad from a trip to California. (Nashville Daily Gazette, 4 Nov. 1852.)

SALLING, John, 110, of Slant, Virginia, in 1956 was one of three surviving Confederate soldiers in the United States. (Daily Herald, 3 Aug. 1956.)

SALTSMAN, Thomas Milton, 7 years 10 days, died yesterday, son of T. F. and S. A. Saltsman. (Nashville Republican Banner, 23 Jan. 1868.)

SAMUEL, Mrs. Zerelda, 86, mother of Frank and Jesse James, died 15 Feb. 1911 on train near Oklahoma City; was on way to see son Frank in Fletcher, Okla. (Maury Democrat, 16 Feb. 1911.)

SAMUELS, Mrs. M., of Nashville, her two daughters and son, were sent yesterday to prison at Alton, Ill., for smuggling; they were arrested on Feb. 1. (Nashville Dispatch, 3 Feb. 1863.) Mrs. Samuels and her two daughters have been exchanged. (Nashville Dispatch, 17 June 1863.)

SANDERS, Charles L., 64, died 14 May 1864; mass to be said at Cathedral. (Nashville Daily Union, 15 May 1864.)

SANDERS, James Andrew, justice of the peace for District 22 in Maury County, was born 20 Jan. 1843; married 1868 to Fannie Dobbins and they had nine children; served in Company G, 1st Tennessee Infantry. (Maury Democrat, 4 July 1895.)

SANDERS, J. M., near Smyrna, was murdered 18 Oct. 1870 by Logan Perry, colored. (Nashville Union and American, 28 May 1874.)

SANDERS, James R., was killed instantly at Shelbyville, Tn, when he fell beneath the wheels of a loaded wagon. (Nashville Republican Banner, 4 July 1868.)

SANDERS, John, 77, died on the 2d instant in Nashville at the home of his son R. A. Sanders. (Nashville Dispatch, 15 June 1862.)

SANDERS, S., blacksmith, formerly of Sumner County but lately of Nashville, died suddenly Feb. 18 of apoplexy, age 45. (Nashville Dispatch, 20 Feb. 1862.)

SANDRUM, General W. J., distinguished Kentuckian, veteran of the Mexican and Civil Wars, died October 11, age 67. (Columbia Herald, 18 Oct. 1895.)

SANFORD, William, Esquire, deceased, of Baldwin County, Georgia, bequeathed $10,000 to Oglethorpe University, $10,000 to Emory University, and $5,000 to Mercer Institute. (Nashville Dispatch, 4 Feb. 1863.)

SAPPINGTON, Captain, Confederate soldier of St. Louis, was killed in the fight at Middlebury, 7 miles from Bolivar. (Nashville Dispatch, 10 Sept. 1862.)

SARDIN, James, age 9, died of gunshot wound yesterday; lived in house where two white women were married to two negro men, Scott Bell and Tobe Blye. He was son of Adaline Bell by a former husband. He was shot by a negro Houston Henry, lover of Maury Hickman, who had married Tobe Blye. (Nashville Republican Banner, 6 Oct. 1868.)

SARGENT, R. W., died suddenly at Sawdust Valley, Maury County, on Friday, age 56; he had worked on his farm Friday morning and died that night; uncle of A. O. McKinnon; wife and five children survive. (Columbia Herald, 17 April 1896.) Confederate soldier, buried at Nebo; served in Company A, 1st Tennessee Cavalry; his pallbearers were his fellow soldiers. (Columbia Herald, 1 May 1896.) Died on April 10 of "intussception." (Daily Herald, Columbia, Tn, 17 April 1896.)

SARGEY, a slave, age 117, died in New Orleans on the 10th; his funeral procession was a quarter of a mile long, mostly composed of quadroons. (Nashville Dispatch, 12 Oct. 1862.)

SAULT. Scranton, Pa., Tues., Feb. 3. A woman named Sault, residing in northern part of Columbia County, murdered on Monday morning, three of her step-children, aged 7, 9 and 14 by severing their heads from their bodies and throwing their remains into the fire. She is now in Columbia County jail. (Nashville Daily Union, 11 Feb. 1863.)

SAVAGE, Mrs. Jesse, of Cathey's Creek in Maury County, has died; she left several children. (Columbia Herald, 28 Feb. 1891.)

SAVAGE, George, father of Colonel John H. Savage, died on the 8th in Coffee County, Tn, age 86. In 1800 he explored the greater part of Middle Tennessee and in 1812 was a soldier from East Tennessee in the campaign against the Indians; Cumberland Presbyterian. (Nashville Union and American, 14 Feb. 1873.)

SAVAGE, Charles, his melancholy and untimely death at Florence, Ala., reported; graduate of the University of Nashville. (Central Monitor, Murfreesboro, Tn, 18 Jan. 1834.)

SAVAGE, Colonel John H., of the 16th Regiment Tennessee, CSA, gave his annual egg nog to the members of his old regiment on New Year's Day. (Memphis Daily Appeal, 9 Jan. 1870.)

SAYERS, Mrs. Maria E., 42, died yesterday; consort of Charles Sayres. (Nashville Daily Gazette, 10 Oct. 1852. N.B. Surname spelled both ways in same obituary.)

SCALES, Mrs. Elsworth P., died at the home of her husband in Williamson County on August 20; sister of the late Governor William B. Campbell. (Whig and Tribune, 2 Sept. 1871.)

SCALES, Henry M., Esquire, of Holly Springs, Miss., died Aug. 1868 in DeSoto County; born Orange County, Virginia, and his parents came early to Marshall County, Miss. He enlisted 9th Mississippi Regiment; was married in 1866. (Memphis Daily Appeal, 16 Nov. 1868.)

SCALES, a low but desperate character, who has been particularly active in arresting Union men and robbing indiscriminately, was wounded in battle 7 miles from Madisonville, Ky, requiring the amputation of his arm. Colonel Fowler commanding the guerrillas was also killed. (Louisville Journal, 10 Nov. 1862.)

SCANLAN, Elizabeth, age 4, daughter of Daniel J. and Ann Scanlan, died on the 4th. (Nashville Daily Union, 5 April 1863.)

SCANLAN, Josephine, daughter of Daniel J. and Ann Scanlan, died on Thursday; "gone to meet her mother." (Nashville Republican Banner, 14 Aug. 1869.)

SCANLAN, Dan J., died July 8 after a long and painful illness. (Nash-ville Republican Banner, 10 July 1869.)

SCANLAN, Captain, was murdered at Stone's River on the Lebanon Pike on Monday night and his body has not been recovered; lived in Scott's Hollow, 10 miles from Nashville; survived by wife and three children, the youngest one only a week old. James Owen, colored, has been arrested for the murder. (Nashville Republican Banner, 26 Feb. 1871.) The body of Capt. B. Scanlan has not been found yet. (Nashville Republican Banner, 28 Feb. 1871.) Capt. B. Scanlan's body, which was found near Ashland City a few days ago, has been brought to Nashville. (Nashville Republican Banner, 17 March 1871.)

SCANLAN, Bartholomew, 7th Pennsylvania, has been charged with bigamy. He married 21 May 1858 in Pittsburgh, Penn., to Bridget Call; married 24 Oct. 1862 to Annie Scanlan. He came here with Buell's Army. His first wife came from Pennsylvania and boarded with Capt. William Driver. (Nashville Dispatch, 5 Aug. 1863.) Scanlan sentenced to serve 4 years; appeals. (Nashville Dispatch, 6 Aug. 1863.)

SCHEIB, Theodore, son of Charles Scheib, age 24 years 6 months 28 days, died on Wednesday. (Nashville Union and American, 24 Sept. 1874.)

SCHEIGLER, Godfrey, was killed Sunday by knife wielded by Frank Lemberdine a desperate character and former sutler for the 29th Indiana Infantry, who had been in prison for larceny but was pardoned by Governor Brownlow. He was killed at Fred Laitenberger's Spring Water Brewery, 6 miles from Nashville on the Chicken Pike. Scheigler came here from Germany a year ago. (Nashville Republican Banner, 7 April 1868.)

SCHNEFF. The following are the particulars of a horrible tragedy which took place in Jefferson County, Wisconsin. A man named Schneff, living in the town of Melford, six miles from Watertown, who has quarrelled a good deal with his wife and children for years, disappeared on the 3d of April. His family manifesting no concern about his absence, and the son having been last seen with him, the neighbors began to be suspicious and instituted a search in the field where the son said he saw the old man last.

There was a large pile of logs and brush which had been burned in the field, and on examing the ashes a quantity of calcined human bones, some suspender buckles, shoe nails, etc., were found, indicating that the elder Schneff had been murdered and his body burned. The son and wife were arrested and taken to Watertown, where great excitement was aroused, and the lynching of the two prisoners was only avoided by the efforts and strategy of the sheriff. (Memphis Avalanche, 18 April 1867.)

SCHNEIDER. W. M. Mayes left for Washington Monday and will bring back the remains of Mrs. Schneider, to be buried at Rose Hill in Columbia. (Columbia Herald, 12 June 1891.)

SCHNURRER, Otto, 21, of St. Florian, Ala., died on the 27th; came here three years ago from Brooklyn, New York. (Florence, Ala., Times, 12 Nov. 1892.)

SCHOFIELD, General John M., commander in chief of the army of the United States, was married at Keokuk, Iowa, Thursday to Miss Georgia Kilbourn of that city. The marriage was performed according to the Episcopal rites and was a quiet one. A lady in Washington, D.C., to whom the general had paid attention, suffered an attack of nervous prostration when she heard of the news. (Florence, Ala., Times, 27 June 1891. N.B. John McCallister Schofield, born 1831, died 1906, graduate of West Point 1853, died at St. Augustine, Fla., 4 March 1906. General Schofield figured prominently in Tennessee history in 1864.)

SCOGGIN, Benjamin M., age 57, died at his home in this county on the 20th instant of pumonary consumption. Pulaski Whig Courier. (The Academist, Lawrence County, 1 April 1846.)

SCHOLES, Joseph, died recently. (Houston County News, 29 May 1891.)

SCHUBERT, John, U. S. Army, married six weeks ago to Elizabeth Ward. (Liz Ward, fair looking girl, considering the fact she had been public property in Nashville for several years.) She became dazzled by shoulder-straps of one who outranked her husband; her husband found out, shot and killed her; then shot himself and has since died. She died 1 Jan. 1863 on Jefferson Street. (Nashville Dispatch, 2 Jan. 1863. N.B. The report of the inquest in the same paper gave her name as Mary Schubert.)

SCHULTZ, Captain, an ex-officer in the Federal army, blew his brains out in the garden of a citizen in Richmond, Va., on the 24th inst., from whose employ he had been discharged. He leaves a family in New York. (Memphis Daily Appeal, 28 Sept. 1868.)

SCHWARZ, Kittie, 18, died yesterday; niece of P. Schwarz. (Nashville Republican Banner, 25 July 1869.)

SCOFIELD, Nathan, of East Haddam, Conn., soldier of the War of 1812, has passed his 100th birthday. (Columbia Herald and Mail, 28 Jan. 1877.)

SCOTT, General Alexander M., who raised a regiment of Federal troops in Kentucky at the beginning of the war, and was formerly of Louisville, died in Chicago Sunday night. (Maury Democrat, 29 Aug. 1895.)

SCOTT, Capt. Alexander, one of the oldest steamboatmen in the West, died at his home in Pittsburg on Thursday. He began his career as a flatboatman and made several trips to New Orleans with Mike Fink. (Nashville Dispatch, 27 June 1862.)

SCOTT, A. M., D.D., shot some months ago in the vicinity of Memphis, died of his wounds Sunday; Methodist; author of some repute. (Nashville Dispatch, 29 Nov. 1863.)

SCOTT, Charles E., born 16 Oct. 1858, married 18 Dec. 1885 to Ida Wagstaff, died 15 Sept. 1893 in Giles County. (Maury Democrat, 26 Oct. 1893.)

SCOTT, Mrs. Francis Ann, consort of David M. Scott, daughter of John B. and Joicey Hagler, aged about 34, died Monday. (Weekly Patriot, Paris, Tn., 4 Sept. 1856.)

SCOTT, Mrs. Joe, 29, funeral to be held at Union Grove, Maury County. (Maury Democrat, 28 March 1889.)

SCOTT, L. B., Company A, 9th Tennessee Infantry, CSA, prisoner of war, died of injuries received by falling of stairs and floors at the Convalescent Barracks Tuesday. (Nashville Daily Union, 1 Oct. 1863.)

SCOTT, Mary Jane, wife of S. M. Scott, died Feb. 5 at 5 p.m., at the home of Mrs. J. G. Brown. (Nashville Daily Union, 7 Feb. 1865.)

SCOTT, Mrs. Martha C., widow of William Scott, died 18 Dec. 1874 of remittent fever near McKenzie Station, formerly of Maury County; born 1796 in Mecklenburg County, Va., married 1816, came to Tennessee in 1830; Missionary Baptist. (Columbia Herald and Mail, 5 Feb. 1875.)

SCOTT, Michael, one of Mosby's guerrillas, was put in prison by the Provost Marshal of Nashville. (Nashville Daily Union, 29 April 1865.)

SCOTT. At Powhattan, Ark., one day last week, Mrs. Morrison aimed a
    blow with a hatchet at the head of "old man Scott," her stepfather
    and killed her mother an old lady of 80 years. (Columbia Herald
    and Mail, 13 Oct. 1876.)

SCOTT. The wife of General Scott died at Rome on 15th ult, age 72.
    She was once a great Virginia belle and rejected General Scott. She
    told him she would marry him when he won a position worthy of her.
    The aged couple have not agreed together very well of late years and
    Mrs. Scott has long lived abroad. (Nashville Daily Union, 11 July
    1862. N.B. The general was not further identified.)

SCOTT-LORD, Mrs., sister of the wife of President Harrison, died at
    Washington on the 10th. (Maury Democrat, 19 Dec. 1889.)

SCOTT, Hon. Robert E., of Fauquier County, Virginia, was killed on 3d
    near Greenwich, Fauquier County, by two deserters, said to be
    Geary's, or Blenker's men, who have been committing many depreda-
    tions through the county. Scott, Winter Payne, and others were
    attempting to capture them at Frank Smith's near Greenwich. In
    approaching the house, Scott and his overseer Dulany were shot dead
    by the deserters. They then broke his gun over him. He was brought
    to Warrenton on the 3d for burial. (Nashville Dispatch, 13 May
    1862.)

SCOTT, Squire Samuel, of Huntington, Indiana, was gored by a bull and
    received fatal injuries. (Lincoln County Herald, 13 June 1894.)

SCOTT, Hon. William, formerly one of the Judges of the Supreme Court
    of Missouri, died near Jefferson City on the 18th. (Nashville
    Dispatch, 24 May 1862.)

SCOTT, William, was killed on 19 July 1872 at Wayne Furnace by two
    boys named Larue, ages 12 and 15. They also wounded William Rhedon;
    they ran away and were captured near old Napier Furnace in Lewis
    County; they were tried and acquitted. Scott had had a difficulty
    with their father. (Columbia Herald, 26 July 1872.)

SCOTT, William Andrew, 1 year 17 months, son of H. B. and Ann Scott,
    died October 13 in Collin County, Texas; he was one of the first
    of a large connection who moved to Texas a year ago to die.
    (Columbia Herald, 24 Oct. 1873.)

SCRIBNER, Walter, son of John Scribner, died on the 15th; married
    Laura Walston 8 months ago. (Columbia Herald, 20 March 1891.)

SCRUGGS, Mrs. Ann M., died yesterday, funeral today. (Nashville
    Dispatch, 27 July 1862.)

SCRUGGS, Burietta Morgan, infant daughter of D. E. and Cornelia A.
    Scruggs, died 23 March 1864 at Goodlettsville. (Nashville Daily
    Union, 25 March 1864.)

SCRUGGS, Mrs. Edna, 89, died yesterday in Columbia at the home of
    Miles Cook. (Columbia Herald, 12 Aug. 1870.)

SCRUGGS. The Improved Order of Red Men paid a last tribute to William
    H. Scruggs, an old citizen, one of the first members of the order.
    A year ago he was bereaved of his reason and taken to the Hospital
    for the Insane where he lived until his death. (Nashville Union
    and American, 11 July 1874.)

SEALEY, Mrs. Ellis, 80, died on the 22d at Hampshire, Maury County.
    (Columbia Herald, 31 March 1871.)

SEALY, John, of Kedron, died April 24 at 3 a.m.; funeral at Blanton's
    Chapel. (Columbia Herald, 1 May 1896.)

SEARCY, Mrs. Amanda E., 47, wife of Col. Anderson Searcy, died on the
    1st. (Free Press, Murfreesboro, Tn., 8 April 1881.)

SEARCY, Miss Frances, died on the 4th. (Tennessee Telegraph, Murfreesboro, Tn., 14 March 1838.)

SEARCY, Mrs., Sarah A. E., wife of Robert Searcy, age 29 years 11 months
31 days, died at her home in Humphreys County on March 14.
(Nashville Republican Banner, 15 March 1870.)

SEARCY, Sophia S., wife of George W. Purvis of the Nashville Banner,
died in Nashville on Saturday. (Whig and Tribune, Jackson, Tn.,
26 April 1873.)

SEARCY, Dr. Reuben M., committed suicide at Tuskegee, Ala., on the
16th. (Florence, Ala., Times, 30 July 1892.)

SEARIGHT, Captain, who deserted the U. S. Army and eloped with a
Southern belle last winter, was killed in a duel by a Spanish
officer near Havana, Cuba. The woman for whom he abandoned fame
and fortune, deserted him and fled with a captain in the Spanish
Army. The duel was fought on a seaside a mile or two from Havana
and Searight fell, pierced to the heart. The Spaniard and the
fair, false one fled to the Isle of Pines. (Nashville Dispatch,
8 July 1863.)

SEATON, Charley, living 10 miles northeast of Camden, Tn., on the
Tennessee River, was shot and wounded in own house by an assassin,
who hid behind a stump 35 steps from the house. (Maury Democrat,
5 Dec. 1889.)

SEATS, Mollie, a keeper of a house of ill fame in Nashville, and at her
house Jacob Flohn, Company F, 45th New York, was shot in the arm
last night, a painful wound. (Nashville Daily Union, 6 June 1865.)

SEAY, John, died a few days ago. (Houston County Times, 28 July 1887.)

SEAY, William Branch, son of George W. and Jennie B., age 1 year 11
months 29 days, died yesterday. (Nashville Republican Banner, 9
Aug. 1870.) Louis Magruder Seay, infant son of George W. and Jennie
B., died yesterday. (Nashville Republican Banner, 10 Aug. 1870.)
Both buried today. (Nashville Republican Banner, 11 Aug. 1870.)

SECKENDORF, Count Alfred, of Russia, took 20 grains of morphine at
the Read House in Chattanooga. His life was saved by a walking.
His money had given out and his friends across the ocean had
refused him further help. (Maury Democrat, 27 June 1889.)

SEDBERRY, Little daughter of Jim Sedberry of Thompson Station, age 3,
died this week of typhoid; buried at Godwin in Maury County by
kindred. (Columbia Herald, 19 June 1896.)

SEDBERRY, Mrs. Lucy, 80, died June 5 in District 20 of Maury County;
Baptist. (Columbia Herald, 11 July 1873.)

SEDBERRY, Sidney, 23, died on the 6th near Carter's Station. (Columbia
Herald and Mail, 12 April 1878.)

SEDGWICK. The dedication of the memorial statue of General Sedgwick
at West Point was held on the 21st. The statue was designed by
Thompson and cast from captured cannon contributed by the nation and
from the Sixth Army Corps. (Memphis Daily Appeal, 8 Oct. 1868.)

SEELEY, Annie Lou, 3, little daughter of Mr. and Mrs. Henry Seeley,
died Sunday; buried at Concord, Maury County. (Columbia Herald,
27 Dec. 1899.)

SEIBERT, Charles, fell from horse, caused concussion, and died Friday.
He was in a race at the Fair Ground in Rutherford County. (Nashville
Republican Banner, 23 Aug. 1868.)

SEIGLER, Dr. William, of Nashville, committed suicide Monday by cutting his throat; suffered from mental derangement. (Clarksville Jeffersonian, 12 Feb. 1853.)

SEIMER, Henry, an old man living near Canton, Miss., was brutally murdered for his money in June. A man living on the place had a dream where the money was he went there and found $3500 in gold 20-dollar pieces. (Murfreesborö Monitor, 28 Nov. 1868.)

SELKIRK, William A., was hanged on the 4th; had been convicted of murder of Adam Weaver of Wilson County. Weaver's son asked for the privilege of adjusting the rope. (Nashville Dispatch, 7 June 1863.)

SELLERS, E. H. (Hart), died May 14 near Williamsport. (Columbia Herald and Mail, 17 May 1878.)

SELLERS, Ison, 77, died April 23 of la grippe. (Maury Democrat, 1 May 1890.)

SELLERS, Mrs. Sarah, wife of E. H. Sellers, died on the 17th of asthma; Presbyterian. (Columbia Herald and Mail, 24 Dec. 1875.)

SELPH, Rev. D. H., formerly of Rutherford County, died near Lexington, Missouri, on the 19th. (Nashville Union and American, 24 Jan. 1874.)

SELVAGE, Thomas, of the Louisville Legion, was killed in battle April 6 at Shiloh. (Nashville Dispatch, 15 April 1862.)

SEMMES, Admiral Raphael, died on the 30th ult., born Charles County, Maryland in 1800; entered the navy as midshipman, attaining the rank of commander in 1855. He saw service during the Mexican War and during the Civil War took command of the steamer Sumter of New Orleans and ran the blockade and the steamer was sunk 19 June 1863, and he was rescued by an English yacht and remained in England until the end of the war. He returned to the United States and practiced law in Mobile. (Columbia Herald and Mail, 14 Sept. 1877.)

SEMPHILL. The following tombstone was found at Williamsburg, Virginia: Sarah Semphill, "who died at the age of 25, slain with her two infant daughters by her own husband." Her husband was John Semphill, a Spanish thief; she was Sarah Jones before her marriage. He shot her in heart and stabbed the two daughters in 1801. He hanged 17 May 1803. (Columbia Herald and Mail, 3 May 1878.)

SENTER, Miss Anna, actress, wife of Harry Langdon, died in Nashville on Wednesday. (Memphis Avalanche, 12 June 1867.)

SEQUOYAH, A Cherokee Indian, was murdered near Fort Smith on the 22d ult. by a party of his countrymen. A man named Vann is suspected. (Nashville Daily Gazette, 13 Nov. 1852.)

SEVIER. The remains of Catherine Sevier, wife of Tennessee's great governor, lie in a moss-grown corner of an abandoned graveyard at Russellville, Alabama. It is proposed to open the neglected grave and place her remains by her husband. (Maury Democrat, __ July 1889; most of date had been torn from paper.)

SEVRES, Baron de, the great pin hunter, of Paris is dead. Among his property found were two large and heavy boxes, which contained, not cash, but hundreds of thousands of pins of all kind. For the last 20 years his regular habit has been to pass along the street and public resorts and pick up pins he found on the ground. (Nashville Dispatch, 14 Aug. 1863.)

SEWARD, Miss Fannie, youngest child of Secretary Seward, died Oct. 29 in Washington City. (Memphis Avalanche, 5 Nov. 1866.)

SEWARD, Mrs. W. H., wife of the Secretary of State, died in Washington on the 21st. (Nashville Daily Union, 25 June 1865.)

SEXTON. Hope Springs Eternal - Mr. Elander Sexton, 98, married Mrs. Craft, 98, at Sergeant, Kentucky last week. (Columbia Herald, 1 Jan. 1897.)

SHACK, Mamie, wife of Tom Shack, died Wednesday and was buried yesterday. (Columbia Herald, 9 Jan. 1891.)

SHACKLEFORD, Mrs. Agnes, beloved consort of Thomas Shackleford of this place, died Sunday last. (Nashville Whig, 2 March 1814.)

SHAFFER, Mrs. Addie P., wife of R. W., died yesterday at home of her father John Guthrie in Williamson County. (Nashville Republican Banner, 10 June 1870.)

SHANE, John, deceased, letters of administration on his estate given by Davidson County court. (Nashville Daily Union, __ Feb. 1865.)

SHANGHAI GEORGE, notorious negro thief at Vicksburg, Mississippi, was killed by Nineon Gibson; he had robbed several families. (Memphis Daily Appeal, 30 July 1868.)

SHANNON, Mrs. Cora, died in Texas; her funeral is to be preached on the fourth Sunday at Union Grove in Maury County. (Maury Democrat, 17 May 1894.)

SHANNON, Thomas S., died in Davidson County on the 4th inst. at the home of Eli Talley; formerly co-editor of the Clarksville Gazette. (Tennessee Watchman, 17 Aug. 1821.)

SHAPARD, William B., 73, died Wednesday. (Columbia Herald, 20 Jan. 1870.)

SHARP, Albert, one of twins, died Sunday of whooping cough. (Columbia Herald and Mail, 12 March 1875.)

SHARP, George Thomas, 2 months 16 days, son of George and Annie Sharp, died June 13 at Edgefield. (Nashville Daily Union, 20 June 1865. Age also appears in paper as 2 months 2 days.)

SHARP, Samuel, of Greenfield Bend, twin of Albert, son of Mr. and Mrs. George Sharp, died of whooping cough. (Columbia Herald and Mail, 5 March 1875.)

SHARP, Thomas A., died in Robertson County; for many years lived in Edgefield; age 40 years; wife and one child survive. (Nashville Daily Union, 30 March 1865.)

SHAULDERS, William, formerly of Wilson County, 6 miles from Lebanon, was murdered by Indians on the 13th. The information was sent by George W. Moore of Lone Tree, Nebraska. (Nashville Republican Banner, 1 July 1869.)

SHAW, Allen, of Giles County, ran away recently with the wife of Curt Owens of Weakley Creek and Peyton Lucas, who has a wife in Lawrence County, ran away with Owens' sister. (Columbia Herald, 3 May 1872.)

SHAW, Major A. M., 70, died in Somerville, Tn., a long time resident. (Nashville Union and American, 26 Jan. 1873.) Major A. M. Shaw, one of the oldest citizens of Somerville, died on the 19th at the age of 74; proprietor of the Eagle Hotel. (Whig and Tribune, Jackson, Tn., 1 Feb. 1873.)

SHAW, Mr., father of Mrs. M. L. Nellums of Spring Hill, died Saturday, at Shaw after a long illness. (Maury Democrat, 28 Nov. 1895.)

SHEA, Thomas, died Thursday night. (Nashville Republican Banner, 18 March 1871.)

SHEEGOG, Mrs. Mary, 64, relict of Robert Sheegog of Oxford, Mississippi, formerly of Hickman County, died in Oxford on Feb. 27. Her son-in-law Daniel W. Jones, 43, died there on the 27th only a few hours later. (Nashville Republican Banner, 1 March 1871.)

SHEEGOG, Nancy R., 76, died Sunday at Thompson Station; married (1) to Constantine Perkins and (2) to Edward Sheegog; at one time lived in the place owned by T. N. Figuers on the Hampshire Pike, now the Maury Jersey Company; maiden name was Cheairs; buried Rose Hill in Columbia. (Maury Democrat, 17 May 1889. Paper torn.)

SHEEGOG, Colonel Edward, 85, died 14 Nov. 1893; born in Ireland in 1816; came to Tennessee at the age of 13 and with the exception of 5 or 6 years had lived in Maury County; served in the Florida war and as a Confederate soldier; for 50 years had been an Episcopalian, in 1844 he married Louise McCormack of Pulaski, who died in 1847, leaving one child; in 1871 he married Mrs. N. R. Perkins, wife of Constantine Perkins; she died 1889; he and three others were the only ones left out of his Florida War regiment; buried St. John's Cemetery. (Maury Democrat, __ Nov. 1893.)

SHEFFIELD, Col. James L., died in Montgomery, Ala., on the 2d. (Florence, Ala., Times, 16 July 1892.)

SHELBY, Jo, the gallant Confederate general, died at his home near Kansas City last Saturday, Feb. 13, of illness of 10 days of pneumonia. (Columbia Herald, 19 Feb. 1897.)

Comrades - While Gen. Joe Shelby was coming down in the elevator at the St. Louis customshouse the other day, the man who was running the car attracted his attention.

"I looked at the fellow," said Gen. Shelby, "and saw that it was Bennet Jackson, a colored man whom I knew in Kentucky 35 or 40 years ago. I touched him on the shoulder."

"See here, don't you know me?"

"Jackson looked at me steadily for a moment and then he brought the elevator up with a jerk and stopped between floors.

"Fo do Lawd's sake!" he exclaimed, "Ef hit ain't Mars Jo Shelby!"

"Then he threw his arms around me and began to sob. The elevator was at a standstill between the floors and the situation was one of the funniest that I ever had anything to do with. It was 27 years since I had seen Jackson, when he turned to speak to me on this occasion. Down in Kentucky years ago, Gratz Brown, Frank P. Blair, Jackson and I were as thick as youngsters ever were, I reckon, when we were all children together." Louisville-Courier-Journal. (Maury Democrat, 29 March 1894.)

SHELBY, Mrs., relict of Dr. John Shelby, octoenarian, recently caught her foot in hearthrug and thrown violently against the floor; she is now improving. (Nashville Republican Banner, 18 Nov. 1869.)

SHELTON, Abner M., 80, father of L. L., died near Erin last Week of la grippe. (Houston County Times, 26 Jan. 1892.)

SHELTON. The oldest mother in Webster County, Ky., and the oldest great-great-grandmother in the history of the United States is Betsy Shelton, mother of 14 children, who has 117 grandchildren, 282 great-grandchildren, and 19 great-great-grandchildren. She was born 1798 in North Carolina and came to Kentucky in 1816. Her husband died 1867. She is in moderate health. (Maury Democrat, 14 June 1894.)

SHELTON, David C., a young lawyer of Columbia, died at the home of his father Rev. W. M. Shelton in Nashville last week. (Whig and Tribune, Jackson, Tn, 7 Dec. 1872.)

SHELTON, De, 26, died 1 Dec. 1874. (Columbia Herald and Mail, 18 Dec. 1874.)

SHELTON, George, died at Wayne Station, Tn., Wednesday of last week. (Maury Democrat, 3 Aug. 1893.)

SHELTON, Harris, private, Company I, 5th Tennessee Cavalry, died 22 Feb. 1864, killed on Calf Killer near Sparta, Tn. (Nashville Daily Union, 24 Feb. 1864.)

SHELTON, M. L., of Nashville, died in Dickson County on the 7th. (Nashville Dispatch, 10 Sept. 1863.)

SHEMWELL, J. E., was murdered at Dover by W. P. Wallace, his three sons, and James Page on 20 June 1890. Three months before J. E. Wallace, brother of W. P. Wallace, had been killed by Shemwell. (Maury Democrat, 17 July 1890.)

SHEPHERD, Ben, formerly of Nashville, but now of Memphis, died there on the 12th of sunstroke. (Nashville Union and American, 14 Aug. 1874.)

SHEPERD (SHEPARD), Uncle Bob, is 84; born in Virginia; moved to Wilson County and later lived in Davidson County, where he was a neighbor and friend of Andrew Jackson; now lives at Beardstown, Perry County. (Linden Times, 13 May 1880.)

SHEPHERD, John H., about 50, leading merchant of Nashville for many years; his body found in mud puddle in Memphis, had gone after medicine and never returned; died under mysterious circumstances. (Nashville Daily Union, 9 Feb. 1864.)

SHEPHERD, Bettie P., infant daughter of Mr. and Mrs. Joseph H. Shepherd, died yesterday in this city. (Nashville Daily Gazette, 4 Aug. 1852.)

SHERIDAN, General Phil, is dead; died August 5 at 10:20. (Maury Democrat, 9 Aug. 1888.)

SHERLOCK, Jimmie, 12, son of James Sherlock, well-known gypsy horse breeder of Nashville, died in court at Guntersville, Ala. Monday. The remains were shipped to Nashville in a metallic coffin but will not be buried until next April. (Columbia Herald, 18 Oct. 1895.)

SHERMAN, General Wm. Tecumseh, his long and stubborn fight with death came to an end Friday afternoon. Southern recollection of General Sherman is not pleasant. In his famous march through Georgia he was stern, terrible and unrelenting, and he maintained that attitude toward the South to the end. His rigid, rugged nature, lacked the milk of human kindness and he was never able to regard with any degree of tolerance the conquered Southerners. He lacked one essential of a great hero: magnanimity. (Free Press, Murfreesboro, Tn., 20 Feb. 1891.)

Three great soldiers died during the year 1891: Von Molke of the German Army, Jos. E. Johnson of the Confederate Army, and William T. Sherman of the Federal Army. (Florence, Ala., Times, 9 Jan. 1892.)

General Sherman at Memphis has ordered that for every boat that is fired on, 10 Secession families will be expelled from that city. (Nashville Dispatch, 23 Oct. 1862.)

General Sherman has returned to St. Louis from his trip to the Rocky Mountains. He reports that the Union Pacific Railroad has been finished 750 miles west of Omaha. (Memphis Daily Appeal, 7 Sept. 1868.)

SHERMAN, General Wm. Tecumseh - Continued
General Sherman has returned to St. Louis from New Orleans much
improved in health. He will leave for Washington in a few days.
(Memphis Daily Appeal, 24 Feb. 1869.)

General Sherman has ordered the discharge of Private Cavanaugh from
Company K, 9th Regulars, for "utter worthlessness." (Memphis Daily
Appeal, 5 July 1869.)

Mrs. General Sherman was a cousin of the Hon. James G. Blaine, who
attended her funeral in New York. (Maury Democrat, 21 Feb. 1889.)

General Sherman goes about New York almost invariably in the street
cars. As a rule one of his daughters accompanies him, and the old
warrior in jumping on and off the stops is as young as many men 40
years his junior. (Florence, Ala., Times, 7 Nov. 1890.)

General Sherman's daughter, Mrs. E. S. Thackara, who is known as a
writer, is said to be engaged on a very ambitious literary work.
(Florence, Ala., Times, 12 Sept. 1891.)

The women of Georgia are still very much against General Sherman.
(Erin Review, 17 Dec. 1881.)

SHERMAN, son of General Sherman, died 6 Oct. 1863 at the Gayoso House
in Memphis, age 11. (Nashville Daily Union, 10 Oct. 1863.)

SHERWOOD, James B., died in New York, formerly of Rutherford County,
Tn., and lived many years in New Orleans; brother of Mrs. James R.
Bruce of Nashville. (Nashville Daily Union, 28 June 1865.)

SHERWOOD, Mrs. Rachel, 63, died on the 10th in Nashville at the home of
her daughter Mrs. J. R. Bruce. (Nashville Dispatch, 11 June 1862.)

SHERRILL, Harvey, 14, was fatally injured in a runaway accident on
Wednesday last; buried Rose Hill Cemetery. (Columbia Herald and
Mail, 11 June 1875.)

SHIELDS, Infant of Mr. and Mrs. A. S. Shields, died Sunday and buried
at Rose Hill Cemetery. (Maury Democrat, 17 June 1891.)

SHIELDS, Oliver Yateman, son of Benjamin and Martha Shields, is to be
buried today. (Nashville Republican Banner, 22 Nov. 1867.)

SHIRK, Charles D., died on the 5th of typhoid in Nashville; native of
Lancaster, Penn., and had lived here for 26 years; for many years
was partner of M. M. Monohan. (Nashville Dispatch, 8 April 1863;
Nashville Daily Union, 8 April 1863.)

SHIRLEY, Jonathan, died 29 Dec. 1893, age 83, on Lisle Road, Oswego,
New York; had son Nathaniel Shirley. He was born 10 Nov. 1810
in Buckinghsire, England, where he was married and his first two
children were born; came in 1836 to the United States and lived at
Oswego for 55 years; father of eight children; brother of William
Shirley of Columbia, who had marble works in Columbia; had been
Baptist for 33 years. (Maury Democrat, 1 Feb. 1894.)

SHIRLEY, Mrs. Manervie, 63, died 22 Feb. 1888 of heart disease, wife of
William Shirley, buried Rose Hill in Columbia. (Maury Democrat, 1
March 1888.)

SHIRLEY, William, 77, died in Columbia, buried Rose Hill. (Columbia
Herald, 6 Feb. 1903.) Mr. Shirley of Columbia says his father
fought under Wellington in the Battle of Waterloo. (Columbia
Herald and Mail, 22 Jan. 1875.) William Shirley has often told me
that he cut the eagle which adorns the finished structure (i.e.
the State Capitol in Nashville). (Maury Democrat, 24 May 1894.)

SHIRLEY, William. Discoverer of Phosphate in Maury Buried. Funeral services were held at Rose Hill Cemetery this afternoon for William Nelson Shirley, 73 years old, stone carver and prospector and the first discoverer of phosphate rock in Maury County.

Mr. Shirley died late yesterday at the King's Daughters Hospital, where he was taken after he broke his leg in a fall on the icy streets here the second week of this month.

It was in 1878 when a lad of 14, that Mr. Shirley, who was then learning his father's trade of stonecutter, did his first prospecting here, seeking onyx, zinc and other ores. However, nothing came of this discovery at the time, it being in the last few years of the nineteenth century before mining was started here and that on new discoveries of much more valuable deposits near Mt. Pleasant.

Mr. Shirley was a stone carver for 57 years, but was never "in the money" in his phosphate deals. A man of visionary mind, he was often planning for new ventures but few of his activities netted him much profit although until his health failed he was a hard worker.

He had been aided for years by friends here, including H. Allison Webster, Sr., who had been associated with him in prospecting years ago. Two years ago he did his last active prospecting for pay, this being the cutting of the stone on the W. P. Morgan farm near here, when a veterans' hospital was being sought.

Living alone, in a poor shack, he was the first person certified for aid under the old age assistance program of the state in Tennessee and the first to receive a check.

Mr. Shirley was born in Nashville, but came here early in life with his parents. (Daily Herald, Columbia, Tenn., 23 Dec. 1937.)

SHIVERS, Mrs. Zilphie, 47, wife of J. C. Shivers, died on the 2d near Nashville after a long and painful illness. (Nashville Daily Union, 11 April 1863; Nashville Dispatch, 11 April 1863.)

SHOOMAN, F. B., private, 4th U. S. Artillery, was shot dead near the square yesterday; he was on his way to jail and broke away from his guard. (Nashville Daily Union, 24 Dec. 1862.)

SHORT, Mrs. Mary Akin, wife of Dr. Thomas Short, died June 25 in Dyer County; she lived most of her life in Maury County; husband and five children survive. (Columbia Herald, 17 July 1896.)

SHOTTS, Florence, 12, died July 18 of typhoid. (Columbia Herald, 24 July 1891.)

SHOUP, Gen. F. A., formerly of Bragg's Army, was ordained a deacon in the ministry of the Episcopal Church at St. Luke's Church, Oxford, Miss. (Memphis Avalanche, 31 Dec. 1868.)

F. A. Shoup has purchased the interest of Dr. George Beckett in the Columbia Institute as of January 30. Beckett, who has been here since 1866, is now 77 and will live in New York. He has resigned as rector of St. Peter's several years aog and remained at the Intitute. Shoup will be called tonight to fill the pulpit left vacant by the death of R. E. Metcalf. (Maury Democrat, 1 Feb. 1894.)

Dr. Francis A. Shoup, died Friday morning at 6 o'clock at the Institute; he had been sick all summer and died of heart failure. Prayers were led in the parlor by Rev. A. J. Killheffer and the body will be taken to Sewanee for burial. He was born 1834 in Indiana and was a West Point graduate, resigned to study law. He came South and joined the Confederate army as an artillery officer.

He was with Johnson at Shiloh. He had been rector at Waterford, New York, Nashville, Tn., Jackson, Tn., and New Orleands and in 1883 went to Sewanee. He was the author of several books. (Columbia Herald, 11 Sept. 1896.)

SHUCK, Rev. J. Lewis, prominent Baptist missionary, spent most of his life in China, died a few days ago at Barnwell Courthouse, South Carolina, age 51; native of Alexandria, Va., educated at the Virginia Baptist Seminary. He married his third wife in 1854 and she survives. (Nashville Dispatch, 2 Oct. 1863.)

SHULL, John, 21, of Mt. Pleasant, was poisoned by taking rat poison last Tuesday; suicide. (Whig and Tribune, 22 June 1872.)

SHUTE, Thomas, old citizen of Nashville, died yesterday after a lingering illness; was deputy sheriff at one time. (Nashville Union and American, 25 April 1873.)

SHY, James, of Sumner County, his body was found Monday; murder or suicide? He was a notorious desperado. (Nashville Republican Banner, 28 Aug. 1869.)

SIGLER, John, 72, died 27 Dec. 1862. (Nashville Daily Union, 29 Dec. 1862.)

SILL, Joshua Woodrow. It seems to be generally conceded that General Sill was killed in action at Murfreesboro, but when or how we could not learn. (Nashville Dispatch, 1 Jan. 1863.) In the great battle at Murfreesboro, Generals Sill, Sheridan and Schafter have been reported killed. (Nashville Dispatch, 2 Jan. 1863.) General Sill was shot through the left eye by a Minie ball. (Nashville Dispatch, 8 Jan. 1863.) The body of General Sill lay in state in the courthouse at Murfreesboro and a guard of honor was stationed around his remains. He was killed by a Minie ball through the head. (Nashville Dispatch, 8 Jan. 1863.) The body of General Sill was brought to Nashville last night from Murfreesboro. (Nashville Dispatch, 7 Jan. 1863.)

At Stone's River, horrible barbarities were practiced on U. S. soldiers. Hundreds were plundered, shoes taken off their feet and the surgeons robbed even while treating rebel suffers. General Sill's body was stripped bare. (Nashville Daily Union, 17 Jan. 1862.) General Sill's body was not violated, but put in a coffin. (Nashville Daily Union, 18 Jan. 1863.)

SIMMONS, Henry, 40th Tennessee, CSA, prisoner of war, died on passage down the Mississippi to Vicksburg. (Nashville Dispatch, 7 Oct. 1862.)

SIMMONS, Mrs. J. B., died on the 23d on Cedar Creek in Perry County, daughter of Joe Newsome of Decatur County; husband and three children survive. (Linden Times, 7 Oct. 1880.)

SIMMONS, Mrs., widow of St. Clair County, Ala., came to Chattanooga three weeks ago, and has been living precariously, going without food for several days and unable to find employment; has a family of eight and three are already dead of starvation. Citizens now have the case in hand. (Memphis Avalanche, 9 Nov. 1866.)

SIMMONS, Mrs., mother of James, Charles, and William Simmons, died in mid-ocean several days ago on a voyage to this country. Her body arrived here yesterday. (Nashville Repbulican Banner, 13 Sept. 1868.) Mrs. Simmons is to be buried today. (Nashville Republican Banner, 20 Sept. 1868.)

SIMMONS, Col. Thomas, of Cedar Creek, Perry County, is dangerously ill. (Linden Times, 5 Feb. 1880.) Died on the 3d at an advanced age at his home on Cedar Creek. (Linden Times, 12 Feb. 1880.)

SIMMONS, Mrs. William, lived on the Brinkley Howell place in the Suck
Island Bend of Maury County, was burned to a crisp one day last week
when her clothes caught on fire. Husband and one child survive.
Buried at Concord. (Columbia Herald and Mail, 2 March 1877.)

SIMMS, Mrs. M. E., died near Wayne Station in District 10, Lawrence
County, on March 31; wife of late P. L. Simms, Esquire; left a large
family of children. (Lawrenceburg Democrat, 20 March 1891.)

SIMONTON. Mrs. Sarah Davis, died near Lawrenceburg on the 27th in her
71st year; born in North Carolina; daughter of John Simonton, who
emigrated to Middle Tennessee at an early period. (Lawrence Journal,
30 Jan. 1873.)

SIMPSON, Charles: "In memory of Dr. Charles Simpson, who was slain
in the night of 4th Jan. 1816 in the 26th year of his age."
(Tombstone inscription in Mt. Moriah Churchyard, Giles County, Tn.)

Proclamation - Whereas it has been represented to me by the Jailor
of Maury county that on the night of the 10th of June 1816, the
following named and described persons did break the jail of said
county, to which they had been committed for safekeeping, and
escaped therefrom and from justice: William Magill, about 30 years
of age, 6 feet high, dark hair and complexion, blue eyes, coarse
features and speaks soft and low, and was recently suspected and
charged with having murdered a certain Charles Simpson of the county
of Giles, for which he was in custody at the time of his escape.
Martin Gurley, about 25 years of age, 5 feet 7 inches high, stout
made, sandy complexion, fair hair, and speaks quick in conversation,
the aforesaid Martin Gurley, was recently suspected and charged
with the crime of Horse Stealing and committed therefor, from which
he escaped. Signed: Joseph McMinn, Governor Tennessee, who
offered reward for the apprehension of these two men. (The
Chronicle, Columbia, Tn, 1 Aug. 1816.)

SIMPSON, B. L., deceased; Josiah Ferriss, administrator, publishes a
notice. (Nashville Dispatch, 26 August 1863.)

SIMS, Washington, age 21, died near Jefferson, Rutherford County.
(Central Monitor, Murfreesboro, 18 Oct. 1834.)

SINGLETON, Mrs. Levenia, 87, died on 28th at home of J. L. Vaughan
in District 7 of Rutherford County; mother of S. H. Singleton;
Primitive Baptist for 60 years. (Free Press, Murfreesboro, 3 Feb.
1882.)

SINGLETON, Mary, woman hermit of Nashville, who had been living at
No. 80 Green Street with four vicious dogs, dies. (Nashville
Banner, 30 April 1904.)

SIPPY, William, killed in railroad accident on the 20th, to be buried
today. (Nashville Republican Banner, 22 April 1869.)

SISTER MARY PATRICIA, funeral held yesterday. (Nashville Union and
American, 29 July 1874.)

SISTER VERONICA died at St. Cecelia's Academy on Monday night of
consumption; one of the youngest Dominican sisters. (Nashville
Union and American, 6 May 1874.)

SITTING BULL. Chief Sitting Bull is a full-blooded Teton Indian, the
Teton being a branch of the great Sioux nation. In stature he is
inclined to be stout rather than tall. In his mocassins he is
5 ft. 8 or 9 inches tall, aged about 48 years. His hair is gray
and his eyes are dark. He is brave, ambitious, clever. He has
long cherished the conviction that he is ordained as the Indian who
must wrest from the whites the country of his father. He has a
great and almost immeasurable hatred towards Americans, as

distinguished from Europeans or Canadians. He is even expert in
detecting who are from the United States and who are not. He is a
polygamist having three wives according to Indian code,but he had
more constancy than Bear Spirit, his brother-in-law, chief of the
Yanktons. His policy: America for the Sioux. (Columbia Herald
and Mail, 9 Nov. 1877.) Sitting Bull's future home is to be Deer
River where he and his band will be guarded by police. (Columbia
Herald and Mail, 16 Nov. 1877.)

SKEGGS, Edwin E., 24, son of T. L. and M. J. Skeggs, died on the 25th.
(Nashville Republican Banner, 27 Aug. 1869.)

SKELLY, James, died and was buried at Cave Spring. (Maury Democrat,
1 Aug. 1895.)

SKILLINGTON, Mrs. Dicy, 95, confined to her bed for five years, died
in District 22 of Williamson County; she had been a member of the
Baptist Church for 25 years. (Columbia Herald and Mail, 10 Sept.
1875.)

SKINNER, John C., 3d Division, 17th Brigade, 15th Regiment Kentucky
Volunteers, Company F, was in General Hospital near Nashville on
January 11; in a letter to his mother he said he was wounded in
right leg and not expected to live. His mother is in Nashville
hunting him. Contact Juliana Skinner at Mrs. Cockrill's hotel.
Jan. 30. (Nashville Daily Union, 31 Jan. 1863.)

SKINNERBURY, James H., private, Squadron C, was killed on an expedition
to Franklin yesterday. (Nashville Daily Union, 3 Feb. 1863.)

SLATTER, Eldridge Greenwood, 2 years 3 months, only son and child of
W. J. Slatter of Winchester, died 6 May 1868. (Nashville Republican
Banner, 24 May 1868.)

SLATTER, D. R., county register of Franklin County, who was disabled
at Gettysburg while in Confederate Army, died Friday at Winchester.
(Clarksville Weekly Chronicle, 23 Oct. 1868.)

SLEDGE, LaFayette M., versus Mary I. Sledge, non-residency notice
published; she lives at Marbuts, Giles County. (Florence, Ala.,
Times, 19 Dec. 1890.)

SLEDMAN, William P., died 18 Oct. 1915 in Washington, D. C.; former
private in 4th Michigan Regiment and the captor of Jeff Davis after
the fall of Richmond, age 79; he had been an employee in the
Department of Agriculture and had lived in Washington for 25 years.
(Columbia Herald, 22 Oct. 1915.)

SLEMMER, little daughter of Adam Slemmer of Monroe township, Allen
County, Indiana, was burned to death on the 10th by her clothes
catching fire and her body was literally wasted. (Nashville
Dispatch, 17 Feb. 1863.)

SLOAN, Amanda E., daughter of John H. and A. E. Sloan, 15 years 2
months, died on the 14th. (Nashville Dispatch, 16 Aug. 1863.)

SLOAN, Mrs. Bettie, 23, died September 12, wife of J. K. Sloan.
(Nashville Republican Banner, 14 Sept. 1870.)

SLOAN, George L., 56, died on September 30. (Nashville Dispatch,
1 Oct. 1862.)

SLOAN, James T., son of James E. and Sophia Sloan, age 8, died and
funeral held today. (Nashville Union and American. 29 July 1874.)

SLOAN, Mr., an aged Union man was assassinated in Davidson County
last summer; Felix Young has been arrested for the killing; he is
a Federal soldier and is believed to have been in the party.
(Nashville Daily Union, 4 March 1863.)

SLOSS, Mrs., wife of Colonel James W. Sloss, President of the Nashville & Decatur Railroad, died Tuesday at Athens, Alabama, her home. (Columbia Herald, 23 June 1871.)

SLOWMAN, Mrs. Jacob, died Wednesday; body taken to Nashville for burial with Jewish rites. (Columbia Herald, 4 Oct. 1872.)

SLY, James Jacob, died 8 Jan. 1865; formerly of Montgomery County, Tn., was executed by Lt. Clark, Company A, 83 Illinois, as a guerrilla and was described as "one of the most murderous of the breeds." (Nashville Daily Union, __ Jan. 1865.)

SMALL, Lt. John G., and Capt. J. E. Scott, both in Union service during the late war, have committed suicide in San Francisco within the past two days. (Memphis Daily Appeal, 28 Feb. 1869.)

SMART, Miss Ann, 72, died 14 July 1870. (Nashville Republican Banner, 15 July 1870.)

SMIDEL, Lt. C. L., died 27 April 1863, 21 st Illinois Volunteers, A.D.C., on staff of General Stanley, died of pneumonia; remains shipped home to his family. (Nashville Daily Union, 28 April 1863. Name also spelled Smeidell in same paper.)

SMILEY, Mrs., living near Chapel Hill, committed suicide on Tuesday of last week by hanging herself. (Columbia Herald and Mail, 14 April 1876.)

SMILEY, Robert, died at Nashville on Sunday. (Tennessee Watchman, Clarksville, Tn., 12 Sept. 1823.)

SMILEY, Dr. Alexander H., died at Trenton on the 21st, age 44; native of Nashville and brother of Thomas T. Smiley; student of medicine under Dr. Thomas R. Jennings; relative of Dr. William Gibson of Pennsylvania University; had lived at Trenton for 20 years. (Nashville Dispatch, 8 July 1862.)

SMITH, Colonel Albert, 49, died 28 March 1871. (Nashville Republican Banner, 29 March 1871.)

SMITH, Andrew Henry, son of General Smith of New Hope, Ala., committed suicide on Thursday by cutting his throat with a razor. (Memphis Daily Appeal, 3 Nov. 1869.)

SMITH, Austin, was murdered four days ago near Franklin, Tn, by William A. and Adam Pewitt in an argument over a fence, and they have been charged with murder. Smith was formerly with the 5th Tennessee Regiment. (Nashville Daily Union, 11 March 1865.)

SMITH, Bob, guerrilla around Okolona, Mississippi, was killed by the Federals in a small action near Lagrange. (Nashville Dispatch, 12 May 1863.)

SMITH, Captain, notorious guerrilla, was killed last Monday on the upper Cumberland. (Nashville Daily Union, 27 March 1864.)

SMITH, Major General C. F., died at Savannah, Tn, on the 25th of dysentery; he was taken sick shortly after the Federal forces under him occupied Savannah; his family has been notified. (Nashville Dispatch, 29 April 1862.)

SMITH, Catherine Robertson, in her 20th year (or 29th year), daughter of Milly Smith, died on the 14th. (Nashville Daily Union, 17 Jan. 1863.)

SMITH, Edward, guerrilla, formerly of Chicago, Illinois, was killed in Maury County. (Nashville Daily Union, 5 Nov. 1863.)

SMITH, E. Kirby. General Grant has written Gen. Kirby Smith granting
him permission to return home on parole and to be placed on the
same footing as other Confederate officers of his rank. General
Smith desires to return and renew his allegiance to the Government
of the United States. (The Monitor, Murfreesboro, Tn, 4 Nov. 1865.)

Gen. E. Kirby Smith, president of Sewanee College, is in New Orleans
undergoing treatment for cancer. (Maury Democrat, 2 Oct. 1890.)

Gen. E. Kirby Smith is one of the three surviving Confederate
generals, the others being Beauregard and Johnston. He is at
present in New Orleans where his erect and soldierly figure, topped,
as it were, with a crown of strong white hair attracts general
attention. (Florence, Ala., Times, 3 Oct. 1890.)

Gen. E. Kirby Smith, professor of math at the University of the
South since 1875, died March 28 at 3:25. His health had been
declining for two years with congestion of the right lung from a
cold. One of his last utterances was a verse from the 23rd Psalm,
"Tho I walk through the valley of the shadow of Death, I will fear
no evil, for thou art with me." He was born 16 May 1824 in St.
Augustine, Florida, and with him closes the list of all generals of
both sides during the last war. His family have participated with
distinction in every war waged in this country since the old French
war. (Maury Democrat, 30 March 1893.) He left a wife and 11
children surviving; his father was a colonel in the War of 1812;
and he had a brother Ephraim killed in the Mexican War. (Maury
Democrat, 6 April 1893.)

SMITH, Eli, of Buena Vista Ferry, found an unknown infant floating in
the river and he buried it on the bank of the Cumberland. (Nashville
Dispatch, 13 Aug. 1863.)

SMITH, Farm, who lived near Rossville, Tn, went coon hunting, and then
rested his head on a steel rail and slept. A train did the rest.
(Columbia Herald, 20 Aug. 1897.)

SMITH, Florence G., infant daughter of Colonel Baxter Smith, 11 months
16 days, died on the 19th and was buried in Gallatin Cemetery.
(Nashville Republican Banner, 20 July 1869.)

SMITH, Harmon W., 70, died March 4 at Carter's Creek Station, Maury
County; had been freight and ticket agent here until recently.
(Columbia Herald, 7 March 1873.)

SMITH, Henderson, well-to-do farmer near Centerville, Hickman County,
while returning from Maury County with a load of corn, fell from
wagon, mashing one side of head, breaking three ribs, one leg and
other injuries; he and a friend, who was with him, had a bottle of
whiskey and they had been drinking. He lived only two days.
(Columbia Herald, 15 Jan. 1897.)

SMITH, Henry Sheffield, 2 months 25 days, died on the 28th, son of
Eugene R. and Minnie V. Smith. (Nashville Union and American, 29
July 1874.)

SMITH, Henry, of Scottsville, Ala., was found murdered near Blocton,
Ala., last week. (Florence, Ala., Times, 15 Aug. 1891.)

SMITH, Mrs. Ida, wife of Robert F. Smith, died Monday at her home near
Blanton's Chapel; had four grown sons. (Maury Democrat, 6 June
1895.)

SMITH, J. T., 5th Georgia Regiment, rebel prisoner, was shot through
head and killed by one of guards at the Convalescent Barracks.
(Nashville Daily Union, 6 Dec. 1863.)

SMITH, Ida, infant child of John L. and Maria Smith, 18 months 13 days
died on the 7th. (Nashville Dispatch, 8 June 1862.)

SMITH, James Hudson, 19 years 8 months, died on 30 Jan. 1870 of smallpox and buried at Elmwood Cemetery, Memphis. (Memphis Daily Appeal,
6 Feb. 1870.)

SMITH, John, formerly a British soldier, died in England on the 4th
ult., 97 years old. (Nashville Daily Gazette, 19 Sept. 1852.)

SMITH, son of John Smith, age 12, who lived near Rock Springs, Maury
County, died Tuesday of meningitis; this is second death in family
in last few days of same disease. (Maury Democrat, 23 Feb. 1888.)

SMITH, John Hugh, 51, died yesterday at 11 o'clock; judge of criminal
court of Davidson and Rutherford Counties; born 1819 in Nashville;
graduate of University of Nashville; Mayor of Nashville 1845, 1850,
1851, 1852, 1862, 1863, 1865; the bell at City Hall tolled from
2 p.m. to 4 p.m. in his honor. (Nashville Republican Banner,
8 July 1870.)
The estate of Judge J. H. Smith is estimated at $30,000. (Nashville
Republican Banner, 10 July 1870.)

SMITH, John J., of Readyville, died of smallpox two weeks ago and since
then a daughter and two sons have died. (Monitor, Murfreesboro,
Tn, 6 Feb. 1873.)

SMITH, J. Stewart, printer, with the Union and Dispatch, died yesterday
of pneumonia. (Nashville Republican Banner, 15 April 1868.)

SMITH, Captain J. Webb, ord. sgt. of Company C, Rock City Guards, will
be buried today. (Nashville Republican Banner, 7 Sept. 1869.)

SMITH, infant, died of whooping cough; child of Joseph and Martha
Smith of Greenfield Bend in Maury County. (Columbia Herald and
Mail, 17 July 1874.)

SMITH, Miss Lucinda, 17 daughter of Rev. Peyton Smith, formerly of
Rutherford County, died near Randolph, Tn, on 3 Sept. 1834.
(Central Monitor, Murfreesboro, Tn, 11 Oct. 1834.)

SMITH, Lieutenant, 3d Ohio Heavy Artillery, was killed when train
thrown from track between Knoxville and Athens. (Nashville Daily
Union, 3 Feb. 1865.)

SMITH, Mark, former conductor of the Mississippi Central Railroad is
to be executed 29 April 1864 in Memphis; he was caught in act of
smuggling 500,000 percussion caps and several hundred pounds of
powder to the rebels. (Nashville Daily Union, __ April 1864.)

SMITH, Mary Alice, 1 year 11 days, daughter of J. T. and Catharine
Smith, died on the 13th. (Nashville Republican Banner, 14 May
1868.)

SMITH, Mary Eliza, 9 months 5 days, infant daughter of Wallace and Ann
Eliza Smith, died on 22d in Davidson County. (Clarksville
Jeffersonian, 4 July 1846.)

SMITH, Mrs. Mary Jane, wife of W. Hy Smith, age 41, died Friday; native
of Campbell County, Va.; daughter of Dr. William L. Glasscock, who
settled in Madison County, Alabama when she was an infant.
(Nashville Daily Union, 22 July 1865.)

SMITH, Maria, infant daughter of Loania V. and Andrew J. Smith, died
on the 21st. (Nashville Dispatch, 24 March 1863.)

SMITH, Maud Craven, age 3, daughter of John Watt and Emily J. Smith,
died in this city yesterday of measles; they lived on Ewing's Row,
Union Street. (Nashville Daily Gazette, 31 July 1852.)

SMITH, Minor, died in Nashville on the 11th; son of Elizabeth Smith of
12 North High Street. (Nashville Daily Union, 12 Jan. 1863.)

SMITH, Nimrod D., 80, buried last week; 1st Lieutenant of 10th Legion in Mexican War; buried at the monument to the Mexican soldiers in the cemetery at Gallatin. (Maury Democrat, 16 Oct. 1890.)

SMITH, Brig. Gen. Preston, was killed at Chickamauga. (Nashville Dispatch, 25 Sept. 1863.) General Preston Smith was killed Sept. 19 at half past seven while leading a brigade from within a few yards of the enemy's line. (Nashville Dispatch, 30 Sept. 1863.) (N.B. He was first buried at Atlanta, Ga., but later moved to Elmwood Cemetery in Memphis.)

SMITH, Robert L., 46, died 21 June 1869, ex-sheriff of Shelby County; died of complication of diseases, mostly yellow jaundice; he fell dead in a store on Front Street. (Memphis Daily Appeal, 22 June 1869.)

SMITH, Mrs. Sarah J., wife of Dr. J. R. Smith of Nashville, died in Nashville on Sept. 10; daughter of Benjamin Warfield of Lexington, Ky. (Nashville Dispatch, 11 Sept. 1863.)

SMITH, son of Stephen Smith of Lincoln County, was struck by a falling tree and instantly killed a few days ago; head was crushed. (Nashville Union and American, 14 Feb. 1873.)

SMITH, Col. Thomas, 73, died October 16 at Hickman on the Arkansas River of typhoid-pneumonia. (Nashville Union and American, 23 Oct. 1874.)

SMITH, Brigadier General William D., died in Charleston on the 5th; body taken to Augusta, Georgia for burial. (Nashville Dispatch, 16 Oct. 1862.)

SMITH, W., was shot by Bob Cotton on Tuesday and died Wednesday; Cotton will probably be acquitted. (Nashville Republican Banner, 31 Jan. 1868.)

SMITH, William, former member of the 4th Tennessee (Federal) Home Guards, formerly of Davidson County, was killed in Marshall County at Joyce's Mill on Duck River on Friday. (Nashville Republican Banner, 5 June 1869.)

SMITH, William, was murdered by George S. Adkins in Stewart County; change of venue to Montgomery County for the trial. (Clarksville Weekly Chronicle, 28 May 1858.)

SMITH, William Hy, 55, editor and late A.P. agent, died April 17 at Nashville. (Whig and Tribune, Jackson, Tn, 26 April 1873.) W. Hy. Smith died suddenly yesterday at 4 o'clock of congestion of the heart. (Nashville Union and American, 4 Feb. 1873.)

SMITH, Williamson, of Huntsville, Alabama, charged with murder of Barry Brown last February had been tried and acquitted. On Saturday night disguised men went to him home, took him out and hung him. (Memphis Daily Appeal, 19 Nov. 1868.)

SMITH, murderer of Burt, was hanged at Corinth, Mississippi, on the 18th before 5000 people, made a full confession. (Free Press, Murfreesboro, 29 July 1881.)

SMITHIMORE. A quarrel took place in a house of ill-fame at Columbia on Saturday night between George A. Kuff and Jake Smithimore, and it resulted in the shooting death of Smithimore. (Memphis Daily Appeal, 30 July 1868.)

SMITHSON, Charley, and his wife Sallie K., died last week; she died on Tuesday at 4 a.m. and he died Thursday at 6 o'clock; six children survive; Methodist; buried in family burying ground on Flat Creek. (Columbia Herald, 10 July 1896.)

357

SMITHSON, Charles, 70, died last week near Park Station. (Columbia Herald, 17 April 1891.)

SNAPP, Sam, called a renegade by the Confederates, and charged with piloting a Federal force into East Tennessee, is under sentence of death as a spy. (Nashville Dispatch, 29 May 1863.)

SNOW, William O., 48, died on the 13th in Edgefield. (Nashville Dispatch, 15 March 1863.)

SNOWDEN, John Bayard, son of J. B. Snowden, age 7 years 11 months 6 days, died yesterday. (Nashville Daily Gazette, 8 Jan. 1850.)

SOLOMON, Hezekiah, of Gallatin, was accidentally killed on the 15th ult., about 8 or 10 miles north of Munfordville, Ky. (Nashville Dispatch, 2 Oct. 1862.)

SOLOMON, Mrs. Angella Carter, died at Lebanon on the 28th; wife of L. D. Solomon, late of Nashville; daughter of W. R. Carter. (Nashville Union and American, 29 Nov. 1874.)

SOMMERVILLE, John, Esquire, 75 years 10 months, died in Nashville on the 26th. (Clarksville Jeffersonian, 2 May 1846.)

SOMERVILLE, Major William Jones, died on the 23d; born in Warren County, North Carolina, son of Jos. B. Somerville, who came to Haywood County early; lawyer; commanded company in Col. Shemmon's Cavalry; practice law in Memphis. (Memphis Daily Appeal, 3 Feb. 1869.)

SOOBY, Col. John, died August 16 at Spring Place; funeral to be held today. (Nashville Republican Banner, 18 Aug. 1870.)

SOUTHALL, Mrs. J. B., funeral to be held today at General Harding's. (Nashville Dispatch, 24 Oct. 1862.)

SOUTHALL, John, was shot on the 25th ult. at Hillsboro, Williamson County, by Sam Dabney. (Nashville Republican Banner, 4 Feb. 1871.)

SOUTHGATE, Mary Elizabeth, daughter of W. W. and P. M. Southgate, to be buried today. (Nashville Republican Banner, 14 June 1870.)

SOWELL, Colonel Augustus, died on the 21st, 6 miles west of Trenton, TN; his horse was fightened by a train, threw him, and his back was broken. (Memphis Daily Appeal, 4 July 1870.)

SOWELL, Louise, daughter of Mr. and Mrs. Wilburn Sowell, died at Rock Spring in Maury County. (Maury Democrat, 22 Aug. 1895.)

SOWELL, Payton, of Williamsport, died last week and was buried in the Russell Cemetery. (Columbia Herald and Mail, 1 May 1874.)

SPAIN. About 80 years ago Wiley Spain, deceased, then a little boy, climbed a tree in Virginia and gathered some mulberries from it. Years after he felled the tree and had a rocking chair made from part of it. Over 50 years ago he came to this country bringing the chair with him. It is now in the possession of Hugh Douglas of Enterprise. (Maury Democrat, 29 March 1894.)

Wiley Spain, three score and 10, died March 4 near Enterprise; he had been living here 30 years; aged wife survives. He had a large family and one son died at Port Hudson. He had been confined to his room for seven years; one of the first settlers here. (Columbia Herald and Mail, 10 March 1876.)

SPAIN, Mr., living near Clarksville, returned home last Sunday and found a man named Hodge in his house and fired upon him, killing him instantly. Spain and Hodge had previously had difficulty growing out of an intimacy existing between the latter and the wife of the former. (Memphis Daily Appeal, 25 Dec. 1868.)

SPALDING, Capt. W. L., formerly of Duke's regiment, Morgan's command, on January 3 attacked a wagon train near Fort Donelson and captured 10 wagons, 40 mules, 10 negroes, and 9 abolition prisoners. The Federals then attacked and he was killed; he was from Nelson County, Ky, and was a member of Morgan's original squadron. He received two sabre cuts at Lebanon last spring. (Nashville Dispatch, 25 Jan. 1863.)

SPARKMAN. Those killed at Port Hudson during the siege were Capt. Fred Weller of Nashville, Lt. Bledsoe of Nashville, Lt. Penix of Nashville, and Capt. Sparkman of Maury County. (Nashville Dispatch, 1 Sept. 1863.) (N.B. The James Madison Sparkman Chapter, UDC, in Maury County was named for Captain Sparkman.)

SPARKMAN, John Thomas, born 20 Nov. 1825 near Franklin; elected justice of the pece in 1860 and for four years a member of the quorum court; in 1872 he was elected chairman of the court; married 1856 to Martha Dodson. (Maury Democrat, 4 July 1895.)

SPARKMAN, Matt, son of Mrs. J. H. Sparkman of Santa Fe, died Monday in Union City. (Columbia Herald, 3 April 1891.)

SPARKS, B. W., old citizen of Tuskegee, Alabama, died on the 1st. (Memphis Daily Appeal, 10 June 1870.)

SPARKS. The following notation was found written in a trembling handwriting in a Bible published 1825 and in New England: "Nancy Ann Sparks born on the 4th January 1752 according to the best of her recollection." (Maury Democrat, 1 Feb. 1894.)

SPARKS, Wash, and Henry Coburn got into difficulty Saturday at Iuka and Sparks was killed. (Memphis Daily Appeal, 16 Sept. 1868.)

SPAUDLING, William, fireman on Engine 61 of L & N Railroad, was knocked from box car at Shepherdsville and run over on Sunday and died instantly. (Nashville Republican Banner, 27 Nov. 1867.)

SPEARS, General James G., well known in the eastern part of the state, died on the 23d near Pikeville, Bledsoe County. (Memphis Daily Appeal, 1 Aug. 1869.)

SPEER, Tom, of Pike County, Georgia, murdered his nine children during the absence of his wife one day last week. (Columbia Herald, 18 Oct. 1895.)

SPEIR, Thomas, is in jail in Pike County, Georgia, charged with killing his eight children by use of poison. (Maury Democrat, 17 Oct. 1895.)

SPENCE, Brent, died yesterday, an aged and esteemed citizen. (Nashville Republican Banner, 24 Nov. 1868.)

SPENCE, William, 86, died on the 16th at home of his son Richard Spencer; he had lived in Rutherford County for 40 years. (Nashville Union and American, 19 Sept. 1873.)

SPENCER, George W., Company K, 42d Tennessee, prisoner of war, died in general hospital at Paducah, Ky, between the 12th and 19th of April. (Nashville Dispatch, 7 Aug. 1862.)

SPENCER. A girl soldier has been discovered in the camp of the 10th Ohio Cavalry at Cleveland; she said her name was Henrietta Spencer from Oberlin, Ohio, and she had enlisted to avenge her father and brother who fell at Murfreesboro. (Nashville Dispatch, 4 Feb. 1863.)

SPENCER, Miss Ida, died of hydrophobia at Dayton, Rhea County, from

the bite of a cat. Several weeks ago a madstone was applied and
it had adhered at the line. (Maury Democrat, Columbia, Tn,
23 Jan. 1890.)

SPENCER, Jeremiah, 94, died recently at New Hartford; was last person
who escaped from the massacre of Wyoming, Pa., in 1778. His two
older brothers were killed. (Nashville Dispatch, 28 Nov. 1863.)

SPENCER, Mrs. Joseph, of Clinton County, Indiana, had four children
born at once on December 29 last. (Maury Democrat, 13 Feb. 1862.)

SPENCER, Thomas S., 80, died October 1 in Hickman County; was born
5 Aug. 1798 in Williamson County. (Columbia Herald and Mail, 2
Nov. 1877.) Col. Thomas Spencer of Leatherwood died last week of
congestive chill. (Columbia Herald and Mail, 12 Oct. 1877.)

SPENCER, Thomas, drowned himself in a barrel yesterday in Nashville;
had been drinking and was under delirium tremens; about 28 or 30
years old; from New York; was a laborer at the Chattanooga Depot.
(Nashville Daily Union, 10 May 1865.)

SPENCER, William, Company H, 85th Ohio Volunteers, fell overboard 12
miles from Cincinnati and drowned on the Sir William Wallace.
(Nashville Dispatch, 31 July 1862.)

SPICER, William T., a gallant soldier of the 30th Virginia regiment,
latterly brakeman on the Virginia Central Railroad, was run over by
cars at Richmond Tuesday last and instantly killed; his body
completely cut in two. (Memphis Avalanche, 14 Dec. 1866.)

SPICER. John and Melissa Spicer have gone to Illinois and abandoned
their six year old child to helpless care of its aged and utterly
destitute grandparents, who live near the Davidson-Sumner County
line. (Nashville Republican Banner, 7 Sept. 1869.)

SPINDLE, Dr. John P., 88, died August 24 on Bear Creek in Maury County,
short and painful illness; erysipilas; buried Rose Hill Cemetery in
Columbia. (Columbia Herald, 28 Aug. 1891.) He was born 1804 in
Rhappohanock County, Virginia; graduate of medical school at Baltimore; in 1828 moved to Mt. Pleasant and in 1841 to Columbia;
married (1) a Miss Gold in Virginia and (2) Mrs. Anna Johnson and
they had two children; he had been a member of Mt. Olivet Methodist
Church for 68 years. (Columbia Herald, 4 Sept. 1891.)

SPIVEY, Jacob, old merchant in Memphis before the war, died on the 19th
in Savannah, Georgia, of lung disease. (Memphis Avalanche, 25 Dec.
1868.)

STACK, John, infant son of Mrs. Kate Stack, to be buried today.
(Memphis Daily Appeal, 10 Nov. 1866.)

STAFFORD, Monroe, has been arrested in DeKalb County, Ala., for
collecting regularly the pension of a Union veteran, who died 10
years ago. (Maury Democrat, 20 June 1895.)

STAGG. The ruins of the oldest settlement on the upper James River
of Virginia were recently discovered and they are supposed to be
the remains of an old store house or fort erected by Col. Thomas
Stagg in 1663. (Columbia Herald and Mail, 2 Feb. 1877.)

STALLWAGON, John, private banker of Buffalo, New York, who suspended
lately, drowned himself in the Erie basin. His body was found
frozen solid. His assets were $119,000; his liabilities $108,000.
(Columbia Herald and Mail, 18 Feb. 1876.)

STANDIAGE, Christian, committed suicide yesterday, son of Mrs. Margaret
Klein and her first husband; age 23. He was born in Bavaria. His
mother came to American and he was left there. He served as

machinist in the French Army and was in many battles around Algiers, where he seduced a girl who had a child. He then came to the United States and had been here 4 months. There was a family argument and he shot himself in the mouth. (Nashville Republican Banner, 27 Aug. 1868.)

STANDLEY, Corporal Moses, Company H, 8th Kansas Volunteers, died 5 Feb. 1863, native of Davidson County, Tn, lived in Ohio, Indiana, and Nebraska. His wife and three children survive, his sons are all in service. (Nashville Daily Union, 10 Feb. 1863.)

STANBACK, ___, was mortally wounded in battle near Washington; in Company C, 14th Tennessee Regiment from Montgomery County. (Nashville Dispatch, 2 Oct. 1862.)

STANFILL, W. J., 33, died Thursday of general debility near Erin. (Erin Review, 3 April 1880.)

STANFORD, John, was killed by George Porter in Hardin County a week or two ago; jealousy was the cause. (Whig and Tribune, 15 Feb. 1873.)

STANLEY, Alexander, private, Company K, 5th Tennessee Cavalry, was killed 22 Feb. 1864 on calf Killer, near Sparta, Tn. (Nashville Daily Union, ___ Feb. 1864.)

STANLEY, Henry M., is engaged to Miss Dorothy Tennant, a young English artist. (Houston County News, 23 May 1890.) Henry M. Stanley is expected to lecture in Montgomery, Ala., at an early date. (Florence, Ala., Times, 21 Nov. 1890.) Henry M. Stanley and his beautiful wife reside quietly at St. Mortiz in Switzerland. (Maury Democrat, 27 Sept. 1894.) Henry M. Stanley, the African explorer, is said to be dying of pleuro-pneumonia at his home in London. (Daily Herald, Columbia, Tn, 11 May 1904.)
(N.B. Sir Henry Morton Stanley, born 1841, died 1904, enlisted 1861 in Confederate Army, was captured at Shiloh, and was in prison at Camp Douglas for two months. He obtained his release by enlisting in the Federal Army, but was discharged in less than a month as unfit.)

STANTON, Frederick P., who once represented Memphis district from 1845 to 1855, and who was Governor Kansas from 1858 to 1861, died 4 June 1894 in Florida at the age of 80 years; he was regarded as one of Tennessee's ablest statesmen. (Maury Democrat, 12 July 1894.)

STAPLES, Robert A., of Farmville, was shot and killed Jan. 27 by Capt. James W. Henley of Amherst in Prince Edward County, Virginia; he was accused by Henley of seduction of his wife while he was absent in service; the court declares if justifiable homicide. (Nashville Dispatch, 2 April 1863.)

STAPLES, Sol., was hung because of his loyalty to the U. S. Government; he was a prominent citizen of Morgan County, Tn; he was taken prisoner by the rebels and hanged in Wayne County, Ky. (Nashville Dispatch, 24 April 1863.)

STAPLES, Tol, Esquire, 60, for many years the clerk of chancery in Scott County, was murdered by rebel soldiers who tied him to a tree and shot him. (Nashville Daily Union, 10 April 1863. N.B. See the listing of Sol. Staples.)

STARLING, Fielding, died 10 Jan. 1863, age 23, of typhoid in Russellville, Ky; Lieutenant in 5th Kentucky Cavalry. (Nashville Daily Union, 10 Feb. 1863.)

STARLING, Lewis, 27, died Pensacola, Florida, formerly of Hopkinsville, Ky. (Nashville Daily Union, 10 Feb. 1863.)

STARLING, Kate, daughter of Lewis Starling, age 5, died in Canton, Miss. (Nashville Daily Union, 10 Feb. 1863.)

STARK, Mrs. Margaret, 85, died at home of her son Col. Jo C. Stark at Springfield, Robertson County, last week. (Whig and Tribune, 21 Dec. 1872.)

STARKEY, Andrew J., funeral to be held this morning. (Nashville Dispatch, 21 June 1862.)

STARKS, Francis, died Saturday night in Bigbyville neighborhood from effects of a bad cold. (Nashville Republican Banner, 31 Oct. 1869.)

STAUDERMAN, John Henry, is dead; born at Bingen-on-Rhine, a well and cistern digger; left no family; addicted to strong drink. (Columbia Herald, 26 Jan. 1872.)

STEADMAN, George, 25, died on the 15th at the Overton Hotel, son of Samuel T. Steadman; had brothers William and Edward. (Memphis Avalanche, 16 Nov. 1866.) Lee C. Steadman, died on the 15th at the Overton Hotel, of which he was proprietor; born in Kentucky; served as private in the Louisiana Guards CSA. (Memphis Avalanche, 20 Nov. 1866.)

STEAMER Sunny Side burned on the 13th opposite Island 16, 28 miles below New Madrid, Mo.; the cotton caught on fire. Of the 13 females on board only 4 escaped and of the 8 children, 6 were lost. Among those lost were Mr. Bride, wife and child of Memphis; sister of Major Bosnell; Mrs. Van Buren and daughter Mattie of Detroit; Mrs. Blake; George Cox and child. (Nashville Dispatch, 17 Nov. 1863.)

STEARNS, "Aunt" Rhoda, celebrated her 101 st birthday at Highgate Center, Vermont, last Tuesday. Despite her great age, Mrs. Stearns rises at 4 o'clock every morning and builds a fire in an old-fashioned box stove. (Maury Democrat, 17 May 1894.)

STEARNS, Miss Mary E., her funeral to be held today. (Nashville Dispatch, 23 Sept. 1862.)

STEELE. A man named Steele had his leg crushed by a freight train yesterday morning and the limb was amputated, but he died at Horse Cave on the L & N Railroad. (Nashville Union and American, 25 July 1874.)

STEELE, Capt. Balie P., Company B, Rock City Guards, CSA, was wounded in the Battle of Perryville on the 8th ult. and has since died. (Nashville Dispatch, 6 Nov. 1862.)

STEELE, Emma Alice, daughter of W. A. and Susan Steele, age 13 years 7 months, died on the 27th ult. of typhoid at Camden, Tn, at the home of Judge W. A. Steele. (Nashville Union and American 12 Oct. 1873.)

STEELE, A. G., prominent Giles County citizen, was murdered by a negro last week. (Columbia Herald, 28 June 1872.)

STEELE, James T., was killed at Buena Vista on Saturday and Gray Butler died Sunday; they were killed by the Taylors. (Nashville Republican Banner, 17 Jan. 1868.)

STEELE, Mrs. Mary J., 47, died on the 5th; wife of John. Lincoln News. (Nashville Republican Banner, 11 May 1869.)

STEELE. Persons indebted to the estate of Thomas Steele, deceased, must come forward. Signed: John W. Bondehamer. (Tennessee Beacon, Pulaski, Tn, 26 Sept. 1834.)

STEGMAN. During Grierson's celebrated raid through Mississippi, General Stegman of the Confederate service was surprised by a squad of Federal troops and in an exchange of shots was mortally

wounded by Henry Dillon, a New Jersey soldier. Before dying he
took from his pocket, his will bequeathing all property and
insurance policy to wife and daughter and intrusted it to his slayer
for safe keeping. Since the war Dillon has advertised in vain for
the owners and finally waited to be sought for. Recently a $500
reward in Alabama papers was offered by Stegman's daughter to
settle the title to the estate, worth $300,000 which spurious heirs
had been trying to get in courts by a forged check. (Columbia
Herald, 10 Nov. 1871.)

STEPHENS, Mr. Hines, of Hickman County, formerly of Maury County, died
at his home on Cedar Creek, 94 or 95 years old. (Columbia Herald,
5 March 1897.)

STEPHENS, ___, was killed by the locomotive a few days since at the
Normandy depot; he was on the track and failed to get out of the
way. (Nashville Daily Gazette, 30 July 1852.)

STEPHENS, Alexander H., monument to him unveiled last week at Craw-
fordsville, Georgia; multitudes of people attended. (Maury
Democrat, 8 June 1893.)

STEPHENS, Mrs. Medora, wife of Dr. J. L. Stephens, died 1 Feb. 1865;
lived 6 So. Cherry Street; daughter of A. C. and Mildred Carter.
(Nashville Daily Union, 3 Feb. 1865.)

STEPHENSON, Benjamin, son of Courtiss Stephenson, died in Nashville,
age 21; brought to be buried in cemetery at Spring Hill. (Columbia
Herald and Mail, 13 April 1877.)

STERNBERGER, Mrs. Fannie, under sentence for killing her husband in
Memphis, died in the hospital. (Clifton Mirror, 27 Oct. 1904.)

STEVENS, Robert L., esteemed citizen of Williamson County, died Feb.
25. (Whig and Tribune, 9 March 1872.)

STEVENSON, Mrs. Hannah, of Brookfield, Massachusetts is 100 years old
and is said to be mentally bright. She has used tobacco and snuff
for last 81 years. (Maury Democrat, 13 July 1893.)

STEVENSON, Capt. Richard, A.Q.M., U.S. Army, funeral to be held today.
(Nashville Dispatch, 5 Oct. 1862.)

STEWART, guerrilla, captured and executed in Franklin, Ky; formerly
in the 13th Kentucky Cavalry. (Nashville Daily Union, 26 March
1865.)

STEWART, Gen. A. P., the Confederate commander, who broke the Union
lines at Chickamauga, on the first day of the battle, is seriously
ill at Chattanooga and not expected to recover; is 80 years old.
(Maury Democrat, 19 Sept. 1895.)

STEWART, Mrs. Agnes W., daughter of Mrs. Elizabeth Humphreys, will be
buried today. (Nashville Republican Banner, 22 Oct. 1869.)

STEWART, Darwin, died night before last; major in the Confederate
Army under Lee; son of E. Pinkney Stewart; he was shot by a negro
dressed in Federal uniform on the Hernando Road; shot on the 6th;
3 miles from town; buried Elmwood Cemetery. (Memphis Avalanche,
9 Jan. 1866.)

STEWART, E. B., of Lagrange, Tn, was killed Saturday by one Kirwin;
buried with Masonic honors. (Memphis Avalanche, 27 Nov. 1866.)

STEWART (or STEWARD), Joe, died Monday at Mt. Pleasant; remains
interred in Hunter's Cemetery. (Columbia Herald, 1 Jan. 1897.)

STEWART, Jerome, deceased; his will admitted to probate Feb. 1865 in
Davidson County. (Nashville Daily Union, ___ Feb. 1865.)

STEWART, John, died of chronic thrombosis Friday last in District 17. (Columbia Herald and Mail, 24 Aug. 1877.)

STEWART, John L., died yesterday. (Nashville Daily Union, 3 March 1863.)

STEWART, Mrs. Margaret, 103, of Plug, Carroll County, Georgia, wants a pension; widow of James Stewart, who fought in Indian War of 1812 under Capt. John Myrick. (Maury Democrat, 28 Nov. 1889.)

STEWART, Aunt Patsy, one of the oldest settlers of District 17 in Maury County, died of consumption on the 9th. (Columbia Herald and Mail, 17 Aug. 1877.)

STEWART, Mrs. Sarah Jane, 21, died Feb. 23; sister of Mr. W. T. Auten (or Anten). (Nashville Daily Union, 26 Feb. 1863.)

STEWART, Mrs. Thomas J., 40, died on the 18th; buried at Rose Hill; husband and three children survive; sister of Sims and John Latta. (Columbia Herald, 23 Jan. 1891.)

STEWART (or STEWARD), William Henry, son of Robert and Sally Stewart, is to be buried today. (Nashville Republican Banner, 30 June 1868.)

STEWART, William, died in this city on the 21st of brain fever. (Nashville Dispatch, 22 Oct. 1862.)

STEWART, William, 45, murdered by Young Alexander, colored, yesterday, shot and killed instantly in West Nashville. (Nashville Republican Banner, 14 April 1870.)

STEWART, William, oldest iron man in Nashville, died in Nashville; had lived there more than 50 years. (Whig and Tribune, Jackson, Tn, 3 Feb. 1872.)

STEWART, William, of Winchester, died a few days ago; once postmaster there; father of Gen. A. P. Stewart. (Nashville Republican Banner, 8 July 1868.)

STILES, Randal, Esquire, fell from a cliff recently at Alleghany Springs, Virginia, and was dashed to pieces; son of the Rev. Stiles of Richmond, Virginia; was connected with the navy when a boy and spent many years at sea. (Memphis Daily Appeal, 5 Sept. 1868.)

STILES, Mrs. Sarah, wife of A. D. Stiles, foreman of Columbia Cotton Mills, died Friday after an illness of several months; Methodist; husband and a daughter survive. (Columbia Herald, 15 May 1896.)

STILL. A respected lady named Still, living near Bowling Green, Ky, was brutally murdered last Monday by a party of negroes. Her head was split open with an axe; money was the incentive. She had $65 in her house. Three have been arrested. (Memphis Avalanche, 3 Nov. 1866.)

STINE, H. J., funeral to be held today in Edgefield. (Nashville Union and American, 28 June 1874.)

STINSON, Kitty, alias Annie Lane, prostitute at 206 Front Row, Memphis died yesterday from taking morphine to commit suicide, age 35; she suffered from heart diease. She had been a woman of great personal beauty and was still attractive up to the hour of her death. Her maiden name was Moreau, or Moro, and her father lives in New York. (Memphis Daily Appeal, 18 Feb. 1870.)

STIRLING, Mrs. Mary, 64, departed this life yesterday morning at home of Dr. Jennings; widow of Henry Stirling of Louisiana. (Nashville Daily Gazette, 28 July 1852.)

STOCKARD, Mrs. Sam, died August 7 near Hopewell, Maury County. (Columbia Herald and Mail, 13 Aug. 1875.)

STOCKARD, Samuel, 70, died of general debility April 10. (Daily Herald, Columbia, Tn, 17 April 1896.) Samuel J. Stockard, died April 10, in his 70th year at 5 a.m. Cumberland Presbyterian; three daughters and one son left to mourn. (Columbia Herald, 17 April 1896.)

STOCKARD. Four persons have been buried at McCain's in five days; Mrs. Sam Stockard, 50, on August 8; the infant of William Lamar; Mrs. Amanda Ramsey, 25; and the 18 month old child of Robert Odom. (Columbia Herald and Mail, 13 Aug. 1875.)

STOCKARD, Reece, 13, son of D. F. Stockard, died Saturday and buried at Glenwood Cemetery. (Maury Democrat, 21 Nov. 1895.)

STOCKS, Ben, was killed near Memphis by his cousin Cullen Stocks a day or two ago; an old grudge and bad liquor. (Nashville Republican Banner, 13 Nov. 1869.)

STOCKSLEY, Captain Charles A., was murdered June 1864 in Tipton County, Tn; John Wise has been arrested, had been living on Island 37 with 40 companions. (Memphis Avalanche, 27 Jan. 1866.)

STOCKTON, George M., his body was found on the 9th in the river near the mouth of Wolf River, sadly disfigured; had been drinking heavily for several weeks; bookkeeper; buried Elmwood Cemetery, Memphis. (Memphis Daily Appeal, 10 Oct. 1868, 12 Oct. 1868.)

STODDAN, Leila Johnston, 5 months 4 days, daughter of George B. and Mary P. Stoddan, died Sunday. (Nashville Republican Banner, 15 March 1870.)

STOKES, Charlie, 4, died June 3, of congestion; buried Rose Hill Cemetery in Columbia; son of Mr. and Mrs. Martin L. Stokes, grandson of Dr. Voss. (Columbia Herald, 5 June 1896.)

STOKES, William C., 2d son of Honorable Jordan Stokes, 22, died at Lebanon on the 2d. (Nashville Republican Banner, 7 Feb. 1869.)

STONE, small daughter of Dude Stone of Big Rock, Stewart County, age 4, died last week of a sore throat. (Stewart Breeze, 4 Nov. 1887.)

STONE, Mrs., wife of Dr. J. M. Stone, District 5 in Davidson County, last Tuesday, met her death by accidental poisoning; she took laudanum instead of a vial of paregoric; suffered with neuralgia. (Nashville Union and American, 14 Aug. 1874.)

STONE. The Stone Family. Sam Stone was on April 23 charged with stealing a horse from Dr. Mallard of Mallard, Tenn., and is in jail at Columbia now. Last Thursday he made the following statement: Three years ago his brother Will went to Kentucky to look after some property and brought a wife back with him. After the girl had been there some time, she wanted to go back home, but Mrs. Stone objected and locked her up and has had her confined ever since. From some cause, Sam says he was locked up two years ago, and has been locked up nearly ever since in one of the rooms; that about the last of March he managed to escape, and taking a horse went to Shelbyville, where he was arrested but not prosecuted on account of his youth (15 years) and that his mother got him back and locked him up again. Escaping once more, he was chased with bloodhounds and to get away from the hounds he stole Dr. Mallard's horse. (N.B. Mallard, Tn, is now Lanton in Maury County.)

Sam wanted to make bond, but refused to sign the conditions and go home, saying that he would rather be in the "pen" than go home, as his mother had threatened to kill him and only wanted to get

STONE - Continued

him home to put him out of the way; that a lot of stolen goods were
concealed in the Stone residence; that the Stone family has taken
things from the following parties: Major Maison, Squire James
Sanders, Frank Fitzgerald, J. T. Bauguss, James Bunch, and others,
that his mother soaked some paper in coal oil and placed it under
Mr. John Moore, Jr.,'s front steps; that his brother Walker set
fire to the paper ball and burned the house about 12 o'clock at
night.

The boy's statement is partially corroborated by Mr. John Moore,
Jr., and his mother-in-law, Mrs. Allen, who say they detected the
odor of burning coal oil and Mr. Moore's watch, which was in the
fire, when found afterwards, had stopped at 12:20. Sam also said
that when their own barn was burned, several years ago, it contained,
groceries, harness, saddles, and a little of everything which they
had taken.

Sam's trial is set for today when he says everything will come out.
Acting on the boy's statement, and suspicions they had held a long
time, the people who lived in the neighborhood of the Stones swore
out a search warrant before Squire Sanders Thursday. The warrant
was given to Constable Tom Parham, who placed guards around the
house Thursday night. Friday afternoon with six deputies and two
neighbors he went to search the premises.

The girl was found but was under no constraint and said she had
never been, that she has always been treated well, and she certainly
was in apparent good health. She said her name before her marriage
was Maggie Campbell, that she had married Will Stone in Louisville,
that they quarrelled and had not spoken for 18 months on account of
some reports circulated about her by Will Moore, her step-brother;
that she and her husband lived in the same house, but did not
speak.

When asked why she had not been seen by anyone for the past six
months, she said she supposed she did not happen to be in front of
the house when people passed. The neighbors say she is afraid if
she talks she will be killed.

Nothing was found Friday which anyone could positively identify as
his own, although several founds things which they thought once
belonged to them. Mr. John Moore, Jr., found some silver spoons,
forks, etc., with the name scratched off, which he thought belonged
to him. He brought them to Columbia claiming this as being part
of the silver he lost when his house was burned. Mr. Moore got out
a warrant against Mrs. W. F. Moore, alias Hulda McConathy, and Will
and Walker Stone, alias Ed and John McConathy, charging them with
arson and burglary. The warrant was issued by Esquire Coleburn
and Sheriff Ragsdale.

Deputies Lunn Erwin, Grigsby McMeens, and Constable Parham arrested
the three and brought them to town Saturday afternoon, when a
large crowd of curious blocked the sidewalk in front of Figures &
Padgett's office, their lawyers, who shortly after went with them
before Esquire Coleburn, who fixed the bonds of the three at $12,000.
H. P. Figures went on their bonds. It is said that Mrs. Moore,
alias Stone, alias McConathy, has plenty of ready money as well as
a good farm and other property sufficient to make good several
"small" bonds like the above. They will appear before the next
term of the Circuit Court which meets here May 13.

In 1870 this family, going under the name of Stone, moved to Maury
County from Nicholasville, Kentucky, and bought the Judge Cooper
place on the Spring Hill pike, seven and a half miles east of
Columbia. From that time to this, none of their neighbors have
entered the house except on two occasions. Once about five years
ago Sallie Stone and her little brother were hunting guinea nests

STONE - Continued

on a mule, the mule had harness on, and scaring at something, threw the little boy off, but the little girl got caught in the harness and the mule, racing around the lot, killed the child against a tree.

Squire Thomas Jamison saw the accident, ran over and caught the mule and carried the child to the Stone residence. That night he alone of all the neighbors were allowed to stay all night. The next morning the body was moved to another house belonging to the Stones, and from there the funeral took place.

The other time was about three years ago when Will Stone brought his wife back from Louisville. The young men in the neighborhood were invited to a reception. The real name of the Stones is said to be McConathy, but when they left Kentucky, they changed it to Stone.

For a long time Mr. Stone got his mail at Columbia under the name of McConathy, instead of at Neapolis, his nearest post office, but the postmaster at that time stopped him. Ever since the Stones have lived at the Cooper place, their neighbors missed harness, bridles, and farming implements and tools of different kind. For a long time they did not know what to think, but at last they suspected that the Stones had a hand in it, and ever since have watched them very closely, but could never catch them.

In July 1885, John Moore, Jr., and his mother-in-law, Mrs. Allen, bought a place just across the pike from the Stone residence. Two months afterwards Mr. Moore's home burned.

Mr. Moore said at the time that the Stones burned him out and wanted to have them arrested, but his lawyer advised him not to. On the night of the fire, Mr. Moore says he caught one of the Stone boys going off with his gun. He also missed part of his silver. Mr. Moore had only $2,000 insurance on the house and furniture, which he valued at a great deal more. He said the place is the Allens, who a short time afterwards sold it to the Stones.

Henry Watterson, editor of the Courier Journal, when visiting Major Campbell Brown and M. C. Campbell three years ago said the Stones were run out of Kentucky where they lived under the name of McConathy, their true name.

Last spring Mr. Stone died, the family said from disease but it is said that a man of Carter's Creek was passing along the pike several nights before Mr. Stone's death, when he was stopped by two men who tried to rob him. He shot at one of them and they ran away. A short time afterwards Mr. Stone died. Six weeks afterwards Mrs. Stone married Esq. W. F. Moore, who lived with her a short time and left, she making application for divorce.

(W. F. Moore, 79, married Mrs. Mary Stone, 60, in chancery court. (Maury Democrat, 14 Dec. 1893.)

When Sheriff Ragsdale went several weeks ago to serve divorce papers on Squire William F. Moore, whom Mrs. Stone had married, Mr. Moore told the sheriff that if he would notice at the Stone place that he would find a certain room in the rear of the house with a padlock on the outside door, and that this room contained the imprisoned woman whom they had so long kept confined, but the sheriff paid no attention to it, as it was none of his business.

On Monday morning Sheriff Ragsdale received the following telegram: "Lexington, Ky, May 6th - Please hold Sam Stone till I get there if he is still in jail. J. McConathy, R. Davis."

The receipt of this telegram together with the article herein republished from the Courier-Journal sent that paper from Lexington, caused the counsel for the prosecution to telegraph Governor

STONE - Continued
Turney not to issue requisition papers if applied for, under any
circumstances, as it looked as though these people wanted to get
young Sam Stone, their best witness out of the clutches of the law
if possible and carry him to Kentucky.

Mr. John Moore, Jr., having attached the Stone property to the
amount of $15,000 charging that his loss by fire at the hands of
the Stones to be at least that much caused ten or a dozen more
warrants to be taken out charging the Stones with grand larceny
by the following neighbors: J. T. Bauguss, T. E. Jamison, J. B.
Chappell, George Fox, J. W. Bunch, Austin Green, and others.
Esquire Sanders issued the papers for the arrest of Mrs. Stone and
her two sons Will and Walker, alias Ed and John McConathy.
Constable Parsham went out and brought them into town late Monday
afternoon and they were carried before Esquire Coleburn, but owing
to the lateness of the hour there was no trial, as the two boys
were sent to jail, while their mother remained at the Guest House
overnight under guard of W. I. Overton and Constable Parham.

Tuesday the preliminary trial was called at 2 o'clock in the courthouse, a large and curious crowd being on hand to see and hear what
they could.

The trial was before Esquire Coleburn, W. J. Webster, and E. S.
Fowler, represented the prosecution, while Figuers & Padgett were
counsel for the defense.

Sam Stone from whom the prosecution expected great things was a
disappointment to them, his testimony was not sensational, as every
one expected, but was favorable for the defendants. On this
account, all but the first two of these cases were dismissed without
a hearing, in the two cases heard, one was dismissed for want of
evidence, in the other Walker Stone was bound over the the Criminal
Court charged with stealing a cow bell, and was let loose on $500
bond.

J. McConathy and R. Davis, the gentlemen, who sent the telegram
to Sheriff Ragsdale to hold Sam Stone till they got here, arrived
in Columbia Wednesday morning. It was reported that they wanted
to take Sam back to Kentucky with them and that he consented to
go provided his Tennessee kinsfolk were not allowed to come after
him. It was also reported that Messrs. McConathy and Davis said that
Mrs. Stone's true name was Hulda Bowen and that her family had a
bad reputation where she came from, that one of her brothers,
named Frank Bowen murdered his wife and after committing other lawless acts, killed himself; that one of her sisters married and was
killed by her husband, and that another sister had her husband put
in prison. Also, that Walker and Will Stone's real names are John
and Henry Hooker instead of McConathy. That Mr. Stone bore a good
reputation when living in Kentucky.

W. I. Overton got possession of some notes and jewelry belonging
to Mrs. Stone by a trick. When she was first arrested and while
being brought to town, he whispered to her that she would be
searched when she got here, so she slipped a little handbag to
him and asked him to keep it for her. Overton brought it and put
it in the bank; it was found to contain about $2,400 in notes and
checks and some jewelry. This was all attached by Mr. John
Moore, Jr.

Was Compelled to Leave - The Lexington, Ky, correspondent, May 5,
Courier-Journal: The arrest of the widow of Jacob McConathy at
Columbia, Tenn., together with two sons charged with arson has
caused a sensation here, where the relatives of Jacob McConathy
live. Jacob McConathy was a son of Acy McConathy and has three
brothers residing in this county--Acy, Nute, and Jim. They are
all quite wealthy and prominent citizens. The father of the

STONE - Continued
McConathy boys was quite wealthy, was a magistrate and director of several turnpikes. Jacob was somewhat wayward, and is said to have been compelled to leave the neighborhood for numerous trifling lawless acts, and located at Columbia, Tenn., where is is said, he changed his name to Stone. The two boys arrested, according to the people who were neighbors of J. M. while he lived in this county, are not his children, but were adopted by him and his wife. (Maury Democrat, 9 May 1895.)

The Stones Again - A special from Lewisburg to Monday's American said that Mrs. Maggie Stone of Maury County accompanied by Detective W. I. Overton and Attorney Voorhies of Columbia were at that place awaiting papers of divorce in answer to a bill filed by Maggie Stone against her husband William Stone, filed on July 25th.

The divorce was granted and Mrs. Stone, now Maggie Campbell, has gone to Milwaukee. Messrs. Overton and Voorhies having returned to Columbia.

The bill filed by Mrs. Stone was rich in its way and she most assuredly deserved a divorce, if what she says is true. In the bill she claimed that her husband deserted her more than two years ago; that since then she had been kept locked up in the kitchen as a household drudge, that she has done all the cooking and washing (when any was done) for the entire family, that her bed has been a pile of rags in one corner of the kitchen and that she was not given clothes enough to cover her body, that she was not allowed to see any one and that she was locked up to prevent her divulging facts which would convict defendant and his mother Mrs. Mary Moore, of various and sundry felonies which they have committed from time to time.

That Mrs. Moore had whipped her with a leather strap and a buggy whip and that the defendant had aided her. That on three different occasions, Mrs. Moore and defendant had tried to poison her to get her out of the way.

She was aided by friends on the night of July 25 to escape and filed the bill for divorce. (Maury Democrat, 1 August 1895.)

Mrs. Stone was found guilty of larceny and sentenced to one year as was her son Walker Stone. (Maury Democrat, 15 Oct. 1896.)

The Stone Cases - The famous Stone larceny cases were settled Saturday by a decree of nolle prosse being entered, this settlement having been made on account of the absence of May Stone, the chief witness for the state and the impossibility of getting her here.

The cases have been in the courts of Maury county since 1896 and have attracted widespread interest.

Jacob and Hulda McConathy lived near Nicholasville, Ky, and had with them besides their own children, a boy named John Hooker. Members of the family were indicted nine times in the Kentucky courts for larceny and they proved so troublesome that they were forced to leave the state.

Jacob McConathy sold his 300-acre farm for $90 an acre in cash and changing his name to Stone came to Maury County and purchased a 600-acre farm on the Spring Hill Pike. There they did not visit their neighbors and never allowed anyone to enter their own house.

Numerous small stealings of arming implements, fowls, etc., began to worry the neighbors and the house of one, Mr. John Moore, Jr., was burned. Mr. Moore suspected the Stones but could get no evidence till 1896 when Sam Stone left home and was arrested on a charge of horse stealing, when he told that his mother burned Mr.

STONE - Continued
Moore's house. She was indicted for arson and Mr. Moore sued her
for $2,000 for damages.

The arson case was nolle prossed on Mrs. Stone, then Mrs. W. F.
Moore, offering to pay the damages demanded. She paid $500 in cash
and gave her notes for $2,000, the greater part of which she never
paid, having signed her married name to the notes which did not
bind her personal estate.

When Sam Stone was caught, he also told that May Stone, his brother's
wife was imprisoned at the house and that his mother and Walker
Stone, alias John Hooker, had stolen some hogs, turkeys, and other
things. Search warrants were issued, May Stone was released and
Mrs. Stone and Walker were indicted on two charges for larceny.

May Stone sued for divorce and for damages for false imprisonment
and was awarded both.

The larceny cases have been in the courts since a verdict of guilty
was brought at one trial, but the supreme court reversed the decision.
A verdict of guilty was brought in at another trial, but the judge
set the verdict aside on account of the improper conduct of some of
the jurors. At another trial the verdict was 11 to 1 for guilty.
(Maury Democrat, 10 March 1898.)

The will of Mary S. Moore was probated Monday; she had a farm worth
$14,175; she willed $5 to sons Walker, Will and Sam Stone, cutting
them off; and left the rest to her sister Mrs. Omie W. Marshall in
Kentucky. (Maury Democrat, 28 Sept. 1899.)

STONELAKE, Henry, 53, died on the 9th. (Nashville Dispatch, 21 Oct.
1862.)

STONELAKE, William Thomas, 17, son of Henry and Mary Stonelake, died
on the 10th in Newark, New Jersey; brought to Nashville for burial.
(Nashville Dispatch, 11 Aug. 1863.)

STOREY. Cochran shot and killed a Mr. Storey, his successful rival,
in Callaway County, Ky, last week. He then went to the house of
the bride's father, shot and killed him, afterward making his
escape. (Lincoln County Herald, 13 June 1894.)

STOUGH, Jacob, died in Tallapoosa County, Ala., on the 28th at the age
of 103 years. (Florence, Ala., Times, 12 Nov. 1892.)

STOUT, Mrs. Catharine T., 75, died in Nashville on the 15th. (Nashville
Dispatch, 17 Sept. 1863.)

STOUT, Dr. Josiah Wilkins, died last Sunday in North Nashville, born
1818 in Nashville; studied medicine under Boyd McNairy and R. C. K.
Martin. In 1850 went to California, but returned the next year. The
following were with him at the Unviersity of Nashville when he was
15:

Isaac Fulton Anderson   William Henry Stephens
Charles Elliott Boddie   Samuel Nichols Stephens
Richard Whitman Hyde Bostick
Richard Owen Currey   (Nashville Union and American,
Frances Dancey, Jr.   27 Oct. 1874.)
Samuel Miller Edgar
Thomas Fletcher
Robert Coleman Foster, 2d
Nathaniel Lawrence Lindsley
James Hardy Maney
William Lawn Murphy
James Clendenning Patterson
Robert Maxingale Porter

370

STOUT. The Odd Fellows paid tribute to their departed brother J.V.D.
Stout yesterday. (Nashville Dispatch, 29 Sept. 1863.)

STOVALL. The wife and three children of Merrit Stovall, who lived
two miles from Fosterville, were found murdered last Sunday;
throats cut, heads split open with axe; Stovall was found in a well.
There were three boys and a girl, the eldest about 16; one boy was
away from home at the time of the murder. The father had been
heard to say he feared that there would be a famine and he would
kill his family; he was about 40 years old. (Murfreesboro News,
26 Sept. 1860.)

STOWELL, Martin, prominent Abolitionist, formerly of Worcester, Mass.,
was lately killed in Tennessee; belong to a Nebraska regiment and
was drawn into ambuscade by Confederates near Paris, Tn, where he
fell mortally wounded. Mr. Stowell was conspicious actor in the
rescue of slave Jerry at Syracuse several years ago and was imprisoned several months in Suffolk County, Mass., for participation
in an unsuccessful attempt to rescue slave Anthony Burns from Boston
courthouse; he also figured in the Kansas troubles. (Nashville
Dispatch, 25 April 1862.)

STRAHL, General. A few years ago you kindly published an article I
wrote suggesting the removal of Brigadier General Granbury's
remains to his adopted state, and the erection of a monument at
the city of Granbury, Texas, so that future generations would know
of his heroic deeds, and for whom that city was named. The suggestion was followed up by you with so much ability in subsequent
articles, that every detail has been successfully accomplished.

I now wish to ask your assistance in doing honor to the memory of
Brigadier General Otho F. Strahl, who was killed while gallantly
leading his command in the battle of Franklin, and was buried in
St. John's churchyard at Ashwood, Tenn., together with Generals
Cleburne, Adams, and Granbury...

I suggest that as St. John's churchyard is only considered as a
private cemetery and is not kept as in antebellum days, General
Strahl should be removed to our Confederate square at Rose Hill,
where a suitable monument should mark his last resting place. The
money for this monument will have to be raised by private subscriptions, for the reason that I understand General Strahl has
neither kith nor kin in any of our Southern states.

I am sorry that I cannot give a good biographical sketch of General
Strahl, b ut hope when you bring this matter before our veterans,
that some one competent to do so, will furnish the facts for the use
of the future historian. Signed Robt. D. Smith. (Maury Democrat,
10 June 1897.)

I read Capt. Robert Davis Smith's article relative to moving the
body of Gen. Strahl that is buried at St. John's church to our
Confederate cemetery at Rose Hill. Gen. Strahl was a Northern man,
it is true, but his blood was shed for Southern liberties and
Southern rights and he died for us. Brothers, let us be true to
his memory. We cannot afford to forget and to cherish his memory
as one of us and let us who live after him see that his memory is
not forgotten.

I assisted in placing the dead body of Gen. Strahl in the ambulance
at the battle of Franklin that brought him to be buried at Ashwood.
I remember that one of his staff was also in the same ambulance
and I have forgotten his name, but if Gen. Strahl is removed, the
same honor and respect should be conferred upon his staff officer
who is also buried at St. John's Church. Signed, Sam R. Watkins,
Ashwood, Tenn., 16 June 1897. (Maury Democrat, 17 June 1897.)

A committee of ex-Confederate soldiers from Dyersburg will arrive

STRAHL, General - Continued
tomorrow and in company with some ex-Confederates from this place
will go to Ashwood for the purpose of disinterring the remains of
General Strahl and removing them to Dyersburg. General Strahl
was a native of Ohio who came to Dyersburg before the Civil War
where he engaged in the practice of law and at the outbreak of
hostilities, he enlisted in the Confederate service. He rose to
the position of Brigadier General and was a gallant soldier. He
was killed at the memorable battle of Franklin 30 Nov. 1864, and his
remains were buried at St. John's at Ashwood where they have lain
since. (Daily Herald, Columbia, Tn, 2 April 1901.)

The disinterment of General Otto F. Strahl's remains which was to
have taken place today has been postponed until tomorrow as the
necessary arrangements could not be made for today. Mr. D. A. Shaw
representing the ex-Confederate camp at Dyersburg arrived today and
in company with a delegation from this place will go down to St.
John's cemetery tomorrow morning and will return with the remains
in the afternoon. They will be taken to St. Peter's Church where
a burial service will take place conducted by Rev. W. D. Capers.
The members of the ex-Confederate camp and the public are invited
to attend the services. (Daily Herald, Columbia, Tn, 3 April 1901.)

The funeral services of the remains of General Otto F. Strahl, which
were disinterred at Ashwood, were conducted yesterday afternoon at
4 o'clock at St. Peter's Church by Rev. W. D. Capers and were
shipped this morning to Dyersburg. The pallbearers were Maj. W. J.
Whitthorne, Dr. W. A. Smith, Messrs. Thos. Fleming, John West,
T. C. Brittain, and Mr. Johnson.

The remains of General Strahl were found to be in poorly preserved
condition, some of the bones being partially disintegrated. Signs
of the walnut casket that had once encased his remains were found
as were also the buttons of his vest; however, no coat buttons
were there, showing that he had evidently been buried without a
coat. Other signs of the clothing he had worn were also found.

The ex-Confederate Briagdier-Generals whose remains were interred
at St. John's were all buried by Gus. Boyd, who lived at this place.
The coffins being made by the old firm of Lamb & Boyd. The senior
member of the firm, Mr. J. R. Lamb, is still living in Columbia.
Mr. Boyd received $1,300 each from the Confederate government for
burying the generals. (Daily Herald, Columbia, Tn, 5 April 1901.)

STRANGE, the youngest child of Mr. and Mrs. James Strange of Suck
Island, died of whooping cough. (Columbia Herald and Mail, 24 July
1874.)

STRATTON, Mrs. Elizabeth A., wife of R. H. T. Stratton, 51, died
yesterday of protracted illness. (Nashville Union and American,
28 June 1873.)

STRATTON, Henry, infant son of W. S. and S. E. Stratton, died 7 March
1864; lived Demumbrane Street. (Nashville Daily Union, 8 March
1864.)

STRATTON, Mrs. Mary E., wife of Col. Madison Stratton, died of diptheria
yesterday, lived on Gallatin Pike. (Nashville Union and American,
8 March 1874.)

STRATTON, Mary has been charged with harboring slave and her case has
been continued. (Nashville Dispatch, 31 Jan. 1863.) Mary Stratton,
free woman of color, has been charged with pedling without license.
(Nashville Dispatch, 1 Feb. 1863.)

STRAUGHAN, John S., died on the 4th. (Nashville Republican Banner,
5 Feb. 1869.)

STREET, Sgt., and Corporal Rose, of the 76th Ohio were killed by
lightning Saturday night near Vicksburg. (Nashville Dispatch, 26
Feb. 1863.)

STREET, William, 88, died in Robertson County, the other day. (Whig
and Tribune, 4 Nov. 1871.)

STRETCH, A., who runs a drug store in Nashville, has been arrested
for unlawful traffic with subjects of rebellious states. (Nashville
Dispatch, 21 June 1862.)

STRETCH, Lillie Nelson, infant daughter of Mr. and Mrs. J. Stretch,
6 months, died on the 4th. (Nashville Dispatch, 3 May 1863.)

STRICKLIN, Rev. John S., died in Culleoka at the home of James S.
Cowden last Sunday; native of Hardin County, had been a pupil at
Webb's School; died 9 Feb. 1873 and buried at Wilkes Cemetery.
(Columbia Herald, 14 Feb. 1873.)

STRONG. President Lincoln has forwarded to the widow of Brig. Gen.
George C. Strong a major general's commission bearing the date of
the battle of Morris Island in which he received a fatal wound.
(Nashville Dispatch, 14 Aug. 1863.)

STUART, General, the Confederate cavalry leader, is to have a noble
monument erected to his memory, and the Richmond, Va., City Council
has already appropriated $10,700 for the purchase of the site.
(Maury Democrat, 25 April 1895.) The brother of Gen. J. E. B.
Stuart has ordered a tombstone for the raider's grave; consequently
the stone contemplated by the Virginia legislature will be set up
over the grave of Gen. Edward Johnson. Ex-President ___ er, whose
grave is also at Hollywood Cemetery is unmarked and will also be
given the tardy honors of a monument. (Columbia Herald and Mail,
25 Feb. 1876. N.B. The name that could not be read was probably
"Tyler.")

STUFFENS, William, of Nashville, well known German citizen, while
intoxicated at a ball given by the Aureaugoura Lodge, stepped from
a balcony on the second story to a speedy death; he was buried with
honors by the lodge. (Memphis Avalanche, 30 Dec. 1866.)

STUTTS. Clifton, Tenn. Walter Stults of the 2nd Tennessee U. S.
Mounted Infantry has been arrested on charge that he together with
Thomas Kennedy and Thomas Brewer, of the same, on April 21 entered
the house of a lady and her two daughters. They demanded money
and the persons of the three ladies were violated, they then hung
them, but let them down before they died. Kennedy and Brewer have
not been caught. (Nashville Daily Union, 12 May 1865. N.B. Stutts
was the correct surname although Stults given in report.)

SUDEKUM, August, foreman of the carpenter shop at the Decatur depot
at Nashville, was run over and killed by a freight train a few
days ago and died immediately; both legs were cut off. (Whig and
Tribune, 15 Feb. 1873.)

SULLIVAN, Andrew J. The Murder of Captain Sullivan. We learn the
additional facts in the case from a reliable gentleman, who was
upon the field after the inhuman tragedy was enacted. Capt.
Sullivan with 23 men were detailed from the railroad to watch the
movements of some rebels in that locality, and while upon duty,
a guerrilla appeared within about half a mile of them, when one of
Sullivan's men made a run after him followed by five or six more.
The guerrilla fell back to the end of a lane, behind the fence of
which his cutthroat companions were in wait, followed by Sullivan's
men, and when even with them, the guerrillas opened fire upon them.
They stampeded back to where Capt. Sullivan and the remaining men
were, stampeding all them save the captain and two men. The
guerrillas seeing them alone rushed up, though receiving from the
little band of three, a warm reception. At length, being over-

373

powered and wounded Capt. Sullivan surrendered, and even after
his surrender his brains were shot out, and he fell a noble martyr
to his country's cause. His corpse was not cold before he was
stripped of everything but his coat and shirt, thus leaving him
unclothed in the presence of a family of ladies. This is but another
instance of "man's inhumanity to man," and is fast leading to an
exterminating mode of warfare. Justice should be meted to those
engaged in such wholesale brutal murder, so soon as can be. The
sad affair took place on Thursday, the 21st, near Baird's Ferry
on the Centerville and Franklin road. Some citizens are implicated.
Columbia Chronicle. (Nashville Daily Union, 5 May 1864.)
(N.B. W. J. Spence's History of Hickman County identifies the
guerrillas as Henon Cross, Dave Miller and one McLaughlin.)

SULLIVAN, Mr. Florence, died on Sept. 16 from a wound in the abdomen
from which the bowels protruded; he had received 7 or 8 wounds;
left a widow and four small children, the oldest under 10 years of
age. Mr. Sullivan and Caleb G. Harrison had an altercation,
Sullivan threw a rock at Harrison and struck him. Harrison then
drew knife and inflicted the wounds. Harrison was found not guilty.
(Nashville Dispatch, 17 Sept. 1863, 18 Sept. 1863, 24 Sept. 1863.)

SULLIVAN, James, of Bigbyville, 45, died Monday morning; funeral to
be held at McCain's; he had walked home from Columbia and the trip
took him 24 hours. (Columbia Herald, 18 Sept. 1896.)

SULLIVAN, Mrs. Mary, wife of John Sullivan, 26, died Friday; daughter
of Mrs. Mary Curran. (Nashville Republican Banner, 27 Feb. 1870.)

SULZBACHER, Martin, 56 years 7 months 22 days, died October 26.
(Nashville Republican Banner, 27 Oct. 1868, 31 Oct. 1868.)

SUMMERFORD, Miss Irene, is very low with consumption; she cannot
recover. (Columbia Herald, 24 July 1891.) Miss Irene Summerford
of Culleoka, died this week of consumption in the full flush of
young maidenhood; buried at Petersburg, Tn. (14 Aug. 1891.)

SUMMERFORD, William, 28, died Tuesday at Culleoka after an illness
with lung disease; buried at Petersburg; wife and one child survive.
(Columbia Herald, 29 May 1891.)

SUMMERS, Walter, son of W. W. Summers of Bedford County, was drowned
while bathing a few days ago. (Nashville Union and American, 22 Aug.
1874.)

SUMMIT, Elizabeth, an unfortunate woman, died in the workhouse on the
11th; she had long been an inmate there. (Nashville Dispatch,
12 Oct. 1862.)

SUMNER, Major General E. V., died March 21 of congestion of the lungs;
died in Syracuse, New York. (Nashville Dispatch, 22 March 1863.)

SUMNER, W. A., funeral to be held today. (Nashville Republican Banner,
11 May 1870.)

SUPPLE, John, brakeman, fell near the Nashville and Decatur junction
on 10 March 1868 and was killed. (Nashville Republican Banner,
15 Aug. 1868.)

SURRATT, Mary, 45, was hanged in Washington, D. C. on 7 July 1865.
The President has issued an order that the remains of Mrs. Surratt
be delivered to her family for decent burial; the petition was
signed by 40 members of Congress and filed in the War Department,
two years ago, but the petition cannot be found. (Memphis Daily
Appeal, 10 Feb. 1869.) Mrs. Surratt was hung once and has been
buried three times. (Memphis Daily Appeal, 20 Feb. 1869.) Mrs.
Surratt's house in Washington has been occupied by several families
since that lady's death by hanging, but none of them stay long and
there is a blood-curdling story that Mrs. Surratt is a ghostly

374

visitant there almost every night. (Memphis Avalanche, 13 Dec. 1866.)

SUTCLIFF, John, 95, a notorious criminal, has died at Steubenville, Ohio. (Maury Democrat, 19 April 1888.)

SUTTON, Samuel, of Helena, Ark., hand was caught in a cotton gin and he died in six hours of the shock; he was related to the Voorhies family of Maury County. (Columbia Herald, 21 Feb. 1873.)

SWAFFORD, Larkin, Esquire, of Bledsoe County, was murdered recently by Champ Ferguson's guerrilla gang. Champ said, Yanks had stolen two fiddles from him and he intended to have ten of their scalps for each fiddle. (Nashville Daily Union, __ March 1864.)

SWAFFORD, Silas, became overheated and dropped dead on the White's Creek Pike in District 21 on Wednesday. (Nashville Union and American, 10 July 1874.)

SWAN, Nathaniel, 80, died in Salem, Mass. He was born, lived all his life and died in the same room in North Salem; never slept but once out of his house; never sick; never needed a doctor until his last illness. (Nashville Dispatch, 13 May 1862.)

SWAN, John Henry, 13 months 17 days, died on the 27th; son of John M. and Mary C. Swan; died of summer complaint. (Nashville Daily Union, 28 June 1865.)

SWAN, Mrs. Mary, of Fayette County, died October 17 at the age of 98 years; she had lived in Tennessee 70 years, in Fayette County for 36 years, and had been a Methodist of 68 years. (Whig and Tribune Jackson, Tn, 4 Nov. 1871.)

SWANN, J. M., deceased, his will admitted to probate in Davidson County in Feb. 1865. (Nashville Daily Union, __ Feb. 1865.)

SWANSON, Col. Richard, 83, died August 13 in Williamson County. (Whig and Tribune, Jackson, Tn, 6 Sept. 1873.)

SWAYNIE, J. A., of the St. Cloud Hotel, died yesterday of brain fever; age 34; had lived here two years. (Nashville Republican Banner, 16 Aug. 1867.)

SWEENEY, Mrs. M. M., 58, died on the 16th, buried Elmwood Cemetery. (Memphis Avalanche, 17 March 1866.)

SWEENEY, Mollie, daughter of G. W. and M. A. Sweeney, age 12, died yesterday. (Nashville Republican Banner, 15 April 1869.)

SWEENEY, George, fireman, was killed when a locomotive exploded at the Nashville & Decatur depot on the 2d; he was hurled 50 feet. (Nashville Republican Banner, 3 Dec. 1867.)

SWEENEY, Mary Worthington, 9, died on the 17th; eldest daughter of James H. and Zerilda Sweeney. (Nashville Union and American, 18 Nov. 1874.)

SWEENEY, Edward P., 3 years 2 months 12 days, died on the 25th; W. H. Sweeney, age 10 years 2 months 15 days, died on the 21st; sons of William and Samantha Sweeney. (Nashville Dispatch, 26 Sept. 1863.)

SWETT. By the recent death of Col. Samuel Swett, Isaac Lincoln is the sole survivor of the Harvard Class of 1800. (Memphis Avalanche, 16 Nov. 1866.)

SWICK. It was reported that David P. Swick had been hanged in Chattanooga by the Federal troops for poisoning his well on the entrance of the Union army. He has arrived in Nashville with his family and has gone to the house of his father-in-law Henry Holt, Jr., 7 miles north of Nashville; he was not hanged. (Nashville Dispatch, 15 Nov. 1863.) David Swick of Chattanooga was hung by the U. S. Army; he had threatened to poison his well when Federals reduced the town. (Nashville Daily Union, 3 Nov. 1863.)

SWINNEA, Yateman, died of pneumonia in Virginia during the Civil War in the Confederate Army. His son Gaines Swinnea, 85, native of Lauderdale County, Ala., died 22 Feb. 1944. (Florence, Ala., Times, 22 Feb. 1944.)

SYLVESTER, James A., 70, who died a few days ago in New Orleans, was the one who captured Santa Ana at San Jacinto on 21 April 1836. He fought Comanche Indians in 1840 at Plum Creek and was the survivor of an ill-fated expedition of Texans to Mier-Mier in Mexico and was one of the prioners who had to draw lots for his life. Those that got black beans were shot in the presence of their companions. (Erin Review, 22 April 1882.)

TABOR, Serina, 27, female spy, has been brought to Nashville; native of Georgia; captured by Federals in Trenton, Ga., when taken she was in full Confederate uniform; unmarried. (Nashville Dispatch, 13 Sept. 1863.)

TAFT, Mr., 72, died recently in Mendon, Massachusetts. "Never told a lie, never was in a city, never rode in a railroad car, and never cheated a man out of a cent." (Nashville Dispatch, 3 Sept. 1862.)

TAIT, Erwin, 19, son of Robert and Mary Jane Tait of South Alabama, died on Sunday the 16th of spinal meningitis. (Nashville Union and American, 18 March 1873.)

TALBERT, Major John R. of Memphis, died in Hernando, Miss., on a visit; typhoid; funeral yesterday. (Memphis Daily Appeal, 5 Sept. 1869.)

TALBERT, Miss, aged 14 or 15, who lived near Huntsville, Alabama, committed suicide Sunday. (Columbia Herald and Mail, 23 July 1878.)

TALKINGTON, William, 103, died near Carlinville, Illinois; native of North Carolina; old soldier. (Houston County News, 19 Oct. 1888.)

TALLEY, Martin, died near Readyville, Rutherford County, 19 Oct. 1875; born Sept. 1770 in Virginia; came to Tennessee in 1796; died at 105 years; had 12 children. (Columbia Herald and Mail, 29 Oct. 1875.)

TALLMAN, Ella Sophronia, daughter of Mr. and Mrs. Peter Tallman, funeral to be held at the Cumberland Presbyterian Church this afternoon. (Nashville Union and American, 28 Aug. 1874.)

TANNEHILL, Wilkins; resolution of respect passed by the Clarksville lodge. (Clarksville Jeffersonian, 16 June 1858.)

TANSEY, William, native of Rosconnon County Ireland, age 28, died suddenly Friday; had been drinking hard for several days. (Nashville Daily Union, 9 July 1865.)

TARDIFF, Thomas Smiley, infant and only son of Justice John and Teresa Tardiff, died after a brief illness. (Nashville Republican Banner, 6 July 1870.)

TARGESON, ___, a Norwegion living at the settlment on the south branch of Watouwan River in Brown County, Minnesota, died on 16th; his house was entered and he and two soldiers were killed by Indians. (Nashville Dispatch, 7 May 1863.)

TARKINGTON, Mrs. W. T., died Tuesday on the farm of Capt. George
Mayberry in Hickman County. (Columbia Herald and Mail, 2 Nov. 1877.)
Mrs. Mary E., died several months ago, wife of Flood Tarkington;
funeral was at Leatherwood last Saturday. (Hickman Pioneer, 28 May
1878.)

TARPLEY, Mrs. Robert, died at her home south of Broad Street last
Saturday, the 18th; born 1782 in Prince Edward County, Virginia;
came to Nashville in 1833; joined the First Baptist Church 1838.
(Nashville Dispatch, 22 Oct. 1862.)

TATE, Eddie, 1 year 1 month 15 days, died June 5 near Santa Fe in
Maury County; son of John C. and Bettie Tate. (Columbia Herald
and Mail, 5 July 1878.)

TATE, George, was killed in Decaturville last Thursday by a man named
Lyle; Lyle is "a man of very bad character"; wilful murder. (Columbia
Herald and Mail, 16 Dec. 1876.)

TAYLOR, child of Mr. Taylor of District 11 in Giles County, fell from
fence, received injuries from which he died. (Memphis Daily Appeal,
7 July 1869.)

TAYLOR, Abram B., Sr., died 21 March 1866 in Crittendon County,
Arkansas, after six months illness of dropsy; age 69 years 10 months
19 days; buried Elmwood Cemetery, Memphis. (Memphis Avalanche,
4 April 1866.)

TAYLOR, Miss Annie, of Memphis, has been ordered deported beyond the
Federal lines by General Washburn; because of her disloyal language
and shameless conduct on hearing of the assassination of President
Lincoln; daughter of respectable parents. (Nashville Daily Union,
10 May 1865.)

TAYLOR, Annie E., granted a divorce from John Taylor for non-support.
(Columbia Herald, 6 Aug. 1897.)

TAYLOR, Colonel, a prominent citizen of Eutaw, Alabama, is dead.
(Florence, Ala., Times, 20 Feb. 1892.)

TAYLOR, Colonel Dick, a son of the ex-president, was so enraged on
coming home from Richmond to find that his plantation had been
ravaged by Federal troops that he forbade all of the neighboring
planters to ship their sugar to New Orleans. (Nashville Dispatch,
12 Oct. 1862.)

TAYLOR, Miss Emma, beautiful young actress, sister of Mary Taylor, died
in New York last week; was playing with Laura Keene's company in
Hartford, Conn., and received accidental internal injury. (Nashville
Daily Union, 8 March 1863.)

TAYLOR, Mrs. Emma, mother of Governor Robert L. Taylor, died in Johnson
City, Tn. (Florence, Ala., Times, 5 Dec. 1890.)

TAYLOR, Col. John C., of Dayton, Ky, has fallen heir to an estate in
Ireland, that will make him the Earl of Tyrone, and better still,
give him property valued at seven million dollars. (Florence,
Ala., Times, 14 March 1891.)

TAYLOR, Col. Julius A., of Memphis, who died last week, was a distinguished lawyer and known all over the state. (Maury Democrat,
8 Aug. 1895.)

TAYLOR, Moses, of Spencer, Indiana, was gored to death by an ox on
Monday night. (Nashville Union and American, 21 Aug. 1873.)

TAYLOR, Thankful. Tennessee Doctors were in council in Nashville last
week. The most exciting subject of discussion that was reported

was the reported living snake in the stomach of Miss Thankful
Taylor, who lives near Christiana in Rutherford County. For a
year this has been engaging the attention of Middle Tennessee
doctors. During her whole life she has been subject to attacks
of illness which were supposed to be epileptic in their nature.
The snake first appeared in the close of the year 1863. She was
then under the care of Dr. White, who treated her for tape-worm.

Dr. Bugar took care of the case in Jan. 1874 and the snake showed
itself several times. The doctor once thrust a pin through it, but
it escaped down her throat. He says he extracted it in June of
1874, and it was 3/4 inches wide and 23 inches in length. There
were sharp discussions in the Rutherford County Medical Society.
(Columbia Herald and Mail, 14 April 1876.)

TAYLOR, Major William, one of the veterans of the War of 1812, died at
his home on Franklin Avenue, Brooklyn, New York, of general debility
he was in War of 1812 and Mexican War. (Memphis Avalanche, 31 Dec.
1868.)

TAYLOR. Death of President. On July 10, General Z. Taylor expired at
30 minutes past 10 o'clock last night. He was surrounded by the
members of his cabinet, members of his family, and attending
physicians. His last words were "I am ready. I Have endeavored
to discharge my duty." (Clarksville Jeffersonian, 16 July 1850.)

New Orleans. The other day a detective was sent to search the
stable where it was understood that arms belonging to the recreant
son of ex-President Taylor were concealed. A variety of weapons
found under the floor, including a sword presented by the State of
Kentucky. It will be sent to General Taylor, brother of the gallant
hero of the Mexican War, only direct representative of Old Zack
whose loyalty is untarnished. (Nashville Dispatch, 29 July 1862.)

TEAGUE, Mrs. Delia, young widow of Medway, Tn, died October 2 at
sanitarium near Tate Springs under mysterious circumstances which
implicate the physicians there and a young man of Mohawk, both of
whom have disappeared. (Columbia Herald, 11 Oct. 1895.)

TEEK. A Frankford, Pennsylvania, maiden, who is growing old, has
applied to the Legislature to change her name. She thinks the one
she bears is hoodoo. It is Ann Teek. (Maury Democrat, Columbia,
Tn, 19 Sept. 1895.)

TEETERS, Sarah B., 23, died 14 March 1868 of consumption. (Nashville
Republican Banner, 20 March 1868. (Nashville Republican Banner,
20 March 1868.)

TEMPLE, Mrs. Billie, born 5 Dec. 1849, died 21 Dec. 1890; Methodist;
four children are dead but husband and two small children survive;
buried Nebo Cemetery; was S. C. McBride, daughter of John and
Hannah C. McBride; 1863 joined Mt. Nebo Church; married 10 April
1868 to W. L. Temple. (Columbia Herald, 28 Feb. 1891.)

TENNESSEE Soldiers. Among the soldiers who died in a Louisville
hospital during the week which ended on 21 Dec. 1862 were:

William Melburn, 2nd Tennessee Cavalry
H. Flynn, 2nd Tennessee Cavalry
J. T. Matthews, 2nd Tennessee Cavalry
L. Aldrich, 2nd Tennessee Cavalry
J. B. Huffacker, 2nd Tennessee Cavalry
N. P. Dunn, 5th Tennessee Infantry
(Nashville Daily Union, 16 Dec. 1862. N.B. These men were not
identified as either Confederates or Federals.)

TENNESSEE Confederates. The following are Confederate soldiers
buried in the Jonesboro Cemetery at Jonesboro, Georgia:

378

J. Auston, Company E
__ Hallingsworth, Company F, 45 Tennessee
R. H. Dooley, Company K, 48th Tennessee
John Whitaker, Company H, 1st Tennessee
J. C. Ballard, Company C, 18th Tennessee
H. G. Renegar, Company C, 41st Tennessee
J. A. Davis, Company C, 12th Tennessee
J. C. Waddell, Company L, 18th Tennessee
Lt. J. Farrell, Company B, 13th Tenesseee
W. D. Swanze, Company E, 3rd Tennessee
R. H. Low, 4th Tennessee
A. B. Callow, Company I, 3rd Tennessee
George Robinson, Company D, 3rd Tennessee
M. S. Chabar, Bates' Escort
A. B. Franklin, Company B
H. A. Johnson, Company F, 134th Tennessee
John T. Woods, 12th Tennessee
Capt. T. E. Cummings, Company K, 47th Tennessee
P. G. Pennegar, Company C, 18th Tennessee
(Nashville Republican Banner, 19 Jan. 1869.)

TERRASS, Hervey Hoge, only son of John W. and Mary Hoge Terrass, died
1 Nov. 1870. (Nashville Republican Banner, 3 Nov. 1870.) Age 3
years 7 months 15 days. (Nashville Republican Banner, 4 Nov.
1870.)

TERRASS, Myra Lenoir, daughter of John W. Terrass, died at Fontenelle
on the 12th. (Nashville Union and American, 14 Nov. 1874.)

TERRELL, Ed, guerrilla, died in City Hospital at Louisville two weeks
ago and buried in a pauper cemetery. His brother John Terrell of
Missouri arrived and caused his remains to be exhumed and buried
in one of the city cemeteries. He hopes to finally have the body
moved to native soil. (Memphis Avalanche, 27 Dec. 1868.)

TERRELL, George Parke, native of New Kent County, Virginia, and a
Confederate soldier, died in Hickman County on the 5th of typhoid
pneumonia; brother of Col. Leigh R. Terrell, who fell in front of
Richmond in command of a brigade of infantry and also of Dr. Arthur
Terrell, killed in battle near Nashville early in 1865. (Columbia
Herald and Mail, 18 Feb. 1877.)

TERRILL, Joe, died on Carter's Creek. (Columbia Herald, 28 Aug.
1896.)

TERRY, Colonel John H., old and respected citizen of Carroll County,
is dead. (Nashville Union and American, 30 Aug. 1874.)

TERRY, Old Man, was shot at Dover on Saturday last; he had quarreled
with one Sexton and Daniel about a trunk put off at Terry's hotel
by a steamer; Sexton shot him through the head. (Clarksville
Weekly Chronicle, 15 Feb. 1861.)

TERRY, Colonel Robert H., of Bedford County, died of heart disease
on the 8th instant. (Nashville Union and American, 14 March 1874.)

TERRY, W. B., of New Orleans, died in Memphis on October 15. (Nashville
Daily Gazette, 21 Oct. 1852.)

TERRY, W. Q., of Amite County, Mississippi, was killed in skirmish
on the 16th in a fight at the Tallahatchie Bridge. (Nashville
Dispatch, 15 July 1862.)

THACKER, Mr., died recently in South Carolina at 138 years. (Columbia
Herald, 3 May 1872.)

THATCHER, William Morgan, 11 months, son of Capt. J. M. and Jennie
C. Thatcher, died August 24. (Nashville Republican Banner, 30 Aug.
1867.)

THIESBES, William, German citizen disappeared on the 10th and suicide is feared; came here from Augusta, Georgia, and he is thought to be the man who walked off the railroad bridge last Tuesday; had been in the Virginia cavalry in the Confederate Army. (Nashville Republican Banner, 19 March 1869.)

THOMAS, Antonio, and his wife were robbed and murdered in Birmingham; their bodies were burned with their house. (Maury Democrat, Columbia, Tn, 22 March 1894.)

THOMAS, David, born 6 July 1806 in Buckingham County, Virginia, died 17 Feb. 1871; once stage agent for the Carter Thomas and Hough stage line; Cumberland Presbyterian. (Columbia Herald, 24 Feb. 1871.)

THOMAS, E. D., correspondent of the New York Herald, was drowned near Stone Inlet, South Carolina, on the 5th; he walked overboard while laboring under a fit of somnanbulism. (Nashville Dispatch, 24 June 1862.)

THOMAS, Mrs. Emily M., her funeral to be held today in Nashville. (Nashville Republican Banner, 23 April 1868.)

THOMAS, Katherine, mother of George L. Thomas, died in France and brought back and buried in New York City. (Columbia Herald, 8 May 1885.) George Lorillard Thomas is cousin to Pierre Lorillard, a millionaire of New York. (Columbia Herald and Mail, 21 Dec. 1877.)

THOMAS, George, young man, shot by accident at Petersburg, Lincoln County, a few days ago, has died. (Nashville Union and American 5 June 1874.)

THOMAS, General George H., died in San Francisco; comrades of his late Army of the Cumberland are to meet at the courthouse in Nashville at noon today for the purpose of paying a tribute of respect. (Nashville Republican Banner, 30 March 1870.) General Thomas left no will and the amount of his personal estate is $40,000. His brothers John W. and Benjamin R. Thomas are still living and his sisters Judith E., Ann, and Frances Thomas live on a plantation near Newsman's Depot, Virginia. (Memphis Daily Appeal, 30 May 1870.) A sister of General Thomas married Dr. Gamaliel Bailey, well known editor of the National Era in Washington. (Memphis Daily Appeal, 6 April 1870.) General Thomas and ex-Confederate General Hood dined together on the 14th in the Louisville Hotel. (Memphis Daily Appeal, 15 Nov. 1866.)

THOMAS, Ed, one of the most dangerous moonshiners in Hardin County, Tn, was killed last week by revenue officers. His brother Gus Thomas later shot and killed the guide who led the officers to the still. (Maury Democrat, 19 Dec. 1895.) Gus Thomas of Hardin County who is in penitentiary for life for murder, escaped, but has been recaptured. (Clifton Mirror, 3 Nov. 1905.)

THOMAS, H., leading grocer at Lynnville, Giles County, died last week; formerly lived in Columbia. (Columbia Herald, 5 June 1891.)

THOMAS, Houston, colored, was hanged on boxwood tree on the public square in Murfreesboro; Miss Mary J. O'Neal is doing very well at present, though for a while it was feared that the brutal treatment she received by Houston Thomas would cause her death. (Free Press, Murfreesboro, Tn, 19 Nov. 1881.)

THOMAS, James, Confederate soldier, was killed in the fight at Hoover's Gap; well known in Nashville. (Nashville Dispatch, 1 July 1863.)

THOMAS, J. Mason, son of Major General George H. Thomas, died Sunday in San Francisco. (Nashville Republican Banner, 17 Oct. 1867.)

THOMAS, John, 83, died last night at Timmons in Maury County; buried
Rose Hill Cemetery. (Columbia Herald and Mail, 31 March 1875.)

THOMAS, John, son of the Honorable James H. Thomas, was found near the
Pulaski Road on the 22d, with his head terribly mutilated and he
was insensible. His horse had thrown him and his skull was
fractured. He had recently married and was on the way to his
mother-in-law's, Mrs. Spain. (Whig and Tribune, Jackson, Tn,
2 March 1872.)

THOMAS, Mrs. Lucie Garrett, wife of James Thomas, Jr., daughter of
Phineas and Margaret Garrett, died on the 9th. (Nashville Republican Banner, 10 Oct. 1868.)

THOMAS, Miss Mattie E., 20, daughter of Wynn Thomas, Esquire of
Daneyville, Tennessee, died on the 2d on Memphis; was on a visit
here; born Mecklenburg County, Virginia. (Memphis Daily Appeal,
9 Nov. 1866.)

THOMAS, Mrs. Phoebe, of Junction City, Illinois, was told by her
doctors she had consumption and there was no hope for her, but two
bottles of Dr. King's New Discovery cured her. Adv. (Columbia
Herald, 8 Jan. 1897.)

THOMAS, William, who died 9 April 1861, was disinterred in July 1888
near Morristown, Tennessee, for removal to a distant cemetery. His
body was found to be in a perfect state of preservation and looked
life-like. The beard, however, had grown considerably. (Maury
Democrat, Columbia, Tn, 26 July 1888.)

THOMAS, William, born in England, died in Columbia on Monday night
and buried in Rose Hill Cemetery. (Columbia Herald and Mail,
26 March 1875.)

THOME, Mrs. Mary C., last surviving witness of the execution of General
Andre, died in New York on the 10th, age 92. Her father was
quartermaster of the Continental Army and was stationed in the
highlands when Andre's capture and execution took place. (Nashville
Dispatch, 17 May 1862.)

THOMASON, James R., deceased, his estate is insolvent. (Columbia
Herald, 17 Dec. 1869.)

THOMPSON, A. C., highly respected citizen, died in this county on
Wednesday. (Southern Flag, Lawrence County, 12 July 1861.)

THOMPSON, Albert E., youngest son of John C. and Rowena F. Thompson,
died 29 November; age illegible. (Nashville Union and American,
1 Dec. 1874.)

THOMPSON, Bethel. Thomas McEwen, a special deputy in Murfreesboro
has killed his third man, a horse thief named Bethel Thompson who
fired on him while he was trying to make an arrest. (Erin Review,
22 April 1882.)

THOMPSON, Grace Elbridge, wife of Mortimer D. Thompson, daughter of
"Fanny Fern" age 22, died in New York on the 13th ult. (Nashville
Dispatch, 11 Jan. 1863.)

THOMPSON, Mrs. Elisabeth, 76, died Thursday; mother of Robert Thompson.
(Nashville Republican Banner, 27 Aug. 1868.)

THOMPSON, Elijah B., died Sunday at the residence of the Rev. F. A.
Thompson; a few years ago moved to Arkansas but returned home
to be nursed by his family. (Columbia Herald and Mail,
19 Jan. 1877.)

THOMPSON, Emma Jane, 5 years 3 months, died in Atlanta on the 20th
daughter of Robert C. and Alice Thompson, formerly of Nashville;
funeral today in Nashville. (Nashville Republican Banner, 23 Jan.
1870.)

THOMPSON, Hill McAlister, infant son of W. Bryce and Ella F. Thompson, 7 months, died Wednesday. (Nashville Union and American, 26 June 1873.)

THOMPSON, Capt. J. D., commander of the Queen of the West when it was a Federal boat, died Feb. 25 in Alexandria, Louisiana, and buried in the city cemetery; was wounded in leg on Atchafalya. (Nashville Dispatch, 8 April 1863.)

THOMPSON, J. W., of Turkey Creek in Maury County, lost his only child to scarletina last week. (Columbia Herald and Mail, 23 March 1877.)

THOMPSON, General Jeff, of New Orleans, died last week at his old home St. Joseph, Missouri, where he was visiting for his health for some months past. (Columbia Herald and Mail, 22 Sept. 1876.)

THOMPSON, Joseph, colored, died on White Oak Creek in Houston County at the advanced age of 100 years and 5 days; born 1 March 1792, died 6 March 1892. (Houston County News, 18 March 1892.)

THOMPSON, L. G., of Franklin and Miss Julia Oden got married August 13 after a courtship of two hours. (Whig and Tribune, 2 Sept. 1871.)

THOMPSON, Lizzy or Lizzy Gabriel, an inmate of a low sink of iniquity, which stands one door above the corner of Vine and Crawford Streets on the west side of Vine, died of overdose of morphine yesterday; long a concubine of a distinguished Army officer, formerly of Lancaster County, Pennsylvania; died in a shanty kept by a negro woman Susan Jones, who had served time for killing a man. Tin Stratton, also an inmate, Carrie Mitchell, and Mrs. Hughes, who live next door were summoned as witnesses for the coroner. This is one of the vilest and most dangerous places in the city as two persons have been shot here. She came here one year ago with some members of the 4th Regulars. (Nashville Daily Union, 3 May 1865.)

THOMPSON, Press; pauper coffin furnished for his burial. (Nashville Republican Banner, 15 April 1870.)

THOMPSON, Robert Fielding, infant son of Richard H. and Cecelia M. Thompson to be buried today. (Nashville Daily Union, 18 Jan. 1863.)

THOMPSON, "I have received $100 for the widow of Sgt. Russel W. Thompson, Company K, 3d Tennessee Cavalry, who was lost on Sultana." Signed, Quartermaster. (Nashville Daily Union, 27 May 1865.)

THOMPSON, T. A. "Black," died at Columbia on Tuesday evening of apoplexy. (Whig and Tribune, Jackson, Tn, 14 June 1873.)

THOMPSON, T. C., stabbed by one Burnam, died Thursday at Decatur, Alabama. (Nashville Republican Banner, 28 Nov. 1868.)

THOMPSON, William, of Nashville, was arrested yesterday on a charge of disloyalty. (Nashville Daily Union, 19 April 1865.)

THORNBURGH, Montgomery, Esquire, of Jefferson County, Georgia died at Planters Hotel in that city on the 13th; he was held as a political prisoner by Confederates, but was on parole at his death. (Nashville Dispatch, 6 July 1862.)

THORNTON, Aaron, colored, to hang December 14 for the murder of Arthur Williams, his wife and two children. (Memphis Avalanche, 21 Nov. 1866.)

THORMAN, William E., of Memphis was murdered last Tuesday on outskirts of Memphis. His mutilated body was found in field between Hatchie Lake and the river and had been stripped; his money was gone. (Nashville Dispatch, 15 July 1862.)

THORP, Clayton, an old and respected gentleman of Flatwoods is dead.
(Columbia Herald, 3 May 1872.)

THROOP, John D., Ferris Center, Montcalm County, aged about 80, has
just completed his own tomb. He is a stone mason and has been for
40 years. Tomb is built of stone, the walls of which are 16 inches
thick, laid in water line, and perfectly impervious to water. The
inscription:
                    Stop, Stranger
                    Did You Know
                    John D. Throop
                    A Free Thinker
                    He was born in Ogdenburg, New York
                    15 Sept. 1815
When his remains are deposited the top will be cemented down. He is
preparing his resting place to suit himself. (Maury Democrat, 23
Aug. 1894. No state given in this entry.)

THRUSTON, Louise Hamilton, 4, only child of Gen. Gates P. and Mrs. R.
Thruston, died in New York City on the 16th of diptheria. (Nashville
Union and American, 26 July 1874.)

THURLOW, Judge, probate judge of Limestone County, Alabama, has died
from effects of wounds he received from a negro mob in Huntsville,
Alabama. (Memphis Daily Appeal, 11 Nov. 1868.)

THURMAN, Allen G., died the 12th in Columbus, Ohio. (Maury Democrat,
19 Dec. 1895.) Allen G. Thurman received his appellation of "Old
Roman" during war times. In midst of a flowery speech by one of the
Senators, Mr. Thurman was characterized as "the noblest Roman of
them all." From this sprang his title "The Old Roman." (Maury
Democrat, 28 Nov. 1895.) Allen G. Thurman is in serious condition
having injured his hip in a fall Thursday in his library. (Maury
Democrat, 14 Nov. 1895.) Allen G. Thurman, The Old Roman, is now
82. He spends his day asleep in his library and reads the entire
night. (Maury Democrat, 18 April 1895.) Allen Thurman's wife is
dying. (Florence, Ala., Times, 21 Nov. 1891.)

THURMAN, Lucy, colored, age 119 years, lives at Clinton, Kentucky.
(Memphis Daily Appeal, 21 Aug. 1869.)

THURMAN, Merida, 77, died in Manor, Texas; born in Giles County and
moved to Texas ten years ago. (Maury Democrat, 16 July 1891.)

THURMAN, Mrs. Polly, of Broadview, Maury County, died Wednesday from
a fall; buried at Gibsonville. (Columbia Herald, 10 July 1896.)

THURMON, Patrick, Company G, 5th Tennessee Cavalry, was killed 22 Feb.
1864 on picket duty near Sparta, Tn. (Nashville Daily Union,
__ Feb. 1864.)

THURMOND, W. W., tribute of respect on his death published by I.O.O.F.,
Tennessee No. 1. (Nashville Dispatch, 21 Sept. 1862.)

THURSTON, Lizzie Blunt, late of New York, wife of Dr. A. Henry Thurston,
died Sept. 8 in Nashville. (Nashville Dispatch, 9 Sept. 1862.)

TIBBALS. When the 20th Connecticut Regiment marched into Dumfries in
December, it halted two or three hours near a farm house, three
miles south of Occoquan River. Cpl. Halsey J. Tibbals of Company
D discovered what seemed to be familiar localities. He remembered
he was born in Virginia and lived there until he was eight, but
had no idea what locality. He soon found that he had found his
birthplace and pointed out the grave of his grandfather. On talking
to the occupants of the house he discovered he was the sole
survivor of the family and heir to property, still called the
Tibbals farm of 300 acres. Tibbals declines to prosecute his claim
as he has a poor estimate of Southern property since the rebellion.

He is also rightful owner of 1000 acres in Texas which fell to him
by death of a relative. (Nashville Daily Union, 27 Feb. 1863.)

TIDWELL, R. C., died on the 10th at the home of his son-in-law, A. J.
Fitzpatrick near Culleoka; buried in the old Baptist Cemetery.
(Columbia Herald and Mail, 24 April 1874.)

TIDWELL, Mrs. Mollie, wife of James Tidwell, of near Wayland Springs,
was overtaken by Train No. 21 on the south end of Sharp's Trestle
on Sunday last and knocked to the guard rail when a car wheel
passed over her foot crushing it. The foot was so badly crushed
that it required amputation at the ankle. She had her baby in her
arms and held on to it til the train passed and she was carried
off the trestle. (Lawrenceburg Democrat, 6 March 1891.)

TILFORD, five months old child of James Tilford of South Columbia died
Saturday. (Columbia Herald, 19 Sept. 1873.)

TILMAN, Abram L., died in Grundy County in the 33rd year of his age;
married 1854 to Miss M. A. Paul, daughter of fellow citizen Isaac
Paul, Esquire. (Nashville Dispatch, 11 July 1862.)

TINDALL, James S., son of William C. and Sarah to be buried today.
(Columbia Herald, 4 Dec. 1870.)

TINNON, Mrs. Susan of Simpson's Chapel, 68, died Friday; buried
Simpson Chapel in Giles County; Methodist; one son is a minister.
(Maury Democrat, 8 March 1894.)

TINSLEY, Old Man, of Beaver Dam in Hickman County has lived to see
the second centennial. (Columbia Herald and Mail, 18 Feb. 1876.)
One of our oldest citizens Spencer Tinsley, 93 years old, has for
the past ten years been working on a perpetual motion and strange
as it may seem has succeeded; he has labored very quietly and
secretly, and now has his model before the public. He will start
for Washington in a few days. He was advised to take it to the
Exposition, but he good naturedly remarked that some Yankee would
steal it before it could be patented. (Columbia Herald, 13 June
1873.)

TISDALE, William S., of District 25 in Maury County, died August 14;
court made provision for his widow Mrs. H. S. Tisdale. (Columbia
Herald, 10 Oct. 1873.)

TITUS, Colonel Silas, of the 12th New York Volunteers, gave a dying
injunction to his son to return a Confederate flag to the Virginia
regiment from which it was captured by Col. Titus in 1862. (Maury
Democrat, 1 Aug. 1895.)

TODD, Alexander A., brother of Mrs. Abraham Lincoln and a captain in
the rebel army, was instantly killed in the late battle of Baton
Rouge (Nashville Dispatch, 3 Sept. 1862.)

TODD, Samuel B., brother of Mrs. Lincoln, died on battlefield from
wounds he received at Shiloh on the 7th. (Nashville Dispatch, 2
May 1862.)

TODD, John N., died on the 29th; his infant son, age 2, died on the
30th and they were buried in the same grave. (Nashville Whig,
2 Nov. 1844.)

TOLAND, Black, of Humphreys County on Tumbling Creek, died lately
leaving $2000 in gold and silver and not owing a dollar nor leaving
any heirs to squabble over his estate. (Columbia Herald and Mail,
3 March 1876.)

TOLBERT, William. About a month ago one of the attaches of this office
went to his mother's home in DeKalb County, Alabama, which is partly

Tolbert, William - Continued
in the mountains. Several days after his arrival an old lady named
Mrs. Tolbert, about 76 years old, walked down from the mountains to
see him, as she had heard he was from Columbia. She told him that
she had a son in the 3rd Confederate cavalry during the late war
and the last she had heard from him he was at a white house, about
two miles from the town on the Shelbyville pike in the year 1863.
He was sick and that was the last she ever heard of him. The years
of anguish she has spent since then, none but a lone widow's heart
can tell. Isolated and cut off from the world by vast mountains,
this old woman had never been able to institute any inquiries about
her son.

The gentleman aforesaid came home and on going to the Confederate
graveyard found the grave and on the headboard was written:
Wm. Tolbert Co. I, Col. Howard's Regiment. In order to satisfy
the mind of the mother of the dead soldier, Mr. H. then went to
Mr. Padgett's and Col. Gordon's, who said they had had so many
soldiers at their houses they could not recollect their names. Mrs.
Padgett recommended him to go to Mrs. James R. Shelton, who was one
of the principal managers of the Confederate Hospital at this place.
That estimable lady told Mr. H. that she recollected Mr. Tolbert
and that he died, but could not recollect the attending circumstances. Mr. H. then wrote all these facts to Mrs. Tolbert. Mr. H.
told her in his letter that he found her son's grave, the 9th from
the first, and zealously care for, having on it a bouquet of faded
flowers. (N.B. In 1979 William Tolbert's grave is No. 9 in the
Confederate plot at Rose Hill Cemetery in Columbia, Tn. Funeral
home records copies by the late historian Frank H. Smith show that
a coffin was furnished and grave dug for him on 21 Feb. 1863.)
(Columbia Herald, 26 Aug. 1870.)
TOLL, Jonathan, 90, has returned from Missouri, as did several others;
he led them off and then led them back. He lived on Swan Creek.
(Columbia Herald and Mail, 29 May 1874.)

TOLLIVER, Ed, died of smallpox on the 13th near Manchester. (Nashville
Union and American, 23 April 1873.)

TOMES, the Rev. Charles, rector of the Church of the Advent in Nashville, died July 11 at noon. (Clarksville Jeffersonian, 17 July
1857.)

TOMES, Henrietta Maria, youngest child of Charles and Henrietta Tomes,
2 years 7 days, died yesterday morning; father is rector of Christ
Church. (Nashville Daily Gazette, 18 Aug. 1852.)

TOMES, young lady, daughter of Mrs. Charles Tomes, died in Gironde in
December; daughter of late Rev. Charles Tomes; brought back to
Nashville for burial. She had been abroad four years seeking
restoration of her health. (Nashville Union and American, 2 June
1874.)

TOMLIN, John, Esquire, gifted poet and author of several novels, is
no more; he died at Charity Hospital in New Orleans recently of
mania apotu, died a raving maniac; had been a resident of this place
19 or 20 years and was at one time in easy circumstances. Jackson
Whig. (Clarksville Jeffersonian, 30 July 1850.)

TOMPKINS, Catharine, died in Memphis November 15; relict of late
elder John G. Tompkins; sister of Philip S. Fall. (Nashville
Daily Union, 1 Dec. 1863.)

TOMPKINS, Horace "Whig", kept saloon on the corner of Cherry and Cedar
Streets and also sang in the theater, died yesterday, age 25;
native of Dubque, Iowa; was in army three years on General
Rousseau's staff; body sent to Dubque for burial. (Nashville Daily
Union, 11 May 1865.)

TONEY, Mrs. Carney, of Kentucky, age 72, was last week divorced from her husband, age 90. They had been married but three years. (Maury Democrat, 13 June 1895.)

TOOMBS. Bob Toombs' monument is having a hard time. The first one was sunk at sea. The second proves to be of defective marble and now a third is being made. (Maury Democrat, 16 Feb. 1888.)

TOON, Eddy, died yesterday; son of R. A. and E. A. Toon; taken to Franklin for burial. (Nashville Republican Banner, 6 Sept. 1870.)

TORBETT, G. C., 4 years, little son of Col. G. C. and Martha Louise Torbett, died on the 4th inst. (Nashville Republican Banner, 5 Jan. 1868.)

TORBETT, Colonel Granville C., respected citizen of Nashville, 62, died on the 14th. (Whig and Tribune, Jackson, Tn, 24 Feb. 1872.)

TORIAN, Alice, infant daughter of Mr. and Mrs. A. G. Torian, will be buried this morning. (Nashville Dispatch, 5 June 1863.)

TORIAN, Ellen, 5 years 12 days, daughter of Mr. and Mrs. A. G. Torian, twin to Alice, died on the 6th. (Nashville Dispatch, 9 June 1863.)

TOUPET, Mlle. Eugenie M., well known and respected, native of France, has died; French instructress; buried Cavalry Cemetery. (Nashville Union and American, 6 Aug. 1874.)

TOURTELLOTTE, Colonel, died a few days ago in Lacrosse, Wisconsin; he was the commander at Altsona, Georgia, to whom General Sherman sent the instruction to "hold the fort." (Maury Democrat, 13 Aug. 1891.)

TRABUE, Louis Horton, son of George W. and Ellen D. Trabue, died; grandson of William D. Dunn of Mobile, Ala. (Nashville Union and American, 28 June 1874.)

TRAINOR, Mrs. John, has been arrested on being associated with her husband in smuggling; arrested in Louisville and brought to Nashville. She bought a lot of medicine in Louisville from C. Tavel. E. R. Davis, Company D, Anderson Troop and Charles Springer were also arrested for being part of this group, which is developing into a most extensive system of fraud and treason. Springer was discharged. Joseph Winborn, Milton Kellogg, Dr. Charles H. Dubois and Mrs. M. E. Trousdell have been arrested for aiding Trainor Dubois and Trousdell have been sent to Alton, Illinois. (Nashville Dispatch, 31 March 1863.) Dr. Pyle, Louisville druggist, has been arrested for selling medicine to Mrs. Trainor to be smuggled. (Nashville Dispatch, 2 April 1863.)

TRAINOR, John, has been arrested as a spy and smuggler. For months he has been active in sending arms, ammunition and medicine to the Confederate Army. He was probably employed by Zollicoffer and others to enter the Federal service. (Nashville Dispatch, 29 March 1863.) John Trainor of Louisville has been convicted as rebel spy and is to be shot in Nashville next Friday. (Nashville Dispatch, 7 April 1863.)

TRANTHAM, Betsy. The McKenzie Times resurrects the following from a biographical dictionary: 'Mrs. Betsy Trantham died in Maury County, TN, 10 Jan. 1834 at the age of 154 years. She was born in Germany, emigrated to British America, and from thence to North Carolina in the year 1810. At the age of 120 years her sight became almost extinct; but during the last 20 years of her life, she possessed the power of vision as perfectly as at the age of 20 years. For many years previous to her death, she was unable to walk. At the time of her death, she had entirely lost the sense of taste and hearing. For 20 years before her death she was unable to distinguish between the taste of sugar and vinegar. At the age of 65

386

TRANTHAM, Betsy - Continued
years she bore her only child, who is now living in 1835 and promises
a long life also.' (Nashville Union and American, 19 Aug. 1873.)

Colonel P. Gordon remembers Mrs. Trantham, who died in this county
in 1834, aged 154 years. Her grandchild was an old man and her son
died soon after her death, a very old man, although she was 65
years old when he was born. Colonel Gordon recollects that they
had to keep blankets around her to keep up animation. (Columbia
Herald, 17 March 1871.)

Betsy Trantham. She was born in German and emigrated to the
British Colonies in America at the time when the first settlement
was made in North Carolina, in the year 1810. At the age of 120
years her eyesight became almost extinct, but during the last
twenty years of her life she possessed the power of vision as
perfectly as at the age of twenty. For many years previous to her
death she was unable to walk, and is said to have required great
attention from her friends to prevent the temperature of her body
from falling so low as not to sustain animal life. At the time of
her death she had entirely lost the sense of taste and hearing.
For twenty years before her death she was unable to distinguish
the difference between the taste of sugar and vinegar. At the
age of 65 she bore her only child, who is now living, and promises
to reach an uncommonly advanced age. (National Gazette, 22 Feb.
1834, quoted in Nashville Banner, 30 May 1908.)

An Interesting Sketch by One of Her Descendants. Fayetteville, Tn,
17 April 1884. To the American: In the issue of the 10th instant
occurs an article from the American Almanac, published at Boston,
in regard to Mrs. Betsey Trantham, in which it is stated that she
lived to the age of 154 years, and that she had but one child. Both
of the statements are incorrect. She was but 149 years old and
was the mother of a large family of children whose descendants are
scattered throughout the Southern and Western States, and the woods
of Williamson, Wilson, and Davidson counties are full of them, with
a few in Lincoln County.

I am now one of the oldest inhabitants, but my father William Peach,
of this place is a great-grandson of Mrs. Trantham, and the facts
here stated he obtained from his ancestors and from her own lips
and may be relied upon as correct.

Betsey Trantham was born in Germany and emigrated to America when
14 years of age, settling first in Virginia in 1702. She soon
afterward married a man by the name of Eppinger by whom she had
eight children. After the death of Eppinger she moved to Carolina
where she married Martin Trantham, by whom she had quite a number of
children.

One of her daughters by this marriage became the wife of one
Steadham, who, with his family were massacred by the Indians at
Ft. Mimms, with the exception of two sons who fought their way
through the Indians and made their escape.

Another daughter, Rachel, married Lawrence, or Larry Burns; and
another daughter Parmelia married Charles Gray. One daughter
Sally, of Charles Gray, married a man by the name of McCallum
and settled at an early day in Indiana. Elizabeth married Luke,
the father of Rev. Robert Happ of New Orleans. A son Robert died
in Arkansas. Another son Charles died in Alabama. All of the
Peaches that are descended from John Peach in Wilson and Davidson
counties and many of the Burns and Grays, are descendants of Mrs.
Betsey Trantham through her daughters Parmelia and Rachel.

My father saw her last in 1832. She was lying on one feather-bed
with another one over her to keep her warm. Jack Peach, an older
brother of my father, knew her well and remembers many incidents

TRANTHAM, Betsy - Continued
in her life, as detailed by her. He is now near 80 years of age.
He has, as a relic of her, a steel thimble, which is probably 175
years old.

The Rev. Mark Gray, now deceased, who was well known in Williamson
and Maury Counties, was a great-grandson of Betsey Trantham.

Martin Trantham, her husband, was the devil raised by Lorenzo Dow
from the pile of tow, as narrated by that eccentric divine, which
those familiar with his book will remember.

In addition to the daughters named, she had a son Martin, who
figured conspiciously in the Revolutionary War. He was with Marion
in South Carolina, and it is told that at time a large force of
Tories held a barn, which they had fortified so strongly that the
Whigs could not dislodge them. Martin allowed himself to be
captured by them and feigned idiocy to such good purpose that they
put no restraint upon him, and he soon made his escape, not however,
until he had obtained all the information in regard to their
strength and means of defense his commander desired; and Weems in his
"Life of Marion" tells how a cannon was improvished from a pine
pole and the barn captured without firing a gun.

My father has seen many erroneous statements in regard to Mrs.
Trantham since her death and is anxious that the few facts here
given should be published. Signed Lewis Peach. (Fayetteville
American, 17 April 1884; this article was in scrap book of R. H.
Gray of Fayetteville in 1942.)

She was a relative of Jesse Gray and W. H. Gray, South Main grocer
of Columbia. (Daily Herald, 19 April 1962.)

The Rev. W. M. Cook of Santa Fe read the history of Mrs. Betsy
Trantham, a pioneer woman, who lived 149 years, according to the
inscription on her tombstone and was buried in Goshen Cemetery when
she died. Billy Gray and Mrs. Charles Shrike, both of Columbia,
were pointed out as descendants of Mrs. Trantham. Both were
present with their families for the services. (Daily Herald,
Columbia, Tn, 2 Oct. 1964.) (N.B. There is no monument to Mrs.
Trantham at Goshen Cemetery as stated in this account.)

TRAVIS. The finding of the decomposed body of an ex-Confederate
soldier Sunday in a lot near the north entrance to the Centennial
grounds has developed into a sensational murder mystery. He was
identified as James Travis of Winchester, Tn. (Columbia Herald,
2 July 1897.)

TRAVIS, Edward, deceased; his land to be sold by I. G. Harris,
executor. (Paris Bee, 11 Dec. 1846.)

TRAWIG, John, notorious guerrilla and robber, who has long infested
Carroll County, Tn, was captured and killed a few days since by
soldiers of Col. Hawkins; regiment; he was noted for inhumane
cruelties practiced upon loyal citizens. Some time ago he called
at the home of Mr. McCaslin, an old man of 63 and compelled him to
get down on his hands and knees, when jumping astride him he
spurred him as he would a horse until his sides were black. He
then took his knife and slit his ears, after which he left him but
after a short time he returned and shot him dead. (Nashville
Daily Union, 27 June 1865.)

TREPPARD, Nina, 4, daughter of Mr. and Mrs. T. J. Treppard, died
April 2. (Nashville Republican Banner, 3 April 1870.)

TRENARY, Frank M., 2, of Nashville, died of hydrophobia. A madstone
had been put on and stayed two hours before it fell off. He died
a horrible death. (Maury Democrat, 7 May 1891.)

TRESILIAM, Colonel, once of Memphis, Chief Engineer on General Logan's staff and once known as "Erin's Hope", died in Hoboken on Tuesday. An accomplished gentleman. (Memphis Daily Appeal, 18 Jan. 1869.)

TREZEVANT. The remains of Major Ed Trezevant of Forrest's old regiment of cavalry, who was killed 6 March 1863, at Thompson Station and buried at Rose Hill Cemetery in Columbia, will arrive this after-noon in Memphis to be buried at Elmwood Cemetery on commemoration day, the 7th. Also to be buried in Elmwood will be Major Charles McDonald, who fell at Farmington. (Memphis Daily Appeal, 4 May 1870.)

TRIBBLE, James C., 80, old and respected, died in Bedford County last week. (Whig and Tribune, Jackson, Tn, 12 April 1873.)

TRIPP, Jimmy, of Lawrenceburg, burned to death last week. (The News, Murfreesboro, 3 Jan. 1873.)

TROLIO, Mary, 21, wife of Peter Trolio, died Feb. 7; a newborn baby survives. (Memphis Daily Appeal, 13 Feb. 1870.)

TROLLINGER, Thomas G., of Shelbyville, was taken ill by cholera on Wednesday last and died last night. (Memphis Avalanche, 20 Nov. 1866.)

TRUELOVE, Mrs. Francis Jane, 74, died Thursday of flux, buried in Jones Cemetery in Maury County. (Columbia Herald, 24 Nov. 1899.)

TRUESDALE, William, 53, died at Bunker Hill, Illinois, on 25 Nov. 1867 of consumption. He was chief of detectives during the Federal occupation of Nashville and "Mercilessly subjected our people to all the rigors of military espionage." (Nashville Republican Banner, 30 Nov. 1867.)

TUBKNET, Mr. and Mrs., of Cisco, Texas, age 80 and 65, have recently become parents of a fine boy. (Maury Democrat, 22 March 1888.)

TUCKER, John D., 52, died 1 mile east of Kedron on Friday; one son, three daughters, three brothers survive. Died of dypsesia. (Maury Democrat, 26 Nov. 1891.)

TUCKER, John M., died yesterday of inflammation of the brain. (Nash-ville Republican Banner, 8 Sept. 1870.)

TUCKER, Mrs. R. H., of West End, died March 27. (Maury Democrat, 5 April 1894.)

TUCKER, Wilson, died on Sixth Street on October 3 at the home of his son-in-law W. F. Tucker; came here at the age of 21; age 84 years 9 months 8 days; buried Rose Hill Cemetery; trustee of the Christian Church. (Maury Democrat, 10 Oct. 1895.)

TURNBOW, John, one of the oldest and wealthiest men on Trace Creek in Lewis County, is low with dropsy. (Maury Democrat, 11 April 1895.)

TURNBOW, Dill, of Lewis County lost by death his son Tommie, age 2. (Maury Democrat, 27 July 1893.)

TURNER, Mrs. Abner, died yesterday; funeral to be held at the Cathedral. Mr. Turner is in danger. All members of the family were seized with violent vomiting at the breakfast table. (Nashville Republican Banner, 20 July 1870.)

TURNER, George S., died in Lafayette, Alabama; had lived in Alabama 34 years; born Oglethorpe County, Georgia. (Memphis Daily Appeal, 27 June 1870.)

TURNER, Mrs. Jessamine, wife of Edward Turner, Esquire, died in

Alexandria, Tennessee, on November 25; daughter of Joshua Flowers, Esquire, of Nashville. (Nashville Union and American, 1 Dec. 1874.)

TURNER, Larkin, of Meriwether County, Georgia, is 106 years old. Mrs. Robertson of the same county is 101. (Columbia Herald and Mail, 21 July 1876.)

TURNER, Milligan, of Chattanooga, tried on charges of murder and bushwhacking, has been sentenced to two years in military prison. (Nashville Daily Union, 11 May 1865.)

TURNER, R. W., his remains were brought up from Wabbasco, Arkansas, on Sunday and buried Monday at the Webster Cemetery at Cross Bridges in Maury County; died of pneumonia; never married. (Maury Democrat, 3 Feb. 1887.)

TURNER, Mr. Yancey, living in Macon County, near the Kentucky line is nearly 128 years old; born 30 Oct. 1746; has 84 grandchildren; still rides horseback. (Nashville Union and American, 16 Oct. 1874.)

TURNEY, George C., Sgt., Company K, 5th Tennessee Cavalry, was killed 22 Feb. 1864 on Calf Killer near Sparta, Tn. (Nashville Daily Union, __ Feb. 1864.)

TUTHERLY, Mrs. Rebecca, of Manchester, New Hampshire, is one of the links in a chain of five generations now living. She is of Scotch-Irish ancestry and was born 4 March 1799 in Elliot, Maine. Her descendants number 151 grandchildren. Her father and mother were natives of Maine and her husband who fought in the War of 1812 died in 1858. She has eight children, 57 grandchildren, 87 great-grandchildren, and 7 great-great-grandchildren. (Maury Democrat, 22 March 1894.)

TWAIN, Mark,(Mr. Clements), the humorist, is now dead broke. He is said to be a failure as a financier. (Maury Democrat, 25 July 1895.)

TWIGGS, General David E., died in Augusta, Georgia; native of Augusta; entered the U. S. Army at 22 years. He had been living in New Orleans before the occupation. General Butler seized his New Orleans residence and sent three of his swords to President Lincoln. (Nashville Dispatch, 25 July 1862.)

TWITTY, Mrs. Nancy, age 115 years, died two weeks ago on Richland Creek in Marshall County; she was a grown woman at the time of the Battle of Lexington in 1775 and up until her death had a vivid recollection of the events of our revolutionary struggle. (Whig and Tribune, Jackson, Tn, 13 July 1872.)

TYLER. No monument, not even a stone, marks the grave of John Tyler, once President of the United States. His body lies buried in an obscure little plot in Hollywood Cemetery, Richmond, Virginia, and the only means of identifying it is by the monument to his daughter, whose grave is next to his. The Civil War was responsible for the neglect. Tyler died in 1862 and the Virginia legislature empowered the Governor to erect a suitable monument. It also requested that he be buried at Hollywood near the grave of James Monroe. In the excitement of the war it was forgotten. It was the President's wish that he be buried in Sherwood Forest beside his wife, but even this wish was not honored. (Columbia Herald, 17 Dec. 1897.)

John Tyler, son of President Tyler, is living in poverty in Georgetown, D.C. He is more than 70 years old. He equipped a regiment and led it in the Mexican War and afterwards entered the Confederate Army. (Maury Democrat, 17 Oct. 1895.) General John Tyler, son of President Tyler, a paralytic, is supported in a modest way by his nephew, who has a position in the treasury department in Washington. He is 75 years old. (Maury Democrat, 26 July 1894.) Col. John Tyler of Virginia, son of ex-President Tyler, is lecturing in Louisville on commerce. (Memphis Avalanche, 17 Dec. 1868.)

TYLER, Mrs. Julia Gardiner, widow of ex-President John Tyler, was buried in Hollywood Cemetery on July 12 between the grave of her husband and that of her daughter, Mrs. Spencer. The funeral took place from St. Peter's Cathedral. The funeral procession was one of the largest ever seen in Richmond. Among the honorary pall-bearers were Governor Fitz Hugh Lee, Major Ellison, Speaker Caldwell, of the House of Representative; all the judges of the city courts and other distinguished citizens. (Maury Democrat, __ July 1889, No. 52.)

TYLER, Dr. Wat Henry, 75, died at his home in Hanover County, Va., eldest son of the first Governor, John Tyler of Virginia and Mary Armstead, who boasted she named him after the greatest rebels who ever lived, Wat Tyler and Patrick Henry. He was among the first to advocate the secession of Virginia from the Union. (Nashville Dispatch, 1 Aug. 1862.)

TYLER, Mrs. Mary E., the original Mary who had a little lamb, is now 82 years old and lives at Somerville, Mass. (Maury Democrat, 4 Oct. 1888.)

TYLER, W. F., died in Birmingham Saturday at the age of 81 of heart failure; buried in the old homestead at Lynnville, Tn. (Maury Democrat, 31 April 1891.)

TYNE, Miss Bridget, funeral to be held today; had brother Lawrence Tyne. (Nashville Republican Banner, 8 July 1870.)

TYNOR, William, sergeant of the 16th Regulars, was shot and killed by a soldier Friday at Chattanooga at a low dance house in a quarrel about a prostitute present. (Memphis Avalanche, 21 Nov. 1866.)

TYREE, Mrs. Bethenia, 102 years, died Sunday in Caldwell County, Ky; born 12 July 1797. (Maury Democrat, 21 Nov. 1899.)

UNDER THE CITY - About 35 years ago, or at least while General Sam Houston was invading Texas, there were found among the Texas Indians an old woman who had a remarkable history. Through her the idea of hidden treasure within the Cumberland Valley was greatly strengthened and renewed efforts were made to discover it.

The Indian name of the old lady was Martaza, which if translated would no doubt be Martha White, or rather White Martha. Her own account of her original name was Martha Sharp so that Marta is a mere corruption of Martha, while is the word for light or bright. The Greeks called the sun huzza, which is high light.

She was, when found among the Indians, very old but still vigorous and strong, retaining her facilities unimpaired. She spoke two or three Indian dialects and still had a smattering of English.

It was not long after the death of the mother when a number of braves returned from a visit to the Valley of the Cumberland and brought a prisoner with them, whom Martaza saw run the gauntlet and at last burned to death.

Up to this time Martaza had retained her knowledge of English pretty perfect, and was allowed to talk with the prisoner; for the Indians made her interpret what the white man said. Among other things he told Martaza a story with respect to a deposit of silver, and lead, and skins, which was to be found on the river in a bluff

near the painted rock. This story became known to a few persons
in this country soon after the revelation was made in Texas some
34 years ago, and I know personally several persons who have made
diligent search for this deposit. Not more than three years ago,
several persons came from Texas and made efforts to find this
treasure on the Tennessee River, no doubt guided by the same legend.

The story of Martaza I have met with in two different forms. One
was that there was a cave upon the river in bluff not far from the
Rising Sun, the mouth of which could be closed entirely by setting
a large flat rock upon its edge, and by this means the entrance to
the cave was so completely closed up that no one would suppose
there was any cave there; but by removing the rock there was a
hole large enough to admit a human body. When once inside, the
cave became large, but in order to get into the main cave, ladders
had to be used. They had to descend a great many feet, and at the
bottom was a large open space, where a rich company kept all their
treasures. On one occasion when all the persons were in the cave,
but one, the giant who inhabited the country, and with whom Uncle
Felty was so familiar, shook the bluff so violently that the rocks
that hung over the hole were shaken down and the entrance was
filled up. The man who was not in the cave was soon after taken
prisoner by the Indians, carried off, and to death. Martaza heard
the story from his own lips the night before he was put to death,
and he told her that by removing a portion of the fallen bluff a
way might be opened to the treasure.

I talked with a man some years ago--one of those mysterious persons
that search all their life long for hidden treasures, who gave it
as his opinion that the cave is under the city of Nashville, and
that the original entrance was near where there used to be a spout
spring or at least between that point and the spot where the City
Hotel is situated. Others, whose named I might give, have looked
for it in all the bluffs between the mouth of Marrowbone and Hays-
borough.

But the legend which is mostly generally believed is this. On the
night before the prisoner who was taken in the Valley of the
Cumberland was put to death, he told Martaza that he knew he was
going to die and would never live to enjoy his treasures. He said
he was connected with three other persons and that they had for
some time been collecting silver in the Valley of the Cumberland
and had been concealing it in a bluff or rocks on the bank of a
river, the name of which he had forgotten. Though she recollected
that it was near a painted rock.

The entrance to the cave was small and not much above high water
mark. When these miners first found it, they undertook to go down
to the bottom of this chasm, and made a long ladder for the purpose
but found that the ladder would not reach the bottom. They then
threw the ladder across the chasm, and went over to explore the
cave beyond and found a number of rooms every way suited to their
purpose. They determined to make their deposits there, and kept
the ladder across the chasm as a kind of bridge, but they were
afraid to go more than one at a time lest it should break. When
they were afraid of the Indians, they would go into this cave and
then pull the ladder after them, so that neither man or beast
could reach them. They had been discovered, that is, their hiding
place, by the smoke which came out of the cave.

After the Indians shot at them, and killed one of the party, their
plan was to get into their cave and pull the ladder after them, and
thus secure themselves. They were so closely pursued by the Indians
that two of them ventured on the ladder at once, and it gave way,
and men and ladder all went into the frightful depths below, while
he, the prisoner, was behind, and consequently captured by the
Indians.

UNDER THE CITY - Continued
   The Indians not knowing but the company that lived in that cave
might be a large one, fled in haste from the place. It has always
been the case, when a small party of Indians once make a strike that
the next thing is to return to their own country, or go so far off
as to be out of harm's way. So the Indians did not remain to make
any examination of the place; they had one scalp and a prisoner and
that they regarded, no doubt, as a success.

So one of the folks was killed at the first fire; two of the
remaining three went down with the broken ladder, and the fourth
and last one was taken prisoner and carried into the Shawnee Nation,
and there burned to death, while the secret of their treasure was
left with Martaza.

The story of Martaza Sharp has possibly reached the ear of some of
my readers, thought I do not recollect of every seeing it in print.
The story that she told to the soldier under General Houston has
gone through several editions among that mysterious class of persons
who are always in search of hidden treasures, and it is by no means
my object to induce persons to go digging down the bluff along the
Cumberland River in order to find this rich deposit. There have
already been time, money and labor enough spent in this fruitless
search. That there is an extensive cave under the city of Nashville
is by no means certain; and if there should be, you will find no
boxes of gold and silver there. If you will only wait until I am
done with my story, you will find the legends with respect to this
subject so numerous and varied that they cross each other in every
direction like network.

The most popular legend of these yet noticed is that of the land-
slide covering the mouth of the cave, which is stated, by the
superstitious, to have been brought about by the displeasure of
Uncle Felty's giants, and, ridiculous as it may seem, many a
mighty rock has been tumbled into the Cumberland in order to find
the entrance to that cave.

It was only a few years ago that an old citizen of Nashville told me,
in great confidence, that if he had the money to purchase a certain
piece of property not far from where the wire bridge now rests on
the bluff at Nashville, that he could find the entrance.

When I told him that it was too far from the great landmark, viz,
the painted rock of the rising sun he took the ground that the
landmark only settled the fact with respect to what river the bluff
was on and not the bluff itself. He said there was not a day in
the year passed over his head but he could hear the hollow earth
respond to the wheels of wagons and carriages as they passed over
this cave; he said he had traced the direction of the cave or caves,
for he said the cavity divided before it reached Market Street and
that he had traced one branch where it crossed Broad Street near
the junction of High Street. He said he had no doubt but it was
an extensive as the Mammoth Cave, and pointed out spots where the
corporation might sink shafts and find sewerage for the whole city--
emptying all the waste water into the cave instead of the river.
When I told him that there was a great many holes in the ground
where there were no boxes of silver, he said if I would listen to
him he would convince me that there was an extensive deposit of
treasure somewhere in the neighborhood of Nashville. (Nashville
Republican Banner, 4 June 1869. This article was not signed.)

UNDERWOOD, J. C., died Wednesday and buried in family cemetery near
   Sharp's Corner in Maury County. (Maury Democrat, 3 Feb. 1887.)

UNDERWOOD, Miss Sallie, died on the 22d in Rutherford County.
   (Columbia Herald and Mail, 29 Sept. 1876.)

UNDERWOOD, Willie, of Rally Hill, died March 23 of pneumonia; buried

UNDERWOOD, Willie - Continued
in Underwood family burying ground; widowed mother survives.
(Columbia Herald, 10 April 1896.)

UNKNOWN.   Skeletons Galore, Waynetown, Ind., Feb. 4. Six miles north
of this place is the village of Whitlock. Some time since the
citizens and farmers of the surrounding country combined to build
gravel roads on the highways entering the village and to get the
necessary gravel they entered the property of Jacob Luce, one mile
west of the village, in a lot of timber where gravel was to be
found in abundance. Soon after opening the pit, a skeleton was
found, and as the pit widened, other skeletons were unearthed
until at least 30 graves have been opened, and many skeletons brought
to light, evidently the remains of an Indian tribe, the Shawnees,
who had villages near that place. One skeleton was found beneath
a large stump and yesterday another was found 12 feet underground.
The grave appeared to be in regular order and the occupants were
buried in a sitting posture. In one grave, three skeletons,
supposed to be that of a woman and two children were found.
Yesterday the largest specimen was unearthed, which in life must
have been a giant. All the teeth are in a perfect state of preservation. One skeleton was a dog by a human skeleton. All the
burials appear to be at least 150 years old, and the oldest settlers
here have no recollection of any burials within their lives.
(Maury Democrat, 7 Feb. 1889.)

UNKNOWN

Giles County White Caps Murder Aged White Tramp at Aspen Hill. -
The man was furnished a house by negroes and said he was employed
by them to organize a band. He got a notice signed by the White
Caps, giving him a day or two to leave. He paid no attention and
on August 5, 25 to 30 men fired at him and his body was found
riddled with bullets. He was an Irishman, about 60 years old. No
one knew his name. (Columbia Herald, 13 Aug. 1897.)

Strange Double Burial at Rock Island, Tn. - A lady whose only son
went into the army when a boy and was killed, preserved his body
in an airtight coffin ever since the war in order that she might
be buried in the grave with him. She kept the body in the house
until the body dried up into a mummy. She went into the room
everyday and took a look through the glass door of the coffin.
When she finally died, they were buried together. (Columbia
Herald, 17 Feb. 1893.)

A young lady in Virginia wears a cross made of the bullets that
killed her father and brother in one of the battles around Richmond.
(Columbia Herald, 19 Jan. 1872.)

Private James K. Bolton, an inmate of the Confederate Soldiers home
near Richmond, Virginia, tells a startling story of the finding in
the hold of the Confederate ram, Merrimac, the skeletons of two
men. Bolton was a member of the Johnson battery during the war and
wounded at Brandy Station. He is now in an almost dying condition.
The discovery of the skeletons has preyed upon his mind for years.
He was engaged as a wrecker in 1873 in getting off the old copper
off the Merrimac. While engaged in this work, Bolton dived into the
forecastles of the Confederate gunboat. There he found the
skeletons of two men manacled to the floor. He supposed they were
members of the crew, who were incarcerated for violation of some
rule of the navy and when the craft was sunk were forgotten by
their comrades and went down to their watery graves. (Maury
Democrat, 28 March 1889.)

UNKNOWN - Continued

At Centerville, Georgia, laborers on the plantation of J. S. Rowland
were felling some trees, 200 to 300 yards from the home, and they
were attracted by a pile of rocks which lay on ground, east and
west, and in somewhat of a grave shape and with the same dimensions
of a grave. They decided to investigate. At the bottom and lying
on its back was the skeleton of a man. The smaller bones were
entirely gone--dissolved into dust--but the skull, a portion of the
pelvis and bones of the limbs were distinct. An ordinary carving
knive, much rust-eaten, flat, foreign-looking brass button, and a
bar of lead rested with the dead. A few rusty nails were found
which indicated the sepulcher once had a coffin. The reasonable
deduction was the deceased was a Confederate soldier, and met his
death in defense of his flag. (Columbia Herald and Mail, 10 Dec.
1875.)

An unknown man, shot through the head above the right eye, was found
on Donaldson Knob on Murfreesboro Pike, 11 miles from Murfreesboro
on Friday. (Nashville Republican Banner, 6 Aug. 1868.)

A dead infant was found in the rear of Dr. H. N. Myers house on the
north side of Cedar at just below Vine Street in Nashville on Sunday
the remains had been eaten by dogs. (Nashville Republican Banner,
18 Feb. 1868.)

"E.S.R., 1824" was tattoo and only identification on a man killed by
the guard on the Lebanon Pike on the 21st. He was dressed in
Federal uniform, aged about 40, and said to be in the 14th Indiana
cavalry. It is believed he was a spy, some say in the 5th Kentucky
Cavalry. (Nashville Dispatch, 23 June 1863.)

A bombshell taken as memento of the war from Overton Hills in
Nashville and deposited in an academy near Cleveland, Ohio, burst
a few days ago when students prodded it with a steel rod. It only
bruised them. (Memphis Daily Appeal, 7 Oct. 1868.)

An unknown woman, aged about 34, was found dead learning against a
tombstone in the Cathedral Cemetery in Philadelphia. The cause of
her death was childbirth. Her infant also found lying dead at its
mother's feet. There has been no clue to her identity. (Maury
Democrat, 5 April 1888.)

A few months ago a man, his wife and five children (the oldest a
girl of 12 and the youngest a boy Willie, age 5) came to Memphis;
the wife sickened and died and was buried in Elmwood Cemetery.
The father had to work as a day laborer to support his family and
he fell from scaffolding and broke some ribs. Relatives from up
the river offered to take the children. When time came for them
to leave, Willie was missing and was gone a long time. He finally
appeared, and said he had been to tell Mama goodbye. (Memphis
Avalanche, 11 Jan. 1866.)

Some two weeks ago two of General Pope's spies were discovered at
Fort Pillow with field plans of the works on their persons and the
poor fellows were taken out immediately and hanged to a tree. They
did not murmur at their fate, but said they could not die for a
better cause. (Nashville Dispatch, 19 April 1862.)

A colored lawyer at Bloomington, Illinois, has filed suit to
recover the price of 12 slaves sold in 1858 by a Tennessee slave
owner to persons at Genevieve, Illinois. (Maury Democrat, 22 Aug.
1895.)

Louisville Democrat, March 8 - Among prisoners that were brought in
on the 7th were two young female volunteers, who entered service in
the 2d Tennessee Cavalry but afterward joined the 27th Illinois
Regiment of Volunteers below Nashville. In Stones River after the
battle of Stones River, they rendered efficient service in administering to the wants of the wounded and dying. (Nashville Dispatch,
10 March 1863.)

A few days ago a mob of Ohio men, women and children led by an
injured wife, stoned a faithless husband from the town of Deshler
and held the woman with whom he had been living beneath the spout
of a railroad water tank until she was almost drowned. (Maury
Democrat, 26 April 1894.)

A Clare County, Michigan man who has made his wife split all the
wood, take care of the cattle, and clean the stable for seven
years, now has to employ a hired man. His wife has disappeared, and
all efforts to induce her to return to her duties have been
unavailing. (Maury Democrat, 26 April 1894.)

A little German girl was buried alive a few days ago in Brooklyn,
Ohio. (Memphis Daily Appeal, 23 Dec. 1869.)

A girl soldier has been discovered in the 10th Missouri Cavalry at
Bolivar, Tn. She had served since the entrance of the regiment in
the field. She was arrested and sent home. (Nashville Dispatch,
20 Feb. 1863.)

The cemeteries in vicinity of Fredericksburg are filled with the
graves of children victims of scarlet fever last winter. In a
population of 4,000, 300 children died during the winter months.
(Nashville Dispatch, 18 May 1862.)

A Hopkinsville exchange of last Saturday says: On respectable
authority, we state that a lady residing at Fairview, in this
county, gave birth some six week ago to a child that was a most
singular compound of man and reptile. The lower portions of the
child are natural in their formation and partake of the characteristic of the genus homo, but the body and the head are similar
to the body and the head of a rattlesnake. The mother every time
she is compelled to give nourishment to the child, is thrown into
convulsions. The singular formation of this creature is thus
accounted for: Sometime during pregnancy a rattlesnake attacked
and greatly frightened the mother of this creature, but fortunately
however, did not injure her. At the date of this writing the child
is still alive. Its parents are among the most respectable people
of Christian County. (Memphis Avalanche, 1 May 1867.)

A melon patch near Orlando, Florida, is said to be haunted by the
ghost of a boy who died after eating some of its fruit which he had
stolen. Persons who pass the place at night claim to have seen a
white figure, and to have heard unearthly shrieks and groans.
(Maury Democrat, 2 Aug. 1888.)

UNKNOWN - Continued

Among the patients in hospitals at Annapolis, Maryland, is a woman wounded in one of the recent battles before Richmond. Her wound is a flesh one in a leg. It is said she followed her husband to the field of battle. (Nashville Dispatch, 7 Aug. 1862.)

An unknown Irishman drowned in the river and his body was found near the mouth of Wilson's Spring branch; had been dead 10 to 15 days. (Nashville Republican Banner, 7 April 1869.)

Unknown baby found in Brown's Creek above the Murfreesboro Pike; had been disemboweled before being thrown in the creek and had been in the creek 10 or 12 days. It was decently buried. (Nashville Republican Banner, 28 April 1869.)

An unknown woman, age 45, weighing about 170 pounds, leaped from Raceway Point in Prospect Park at Niagara Falls on June 14. Her body was carried immediately over the American Falls. (Maury Democrat, 20 June 1889.)

A fly bit a man in California and killed him. (Columbia Herald, 15 Sept. 1871.)

Tombstone at Knightstown, Rush County, on a son's grave: "He died at nashville, tennessee, he died of kronic diarea, it trooly paneful must have bin to die so fur away from home." (Nashville Republican Banner, 29 April 1869.)

Cornersville, Giles Co. - A young couple were on the point of getting married and her brother was opposed to the match. He shot through the window, fatally killing the groom. Before the man died, however, he insisted on having marriage ceremony completed. (Memphis Daily Appeal, 2 Feb. 1869. N.B. Cornersville is now in Marshall County.)

Last Wednesday while a man was digging cellar under the house of Mr. Winfrey at Johnsonville, he struck a coffin in which he found a skeleton. Upon striking the bottom of the grave he found a boiling spring under the coffin. (Nashville Republican Banner, 25 Sept. 1869.)

A woman was arrested at Catania, Sicily, charged with killing 23 children by giving them wine poisoned with phosphorus. (Maury Democrat, 17 Oct. 1895.)

A child was born a few days ago in Heard County, Georgia, that had two heads and three legs. (Nashville Union and American, 12 May 1874.)

Negro was lynched in Giles County for rape on Mattie Hendricks on October 11. Eight hundred to 1000 people attended. (Linden Times, 16 Dec. 1880.)

Among the wounded soldiers who arrived at St. Louis on the 18th on the steamer Empress was a woman who had followed her husband to war and received a gunshot wound in the battle of Pittsburg Landing.

On way up the Mississippi she gave birth to a daughter, whom she named Empress. Her husband was killed in the battle. (Nashville Dispatch, 1 May 1862.)

In August last a little girl living near Oswego, New York, left her home to pick berries, and never returned. On Tuesday last, five or six lads went out hunting and during the day came upon a spot where a large number of snakes were discovered and killed. Near this they discovered an opening, containing a human skeleton, from which every particle of flesh had been taken, leaving the bones as white as ivory. There can be no doubt these were the remains of the missing child, who, probably, being tired, seated herself near this horrid den, and was attacked by the reptiles in numbers and killed. (Memphis Avalanche, 5 April 1867.)

The Chattanooga Union of the 30th: Last Tuesday morning a farmer named Wilkins, living in Walker County, Ga., whose hogs had strayed away, was searching for the lost animals among the mountains in the vicinity, when he discovered two newly made graves on the extreme summit of a hill far away from any known habitation.

Marking the spot, he continued his search, and on his return home, having informed a neighbor of the strange sight which he had seen on the lonely mountain's peak, the two started off next morning to examine the mysterious graves.

Having turned up the earth over the graves, they exhumed two pine coffins, which on being open were found to contain the bodies of two infants about three weeks old. The fact that they were buried far away from any human habitation excited the surprise of the two farmers, and they proceeded to explore the vicinity.

After an hour's search, they found an opening in the side of the mountain, in which, upon entering they were horrified to find the lifeless remains of a woman lying on the floor of the cavern.

The features of the dead were unknown to the farmers, who, after giving the remains Christian burial, returned to their homes. No clue to the mystery which enshrouds the cause of the poor woman's fate has yet been found. (Memphis Avalanche, 3 Nov. 1866.)

UNMASONIC CONDUCT. Notice to all Free Masons--Benton Lodge III: William Gray, master mason, has been expelled for highly immoral and unmasonic conduct, viz, the seducing and running away with a young (and hitherto supposed to be innocent girl); and by marriage his own neice; leaving a wife in great mental as well as pecuniary distress. He weighs about 175 pounds, 23 years old, fair complexion and 6 feet high. Papers in Missouri and Southwest please copy. Signed Cavel B. McLean, Secretary, 15 Jan. 1846. (The Academist, Lawrenceburg, Tn, 18 March 1846.)

URSERY, John, was killed by W. W. Briggs, grocer, at Campbellsville on April 10; murderer headed for Mt. Pleasant. (Columbia Herald and Mail, 12 April 1878.)

USSERY, Mrs. Mary, 85, died Wednesday at Lynnville of heart failure; mother of the Rev. W. T. Ussery; three sons and three daughters survive. (Columbia Herald, 8 Jan. 1897.)

VAN BUREN, Martin. Ex-President Van Buren, now 80, is suffering from
dangerous affection of the throat of bronchial organs. (Nashville
Dispatch, 27 June 1862.) Ex-President Van Buren reportedly very
sick at his residence in Kinderhook, New York. There is slight
hope for his recovery. (Nashville Dispatch, 9 July 1862.) The
funeral of Martin Van Buren was held at Kinderhook on the 28th. His
remains were buried in public cemetery near village of Kinderhook.
(Nashville Dispatch, 3 Aug. 1862.)

Van Buren's Visit. It had already been announced that the President
would stop at the Eagle Hotel on the east side of South Main street
near 8th street. That old hotel is said to have been built of
brick and as large as the Bethell house. Built by a company the
hotel was long since destroyed by fire. The Tennessee Democrat
12 May 1842 has the following:

Mr. Van Buren's Visit to Columbia - On Saturday last Mr. Van Buren
accompanied by Mr. Paulding visited our county and town. Having
declined to accept a public entertainment he was received very
cordially by our citizens but without form or ceremony. A larger
number were assembled to welcome him than had for many years, if
ever, been assembled in the town at any one time. He was met
several miles from town by a large concourse of citizens in carriages and on horseback and was escorted by them to the village.

He stopped at the Eagle hotel, where lodgings had been prepared for
him. Hundreds of people, without distinction of party, thronged
the large hall of the hotel, and were personally introduced to
himself and Mr. Paulding. The crowd, however, soon became so dense
that it would found to be impossible for all who pressed forward
to take the distinguished strangers by hand--to have an opportunity
to do so and at the suggestion of many persons present, they were
conducted to the open court square where they remained an hour--
receiving the salutation of the people and being personally
introduced to them. They dined at the hotel with several hundred
citizens, but there were no toasts--no form, no ceremony. At six
o'clock in the afternoon on the invitation of the Rev. Rector Mr.
Smith, they visited his school and spent the evening with Governor
Polk at his residence (now Dr. A. L. Pillow's) where they were met
by a large number of ladies and gentlemen.

The weather was fine, perfect order and decorum prevailed among the
immense multitude who were assembled throughout the day, and the
occasion passed off as far as we have learned, without the occurrence
of a single unpleasant incident. The distinguished strangers left
early Monday morning and proceeded to the Hermitage--where we understand they will remain a few days--and then proceeded on their
journey.

They have declined, we learn, to accept invitations which had been
forwarded to them by committees of citizens to visit Huntsville,
Ala., Pulaski, and other places.

Mr. Van Buren's personal appearance greatly and agreeably surprised
many who had heard him represented as a person of diminutive stature,
and foppish appearance. Instead of this they found him to be a man
rather over the commonplace, perfectly plain in his dress--easy
affable and familiar in his manners. But few men we have ever seen,
mingle with more ease and familiarity in a crowd than Mr. Van Buren.
Hundreds who had heard a very different account of him, were astonished to see it, and all we believe without distinction of party,
agree that he has been greatly mispresented..." (Maury Democrat,
9 Aug. 1894, quoting the Tennessee Democrat, 12 May 1842.)

VAN BUREN, John, son of the late ex-president, is said to be in a very
delicate state of health; he has been an invalid for nearly two
years. (Nashville Dispatch, 7 Aug. 1862.)

VANCE, Capt. Samuel, died yesterday in Memphis, to be buried in the
    family vault in Nashville, age 45. (Memphis Daily Appeal, 24 Nov.
    1868; Nashville Republican Banner, 25 Nov. 1868.)

VANCEIL, W., 2d East Tennessee Mounted Infantry, and Morris Brean, 2d
    Massachusetts Heavy Artillery, escaped from the rebel abomination at
    Andersonville, Georgia, and have arrived at Chattanooga. (Nashville
    Daily Union, 15 March 1865.)

VANDERBILT, Commodore, the great railroad king is dead, died yesterday
    morning; born on Staten Island May 1794, the son of a kitchen gar-
    dener; a remarkable man. (Columbia Herald and Mail, 5 Jan. 1877.)
    Vanderbilt had 15 children by his first wife, 11 of them daughters.
    (Columbia Herald, 23 Sept. 1870.)

VANDERGRIFT, Adam, private, Company I, 5th Tennessee Cavalry, was killed
    22 Feb. 1864 on Calf Killer near Sparta, Tn. (Nashville Daily
    Union, __ Feb. 1864.)

VANDEVER. The infant of Mr. and Mrs. Dave Vandever, died August 13.
    (Columbia Herald, 21 Aug. 1891.)

VAN DORN, Earl. (Refer also to George B. Peters listing.) May 9--
    It was reported by a gentleman who has just come through the lines
    that General Van Dorn was shot and instantly killed by Dr. Peters
    of Maury County. Dr. Peters discovered Van Dorn in criminal inter-
    course with the wife of Dr. Peters. (New York Times, 10 May 1863.
    N.B. This paper was in the possession of Norris Hunter of Columbia,
    Tn.)

The killing of General Van Dorn by Dr. Peters has been confirmed.
Dr. Peters has arrived in this city and from him we learn that the
cause of Van Dorn's death was an interview held 30 hours previous to
the killing in which the latter agreed on his honor to give Dr.
Peters a written statement the next day setting forth four distinct
facts.

Dr. Peters said to him that upon the fulfillment of this promise he
would spare his life to his wife and children although Van Dorn had
said he cared nothing for his own wife.

The next day Dr. Peterswas sick and did not call on Van Dorn until
the second day, Thursday morning, about 8 a.m. and demanded of Van
Dorn a compliance with his promise, which he seemed not inclined to
do. Dr. Peters then said that he would give him half an hour in
which to comply and distinctly notified him that, in case of failure,
his life would be forfeit. He then walked up into the village. On
his return Van Dorn read to him what he had written.

The first clause fully complied with his promise, the second was an
entire misrepresentation and the other two acknowledgements he
refused to make.

Dr. Peters then denounced him for his bad faith. When Van Dorn
cursed him for a "cowardly dog" and ordered him to leave the room, or
he would kick him out. Dr. Peters then drew his pistol and fired,
the ball taking effect in the left side of the head, producing
instant death.

Dr. Peters picked up the statement Van Dorn had prepared, and has
preserved it as circumstantial evidence, and mounting his horse rode
off.

Avoiding the pickets at Hurt's, he crossed Duck River and arrived
at Shelbyville where he learned that General Polk, to whom he had
intended surrendering himself, had issued an order for his arrest.

The next morning he left for Winchester, disguised, and passing

VAN DORN, Earl - Continued
through Gainsboro and Gallatin arrived at this place Monday afternoon.

Dr. Peters says it is not true he detected Van Dorn in a criminal
act with his wife. He refuses to reveal the history of the 30 hours
previous to the tragedy, and will only do so in a court of justice
in justification of the course he felt it his duty to pursue.

Dr. Peters was for a number of years a distinguished practitioner
of medicine in West Tennessee and was a member of the Senate of this
State one or two sessions. His present residence is in Mississippi
where he is regarded as a wealthy planter. (Nashville Dispatch,
13 May 1863.)

A correspondent who having coming from Spring Hill says Dr. Peters
called on Van Dorn and asked for "a pass to go to Nashville" and that
Dr. Peters shot him from the back. Dr. Peters was five days making
a circuitous route from Spring Hill to Nashville.

Rumors of the conduct of Van Dorn not only in this one instance but
in others near Columbia have been prevalent for some time. Without
a doubt he acted very badly. My informant tells me that he has
degraded the cause and disgusted every one by his inattention to his
duties and his constant devotion to the ladies--and that to the
exclusion of all else. Wine and women have ruined him, as they have
ruined many another brilliant but reckless man.

Van Dorn was a man of daring genius there can be no doubt. Being
handsome with dark, flashing eyes, a magnificent moustache--a
superb rider, showy address, quick-witted, and graceful; he was also
a man of sagacious foresight, keen, intelligent, but he was wholly
and thoroughly unreliable. He always sacrificed his business to
his pleasure. He was never at his post when he ought to be. He was
either tied to a woman's apron-strings or heated with wine.
(Nashville Dispatch, 24 May 1863.)

A rumor was circulating in the city yesterday that General Van
Dorn had been shot and instantly killed by Dr. Peters, formerly a
Senator in the Tennessee Legislature from the Hardeman District, at
Spring Hill in Maury County on the 7th. Parties who came in from
the neighborhood of Triune in Williamson County yesterday had heard
nothing of the affair. (Nashville Dispatch, 10 May 1863.)

General Van Dorn was a member of the West Point Class of 1842 and
among his mates were William S. Rosecrans, Gustavus W. Smith,
Mansfield Lovell, John Pope, Seth Williams, Abner Doubleday, D. H.
Hill, James Longstreet, "Van" was a poor scholar and in a class of
56 stood 52 in the order of merit. (Nashville Dispatch, 15 May
1863.)

Van Dorn's staff has published a card denying that domestic difficulties in Dr. Peters' family had anything to do with the assassination of their General. (Nashville Dispatch, 28 May 1863.   N.B.
This card was published in the 30 May 1863 issue of the Nashville
Dispatch.)

A Memphis dispatch of the 12th says that Dr. Peters, who killed Van
Dorn, is here. He denounces the card published in Mobile by Van
Dorn's staff relative to the affair as a tissue of falsehoods and is
on his way South to stand trial. (Nashville Dispatch, 17 June 1863.)

St. Peter's Episcopal Church Records, Columbia, Tn: May 8th 1863 -
Burials - In Columbia. Held funeral services over remains of Maj.
Genl. Earle Van Dorn, C. S. A., before their deposit in a vault
preparatory to their removal South.

Lamb and Barr interment records, copied by the late Frank H. Smith
and published in Frank H. Smith's History of Maury County: "May
1863 - Gen. Van Dorn, paid by Maj. Paul, $175.00."

VAN DORN, Earl - Continued
Interview with Joseph H. Fussell, 18 Oct. 1906, Frank H. Smith, and
published in Frank H. Smith's History of Maury County, page 119:
Gen. Joe H. Fussell was first man to reach Van Dorn after Peters shot
him. Van Dorn's headquarters were in Martin Cheairs brick house,
Spring Hill. His private office was in a rear room opening on the
central hall.

Fussell's company was in the saddle when Gen. Frank (Armstrong) told
Fussell to go at once to Van Dorn's Headquarters. Fussell's command
was then about __ yards north of the headquarters. The command
went in a gallop through the streets. Command halted in front of
house; he went in alone.

Fussell met Mrs. Martin Cheairs and negro woman cook in hallway and
was told that Van Dorn was shot. When Fussell went in, Van Dorn
was sitting at desk, arms on desk, head bent forward, still breathing.

Pistol ball had entered back of head, near base of brain. Did not
come through face but lodged just above eye. Eye protruded.

Fussell lifted up head and blood ran out of wound on collar and back.

Negro cook, or Mrs. Cheairs, told Fussell that Dr. Peters had shot
Van Dorn and left the house by the rear with pistol still in hand,
as if going to his own home east. Fussell sent details east and
elsewhere to look for Dr. Peters. Unsuccessful.

Fussell later learned that the detail sent east did not want to
catch Peters.

Hatred against the Mississippians was so great and bitter at
Pulaski that when Van Dorn was killed, people said on the streets
they wanted his whole command served in that way. (Nashville
Daily Union, 5 Aug. 1863.)

VANLEER, Anthony, died in his 80th year in this city last night.
(Nashville Dispatch, 10 July 1863.)

VANNOY, Mason, 73, died near Manchester on his farm. (Nashville
Dispatch, 29 April 1863.)

VAUGHAN, Issaac L., Esquire, 44, died 5 May 1863 in Williamson County.
(Nashville Dispatch, 8 May 1863.)

VAUGHAN, John, 104, probably the oldest man in Kentucky, has died at
Big Hill, Madison County. (Maury Democrat, 28 March 1895.)

VAUGHAN, Mrs. Martha, died near Chattanooga recently aged 103 years.
(Maury Democrat, 27 Dec. 1894.)

VAUGHN, ___, notorious bad man of near Triune, Tn, divorced his wife
and married again. He tried to separate from his second wife.
His body was found in the woods with nine bullet holes in it.
(Nashville Republican Banner, 4 June 1869.) J. B. Vaughn was killed
in West Rutherford County; he had been blindfolded and killed by
masked parties. His body was left in a sinkhole. He had been
trying to cause insurrection among negroes. (Nashville Republican
Banner, 5 June 1869.)

VAUGHN, Randall, of Paulding, Georgia, was wounded in battle of
Waynesboro in 1864, the rifle bullet entered his body below the
breast-bone and point of heart. Four years ago an abscess formed
in the abdomen about 14 inches from where the ball entered, and the
other day the ball was extracted from abdomen. Mr. Vaughn is
recovering. (Houston County News, 7 Aug. 1886.)

VAUGHN, Mrs. Rhoda, daughter of Capt. John Holder, was the first white
woman born in Kentucky and lived near Lexington many years.
(Columbia Herald, 24 Jan. 1873.)

VAUGHN, Walter, 7, was killed by freight train in East Nashville. He
lost his footing as he was trying to get on train; was a messenger
and a caller. (Daily Herald, Columbia, Tn, 2 Aug. 1900.)

VAUGHN, W. R., of Omaha, Nebraska, is trying to procure $400,000,000 in
pensions for the surviving ex-slaves in the South and is much
encouraged by ex-Minister Fred Douglas. (Florence, Ala., Times,
29 Aug. 1891.)

VAUGHT, S. D., was murdered while sleeping in a chair by John James,
a relative, near the Cannon County line on Friday. They had been
drinking together and James beat him over the head until he was
dead. James is now in jail. (Monitor, Murfreesboro, 21 Nov. 1868.)

VAULX, Mary, wife of William Vaulx, died in Nashville on 31 Dec. 1829.
(Western Mercury, Columbia, Tn, 13 Jan. 1830.)

VAUPEL, Willie, age 2, died on the 26th; son of Christian and Catherine
Vaupel. (Nashville Republican Banner, 27 Sept. 1868.)

VEAL, John, late of Nashville, died in Rome, Georgia; found dead near
railroad; found on the 17th and he had been dead three days.
(Nashville Republican Banner, 27 Nov. 1870.)

VEST, Peter, Union man at Wartrace, Tn, was hanged a few days ago.
(Nashville Daily Union, 9 Sept. 1862.)

VESTAL. The funeral of J. T. Vestal and Betty Vestal will be
preached the first Sunday in August at Mt. Zion. (Columbia Herald
and Mail, 6 July 1877.)

VESTAL. Among the brave boys who fell at Perryville was my dearest
brother Henderson Vestal...he left his old home and went out to
endure the hard life of a soldier...I still reside at the old home
he left. Our dear father and mother have long since been laid to
rest in the old family graveyard, and O how often have I wished that
he was beside them there; but alas! his remains be on the distant
battlefield of Kentucky. Signed, Mary J. Fitzgerald. (Columbia
Herald, 6 Sept. 1895.)

VESTAL, Jay, Jr., 30, died Sunday at the home of grandfather Jay
Vestal, Sr., on Snow Creek; died of consumption. (Columbia Herald
and Mail, 23 March 1877.)

VESTS, William, was killed last week in Nashville by John Coussens, who
escaped. They were aruging about the causes of the Civil War when
Coussens shot Vests. (Maury Democrat, 27 March 1890.)

VICK, Mrs. Hannah, of Tennessee, is 107 years old and still draws
pension of her husband who was in Revolutionary War. (Memphis Daily
Appeal, 20 Oct. 1868.) Mrs. Dinah Vick of Williamson County draws
a pension as Revolutionary War widow as does a Mrs. Guthrie.
(Memphis Daily Appeal, 1 May 1870.)

VICKERS, Lindsey P., private, Company I, 5th Tennessee Cavalry, was
killed 22 Feb. 1864 on Calf Killer near Sparta, Tn. (Nashville
Daily Union, __ Feb. 1864.)

VINCENT, Benjamin Perry, 58, died on Thursday on 10th Street; had only
lived in Columbia a short time; died Oct. 17 of flux; buried Rose
Hill. (Maury Democrat, 24 Oct. 1895.)

VINCENT, John, 22, was killed on the 2d by his brother Robert G.
Vincent, 19; he was shot several times; they were sons of Clement N.

Vincent of Huntsville, Alabama; they were 12 miles from town. (Murfreesboro News, 17 Oct. 1860.)

VINCENT, Elisha, lived near Kelly's Ford on Richland Creek, Giles County, and died of hydrophobia on the 6th; had been bitten two months ago. (Whig and Tribune, Jackson, Tn, 20 Sept. 1873.)

VINEYARD, Frank, 3d East Tennessee Cavalry, drowned in Cumberland River; fell off his horse. (Nashville Daily Union, 23 June 1863.) Frank Vineyard and John McCullough, 3d East Tennessee Cavalry (U.S.A.), drowned in Cumberland River while watering their horses. (Nashville Dispatch, 23 June 1863.)

VINTON, Honorable Samuel P., of Ohio, died in Washington, D.C., on the 11th after a brief attack of eryiseplas; wwas a representative many years and had recently been appointed commissioner of emancipation. (Nashville Dispatch, 18 May 1862.)

VIVRETT, Thomas, was fatally stabbed in abdomen by McFall brothers at Green Hill Saturday. (Nashville Republican Banner, 12 Oct. 1869.) Thomas Vivrett, 24, of Wilson County originally and son of Thomas Vivrett who was killed a few weeks ago, was shot by Ben Snowden and there is little hope for recovery. (Nashville Republican Banner, 13 Nov. 1869.)

VON ADELUNG, Mrs. Selmer, died November 14 in New York; for a number of years she and her husband taught music at the Athenaeum in Columbia. (Columbia Herald, 17 Nov. 1899.)

VOORHIES, Mrs. Sackey, has died; joined the church at Peters Camp Ground August 1819. (Columbia Herald, 18 April 1873.)

VOORHIES, Colonel William Milton, died yesterday; was colonel in the 48th Regiment. (Columbia Herald, 26 June 1896.)

VOORHIES, William Milton, Jr., died May 6 in Pulaski; born 3 Oct. 1843 in Maury County; Presbyterian; served four years in Confederate Army. (Maury Democrat, 10 May 1894.)

VOSS, Dr. Elihu Crisp, died October 13 on Garden Street in Columbia; born 2 July 1821. (Maury Democrat, 17 Oct. 1895.)

WADE, Mrs. Clement W., died Feb. 22 in Williamson County; daughter of late Claiborne H. Kinnard; seven children survive. (Whig & Tribune, Jackson, Tn, 8 March 1873.)

WADE, Colonel D. Fount, died recently near Nashville; buried at Mt. Olivet Cemetery; he was wounded at Fort Ionelson during the Civil War and later severely wounded by bushwhackers in North Alabama; married Margaret Pillow, daughter of General Gideon J. Pillow and lived in Nashville until his death. (Columbia Herald, __ Jan. 1891.)

WADE, Mrs. Elizabeth L.', 86, who lived on the headwaters of Enon Creek, died 10 April 1897; had been a widow for 40 years; mother of 11 children, six of whom survive; buried in family cemetery by her husband. She had been paralyzed several years and helpless. She was a Miss Pointer before her marriage. (Columbia Herald, 16 April 1897.)

WADE, Mary, little daughter of Mr. and Mrs. D. F. Wade, her life is despaired of. (Columbia Herald and Mail, 13 March 1874.)

WADE, John, Sr., deceased; his debtors are asked to come forward. (Tennessee Telegraph, Murfreesboro, Tn, 12 Sept. 1840.)

WAECHTER, Mrs., proprietor of a beer saloon in Memphis hanged herself from the transom over a door with a clothes-line. Her husband died

last fall of yellow fever, she also had it and had never fully
recovered. She had made two other attempts to destroy herself.
(Nashville Union and American, 21 May 1874.)

WAGGONER, Arilla, administratrix, petitions court for widow's dower of
land and division among the heirs of Abraham Waggoner, deceased,
in Davidson County. (Nashville Dispatch, 27 Nov. 1863.)

WAGGONER, Cornelius, 83, died near Nashville last week. (Whig and
Tribune, Jackson, Tn, 10 May 1873.)

WAGGONER, Rev. T. J., was murdered by Beverly "Bose" Haley in December
he was 55 last July 2. (Nashville Dispatch, 16 April 1863.)

WAGGONER, William, aged gentleman, arrived on train from Louisville
yesterday to see a sick friend in the 21st Indiana Battery; he fell
dead one hour after arrival; from South Bend. (Nashville Daily
Union, 25 Dec. 1865.)

WAGNER. Party of guerrillas roaming through Robertson County on last
Saturday, went to house of an old man named Wagner, a preacher,
robbed him of $300 and shot him dead. (Nashville Daily Union, 25
Dec. 1862. N.B. See T. J. Waggoner listing before.)

WAGNER, Widow, of Rev. Mr. Wagner, (Murdered some months ago near
White's Creek), died last week of jaundice. She had been paralyzed
for a long time. (Nashville Dispatch, 6 Oct. 1863.)

WAGONER, Cornelius, 83, died on Buena Vista Pike yesterday. (Nashville
Union and American, 3 May 1873.)

WALCON, Francis M., prisoner of war, jumped overboard from steamer
B. M. Runyan on the 15th, en route from Alton to St. Louis and
drowned. He had been sentenced to confinement for the remainder of
the war. (Nashville Dispatch, 23 Aug. 1863.)

WALKER, Mrs. Ann, daughter of John G. Ramsey, married William Walker of
Giles County three years ago, died January 20. (Columbia Herald,
6 Feb. 1891.)

WALKER, Asa.

Former Maury Countian Figured in Historic Battle of Alamo in 1836.
Through the courtesy of a New York friend, Mrs. Izora Andrews has
received a newspaper clipping which gives an account of new light
thrown on the fall of the Alamo by a Texas lawsuit in which a former
Maury Countian figures.

William W. Gant mentioned in the article was an uncle of Dr. H. A.
Gant of Columbia and was a member of the first Congress of the
Republic of Texas. His father William Gant is buried on the Ocey
Gordon place on Carters Creek and his mother Mrs. Lesey Norwood
Gant is buried in old Greenwood Cemetery at Columbia. Mr. Gant
fought under Sam Houston at San Jacinto and Dr. Gant has letters
written by him to his father John Isom Gant during the period 1835-
1837.

The newspaper clipping which was written by Bob Davis of Houston,
Texas, is as follows:

"After a lapse of 96 years there comes to light a new chapter that
has to do with the Alamo, the historic shrine at S. A. de Bexar where
182 Texans under the command of Lt. Col. Travis, beseiged by 6,000
Mexicans under Santa Ana were driven to bay and massacred to the
last man on 6 March 1836.

"This new chapter presented for the first time is best told in the
words of F. C. Proctor, a Texas born, who has practiced law throughout Texas for half a century. Here is his story: 'About 30 years

ago,' said he, 'I represented the defendants in a suit brought in
federal court in San Antonio by the heirs of Asa Walker to recover
a tract of land granted them by the Republic of Texas by virtue of
the fact that Walker had been killed in defense of the Alamo. The
defendants claimed title through a sale of this land in an administration had on his estate. The issue was whether this administration was valid and whether there was a debt that justified the
opening of the administration upon his estate and sale of property
thereof to pay a debt.

'"In a musty old file in probate records in Washington County, Texas,
there was found proof of the existence of this debt and incidentally
in the form of a letter. Evidence of the most gallant declaration
that my perusal of Texas history has disclosed--this proof was in
the form of a letter from Asa Walker to Wm. W. Gant. Here is the
epistle in full:

> "'Mr. Gant--I take the responsibility of taking your
> overcoat and your gun. Your gun they would have any-
> how and I might as well have it as anyone else. If I
> live to return, I will satisfy you for all, if I die
> I leave you my clothes to do the best you can with.
> You can sell them for something. If you overtake me,
> you can take your rifle and I will trust to chance.
> The hurry of the moment and my want of means to do
> better are all the excuse I have to plead for fitting
> out at your expense. Forgive the presumption and
> remember your friend at heart.
> A. Walker

"History records that Walker reached the Alamo and joined the Texans
under the command of Travis. Tradition has it that he was the last
man killed. Clutched in his hand was the gun borrowed from William
Gant. The barrel was empty as a result of the firing of the last
shot. The stock of the weapon he had used as a club. At the feet
of Asa Walker in a semicircle lay seven dead Mexicans. Walker upon
departing for the Alamo announced that if deprived of his arms he
would fight the enemy with his fists   The mortal clay that fell
under his rifle butt proves that Asa kept his word.

"Attorney Proctor left his chair, walked to an open window of his
office on the 20th floor of the Gulf Building that towers over Houston
and looked out upon a peaceful and prosperous land. 'Asa Walker did
not die in vain,' he said, 'more is the pity that coming to Texas as
he did in 1835 from Columbia, Tennessee, with his friend Gant he
should have been cut down the following year.'

"Among the papers filed in a case was a note for $37.87 1/2 for
transportation from Tennessee to Texas paid by Gant. There was also
a claim for $35 for the rifle and $10 for the overcoat. The letter
that I have quoted was the particular important evidence upon which
Judge T. F. Maxey rendered a decision for the defendants.

"Judge Maxey said that he had tried hard to find a way to award the
land to the plaintiffs because they had not had the benefit of the
bounty that the republic had intended for them and that the land had
been sold to pay a trifling debt. But was nevertheless an honest
debt and the title had passed from the plaintiffs.

"Gant from the death of Walker served in Capt. J. Calder's company
at the Battle of San Jacinto when the Mexicans were defeated by
Sam Houston and Santa Anna was taken prisoner. In connection with
the Walker-Gant case, it is a curious coincidence that while presenting my argument before the federal court justice at San Antonio
I would see past Judge Maxey through an open casement to the very
room on the second floor of the Alamo where Asa Walker, after
accounting for seven of the enemy, fell and died. I shall never
forget the sensations I experienced on that occasion, an extra-

WALKER, Asa - Continued
ordinary link between the quick and the dead." (Maury Democrat,
Columbia, Tn, 3 March 1932.)

(N.B. William W. Gant's mother Lesey Norwood Gant married 1831 to
Jonathan Webster of Maury County; she is buried at Greenwood
Cemetery in Columbia where he stone reads: Mrs. Lesey Webster,
9 Sept. 1772-17 Nov. 1862. Her husband is buried on the Carter's
Creek Pike in a small cemetery.)

WALKER, David Charles, infant son of Peter and Margaret Walker, died
last night at 10:25. (Nashville Republican Banner, 10 July 1870.)

WALKER, Hampton, citizen of DeKalb County, was arrested yesterday by
Department HQ and confined in military prison. (Nashville Daily
Union, 21 Feb. 1865.)

WALKER, Hiram K., died on the 2d; editor of the Republican Banner and
member of I.O.O.F. (Nashville Dispatch, 3 Aug. 1862.)

WALKER, Hiram K., infant son of late H. K. Walker, 11 months, died
April 7; son of Mrs. M. J. Walker, a daughter of Mrs. Austin.
(Nashville Daily Union, 8 April 1863.) Hiram K. Walker, son of late
H. K. Walker, former editor of Nashville Banner, died April 7 at
11 months; son of Mrs. Mary J. Walker. (Nashville Dispatch, 8
April 1863.)

WALKER, James T., noted bushwhacker, was killed in Lafayette County,
Missouri, near Lexington on 31 March 1864, by a detachment of Company
F, 1st Missouri State militia; formerly with Quantrell and he boasted
he killed 14 during the massacre at Lawrence. (Nashville Daily
Union, __ April 1864.)

WALKER, Joel, died at home of Thomas Berton over the river on October
14; born Fluvanna County, Virginia, and was in his 83d year; father
of Joseph A. Walker and Mrs. Mary Berton; buried Greenwood Cemetery
in Columbia; served in War of 1812. His grandchildren were Joseph
A. and Crawford Irvine, Joseph N. Walker and Mrs. Theo Lipscomb.
(Columbia Herald and Mail, 30 Oct. 1876.)

WALKER, Judge Pleasant, died of apoplexy near Centerville, Tn, on the
13th. (Nashville Republican Banner, 16 June 1870.)

WALKER, Col. J. Knox, died in Memphis about the 24th. (Nashville
Dispatch, 29 Aug. 1863.) Col. J. Knox Walker, died on the 21st in
Memphis; first private secretary of President Polk; once state
senator; opposed to secession but raised a regiment of which he
was elected colonel; then resigned. Survived by several children.
(Nashville Dispatch, 1 Sept. 1863.) Maria Armstrong, late wife of
General Frank Armstrong, daughter of the late J. Knox Walker, died
in Springfield, Missouri, after a long illness. (Columbia Herald,
30 Aug. 1872.)

WALKER, Miss Mary, died September 9 in Nashville buried at Zion Cemetery
in Maury County. (Maury Democrat, 19 Sept. 1895.)

WALKER, Lucius Marshall, brigadier general, CSA, nephew of President
James K. Polk, brother-in-law of Frank C. Armstrong, born 18 Oct.
1829 in Columbia, Tn, was shot 6 Sept. 1863 at Little Rock,
Arkansas, in a duel with General John S. Marmaduke and died the
next day. His remains were deposited at Elmwood Cemetery in Memphis
yesterday afternoon. (Memphis Avalanche, 20 Feb. 1866.)

General L. Marsh Walker, buried in Lot 257, Chapel Hill Section,
Elmwood Cemetery, Memphis. Tombstone inscription: born 18 Oct.
1829, died 7 Sept. 1863.

The last duel of note to be fought in Arkansas was between two
generals in the Confederate Army, J. S. Marmaduke and L. M. Walker,

WALKER, Lucius Marshall - Continued
who fought with pistols 6 Sept. 1863, a few miles east of Little
Rock. Walker held a superior title and Marmaduke was his sub-
ordinate. During the defense of Little Rock, Marmaduke voiced some
harsh criticism of Walker's lack of courage and his military
direction. When this was reported to Walker, he demanded an apology,
which Marmaduke refused. Forgetting that the safety of the capital
city lay in their hands, these two cavalry officers arranged a duel.
General Walker fell at the first shot and lived but a short time
after being taken to a Little Rock Hospital. He died at the home of
Mrs. Cates at Little Rock on 7 Sept. 1863. (Note found in the
Craig Mathews papers in the UDC Collection, Tennessee State Library
and Archives.)

Col. Robert H. Crockett was the second in the duel. Walker fell at
the first shot, the ball passed through the right kidney and lodged
in the spine, causing paralysis of the lower extremities. He was
carried to Little Rock in the ambulance. After a night's travel,
he reached Little Rock and stopped at the residence of Mrs. Cates
where he was cared for and lived until the next morning. "I was
sitting with him there by his dying bed," said Col. Robert H.
Rockett at Eureka Springs, Ark. (Houston, Texas, Chronicle, 26
Sept. 1920.)

Elmwood Cemetery burials; Maj. Gen. Marsh Walker, buried 19 Feb.
1866; Anna McNeil, Walker, age 7, buried 19 Feb. 1865.

WALKER, Mrs., Judge Samuel P. Walker's wife died in Memphis last Friday.
His mother was Miss Wormly of Maury County and his father was Samuel
Polk Walker, son of Mrs. James Walker of Columbia, sister of
President Polk. (Columbia Herald and Mail, 23 March 1877.)

WALKER, Mrs. Samuel P., 72, widow, died 20 June 1889 of paralysis in
Columbia and taken to Memphis for burial. (Maury Democrat, __
June 1889.)

WALKER, Colonel Samuel P., died at Bailey Springs, Alabama, where he
had gone for his health. He was a leader of the Democratic party
in Shelby County, Tennessee, and nephew of President Polk.
(Columbia Herald, 11 Nov. 1870.)

It is with pain that we record the death of Col. Sam P. Walker, which
event occurred yesterday at Bailey Springs, Alabama, where he had
some weeks ago gone for his health. Col. Walker was one of the
oldest members and the oldest leader of the Democratic party of
Shelby County, Tn. Twenty-five years ago he came to Memphis from
Columbia; he was a nephew of President Polk and in the late J. Knox
Walker had a brother distinguished as a brilliant politician and
able lawyer. He was about 60 years of age and died in the communication of the Protestant Episcopal Church. (Columbia Herald,
11 Nov. 1870.)

WALKER, Mrs. Sallie, 76, died at Williamsport of general debility.
(Columbia Herald and Mail, 14 Aug. 1874.)

WALKER, Mrs. Sallie S., 26, died April 5, husband and one son survive.
(Columbia Herald and Mail, 10 May 1878.)

WALKER, Mrs. Sarah S., about 70, died on the 10th; widow of Griffith
Walker. (Columbia Herald and Mail, 14 Aug. 1874.)

WALKER, William B., "Uncle Billy," died April 28 near Ashland, Wayne
County of pluro-pneumonia, age 84 years 2 months 7 days. His wife
survives at 80 years; they had lived together 60 years. Of their
six sons who survive, four are Cumberland Presbyterian ministers.
(Columbia Herald, 23 May 1873.)

WALKER, Mrs. William H. T., wife of late Major General of the
Confederate Army, died in Albany, New York, a few days since.
(The Monitor Murfreesboro, Tn, 16 Jan. 1869.)

WALL, D. B., 23, unmarried, of Williamson County was mortally wounded
in a duel at Norfolk Landing, Miss., 28 miles below Memphis; he was
able to fire and mortally would his assailant, a negro named Reed.
(Columbia Herald, 14 Aug. 1891.)

WALL, Colonel T. N., and Colonel Lee Willis of the Texas Legion, were
seated pleasantly in shade at fort near Vicksburg.Miss., when a
shell exploded in their midst, killing them and literally blowing
them to fragments. (Nashville Dispatch, 12 June 1863.)

WALLACE, Aden, of Iuka, Mississippi, was seized with lockjaw a few
days ago and died. (Memphis Daily Appeal, 6 Dec. 1869.)

WALLACE. Fund being raised at Huntsville, Alabama, for disinterring
and bringing home the remains of Edwin Wallace, Esquire, killed at
Parker's Cross Roads in 1863; a true soldier. (Memphis Avalanche,
12 Dec. 1866.)

WALLACE, James, of Nashville, was shot Thursday last by a man named
Tolles; the ball went through the brain; Tolles says it was in
self-defense. (Weekly Times, Murfreesboro, Tn, 19 Sept. 1840.)

WALLACE. Constable J. E. Shemwell of Stewart County attached a raft of
logs belonging to James Wallace to satisfy a judgment. Wallace took
an axe to Shemwell, who drew pistol and shot Wallace, who died in
two hours. He was survived by a wife and seven children. Much
feeling among relatives and more trouble is expected. (Maury
Democrat, Columbia, Tn, 27 March 1890.)

WALLACE, Capt. Jones, of an Ohio Regiment, was mortally wounded at
Fredericksburg. His fiance Henrietta Schneider of Canton, Ohio,
went to him. His leg was amputated and they were married after the
operation. He died and was taken to Canton for burial; 2,000
people attended his funeral. (Nashville Dispatch, 7 Feb. 1863.)

WALLACE, General, was wounded about 4 p.m. Sunday the first day of the
battle at Shiloh; in confusion of retreat, he was left behind on
the battlefield and lay there for 20 hours before he was discovered.
He was found in an insensible condition and was conveyed to
Savannah, Tn, where he was cared for by his wife who had arrived
at Pittsburg Landing on Sunday. He lingered until 7 p.m. Thursday
when he died in state of consciousness. (Nashville Dispatch,
23 April 1862.) The body of General William H. L. Wallace, killed
in battle near Pittsburg Landing, has arrived at his home in
Illinois. (Nashville Dispatch, 20 April 1862.)

WALLACE, General Lew, has realized over $190,000 from the sales of
"Ben Hur." (Florence, Ala., Times, 23 Jan. 1892.)

WALLENSPIEL, barkeeper at the Galt House, was killed last December
by Dr. W. P. Headington, surgeon in the Confederate Army, in St.
Louis. The doctor was known as "Foot Wetmore." (Nashville
Republican Banner, 24 Jan. 1867.)

WALLER, S. L., has been appointed administrator of the estate of
Catharine Watson, deceased. (Nashville Republican Banner, 21 June
1868.)

WALSH, James O'Hanlon, 14 years 3 months, son of Thomas H. and Rose
Walsh, died on the 6th. (Nashville Republican Banner, 9 Dec. 1868.)

WALSH, Jeremiah, was shot and killed by Capps, the bugler of the 10th
Michigan Volunteers, by mistake. (Nashville Dispatch, 11 July
1863.)

WALSH, Thomas, Catholic priest, died very suddenly of apoplexy during a service on the 15th at Cairo, Illinois. (Nashville Dispatch, 19 March 1863.)

WALTHALL, City Marshal Robert, died at his home in Clarksville on Sunday; universally popular. (Erin Review, 3 June 1882.)

WALTHAM, Brigadier General, of Mississippi was killed at Chickamauga. (Nashville Dispatch, 26 Sept. 1863.)

WALTINGTON, H. S., was killed by W. T. White at Aberdeen, Mississippi, a few days ago. (Nashville Daily Gazette, 25 Sept. 1852.)

WALTON, Robert J., died 17 Dec. 1862, funeral at First Presbyterian Church. (Nashville Daily Union, 18 Dec. 1862.)

WARD, Capt. A. E., was killed when the steamer Quaker exploded at Beard's Mill on Willow Bayou near New Orleans on Tuesday; he was buried in Burthood's graveyard near the place where the accident happened. (Memphis Daily Appeal, 31 July 1868.)

WARD, Allen, negro charged with burning Thomas Bond's home near Thompson Station, was taken by 30 masked men and shot. (Whig and Tribune, 12 July 1873.)

WARD. News wanted on Major Frank B. Ward of Anderson's Cavalry, who was among the seriously wounded in skirmish December 29; he is supposed to be in a private home in Nashville; his brother wants information about him; leave word for brother at the Commercial Hotel. (Nashville Dispatch, 10 Jan. 1863; Nashville Daily Union, 10 Jan. 1863.)

WARD, Silas of Texas prisoner of war at Camp Douglas died on the 1st; he was brother of Rev. W. E. Ward of Nashville. (Nashville Dispatch, 6 July 1862.)

WARDEN, Elder C. K., 54, died six miles south of Campbell's Station in Maury County on January 31; consumption; he taught school at Campbell Station for a number of years; married Janie McCain, daughter of Hughey McCain. (Columbia Herald, 20 Feb. 1891.)

WARDSWORTH. At Harris Station near Athens, Alabama, last summer one Wardsworth seduced Miss Sue McKibbon. Her brother killed Wardsworth at Harris Station on Thursday. (Memphis Daily Appeal, 7 Dec. 1868.)

WARE, A. C., versus J. P. Ware, suit for divorce; J. P. Ware is nonresident of Tennessee. (Houston County News, 8 Jan. 1887.)

WARE, Rowland, age 102 years 2 months 2 days, died at Athens, Tn, on March 22; soldier of the American Revolution and drew a pension until the commencement of this war. (Nashville Dispatch, 23 April 1863.)

WARFORD, Mrs., 53, attempted to poison herself Monday by taking two doses of laudanum; husband is a baker; unhappy domestic relations; no hopes for her recovery. (Nashville Union and American, 24 June 1874.) Mrs. Warford died yesterday; she had taken both laudanum and morphine; she had gone from wealth to poverty; she ran away and married Warford, her father's coachman. She inherited $50,000 from her father's estate and they ran through it. They came to Nashville in 1866. Her father was Francis Smith, wealthy manufacturer of Manchester, England. Her mother still lives there at 90 years of age. (Nashville Union and American, 25 June 1874.)

WARNER, George. 3d Ohio Cavalry, private, on the 2d was arrested for desertion at Newark, Ohio; he was taken to the depot; said he would never enter the ranks alive; drew a pistol from pocket and placed it at his heart and fired. He was killed instantly. (Nashville Dispatch, 7 March 1863.)

WARNER, Sarah, 96, died near Gardner, Tn; widow of Major Mears Warner; at 50 she gave birth to a son who lived 16 months. (Memphis Daily Appeal, 25 Sept. 1870.)

WARNER, William, train-boy on L & N, was killed Monday at a water station this side of Louisville; his head came in contact with a water-tank. (Nashville Dispatch, 7 Oct. 1863.)

WARREN, Elijah E., died 26 Dec. 1884 at Murfreesboro, Rutherford County, Tn.; married Maria Oliver, the daughter of Smith and Sarah Ann (Sanders) Oliver, on 29 April 1858 in Rutherford County, Tn. Maria Oliver was born 18 March 1835. (From family records of Polly C. Warren, Columbia, Tn.)

WARREN, Goodlow, died in this county Wednesday last; worthy and respected citizen. (West Tennessean, Paris, Tn, Henry County, 5 Sept. 1835.)

WARREN, John, deceased; administrator's notice published by Thomas Garner. (Central Monitor, Murfreesboro, 6 Sept. 1834.)

WARREN, John P., of the 2d Tennessee, CSA, died recently in Murfreesboro. (Nashville Union and American, 3 March 1873.)

WARREN, Miss Letitia, died August 17, near Sulphur Spring, sister-in-law of William Miller, (Columbia Herald, 21 Aug. 1891.)

WARREN, Georgetta Baxter, infant daughter of P. G. and N. L. Warren, died June 30. (Nashville Daily Gazette, 4 July 1852.)

WARREN, Peterson Gurley, known as "Uncle Peter," Nashville printer, died Sunday. He was born 1812 in North Carolina and moved to Rutherford County at the age of 8 years; apprentice to Mr. Sublett in Murfreesboro; went twice to Mexico, first time in Col. W. B. Campbell's regiment and the second time under Colonel Whitfield, and he was severely wounded in Mexican War. He was stabbed a few years ago by a printer called Col. Heard. He was buried at Todd's Knob burying ground. On Friday a son, age 13, died of brain fever and a daughter now lies at the point of death. (Nashville Union and American, 28 July 1874.)

WARREN, S. G., died Wednesday in Hickman County while at work in the field; Methodist. (Columbia Herald and Mail, 24 March 1876.)

WARREN, Mrs. Susan, 72, relict of late Thomas S. Warren, died January 15 in Shelbyville, Tn; native of Nashville; daughter of John and Elizabeth Synder. (Nashville Dispatch, 29 March 1863.)

WASH, Lucien, Esquire, formerly of Nashville graduate of University of Nashville in 1850, died in his 25th year in Cumberland County, Kentucky. He was married only four times. (Nashville Daily Gazette, 7 July 1852.)

WASH, Captain, a noted rebel in 1862, went into Greasy Cove, Washington County, with a squad of guerrillas and shot an old esteemed Union man named Tinker; seven balls passed through the old man's body. Wash, forgetful of the crime, returned to Jonesboro, the county seat, last week. He was promptly arrested and will be tried. (Nashville Daily Union, 15 June 1865.)

WASHBURN, General Peter T., Governor of Vermont, died at his home Woodstock, Vermont, on the 7th. (Memphis Daily Appeal, 12 Feb. 1870.)

WASHINGTON, George, nephew of the great Washington, died a few days ago in Wilmington, Ohio. The remains were taken to Prince Edward County, Ga., for interment. (Memphis Avalanche, 2 Dec. 1866.)

WASHINGTON, Hon. John N., grandson of General George Washington's
uncle Lewis, died at Newbern, N. C., last week; 1841 graduate of
Yale University. (Memphis Daily Appeal, 5 March 1869.)

WASHINGTON. Washington, Georgia was first place to be named for the
Father of His Country. (Maury Democrat, 15 June 1893.) A visitor
to Mt. Vernon had a fight with the keeper because he wasn't shown
the tree George Washington cut down. (Memphis Daily Appeal, 27
Feb. 1870.)

George Washington's nearest living kin is Mrs. Fanny Washington
Finch, a great-grand niece. She is a tall, majestic woman and in
features resembles the portrait of her distinguished relative.
(Florence, Ala., Times, 19 Sept. 1891.)

Fredericksburg, Va., Mar. 2 - Within the precincts of this city is
the grave of the mother of George Washington. The site of the old
farm house in which she died is also in this vicinity, and the
ground is everywhere sacred with historic memories. Hither Washington came on his way to his first inauguration as President to bid
his mother a last farewell, just before her death. Pilgrim tourists
have come here to view the spot, and the propriety of erecting
suitable monuments over the ruins of the old homestead and the
grave has again and again been discussed, but thus far without
practical results.

It will shock the whole country to learn that the grave of Washington's mother is likely to be sold at auction next week. During the
administration of President Jackson, the corner-stone of a monument
was laid but it has never been completed. Messrs. Colbert and
Kirtley, real estate agents of this city, will offer for sale at
Washington March 5, at public auction, twelve acres of land on which
is the tomb of Mary, the mother of Washington. Will the patriotic
women of America save this sacred spot and keep it from falling into
the hands of speculators? (Maury Democrat, 7 March 1889.)

WASHINGTON, Thomas, died on the 18th; born in Brunswick County,
Virginia on 1 Jan. 1788; lived here 50 years. (Nashville Dispatch,
22 Dec. 1863.) For many years head of the Nashville bar. (Nashville Dispatch, 19 Dec. 1863.)

WATERS, Warren, of Monticello, Georgia, set upon by Henry and Dick
Watson and was literally cut to pieces while on the way to church;
he had assaulted their mother. (Maury Democrat, Columbia, Tn,
11 July 1889.)

WATKINS, David and Annie, who lived together as man and wife for 57
years, died last week at Warren, Mass., and were buried in one grave.
(Memphis Daily Appeal, 20 Jan. 1870.)

WATKINS, Laura Matilda, wife of James B. Watkins, died November last in
Haywood County; native of Maury; daughter of Mr. and Mrs. Lankford,
early pioneers of West Tennessee. (Columbia Herald and Mail, 6
Feb. 1874. N.B. Item not clear if Mrs. Watkins or her husband
were native of Maury County.)

WATKINS, Virginia, sues John Watkins for divorce in Rutherford County.
(Central Monitor, Murfreesboro, 6 Sept. 1834.)

WATKINS, William, old and popular citizen, lived 2 1/2 miles north of
Mt. Pleasant, died August 1, age 75; Methodist. (Columbia Herald
and Mail, 20 Aug. 1875.)

WATKINS, William A., born 4 May 1831, died 31 March 1899 at St. Florian,
Lauderdale County, Alabama; son of Robert Watkins, born in Virginia.
He married 4 August 1853, Mary A. (Polly) Grimes, the daughter of
George and Hettie Hough Grimes. (Family records of Polly C. Warren,
Columbia, Tn.)

WATKINS, William E., 77, died on the 28th, lived 6 miles from city on
Charlotte Pike; old and respected citizen. (Nashville Dispatch,
29 Nov. 1863; Nashville Daily Union, 29 Nov. 1863.)

WATSON, Charles F., died on the 6th in New Orleans; son of Matthew and
Rebecca Watson; burial to be in Nashville. (Nashville Republican
Banner, 11 Feb. 1869.)

WATSON, Mrs. Charlotte M., wife of Samuel Watson to be buried today.
(Nashville Republican Banner, 5 Aug. 1869.) Mrs. Charlotte Morton
Watson, died 4 Aug. 1869 in Columbia; wife of Judge Samuel Watson;
mother of four children; daughter of late Marcus Morton, Governor
of Massachusetts; age 50; Episcopalian. (Nashville Republican
Banner, 8 Aug. 1869.)

WATSON, George W., well known citizen of Giles County, died last week.
(Whig and Tribune, 23 Sept. 1871.)

WATSON, Mrs., an aged lady of Knob Creek in Maury County, age 82, died
Wednesday evening. (Maury Democrat, Columbia, Tn, 22 Feb. 1894.)

WATSON, J. W., died March 22. (Columbia Herald, 15 May 1896.)

WATSON, Lewis, 72, died in Shelby County, Alabama, last week.
(Florence, Ala., Times, 9 July 1892.)

WATSON, Sydney Y., prominent lawyer of Memphis, died February 2 of
small-pox. (Nashville Dispatch, 8 Feb. 1863.)

WEAKLEY. We learn with deep regret that Col. R. L. Weakley the head
of a numerous and interesting family; was killed on Sunday night in
an encounter with a man named Bowman, who is in custody. The deed
was committed with a pistol, and the death of Col. W. was almost
instantaneous. Banner. (Maury Intelligencer, Columbia, Tn, 22 Dec.
1848.)

WEAKLEY. R. L. Weakley's fine racer Mollie Muggins died Monday night
of congestive penumonia, three years old. (Nashville Union and
American, 6 May 1874.)

WEATHERLY, James, of Phillips County, Arkansas, was killed in self
defence on the 31st ult, by Lt. J. C. Wallace of Forrest's
Cavalry. (Nashville Dispatch, 15 April 1862.)

WEATHERSPOON, Col. John, 70, died on the 14th ult. in Wayne County at
the house of William B. Ross, Esquire; old esteemed soldier of the
Revolution and participated in the Battle of King's Mountain.
(Western Weekly Review, Franklin, Tn, 14 Feb. 1840.)

WEAVER, John, 98, died in Coffee County last week. (Nashville Union
and American, 26 Jan. 1873.) John Weaver, 98, who lived five
miles south of Tullahoma, died recently. (Whig & Tribune,
Jackson, Tn, 8 Feb. 1873.)

WEAVER. The oldest living trapper in Arizona at this day is Pauline
Weaver from White County, Tn. His name is carved in the Casa
Grande, near the Pima Villages, on the Gila River, under the date
of 1832. (Monitor, Murfreesbor, Tn, 4 Nov. 1865.)

WEBB. Wanted information about the heirs of James Webb, who was
killed with Colonel Fannin at the Goliad Massacre in March 1836.
Signed, S. Engelhing, Austin County, Texas. (Maury Democrat, 29
May 1889.)

WEBB, Ridley, 65, faithful servant of Grey P. Webb fell dead a few
days ago at Williamsport. (Columbia Herald and Mail, 14 Jan. 1876.)

WEBB, Colonel, 77th Illinois, was recently killed in Louisiana; former editor of the Peoria Transcript. (Nashville Daily Union, 5 May 1864.)

WEBER, Albert M., of Madison, Wisconsin, died of consumption there on March 14; formerly worked in Nashville. (Nashville Republican Banner, 30 March 1869.)

WEBSTER, Capt. A. G., of the Federal Army was hanged at Richmond on Friday last. (Nashville Dispatch, 16 April 1863.) Capt. A. Webster has been tried and sentenced to hang April 2 in Richmond for the murder of Capt. Simpson of the Confederate Army. (Nashville Daily Union, 31 March 1863.) Name is given as Capt. Alphonso Webster. (Nashville Dispatch, 30 April 1863.)

WEBSTER, C. P., of Nashville has died; lived in Clarksville for several years. (Clarksville Jeffersonian, 15 Oct. 1851.)

WEBSTER, Col. Fletcher, who died of wounds received in Virginia, was the oldest son of Daniel Webster. His younger brother was in army in Mexico and died in service there. His sister Mrs. Appleton died some years ago. There is none left of the blood of "Webster." (Nashville Dispatch, 16 Sept. 1862.)

WEBSTER, James, supposed to be the last of the Waterloo veterans in Toronto, died on Tuesday. (Columbia Herald and Mail, 27 July 1877.)

WEBSTER, Mrs. Jennie, died at home of her brother Gid Polk and buried at Concord Cemetery. (Maury Democrat, Columbia, Tn, 23 Aug. 1894.)

WEBSTER, Timothy was hung as a spy in Richmond on the 29th ult. (Nashville Dispatch, 8 May 1862.)

WEED, A. F., died. (Nashville Republican Banner, 24 April 1870.)

WEIDENBACKER, Andrew F., 30 years 10 months, died on the 21st. (Nashville Republican Banner, 22 Feb. 1871.)

WELCH, Daniel, master's mate of Chicago, died on passage of the Rattler on the Tallahatchie River of climate disorder. (Nashville Dispatch, 27 March 1863.)

WELCH, Mrs. Henrietta Armstrong, died July 2 near Chestnut Hill. (Nashville Republican Banner, 8 July 1870.)

WELLER, Ben S., one of the oldest citizens of Nashville, died in Nashville on the 12th of heart disease. (Whig and Tribune, Jackson, Tn, 21 June 1873.)

WELLS, George, an orphan boy of this neighborhood (Williamsport), died of putrid sore throat Saturday morning. (Columbia Herald and Mail, 29 Oct. 1875.)

WELLS, Sam Watkins, infant son of George W. and Catherine Wells, age 2 months 5 days, died on the 18th. (Nashville Union and American, 19 Aug. 1874.)

WELLS, Rufus, prominent citizen of Lincoln County, was found dead near Fayetteville last week; found dead in the road. (Nashville Union and American, 18 Aug. 1874.)

WELLS, William H., 81, once a well-to-do farmer of Williamson County, but ruined by dissipation, died suddenly while riding along from Lewisburg Pike in a wagon last week. (Whig and Tribune, 24 Feb. 1872.)

WELLS, J., Company D, 19th Alabama Infantry, CSA, prisoner of war, died of injuries received in falling of the stairs and floors at the Convalescent Barracks on Tuesday. (Nashville Daily Union, 1 Oct. 1863.)

WELLS, Sgt. Noah, Company A, 4th Tennessee Cavalry, was killed about
29 Feb. 1864 in Mississippi on an expedition out of Memphis; was
from Greene County and had been imprisoned once for bridge burning.
(Nashville Daily Union, ___ March 1864.)

WENDEL, Mrs. Lucy A., wife of Col. W. H. D. Wendel, daughter of L. P.
C. and R. C. Burford of DeSoto County, Miss., died on the 5th in
Memphis. (Memphis Daily Appeal, 7 Feb. 1870.)

WENDELL, D. D., one of the oldest citizens of Murfreesboro, died on the
29th ult. (Nashville Union and American, 2 May 1873.) David D.
Wendle, Esquire, age 63, died April 29 in Murfreesboro. (Whig and
Tribune, Jackson, Tn, 17 May 1873.)

WENDELL, Mrs. David D., died in Murfreesboro recently. (Nashville
Union and American, 23 March 1873.) Mrs. Sarah Wendle, 58, wife of
David D. Wendle of Murfreesboro died on the 18th. (Whig and
Tribune, Jackson, Tn, 29 March 1873.)

WENDELL, Susan Amanda, daughter of David D. and Sarah Wendell, age 1
year 6 months 17 days, died at Murfreesboro on the 22d. (Nashville
Daily Gazette, 28 Sept. 1852.)

WENDELL, Mrs. Jane C., died Feb. 14 at Murfreesboro, wife of Dr. R. W.
Wendell and eldest daughter of the Hon. E. H. Ewing. (Nashville
Republican Banner, 15 Feb. 1871.)

WENTWORTH, Long John, of Chicago, flatters himself that he is the last
survivor of the battle of Thomas on 13 Oct. 1813 where Tecumseh was
killed. (Erin Review, 17 Dec. 1881.)

WESLEY, John. John Wesley's Church. Christ Church, the oldest church
in Georgia, founded by John Wesley before he promulgated the
Methodist faith, burned almost to the ground May 22 at Savannah.
The building contained all the records of Savannah and practically
all of Georgia since 1825 and the building was a total loss; considered the mother of the Episcopal Churches in Georgia. The first
church was built 1743 but not completed until 1750, and in 1785
was destroyed by fire. It was rebuilt in same plan 1803, and in
1804 almost demolished by a hurricane and not rebuilt until 1810.
This was torn down and in 1838 the cornerstone laid to the present
church and completed 1840. It was founded by the Rev. Henry Herbert,
who came over from England with Oglethorpe. John Wesley was its
third rector and chaplain to the colonists. (Columbia Herald, 28
May 1897.)

WEST, James P., deceased, estate is insolvent; M. V. West, administrator.
(Nashville Republican Banner, 20 May 1870.)

WEST, Mary, 32, died in Nashville on the 5th; the funeral held at the
home of her mother Martha Miller in West Nashville. (Nashville
Dispatch, 7 Nov. 1862.)

WEST, Mrs. Mary R., wife of the Rev. J. B. West, once minister of
First Methodist Church in Columbia, died in Nashville and taken to
Clarksville for burial. (Columbia Herald, 8 Jan. 1897.)

WEST, Mr., was killed in Tallahatchie County, Miss., a few weeks ago
by C. E. Mooney and the government offers reward for Mooney.
(Memphis Daily Appeal, 28 Feb. 1870.)

WESTBROOK, Thornton of Williamson County, died recently. (Whig and
Tribune, Jackson, Tn, 17 Feb. 1872.)

WESTERVELT, Pirden Henry, 2 months 1 day, son of Dr. P. A. and Ann W.
Westervelt, died June 6 of dropsy. (Nashville Dispatch, 8 June 1862.)

WESTMORELAND, Sallie, daughter of Fisher Westmoreland of Mason's Depot, age 21, died at Pulaski of consumption. (Whig and Tribune, 19 April 1873.)

WESTON, Mrs. E. T., died at Greenfield, New Hampshire on July 5 at the age of 104 years 5 months. (Erin Review, 15 July 1882.)

WETMORE, Jennie Elise, 4 years died on August 29; daughter of M. W. and J. E. Wetmore. (Nashville Daily Gazette, 2 Sept. 1852.)

WHALEN, Mrs. Lucy, 53, niece of the Mormon prophet Joseph Smith, died at Burlington, Iowa. (Maury Democrat, 27 Oct. 1892.)

WHARTON, Elvira, daughter of Robert and Sarah Wharton, died on the 7th. (Nashville Republican Banner, 8 July 1868.)

WHARTON, Jesse D., of Hagerstown, Maryland, rebel prisoner, was shot in Washington, D. C., by a sentinel, who could not stand the repeated epithets Wharton called him. (Nashville Dispatch, 26 April 1862.)

WHEAT, Capt. John Thomas, who fell at Shiloh, remains accompanied by his parents the Rev. and Mrs. Wheat, reached Nashville Wednesday. (Memphis Avalanche, 25 May 1867.)

WHEAT, Major, of Louisiana battalion, who fell in battle at Gaines Mill on the 30th ult., funeral held from Monumental Church, Richmond, Va. Buried in Hollywood Cemetery. (Nashville Dispatch, 24 Feb. 1863.)

WHEELER, Rev. John, D.D., 64, died at Burlington, Vt., on the 16th; president of the University of Vermont. (Nashville Dispatch, 27 April 1862.)

WHEELER, Thomas H., son of General Joe Wheeler, and Lt. Kirkpatrick dorwned last week. (Columbia Herald, 16 Sept. 1898.)

WHEELER, Mrs. Sallie, 66, died 18 Jan. 1864. (Nashville Daily Union, 19 Jan. 1864.)

WHEELER, William C., private in Neel's Tennessee Regiment, CSA, died of smallpox on the 12th ult. in military prison at Alton, Illinois. (Nashville Dispatch, 16 Sept. 1863.)

WHELESS, Mrs. Ellen, wife of William T. Wheless of Nashville, daughter of W. B. Shapard, died at Cleveland, Tn, on Feb. 17 of inflammation of the stomach. (Nashville Dispatch, 5 March 1863.)

WHELESS, General John F., died in Nashville yesterday; born 2 Feb. 1839 in Montgomery County; his parents died when he was six and he moved to Nashville soon afterward; brave Confederate soldier, wounded several times and was left for dead on the battlefield at Perryville. (Progressive Democrat, Clarksville, Tn, 12 Aug. 1891.)

WHELESS, Percy, 1 year 3 months, son of John F. and Fannie A. Wheless of Nashville, died in Fayetteville on the 26th. (Nashville Republican Banner, 28 Aug. 1870.)

WHITE, Mrs. Ann, died yesterday in Edgefield. (Nashville Republican Banner, 23 April 1870.)

WHITE, Andrew Jackson, who murdered James T. Clardy near Charlotte, Tn., in January was to have been hanged on the 26th at Charlotte; he is 22. Clardy was a bachelor, aged 65 to 70. The case has gone to the Supreme Court. (Erin Review, 10 Sept. 1881.)

WHITE, Eddie, 13, died of lockjaw on July 6; son of Sumner White of Maury County. (Columbia Herald, 11 July 1873.)

WHITE, H. A., of near Kingston Springs, was murdered 3 Dec. 1866 by
John Patterson who fled. Patterson returned a few nights ago and
was arrested. (Nashville Republican Banner, 23 June 1869.)
H. A. White of Kingston Springs lost a horse and a man named
Patterson was suspected; Patterson clubbed White to death and then
made his escape. (Memphis Avalanche, 8 Dec. 1866.)

WHITE, H. L., of Hickman County, noted troutline fisherman, died
Friday in Centerville. (Columbia Herald and Mail, 25 Aug. 1876.)

WHITE, Mrs. Isaac B., died suddenly on Saturday. (Columbia Herald,
15 Oct. 1869.)

WHITE. On Wednesday evening the 13th inst., Mr. and Mrs. James M.
White celebrated their golden wedding. James M. White was born
2 March 1802, and his wife was born 17 Aug. 1806, and they were
married 13 Sept. 1821. They have 16 children, 12 boys and 4 girls;
lost three children by death; there was present one person who was
at the wedding fifty years ago, Richard Johnson. Mrs. Jas. R.
Shelton, who was one of the selected waiters 50 years ago, but
who was prevented by sickness from being present, was also present
on this occasion, and gave the loan of a table cloth over 50 years
old, upon which to spread the supper. (Columbia Herald, 1 Sept.
1871.)

WHITE, J. Beverly, son of St. Ledger (Gosh) White, killed his wife and
himself about May 10 in Houston, Texas, by shooting. She was
getting a divorce. (Maury Democrat, 17 May 1894.)

WHITE, J. H., of Milton, Tn, committed suicide by shooting himself in
the head last week; he was to have been married soon. (Columbia
Herald, 11 Nov. 1870.)

WHITE, Dr. James D., "murdered" four miles northeast of Lebanon on
Wednesday by one of his own slaves with an axe. He was in bed with
his wife at the time. The slave attempted to murder the small son
and wounded him severly. Mrs. White died of her wounds and there is
little hope for Dr. White's recovery. (Nashville Daily Union, 24
Jan. 1865.) Later his name is found as A. D. White and he was
reported as still being alive but his son will be crippled for life
as his spinal column was badly injured. (Nashville Daily Union,
27 Jan. 1865.)

WHITE, James Thomas, 17, died of bronchitis. (Maury Democrat, Columbia,
Tn, 20 May 1886.)

WHITE, Honorable John J., of Gallatin, died a few days ago; had lived
to a "green old age"; member of the Tennessee Constitutional
Convention. (Nashville Daily Union, 14 April 1863.)

WHITE, Honorable John J., distinguished lawyer and onetime judge, died
on the 12th in Gallatin; upwards of 70 years of age. (Nashville
Dispatch, 14 April 1863.)

WHITE, John Campbell, soldier, 28th Indiana, was killed by John
Williams, private in the 45th Infantry, in a negro bagnio near
Ash Barracks from a blow on the head. (Nashville Republican
Banner, 11 Dec. 1868.)

WHITE, Dr. J. P., resolution of respect on his death; member of the
2d East Tennessee Volunteer Infantry, died of wounds received at
Murfreesboro. (Nashville Daily Union, 4 March 1863.)

WHITE LOON, age 107, died recently at Roanoke, about the last of the
Miami Indians, once very powerful in this section. He was born 1769
where Peru, Ind., is at present situated, when the famous chief
Richardville, the Shawnee, was in command. He remembered Tecumseh
distinctly and recalled the building for Fort Wayne, which he
always called Kekionga. He knew only the languages of the Miamir. He
lived for many years on the "Resevers," 16 miles west of Fort Wayne

in Lafayette Township. From Fort Wayne Sentinel. (Columbia Herald and Mail, 10 Nov. 1876.)

WHITE, Mrs., died last Thursday at Park Station and buried at Friendship Church at Culleoka. (Maury Democrat, 3 June 1889.)

WHITE, Molly, who keeps a house on Sumner Street, near the cemetery, Lucinda Lowry, Mollie Trainor, have all been charged with disorderly conduct. The house is in bad repute, and soldiers and citizens are seen at all hours passing into the house. She was fined $10. (Nashville Daily Union, 24 May 1865.)

WHITE, Mr., was stabbed in Hardin County three weeks ago by Monroe Wyrick, who was recently tried in Savannah and got three weeks. Wyrick was raised in Lewis County. (Columbia Herald and Mail, 1 Feb. 1878.)

WHITE, Mrs., of Maury County, who lives 10 miles from Spring Hill, gave birth yesterday to four male children, weighing 23 pounds. She is 22 and has been married three years. (Memphis Daily Appeal, 31 Aug. 1868.)

WHITE, Robert Gardner, infant son of Robert L. and Rosalie W. White, died on the 3d of brain fever. (Nashville Dispatch, 4 Nov. 1862.)

WHITE, Mrs. Reuben, was buried Saturday in the Williamsport Cemetery. (Columbia Herald and Mail, 31 March 1876.) Letitia S. White, age 54, died 23 March 1876. (Columbia Herald and Mail, 7 April 1876.)

WHITE, Mrs. Susan A., native of Maury County, died near Paris, Tn, on 2 Sept. 1871. (Columbia Herald, 15 Sept. 1871.)

WHITE, Tom, remembered by many of our citizens as a school teacher and barber, died Wednesday at Macon, Miss. He was at one time the circuit court clerk of Noxubee County. (Columbia Herald and Mail, 4 May 1877.)

WHITE, Thomas, postmaster at Campbell Station, died on the 13th at the age of 67; born 22 Nov. 1827; for 13 years had been merchant and postmaster and station agent. (Maury Democrat, 15 June 1893.)

WHITE, Thomas B., died 1854 in Davidson County, leaving a will. His widow Sally White and his next of kin, two sisters, engaged in a lawsuit and a decision was finally reached in 1871. (Nashville Republican Banner, 4 Jan. 1871.)

WHITE, Miss Mattie, 15, daughter of Mrs. Dr. Thomas C. White of Pulaski, was burned to death last night when a kerosene lamp exploded. (Nashville Union and American, 1 Oct. 1874.)

WHITE, Dr. Alfred H., died in Giles County on the 22d inst.; funeral at Brick Church. (Columbia Herald, 29 March 1872.)

WHITE, Thomas C., resolution of respect on his death published by the Tennessee Lodge No. 1, I.O.O.F. (Nashville Daily Union, 12 Feb. 1863.)

WHITE, William, of Memphis Transfer Company, was so severly injured by a recent accident on the Mississippi and Tennessee Railroad at Nonconnah Creek, that he died yesterday after many days of intense suffering. (Nashville Republican Banner, 19 Jan. 1871.)

WHITE, William, 78, of Park Station, is very sick and cannot live long. (Maury Democrat, 27 May 1889.)

WHITE, William, was murdered near Eagleville on the 20th of last month; J. N. Puckett has been arrested. (Nashville Union and American, 20 March 1874.)

WHITE, William, born 12 Jan. 1800, Jackson County, Tn, lived in Mc-
Minnville until the fall of 1862, died 10 Dec. 1863; president of
Burk's Bank. (Nashville Daily Union, 11 Dec. 1863.)

WHITE, Mrs. William, died on the 22d at the late residence of Richard
Finch on Leiper's Creek in Maury County. (Columbia Herald and Mail,
1 Dec. 1876.)

WHITELEY, Nathan of Covington, Georgia, is 102 years as shown by a
record in his family Bible; as hale as a man of 60. (Erin Review,
17 Dec. 1881.)

WHITESIDE, Milton, 66, died Wednesday at Isom. (Columbia Herald and
Mail, 1 June 1877.)

WHITFIELD, Capt. Edward, was shot and killed on the streets of Memphis
yesterday by S. A. Coran; son of T. E. Whitfield; age 28; buried
Elmwood Cemetery. (Memphis Daily Appeal, 10 Jan. 1869.) 200 men
accompanied his body to the grave. (Memphis Daily Appeal, 11 Jan.
1869.)

WHITFIELD AND Bender, noted horse thieves, both aged about 24, both of
Memphis, were hanged by a mob at Raleigh. (Memphis Daily Appeal,
1 Aug. 1868.)

WHITING, James, Sr., colored, to be buried today. (Nashville Republican Banner, 13 July 1869.)

WHITINGHAM, Henry, bookbinder, died of heart attack on Broad near
Vine; his last word was "Locust," which is the name of the street
where he lived; wife and two daughters survive; originally from New
York. (Nashville Republican Banner, 26 Jan. 1868.)

WHITLEY, Samuel, of Henderson County, on Wednesday threw his two
young children in a well and jumped in after them. Terrible shrieks
were heard, but they drowned. He was rescued, but in a critical
condition. Insanity is hereditary in the family; he is brother-
in-law of Col. John M. Stone of Iuka, Miss., one of the bravest men
that did service for the lost cause. (Memphis Daily Appeal, 20
Dec. 1869.)

WHITLOW, Solomon, 21, died in Madison County on the 28th; Mexican War
soldier. (West Tennessee Whig, 4 May 1849.)

WHITNEY, Major General, rebel, died at Governor's Island, New York on
March 10. (Nashville Daily Union, 11 March 1865.)

WHITTAKER. The mother of Walker Whittaker, Esquire, of Turkey Creek,
Maury County, died last week at an advanced age. (Columbia Herald
and Mail, 8 Oct. 1875.)

WHITTAKER, Mrs., of Fayetteville, on returning home after a couple of
days on a bridal tour, fell dead as she descended from the
carriage. (Memphis Avalanche, 20 Oct. 1867.)

WHITTEN, F. M., was shot 4 June 1889. (Maury Democrat, 25 July 1895.)
James Kelley was arrested in Alabama for the murder of Fernando
Whitten of Wayne County and brought to the jail in Columbia. In
1889, Kelley and one Brown were arrested for illicit distilling
whiskey and they thought Whitten led officers to the still. Whitten
was called to the door and shot. Brown was arrested in Arkansas.
Kelley has been brought here until the new jail at Lawrenceburg
is completed. (Maury Democrat, Columbia, Tn, 30 May 1895.)
On 27 May 1889 Revenue Officer C. C. Tansel, George Shaw, J. B.
Davis, and J. G. Haggard raided a wildcat still in Wayne County,
belonging to Jim Kelley, Jim Brown, Jack Miller, and Thomas
Wilson. The still was destroyed. It was said that F. M. Whitten
led them to the place and on the fourth night Whitten was called

to his door and shot. The men disappeared. Brown and Wilson were
captured in the Choctaw Nation. Brown confessed. It took six
years but all have been captured and will be tried. (Maury
Democrat, 20 June 1895.)

WHITTHORNE, Dr. A. J., druggist and doctor of Pulaski, died last Friday
in Pulaski; brother of W. C. and W. J. Whitthorne of Columbia.
(Columbia Herald, 15 Sept. 1871.)

WHITTIER, Mrs., is the oldest lady in Shelby County, Tn; came here
1811. (Memphis Daily Appeal, 28 Oct. 1869.)

WHITWORTH, Mrs. Ann, 74, died October 3 in Sumner County; mother of the
Honorable James Whitworth. (Nashville Dispatch, 6 Oct. 1863.)
She was born 1790 in Virginia and came with her parents to Barren
County, Ky; at 18 married James Whitworth and moved to Sumner County.
She had been a widow for 35 years. (Nashville Dispatch, 7 Oct.
1863.)

WHITWORTH, Abe, formerly of Williamsport in Maury County, died near the
Tennessee River recently. (Columbia Herald and Mail, 29 Oct. 1875.)

WHORLEY, Edward, age 3, son of Lewis and Augusta C. Whorley, died on the
14th. (Nashville Republican Banner, 16 Jan. 1868.)

WIGGINS, Acting Master, brother of Capt. Wiggin of the gunboat Kinsman,
mortally wounded and died in New Orleans at St. James Hospital;
wounded in fight on Teche. (Nashville Dispatch, 14 March 1863.)

WILCHER, Thomas, Federal soldier, killed on picket duty near Sparta,
Tn, on 22 Feb. 1864; Company G, 5th Tennessee Cavalry. (Nashville
Daily Union, __ Feb. 1864.)

WILDER, General John T., who fired the first hostile shot into
Chattanooga from Stringer's Ridge in 1864, has been elected Mayor
of Chattanooga. (Columbia Herald, 24 Nov. 1871.)

WILD MAN. Walker County, Georgia, in the vicinity of Chattanooga and
as far south as Pond Springs is all torn up over the reappearance of
the celebrated wildman of Lookout. He was seen a few days since and
he is a most remarkable being. His hair and beard are described as
flowing to the waist, his finger and toe-nails are long, giving
his hands and feet the resemblance of claws; he wears trunks of
bearskin with a bearskin robe thrown over his shoulders. He carried
an ugly bludgeon and avoids coming in contact with anybody. The
timid people are greatly alarmed and there is little traveling about
at night though he is generally believed to be harmless. This
strange creature has been haunting the caves and fastnesses of
Lockout Mountain and elevations in lower East Tennessee for years
and nothing is known of his identity. He has never been known to
harm anybody and there has been no occasion to arrest him. He is
said to now occupy a cave near Pond Spring, Georgia. (Maury
Democrat, 14 March 1889.)

WILEMAN, Major, of the 18th Kentucky, wounded at Chickamauga, returned
home to recover and was taken from his house at Pemberton County,
Kentucky, on Monday, stripped of his clothing, tied to a tree and
shot. Five of the murderers have been caught. (Nashville Dispatch,
9 Oct. 1863.)

WILES, James, charged with the murder of John N. Morgan in the fall
of 1862, has finally been brought to trial. (Nashville Republican
Banner, 29 Jan. 1868.) James Wiles found not guilty of the murder
of John Morgan in Sept. 1862. (Nashville Republican Banner,
1 Feb. 1868.)

WILEY, Hamilton, of Lincoln County, was baiting a fishing piece in
Elk River when he fell in and drowned. (Rutherford Telegraph,
Murfreesboro, 10 March 1849.)

WILEY, Mrs. Mary, 81, sister of Losson Berry, the oldest printer in the
United States, died near Hampshire, Maury County, on the 23d.
(Columbia Herald, 31 March 1871.)

WILEY, Thomas H., died December 2 in Nashville; native of Georgia and
later of Washington, D. C.; 70 years. (Nashville Daily Union, 4
Dec. 1863.)

WILHITE, John, old and valuable citizen of Bedford County, died last
week of congestion of the brain. (Whig & Tribune, 9 Sept. 1871.)

WILHOITE, Mrs. Betty, 49, died 23 Nov. 1899; Cumberland Presbyterian;
buried at Murfreesboro; wife of James Wilhoite. (Williamson County
News, 30 Nov. 1899.)

WILKERSON, Henry A., son of James F. and America Wilkerson of
Nashville, died near Helena, Ark., on the 8th; funeral to be held
today in Nashville. (Nashville Republican Banner, 11 Nov. 1870.)

WILKES, Ann Eliza, died November 2; buried Zion Cemetery. (Columbia
Herald and Mail, 9 Nov. 1877.)

WILKES, Nathaniel Robards, born July 1833 in North Carolina, died 10
April 1896 in Columbia; moved here 1837; educated at old Jackson
College; admitted to the bar 17 March 1856; died of complication of
diseases; married (1) sister of Vance Thompson and (2) Mrs. Nannie
Baird. (Daily Herald, Columbia, Tn, 17 April 1896.)

WILKINS, Mrs. James, aged, is very sick. (Columbia Herald, 14 Feb.
1873.)

WILKINSON, Captain, sutler of a Michigan regiment, was shot and killed
by bushwhackers near Franklin last Wednesday. (Nashville Dispatch,
11 July 1862.)

WILKINSON, Mrs. Mattie, widow of Robert Wilkinson of West Lauderdale
County, Alabama, died at Pulaski, Tn, last week buried near Waterloo; daughter of late Horace Summerhill; sister of Mrs. Rebecca Amis
of Pulaski. (Florence, Ala., Times, 12 Sept. 1891.)

WILKINSON, W. H., Justice of the Peace in Davidson County, died March
21 of pneumonia. (Whig and Tribune, Jackson, Tn, 12 April 1873.)
William Henry Wilkinson, Esquire, died in South Nashville yesterday
of pneumonia, age 61; held many offices, had been city marshall,
recorder, and member of board of aldermen. (Nashville Union and
American, 22 March 1873.)

WILLETT, Miss Sallie Wilson, died 25 May 1891 of consumption, buried at
Springville, daughter of David L. and Jane A. Willett. (Houston
County Times, 29 May 1891.)

WILLIAMS, Anthony, colored, who outraged and murdered Miss Rene
Williams, 17, last week, has been captured; a mob took him on the
road from West Point in Lawrence County, the scene of the crime, and
one felled him with a stone, then volley after volley of shots rang
out. A bon-fire was built and the carcas was burned to ashes. She
was beautiful young lady and was to have been married August 7 to
Will Perdue. (Columbia Herald, 23 July 1897.)

WILLIAMS, Aaron, died on Friday four miles south of Mt. Pleasant.
(Columbia Herald and Mail, 10 March 1876.)

WILLIAMS, Mrs. A. C., wife of the Rev. J. R. Williams, died Oct. 30
in Henry County of typhoid, age 49. (Whig and Tribune, Jackson,
Tn, 22 Nov. 1873.)

WILLIAMS, Andrew J., young son of Willo. Williams, died in this county
on the 20th from the effects of wounds received at the hands of one
Kimbro Sunday in a personal difficulty. (Nashville Dispatch, 22
April 1863.)

WILLIAMS. Murder in Cherokee County, Alabama. Near Cedar Bluff. On the 15th Arthur Williams of Georgia was moving to Texas and he camped two miles from Cedar Bluff on the Chattooga River. He and two children were found dead and on fire; they had been killed with an axe. Mrs. Williams was found with her left eye destroyed, her jaw broken, and her clothes on fire, but alive. The deed was committed by a bare-footed negro. (Memphis Avalanche, 27 Oct. 1866.)

Mrs. Arthur Williams died a few days after her family was killed at Cedar Bluff, Cherokee County, Alabama; the family was camped at a ferry; they were from Cass County, Georgia. (Memphis Avalanche, 12 Nov. 1866.)

WILLIAMS, Colonel, hanged at Franklin, Tn, was Lawrence Orton Williams, son of an old army officer of that name, who was killed at Cerro Gordo. He changed his name to Lawrence Williams Orton. One of the 2d Regiment Cavalry and at one time a member of General Scott's staff. The other was Lt. Dunlap of little notoriety. (Nashville Dispatch, 11 June 1863.) Two rebel officers in Federal uniforms, Colonel Williams and Lt. Peters, were arrested at Franklin inspecting the orifications at that place. They were hanged about 9 o'clock yesterday. (Nashville Dispatch, 10 June 1863.)

Lawrence Orton Williams was one of the most honorable officers in this service. He was recently married to Mrs. Lamb, formerly Miss Hamilton of Charleston. This expedition was taken on his own account. Chattanooga Rebel. (Nashville Dispatch, 20 June 1863.)

WILLIAMS, Honorable James, died of apoplexy in Austria at the home of his son-in-law, Baron Kavanaugh, Grate, Austria, Schutzenhof Villa; died on the 10th; son of Etheldred Williams of Grainger County, Tn; educated at West Point; served in Mexican War; editor of the Knoxville Post; served in General Assembly; formerly of Nashville and had brother William Williams of Nashville. (Nashville Republican Banner, 30 April 1869.)

WILLIAMS, Ed, buried another child on Tuesday, diptheria. (Columbia Herald and Mail, 29 March 1878.)

WILLIAMS, Emily Polk, age 1 year 2 months, daughter of J. Minnick and Emily P. Williams, died at Minnick Grange on the 27th. (Nashville Dispatch, 29 Oct. 1862.)

WILLIAMS, Fanny Mary, wife of Henry P. Williams, died January 24 in Kentucky; sister of F. M. Brannan of Nashville. (Nashville Republican Banner, 26 Jan. 1869.)

WILLIAMS, Mrs. Fannie Champlin, 19, wife of Henry O. Williams, died Oct. 21. (Memphis Avalanche, 4 Nov. 1866.)

WILLIAMS, George and George Lyles were hung in Murfreesboro on the 18th for the murder of a Mr. Weaver at the same time and on the same scaffold; they were well-known desperadoes and 5,000 people witnessed the hanging. (Nashville Dispatch, 19 June 1863.)

WILLIAMS, Rev. J. C. R., of Hampshire was bitten two weeks ago by a mad dog and is having symptoms of hydrophobia. He has spasms every hour or so. (Columbia Herald, 10 Nov. 1871.)

WILLIAMS, infant of Mr. and Mrs. Jake Williams died today and buried in Rose Hill Cemetery. (Columbia Herald, 20 Dec. 1899.)

WILLIAMS, John, late of the old 15th Tennessee Regiment to be buried today in Memphis. (Memphis Daily Appeal, 7 May 1869.)

WILLIAMS, John, of a North Carolina regiment, died a few days ago in a private residence in Louisville; he was wounded at Perryville. (Nashville Dispatch, 1 Feb. 1863; Nashville Daily Union, 1 Feb. 1863.)

WILLIAMS. Information wanted. - In Sept. 1814 Major John Williams, who occasionally acts as a Baptist preacher, moved from Martin County, North Carolina, to the western country, where to is not known. William A. Williams, an only son, who was thought to have died at sea, but has recently returned to the United States after a long confinement in the dungeon of Spain, is anxious to find out his residence and takes this method to apprize him of his existence, and that he is now at the house of Mr. Claiborne Goodman, about 14 miles from Nashville, where he will remain for a while in hopes of hearing from his father. Sept. 12. (Town Gazette and Farmers Register, Clarksville, Tn, 4 Oct. 1819.)

WILLIAMS, Colonel Kitt, of Memphis was killed at the battle of Shiloh. (Nashville Dispatch, 30 April 1862.)

WILLIAMS, Lizzie, daughter of J. M. Williams, died in Nashville; niece of Mrs. Campbell Brown. (Columbia Herald, 10 July 1891.)

WILLIAMS, Rev. Melancthon M., 92, died recently in Cambridge, Mass., the oldest living graduate of Princeton College. (Maury Democrat, 2 Jan. 1890.)

WILLIAMS, Mr. and Mrs., were killed on the 9th by lightning at Flat Creek in Bedford County. (Nashville Republican Banner, 11 July 1868.)

WILLIAMS, Mr., of Giles County, returned last week from war, had been gone 11 years. He had been taken prisoner and nothing heard further of him. He found his lawful wife the lawful wife of another man and with two little children. (Columbia Herald, 10 Jan. 1873.)

WILLIAMS, Miss Octavia, formerly of Williamsport, moved to Winchester 12 to 18 months ago, died recently of consumption. (Columbia Herald and Mail, 17 Nov. 1876.)

WILLIAMS, R. G., 8th Regiment, and T. W. Tays, 4th Regiment, died recently at Camp Douglas. (Nashville Dispatch, 3 April 1863.)

WILLIAMS, Miss Rene, 18, of West Point, her mangled body was found July 13. She had been blackberry picking and had been dead several hours when founds; she had been outraged and murdered. Sister of David Williams, telegraph operator at West Point in Lawrence County. (Columbia Herald, 16 July 1897. Refer also to Anthony Williams entry.)

WILLIAMS, Mrs. Robert, 50, died of pneumonia April 14 at Mt. Pleasant. (Daily Herald, Columbia, Tn, 17 April 1896.)

WILLIAMS, Sarah Jane, wife of Allison Williams of Manchester, died on the 3d at home of her father John Herribord in Nashville. (Nashville Republican Banner, 4 Sept. 1870.)

WILLIAMS, Mrs. Sarah P., 58 years 5 months 8 days, wife of Samuel H. Williams, died at Centreville; sister of Colonel Thomas S. and E. H. Spencer. (Columbia Herald, 20 Dec. 1872.)

WILLIAMS, Mrs. Sinah, 73, died yesterday. (Nashville Dispatch, 6 Feb. 1863.)

WILLIAMS, Mrs. Steven, 79, died on Wednesday; buried in family cemetery on Knob Creek; her husband survives and is 86 years old. (Columbia Herald, 20 Feb. 1891.)

WILLIAMS, Thomas Otho, 23, died in Columbia Feb. 2 of consumption. (Maury Democrat, 3 Feb. 1887.)

WILLIAMS, Bvt. Lt. Col. Thomas C., 19th U. S. Infantry, died in Little Rock a few days ago; was husband of Miss Saunders, step-daughter of

Governor Aaron V. Brown, postmaster general in Buchanan's cabinet. (Memphis Daily Appeal, 10 Jan. 1870.)

Capt. Thomas C. Williams, A.D.C., Major General Rousseau's staff, was married yesterday to Miss Cynthia Saunders, daughter of Mrs. A. V. Brown. (Nashville Daily Union, 30 May 1865.)

A most interesting will case has just been decided in Nashville. Miss Cynthia Saunders, the daughter of Mrs. Aaron V. Brown, was married during the war to a Col. Williams, a Federal officer. He won her affections whilst affording some protection to her family's property during the war. He no sooner married her, according to some of the witnesses, than he coerced her by his treatment into his trembling and wretched slave, instead of his wife.

In this condition he moved her to his mother's home in Philadelphia, where she pined away and died. Whilst thus tortured, he is alleged to have coerced a will whichleaves all the property to him and his heirs in perpetuity, proscribes from its benefits her fond mother and loving sister and brother.

Before dying, he sent her mother a blasphemous dispatch informing her of the approaching dissolution of her daughter, his wife. Mrs. Brown hastened to Philadelphia where she was subjected to the most cruel indignities, such as humbling herself on her knees before he would permit her to see her dying daughter.

When she reached her room, her daughter was insensible. This was the close of this ill-fated woman's career. We knew her as a lovely young school girl, the favorite of all who visited her family circle, and afterwards as she blossomed into lovely womanhood, and can sympathize with her relatives in the deep misery which her marriage entailed. The jury found against the will. Williams resorts to the usual devices of a desperate and defeated litigant-- the gross misconduct of a juryman and that other howl, so fashionable in these days of undue outside pressure, because he is an ex-Federal officer. (Memphis Avalanche, 26 June 1867.)

Thomas C. Williams versus Narcissa C. Saunders, lawsuit on the probate of the will of his wife Cynthia P. Williams, comes to court. (Nashville Republican Banner, 26 Nov. 1867.) Thomas Williams probated his wife's will in Pennsylvania, which was not her residence, although she died there on a visit, she was from Davidson County. Williams appeals the suit to the State Supreme Court. (Nashville Republican Banner, 3 Dec. 1867.)

The Supreme Court decided in favor of Colonel Williams in his suit versus John R. and Narcissa P. Saunders. (Nashville Republican Banner, 14 March 1868.)

Thomas C. Williams is suing for part of the estate of Mrs. Cynthia P. Williams in the case Williams vs. Saunders. There is to be an inquiry into the personality of the late Mrs. Williams. (Nashville Republican Banner, 29 May 1868.)

Miss Narcissa Pillow Saunders, belle of Washington during President Buchanan's administration, died in Nashville 30 June 1913; stepdaughter of Governor Aaron V. Brown, niece of General Gideon J. Pillow; last surviving member of a once wealthy family. (Maury Democrat, Columbia, Tn, 3 July 1913.)

Following a long illness, Miss Narcissa Pillow Saunders, died at 10:30 o'clock Monday night at her home 927 Montrose Avenue. She was the daughter of the Hon. John W. Saunders. Her mother was Cynthia Pillow, sister of General Gideon Pillow. Mrs. Saunders was left a widow with three children, Narcissa, John Edward, and Cynthia. The family then resided at "Melrose," near Nashville and it was there these children were reared. Afterward, Mrs. Saunders married Gov. Aaron V. Brown. Miss Narcissa had at that time

424

blossomed into a lovely type of young womanhood and she was known throughout the South for her beauty.

At Washington during the time Gov. Brown was Postmaster-General, she was the reigning belle of the nation's capital. She and the lovely Harriet Lane, also famed for her beauty, were inseparable companions. Miss Lane was the niece of President Buchanan and presided over the White House, where she died. Gov. Brown had been appointed Postmaster-General by President Buchanan and during his residence in Washington, Mrs. Brown became a leader in the social circles of that city. An entertainment given at the Brown residence in Washington was attended by the elite of the capitol, including members of the Diplomatic Corps...A writer of that time said of the affair:

"Mrs. Brown, an elegant looking woman, is dressed in rose-colored brocade with an exquisite resemblance of lace stamped in white on either side, a point lace cape, a head-dress of fleecy whiteness, with a few ornaments tastefully arranged completed her attire. But it was the lovely girl at her side we wish to draw your attention to, as she receives the salutations of her mother's guests. A white tissue embroidered in moss roesebuds, a circlet of pearls on her hair and natural flowers on her bosom, present an appropriate and beautiful contrast to her mother's more elaborate and gorgeous toilet. The charm of Miss Narcissa Saunders is her simplicity of character in the highly artificial society of Washington. This sweet girl performs on the harp beautifully, with arms as white as those Venus might have lifted above the sea-foam, and little pin-tipped fingers, so delicate and tapering, that one feels that it is marvelous how they can pinch the cords so as to produce such full-sounding, pleasing notes as they do. Young lovely, and an heiress, like Elizabeth of old, whichever way she turn, people will assume an attitude of devotion. Her fortune will insure her suitors of various nations."

After the death of Gov. Brown, the family returned to Nashville and again occupied the beautiful home of Melrose where they remained til the misfortunes that overwhelmed the South in the sixties, robbed them of that splendid estate. (Undated clipping from Nashville newspaper found in the papers of Miss Lizzie Porter, Columbia, Tn, given to the Maury County Historical Society.)

Married on the 16th inst. eveing by Rev. J. T. Wheat, Hon. A. V. Brown, Governor-Elect of Tennessee, to Mrs. Cynthia Saunders of Davidson County. (Clarksville Jeffersonian, 20 Sept. 1845.)

WILLIAMSON, Col. George, 78, of Green Hill, Wilson County, died December 15. (Whig and Tribune, Jackson, Tn, 8 Jan. 1872.)

WILLIAMSON, Richard, 66, died on the 13th in the Windrow district of pneumonia. (Free Press, Murfreesboro, Tn, 23 April 1880.)

WILLIAMSON, Mrs. Tabitha R., 74, died and to be buried in Saddlersville, Robertson County. (Nashville Union and American, 22 Oct. 1874.)

WILLIAMSON, Capt. Thomas C., is the oldest Odd Fellow in the United States; he was initiated into the order 1824 at Detroit. He is now more than 90 years old and full possession of his faculties. (Maury Democrat, 29 Aug. 1895.)

WILLIS, Mr. Marcus A., a young man, died at the home of his grandmother Mrs. Wilson on High Street, age 23, the fireman of Nashville will attend the funeral at McKendree Church. (Nashville Daily Gazette, 4 July 1852.)

WILLIS, Mrs. Mary Magdaline, 94, of Duck River Station, died Wednesday. (Columbia Herald and Mail, 1 Feb. 1878.)

WILSFORD, Mrs., was buried at Buford Station, Giles County, Sunday; mother of Mike Wilsford of Columbia. (Columbia Herald, 24 July 1891.)

WILSON, Sgt., Company G, 2nd Indiana Cavalry, died 29 Nov. 1863; his boat overturned in Caney Fork near Smithville, Tn. (Nashville Daily Union, __ Dec. 1863.)

WILSON. Governor Yates has appointed young Wilson of the 8th Illinois, who had his jaw partly shot away on the bloody field of Donelson, the position of post quartermaster of the Peoria camp. (Nashville Dispatch, 10 Aug. 1862.)

WILSON, Dr., of Centerville, Hickman County, died Monday; brother-in-law of J. D. Moore of Clarksville. (Clarksville Democrat, 24 July 1890.)

WILSON, Mrs. Eleanor, 72, died on the 7th. (Columbia Herald, 8 Jan. 1871.)

WILSON, Mrs. Elizabeth, died near Norfolk, Virginia, Thursday at the age of 107. (Memphis Avalanche, 21 Dec. 1868.)

WILSON, Miss Emma E., died this morning; buried at Rose Hill Cemetery; daughter of Flav Wilson, killed at Shiloh. (Columbia Herald, 1 Dec. 1899.)

WILSON. A man and a woman were shot dead Friday at the old Dickens Place, 3 miles northeast of Raleigh Springs, 12 miles from Memphis; were murdered outright. Col. Tom Dickens and his ex-slave Nancy and two other men while eating supper, and Green Wilson, who was riddled with eight shots and nearly cut in two and had five Bowie knife wounds. Nancy was killed. The murderers plundered the house of $200, stole a horse. There had been bad blood between Col. Dickens and his son Dr. Sam Dickens and a Capt. Patterson. (Memphis Daily Appeal, 21 Feb. 1869.) Tragedy on Feb. 19 at old Dickens place. One Inman and Morgan had been paid to murder Green Wilson, Nancy Dickens, Col. Tom Dickens, and Tom Humphries. Inman's mother lived near Frankfort, Alabama, and on Wednesday night two weeks ago, a band of disguised men took Inman and one Addison out of jail at Frankfort and shot them on the Tuscumbia Road. Addison was killed and was also the same person as Morgan. Both were hired killers. (Memphis Daily Appeal, 17 June 1869.)

WILSON, Henry, Company B, 85 Ohio Volunteers, fell of the steamer Sir William Wallace and drowned Sunday night at Cincinnati Landing. (Nashville Dispatch, 31 July 1862.)

WILSON, James H., is to be buried today in Williamson County. (Nashville Republican Banner, 24 Aug. 1869.)

WILSON, James M., died at the home of Major James H. Akin near Hampshire, Maury County; a cordwainer; no relatives can be ascertained. (Columbia Herald, 18 April 1873.)

WILSON, Major Jerome P., has died of cholera on Wednesday; was a Confederate soldier; Bishop Quintard conducted his funeral. (Memphis Avalanche, 28 Dec. 1866.)

WILSON. Information wanted - on Johanna Wilson, daughter of Mark Sweeney and wife of Thomas Wilson; born Limerick County, Ireland; she is heir to an estate. (Maury Democrat, Columbia, __ July 1889, Issue No. 2.)

WILSON, John, age 90, of Nelson County, Virginia, has gone on a deer hunt. (Memphis Avalanche, 19 Dec. 1866.)

WILSON, John W., Sr., died near Nashville on the 5th; served in War of 1812 and was one of the oldest Masons in the state. (Nashville Union and American, 8 July 1874.)

WILSON, John, killed his wife with a pocket knife yesterday around

4 o'clock; lived on Hernando Road; has a daughter Martha 18. (Memphis Avalanche, 17 Feb. 1866.)

WILSON, Dr. Lafayette, well-known physician hanged himself at the home of his brother Arthur on the Louisville Pike. He was arrested by Andrew Johnson while he was military governor and this unsettled his reason. He had to be taken to the Lunatic Asylum. He was buried yesterday in the family graveyard. (Nashville Republican Banner, 6 Oct. 1867.)

WILSON, Madeline, died November 28 of scarlet fever; daughter of Willie Wilson of Mt. Pleasant. (Maury Democrat, 5 Dec. 1895.)

WILSON, Mrs. Nancy, 76, wife of J. W. Wilson of the Nolensville Pike, age 77, died on the 12th. (Nashville Republican Banner, 13 Aug. 1867.)

WILSON, Napier, is lying low at his son-in-law's I. M. Powell. (Columbia Herald and Mail, 12 March 1875.) Napier Wilson died last week, War of 1812 soldier, buried in Greenwood Cemetery in Columbia. (Columbia Herald and Mail, 26 March 1875.)

WILSON, Robert, prominent Stewart County citizen, committed suicide because of financial reverses. (Maury Democrat, 22 Oct. 1896.)

WILSON, Mrs. Sallie, of Rally Hill, died on the 3d of puerperal fever. (Columbia Herald and Mail, 28 May 1875.)

WILSON, Mrs. Sallie E., wife of Hon. W. B. Wilson, died on the 6th. (Columbia Herald, 11 Nov. 1870.)

WILSON, T. S., 20, found dead in bed in Nashville; died of epileptic convulsion, but mother attributes his death to excessive use of cigarettes. (Maury Democrat, 20 June 1895.)

WILSON, Colonel William T., 7th Georgia Regiment, was killed in battle on August 30 at Manassas. (Nashville Dispatch, 23 Sept. 1862.)

WILTON, John Hall, well known in United States, was found dead in bed December 18 at Sidney, Australia. He was a great traveller and agent for Barnum and had just completed engagement for Jenny Lind in this country. He once was in the English Army. (Nashville Dispatch, 14 March 1863.)

WIMBERLY, Mr., and his two sons and a Mr. Clark, 80, and his son were in a shooting and stabbing affray at Abbeyville, Miss. Clark was shot in the head. Wimberly, Sr., was Clark's son-in-law. Old family feud. (Murfreesboro Monitor, 30 Jan. 1896.)

WINBOURN, John A., son of William M. and Mary R. Winbourn, died on the 13th. (Nashville Republican Banner, 15 Jan. 1870.)

WINBOURN, Mrs. Mary E., 21 years 1 month, wife of James R. Winbourn, daughter of B. F. Brown, died on the 14th of consumption. (Nashville Dispatch, 15 Aug. 1863.)

WINBURN, Agnes, 3 months 2 weeks 1 day, daughter of James E. and Mary E. Winburn, died on the 25th.

WINCHESTER, Dave, 88, died 11 Jan. 1897 at Kedron, Maury County; came here from Massachusetts. Buried Blanton Chapel Cemetery. (Columbia Herald, 15 Jan. 1897.)

WINCHESTER, Lula Malinda, infant of Mr. and Mrs. James Winchester, died on the 11th and buried at Blanton's Chapel. (Columbia Herald, 24 July 1891.)

WINDER, Brigadier General Charles S., killed in the battle of Southwest Mountain on Saturday; nephew of Brig. Gen. Winder, military commandant of Richmond. (Nashville Dispatch, 26 Aug. 1862.)

WINDER. The rebel general Winder, the great Southern savage is dead. He died on the 6th at Florence, South Carolina, where he was engaged in that pleasant task, to him, of starving Union prisoners. His pupil Bob Fox, the Knoxville jailor, and marshall preceded him a few days. Hell has never welcomed a meaner brace. (Nashville Daily Union, 13 Feb. 1865.)

WINDES, Col. F. M., formerly of Roddey's command of North Alabama, died around the 17th of disease contracted by exposure in Confederate service; died Lynchburg. (Memphis Daily Appeal, 26 Sept. 1868. No state given for place of death.)

WINHAM, Capt. William, 73, died in Sandersville, Tn, on May 30, an old and respected citizen of Sumner County; served with distinction in War of 1812 and rose to captain before the Battle of New Orleans. (Nashville Republican Banner, 2 June 1868.)

WINN, Dr. C. W., died Sunday in Nashville; at one time a practicing physician at Bigbyville in Maury County; married (1) Sadie Lawrence of the Hermitage; (2) Minnie Branch, daughter of Mrs. M. P. Branch. (Maury Democrat, Columbia, 19 Jan. 1893.)

WINN, Rev. G. W., died near Nashville a few days ago; born near Culleoka 50 years ago; itinerant Methodist preacher; during the war he was one of General John Morgan's favorite scouts. (Maury Democrat, 25 April 1895.)

WINSHIP, Mrs. Susan A., died at Murfreesboro on the 11th instant, consort of Frank Winship. (Nashville Dispatch, 24 Aug. 1862.)

WINSTON, Dr. John D., died in Nashville last week. (Whig and Tribune, Jackson, Tn, 4 Oct. 1873.)

WINTERS, Mr., who was shot on the 30th in a fracas on Bridge Street, died from the effects of the wound on the 8th. (Nashville Daily Gazette, 10 Nov. 1852.)

WISE, John J., of Norfolk, Virginia, a brother of the ex-governor, died last week. (Memphis Avalanche, 5 Nov. 1866.)

WISE, Miss Medessa, the betrothed of a young soldier Dennis Stull (who died from wound received in battle) committed suicide at Frederick, Maryland, by an overdose of laudanum. At his funeral she placed her likeness under his head and when she was found, his photograph was found under her head. (Nashville Dispatch, 5 June 1862.)

WISE, Richard H., son of E. and J. F. Wise, to be buried today. (Nashville Republican Banner, 8 Feb. 1870.)

WISEMAN, B., and Thomas Dowal had an altercation on one of the roads leading from Camden, about one mile out. Dowal (or Dowel) shot Wiseman three times and turned to run; Wiseman shot him. Dowel died the next day and Wiseman is not expected to recover. (Paris Gazette, 10 April, 1878.)

WISENER, Mrs. Elizabeth, 83, died on the north side of the river on the 10th; wife of Alexander Wisener. (Columbia Herald, 14 Oct. 1870.)

WITHERS, Colonel Bob, was killed by Sam Doxey at Hendersonville; shot in the groin; was lieutenant colonel in Carter's Regiment, CSA. (Nashville Republican Banner, 29 Nov. 1868.)

WITHERSPOON, Major John W., 76, died Feb. 5 near Cleburne, Texas, born 1815 in Maury County; moved to Texas in 1877 and settled in Johnson County; three children survive. (Columbia Herald, 28 Feb. 1891.)

WOLFF, Claus, resolution of respect on his death published in paper. (Nashville Republican Banner, 16 April 1870.)

WOLFF, Leila, infant daughter of E. and S. B. Wolff, died on the 7th. (Nashville Republican Banner, 9 April 1870.)

WOLFORD, General Frank L., died Friday at Columbia, Ky, age 78; he had suffered constantly with wounds received in the war. (Maury Democrat, 8 Aug. 1895.)

WOLLARD, Marion, died on the 3d in St. Francis River, Arkansas; his remains returned to Maury County and buried on Leiper's Creek. (Columbia Herald and Mail, 19 March 1875.)

WOLVERLIN, John, section foreman on the Northern Pacific near Spokane Falls, was scalped by two drunken Indians who demanded liquor. (Maury Democrat, 11 Sept. 1890.)

WOMACK, John B., Company E, 16th Tennessee Regiment, killed at Franklin on 30 Nov. 1864; stone in the Confederate Cemetery at Franklin. (Columbia Herald,16 Aug. 1895.)

WOOD, Mrs. Amy E., died 18 Oct. 1893 in Nashville; born 18 April 1815; two sons and three daughters survive; buried Rose Hill, Columbia. (Maury Democrat, 26 Oct. 1893.)

WOOD, J. H., 98, of the Confederate Soldiers Home is the oldest former Confederate soldier alive; born 1815 and served in Company B, 42 Georgia Infantry; severely wounded at Battle of Franklin; after the war settled near Nashville. (Maury Democrat, 5 June 1913.)

WOOD, Mrs. James, of Jefferson County, Alabama, is 106 years old. (Florence, Ala., Times, 14 Nov. 1891.)

WOOD, Lt. C. N., 74th Illinois, and Captain Eerheart of the 35th Ohio, died on 12 Aug. 1863 at Winchester, Tn; the latter died of an attack of cholera. (Nashville Dispatch, 14 Aug. 1863.)

WOOD, Lieutenant, killed in Memphis, was in Forrest's Cavalry. (Nashville Dispatch, 8 Feb. 1863.)

WOOD, Lillian, youngest daughter of Mr. and Mrs. W. H. Wood, age 15, died in southeast Columbia. (Maury Democrat, 12 Sept. 1895.)

WOOD, Mrs. Major General, was struck with paralysis through the entire right side Thursday and it was thought that the attack would prove fatal. (Memphis Avalanche, 4 Nov. 1866.)

WOOD, Captain Will T., 43, died in Memphis 7 April 1869. (Memphis Daily Appeal, 8 April 1869.)

WOOD, William H., died 18 August 1869 near Pinewood in Hickman County. (Nashville Republican Banner, 21 Oct. 1869.)

WOODARD, Mrs. Ann, 89, died near Clarksville last week; member of the Hoskins family. (Maury Democrat, 23 July 1891.)

WOODARD. Monday in District 4 of Giles County, Asa Foster and Fields Woodard were engaged in a fight; Foster's 19 year old son Morgan Foster shot Woodard in the head, killing him. James McGill and Ben Aymett, deputy sheriffs, attempted to arrest him, young Foster drew pistol, but McGill shot him through neck and it is thought a fatal wound. (Columbia Herald, 31 Dec. 1897.)

WOODARD, Lt. Col., of Ben Hardin Helm's regiment, was killed while the 50th Regiment of Indiana Volunteers were in Hopkinsville last winter. Woodard was on a clandestine visit to his home; they surrounded the house and fired up repeatedly at the windows. (Nashville Dispatch, 8 Aug. 1862.)

WOODS. In the case of the dependent mother of Abraham Woods of the 22d New Jersey Volunteers, who died in service, the Department of Interior hold that where the father and mother of the soldier are without property and the father is unable to support the family the parents are entitled to aid. (Columbia Herald, 1 March 1898.)

WOODS, Samuel, died of injuries received in a stabbing affray on Saturday; stabbed his brother James Woods, who stabbed him; died yesterday. (Nashville Union and American, 26 Sept. 1874.)

WOODS, W. J., was shot in the face with a squirrel shot by William Smith in Lincoln County a few days ago; the wound is ugly, but not dangerous. (Nashville Union and American, 7 Nov. 1874.)

WOODS, Warren and William David of Wayne County were struck by lightning near the entrance to an ore bank and were rendered speech-less and remained so until the next day. (Nashville Union and American, 20 Sept. 1874.)

WOODWARD. On Feb. 24 a Southern Railway train at Avondale Crossing near Chattanooga, hit a covered country wagon on the track, killing Mrs. W. J. Woodward and her eight children. A grandchild was the only one to escape. The engineer is prostrate over the shocking event. (Columbia Herald, 26 Feb. 1897.)

WOODY, Mrs. Emma, wife of Rufus Woody, was buried Sunday on Leatherwood Creek; died of consumption; husband and three children survive. (Maury Democrat, Columbia, Tn, 21 Nov. 1895.)

WOODY, the seventeen year old daughter of William Woody of Santa Fe died suddenly and unexpectedly of diptheria; she was sitting up in a chair when she died. (Columbia Herald and Mail, 5 Nov. 1875.)

WOOLDRIDGE, Elizabeth; 108 acres on the north side of Duck River are for sale, land where Mrs. Elizabeth Wooldridge lived at her death. (Columbia Herald, 29 Oct. 1869.)

WOOLFOLK, Tom, murderer of nine members of his family, hanged in Perry County, Georgia, on the 29th. (Florence, Ala., Times, 31 Oct. 1890.)

WOOLFORD, Brigadier General, of Louisiana, was killed at Chickamauga. (Nashville Dispatch, 26 Sept. 1863.)

WOOLSON, Albert, 109, died; the last member of the Union Army. President Eisenhower said: "The American People have lost the last personal link with the Union Army." (Daily Herald, Columbia, Tn, 3 Aug. 1956.)

WOOTEN, James, a noted fighter of Hickman County, was shot Saturday night at some point in Hickman County it was rumored. (Nashville Republican Banner, 27 Nov. 1871.)

WORKS, Major J. L., cut his throat in Mrs. Flake's boarding house, 42 South Cherry Street; aged about 60; remains sent to Bowling Green. (Nashville Republican Banner, 12 Nov. 1867.)

WORLEY, child of Capt. Worley of Bradshaw Creek, Giles County, was drowned in a tub of water. (Memphis Daily Appeal, 7 July 1869.)

WORMICK. N. P. Garrett, formerly of Florence, Alabama, now city marshal of Covington, Tennessee, killed a bad character named W. A. Wormick in that town last week; it was justifiable. (Florence, Ala., Times, 8 Oct. 1892.)

WORTH, the Paris dressmaker, died on March 12. (Maury Democrat, 14 March 1895.)

WORTHAM, Mrs. Lou, 61, died October 1 of typhoid; husband J. D.
Wortham, aged; lived at Andrews in Maury County. (Maury Democrat,
10 Oct. 1895.)

WRENN, ___, age 60, was hung near Glaze Bridge, Arkansas, for being
a Union man; body hung three days before it was taken down. Five
Union men from Wittsburg were shot at Little Rock a short time since
by the order of General Hindman. The Charleston papers report that
he executed 10 Yankee officers in retaliation of the McNeil butchery.
(Nashville Daily Union, 14 Jan. 1863.)

WRENN, Mrs. Mildred B., wife of Thomas W. Wrenn, 73, died near Santa
Fe Monday and buried in family graveyard. (Columbia Herald,
8 Jan. 1897.)

WRENN, Peter, Esquire, 70, died on April 2 while returning home from
Nashville; Cumberland Presbyterian; formerly lived in Maury County
but now lived at Pinewood in Hickman County. (Columbia Herald and
Mail, 10 April 1874.) Peter Wrenn, of Pinewood, aged and
respected, left Nashville in a wagon and a few miles out of Nashville he got out and walked up a hill. He was found lying dead
in wagon soon after. He was nearly 80. (Nashville Union and
American, 4 April 1874.)

WRENN, Uncle Tom, who is a crippled, fell last week and is in critical
condition. (Columbia Herald, 14 Aug. 1896.) Thomas Wrenn of
Water Valley died Sunday, age four score years; buried in family
burying ground. (Maury Democrat, 28 Sept. 1899.)

WRIGHT, Alex of White Bluff, Dickson County, was killed in a train
wreck, 14 miles from Nashville on Monday. The train went through
the bridge into the river, three coaches, the smoking car, the
ladies car. It went 25 feet down into the river. Deputy Sheriff
Pendergrast was also killed. (Columbia Herald, 7 July 1871.)

WRIGHT. Alfred Wright's little boy was drowned in Stone's River a day
or two ago. It is said two men stood upon the bank and saw him
drown without offering any assistance, when they could easily have
saved him. (Nashville Republican Banner, 15 Sept. 1870.)

WRIGHT, Bobby, 70, died Sunday; lived near Leftwich in Maury County.
(Columbia Herald, 21 March 1873.)

WRIGHT, Captain Eldridge E., was killed in the Battle of Murfreesboro;
son of the Honorable Archibald Wright of Memphis. (Nashville
Daily Union, 25 Jan. 1863.)

WRIGHT, Egbert G., died Tuesday at his home on the Campbellsville
Pike; buried Reece's Cemetery; his wife has been dead several
years; she was the widow of Alexander Terry. (Columbia Herald,
19 June 1896.)

WRIGHT, General, is among the killed at Culpeper, Virginia.
(Nashville Dispatch, 16 June 1863.)

WRIGHT, John Samuel, 31, son of Mrs. John Wright, died on the 31st
ult. (Nashville Republican Banner, 2 Feb. 1870.)

WRIGHT, John, 98, died at Hopewell last Sunday; father of A. R. Wright
of Memphis. (Nashville Union and American, 1 May 1874.)

WRIGHT, Captain, 28th Tennessee, was killed at Murfreesboro.
(Nashville Dispatch, 8 Jan. 1863.)

WYATT, Miss Meadia, died on the 28th in District 11 of Rutherford
County. (Free Press, Murfreesboro, 6 May 1881.)

WYNDHAMMER, Josephine, sister of Mrs. H. Bollinger of Peoria, Illinois,
was treated with great cruelty by her sister, who whipped her and

kept her locked away in filth and endeavored to starve her to death.
She was kept in an attic in the winter and her feet were frozen.
The sister claimed she was sickly. (Nashville Dispatch, 6 Feb.
1863.)

WYNN. Last Saturday, James Wynn took double-bit axe and murdered his
wife in bed in Dickson County. Her 12-year old daughter was next
assaulted. He severed her fingers and crashed her brain and it is
thought she would die. He tried suicide but was lynched. Mob took
him from sheriff near the old Spicer place, two miles from Burns,
and hanged him. Mrs. Wynn was the Widow Anderson before she married,
and the mother of Will Anderson. (Dickson Press, 28 July 1892.)
Wynn, wife murderer, was lynched by the people of Dickson, Tennessee.
(Florence, Ala., Times, 6 Aug. 1892.)

YAKELY, Henry, was murdered by Vaughn's command at Laurel Gap, Tn.
(Knoxville Whig, 4 Jan. 1865.)

YALLERY. Margaret Yallery arrived at Detroit last week from the
wilderness. She had started with her father and mother and was
captured by Comanche Indians on the plains and she had been a
captive for 40 years. The parents purchased their liberty and are
living at St. Joseph, Missouri. She was treated brutally. At the
age of 20 she married David Ward, Irishman, and had three children.
Ward was burned at the stake. After this a young Indian married
her and she had six children. The Indian was killed. She was
freed June 1870. (Columbia Herald, 18 Aug. 1871.)

YANCEY, William L., 48, died of an affection of kidneys. (Nashville
Dispatch, 11 Aug. 1863. This is not a Nashville area death, but
no place given.)

YANDELL. The rebel guerrillas recently stole from old John Yandell of
Gibson County all his horses, except one which was worthless, and
the clothing of his daughters. Yandell is between 75 and 80 years
of age, and was a soldier in the War of 1812. (Nashville Daily
Union, 10 Nov. 1863.)

YANDELL, Dr. David, offers his professional services to the citizens
of Davidson County. His residence is on the Gallatin Turnpike,
four and a half miles from Nashville, at the place formerly owned
by the late Josiah Williams, Esquire. (Nashville Union, 3 Nov.
1852.)

    Louisville Journal: It is said that Dr. David W. Yandell, late
    of this city, but more recently of the rebel army, departed this
    life recently in Chattanooga, Tn. (Nashville Dispatch, 21 Feb.
    1863.) Dr. Yandell was alive and well on the 17th in Chattanooga.
    (Nashville Dispatch, 26 Feb. 1863.) (Dr. David Wendel Yandell
    died 2 May 1898--family records of Ted Garrett, Columbia, Tn.)

YANDELL, Dr. L. P., Sr., a celebrated physician, died at Louisville
last Monday in his 83rd year. (Columbia Herald and Mail, 8 Feb.
1878.)

YANDELL, Dr. Lunsford, a physician of Louisville, Ky, died in that city
last week. He was a native of Rutherford County and was a brother
of the celebrated Dr. David W. Yandell. (Hickman County Pioneer,
21 March 1884.)

YANDELL. Notes on the estate of Dr. Wilson Yandell, deceased, are to
come in; signed by Lunsford P. Yandell, executor, Nov. 29.
National Vidette, Murfreesboro, 10 Jan. 1828.)

YANDELL, Henry. Dr. Henry Yandell, having located himself in Mur-
freesborough, tenders his services to the people of Rutherford

County; shop is one of the rooms of Col. Smith's former tavern and his dwelling house is one door below the Printing Office. (Central Monitor, Murfreesboro, 25 Jan. 1834.)

YARBROUGH, Margarette, wife of S. J. Yarbrough, died in DeKalb County on the 22d; funeral to be held in Nashville; daughter of James B. Parrish. (Nashville Republican Banner, 25 July 1869.)

YARBROUGH, William, first lieutenant of the night police, died on the 4th of congestion of the lungs. (Nashville Dispatch, 5 Aug. 1862.)

YARNELL. Senate Bill 33 for the benefit of Isabel J. and Henry T. Yarnell to consider them legitimate as born in wedlock before the General Assembly on the application of the father; the bill was passed and later rejected. (Nashville Daily Union, 29 April 1865.)

YEADON, R., Jr., killed. Richard Yeadon, editor of the Charleston Courier, writes about the Battle of Chickahominy, "the accursed Yankees have slain my nephew and namesake; he was killed between 3 and 5 o'clock; shot through the head and died instantly; in the Washington Light Artillery." (Nashville Dispatch, 15 June 1862.)

YEATMAN, Mrs. Eliza, formerly of Nashville, died in New York City wife of the late John Yeatman. (Nashville Republican Banner, 27 May 1870.)

YEATMAN, Nellie Fortier, wife of J. W. Yeatman, died October 20 in Canada of consumption. (Nashville Republican Banner, 21 Oct. 1869.)

YELLOW WOLF, aged Kiowa, died on the 4th in Washington and buried in the Congressional Graveyard by the side of a Ponca Indian, who was buried there a few years ago. (Nashville Dispatch, 14 April 1863.)

YOHE, David, of Pigeon Creek, Washington County, went to the battle-field at Fort Donelson and had the body of his son disinterred; son had been wounded and died and buried. The body was taken home and buried. All thought it was his body except one sister. Last week they got a letter from him--alive. He had recovered from his wound and was going to rejoin his outfit. (Nashville Dispatch, 1 June 1862.)

YORK, John, Esquire, old and well known citizen of Edgefield, died yesterday of bilious fever. (Nashville Republican Banner, 19 July 1868.)

YOUNG, Abe, of Rally Hill in Maury County, was found dead in Duck River on May 2 at Hardison's Mill. He was to be a witness for the grand jury against a number of parties, and he was killed to keep him from testifying at the next term of court. (Maury Democrat, 9 May 1889.)

YOUNG, F. G., died near Culleoka; heart disease; buried on the 8th. (Columbia Herald, 19 Aug. 1870.)

YOUNG, George, colored, one of the best waiters at the Maxwell House, died Sunday. (Nashville Union and American, 18 Aug. 1874.)

YOUNG, Joseph, of Company A, 47th Tennessee Regiment, died at St. Louis on the 1st as prisoner of war. (Nashville Dispatch, 11 July 1862.)

YOUNG. Male Thief Caught. - Mr. John T. Sullivan of Humphreys County came to our city last Monday or Tuesday, and told the Sheriff that a man named George Young had borrowed his horse, and ran away with it. On Tuesday morning, Deputy Sheriff Harris concluded he would go down in the direction of Cross Bridges but failed to carry any weapons with him. When he reached Mr. Park's gate, near the Hampshire crossing, he met a man whom he recognized as the mule

thief, from the description which Mr. Sullivan had given. Mr.
Harris immediately feigned that he had lost some papers, and asked
Young if he had seen any along the road he had come, who replied
that he had not, whereupon Mr. Harris remarked that he believed
he would also go back to town, and give up the papers as lost for
good. On the way back to town, Young offered to sell the mule to
the Deputy Sheriff, which completely satisfied the latter's mind
that he was in company with the man who had stolen Sullivan's
mule. They took their steeds to McGaw's stable, and Harris soon
managed to arrest Young. The prisoner says he is a native of
Virginia, but whether from Buckingham or Cumberland County, we are
not able to learn. (Columbia Herald, 14 Oct. 1870.)

ZADING, Mr., his body has been recovered near wreck of the steamer
United States at Louisville; formerly of Nashville, now merchant
of Pulaski. (Nashville Republican Banner, 15 Dec. 1868.)

ZELLNER, Mrs. Martha, died May 22 in Williamson County; wife of
Henry Zellner. (Maury Democrat, 29 May 1889.) Mrs. Henry Zellner's
remains brought and buried in family burying ground at Timmons in
Maury County; had been married 50 years and 1 day. (Maury Democrat,
27 May 1889.)

ZELLNER, Henry, 86, died this morning near Brentwood; buried in
cemetery at Timmons in Maury County. (Columbia Herald, 4 Nov. 1899.)

ZOLLICOFFER, Rev. Daniel, of Carroll County, Maryland, died recently
at an advanced age. He was son of a Swiss noble and had been
bred to arms in France. He was son of John Conrad Zollicoffer, who
received a commission from the Governor North Carolina during the
Revolution, settled at Baltimore and died there. He was the oldest
member of his family in this country, of which the late General
Felix K. Zollicoffer was one, and he was by courtesy Baron Zollicoffer of St. Gauts, Switzerland. He received an annuity from
Switzerland in Virtue of this dignity, which now passes with baro-
netcy to the son of a brother, the late distinguished Dr. William
Zollicoffer. (Nashville Dispatch, 1 Jan. 1863.)

ZOLLICOFFER, Felix Kirk. The Paris Intelligencer has been given by
Cornelius Peden a part of the press owned and used by General
Zollicoffer many years in Paris, Tn. It is also the first printing
press used in Nashville. (Memphis Daily Appeal, 4 July 1869.)

Quartius C. Rust, a veteran of prominence in the Mexican and Civil
Wars and an original character, known among the G.A.R. people in
all the Central States, was found dead today (Aug. 21) on the old
National Road, 15 miles west of Indianapolis. He was lying at the
bottom of a 14-foot embankment with his head crushed under his buggy,
his horse dead also. There is nothing to explain the mystery of
his death, theories of murder and accident being both entertained.
"Quart" Rust, as he was called in the army and ever since, was
widely known for his claim, never disputed, that he killed the rebel
General Zollicoffer in the battle of Perryville, Ky, in 1862.
Until the war he was a Democrat and so popular in this district
that he ran for the Congressional nomination against the late Senator
Joseph E. MacDonald, and was beaten by one one vote. This was
immediately after his return from the famous trip across the plains
with General Fremont, wherein Rust gained special praise from
Fremont. (Indianapolis News, Maury Democrat, 30 August 1894.)

ZOLLICOFFER, Mrs. Louisa P., wife of General Felix K. Zollicoffer, died
in Nashville on Monday last. (Clarksville Jeffersonian, 10 July
1857.)

ZUCCARELLO, Mary Erwin, infant daughter of Mr. and Mrs. James
Zuccarello, died at Pulaski last Monday. (Columbia Herald,
11 Sept. 1896.)

Compiled By:
Ella E. Lee Sheffield
Texas City, Texas 77590